The Shan
Culture, Art and Crafts

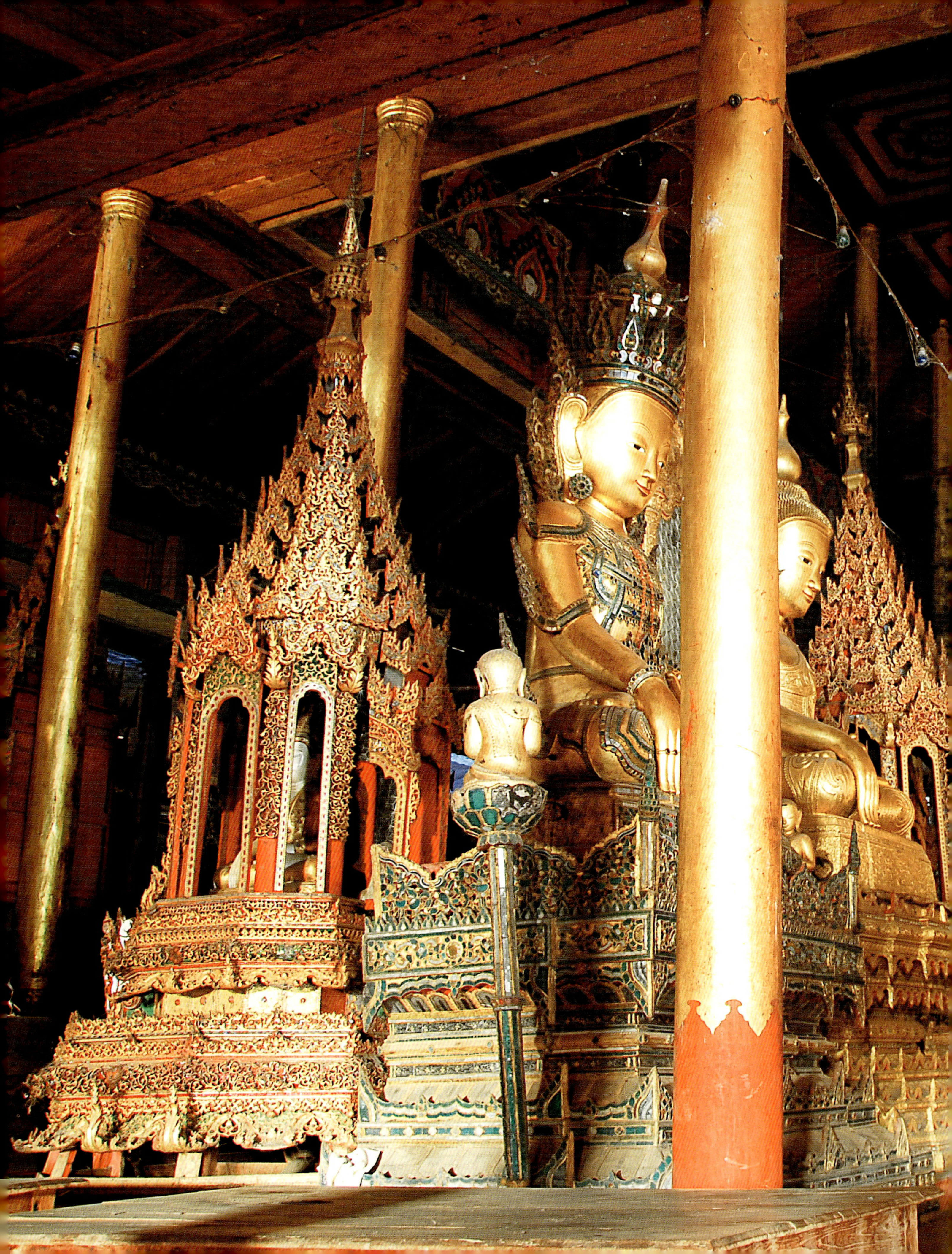

The Shan

Culture, Art and Crafts

Susan Conway

RIVER
BOOKS

For my father who loved Burma and the Shan States

Acknowledgements
Many people have contributed to this publication, particularly surviving members of the Shan royal family. They include Sao Hkam Hip Hpa (Ivan) and his sons, Sao Nang Sumpee (Eleanor), Sao Sein Myint (Elaine), Sao Cheo Muong, Sao Noan Oo (Nel), Sao Sanda Sim and Sao Phong Keau (Ouie). My thanks also go to William Klausner, Eric Booth and Jane Puranananda of the James H. W. Thompson Foundation, Bangkok. I acknowledge the help and advice of Ruth Barnes (Ashmolean Museum, Oxford), Richard Blurton (British Museum, London), Henry Ginsburg and John Falconer (The British Library, London), Rosemary Crill and Frances Franklin (Victoria and Albert Museum, London), Alexandra Green (Denison University, Granville, Ohio), Helen Mears and Sarah Posey (Green Centre for World Art, Royal Pavilion, Libraries and Museums, Brighton), Mattiebelle Gittinger (Textile Museum, Washington) and David Lyman and Khun Wipawee (Tilleke and Gibbens Textile Collection, Bangkok). I am also grateful to the staff of the Shan Palace Museum, Yawnghwe, Shan States.
In Thailand, Akadet Nakbunlang, Duangjit Thaveesri, Somchai Songwattana, Cherie Aung-khin and Paothong Tongchua gave advice and allowed me to photograph their dress and textile collections. Others who contributed to this edition wish to remain anonymous.
I am deeply appreciative of the help provided by my publisher M. R. Narisa Chakrabongse, Khun Paisarn Piammattawat and Khun Oraphan Chaivorarat of River Books.

First published and distributed in Thailand in 2006 by
River Books Co., Ltd.
396 Maharaj Road, Tatien, Bangkok 10200
Tel: (66) 2 225 4963, 225 0139, 622 1900
Fax: (66) 2 225 3861
Email: riverps@ksc.th.com
www.riverbooksbk.com

Editor Alexandra Green
Design Narisa Chakrabongse and Suparat Sudcharoen
Project Coordinator Oraphan Chaivorarat
Production Paisarn Piammattawat

ISBN 974 9863 06 2

Printed and bound in Thailand by Bangkok Printing Co., Ltd.

Frontispiece: Shan temple interior, Inlay Lake.

Opposite: *Hti* with *hintha* bird, Inlay Lake.

Page 6: Monk's preaching throne, Inlay Lake.

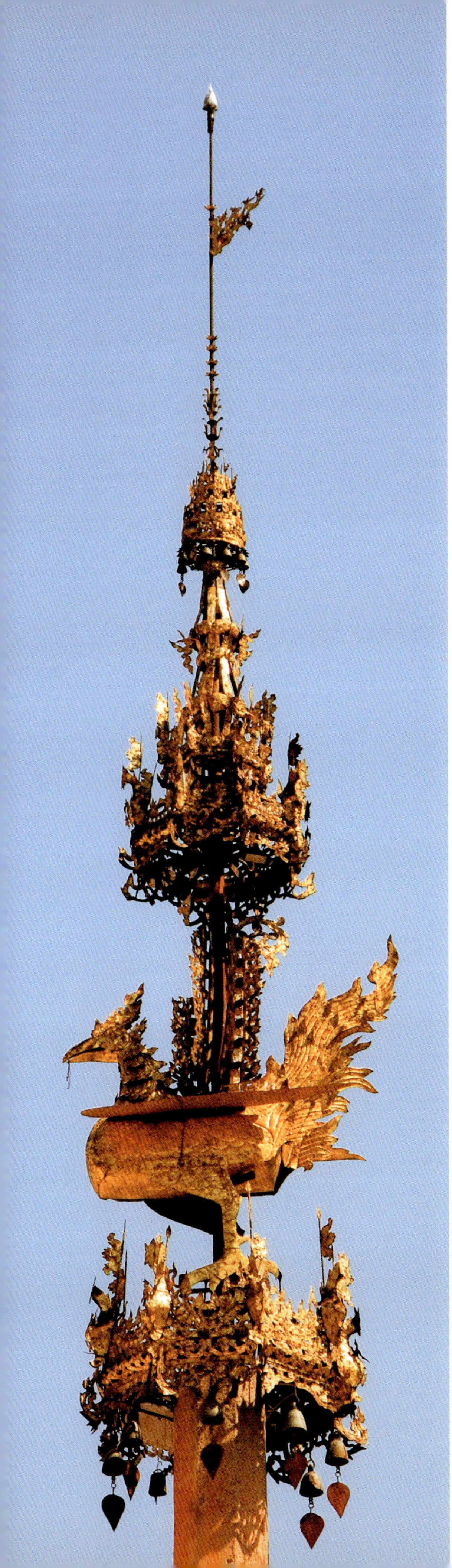

Contents

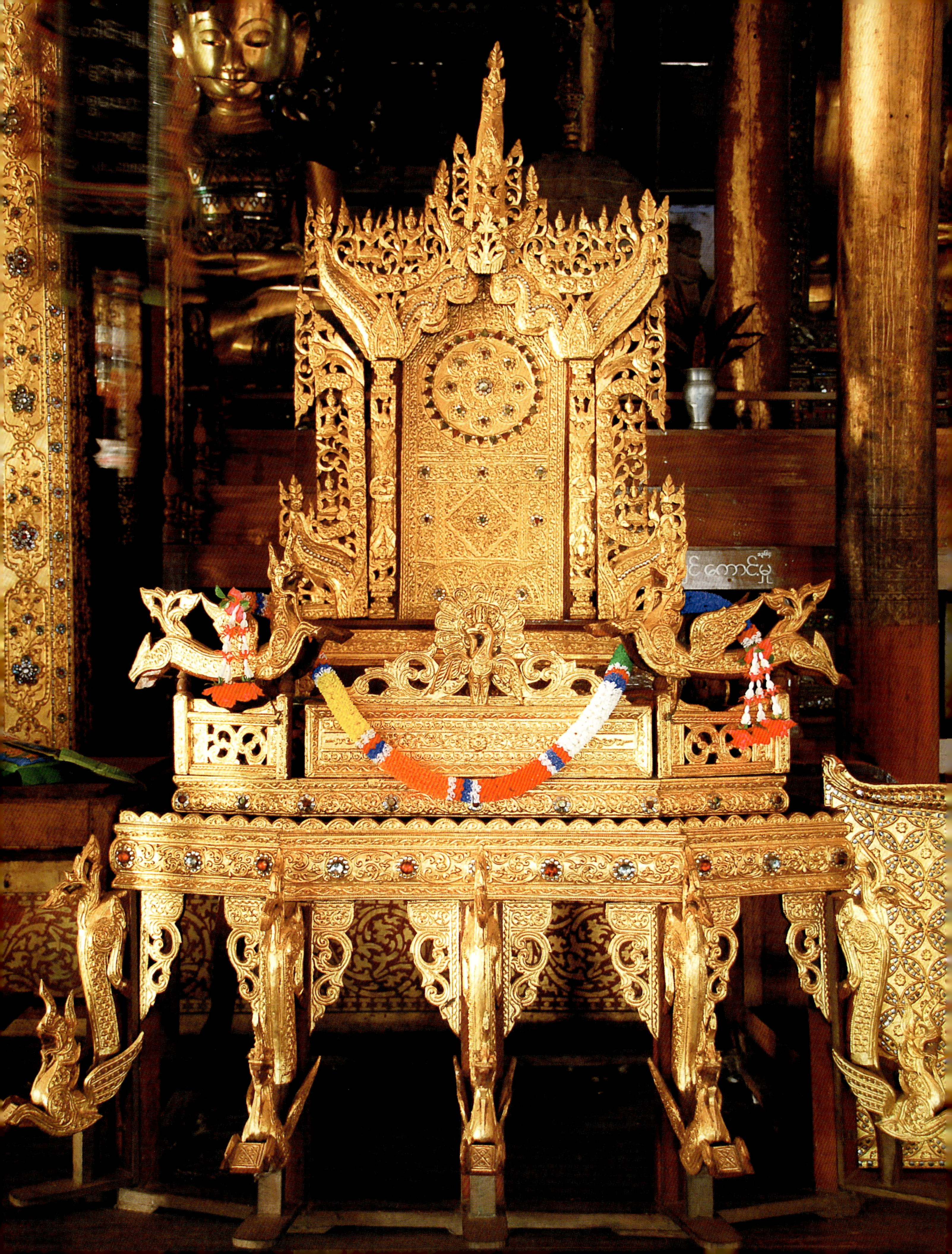

Preface

If you look at a topographic map of Asia you will see that four great rivers have their origin in a tight cluster at the eastern end of the Himalayas. To the west lies the Brahmaputra, in the centre the Salween and Mekong and to the east the Yangtse. From this common origin the rivers spread out to form an almost perfect fan, cutting through the mountain ranges before descending to the flood plains and then on to the Bay of Bengal or the South China Sea. The apex of the fan, high on the Tibetan plateau, has its own character and mystery and has long excited the attention of explorers and writers. At its widest the fan encompasses the hinterlands of the great Asian cities of Dacca, Yangon, Bangkok, Phnom Penh, Saigon, Hanoi, Canton and Shanghai. It is the middle swathe of the fan that is less familiar. Here the original rivers are joined by their tributaries and by the Irrawaddy, the Chao Phraya, the Ho and the Hongshui. Together they dissect the mountain ranges into small valleys, forming a distinctive landscape which extends over thousands of square miles.

The focus of this book is the section of the middle fan referred to as the Shan States. This is a region with a beautiful landscape but its appeal does not come from the grandeur of high mountain ranges or the sweep of the sky over the plain. The hills and valleys are on a human scale and they have nurtured humans for many thousands of years, providing a fertile environment where a unique culture has developed and flourished.

The Shan States are at the crossroads of inland Southeast Asia and for over a thousand years the surrounding super powers, particularly China and Burma (Myanmar), have crossed this territory to wage war, to trade and to influence local politics. Although as this book will show, their presence affected some aspects of local life, the Shan States maintained a distinct culture. This sophisticated culture developed spontaneously within the world of inland Southeast Asia, sharing common features with the surrounding inland polities of Lan Na (north Thailand), Sipsong Pan Na (Xishuang Banna, Yunnan Province, China) and Lan Xang (western Laos). This was manifested in religion, in language and literature, in politics and in arts and crafts. Intermarriage was common among the ruling elite in the valleys and hills and interaction was an important factor in the way the culture developed.

Chapter one sets the scene by examining the culture and traditions of the Shan States within the context of the landscape, people, their religion, their arts and crafts and their politics. This involves the valley dwelling Tai, the Wa (Lawa), the Karen, the Kachin and other groups of hill-dwellers, such as the Palaung. The Tai are defined in this book as Tai Yai, Tai Lue, Tai Khoen and Tai Neua, but when they are referred to in the text as a group, they are called Shan, a convenient geographical term to differentiate them from the Tai living in the surrounding inland states of Lan Na, Sipsong Pan Na and Lan Xang. As will be evident, in many inland principalities various Tai groups lived in communities or in adjoining settlements. The Tai people of the Shan States developed an endogenous culture in the thirteenth and fourteenth century, based on wetland rice cultivation, Theravada Buddhism and spirit religion. Some groups of Karen, Kachin and Wa had inhabited the land long before the Tai arrived, and some had converted to Buddhism although neither they, nor the Tai rejected spirit religion beliefs.

There are references in this book to historic and cultural links that existed, and continue to exist, between the Shan States and the surrounding inland states of Lan Na, Lan Xang and Sipsong Pan Na. How the people organised themselves politically and their relationships with China, Burma, Siam and later Britain, are also explored in the text.

Chapter one also examines the role of women in local society. Although they were viewed as potential polluters of men, and merely "followers" in religious terms, they maintained a high level of social and economic freedom, uncommon in many areas of Asia. This chapter also identifies the unique form of Theravada Buddhism that co-existed with a form of spirit religion that was endorsed and celebrated by the ruling classes and in some instances, supported by Buddhist monks. Shan architecture and interior decoration is introduced in the context of religious buildings, palaces and village houses. A link is established between the annual sequence of rice production and Buddhist festivals, and the cycle of textile production. Issues concerning dress and ethnicity and dress and politics are set in the context of relations between hill and valley societies, of tributary relations and sumptuary law. The chapter concludes with the notion of a land where complex family networks and political alliances enabled hill and valley people to interact socially, politically and economically and at times to quarrel and go to war.

Chapter two begins with an early history of the people passed down from generation to generation through creation stories and later recorded by Buddhist monk scribes on palm leaf manuscripts, referred to as chronicles. From supernatural beginnings the Shan Chronicles chart the history of states that it is claimed were founded before the birth of the Buddha. The Shan principalities were tributary to Burma, Siam or to China but by the end of the thirteenth century were a strong force in their own right. Their main difficulty was that they were targets for powerful predatory rulers, as in the sixteenth century when the king of Pegu subjugated them. Nevertheless the ability to play Burma off against China enabled the Shan to bargain for a degree of independence, especially when the super powers were preoccupied with events elsewhere. Their relationship with their neighbours in Lan Na and Siam is examined in the context of the eastern Shan state of Keng Tung and the Lan Na state of Chiang Mai.

In the nineteenth century the colonial ambitions of Britain and France began to impact on the Shan States and this affected the political climate and administration. The British replaced the Burmese as the major power and the Shan rulers swore allegiance to Queen Victoria.

Independence from Britain in 1947 led the Shan to join the new Burmese parliament, an important era that came to an end in 1962. The chapter ends with the return of Burmese military rule and the subsequent events that led to the disappearance or exile of many Shan leaders.

Chapter three considers male dress and body decoration in the nineteenth and early twentieth centuries, a particularly interesting time when, although the finest clothing was reserved for royalty, villagers wore colourful clothing and textiles on festive occasions. With his long hair coiled in a knot and wrapped with a turban, with his sarong hitched high on his hips to reveal extensive leg tattoos, a man from the Shan States could make a dramatic impression. In winter his heavy turban and glazed indigo coat, possibly lined with fur, and his loose-legged trousers secured with a sash, created a unique style.

The Shan male elite also wore striking forms of dress that reflected ethnic allegiance and the complex politics of tributary relations. In the nineteenth century the princes and chiefs were photographed in Chinese hats and silk dragon robes, or gilded Burmese crowns and highly embroidered coats and jackets. With the arrival of the British they added medals and decorations. On other occasions they dressed in a distinctly Shan court style. Male dress included locally produced hand spun and hand woven textiles, as well as imported yarns and textiles from India, China and Burma. As will be evident men modified their dress to suit prevailing political and economic circumstances. As society adapted to change, so did the way they dressed.

Chapter four examines female dress in the same period, concentrating on the Tai groups living in the Shan States, but also referring to the Palaung and Karen. One of the terms generally associated with female dress in Southeast Asia is "traditional", meaning that the way women dressed was linked to a particular ethnic group or homeland, and had been worn in that style for an extended, although often undefined, period of time. Female members of the Shan royal families wore some of the most beautiful textiles produced in inland Southeast Asia. Like their male counterparts, princesses also wore clothing and textiles associated with sumptuary laws, particularly when they attended lavish ceremonies held at the Burmese court.

Chapter five highlights the customs and life style of the royal courts of the Shan States, from the most powerful Tai princes to hill dwelling chiefs. Shan palace architecture and regalia were subject to sumptuary laws that affected all levels of the hierarchy. The number of tiers on the roof of a palace, the design of the throne and the royal umbrellas, and the style of animal trappings all depended on one's place in the social order. The arrival of Europeans, particularly the British in the late nineteenth century, brought new developments in Shan architecture and design.

Chapter six is concerned with artisans and their products. This includes the work of spinners, weavers and dyers, embroiderers, lacquer workers, metal workers and gilders, painters and scribes, wood carvers and umbrella and basket makers. Many objects produced by Shan artisans in the nineteenth and early twentieth centuries, for example silverware and lacquer, were recognised for their high quality and were exported to other parts of Southeast Asia. This chapter ends by examining the current state of arts and crafts, with photographs of artisans working today.

Chapter seven looks at trade in the Shan States with particular reference to textiles, dress and raw materials. Textile history in Southeast Asia has generally focused on ocean trade with India as the point of convergence but because of their inland location the Shan States relied on overland trade that restricted the amount and type of goods that were available, in comparison to countries with thriving ports, like Siam and Burma. Transporting goods long distances overland was expensive and made imported goods generally the privilege of the elite. Nevertheless some foreign goods, particularly from China and Burma, penetrated far inland and were distributed at the level of village markets. In the nineteenth century caravans of Yunnanese (Ho), Shan and Burmese traders travelled the inland routes to and from south China and Burma and to and from the Shan States. Human porters were used on some routes. Regional trade was in the hands of villagers, mostly women, and involved goods sold at local markets. This chapter also charts the changes in textiles and dress as imported mass-produced items, such as dyes and mill cotton, replaced locally produced materials.

Chapter eight is the conclusion and considers the state of Shan culture in the current political climate.

Sources

This book is based on a number of historical sources, including Tai chronicles inscribed on palm leaf or written on Shan paper in *tham* script. These manuscripts were copied and recopied over the centuries and were revised by Buddhist monks, often under the instruction of local royalty. In the Shan States the manuscripts are stored in monastery libraries where they are under the protection of Buddhist monks. Some manuscripts have been translated into English, central Thai, or other Southeast Asian languages.

Other written sources referred to in this book include accounts by British and French officials who travelled in the Shan States in the nineteenth century. From the 1830s the British and French were engaged in exploring and mapping the inland states with a view to expanding trade and colonial influence in the region. The British were particularly interested in a proposed railway line from Burma via the Shan States to China. Dr. David Richardson and Captain William Couperus McLeod wrote of their travels that began in the 1820s and ended in 1846. The French explorers Francis Garnier and Louis de Carné recorded the tour of the Mekong Exploration Commission (1866 to1868) and E. Lefèvre wrote of his expedition from 1894 to 1896. James George Scott K. C. I. E. was appointed Resident for the Northern Shan States in 1891 and remained in the region until he retired in 1910. His descriptions of life in the Shan states are quoted in the text.

The American Presbyterian missionaries established a station in Keng Tung in 1910, and William Clifton Dodd published a book of his experiences of local life as a missionary in the field. Mrs Leslie Milne and the Reverend Wilbur Willis Cochrane also contributed to this genre. In the 1930s Maurice Collis toured the Shan states as a guest of the princes and wrote some moving accounts of life during that period. The published memoirs of surviving members of the Shan royal family, including Nel Adams and Inger Sargent, provide a personal glimpse of life at the Shan courts. These and other sources are in the bibliography.

The artist Delaporte travelled with Francis Garnier on the Mekong Exploration Commission. Delaporte produced a series of drawings and sketches of the courts of Sipsong Pan Na that were later produced as etchings in a series of articles in *Le Tour du Monde.* Many of the black and white photographs in this book come from the collections of James George Scott, now in the archives of the Oriental and India Office Collections, The British Library. Other photographs come from the Colonel Green Collection at The Green Centre for World Art at the Royal Pavilion Art Gallery and Museums, Brighton and The Museum of the Chiefs, Yawnghwe Museum, Yawnghwe. Members of the Shan royal family also allowed access to their private photographs.

There is a strong tradition of oral history in the Shan States. Descendants of the Shan royal families living in Thailand, Britain, and North America provided important information on court life, and they are named in the acknowledgements. Some generously donated photographs, or allowed me to photograph textiles and dress, heirlooms from the Shan courts.

Establishing the correct Shan usage of words and their spelling is a complex task. For example the word *nat* (spirit) is Burmese but is used in parts of the western Shan States. In other areas *phii,* the Tai word for spirit is common, particularly in the eastern Shan States. The Shan word for a prince is *saohpa* but *sawbwa* is the Burmese form and was used by the British. The spelling of the states and towns also varies according to who is writing. Where possible I have used the forms suggested to me by Shan advisers. The glossary gives Shan, Burmese and English spellings. Another difficulty arises over the umbrella term "Shan" to describe the people. As mentioned, in this context it includes the Tai Yai (often referred to as Shan Proper), the Tai Khoen, Tai Lue and Tai Neua. I have used the term Shan to denote the Tai living in the Shan States, and have identified individual Tai groups where it is appropriate. The hill dwellers are identified in four main groups, the Wa, the Karen, the Kachin and the Palaung. There are many other groups and sub-groups living in the hills but they are less relevant in the context of this book.

Descendants of Shan royalty have given generous support during the production of this book, helping with family history and allowing me to reproduce photographs from their private collections. I have also drawn on textile and dress collections in museums and private collections in Britain, the USA and Thailand. The sources are listed in the acknowledgements.

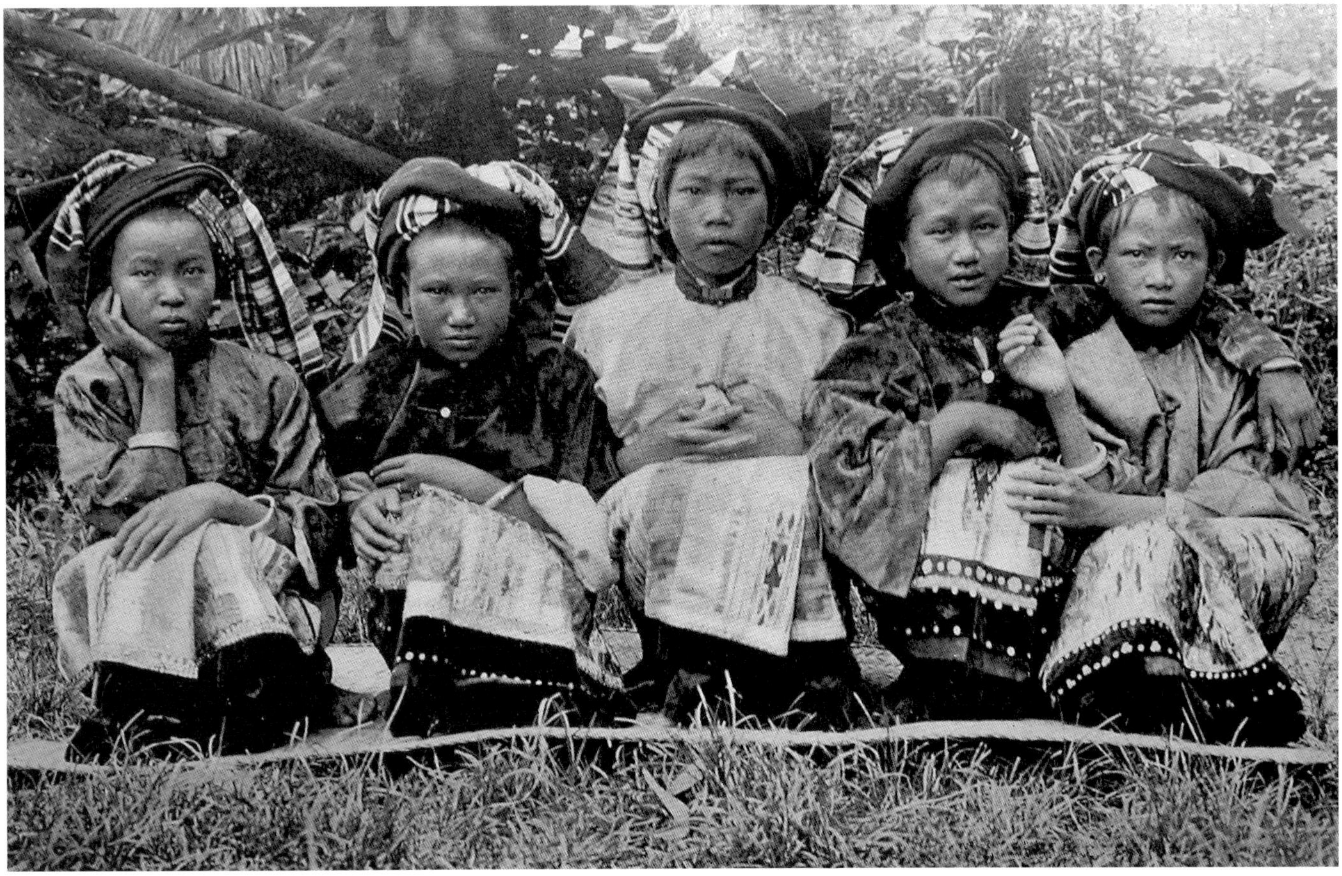

Group of Shan girls, Milne & Cochrane, 1910.

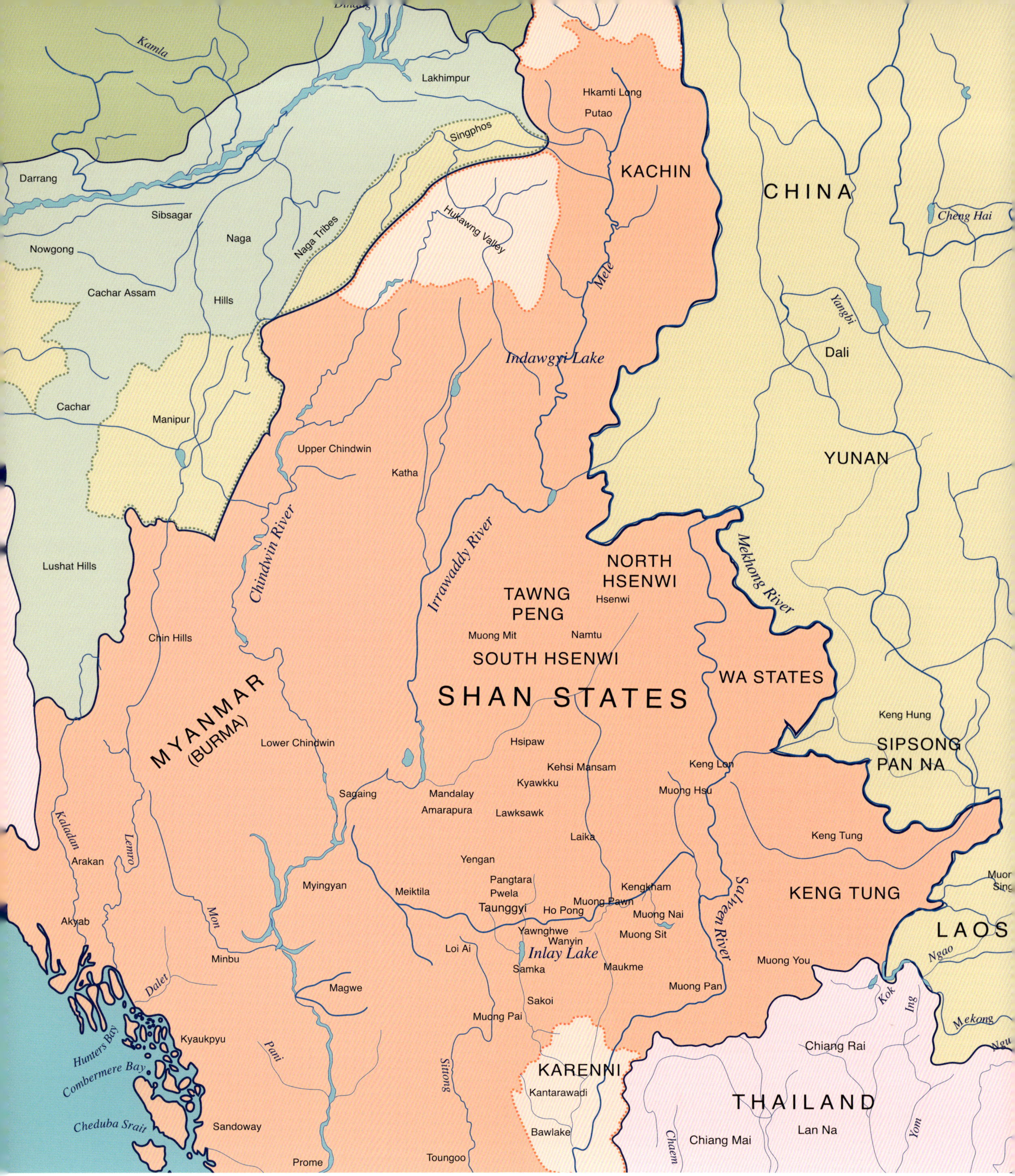

1 Map of the Shan States and border regions.

Chapter 1
Setting the Scene

The Shan States together comprise 160, 000 square kilometres, almost a quarter of the country known today as Myanmar or the Union of Burma. The States are bordered by China and Tibet in the north, Laos and Thailand to the east, and Myanmar to the south and west. Over the centuries the number of principalities and chiefdoms has varied. Power centres formed groups under one ruler or split into small units, often reforming later as political circumstances changed. In the nineteenth century the state of Keng Tung was about the size of Belgium. Hsenwi to the north was comparable to Wales. Some states were tiny, comprising as little as sixty square kilometres. At the end of the nineteenth century, the total population of the Shan States was estimated to be over one million.[1]

The Shan landscape consists of upland valleys and rugged river gorges intersecting an undulating highland plateau. In the winter months the weather is cool, and the temperature may drop at night below freezing. The hot season begins in March, and in June clouds begin to gather, heralding the start of the monsoon. Irrigated wetland rice is grown in the valleys and on terraced slopes, while soft fruit, sugar cane, citrus and vegetables are cultivated on the highland plateau. The hill slopes are planted with tea. In the nineteenth century, cotton was a major crop and until the advent of synthetics, a range of dyes and mordants were cultivated or gathered from the wild. Hemp was grown in the hills. Sericulture was practiced in areas where the soil and climate were suitable for cultivating mulberry. In 1906 the British Commissioner Sir George Scott reported that opium poppies were grown extensively.[2] The Shan States are rich in natural resources including precious metals and gems, timber and forest products, although the latter are now being rapidly depleted.

In 1846 a Siamese government official Thao Sittimongkhon described his diplomatic mission to the Shan States. Travelling involved hiring elephants and oxen to carry loads and, where the paths were steep and too narrow for large pack animals, ponies and human porters. Attack from wild animals was a serious threat, particularly in areas where tigers roamed, and travellers erected platforms in the trees when sleeping on the ground was too dangerous. They had also to keep watch for dacoits (robbers) who ambushed convoys. By far the greatest danger came from exposure to malaria and other debilitating tropical diseases. Long journeys were usually undertaken in the dry season, as during the monsoon many paths became impassable and villages and towns were isolated for long periods.

In the nineteenth century European cartographers compiled maps of the Shan States, marking watersheds and land gradients. Shan maps of about the same period show a completely different mind-set in mapping the terrain.[3] They are not drawn to scale but represent the land in sweeping outlines that resemble Lan Na (northern Thai) Buddhist mural paintings. Rows of undulating brush strokes symbolize the hills, narrow winding ribbons of paint represent rivers and streams, and wide bands of blue paint, often outlined in black, mark the Salween, Irrawaddy, or Mekong rivers.[4] Splashes of green signify river valleys and red squares mark fortified towns; villages are indicated in lozenge shapes or in circles. The broken lines running between them denote footpaths. There are clusters of Buddhist monuments (stupa) in the valleys and single stupa on the hilltops, drawn in a distinctive, elongated shape that is typical of Shan architectural style. Burmese or Shan script written on the paths provide information on the number of days or nights it takes to journey between towns and settlements. These simple maps enabled travellers to follow well-worn and relatively safe paths from one settlement to the next and were used by many, including Buddhist pilgrims visiting holy sites. Maps that marked footpaths were particularly important because the Salween (Nam Khong) River and its tributaries were not navigable by boat due to swift currents and dangerous rapids. Hilltop stupa made excellent landmarks and proved useful to nineteenth century European explorers, like the British officer Captain William Couperus McLeod.[5]

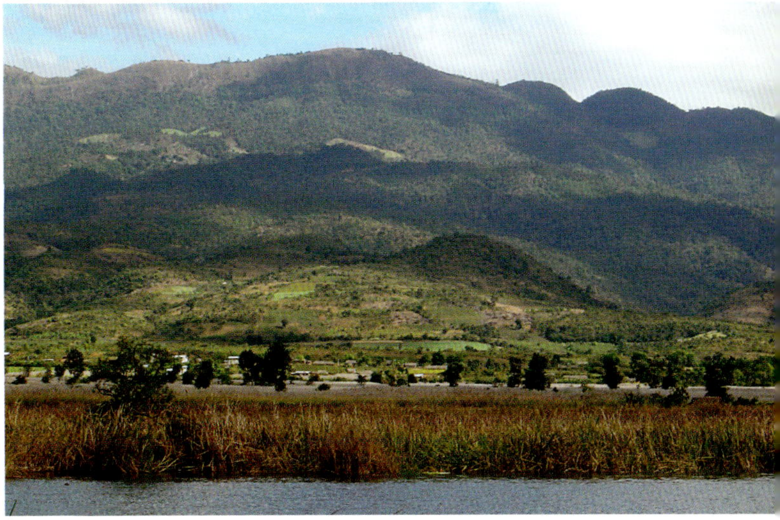

2 A typical Shan landscape. People from the hills and valleys have interacted socially, economically and politically since settlement first began.

Indigenous maps also provided interesting information about human settlements. One in the collection of the British Library illustrates the course of a meandering river, probably in Sipsong Pan Na (Xishuang Banna, Yunnan Province, China) where Chinese-style houses were common.[6] Men fish on the river, and there are men on the riverbanks dressed in Chinese robes and hats (see fig. 5). The women are portrayed in ankle length skirts painted in the style of Burmese *luntaya* (tapestry weave) designs. Others wear ankle-length skirts (*phasin*) in a style worn by Tai women. Based on the style of dress illustrated here we can assume that the river valley was home to more than one ethnic group, a common occurrence in the world of nineteenth-century inland Southeast Asia where river valleys were a main source of livelihoods.

The concept of mapping and the use of maps became a controversial issue in the nineteenth century when European interests began to focus on the region. European mapping systems that marked boundaries according to watersheds challenged the culture of the inland states where

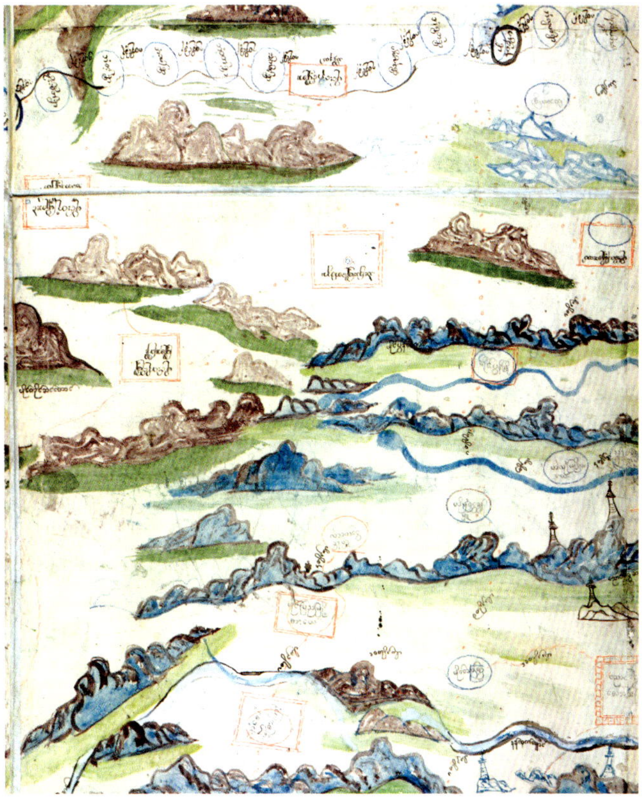

3 A hand-drawn and painted nineteenth-century Shan map. *(The Oriental and India Office Collections, The British Library, London, C1076-01)*

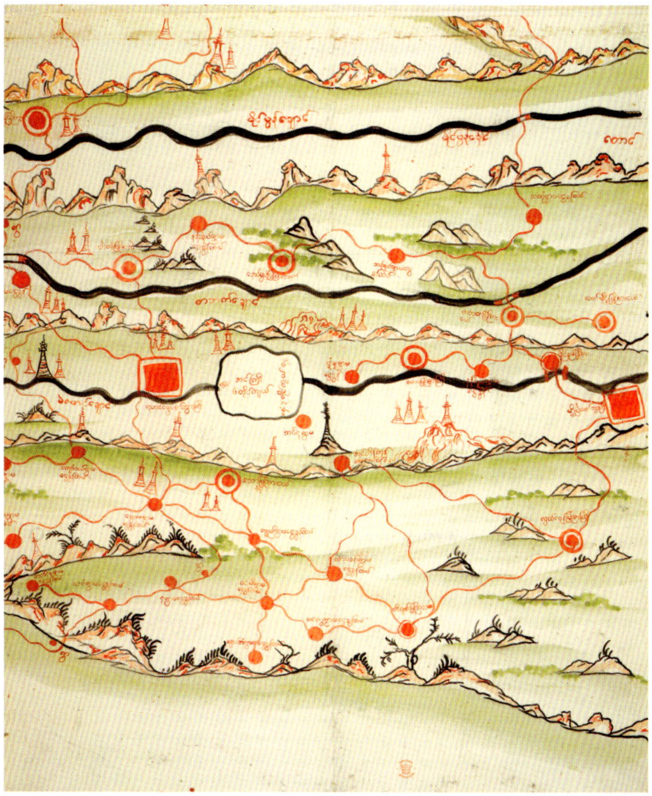

4 A hand-drawn and painted nineteenth century Shan map. The Shan stupa are associated with pilgrimage and in some cases acted as boundary markers for travellers. *(The Oriental and India Office Collections, The British Library, London, C1076-02)*

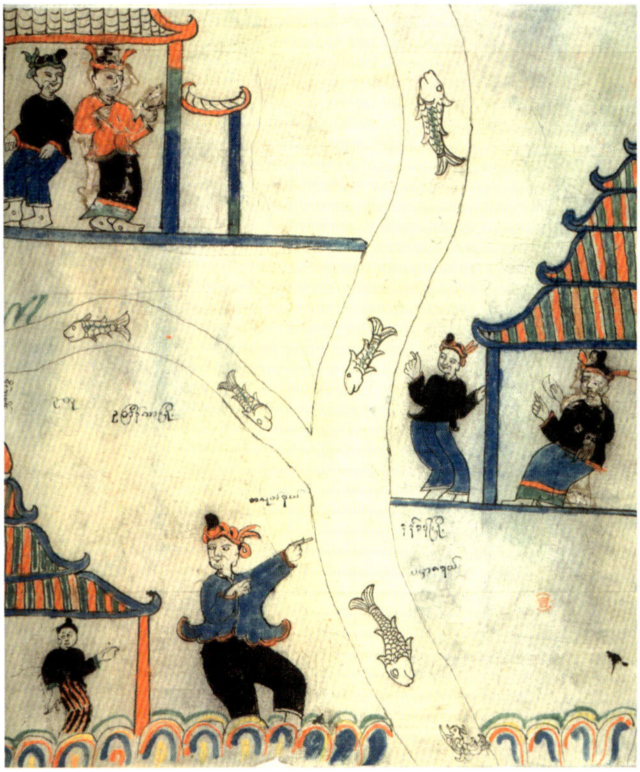

5 Detail of a hand-drawn and painted map showing Chinese homes along a river bank. The men and women wear Shan and Tai Lao dress. *(The Oriental and India Office Collections, The British Library, London, C1076-03)*

land was measured according to the Tai *muong* system that involved spheres of influence. The concept of a linear territorial boundary was foreign. Henry Burney, British Political Resident at the court of Ava in the 1830s understood this and argued that the Salween River should not be defined as an official boundary between Burma, Siam and Lan Na (Chiang Mai) because local people had always crossed backwards and forwards without restriction.[7] That did not mean that there were no boundaries. The Sipsong Pan Na Chronicle states in its opening paragraphs that Sipsong Pan Na was marked and named.[8] The difference between "marked and named" and the linear boundary system imposed by the Super Powers was to cause anger and resentment in inland Southeast Asia. In 1837 the Prince of Muong Long had brought his own map of Sipsong Pan Na to show to Captain McLeod but requested that he did not reveal it to any other person. It probably resembled the painted maps illustrated here. The fundamental difference was that most of inland Southeast Asia was under-populated or even uninhabited in many areas and attempts to gain power were not primarily concerned with grabbing land but with appropriating people. Labour was in such short supply that powerful rulers raided other states for workers to tend their fields, harvest crops, extract timber, to build, decorate and maintain Buddhist temples and monuments, and to work in their palaces and households.

The main ethnic groups living in the nineteenth-century Shan States are identified in ethno-linguistic and geographic terms as Tai, Wa, Karen and Kachin, although many other terms (listed in the appendix) are used to describe them. The Chinese had the advantage of written records and were able to register for posterity that the people on their southern borders were "barbarians". The Chinese also noted that the people wore "skin garments" interpreted later as meaning that they were tattooed. Missionaries, British and French colonial and military officers, anthropologists and ethnographers divided those living in the Shan States into groups and sub-groups and recorded the names that local people used to describe themselves and to define others.[9] Many of these terms when translated from local languages and dialects meant only "people" or "people of this land" and like the Chinese they used terms like "savages" and "strangers" to describe others. Foreigners often recorded these terms verbatim and duly entered them into official reports. One linguistic surveyor commented that the inland states of Southeast Asia reminded him of "a dish cloth which has traces of everything it has wiped."[10] During the nineteenth century government officials aided by anthropologists and ethnographers attempted to create their own sense of order by formulating a classification system that incorporated physical characteristics, cranial measurements and specific cultural traits including the way hill and valley people dressed. Some included what they considered to be character traits. The anthropologist Edmund Leach challenged the value of this research with his 1950s study of hill and valley dwellers which showed how migrating hill people often adopted the dress codes, language and farming methods of valley inhabitants and could merge with them completely in the course of a few generations.[11] His research is particularly relevant in the context of this book which aims to show how dress codes changed according to political, social and economic conditions.

Some researchers concluded that assertions about ethnic origin were better understood if they could be connected to creation myths.[12] In the Shan chronicles Buddhist princes are descendants of heavenly beings sent to earth from the Tavatimsa Heaven, while their subjects are said to have emerged from a giant gourd. Kachin myths involve ancestors who were the descendants of powerful elemental spirits. Wa mythology claims origins from a lake at Nawngkheo where their people evolved from frogs to ogres and then to humans. The ancient saying quoted below gives an interesting insight into how the people of the Shan States thought of each other:

The Shan nourish Buddhism
The Wa nurture the spirits
The Karen care for their friends.[13]

The valley people of the Shan States, who are the main subject of this book, are defined as descendants of the Tai who originally inhabited south China from at least the ninth century BC. Their migration to the Shan States may have begun as early as the first century AD.[14] They also moved into north Thailand (Lan Na), Laos, north Vietnam and Assam. The Tai are identified throughout inland Southeast Asia as people who inhabit upland valleys and practise wetland rice cultivation. They are Theravada Buddhists and maintain older beliefs based on spirit (*phii*) rites. Tai people share a monosyllabic, tonal language and although there have been changes in dialect and accent over the centuries, today there is still a high degree of mutual understanding. Passing from one valley to the next it is also possible to identify similarities in religious and domestic architecture.[15]

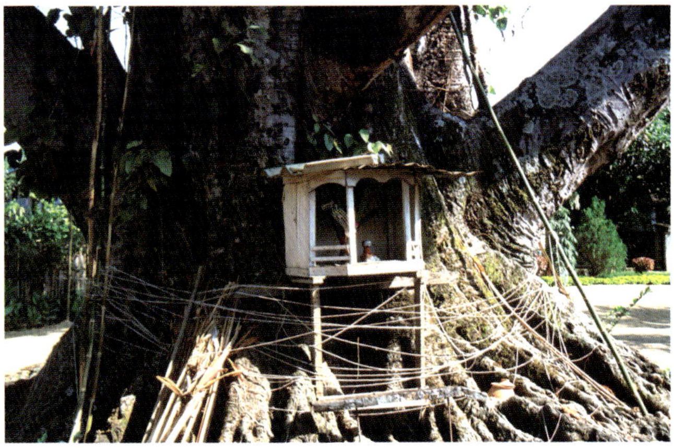

6 A wooden spirit shrine in a village on the outskirts of the city of Keng Tung. White cotton thread circles the tree to mark the sacred space.

The Tai who settled in Lan Na, the eastern Shan States, Sipsong Pan Na and western Laos (see page 10) developed a similar culture that by the fifteenth century included a religious script called *tham* or "muong letters" also employed in secular correspondence.[16] The script is still in use in some religious communities and schools.[17] The Tai in this region practised a distinct form of Buddhism known as the Yuan Sect and observed rites associated with guardian spirits. Today they preserve in their folk tales and traditions a sense of common origins. In terms of governance and the arts, a loose comparison can be drawn with the principalities of Renaissance Italy where powerful ruling families commissioned fortified cities, palaces and places of worship from artists, architects and artisans hired to design and build them. The Italians created buildings in brick and stone and paintings in wet stucco, and although some people in the Shan States worked with brick they also used wood and bamboo for buildings and dry stucco for wall paintings, materials that fit the Buddhist concept of the impermanence of life, slowly disintegrating over the centuries leaving only a glimpse of their former beauty.

In their own language the Shan call themselves Tai and refer to the Shan States as "Muong Tai" (land of the Tai). The Burmese, and later the British, used the term Shan to define all the Tai people living in the Shan States and further categorised them according to tributary systems.[18] Adding to the confusion, the French and Americans often used the term "Lao". The people who call themselves Tai Yai or Ngio were named Shan Proper or Western Shan by foreigners because they formed the largest group of Tai in the Shan States. Probably because of their proximity and interaction with Burma, they use many Burmese words in their speech. Those who call themselves Tai Lue live in the valleys of Sipsong Pan Na and the eastern Shan states with important cities at Muong Yong, Muong La and Keng Hung. In 1918 it was calculated that about fifty thousand were living in Keng Tung.[19] Those identified as Tai Khoen inhabit the central and eastern Shan valleys and in the nineteenth century were the majority population on the plain of Keng Tung, where today they retain their particular form of language and script. Their dialect is similar to neighbouring Chiang Mai. Interestingly, the Khoen and Lue are particularly closely allied in terms of culture, although

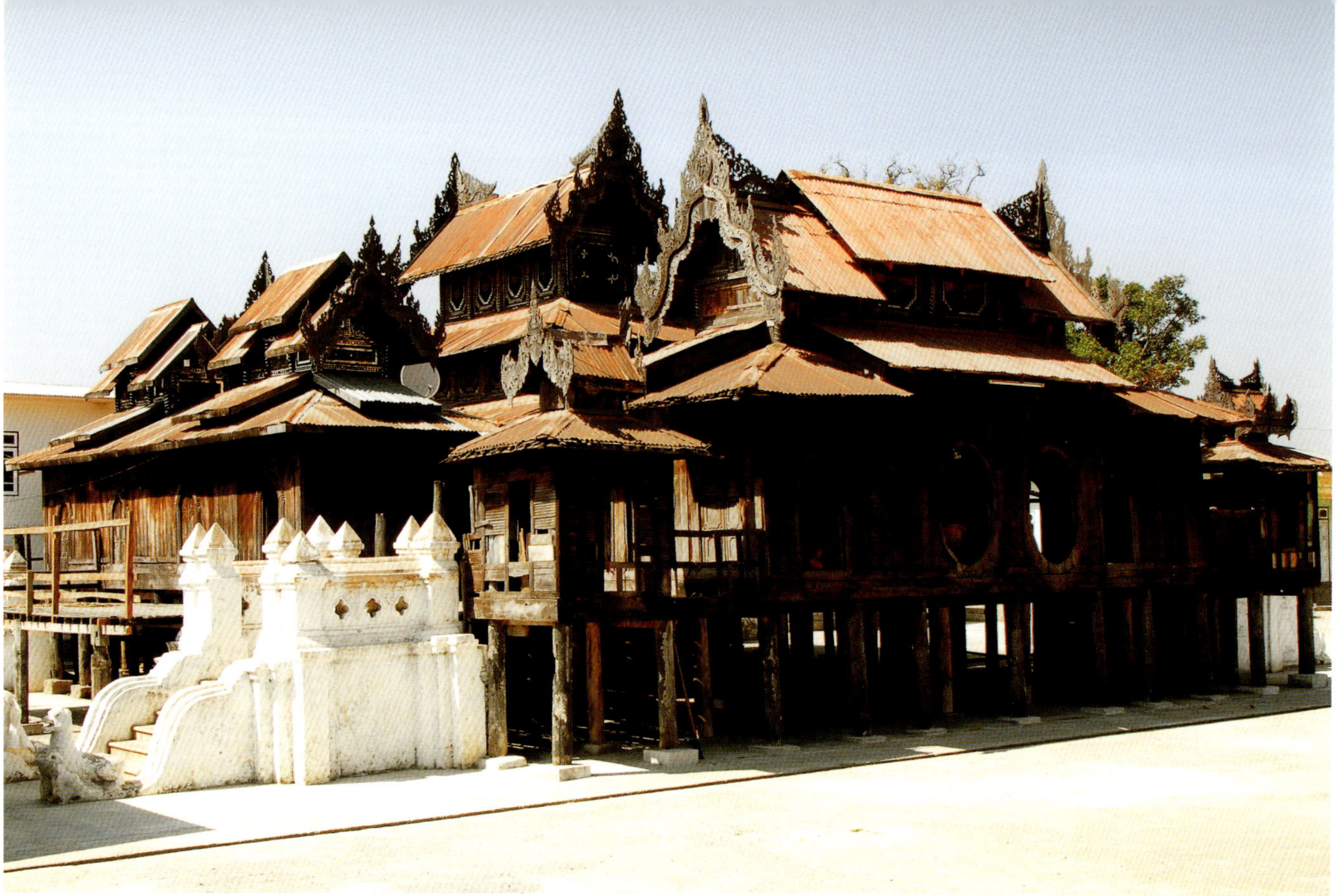

7 A monk looks out of the teak monastery of Shwe Yan Phye, Yawnghwe, built in the late eighteenth century.

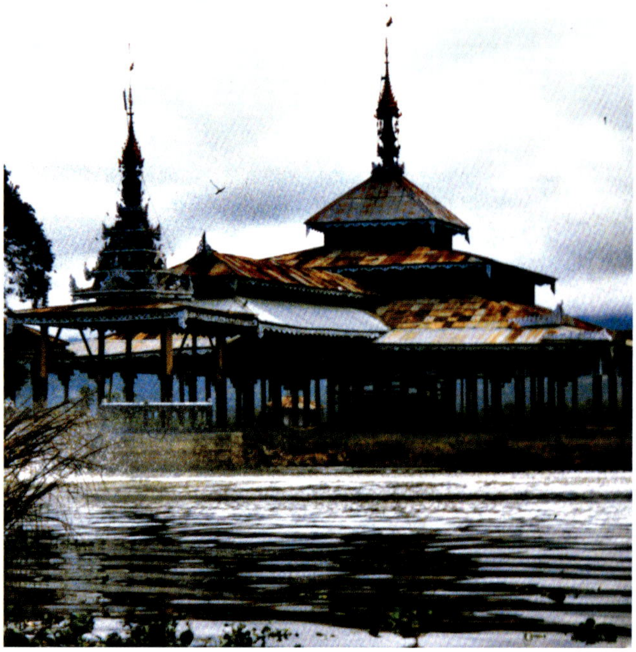

8 The monastery Na Phe Chaung on Inlay Lake.

there are variations in women's dress. They are closely related to the Tai Yuan of Lan Na. Those calling themselves Tai Neua live mainly in Sipsong Pan Na.

According to oral history, the Wa (called Lawa by the Burmese) preceded the Tai in the valleys of the Shan States and neighbouring Lan Na.[20] They claim to have journeyed thousands of years ago northwards along the Mae Ping River settling for a long period in what is now the Chiang Mai valley. Ruins of ancient Wa settlements discovered in Chiang Mai Province provide evidence that authenticates their oral history. In the nineteenth century, they were living between the Salween River and the Mekong River on the slopes of a series of mountain ranges. There were many settlements around Keng Tung. They practised swidden (slash-and-burn) agriculture, cultivated cotton and sugar cane, traded in cattle and extracted iron from the hills to make swords and muskets and everyday items such as knives and cow bells. Most lived in settled communities and cultivated fields some distance from their villages. Their reputation in the nineteenth century rested on their headhunting rituals. The Chinese who traded with them, divided them into "Wild Wa" who took heads from strangers and anyone vulnerable and Wa who took heads for ritual purposes only. When he came into contact with the Wa, the British official Sir George Scott argued that they took heads for ritual purposes and when their homesteads were threatened.[21] Their reputation was certainly a deterrent to intruders and helped stop encroachment on their lands. Whatever the truth about headhunting, the Wa had a great reputation for robbing trade caravans. The Tai respected them and acknowledged that they were the original inhabitants of the land. The Keng Tung Chronicle states that in the thirteenth century King Mengrai sought Wa allegiance to ensure the successful establishment of a powerful Tai dynasty in Keng Tung. Whenever a Shan prince was consecrated, a Wa chief was invited to sit on the throne and then was symbolically removed as part of the ritual. This ceremony was recorded in the fourteenth century and was last performed in 1897 when Prince Lonkeau, Saohpa Long of Keng Tung was consecrated.[22] A similar ceremony was performed at the court of Chiang Mai.[23]

Powerful Kachin groups lived in the hills and in the outer reaches of Shan territory and were controlled by their own rulers. Kachin is a Burmese term loosely translated as "barbarians of the north-east."[24] Subsequently the term Kachin was used to define a group of people with specific cultural characteristics who lived on the mountain ridges in the hills of the northern Shan States and in the region of Bhamo and Katha. By the early nineteenth century there were Kachin in the southern Shan States. Many other terms have been used to describe them and their sub-groups but they called themselves *pak ayor* or *chingpaw* meaning simply "men" or "people".[25] British military officers and missionaries interpreted the term as *jinghpaw* and used it in their reports.[26] From their elevated strongholds the Kachin levied taxes on valley dwellers, collected in the form of silver, cattle and agricultural products.[27]

The Shan chronicles state that in order to maintain peace, valley dwellers made treaties with the Kachin and agreed to pay their levies annually. When relations were good, there was a great deal of mutual respect and the Kachin chiefs *(duwa or dwa)* attended important Shan ceremonies, including weddings and the funerals of senior royalty. Nevertheless the relationship was always complex and subject to the power struggles of the time. A series of Kachin chiefs ruled Hkamti-Long in the northern Shan States and paid tribute to a succession of Shan princes, but when a Burmese king usurped Shan authority, the Kachin became nominally subordinate to Burma.[28] Whatever their relationship with the Shan, the Kachin were powerful enough to come down from the hills at regular intervals to demand tribute.[29] We know from oral history that the rulers of the Shan state of Hsenwi paid the Kachin chiefs large quantities of silver every year as a way of preventing devastating raids that might include sacking and torching a palace compound.[30] Shan villagers were so frightened of Kachin ambushes that they only travelled in well-armed groups.[31] In some districts where the Kachin were particularly active, the people chose to sleep in boats so that they had a chance to escape by river.[32]

The Karen (also called Karenni, Tongsu, Nyang Daeng, Sgaw, Pwo, Pa-o, Thaung-thu or Kayah) were hill dwellers. Their villages can be found throughout the hills that border the Salween and the Pai River and in western Lan Na. They practise swidden (slash and burn) agriculture. Some Karen groups settled at lower altitude and lived in permanent villages. Colonial officers and missionaries documented their cultural practices in the nineteenth century, and the Karen leader San C. Po produced an account of their culture and traditions in the 1920s.[33] The Karen practised spirit religion and Theravada Buddhism but in the nineteenth century many were converted to Christianity. They traded agricultural produce and village crafts with the Shan. They had a reputation as kidnappers and slave traders but by the end of the early twentieth century appear to have restricted their activities to cattle rustling.

There were other groups who produced charismatic rulers, particularly the Palaung (also called Palé, Ngwe, Ta-ang and Rumai) of Tawng Peng, a northern Shan state.

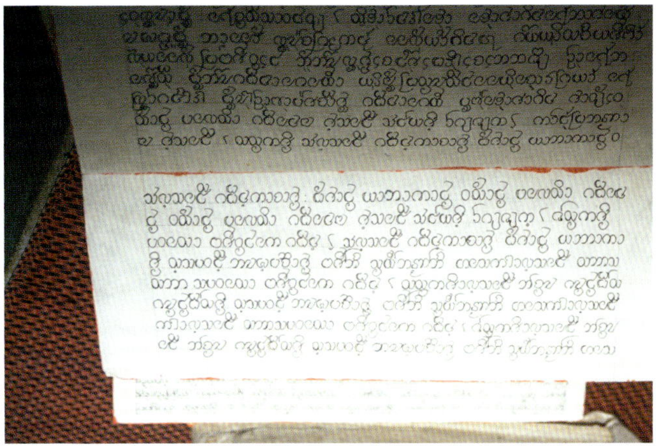

9 Shan script on mulberry paper, forming part of a folding manuscript.

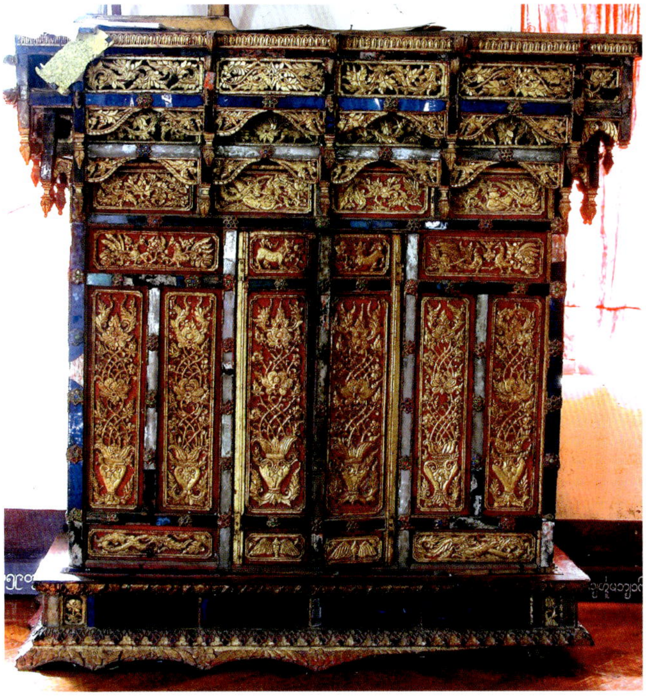

10 An ornate lacquered and gilded manuscript chest in a Keng Tung monastery.

According to Sir George Scott their spoken language was allied to Wa, although he said they denied the connection. There were also Akha, Lahu and Lisu people living in the hills, although they appear to have had less impact on nineteenth century Tai valley dwellers.

The ethnic and cultural identity of Tai royalty living in the Shan States is one of the major themes of this book, but there was a great deal of intermarriage between groups so there is no claim of ethnic purity. Tai royalty took brides from powerful hill tribe families as a way of creating political alliances and maintaining peace. Scott wrote in the nineteenth century that Hkun Hsang Ton Hung, Prince of North Hsenwi (ruled 1888-1913) was of Shan and Wa descent, and one of the most powerful Kachin chiefs had married a princess from Hsenwi. The Palaung ruler of Tawng Peng had a minor wife who was Shan. This book

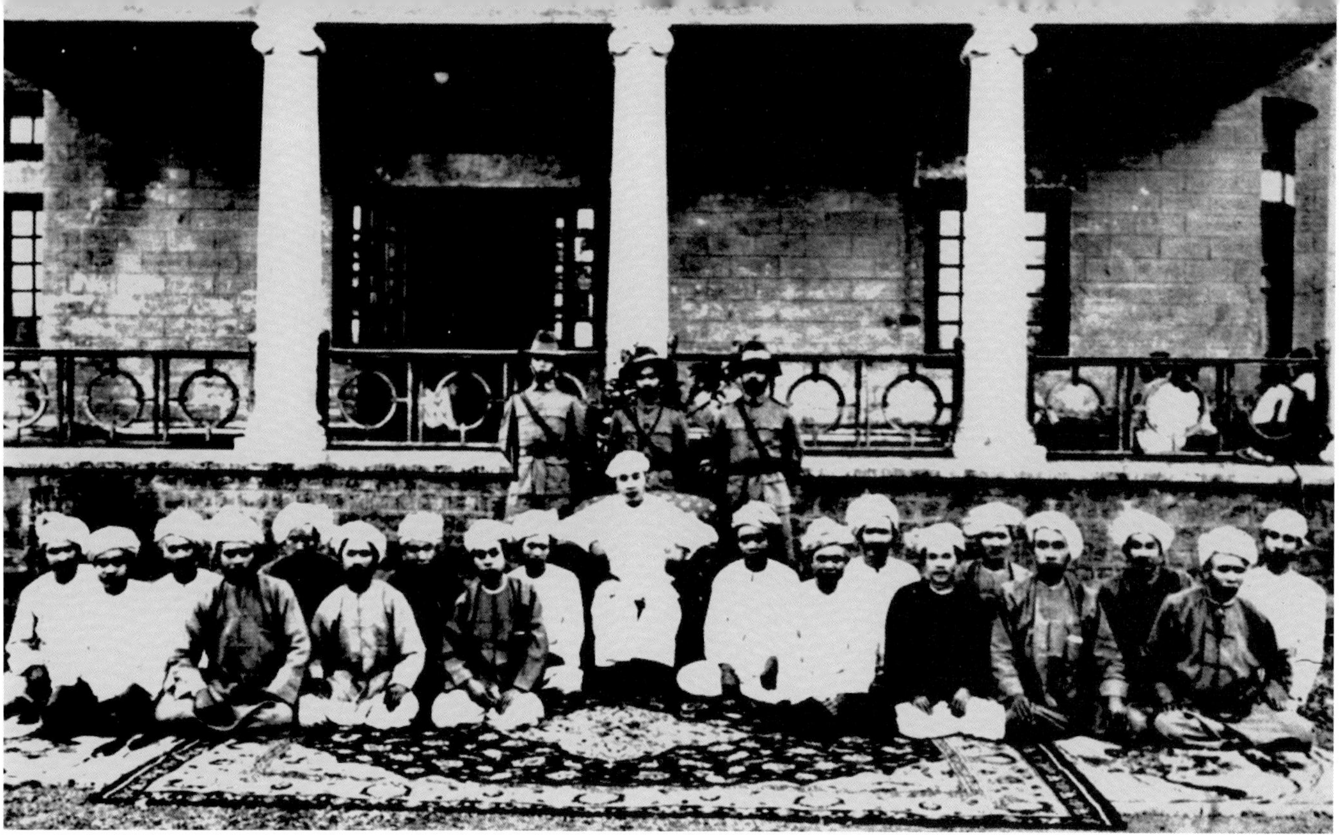

11 Prince Hom Hpa of Hsenwi seated with his officials outside a colonial style building, Shan Palace Museum, Yawnghwe.

contains many nineteenth-century photographs of the princes and chiefs with their consorts in the dress of their hill and valley homelands. These dynastic marriages were celebrated as important political unions but later, at a time when ethnic purity was a political issue, people of mixed race often chose to hide their identity.

Tai royal families in the Shan States intermarried with other Tai from Lan Na, from Sipsong Pan Na and from Laos and they sent their daughters as consorts to the kings of Burma. Princesses of Burmese descent married Shan princes, and it is documented that in at least one instance this led to a Shan consort assuming Burmese kingship.[34] In the nineteenth century the Burmese term *Danu* was reserved specifically for those of Burmese-Shan origin. The Shan chronicles record that the lives of powerful valley dwellers and hill groups were linked through an intricate web of political treaties and marital alliances and also through trade, although local feuds and fighting between them was common.[35]

In these complex circumstances how did the people organise themselves? One of the defining cultural characteristics of the Tai inland valley states is the *muong* (also written as *möng*, *muang* or *mueang*), a term that describes a primary unit of political and social organisation. It has been used to mean a city, a city with village dependencies, or a large, important village. In a geographical sense *muong* means a territorial unit centred in a river valley. A *muong* ruler came from a prominent local family who had acceptable claims to sovereignty. In general a *muong* had one main city where the ruler lived, possibly some smaller towns if it was a large *muong,* and many great and small village settlements. In political terms, *muong* describes a valley society based on mutually beneficial relationships with people coming together for water management, agricultural labour and trade, for defence and for social interaction. The Tai used the term *muong* in the broadest terms when they referred to the Shan States all together as "Muong Tai." The princes who controlled the more powerful *muong* appointed a number of officials to collect tribute (taxes) and report to them at least once a year. The photograph of Prince (*saohpa*) Hom Hpa seated in the middle of his administrators, collectors and village headmen gives a sense of how the system was organised within a *muong* (fig. 11). The seating arrangement and the presence of military guards is an indication of the deference due to him.

The Shan Chronicles provide examples of how the system functioned socially. At the funeral of Prince Mahakhanan of Keng Tung (1781-1857), his son Prince Saenmong, his state ministers, his senior officials and junior clerks with their consorts, performed the invitation ceremony by placing the prince's remains in the coffin. Officials from smaller *muong* who were tributary to Keng Tung, villagers and palace staff slept in the temple compounds and took part in a night's vigil. Official delegations attended from the major *muong* of Muong Nai and from the court of Ava to which the prince of Keng Tung paid tribute. Crown Prince Saenmong led the funeral procession followed by his family, palace officials, royalty from foreign *muong* and officials and representatives of tributary *muong*. Senior princes were mounted on elephants and wore their state regalia.[36] Lay worshippers prepared meals for the public in a thatch and bamboo cookhouse and palace slaves drew the water and prepared the kitchen fires. People from the hills and from the tributary states fed the funeral guests. The ferry workers and fishermen gave one hundred strings of cowrie shells and betel nuts as ceremonial offerings. The tiered roof (*prasad*) of the funeral chariot was provided by tributary *muong* and lay religious communities.

Over the mountains in the next Shan valley there would be another *muong* that might be dominant or be a satellite of a powerful *muong*. As an example, in the nineteenth century the principalities of Muong You and Muong Yong were subject to the authority of Keng Tung that was the greatest power in the region and the princes sent tribute there annually. Keng Tung in turn paid tribute to Burma. Europeans travelling in the inland states had great trouble comprehending the *muong* system. A French expedition in the 1860s was held up for some time because they had assumed that the princes of Muong You and Muong Yong could grant them travel permits for the region but they were told to apply to the Prince of Keng Tung. Their confusion increased when Burmese officials tried to control access to him. A Burmese official wrote to the leader of the expedition accusing him and his team of bad behaviour for not presenting themselves directly at the court of Keng Tung. He ended with the biting statement, "we therefore do not admit people who are so ignorant of good manners."[37] Louis de Carné, an officer with the French party, noted that rivalry for influence and dualism of authority was common in the Shan States, and he stressed that it was essential to be accompanied by an experienced negotiator who understood local politics. Foreigners also needed a great deal of patience. In 1853 an American Baptist minister, Dr. Bixby, tried to circumvent the system by securing passes from the King of Burma and the King of Siam to permit safe passage throughout the Shan States.[38] His Burmese pass was inscribed on a narrow strip of palm leaf about four feet long and was carried in a cloth-covered bamboo container.[39] It is not clear if this prevented the complications experienced by the French.

Further confusion occurred when less powerful states changed allegiance from one Shan state to another. Until 1788 the Shan state of Lawksawk was tributary to the Prince of Yawnghwe but was then granted separate status with a governor (*myosa*) installed as ruler. The *myosa* died without issue and Lawksawk returned to its previous relationship with Yawnghwe. After a number of years Lawksawk changed allegiance to the Prince of Laikha, but on his death, years of uncertainty followed as rival princes fought for sovereignty. Eventually Lawksawk returned to be tributary to the Prince of Yawnghwe, who sent one of his relatives as *myosa*.[40]

The relationship between the Shan States and the surrounding super powers of Burma, Siam and China was also based on a system of tribute. The token of tribute to a superior power was two small trees, one made of gold, the other of silver.[41] The branches of the tree were interpreted as a symbol of the protection that extended over those paying tribute. Powerful kingdoms claimed a percentage of local goods, such as forest products, wood oil, cutch and lac, or were paid in silver. Their main demand was for manpower, particularly conscripts in times of war. Some northern Shan States paid tribute to the Governor of Yunnan as the formal representative of the Emperor of China. The rest paid tribute to Burma or Siam, although in practice the system was more complex. In some cases the princes paid both Burma and China or Burma and Siam (through Lan Na, north Thailand) or China and Lan Na, because they were coerced or because they wanted the super powers as allies and at times, to play them off against each other. These relationships were not stable in the long-term as many princely states changed loyalty as centres of power weakened or strengthened. The Burmese and Chinese were anxious to be on good terms with the most powerful princes and sent them sumptuous tribute exchange gifts. In the early nineteenth century the King of Burma lavished gifts on Prince Mahakhanam of Keng Tung as a reward for not allying himself with neighbouring Chiang Mai, which paid tribute to the King of Siam, a staunch enemy of the Burmese.[42] Interestingly, when the British first established authority in the Shan States, they were presented with tribute. A list of the items accepted by Sir George Scott on behalf of the British Colonial Office included the traditional gold and silver trees, bolts of silk and articles of clothing, animal trappings, candles and spear handles.[43]

Tribute ceremonies (*kadaw*) were occasions when the princes were summoned to the court of Burma to pay respect to the king, and they were lavish affairs. The king, appeared in heavy gold robes encrusted with jewels, and the princes added to the spectacle in their court dress woven and embroidered with gold and silver thread, semi-precious stones and sequins. They and their senior consorts were seated according to strict rules of precedence with minor princes and chiefs placed behind them. The king presented tributary exchange gifts that were graded according to sumptuary law administered by the Burmese court chamberlain (*akyok-won*). Sumptuary law established the type of fabrics, the style of dress, the value of regalia and the jewellery allocated to the princes, their senior consorts and court officials.

Paying tribute to Burma often involved being absent from home for an extended period of time and made the Shan princes vulnerable to coup d'etat, often carried out by rival factions in their own families. In contrast to their obligations in Burma, the Shan princes who paid tribute to China did not go to the Forbidden City (Peking) but only went as far as Yunnan where the Governor accepted the gifts on behalf of the Emperor. Tribute exchange gifts came via Chinese emissaries and included inscribed golden seals, Chinese dragon robes, bolts of silk and jewelled hats.

When they first came to power the British used the tribute system as a way of defining Shan groups. They called the Shan who paid tribute to China "Chinese Shan," those who paid tribute to Burma, "Burmese Shan" and identified the people of Lan Na (north Thailand) as "Siamese Shan" because they paid tribute to Siam. Sir George Scott who lived and worked in the Shan States in the late nineteenth century, attempted to understand the intricacies of the tribute system which he described as "haphazard," and he noted that the Shan princes who paid tribute to Burma frequently ignored sumptuary laws and assumed the regalia and court rituals of the Burmese kings to which they were not entitled. He claimed that they called themselves prince (*chao fa* or *saohpa*) whether or not the Burmese considered them worthy of the title. Scott was assuming that the Shan princes were happy to operate within a system imposed from outside when clearly at times they were not. The ability to flout sumptuary laws depended on a calculation as to whether the King of Burma would and could intervene. In the first half of the eighteenth century the Shan princes had experienced a particularly liberal period when the court of Ava was preoccupied with incursions from Manipur and a Mon rebellion, and the king paid little attention to them. After the British exiled King Thibaw of Burma in 1885, the Burmese system of sumptuary laws collapsed and the princes worked to their own rules of hierarchy. Many Burmese manuscripts that codified sumptuary laws were taken from the Mandalay palace. Scott complained, and it also troubled administrators of the British Empire in India, that Shan rules of precedence had become indiscriminate. Any type of political system that was disorganized made it difficult for the British to assess where the real power lay.

As part of marriage treaties, the Shan princes were expected to give daughters as ladies-in-waiting and as minor consorts to members of the Burmese royal family. If a Shan princess caught the attention of a Burmese king and became one of his four chief consorts or was given the rank of a favoured minor consort, the status of her father and brothers was raised, and they were granted a special audience with the king. During the reign of King Mindon (ruled 1853-1878), a princess from Muong Nai was promoted in this way and her father was given land concessions. In a similar arrangement, senior Shan princes were presented with the daughters of minor Shan rulers who might also be promoted to senior consort status. Other ways of gaining favour with the king of Burma included the presentation of rare gifts. The Prince of Hsawnghsup was rewarded with land, when in 1858, he gave a rare white elephant, considered highly auspicious, to King Mindon.[44]

Many Shan princes can trace their ancestry to before the twelfth century, although local myths and legends give a much earlier history that links them to heavenly beings in the Buddhist Tavatimsa Heaven. According to Buddhist cosmology, a prince was a *bodhisattva* (a being on the way to Enlightenment) who resided in a royal palace built as a symbol of a celestial mountain. He should have a tiered and canopied throne and a tiered crown, symbols of cosmological and protective forces. Only powerful Shan princes reached such elevation and many dwelt in humble circumstances with modest regalia to represent their status. Nevertheless when visitors entered any palace compound, they were expected to respect established rules of obeisance by dismounting from their horses and elephants and closing their umbrellas. When going into the palace itself, they removed their shoes.

Shan social organisation was feudal. A senior Shan prince was addressed as *chao fa* or *saohpa* (*sawbwa* in Burmese), titles that translated into English as "Heavenly Lord" or "Lord of the Sky" or "Lord of the Sunset."[45] If he was particularly powerful he might use the Pali title *raja* or *maharaja*.[46] A prince who ruled over a small principality was often referred to as *chao* or *saohpa-awn* (little *saohpa*). A senior prince had the power of life and death over his subjects and his authority was rarely challenged except by occasional appeals for clemency from senior Buddhist monks. The chief consort of a prince was called *chao* or *mahadevi*, translated as "Great Queen." *Sandadevi* and *nandadevi* were titles that could be bestowed by the Burmese court, according to a code of ranking established in Burma. A senior Shan prince ruled with a deputy and three other princes who had titles indicating their personal loyalty to him. As the princes practiced polygamy, the line of succession was often disputed. The eldest son born to the senior prince and his chief consort was considered the first in line, but the son of a junior wife might challenge him if the eldest son was considered unworthy or incapable of governing. Conflicts arose between brothers making rival claims and in some cases ended in the death of several claimants.

At the township level there were senior officials (*myosa*) who claimed their positions by hereditary right. They supervised local affairs and collected taxes. The Burmese are said to have introduced the term *myosa* ("eater of the town") and it was used by the British when they wrote their reports. The wife of a *myosa* was given the title *thakin-ma*, generally translated as "madam." There were also chiefs called *ngwegunhmu* and *duwa* who ruled over the Karen and Kachin and other hill residing people. Important officials (*amat*), often spoken of as "minor lords," had the power of local justices and travelled with retainers acting as bodyguards.[47]

All officials came to take an oath of allegiance to their ruler at the time of the Buddhist New Year in March or early April, dependent on the phases of the moon. Although the princes ruled a feudal society, the way *muong* were actually administered on a day-to-day basis depended on individual personalities, and in the nineteenth century, on the amount of outside interference in local affairs.[48] It is claimed that the rulers were not oppressive because there was always a shortage of labour and people could choose to migrate to another *muong* where conditions were more favourable. This worked for those subjects who were able to move but many were forced to live their lives in servitude. Every villager was considered the subject of a prince or chief, and farmers paid tribute assessed according to the number of rice fields and buffalo they owned. Tribute was paid as a percentage of farm produce and included rice, orchids, vegetables, fruits, cotton and more unusual commodities such as mineral and vegetable dyes, flares and torches. Forest products such as animal skins, musk and deer antlers were also deemed acceptable. Some villages supplied labour for the ruler's fields while others provided household staff, including mahouts to work the elephants, gardeners for the palace grounds and women to weave, embroider and maintain royal clothing. Metalworkers, carpenters, gilders, painters, lacquer producers and other artisans with specialist skills worked for the princes. Some privileged families had a hereditary right to send their sons as palace guards. They received land in lieu of service.[49] Every male subject fit to serve might be called on for military duty. The system was subject to interference when the Burmese demanded Shan conscripts to fight in their wars, and they forcibly removed artisans and labourers to work for them. The Shan princes were at times compelled to impose heavy taxes on their subjects under instruction from the Burmese court and this created dissatisfaction and unrest.

Although the princes had special status in Shan society, the tenets of the Yuan sect of Theravada Buddhism viewed the destiny of a ruler as dependent on religious merit and not divine incarnation. Shan royal families were not exempt from the Buddhist cycle of death and rebirth and in order to be re-born as senior members of society they had to earn merit. The concept of merit involves reaching a virtuous state of mind in this life and gaining spiritual grace for the next. A prince spent at least one Buddhist Lent in a monastery as a novice monk and throughout his reign he was responsible for merit making by building Buddhist monuments and monasteries and paying for repairs. He financed the installation of gilded umbrellas (*hti*) on the top of *stupa* and paid when it was time for re-gilding. A prince was expected to oversee the well being of the monks and to offer them gifts, and it was his duty to lead the lay

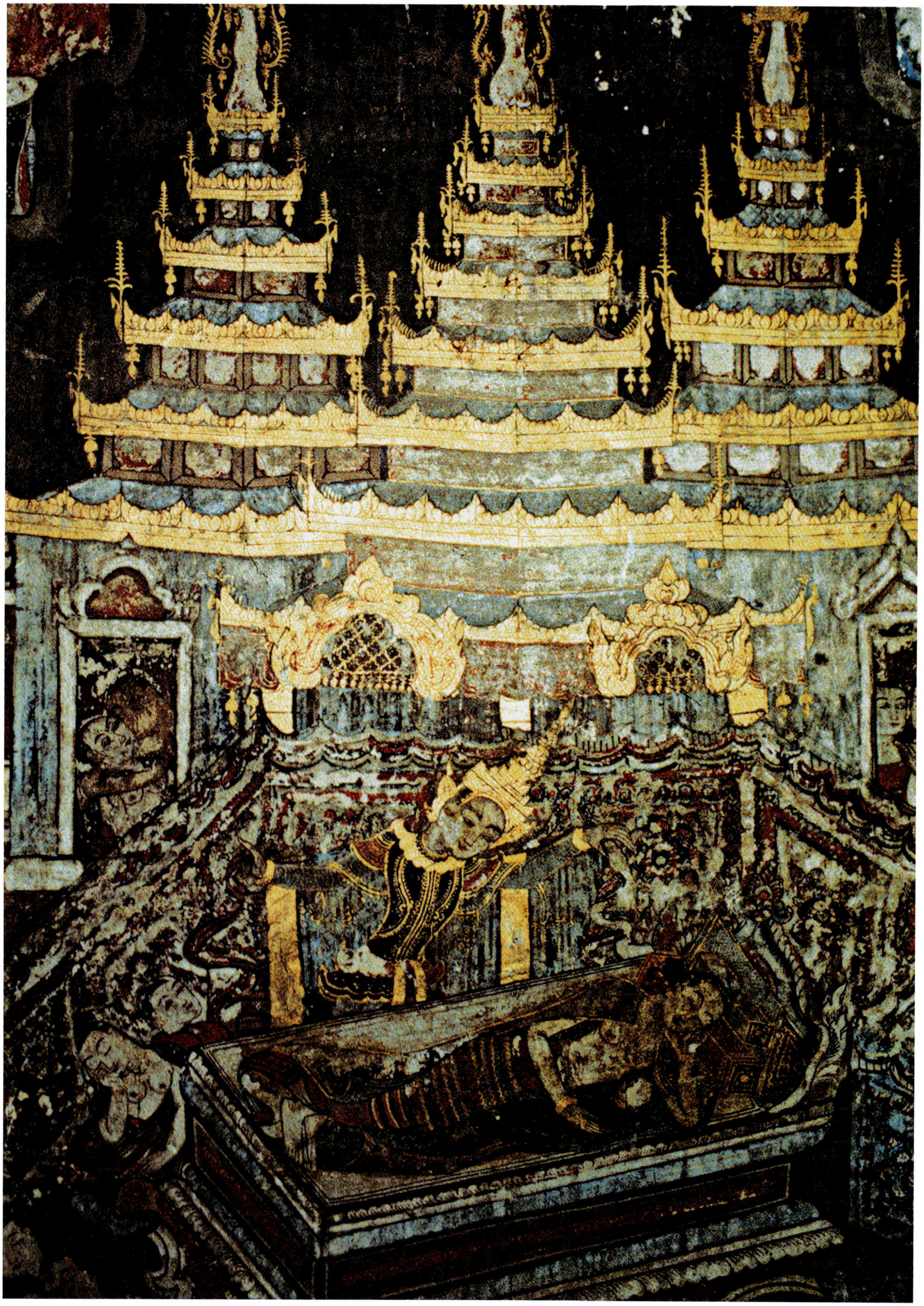

12 Prince Siddhartha gazes on his wife and child before departing from the palace to seek Enlightenment. The palace in the background of this mural painting is in Shan style. Wat Buak Khrok Luang, Chiang Mai.

community in seasonal Buddhist rites. Acts of merit making and gifts to monasteries were recorded on palm leaf manuscripts or on folded paper manuscripts. They listed donations such as Buddha images, temple shrines, monk's robes, blankets and food bowls, woven and embroidered Buddhist banners to hang in the temples, and sets of palm leaves prepared for future manuscripts. The Keng Tung Chronicles record that in the nineteenth century, Prince Mahakhanan of Keng Tung made merit by donating one hundred sets of monks robes and one hundred sets of palm leaf manuscripts, and he financed a rocket festival.

The princes had obligations associated with the guardian spirits of the *muong* (*phii muong*). They officiated at rain making ceremonies intended to guarantee crop fertility and they paid tribute to ancestor spirits (*chao muong*). The main ceremony was held at the time of the Songkhran Festival when the prince went in procession to pour water at the site of the main city shrine, thus ensuring the well-being of the *muong* and all its inhabitants. The princes led other events that included processions to visit important shrines within the principality, the witnessing of ritual sacrifices and the funding of firework displays. Many rituals were localised as in Muong Singh where the prince presided at the sacrifice of a buffalo in a ceremony intended to predict the destiny of the *muong*.[50] When a member of the royal family died the senior prince oversaw the funeral that involved a long and complex series of ceremonies.

Although there was rivalry and skirmishing between states there was also a long tradition of political discourse and trade. Inter-state relations can be judged by the exchange of letters that passed between courts, proving a high degree of literacy and linguistic knowledge among the elite. Many princes spoke Burmese or Chinese, as well as Shan. During the British occupation they learnt English. Each ruler had a distinctive seal that was stamped on all his correspondence (see figs. 173 and 174). Diplomatic missions between states were common and the princes built temporary guesthouses (*tawmaw*) to house important visitors if they could not be accommodated in the palace compound.[51]

The role of women in Shan society is a particularly interesting subject because there are many contradictions. Princesses and the wives of minor chiefs were referred to in the Tai Buddhist chronicles as "followers."[52] In general, when women were referred to in a religious context they were identified as the dependents of men, living as homemakers, nurturers and pious Buddhists.[53] Viewed as potential polluters of monks and men, they were denied access to many rituals. However the power to weaken men could be turned to good effect as shown by the story of Queen Camadevi of Lamphun who, according to legend, wore a white petticoat that became contaminated with menstrual blood. She washed the petticoat and cut it up to make a turban which she sent to an enemy prince. He wore it in battle and was defeated. The Keng Tung Chronicle claims this is the reason why Tai Khoen women wear petticoats under their ankle-length skirts. Myths and legends of this kind appear in all aspects of Shan textile and dress history and even today women's undergarments are feared because of their capacity to weaken men.[54] They are usually laundered separately and hung to dry away from an area where a man's head might accidentally come into contact with them.

The Buddhist interpretation of women as dependents cannot be applied to women in their working lives. Village women were free to choose their marriage partners and

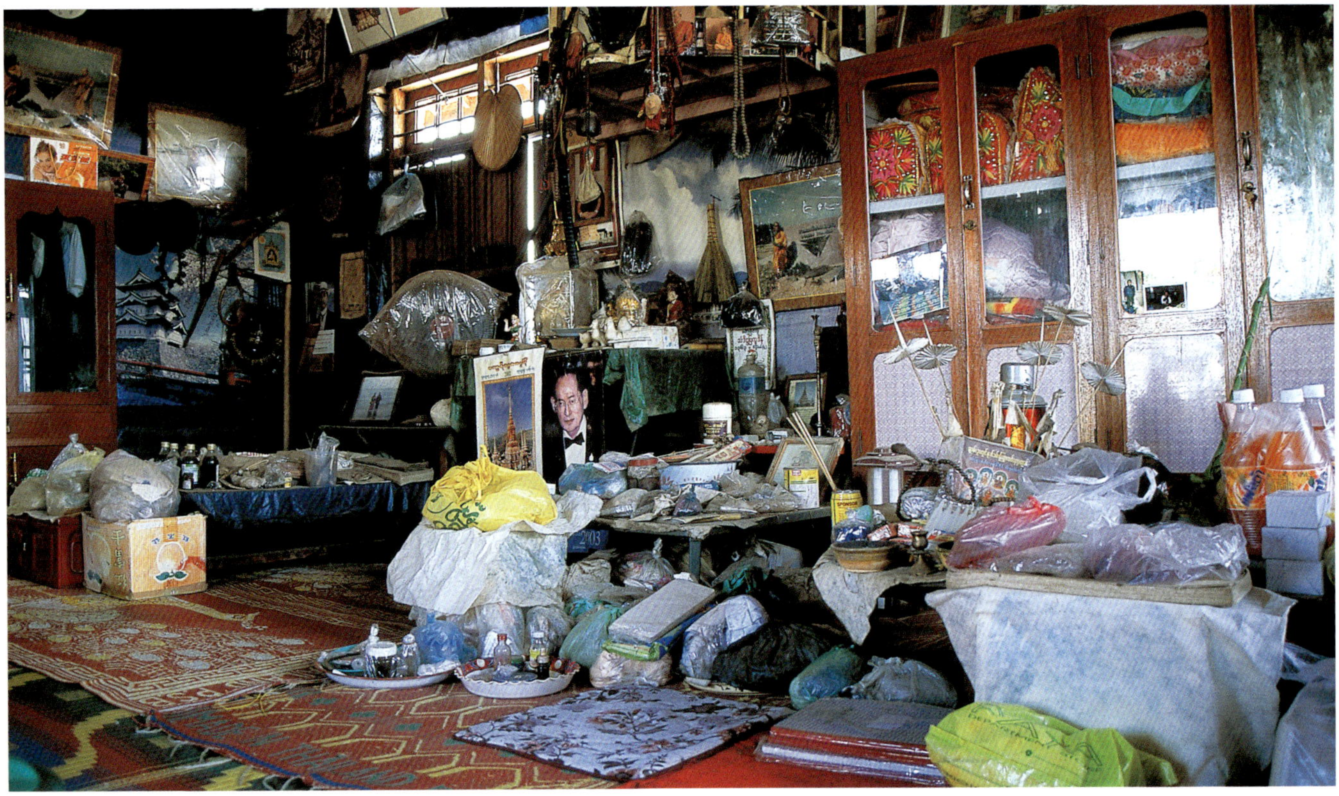

13 The audience room of a shaman in the Shan States.

were not confined in the home. They travelled to early morning markets on a regular basis to sell their produce and they shared heavy physical labour with men in the rice fields. There were female pilots operating on the rivers and female porters carrying heavy loads. This evoked mixed feelings among male European travellers who were surprised and sometimes embarrassed when women arrived to carry their packs. They were probably not aware that women dressed as men had fought bravely in the First Burmese War (1824-1826) against the British.

> *These Amazons, dressed in warlike costume, rode constantly among the troops, inspiring them with courage and ardent wishes for an early meeting with their foe...... Another of the Shan ladies was here observed flying on horseback with the defeated remnant of her people but before she could gain the opposite bank of the river, where a friendly forest promised safety and protection, a shrapnel exploded above her head....*[55]

Some European men openly admired the accomplishments of Shan women. Maurice Collis commented on the ferrywomen working on the River Nam Pang, a wide tributary of the Salween.[56] Women had many opportunities to prove their courage, physical strength and shrewd marketing skills. One of their most significant roles was as spirit (*phii*) mediums and healers; if they needed to invoke a male spirit they dressed as men. Although they are fervent Buddhists women were and remain, deeply involved in spirit propitiation.[57] Having power over the spirits gives them authority at village level and in many cases, influence among the elite.

In judging the overall freedom of men and women in Shan society it is important to take account of the tribute system. Women were subject to the authority of the prince rulers in the same way as men. They might be called to work in a ruler's house or in his fields, or be forced to pay tribute in the form of farm produce and household goods. Those women not called on for labour were often left at home to bear the brunt of farm work when a ruler summoned men. In contrast to village women, princesses were often betrothed when they were as young as six and might be married as early as fifteen. Marital alliances were arranged according to an ancient system of hierarchy. Shan manuscripts record that in 751 BE (1389 AD) the Prince of Maw, a Shan state in the Mogaung area, presented his graceful and virtuous daughter Princess Shinminauk to the King of Burma as a sign of submission. The king consulted a court minister who advised him that the princess was not senior enough to be his wife and she was given instead to one of the kings' younger sons.[58] When they married the Shan princesses had to tolerate a system of polygamy. This led to jealousy, rivalry and intrigue between consorts and their children. Many endured these conditions far from home and rarely had an opportunity to visit their relatives.

However on a more positive note some princesses were major traders owning packs of animals and human porters. In the absence of a suitable male, some princesses managed state affairs. Nang Keng Kham, mother of the *myosa* of Hopong administered the state while her son was a minor, and in the 1830s a female regent ruled Keng Hung. The impressive Princess Tip Htila, daughter of Prince Chotikong of Keng Tung ruled for two years until her brother Prince Intaleng came of age and then assisted him in skirmishes with the Chinese. Later she married the *myosa* of Keng Kam and ruled there for eleven years following his death. The British colonial magistrate and writer Maurice Collis wrote:

> *....during half a century she had commanded men. She knew all about men, their fighting, their greed; she knew how to dominate and how to deceive them.*[59]

Following her time as regent Princess Tip Htila set up business as a merchant, using elephants to transport goods, and she also controlled a band of muleteers, riding at the head of convoys armed with a rifle (fig. 283). She was not the only trader, as other Shan princesses managed forestry concessions, and in the late nineteenth century traded with the Bombay-Burma Company. At some courts there were princesses acting as interpreters.[60] The active participation of female royalty in politics, in commerce and in the rites of spirit religion led to a more egalitarian form of society than existed in many Asian and European courts.

The religion of the Shan States is Theravada Buddhism that remains relatively faithful to the original teachings of the Buddha. This involves the concept of human life in a continuing process of change. The aim of religious practice is to free oneself from the materialism of the world, a goal expressed in the rules that govern the life of Buddhist monks. The ultimate aim is to reach nirvana, the extinction of the suffering embodied in the cycle of birth and rebirth. Lay members of the community accept a number of precepts that include attending temple ceremonies and feeding and clothing the monks. In this way the lay community make "merit." The concept of merit involves reaching a virtuous state of mind in this life and gaining spiritual grace for rebirth.

The Shan form of Theravada Buddhism was known as the Yuan sect and, according to the Chronicle of Hsenwi, was established in the northern Shan States by monks from Chiang Mai who also introduced the Yuan religious script. The Yuan sect flourished until the early Konbaung period (1752-1819) when Burmese monks were sent to teach Thudhamma Burmese Buddhism. Many Shan people continued to favour the Yuan sect and disdained court Brahmanism, accepted as part of the Burmese form of Buddhism.[61] It has been argued that the introduction of the Thudhamma sect affected the religious language and writing

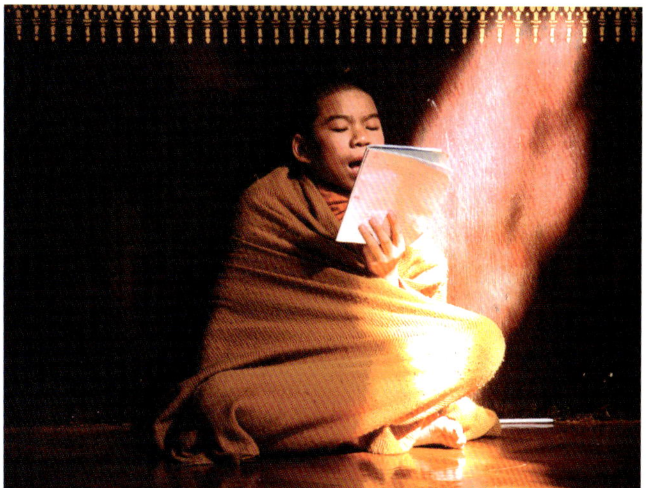

14 A young novice monk chanting in the morning light, Keng Tung.

systems of the Shan and separated them from other Tai Buddhists practicing in inland Southeast Asia. However, Shan rulers like the princes of Hsenwi and Keng Tung, and many abbots and monks continued to support indigenous monastic traditions and the use of local scripts even if they were abandoned elsewhere. The manuscripts deal with more than religious texts, they are also concerned with local history and indigenous folk tales, astrology, herbal medicine and magic formulae. Yuan, Lue and Khoen manuscripts, written on Shan paper and on palm leaf, were still being produced at the beginning of the twentieth century, particularly in Hsenwi, Keng Tung and in the Chinese Shan States. The Khoen dialect and script is still flourishing in Keng Tung where it is considered to be a special gift of the Buddha.[62]

Shan monasteries enjoyed a great deal of autonomy and in the cities were supported by royalty and citizens, while village communities sustained smaller religious centres. In the nineteenth century the monks made up about three per cent of the population. Although they lived separately from the lay community, they were not isolated from local affairs and functioned as intermediaries between the ruling elite and the people. Some senior monks intervened when they felt that there was injustice and appealed for the lives of those threatened with execution. They pleaded for remission of taxes in times of famine and natural disaster, and they appealed to officials against the unfair confiscation of land. The monastery was the place where local people entrusted their valuables and family heirlooms in times of war and forced migration.

Throughout inland Southeast Asia the Tai built elegant monasteries from teak (*Tectona grandis*) and from red brick. For interior and exterior decoration the wood carvers used *yamane*, a hardwood from Mogaung, and *yindaik* similar in texture to ebony and sandalwood.[63] There were no nails in the construction as carpenters used tenon and mortise joints. Vertical teak pillars formed the basic structure and were set on brick or stone bases. Floors were added above ground level allowing for air circulation and to prevent flooding of the interior in the monsoon season. Woodcarvers worked on the roof decoration, door lintels, doors, window blinds, balustrades and verandahs. They produced exquisite floral and foliage motifs that twisted and curled in two and three- dimensional forms, interspersed with Buddhist iconography and with graceful images of animals, birds and characters from Shan legends. They come to life in the extremes of intense light and deep shadow associated with tropical landscapes.

Maurice Collis wrote:

> *On the following morning I went to see the Temple of Heaven. In Shan this is called Wat In and it is the most famous monastery in Keng Tung. The monks…live in houses in the compound of the main structure. The appearance of the exterior supports what I have said about the existence of a Kengtung style. The architecture is neither Burmese Siamese nor Chinese and appears to be a creation of a genius loci. On the pillar of the main gate… is a tiger and a celestial daughter…The porch between two dog-lions is rustic and leads to a paved way and on to the entrance door of the main building, which is constructed of old brick and roofed with tiles made in the town…..as you enter the great hall you are amazed at the colour, pillars decorated in red and gold with ecclesiastical designs and golden spirits painted on the walls.*[64]

Monasteries were repositories for manuscripts written in local scripts and for indigenous Buddhist art and crafts. Shan artisans created distinctive Buddha images that were carved from wood and gilded with thin sheets of gold leaf. Monastic furniture, including preaching chairs and stands were produced in a similar way. Manuscript chests were also carved from wood and decorated with gilded moulded lacquer (fig. 17). Items such as small Buddha images, monk's fans and bowls, and manuscript covers were lacquered and gilded. Some decoration in the temples, including stands for Buddha images, were inlaid with semi-precious stones and coloured glass cut in geometric patterns. Shan artisans also produced metal bells that were suspended on frames with separate wooden or metal strikers (figs. 19 and 20). They were sited either in the grounds of the temple or in the main building. They were sounded by the faithful at the time of merit making and used by the monks to mark their pre-dawn rising, their devotions, meal times and retirement in the evening. Many are ancient. According to the monks of Wat Maha Kaew, Keng Tung, the main monastery bell has been in use for over five hundred years.

As many Shan monks reside in the main monastery building where religious ceremonies are held, space has to be allocated for worship and for living quarters. There is a main shrine room (*pyathat-hsaung*) where Buddha images are set on a raised dais; this area is marked on the outside by a multi-tiered spire (*pyathat*). The abbot or presiding monk has a separate area for study and for sleeping. A large reception hall (*hsaung-ma-gyi*) serves as a multi-purpose room that can

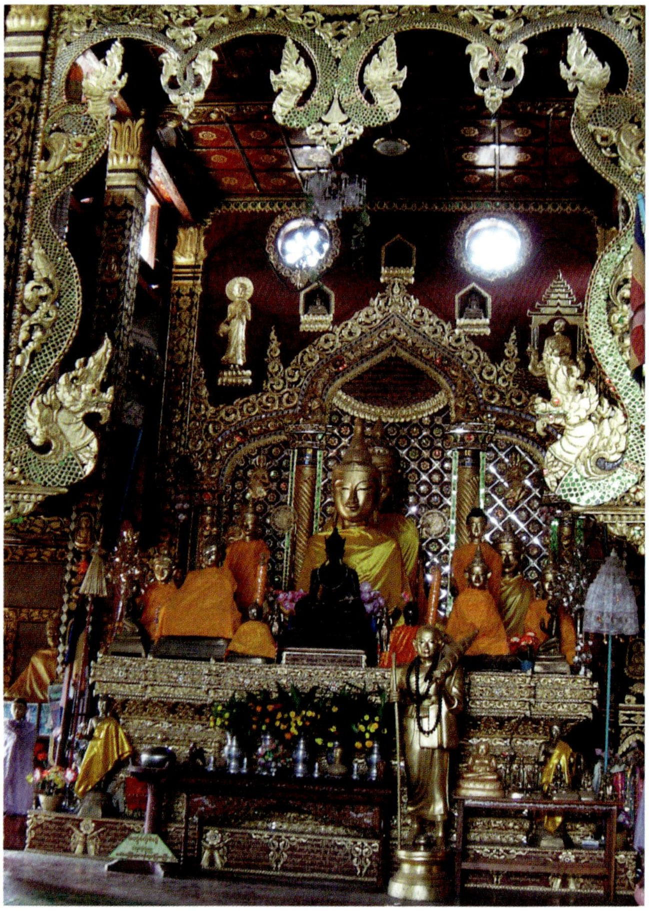

15 A lacquered and gilded altarpiece in a Shan monastery, Keng Tung.

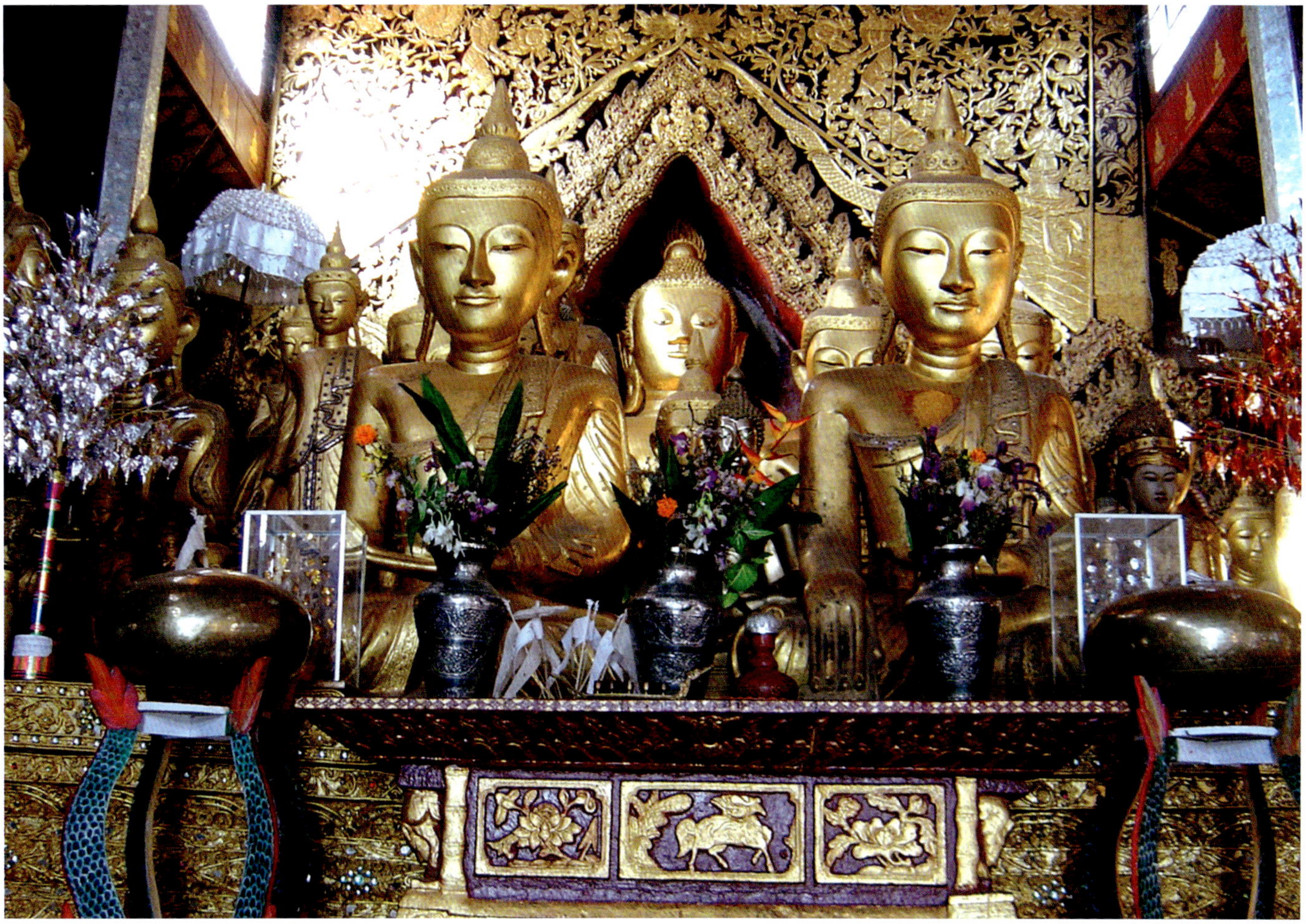

16 Gilded Buddha images on the altar of a temple in Keng Tung.

18 A gilded and inlaid monk fan and stand carved in the shape of a peacock.

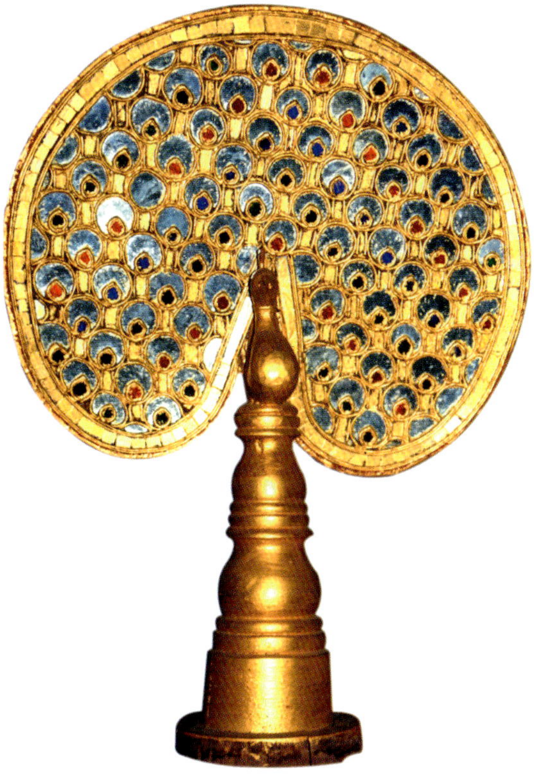

17 Detail of a lacquered, gilded and inlaid manuscript chest in the collection of the Shan Palace Museum, Yawnghwe.

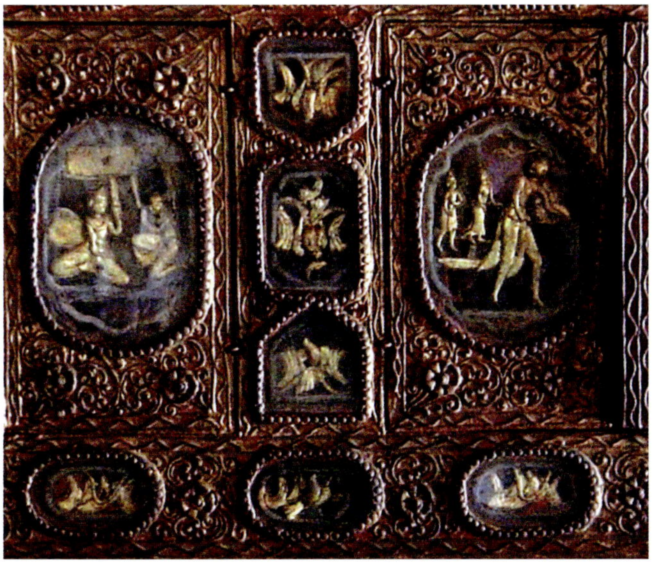

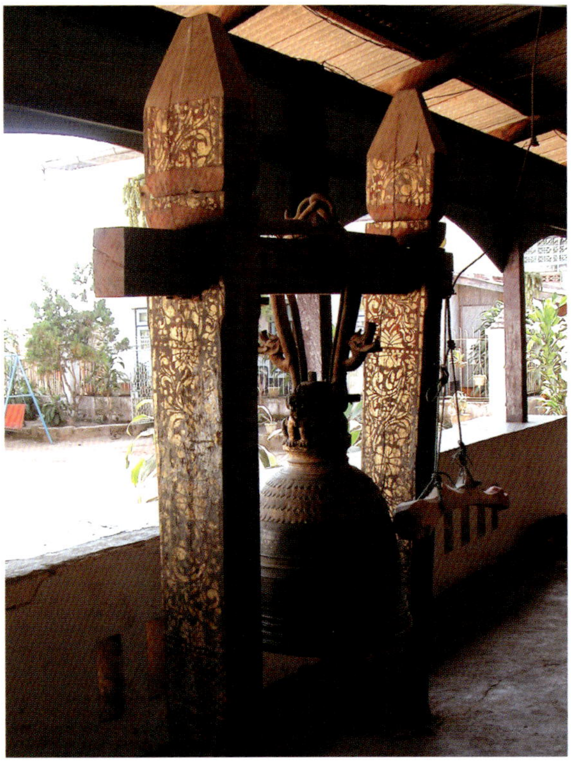

19 A bronze temple bell on a gilded and stencilled wooden stand, with a separate wooden striker, Keng Tung.

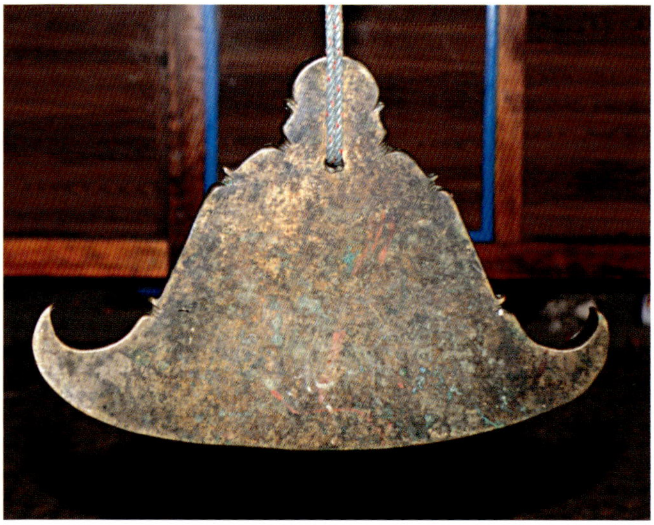

20 A metal striker for the temple bell at Wat Maha Kaew, Keng Tung. The striker is said to date to the sixteenth century.

be divided to provide sleeping quarters for the monastic community, an area where novices are instructed and a zone where visitors can be received. Behind the reception hall is a store where the monks also keep their few belongings. A wide veranda circles the entire building. Shuttered windows can be adjusted to allow air to circulate while blocking out intense light. In the monasteries of Keng Tung and the eastern Shan States, monks usually resided in separate wood or brick buildings, and there were separate storerooms.

Shan villagers decorate the monasteries at the time of seasonal rites, particularly during the Kathin Festival and the Bun Phrawes merit-making ceremony that occurs after the rice harvest. The area of the temple where the lay community worship is decorated with flowers, streamers and banners. In the temple grounds long woven banners are strung on bamboo poles taller than the trees that surround them. As they spin in the breeze, the banners are viewed as symbols of merit, drawn spiralling upwards to Heaven. They also act as a landmark so that everyone can see from a distance that a festival is taking place. The people use such occasions as an opportunity to appear in their best clothes and jewellery.

One of the most important events for a family is the time at the beginning of the Buddhist Lent, when a young man is ordained as a novice monk. This act makes merit for the family and particularly for his mother. On the day of his ordination he travels to the monastery on horseback, or in a specially constructed chariot. He is dressed as a prince in a sequined robe, shoes and hat, and a gilt umbrella is held over him. His family and sponsors carry his monastic robes, his bed linen, sandals, his bowl for collecting food and a palm-leaf fan. Before the ceremony of acceptance he is divested of his princely robes, his hair is cut, his head and eyebrows are shaved and he takes a ritual bath. Clad as a novice, he becomes part of a monastic community for about three months, the period of the Buddhist Lent.

Although Buddhism is the mainstay of life, the people also pay great respect to the spirits. The Shan princes and chiefs were responsible for the appointment of official representatives to supervise spirit guardians to protect and maintain important spirit shrines and prepare them for seasonal festivals. One of the most important aspects of spirit religion involves appeasing the water spirit. According to local legend, in ancient times when irrigation systems were first constructed, a human sacrifice to the water spirit was made at every weir.[65] In pity for the victims of this cruel practise, the sister of a Shan king intervened and gave her life as a way of ending the custom. From that time, carved wooden images of the princess, overlaid with gold leaf, were placed in all the shrines situated by major weirs, and they became a focus for other images, including attendant guardian figures.

This legend is similar to another Shan myth involving a female guardian spirit in the form of a serpent (*naga*), whose carved wooden image was appeased at seasonal rainmaking ceremonies and land fertility rites. In some instances the image took a male form and was known as "the great father." With grotesque features, bulging eyes, a long nose and exaggerated nostrils, the image was crowned with a five-tiered diadem and covered in gold leaf. It was considered to be so potent that it was kept hidden in a shrine behind locked doors. Once a year the spirit guardian opened the doors briefly so that villagers could make offerings, although many chose to avert their eyes from the image in fear of its enormous power. Even when the image was firmly locked away, the shrine was the subject of intense superstition and villagers who passed dismounted from their ponies, climbed out of their bullock carts and took off their shoes. If they failed to perform such obeisance, they feared sickness and bad luck.

Another famous shrine on the outskirts of Keng Tung commemorates a Shan princess and her brother. She was the daughter of the *saohpa* of Hsipaw and married King Anawrahta of the Pagan Dynasty (1044-1077). The king's

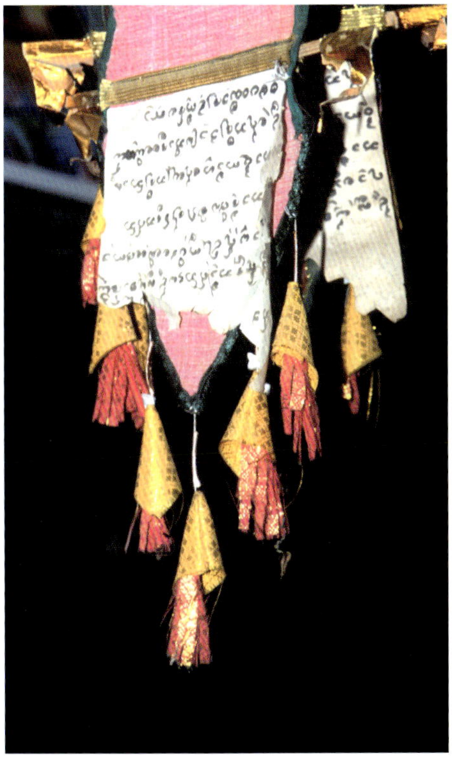

21 The decorative border of a temple banner, Wat Zom Khum, Keng Tung.

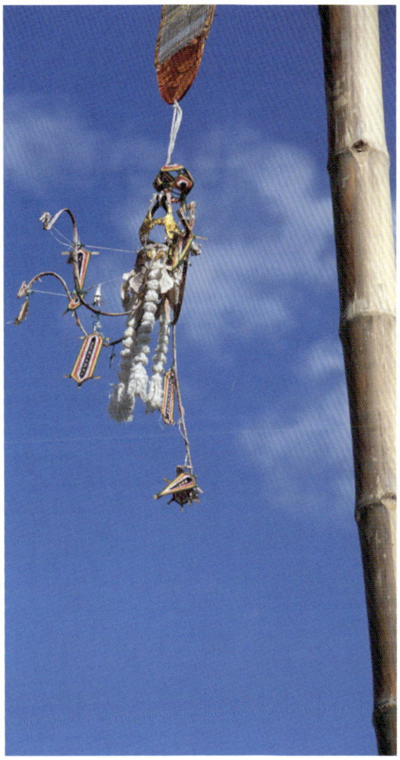

22 A banner flying from a bamboo pole in the grounds of Wat Ho Ko, Keng Tung.

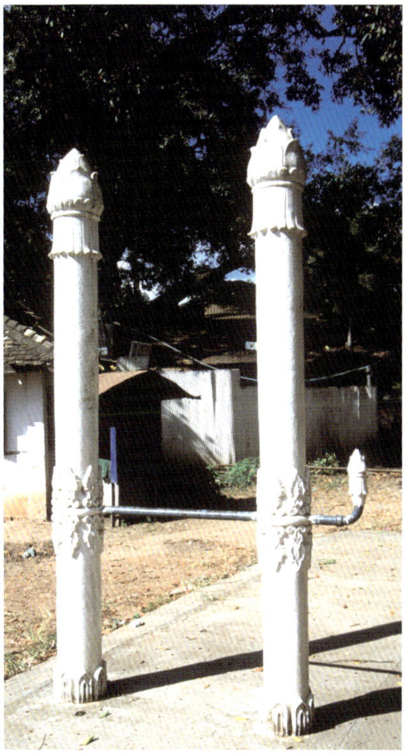

23 The stand for the town drum used during the *pwe leun ha* festival. It is situated near the spirit shrine of Keng Tung.

other consorts did not like this Shan princess because her diamond earrings sparkled at night and they suspected that she was an evil spirit. They persuaded the king to have her killed by burning on a pyre. When the pyre was lit, her brother jumped on with her, and both perished.

In years when spirit rituals failed to bring rains, villagers made more offerings of rice wine, chicken, pickled tea and eggs. A male intermediary recited incantations appealing for water, peace and deliverance from all evil. When the rice is harvested it is customary to make similar offerings of thanks to the rice goddess, particularly before the rice is threshed. Vegetables, rice, curry and liquor are also prepared for other spirits who are summoned to accept the offerings and protect the rice barns where the grain is to be stored.

Although they can bring good fortune, spirits can also be cruel and vindictive and are propitiated at every stage of life and in death. Many are considered to be the spirits of humans who have died in tragic circumstances. Their effigies are reproduced with specific gestures and attributes and dressed in a way that makes them instantly recognisable. As in other regions of inland Southeast Asia, the Shan spirits take particular forms. Their invocation involves music, song, dance and drama performed at ceremonies and festivals. At village level a local medium might be called to a house where someone is thought to be possessed. The family prepares a special bamboo altar with offerings of meat, rice, vegetables and fruit. The medium invokes the spirit by placing a copper or brass plate near the altar and studying it carefully until the shadow of the spirit appears. She dances until she gradually enters a state of trance. The person thought to be possessed also enters a trance, which is viewed as a way of aiding the exorcism.

Astrologers also contributed to the general well-being of society with their predictions of, and remedies for, unusual incidents. In the fourteenth century there was a severe drought in the state of Keng Tung and the reigning prince consulted his astrologers. They calculated that Keng Tung belonged in the Monday planet but the ruling family were Tai Yuan people from the Wednesday planet, a disharmony creating a planetary clash that caused the drought. Twenty-four Tai men from Muong Yang were summoned to Keng Tung to beat the auspicious drum that hung inside the compound of the main spirit shrine. They were dressed in red and white robes and by order of the astrologers the drumbeat was to continue for two days. The drum was then carried in procession, followed by a man on horseback dressed in the robes of the guardian protector of Buddhism. The procession followed a prescribed route to a local river creek. Villagers lined the route to sprinkle scented water as the procession passed. A clay statue of a frog and a crescent moon, representing the Monday planet was constructed in readiness on the bank of the creek, and when the procession arrived the town elders recited from the Buddhist scriptures. The frog and moon were pushed into the creek and the procession made its way to a point near the Maha Muni Pagoda in the city of Keng Tung, where four monks recited from the scriptures. The drum was taken to the Keng Zan monastery, and when it was installed the rains began and the drought ended. This ceremony is still performed in Keng Tung and the drum remains one of the most important artefacts in the city.[66] The stand is situated in the vicinity of the spirit shrine.

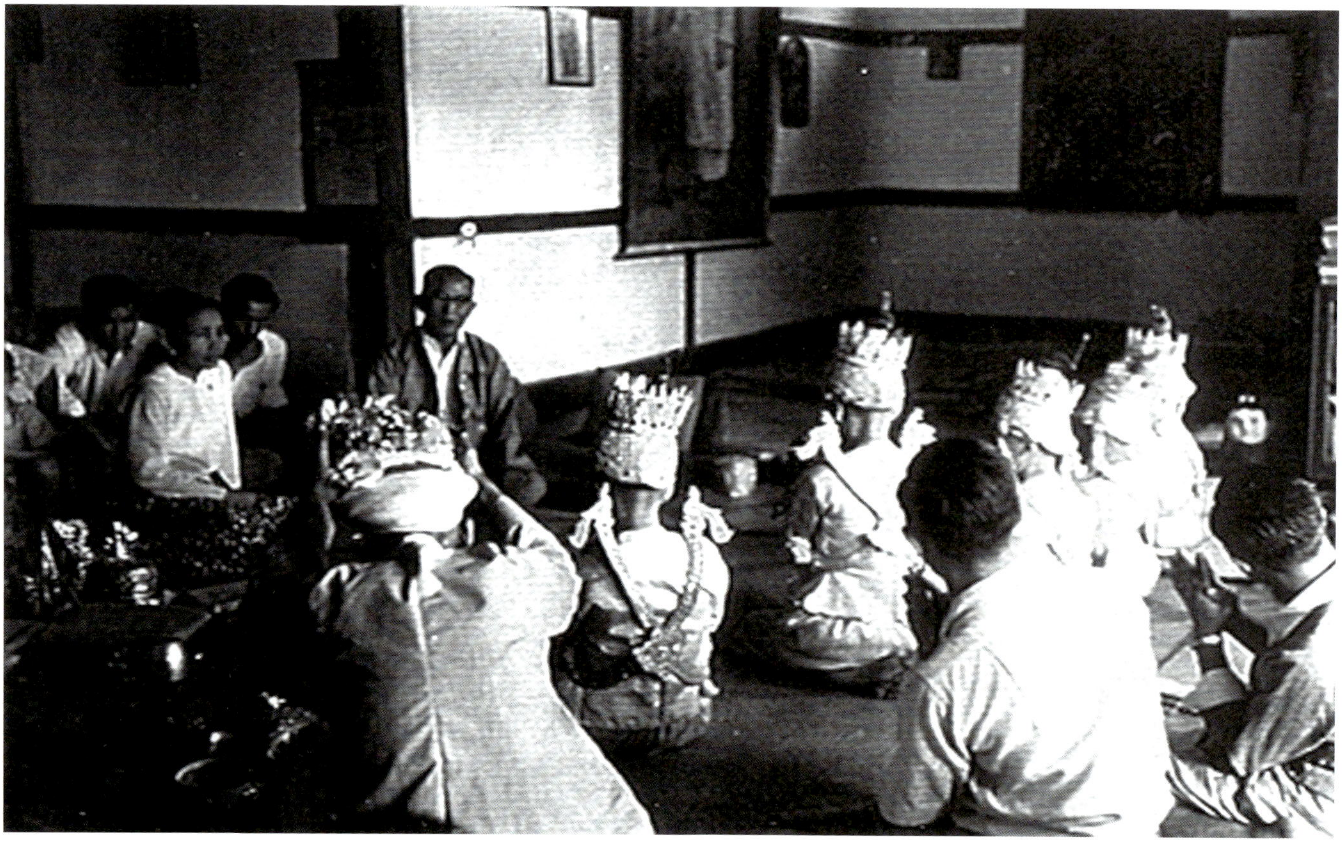

24 An ordination ceremony with the young prince Sao Hkam Vai Hpa of Hsenwi among the novices, circa 1960.

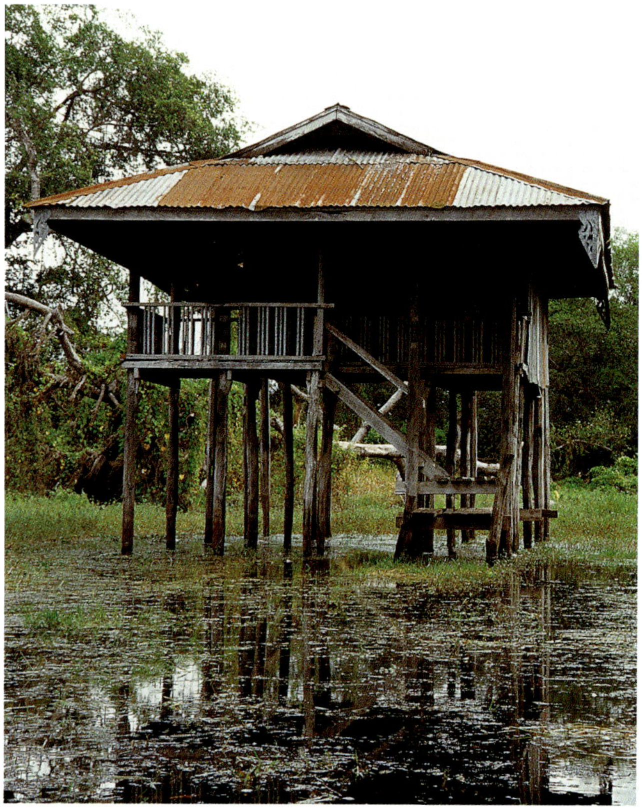

25 A spirit shrine on Inlay lake. Visitors arrive by boat.

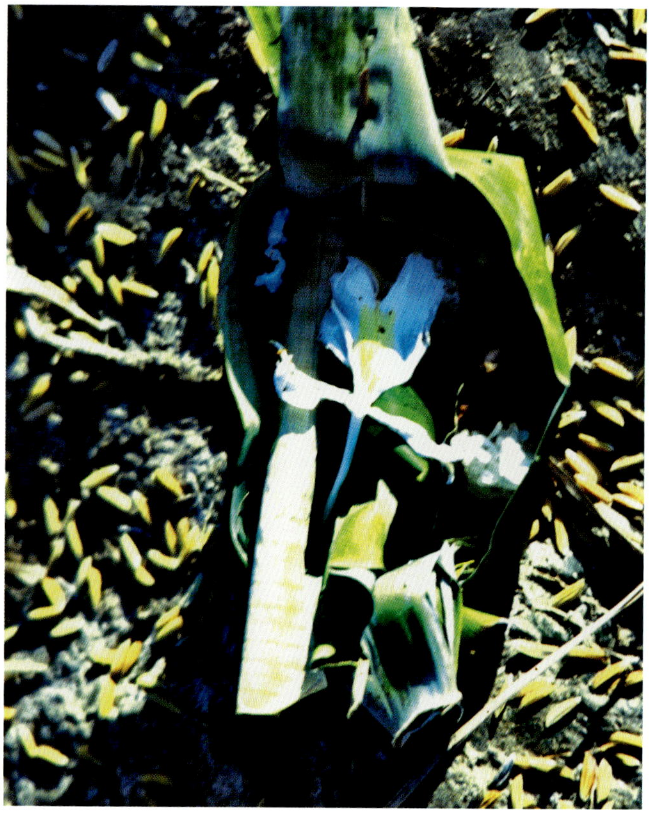

26 An offering to the rice goddess *(mae posop)* placed among the rice grains.

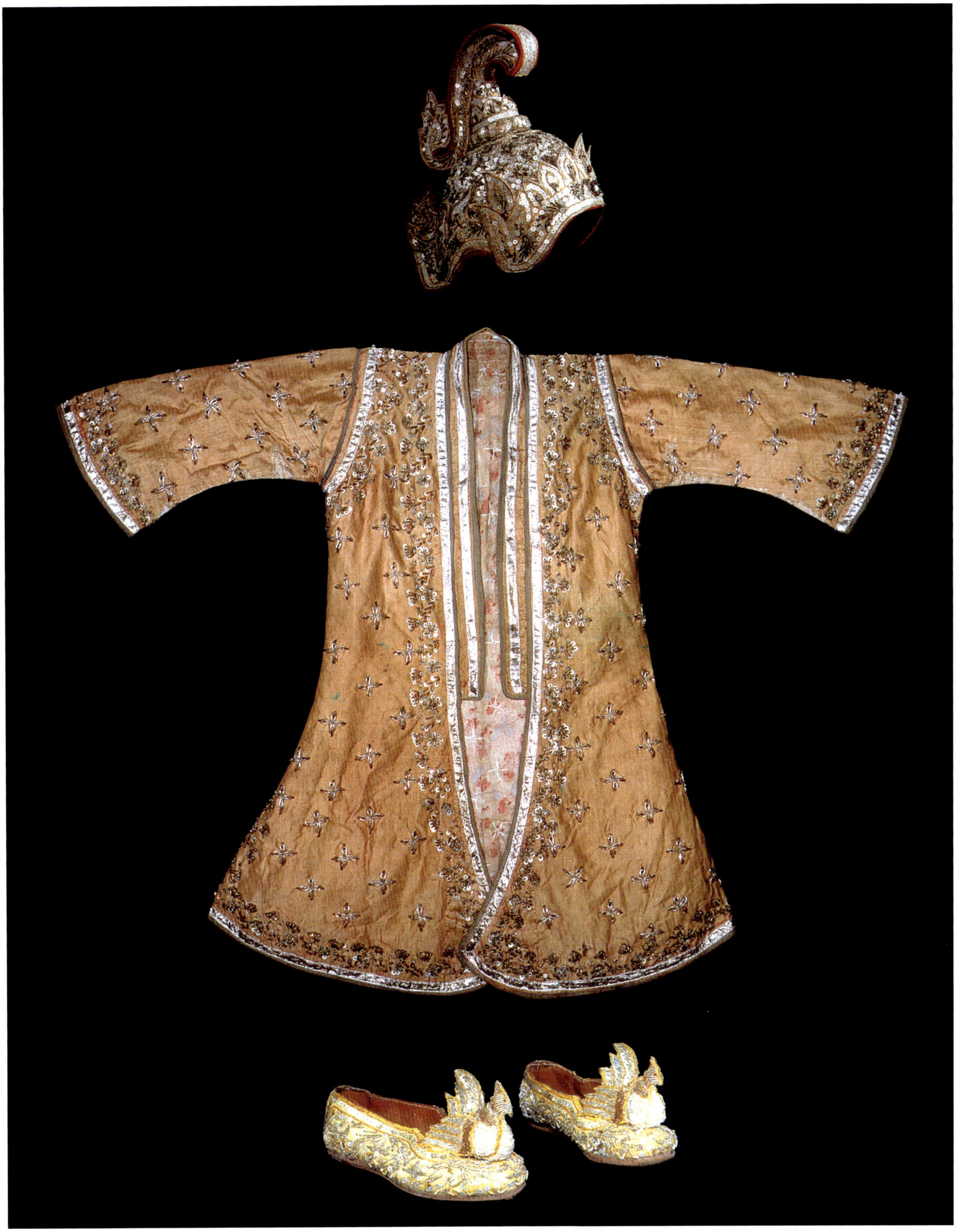

27 A crown, robe and shoes worn by a novice monk in the ceremony before his entry to the novitiate.
(Akadet Nakbunlung collection)

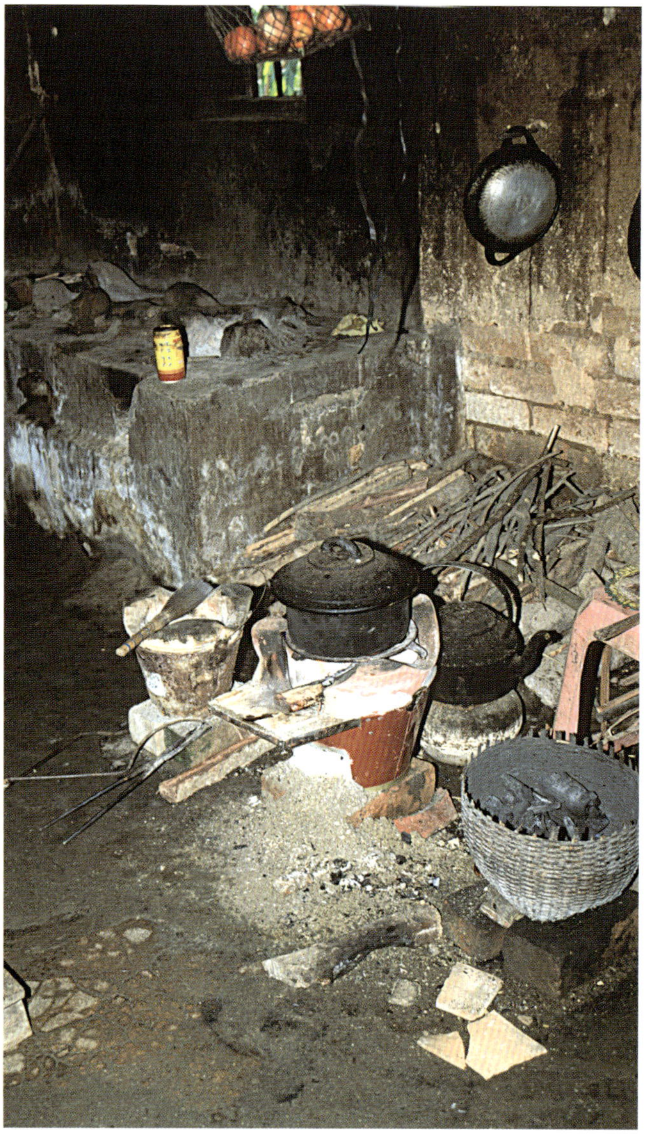

28 The kitchen in a Shan village house.

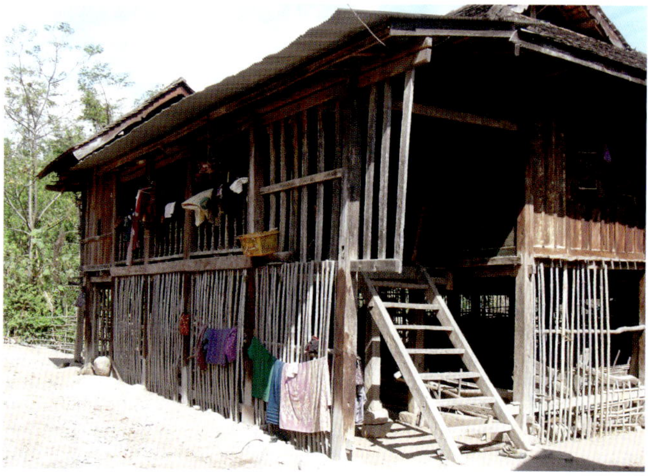

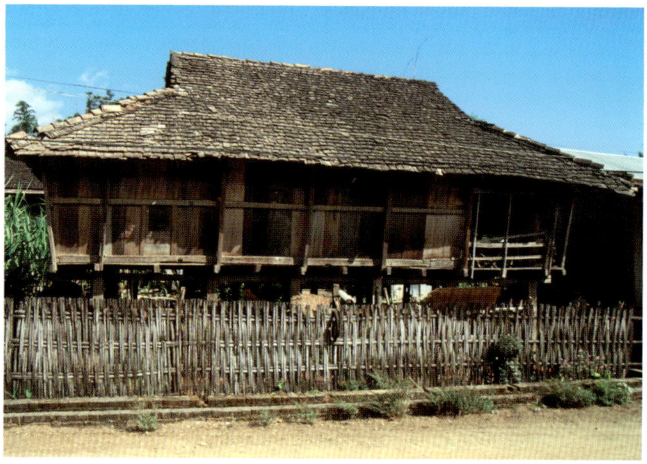

29 and **30** Wooden Shan houses in a village in the Keng Tung valley. To enter the living quarters one goes up a wooden ladder. The area under the house is used to store agricultural equipment, to dry crops, to keep small animals and is also the area where women set up their looms.

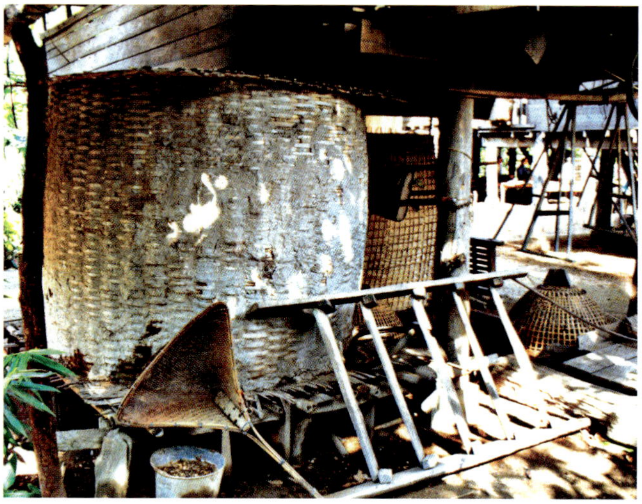

31 A rice granary made of plaited bamboo, rice straw and mud.

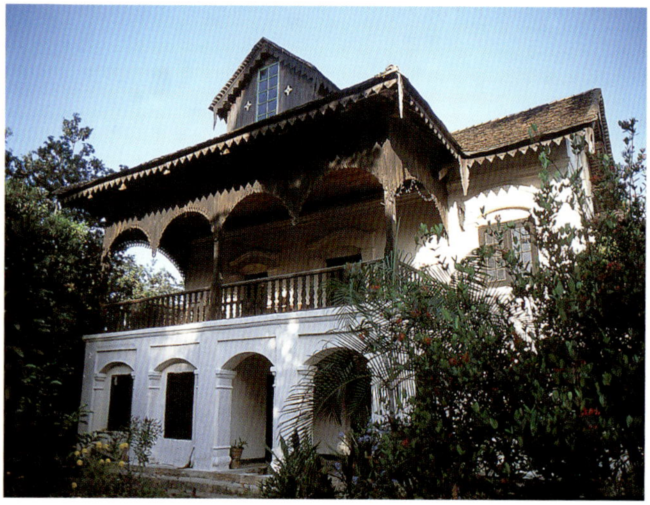

32 The palace of Prince Wun Wat, son of Prince Inthaleng of Keng Tung. It was situated next to the palace of Keng Tung, that was demolished in 1991.

Shan shaman and astrologers attained their qualifications by serving an apprenticeship with a recognised master. This often involved dieting and wearing white clothing.[67] A shaman might be inducted by drinking water mixed with the ashes of magic scrolls and specially prepared supernatural potions. In many cases their bodies were tattooed with mystical symbols and diagrams. The Yuan sect of Theravada Buddhism allowed some Shan monks to be practitioners by reaching the status of "esteemed teachers."[68] Some monks also learnt the arts of astrology and fortune-telling. It is probably due to their intervention that images of the Buddha, his disciples and attendants (*deva*) were incorporated in mystical diagrams. Many monks were prepared to add a blessing to amulets, charms and magic cloths created by spirit priests, and interestingly many Shan people believed that a monk's blessing was essential for a charm to reach its full potential. Monks were expected to use magical powers only for good, particularly for protection.

Shan village architecture involves building on wooden piles. Roofs are made of clay tiles fired locally or of thatched rice straw. The walls are made of wood or woven split bamboo, either coated with a mixture of mud and straw or varnished. Wealthier families build their houses with locally fired brick. The space under the house is used to dry farm produce, raise farmyard animals and is the place where the loom is set up in the weaving season when women's labour is not required in the fields. There is a separate rice granary, built of wood or woven bamboo, raised above ground to prevent rats from entering. The garden may have a well, plots for vegetables, herbs and flowers and mulberry, if the household is engaged in sericulture. A bamboo fence surrounds the garden. To enter the house one removes shoes and passes up a wooden staircase and onto a covered veranda. Well-shaded from the sun, yet open to the breeze this is the place where casual visitors are received, sitting on woven rush mats. The interior of the house has a living room where more formal visits take place. There is a kitchen with a simple hearth, or a charcoal-burning stove. The sleeping room or rooms are off the living room, although they may only be separated from the main living area by curtains. Sleeping mattresses are laid out at night, each with a mosquito net and pillow, sheets and blankets, which are all put away during the day. There is a space at the back of the house for washing and for laundry.

Shan palaces were constructed in a similar way to monasteries with the audience hall of the prince, like the main shrine room (*pyathat-hsaung*) marked on the exterior by a multi-tiered roof. The private quarters of the senior prince and his chief queen were situated in the front of the building, on a higher plane than the residences of the minor consorts who were housed at the rear where kitchens and storerooms were also located. Palace interiors and roof structures were decorated with exquisite woodcarving, and teak pillars and door lintels were stencilled with gold paint, gold leaf and cinnabar. Although many wooden Shan palaces were masterpieces in terms of construction and the quality of the woodcarving, they were not deemed important in the opinion of many foreign scholars of Southeast Asian art who focussed attention on stone and brick buildings and stone and metal sculptures. It was somewhat in line with this judgement that Captain McLeod described the palace of Keng Tung.

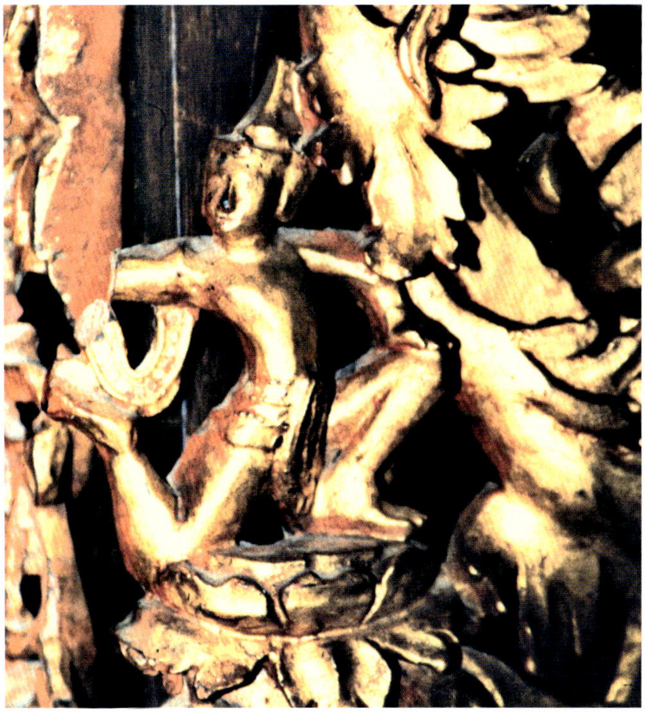

33 Detail of a carved and gilded wooden figure forming part of the interior decoration in a Shan palace.

> *On the 22nd of February I was introduced to the Tsobua [saohpa] ...On arriving at the gate of the palace enclosure the officer with me asked me whether I would dismount as no person ever entered it on horseback; knowing their customs I immediately complied with his request. On entering the gate I could not help observing the total absence of care and neatness in the compound. It was overgrown with grass and the outhouses in a dilapidated state, and the whole surrounded by a brick and mud wall of eight feet high. The palace itself, a shabby looking pile of wood, raised about fifteen feet from the ground on high pillars. After ascending the steps, and on reaching the door of the hall, the Tsobua's two sons came forward and led me to a seat in front of the Tsobua, where carpets had been spread for me and my followers.*[69]

The Shan princes also built less substantial, temporary accommodation (*tawmaw*) when large numbers of guests were to be accommodated.

The Shan palaces and the regalia associated with authority were graded according to rank and sumptuary law. There are important issues concerning the control of this system. Burmese sumptuary law was administered through the court of Ava in the late eighteenth century and from Mandalay in the nineteenth century by the office of the Lord Chamberlain (*akyok-won*). Burmese and Shan manuscripts illustrate in detail what members of the Burmese royal family, tributary state rulers and officials were entitled to use on ceremonial occasions. Writing in 1795 the British envoy Major Michael Symes claimed that the *saohpa* and *myosa* were told how many tiers the roofs of their palaces should have, how many white or gold umbrellas they were entitled to use and how many articles of royal regalia they were allowed to display. He wrote that almost every article that the princes wore on official occasions, and the regalia that decorated their palaces were allocated according to rank.[70] Symes was describing the system at the height of

Burmese power and as it was viewed from the court of Ava. As was stated earlier Sir George Scott complained of its ineffectiveness in the Shan States. Far away from the Burmese court the princes maintained their own ranking system.

According to an ancient Tai legend, passed from generation to generation through story telling, eight guardian spirits taught women how to cultivate cotton and spin and weave cloth. There are other legends involving Khun Borom, a ruler from Sipsong Pan Na, Laos or Lan Na, depending on where the story is being told, who proclaimed that weaving was a household duty to be carried out with skill and diligence, to bring respect in this life and spiritual merit in the next. Shan hand-woven textiles were a symbol of the well-balanced rhythms of social and religious custom and an expression of women's creative talents. Weaving fitted into the yearly cycle of rice production and Buddhist festivals. It was valued as a household duty to be carried out with skill and diligence, to bring respect in this life and spiritual merit in the next.

Stone and wooden artefacts and temple mural paintings give a sense of dress in early times. By the nineteenth century dress and textile designs had evolved and changed to assimilate the designs of indigenous hill and valley dwellers. Chinese, Burmese and Indian traders enriched the supply of yarns, fabrics and trimmings available in the Shan States. The choice of yarn, the type of weaving patterns, the colours, the use of imported as well as locally produced fabrics, the chosen style, whether tailored or created by wrapping and tucking around the body, and the choice of trimmings helped to define nineteenth century dress as belonging to a particular ethnic group. Although some items of dress were consistent, many groups did not have strict codes and purchased items of clothing from other groups, particularly in years when there was a good harvest and excess money or materials for barter were available. Changes in fashion affected even remote hill tribe outposts. Those who were resettled away from their homelands either continued to wear their usual form of dress or were forced to adapt to new circumstances.

Although there was a great deal of adaptation and change, "traditional" dress was used as a way of displaying ethnic allegiance and political solidarity. Tai Khoen women from the Shan state of Keng Tung who were resettled in Chiang Mai in the early nineteenth century continued to wear Khoen dress as a symbol of their separate identity from the Tai Yuan community.[71] It was customary for princesses to wear the dress of their homeland when they married into a foreign royal family. If a prince gained a number of consorts particularly from more powerful states and from different ethnic groups, then bringing them together publicly signalled the extent of his influence.

While women often maintained "traditional" dress, the Shan male elite adapted their dress to suit prevailing political authority. When tributary to Burma they wore Burmese ceremonial dress and regalia that was allocated to them according to sumptuary law. If tributary to China, they received and wore Chinese textiles and robes. Many reserved this dress for specific rituals and wore indigenous court dress, considered prestigious by the standards of local society, on other occasions. This often included imported Chinese, Siamese and Burmese fabrics mixed with locally woven and embroidered cloth and worn in local style. The allocation of dress and regalia to subordinates depended on the power and hierarchical nature of individual courts. Body decoration, particularly tattooing, an important custom among men, was not hierarchical and there were no particular symbols to denote rank.

In the late nineteenth century the people of inland Southeast Asia were under pressure from Great Britain, China, Siam and France who were extending their authority in the region. In this atmosphere dress became a potent symbol of cultural characteristics that bound individual ethnic populations, expressed their desire for recognition and, in some cases, for independence. Such behaviour is seen today among minority groups like the Kachin and Karen who frequently express nationalism through "traditional" forms of dress.[72]

Some expatriates working in the Shan States in the nineteenth and early twentieth centuries built collections of dress and textiles and at a later date, many were donated to museums in Europe and the USA. They are a helpful tool in understanding the range of dress and textiles worn by hill and lowland groups, but the collectors often classified ethnic groups and sub-groups by the colours, stripes and weaving patterns of their clothes which has left a confusing and contradictory legacy.[73] They were gathering material in a particular place and in a specific time frame, although the collections were often treated as a benchmark for "correct" dress. The people of the Shan States were constantly modifying their dress to suit political and economic conditions, and this phenomenon is represented in Shan court collections. These issues challenge the concept of "traditional" or "correct" ethnic dress and force us to think in terms of continuity and change, themes that will be examined in chapter four.

In order to maintain court ceremonies, the princes required regalia that was produced either within the confines of the palace compound, or by groups of artisans working in close proximity in the town or a nearby village. In the nineteenth century there were wood carvers, metal workers, goldsmiths, silversmiths, lacquer makers, inlay specialists, painters, weavers and embroiderers and many other artisans working in the Shan courts and in the villages, producing beautiful objects in a specific Shan style.

The Shan States were a complex network of principalities operating under the traditional Tai *muong* system with people in the outlying areas controlled by their own leaders. As observed by officials from Burma, Siam and China, and later from Britain and France, the Shan States appeared as a complicated world of fragmented ethnic categories but in fact it was also a land where sophisticated political networks and alliances operated. The major powers tried to control the region but were hampered by poor roads and rivers that were not navigable in many states. As will be evident in chapter two, the Shan were able to repel or seriously undermine many invasions, although they suffered loss of population due to forced resettlement particularly following defeat in war. What held them together was their unique culture. It was expressed through language and written scripts, through a distinctive form of Theravada Buddhism and spirit religion and a *muong* political system. It is also evident in religious and domestic architecture, and in their beautiful arts and crafts.

Endnotes

[1] J. G. Scott, *Burma, A Handbook of Practical Information*, London 1906, reprint, Orchid Press, Bangkok 1999.
[2] *Ibid*.
[3] Sir Arthur Phayre Collection 13th Nov 1886, OR3478 A-1, India Office Collections, The British Library, London. Arthur Phayre was Chief Commissioner of British Burma, 1862-1867.
[4] India Office Collections, The British Library, Map OR3478A and Map OR3478B.
[5] Capt. McCleod 1837, quoted in Grabowsky, V. and Turton, A., *The Gold and Silver Road of Trade and Friendship*, Silkworm, Chiang Mai, 2003, p. 364.
[6] India Office Collections, The British Library, London, Map 3478E.
[7] Letter from Burney to Blundell dated Rangoon June 20th 1834, ORC BUR MSS 2, India Office Library, The British Library, London.
[8] Excerpts from The Sipsong Pan Na Chronicle translated by Pen Suwannarat, Chiang Mai, 2003, n.p.
[9] Frank M. Le Bar, Gerald C. Hickey, and John Musgrave, *Ethnic Groups of Mainland Southeast Asia*, New Haven: Human Relations Area Files Press, 1964, pp. 95, 193-215; Dodd, William Clifton, *The Tai Race: Elder Brother of the Chinese*, The Torch Press, Cedar Rapids: 1923, reprint, White Lotus Press, Bangkok 1996, pp. 170-274.
[10] Sir George Grierson, quoted in J. G. Scott, *Burma and Beyond*, London, 1932, p. 26.
[11] Edmund R. Leach, *Political Systems of Highland Burma*, G. - Bell, London, 1954, p. 41.
[12] Charles Keyes, 'Kin Groups in a Thai-Lao Community', in G. William Skinner and A. Thomas Kirsch (eds.), *Change and Persistence in Thai Society: Essays in Honor of Lauriston Sharp*, Cornell University Press, Ithaca, 1975.
[13] An adaptation from a Shan legend, oral communication, Chiang Mai, 2002.
[14] D. G. E. Hall, *A History of South-East Asia*, Macmillan, London, 1955, reprint, 1968, pp. 10-11.
[15] W. C. Dodd, *The Tai Race: Elder Brother of the Chinese*, The Torch Press, Cedar Rapids, 1923, Zhu Liangwen, *The Dai*, D. D. Books, 1992.
[16] Tawee Sawangpanyankoon, Chiang Mai University, n. d.
[17] Recently the Chinese government has introduced a new alphabet for the Sipsong Pan Na (Xishuang Banna) region to replace the old Tai Lue alphabet.
[18] Today the Shan comprise 10-15% of the population of the Union of Burma (Myanmar).
[19] Maurice Collis, *Lords of the Sunset: A Tour in the Shan States*, Faber and Faber, London, 1938, reprint, Bangkok, 1996.
[20] George Young, *The Hill Tribes of Northern Thailand*, The Siam Society, Bangkok, 1962.
[21] Scott, 1906.
[22] Sao Saimong Mangrai, *The Padaeng Chronicle and the Jengtung State Chronicle* translated, University of Michigan Papers on Southeast Asia, no. 19, University of Michigan, Ann Arbor, Michigan, 1981.
[23] Susan Conway, *Silken Threads Lacquer Thrones*, River Books, Bangkok, 2000.
[24] Leach, 1954.
[25] Scott, 1906.
[26] Mandy Sadan, 'The Kachin Photographs in the J. H. Green Collection: a contemporary context', in *Burma Frontier Photographs* Merrell, London, 2000, p. 187.
[27] O. Hanson, *The Kachins: Their Customs and Traditions*, American Baptist Mission Press, Rangoon, 1913, p. 12.
[28] J. G. Scott and J. P Hardiman, *Gazetteer of Upper Burma and the Shan States*, 5 vols., Rangoon, 1900, Vol. I. pt. II, p. 124.
[29] *Ibid*.
[30] Interview with Eleanor Gaudoin, member of the royal family of Hsenwi, Brighton, 1993.
[31] Milne and Cochrane, *Shans at Home*, London 1910, reprint, Paragon London, 1970, pp. 187-188.
[32] Scott, 1906.
[33] San Po, *Burma and the Karens*, 1928, reprint White Lotus, Bangkok, 2001, Scott, 1906, Gilhodes, A., *The Kachins* 1922, reprint, White Lotus, Bangkok, 1996.
[34] Dr. Richardon noted that the saopha of Muang Pai paid allegiance to a powerful Karen chief.
[35] Sir Arthur Phayre, *History of Burma*, London 1883, reprint, London, 1967.
[36] Rujaya Abhakorn, 'Chiang Tung and the Thai State Before 1948', Proceedings of the 16th Conference of the International Association of Historians of Asia, Kota Kinabalu, Sabah, Malaysia, 2000.
[37] Sao Saimong Mangrai, *The Shan States and the British Annexation*, Data Paper no. 57, South East Asia Program, Cornell University, Ithaca, New York, 1965, p. 263.
[38] Louis de Carné, *Travels on the Mekong*, Paris, 1872, reprint White Lotus, Bangkok, 2000, pp. 181, 191.
[39] Dr. Bixby first went to Burma as a Baptist missionary in 1853. He left for the US in 1856 and returned to the Shan States in 1861.
[40] From the archives of Denison University, Granville, Ohio.
[41] Scott and Hardiman, 1900.
[42] Capt. Henry Yule, *A Narrative of the Mission Sent by the Governor-General of India to the Court of Ava in 1855*, London 1858, reprint Oxford University Press, Kuala Lumpur, 1968.
[43] de Carné, 2000, pp. 191-196.
[44] Scott, 1906.
[45] Vincenzo Sangermano, *The Burmese Empire A Hundred Years Ago*, Westminster, London, 1893.
[46] Contary to received wisdom, this included many British officers visiting the palaces.
[47] Maurice Collis used the term "Lord of the Sunset".
[48] The title *cherand daw* or *cheyin daw* that in English translates as "Royal Presence" or "Royal Feet" was reserved for the King of Burma. The supreme title *bawashin mintaragyi*, translated as "Lord of Life and Great and Just King" was also reserved for the King of Burma.
[49] Collis, 1996, p. 131.
[50] Scott, 1906.
[51] Mangrai, 1965.
[52] Thipmuntali Khampaeng, 'The Tai Lue of Muang Singh' in Grant Evans (ed.), *Laos Culture and Society*, Silkworm Books, Chiang Mai, 1999.
[53] C. M. Wilson and L. M. Hank, *The Burma-Thailand Frontier over Sixteen Decades*, Monographs in International Studies, Southeast Asia Series, no. 70, Ohio University, 1985, p. 12.
[54] Interview with Dr. Roongruangsiri, Chiang Mai University, February 1997.
[55] Michael Rhum, *The Ancestral Lords*, report no. 29, Monograph Series on Southeast Asia, Center for Southeast Asian Studies, Northern Illinois University, De Kalb, 1994, pp. 156-157.
[56] Mangrai, 1981.
[57] J. J. Snodgrass, *Narrative of the Burmese War,* London, 1826, reprint 1997, Bangkok, pp. 231-235.
[58] Collis, 1996.
[59] Melford E. Spiro, *Burmese Supernaturalism*, Prentice Hall Inc. New Jersey, 1967, p. 59.
[60] Parabaik 26, ORC BUR MSS 2, India Office Collections, The British Library, London.
[61] Collis, 1996, pp. 293-295.
[62] de Carné, 2000, p. 198.
[63] David Steinberg (ed.), *In Search of Southeast Asia*, 1971, reprint University of Hawaii Press, Honolulu, 1987.
[64] Observations by the author in Keng Tung, November 2004.
[65] Harry L. Tilly, *Wood-carving of Burma*, Superintendent of Government Printing and Stationery, Rangoon, 1903, p. 1.
[66] Collis, 1996, pp. 281- 282.
[67] R. Grant Brown, 'The Lady of the Weir', *Journal of the Royal Asiatic Society*, July 1916, pp. 491-496.
[68] From a phamphlet compiled by U Sai Lone Seng Lung, Secretary, Gon Shan Literature and Culture Committee, Keng Tung, n.d.
[69] Oral communication with a shaman, Keng Tung, November 2004.
[70] Charles Keyes, 1971, 'Buddhism and National Integration in Thailand, in *Visakha Puja*, B.E. 1514, Bangkok, pp. 22-34.
[71] Captain McLeod, 22nd February 1837, quoted in V. Grabowsky, and A. Turton, *The Gold and Silver Road of Trade and Friendship*, Chiang Mai, 2003, p. 344.
[72] Micheal Symes, *An Account of an Embassy to the Kingdom of Ava sent by the Governor-general of India in the year 1795*, London, 1800, reprint, Madras, 1995, p. 310.
[73] Dodd, 1996, p. 201.
[74] Sandra Dudley, 'Whose textiles and whose meanings', in *Textiles from Burma*, E. Dell and S. Dudley (eds.), Philip Wilson Publishers, 2003, pp., 37-47.
[75] Scott, 1999, pp. 75-76.

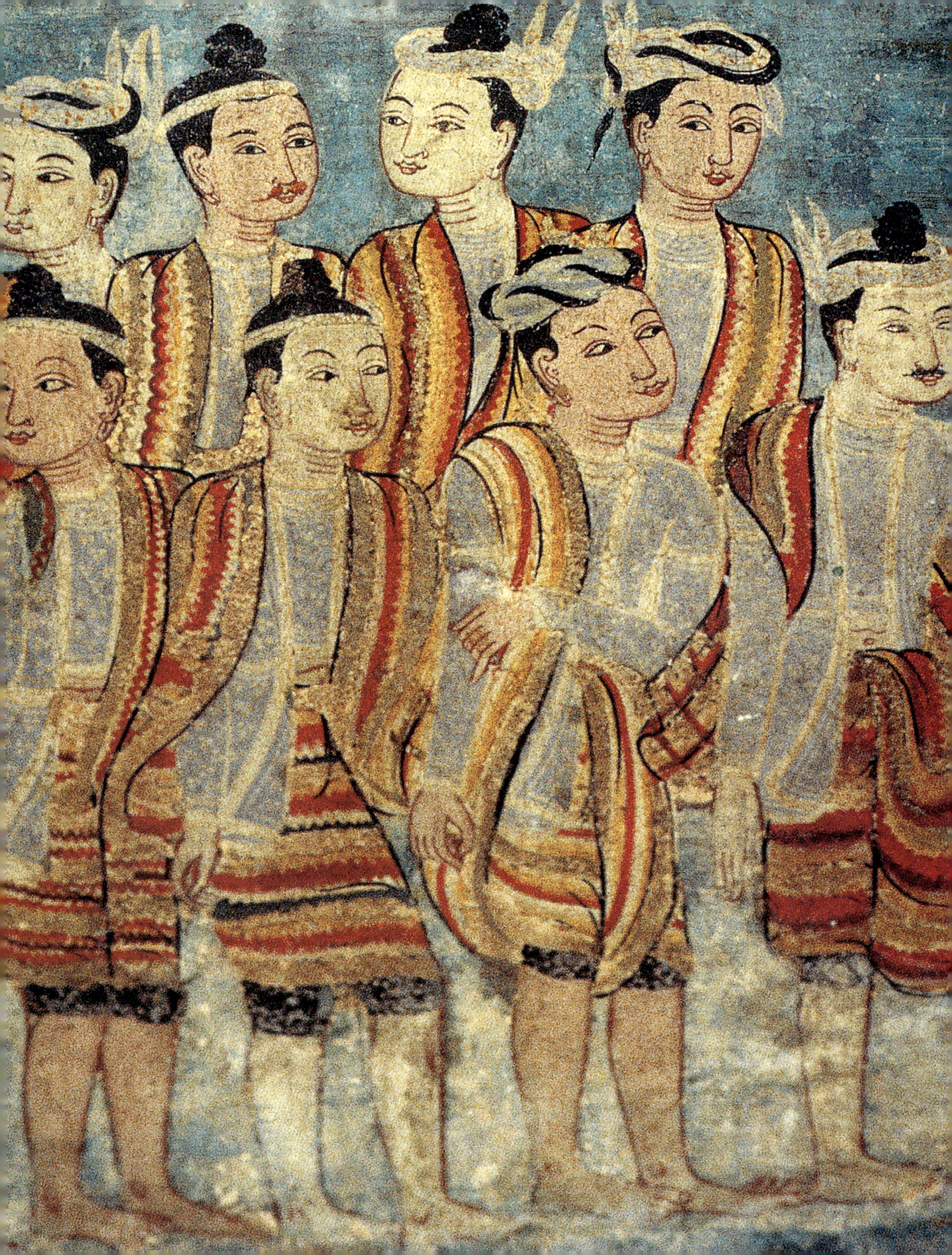

Chapter 2
The Shan States: History

The history of the Shan people is a potent blend of fact and fantasy, passed down through oral history and recorded by monks in the form of manuscripts (*parabaik*) written on palm leaf or on mulberry paper. Usually referred to as "chronicles," they were copied generation after generation by monk scribes. Like other rulers in Southeast Asia, the princes of the Shan States made grand claims about their ancestry, their pious deeds and military achievements. Each generation commissioned new copies to add their contributions to the history of the region. The chronicles were stored in Buddhist temple libraries and palace archives; wealthy Shan families also sponsored copies, kept in manuscript chests in their homes. According to the Keng Tung Chronicle, the first ruler was a cowherd who gained a kingdom with the help of a flock of crows.[1] They transported him through the air in a basket and set him down in a palace where he donned a set of royal robes and was crowned king at sunrise. The manner of his arrival caused suspicion among the people and astrologers were summoned to decide on his fate. They pronounced that no harm would come to the state if the cowherd remained as king. As time passed the king forgot his debt to the crows who in anger, plotted against him. They tempted the king with tales of great riches in another kingdom and they offered to take him there. Driven by greed, the king was carried off and the vengeful crows abandoned him. Alone and powerless the king took the form of a golden crab and became one of the guardian spirits of Keng Tung. A dragon (*naga*) lady also guarded the state from her lair in the hills. The chronicles say that from that time Shan rulers led the people of Keng Tung in ceremonies to appease the guardian spirits. These ceremonies, associated with rain-making and crop fertility, were led by ruling families throughout the Shan States until the end of the Shan Dynasty in the mid twentieth century. The crow became an important symbol in the iconography of Keng Tung and was depicted in woodcarving and in lacquer ware.

The Shan chronicles also recount stories of heavenly beings descending to earth from the Buddhist Tavatimsa Heaven. The Shan people regarded their coming as auspicious and asked them to stay on earth.[2] The heavenly beings agreed and were taken in golden chariots to palaces where they donned supernatural clothing and regalia and conducted state affairs while seated on gem-studded thrones.[3] The concept of a ruler whose ancestors came from heaven was interpreted in Shan court dress and regalia. The sight of a prince with the rays of the sun reflecting off his golden robes or a princess with the tropical light shimmering off her dress lured even foreign visitors to speculate on the supernatural.[4]

According to the Shan chronicles, the heaven-sent rulers and their descendants organized the construction of towns and villages, established boundaries between principalities and appointed honourable men as ministers and officials. From these supernatural beginnings the chronicles chart the history of the Shan people, recorded generally in terms of

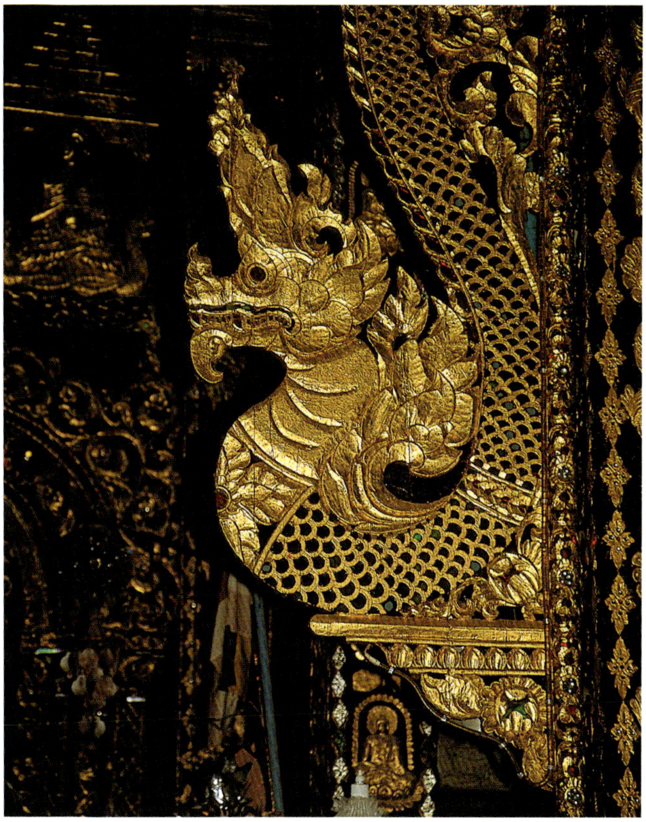

35 Carved and gilded wooden bracket in the form of a *naga*.

settlement. It is claimed that Hsawnghsup was established three hundred years before the birth of the Buddha in the mid sixth century BC.[5] Hsen-Hse-Manse to the south-east of Bhamo had settlements from the time of the Buddha's birth. The states of Muong Nai and Hsipaw declare a history beginning in 519 BC and Hsenwi claims its origin to have occurred in 441 BC. A chronicle preserved in Manipur states that there were Tai living in the Irrawaddy River region from the first century AD.[6] Although early histories mix fact and fantasy, some rulers, can with substantial evidence, trace their ancestors to the twelfth and thirteenth century and some genealogy charts are reproduced in this book (see pages 190–93). The rulers of the far northern state of Singkaling Hkamti claim a continuous family line back to the twelfth century and two women rulers are listed among them, one the daughter of a senior prince, the other a queen consort who ruled after her husband's death. Keng Tung has a recorded genealogy from the thirteenth century, and the genealogy of Yaunghwe begins in the fourteenth century with Prince Si Hseng Hpa. Thirty-three rulers are listed following his reign. The last prince was Sao Shwe Thaike whose reign ended in 1959. Some nineteenth-century princes and princesses, descendants of these ancient hierarchies, feature in later chapters.

The Shan chronicles record the pious deeds performed by royalty who built Buddhist temples and monuments, paid to gild their exteriors, made donations to support

34 (Opposite) A mural painting of Shan and Burmese officials. Wat Phra Singh, Chiang Mai.

communities of monks and propitiated the guardian spirits in seasonal rituals. The role of Burmese kings in the founding of Shan cities is acknowledged in the chronicles with a claim that in the twelfth century King Narapati of Pagan sailed to Muong Nai in a golden barge and created a new city by resettling a population of Shan people from the surrounding countryside. Narapati ordered the construction of wells and during their excavation an ancient Buddha image was discovered.[7]

Although the chronicles refer to a long history of settlement the Shan were not the first people to occupy the land and in many cases they displaced existing inhabitants, like the Wa (see chapter one) who were driven to the outer reaches of the upland valleys and into the hills. When they established their power centres, the Tai princes negotiated with the Wa and with other influential hill-occupying people, like the Karen and Kachin, who had ancient claims to the highlands. The chronicles give an insight into the complex relationships existing between hill and valley dwellers with peace treaties and marital alliances arranged between periods of skirmishes, raids and outright war.

The Shan principalities operated in the milieu of inland Southeast Asia, maintaining a degree of independence from China and Burma who competed for authority in the region. Political and military action was generally motivated by individual states as they struggled for supremacy. In early Chinese records, the Shan are listed among many groups who paid allegiance to China.[8] In the eighth century AD, a Chinese envoy escorted by sixty-five horsemen, their harnesses set with cowrie shells and decorated with gold leaf, conferred a golden seal on a tributary Shan prince.

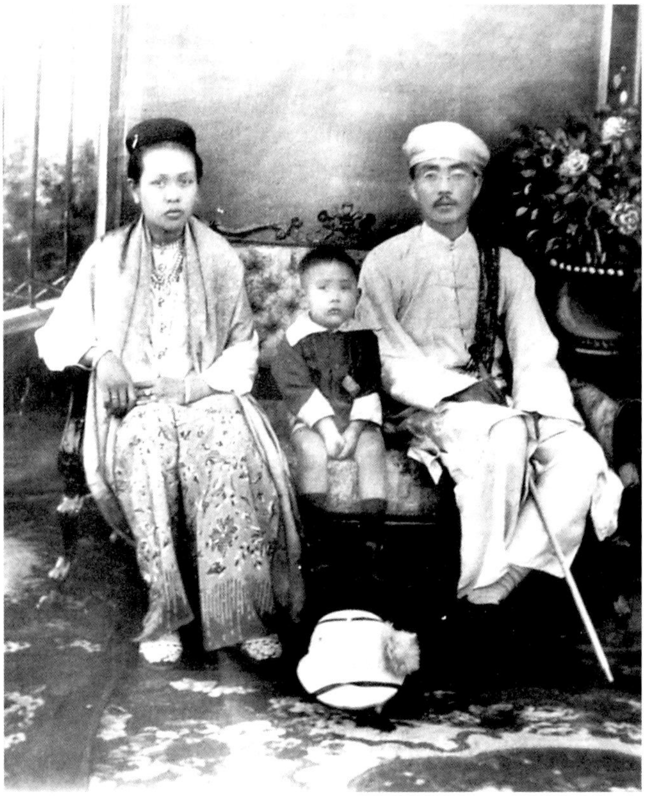

36 Prince Sao Shwe Thaike, *saohpa* of Yawnghwe with *mahadevi* Sao Nang Yi and their eldest son, Sao Hseng Hpa, circa 1928. *(Shan Palace Museum, Yawnghwe)*

He wore a coat of chain mail and a tiger skin. Twelve elephants led the procession of cavalry and foot soldiers carrying spears. The prince bowed twice and prostrated himself on the ground facing north in the direction of China. The Chinese envoy then presented the prince with gifts that included textiles and dress.[9] Although there are no details it is likely that bolts of Chinese silk and embroidered robes were included, as they were many centuries later.

In the thirteenth century, Mongol invaders led by Kublai Khan demanded submission from all tributary states as recorded in the Imperial Chinese archives, and he sent envoys demanding that they pay homage to him. The Burmese king of Pagan refused to comply and his defiance led to an invasion, dispatched by the Governor of Keng Hung (Dali), capital of Yunnan. Pagan was defeated and forced into submission. The weakening of Burmese authority at Pagan enabled the Shan princes to fortify their position in the Irrawaddy River valley and to play a more prominent role in the region.[10] They strengthened personal relationships with Burma through marital and political alliances. Shan success can be gauged at the end of the thirteenth century when the king of Pagan officially recognised Shan principalities in the Kyauksè rice-growing area to the south-east of Mandalay.

The Burmese chronicles refer to three Shan Brothers who in 1301 helped to expel the Mongols from Burma and who later sent tribute delegations to China. Table 1 (see page 35) gives the names of the three princes and their descendants who ruled at Pinya and Myinsaing in the late thirteenth and fourteenth centuries.[11] In 1312 the son of Prince Thi-ha-thú Ta-tsi-sheng (Thihathura) is said to have established another power centre across the Irrawaddy at Sagaing. The extent of Shan authority in Sagaing has been disputed but there is evidence of their presence in the area, marked by the graceful Shan style Soon U Ponnya Shin Paya stupa, constructed in 1312, and the nearby Ponnya Shin stupa. Situated high in the Sagaing hills, the stupa sites provide an excellent vantage point to survey the Irrawaddy River valley far below.

In 1364 Thadomengbya (Thadominbya), a stepson of the prince of Sagaing, established a power centre at nearby Ava (In-wa) that was to become the capital of upper Burma. The city had fortified outer walls and contained Buddhist monuments, monasteries and a palace complex. The layout was modelled on the ancient city of Pagan and city inscriptions were written in Burmese. Shan princes who were loyal to Ava ruled surrounding power centres (*muong*), and local officials with special titles administered outlying regions, a system of government that was still functioning in the nineteenth century. In keeping with tradition, Thadomengbya claimed that his ancestors were linked to the legendary kings of Tagaung, an ancient civilisation to the north of Mandalay, a claim intended to reconcile Burmese national sentiment.[12] Interestingly centuries later the powerful Shan *saohpa* of Yawnghwe was to claim descent from the Tagaung Dynasty.

In the middle of the fifteenth century during a period of relative peace, the Ava kings established relations with the centre of Theravada Buddhism at Kandy, Sri Lanka. In 1456 King Narapati of Ava acquired land for a monastery complex intended to house the monks who visited Kandy for instruction. Although there are references to peaceful times the chronicles generally portray the fifteenth century

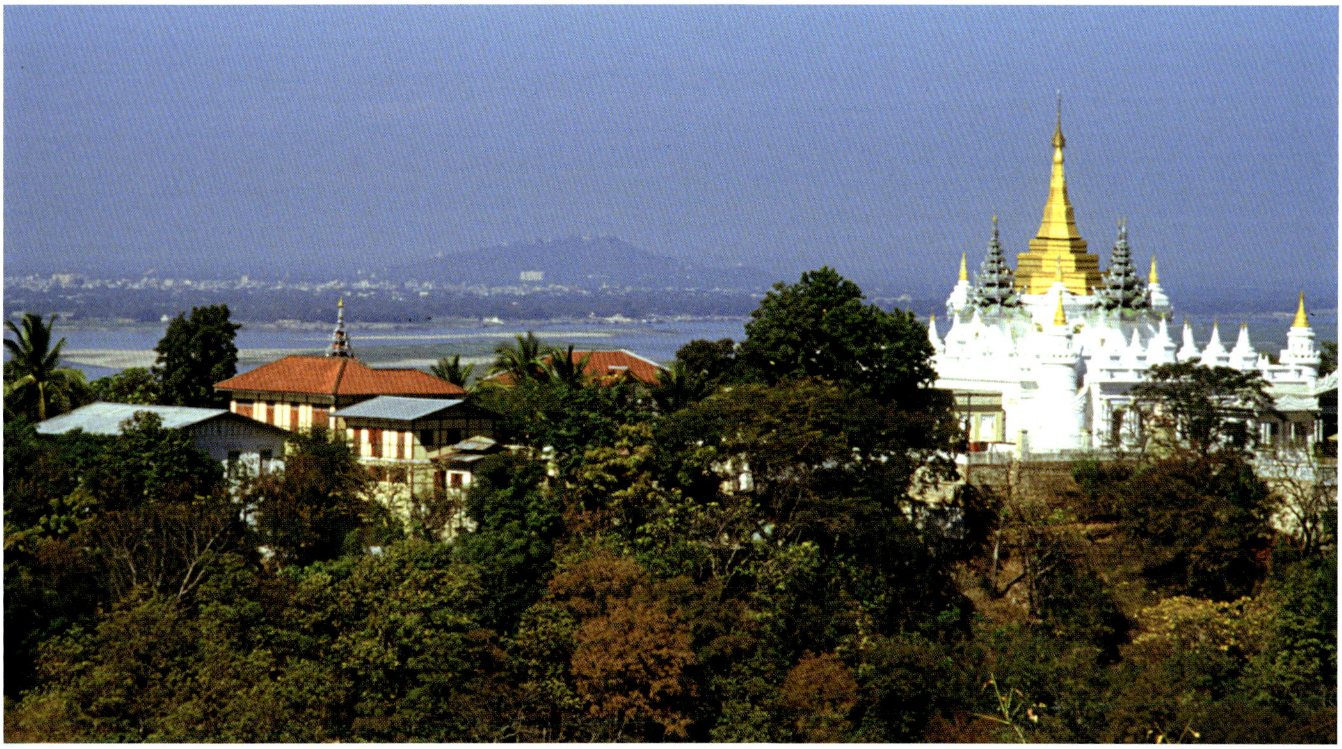

37 Late eighteenth century monastery of Shwe Yan Phye in the Sagaing Hills.

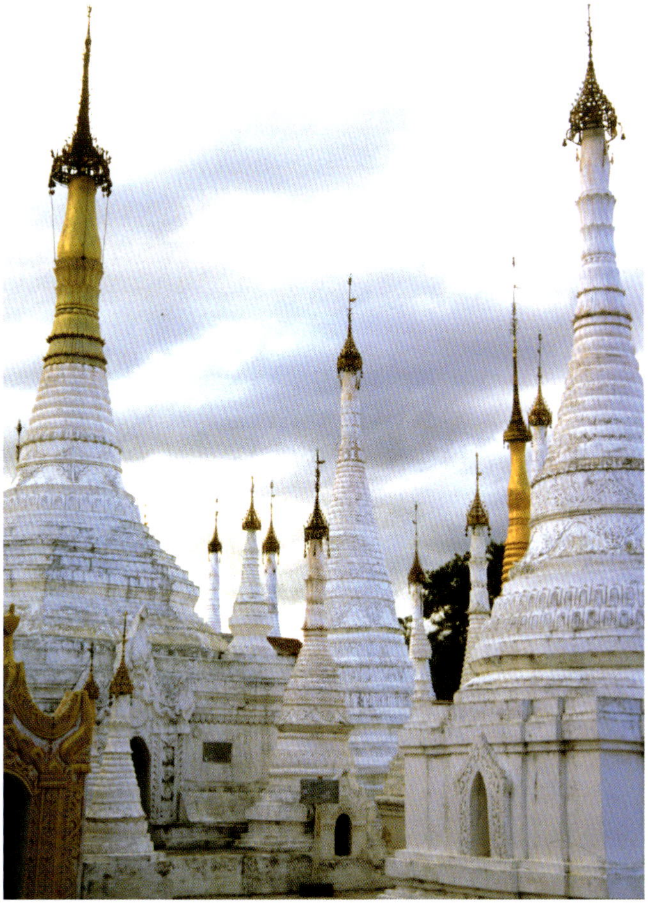

38 A group of seventeenth century Shan stupa, Yawnghwe.

TABLE I

Names of Shan princes who reigned at Myin-saing and Pinya	Date	Relationships
A-theng-kha-yá Rá-dzá-theng-gyan Thi-ha-thú Ta-tsi-sheng	1298 -1312 AD	Three Shan brothers who ruled with equal power
Thi-ha-thú Ta-tsi-sheng	1312-1322 AD	The youngest brother rules alone at Pinya
U-za-ná	1322-1342 AD	The adopted son of Thi-ha-thú Ta-tsi-sheng
Ngá-tsí-sheng Kyau-tswá	1342-1350 AD	Son of Thi-ha-thú Ta-tsi-sheng
Kyau-tswá	1350-1359 AD	Son of Ngá-tsí-sheng Kyau-tswá
Na-ra-thú	1359-1364 AD	Brother of Kyau-tswá
U-za-ná byaung	1364 AD	Brother of Na-ra-thú

TABLE II

Names of Shan princes who reigned at Sagaing	Date	Relationships
A-theng-kha-yá Tsau Ywon	1315 AD	Son of Thi-ha-thú Ta-tsi-sheng (see Table 1)
Ta-ra-bya-gyi	1322-1336 AD	Stepson of Thi-ha-thú Ta-tsi-sheng
Shwé-daung-tet	1336-1339 AD	Son of Ta-ra-bya-gyi
Kyau-tswá	1339-1349 AD	Son of A-theng-kha-yá Tsau Ywon
Nau-ra-htá Meng-rai	1349 AD	Brother of Kyau-tswá
Ta-ra-bya-gyi	1349-1352 AD	Brother of Nau-ra-htá Meng-rai
U-za-ná byaung	1352-1364 AD	Brother-in-law of Ta-ra-bya-gyi

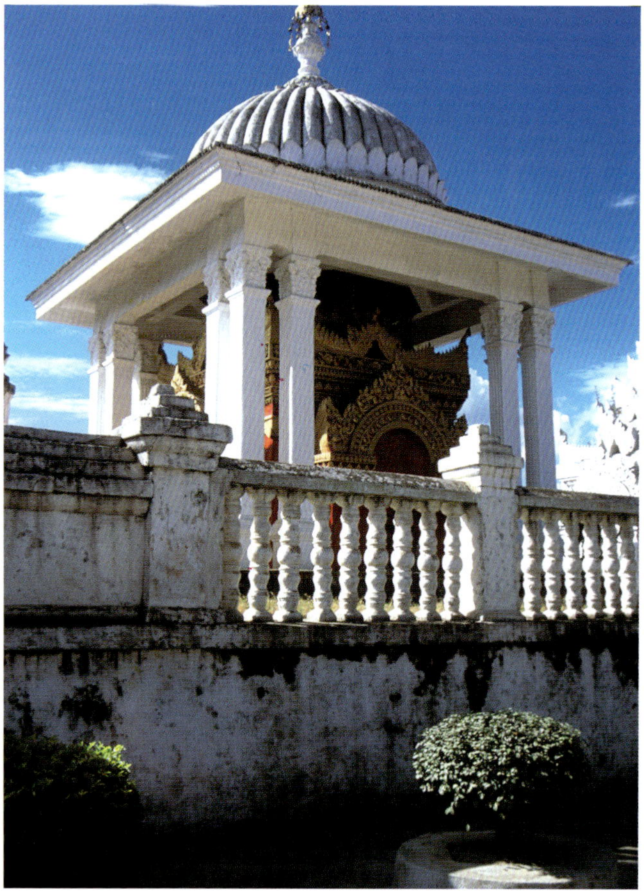

39 Tomb of a Shan prince in the cemetery of Keng Tung.

Shan States as far from quiet. The *saohpa* of Kale, Monyin, Mogaung, Yawnghwe, Momeik, Bhamo, Muong Nai, Hsipaw and Muong Pai were constantly at war. The senseless slaughter went on for several generations and prevented consolidation of a powerful Shan force. During this period successive kings of Burma took advantage of Shan disunity and posted Burmese military officers and administrative officials in the Shan States, although they were withdrawn at times to be deployed in quelling rebellions in other regions, for example on the north-west frontier with Assam. In their absence the Shan princes tried to overthrow Burmese rule. In one instance, an example was made of a rebellious Shan prince who, according to legend, was publicly humiliated outside the gates of Ava. He was shackled in chains of gold and his men were sold as slaves to foreign merchants.[13]

The Shan princes never created a united force and continuing skirmishes made them an easy target for predatory rulers. In 1556, King Bayinnaung of Pegu overpowered them. Bayinnaung was a commoner who had risen through the ranks of the military; he was a brilliant military strategist and had experience in commanding advance units in battle. He subdued the Shan states of Hsipaw and Muong Nai on his way east to conquer the capital of Lan Na (north Thailand) at Chiang Mai. The Shan princes were fearful of Bayinnaung and his mighty army and they hastily swore allegiance to him. Those who accepted tributary status are listed in table III, arranged in alphabetical order. The last Shan state to submit to him was Hsenwi.[14]

TABLE III
Shan Princes who accepted Tributary Status

Hopong, Hsahtung, Hsamongkham, Hsawnghsup, Hsenwi, Hsipaw, Kehsi Mansam, Kengkham, Keng Lon, Keng Tung, Kyawkku, Kyong, Laikha, Lawksawk, Loi Ai, Loi Long, Loi Maw, Manglon, Maw, Mawkmai, Mawnang, Mawson, Muong Hsu, Mongkung, Muong Mit, Muong Nai, Muong Nawng, Muong Pai, Muong Pan, Muong Pawn, Muong Sit, Namkhai, Namkhôk, Nam Tôk, Nawngwawn, Pangmi, Pangtara, Pwela, Sakoi, Samka, Singkaling Hkamti, Wanyin, Yawnghwe, Yengan.

Although he gained authority over the Shan princes, Bayinnaung did not interfere with their feudal rights, allowing them to keep their royal regalia and to conduct traditional Shan spirit rites. He is said to have introduced Burmese customary law "as far as it was compatible with customs and practices of Shan feudal society."[15] He dispatched Burmese monks from the Buddhist Thudhamma sect and ordered the Shan princes to support them, although they continued to practise their own form of Theravada Buddhism. He introduced a Burmese system of weights and measures, and he taxed Shan revenues from forestry and mining that included precious metals, jade and gemstones. The Shan princes were also required to provide military conscripts, and as part of tribute payments, they sent to Bayinnaung silver and gold trees, ceremonial bowls and lengths of silk. The king encouraged intermarriage between Shan and Burmese. The prince of Keng Tung sent Bayinnaung a princess as a consort, and the king reciprocated with white umbrellas, items of dress and textiles and royal regalia.[16] Some of the claims made about Bayinnaung are dubious and aim to create a picture of a fair and just king. He is credited with prohibiting human and animal sacrifice among the Shan.[17] This type of claim was common as powerful rulers sought to establish their place in history by implying that the people they conquered were primitive and in need of "civilising."

Bayinnaung's edicts and the demands he made give the impression that he was able to control the Shan princes, but in reality his power did not extend far beyond the foothills and his suzerainty was seldom more than nominal. His challenge to the Yuan sect of Theravada Buddhism was not effective, and the Shan princes frequently rebelled against the heavy taxes and conscription demands he imposed, appealing to China for help. Successive kings of Burma were reluctant to incur the wrath of the Chinese so this strategy was relatively successful. In 1562, Bayinnaung set out with a huge army to increase his conquests in the northern Shan states of Mongmau, Hsikwan, Muong Nai, Sanda, Hohsa, Lahsa, Mongwan, Kungma and Monglem. An oath of allegiance was administered to every prince who became a vassal but they were excused from tribute payment, probably seen as a way of securing their loyalty. Successive kings of Burma ruled from Ava or Amarapura until 1857, when the capital moved to Mandalay. They posted troops and officials

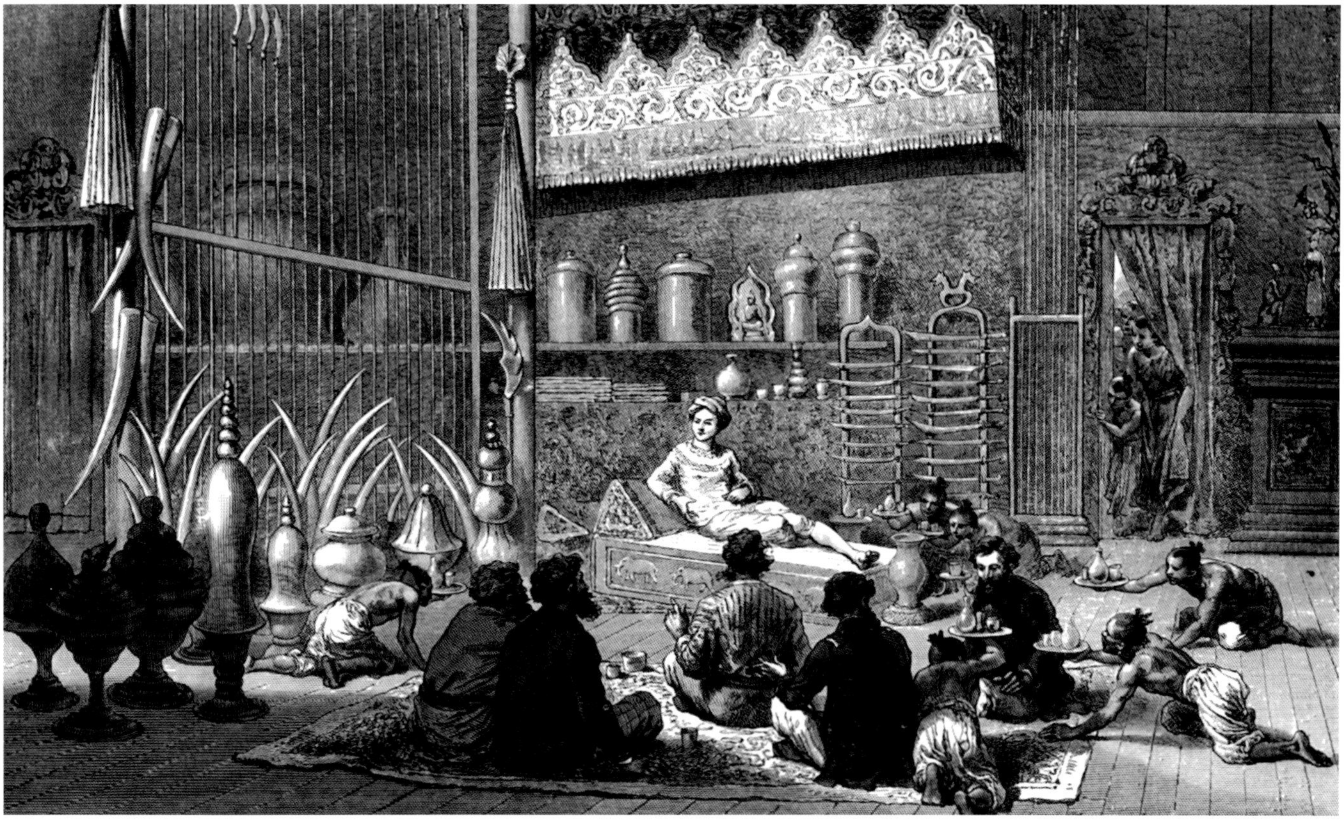

40 The Prince of Muong You holding an audience with a delegation from the French Mekong Exploration Commission. Etching based on a drawing by Delaporte, in Garnier (1885). *(White Lotus Press)*

in the Shan States and by 1840 one and a half thousand Burmese soldiers were stationed in Muong Nai to keep an eye on the Shan. The Burmese exercised a measure of control by influencing succession issues, and they attempted to prevent combined rebellion against their authority. In 1846, the Siamese diplomat Thao Sitthimongkhon, who travelled in the region, listed seventeen Shan towns on the west bank of the Salween River that were tributary to Burma, and he estimated that twenty thousand Shan males were eligible for military service.[18]

Successive Burmese kings insisted that some sons and brothers of Shan rulers live at the Burmese court, basically as hostages for good behaviour. They were expected to learn Burmese customs and to develop a sense of loyalty to the king of Burma. Shan princesses also served at court as attendants and consorts. In some cases they rose to the rank of queen, adding to the prestige of their family, as happened to Princess Sao Lai, sister of the Prince of Muong Nai, who became a consort of King Mindon (ruled 1853-1878).[19]

In 1857 King Mindon moved his court from Ava to Mandalay where he constructed a large palace compound. The Shan princes then paid tribute at the court of Mandalay and were held there if payment was not forthcoming. Because journeys from some states were long and hazardous, King Mindon offered the alternative of paying through an administrative centre operating in Muong Nai. Unless they were incapacitated, the senior princes were expected to attend court to pay respect (*kadaw*) to the king. *Kadaw* ceremonies were an amazing sight with the dress and regalia worn by all those who attended allocated according to sumptuary laws. The Shan princes and their senior consorts added to the spectacle in their court dress embroidered with gold thread and set with semi-precious stones, coloured glass, beetle wings, silver and gold sequins and mother-of-pearl beads.

Burmese bureaucrats were deployed in the main Shan principalities in the nineteenth century, as witnessed by foreigners such as the British officer Captain McLeod in the 1830s and by French delegations that included Dr. E. Lefèvre, Louis de Carné and Francis Garnier in the 1860s to 1890s. They gave varying accounts of the role played by these officials. Francis Garnier judged that their main purpose was to collect taxes; de Carné described strained relations between the princes and Burmese officials who attempted to regulate their affairs. He also noted that similar tensions existed between major and minor Shan states, and his party were often confused when they tried to establish where the real power lay. In Keng Tung, de Carné described a "grand Burman mandarin" who reigned by the side of the prince, but he also noted that the king of Burma was careful in his treatment of the more powerful princes. This cautious attitude penetrated all levels of court life and was expressed in oral history, poetry and prose. In a well-known Burmese palace story, a legendary king of Mandalay muses that the Shan are always ready to rebel and he expresses anxiety in case he might upset them.[20]

One of the main Shan grievances against Burma was the demand for military conscripts. The Shan princes also complained to the king when Burmese soldiers behaved in an undisciplined way in their territory. At times there were serious disputes. One occurred in the 1870s in the state of Keng Hung that paid tribute to Burma and to China, although it was the prince of Keng Tung who had the right to nominate the ruler. King Mindon ignored this prerogative and nominated his own candidate. In retaliation the prince of Keng Tung ordered the massacre of Burmese subjects in his territory, removed the king's chosen candidate and installed his own nominee in Keng Hung. King Mindon died before there was time to punish the prince, and his heir King Thibaw (ruled 1878-1885) was too weak to act.

Shan Relations with Lan Na and Siam

The eastern Shan States and the Lan Na kingdom of north Thailand had strong political links dating from the thirteenth century, when King Mangrai (1259-1317) ruled both Lan Na and Keng Tung. From the thirteenth to the sixth century Chiang Mai regarded Keng Tung as a "younger brother" state or at times, as a dependency. The Chiang Mai Chronicles record the political power struggles and skirmishes and also the marital alliances that took place between these two power centres. In peacetime it was customary for the Chiang Mai ruler to send gifts to Keng Tung, including textiles and regalia, when a prince was consecrated or when there was a royal funeral. Keng Tung responded in similar fashion to events in Chiang Mai.

In the late eighteenth century the Siamese defeated the Burmese and drove them out of the Lan Na principalities. The Lan Na princes then looked south to establish tributary relations with the Chakri Dynasty in Bangkok. Although the Siamese were victorious, the Burmese army continued with skirmishes and incursions into Lan Na territory. The Burmese used Keng Tung as a staging post for attacks on Siam, while the Siamese used Chiang Mai as a base for counter attacks. Peace came when the Burmese army was finally routed, but there were serious consequences. The long war waged across Lan Na territory had destroyed the towns and devastated the population, leaving the country in a state of dereliction. In order to repopulate towns and villages, the Lan Na princes organised raids into the Shan States, Sipsong Pan Na and Burma to take captives for resettlement.

In 1807 the second prince (*uparat*) of Chiang Mai led a military mission to Keng Tung. The ruling Prince Mahakhanan fled with his most loyal followers to Muong Yang but hundreds of families moved to Chiang Mai and transferred their allegiance to Prince Kawila of Lan Na (ruled 1781-1813). Over an extended period of time, members of the Keng Tung royal family and many commoners were captured and taken to Chiang Mai where they were resettled on the outskirts of the city.[21] They included many skilled artisans, a loss that had serious consequences in Keng Tung (see chapter six). The Keng Tung Chronicle recorded,

> *Jengmai* [Chiang Mai] *brought up an army and attacked Jengtung* [Keng Tung] *and captured the person of the prince, members of the royal family and subjects of the state and took them all down to Jengmai* [Chiang Mai], *with the exception of Prince Dongsaeng* [Mahakhanan].[22]

41 Mural painting showing Shan and Siamese soldiers preparing for battle. Wat Buak Khrok Luang, Chiang Mai.

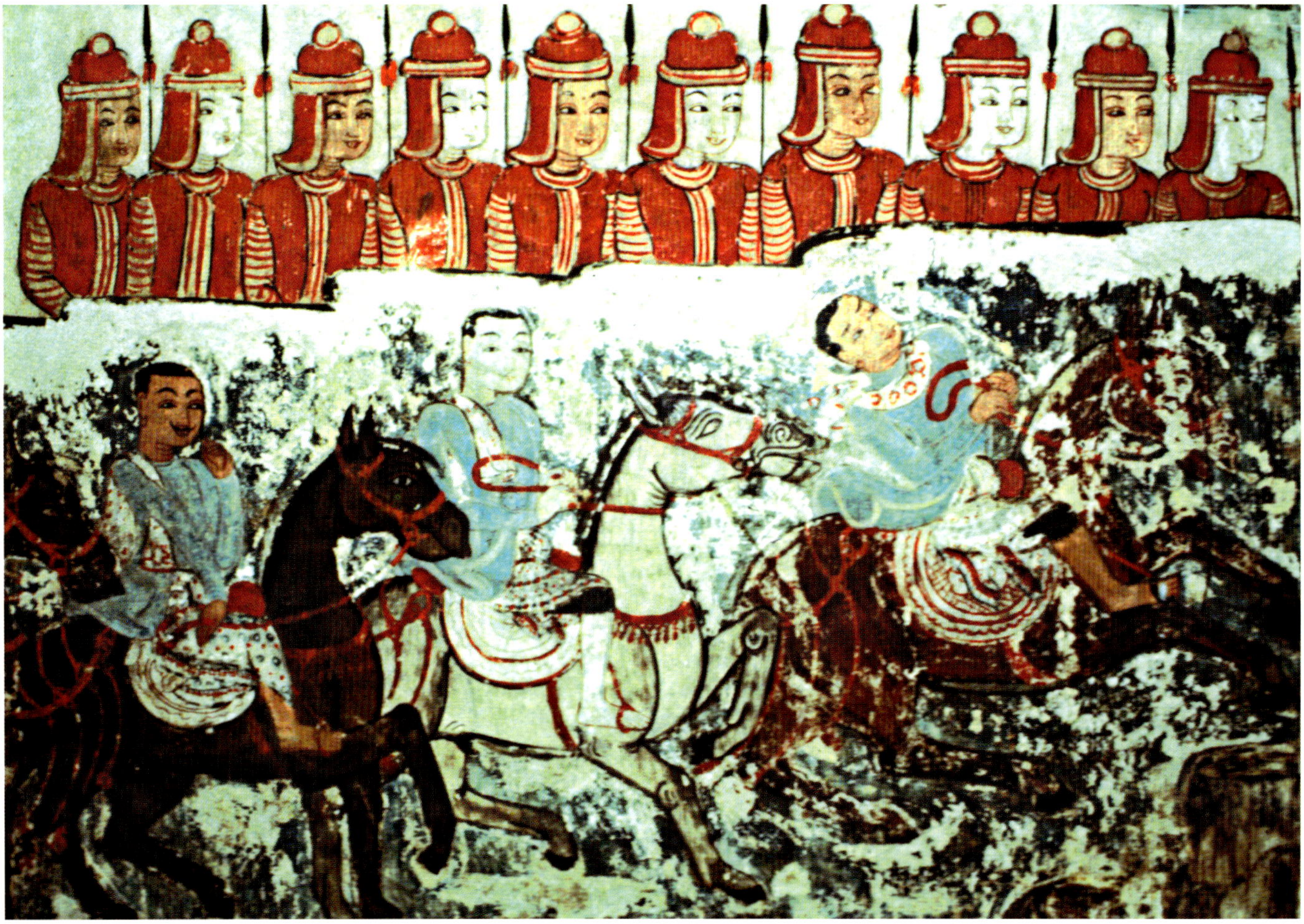

Tai Khoen royalty were allowed to build residences outside the Chiang Mai gate on the south side of the city. Following resettlement, a marriage was arranged between Princess Chantima, daughter of Prince Sethi Kham Fan of Chiang Mai (ruled 1822-1825) and Prince Mahaphrom, younger brother of Prince Sirichai of Keng Tung.

In 1839 the *uparat* again led raids to Keng Tung with a deputy called Nai Phimsan.[23] The eastern Shan States experienced major losses in population and the city of Keng Tung was almost deserted. The Lan Na princes began to resettle people in Chiang Rai, an area close to the Shan border. The Burmese suspected that Chiang Rai was intended as a launching stage for future attacks on Burma. Fears increased when the man put in charge of the settlement was Deputy Nai Phimsan. The Burmese responded by setting up border posts on the banks of the Salween and sending troops to patrol the area.[24] In order to allay further tension the prince of Chiang Mai attempted to broker a new relationship with Keng Tung, suggesting that they should become "brothers" and expand trade between them. While Chiang Mai and Keng Tung spoke of friendship, the Bangkok kingdom prepared for further invasion. During the reigns of Rama III (ruled 1824-1851) and Rama IV (ruled 1851-1868), Siamese troops were dispatched to the north in an effort to bring Keng Tung and Keng Hung under Bangkok's authority.

Siamese expansionism was taking place at a time when the British and French were becoming important players in the region, and the British were gaining authority in Burma. Fear of confrontation with the British impeded Siamese ambitions, although it did not stop them attempting to extend their borders to the Salween River. The general attitude in Bangkok seemed to be that Siam should take Keng Tung while British power did not extend as far as the Shan States. The Siamese Commissioner to Lan Na, Krom Mun Phichit Prichakon, wrote in the careful language of a diplomat.

> *....regarding Keng Tung it is most unfortunate that it lies nearer to us than Burma, that it is well-watered and rich in rice... The younger brother of the ruler of Chiang Mai could be sent to look after the country.*[25]

Meanwhile Prince Mahakhanan (1781-1857) continued to lead raids against the Burmese. He eventually accepted that this strategy was imposing too much hardship on his followers, and he accepted Burmese authority. He then rebuilt the city of Keng Tung. He probably calculated that he could keep a degree of sovereignty from Burma as the closest Burmese station was in Muong Nai, a difficult journey from Keng Tung. Mahakhanan's decision proved to be wise, and he was able to maintain a level of independence from Burma and Siam. His loyalty to Burma was rewarded with lavish gifts from the king. They included golden regalia, umbrellas of state, musical instruments and a gilded carriage and chair. The ultimate prize was Princess Ratanadevi, sister of King Mindon.[26] As part of tribute payments to Burma, Keng Tung sent gold and silver trees, ceremonial bowls and local silk. As had been the tradition in earlier centuries, the Burmese taxed forestry revenue and profits from mining precious metals, jade and gemstones. The Keng Tung royal family was also required to attend tribute ceremonies (*kadaw*) at the Burmese court and to provide conscripts in times of war, a condition that was always resented. Having opted to stay loyal to Burma, Mahakhanan proved to be a skilful politician and diplomat, and he improved relations with the court of Chiang Mai where many of his relatives and subjects were now settled.

Shan Relations with Sipsong Pan Na and China

Shan relations with Sipsong Pan Na and China were as complex as they were with Burma. In the thirteenth century the Chinese emperor had claimed tribute payments and sent an army that was eventually repulsed "by lightening induced through invocations and abnormal rites." In reality the troops were probably brought down by disease and demoralised by the difficult mountainous terrain that crippled supply lines. Chinese-Shan relations had been curtailed in the sixteenth century when King Bayinnaung of Burma (1551-1581) invaded the Shan States, although when they felt they were paying too much tax in the Burmese tributary system, the Shan princes appealed to China for help. The Shan were clever at playing the super-powers off against each other, and from time to time the Chinese challenged Burmese authority by sending troops via Yunnan to states west of the Salween River which they claimed to be under their jurisdiction. In 1659 they penetrated as far south as Ava before being repulsed. Disaffected Shan princes gave their support to incursions.

At times the Chinese looked for provocation as a justification to invade. One opportunity came in 1765 when a drunken brawl in Keng Tung led to the death of a Chinese citizen. The prince of Keng Tung offered compensation to the family and undertook to arrest and punish the murderer. The governor of Yunnan was not satisfied and demanded that the accused be handed over to him. The prince refused. This was used as the reason to invade Keng Tung with a large army. Captain McLeod who visited Keng Tung in the 1830s, was told the story of what happened to the Chinese soldiers. Their supply lines had been cut by local hill tribe gangs who had stolen their horses and eaten them, causing the soldiers to retreat to the Mekong River.[27] The governor of Yunnan was held responsible for this debacle, and in shame and humiliation he committed suicide. A new governor was appointed with orders to subdue the Shan, although his attempts were unsuccessful and the Chinese force was again defeated. In 1767 the Chinese invaded Hsenwi and executed the prince, but were eventually repulsed. In total the Chinese were defeated four times in four years. In 1770 a peace treaty was signed between all the parties and trading relations were restored. It proved to be an uneasy peace as bands of Chinese Muslims (Haw) plagued the Shan States in the nineteenth century, disrupting agriculture and trade and destabilising village life.

In the nineteenth century foreigners needing permits had great difficulty travelling between the northern Shan States and Yunnan and between Yunnan and China, as they were often not sure where to apply. Francis Garnier noted that in spite of Chinese-style architecture and Chinese dress worn by people in the far northern Shan States and Sipsong Pan Na, he was not dealing with officials whose power related directly to China, but with bureaucrats whom he surmised had been promoted by local rulers to the rank of "mandarin."[28] He was sure they had no significant relationship with Peking (Beijing). Dali and Muong La (also

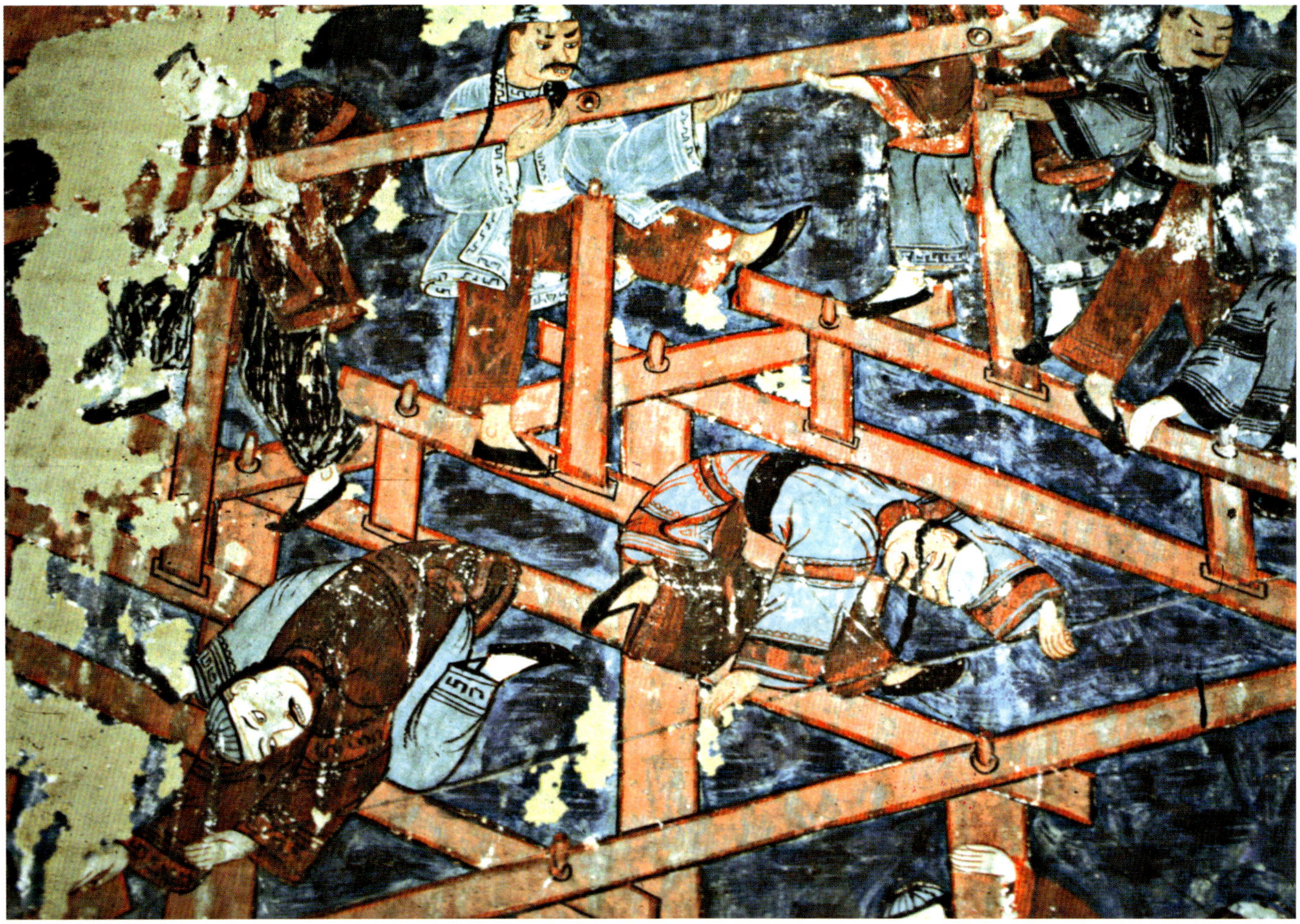

42 Mural painting of Chinese labourers building a house. Many Chinese workmen travelled south during the dry season and returned home in the monsoon season. Wat Buak Khrok Luang, Chiang Mai.

called Semao) were powerful independent kingdoms and had often fought with success against Chinese invaders. Garnier judged that the division of the region into Chinese administrative districts was a nineteenth-century phenomenon. There was general confusion over the terms used to describe the Tai living in the region who called each other Yai (Ngio) Neua, Khoen or Lue and described the area by the general term "Muong Tai." The British described the area as the Chinese Shan States and spoke of the people as Chinese Shan.

Officials like Captain McLeod who travelled extensively in the Shan States reported on the complex nature of tributary relations. Many Shan princes in the north sent the same tribute to Burma as they paid to China. This consisted of one gold cup, "tinsel" cloth, silk cloth, a pair of shoes, a cake of salt, a viss of tea and a viss each of candles covered with gold leaf, candles covered with silver leaf, candles decorated with gold flowers and candles decorated with silver flowers.[29] He also noted the presence of itinerant Chinese labourers and craftsmen who came in search of work in the dry season and returned home before the rains. In Keng Tung, Chinese merchants were key agents in trading companies owned by the prince and his family, and some actually resided within palace enclosures. McLeod often spoke of the Shan-Burmese-Chinese phenomenon in terms of manuscripts, languages and dialects. In Keng Hung, he acknowledged the dominance of Chinese culture when he was informed that only one official in ten spoke Tai, although those who did spoke a dialect similar to that spoken in Keng Tung and Chiang Mai. He noted that few scribes could write Shan script, although when he saw it written McLeod recognised that it had the same characters as Keng Tung and Chiang Mai scripts. He also discovered that only one official in a hundred understood Burmese and that Chinese was the official language spoken at court.

In 1910 the American missionary William Clifton Dodd set off on a tour of Sipsong Pan Na and Yunnan and estimated that the Tai were the majority population along the southern and western borders of Yunnan. He argued that the Tai had ruled as far as Kwangsi before the Chinese took the area and built on the sites of old Tai palaces. He wrote:

> *For a moment the curtain rises and we get a glimpse of a struggle between the Chinese and the vigorous Shan* [Tai] *race for the possession of southern China.*[30]

Interestingly he noted the complaints made by local Tai people who resented Chinese hegemony.

> *They were of the opinion that everyone should be allowed to follow his own religion, theirs was that women should dress in tunics and skirts, and not in sacks and trousers.*[31]

Relations between the Shan, the Burmese, the French and the British

Tributary relations were further complicated in the late nineteenth century when British and French colonial ambitions impacted on the politics of the inland states. The British had turned their attention to Burma at the beginning of the nineteenth century, at a time when they were rapidly expanding their Empire eastwards from India. They created conflict with King Bodawpaya (ruled 1819-1853), leading to the first Anglo-Burmese War of 1824-1826. The ensuing peace treaty, ratified at Yandabo, forty-five miles from Ava, gave the British the southern province of Tenasserim, control of the port of Moulmein and the states of Assam and Manipur. In addition to making these large territorial concessions, the Burmese paid a crippling indemnity. The defeat of the Burmese and the British presence at the mouth of the Salween weakened Burma, a situation that the Shan princes were quick to exploit. A second Burmese War with the British in 1852 further undermined Burmese authority, although the accession of King Mindon (ruled 1853-1878) led to a period of relative calm and negotiation with the British government of India in Calcutta. Mindon resented the fact that he was not able to negotiate directly with Queen Victoria and the British government in London. In 1872, he was slighted when his chief minister visited London and was introduced to the Queen by the secretary of state for India and not by the British foreign secretary, as he had expected. After Mindon's death any good will that had existed between the two nations was lost. His successor at the Mandalay court was the weak King Thibaw, and during his reign the Shan princes set up independent states and confederations and freed themselves from the taxes imposed by the Burmese court. Some Shan chiefs began to engage in banditry, and marauding bands of men, grouped around local leaders, took a share of the spoils.

In 1885 the British intervened to oust King Thibaw and to end the Kon-baung Dynasty. The Keng Tung Chronicle describes the arrival of the British (*Gala Ingalik*) by steamer, an event predicted by Shan astrologers. The Chronicle states that twenty thousand English soldiers surrounded the palace. King Thibaw, his consorts and their attendants were taken prisoner and boarded onto a river steamer, going by stages to Rangoon (Yangon) and then on to exile in Ratnagiri, India. The Royal Audience Hall became the garrison church and most palace apartments were whitewashed to become offices for British army personnel. The removal of Thibaw and his court meant that many highly skilled artisans, musicians and entertainers were made redundant. The knowledge and skills passed from one generation to the next were in jeopardy. Some artisans found new patrons at the Shan courts, while others survived by producing goods for the Burmese middle classes and, as their numbers grew, for British colonial officers and their families.

The Shan princes experienced freedom when King Thibaw was exiled, and they had no intention of loosing it in submission to British authority. Their aim was to elect a Burmese king who would not interfere in their internal affairs, make demands on local labour or impose crippling taxes. Their choice for this role was the Limbin Prince, son of the Crown Prince (younger brother of King Mindon) who had been murdered by his nephews. The Limbin Prince was residing in Moulmein when a deputation of Shan princes arrived to offer him the Burmese throne, if he agreed to support their cause for greater freedom. The prince of Keng Tung wrote to the prince of Hsipaw.

> *As King Thibaw did not rule his Empire justly the Sawbwas [saohpa]...invited the Prince Limbin, then residing in British territory, to come and wrest the crown from King Thibaw.* [32]

The Shan princes returned from Moulmein accompanied by the pliant Limbin Prince who proceeded to lavish titles on his Shan supporters in what turned out to be a short term in office. In the meantime an anti-Limbin league had formed among disaffected Shan princes, and in 1886 fighting broke out between the two factions, creating the most appalling chaos. Cities were burnt and hundreds of villagers fled to hide in the forest. In January 1887 the British sent a column under Colonel Sir Edward Stedman to establish a garrison and fortified post at Yawnghwe that was named Fort Stedman. H. Thirkell, a political officer reported:

> *The country was to a great extent deserted, villages had been abandoned and many inhabitants had fled to the neighbouring states...Much of the land had been left uncultivated, the road was neglected and overgrown with grass....I learnt that the rest of the country was the same.. .* [33]

Some Shan states, like Ho Pong, suffered particularly badly during the disturbances because they lay in a direct path between the hostile powers of Muong Nai and Yawnghwe. In 1887, the city of Ho Pong was burnt to the ground; Laikha was looted and pillaged and the people fled with the royal family to take refuge in the hills. The following year there was a famine that took the lives of many survivors.

By June 1887 the British had established a degree of order and gained the submission of all the southern Shan States. They also negotiated with the Karen and Kachin who did not want Shan officials imposed on them. From 1887-1888, the newly appointed Superintendent, Mr. A. H. Hildebrand, embarked on a tour with a considerable military force. In Muong Nai he held a durbar with most of the *chao fa*, *saohpa* and *myosa* present and negotiated a reconciliation between the followers of the Limbin Prince and his adversaries. The Limbin Prince surrendered to the British in Muong Nai in May 1887. He was the subject of some ridicule; his palace described as "a mat shed decorated with shiny paper, his throne a rough wooden dais."[34] Like King Thibaw before him, he was sent under escort to Rangoon, and at his own request, he was allowed to settle in India with members of his family.

The British established an administrative centre at Taunggyi and appointed a British Commissioner and six Superintendents as his assistants to liaise with the princes and *myosa*. They were to swear allegiance to Queen Victoria and British officials, and then be issued with patents of appointment recognizing their right to rule. Each prince was to administer his own state with the aid of a prime minister, departmental ministers and a state judge. Members of the British administration and the princes and *myosa* formed the Governing Shan State Council. Wooden bungalows built on stilts, and referred to as *haw* (palaces), were provided as formal residences while they attended sittings in Taunggyi. On their part, the British agreed not to interfere in local traditions and customs which they considered just and not contradictory to the laws of British India. The British maintained civil order and controlled foreign affairs and state revenues. For administrative purposes the British divided the Shan States into two main blocks of north and south.

TABLE IV

The Northern Shan States

Hsipaw, Manglon, North Hsenwi, South Hsenwi, Tawng Peng.[35]

The Southern Shan States

Ho Pong, Hsahtung, Hsamongkham, Kehsi Mansam, Kengkham, Keng Lon, Keng Tung, Kyawkku, Kyong, Laikha, Lawksawk, Loi Ai, Loi Long, Loi Maw, Maw, Mawkmai, Mawnang, Mawson, Muong Hsu, Muongkung, Muong Nai, Muong Nawng, Muong Pai, Muong Pan, Muong Pawn, Muong Sit, Namkhai, Namkhok, Nam Tok, Nawngwawn, Pangmi, Pangtara, Pwela, Sakoi, Samka, Wanyin, Yawnghwe, Yengan.

Muong Mit, Hsawnghsup, and Singkaling Hkamti, listed earlier in this chapter, were administered as part of Burma. The last Shan state to pass under British administration was Keng Tung, and Sir George Scott was sent there to present the prince with his patent of appointment. Scott wrote of his journey,

> *Part of the way ran along the side of a precipice. The ledge to be traversed was so narrow that the mules, striking their loads against angles, were many times in danger of being driven over the outer edge into the abyss below.*[36]

After an eventful time in Keng Tung, including a drunken brawl involving some of his muleteers, Scott gave the *saohpa* his Order of Appointment.

The British held a series of durbars up-country with the Shan princes, *myosa* and *ngwegunhmu*. Following local tradition, temporary buildings (*tawmaw*) were constructed as meeting places and accommodation for visiting officials. Sir George Scott photographed them at the durbars they attended in the 1890s and 1900s, Colonel James Henry Green photographed from 1918 to1935. These photographs are an important resource for textile and dress historians, as they show the range of dress, textiles and regalia worn by members of the Shan royal family, officials and staff who attended the durbars.

43 Durbar house (*tawmaw*) in Keng Tung where villagers can be seen sheltering under the raised floor, circa 1890. *(The Oriental and India Office Collections, The British Library, London, 92/3 (13))*

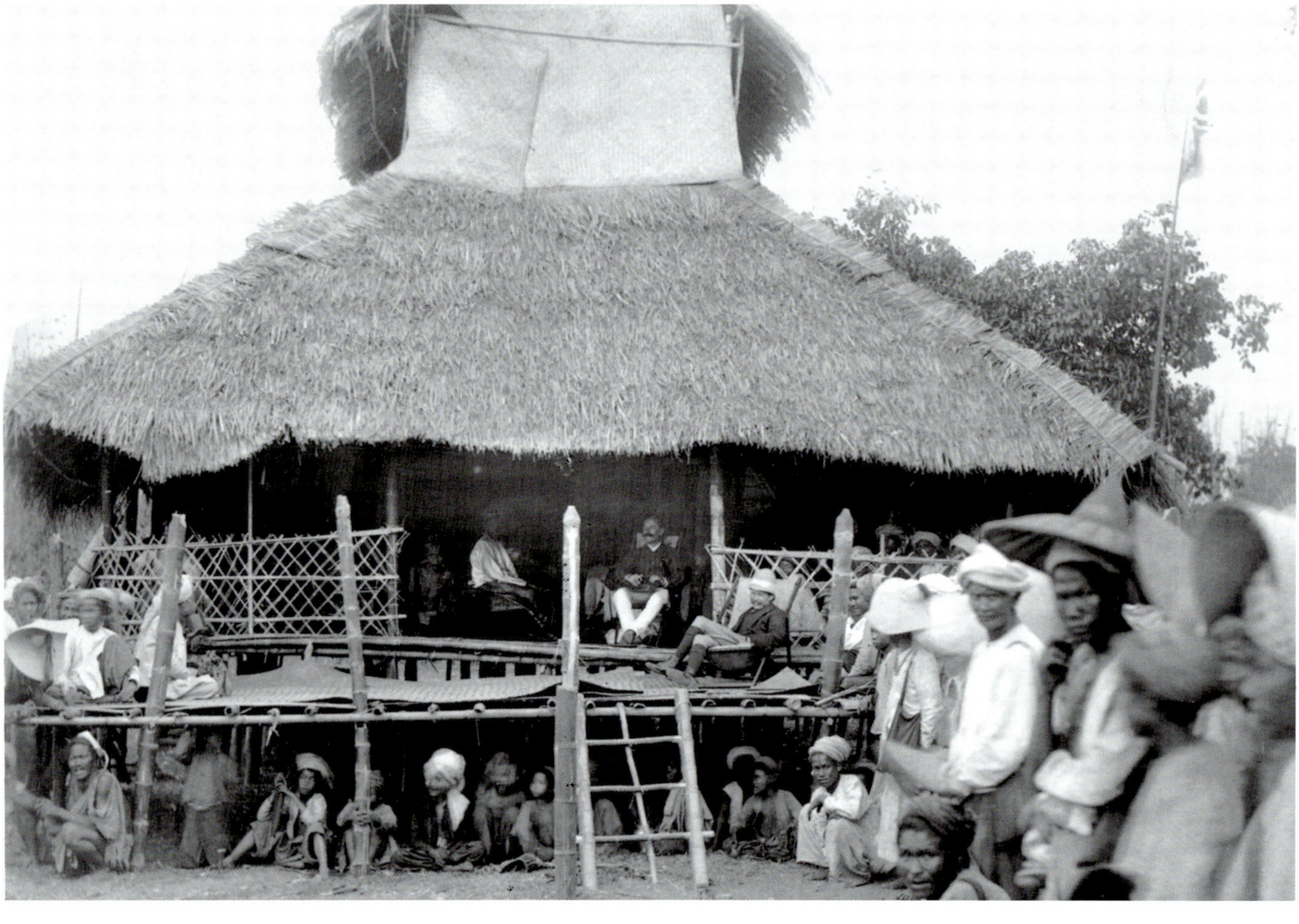

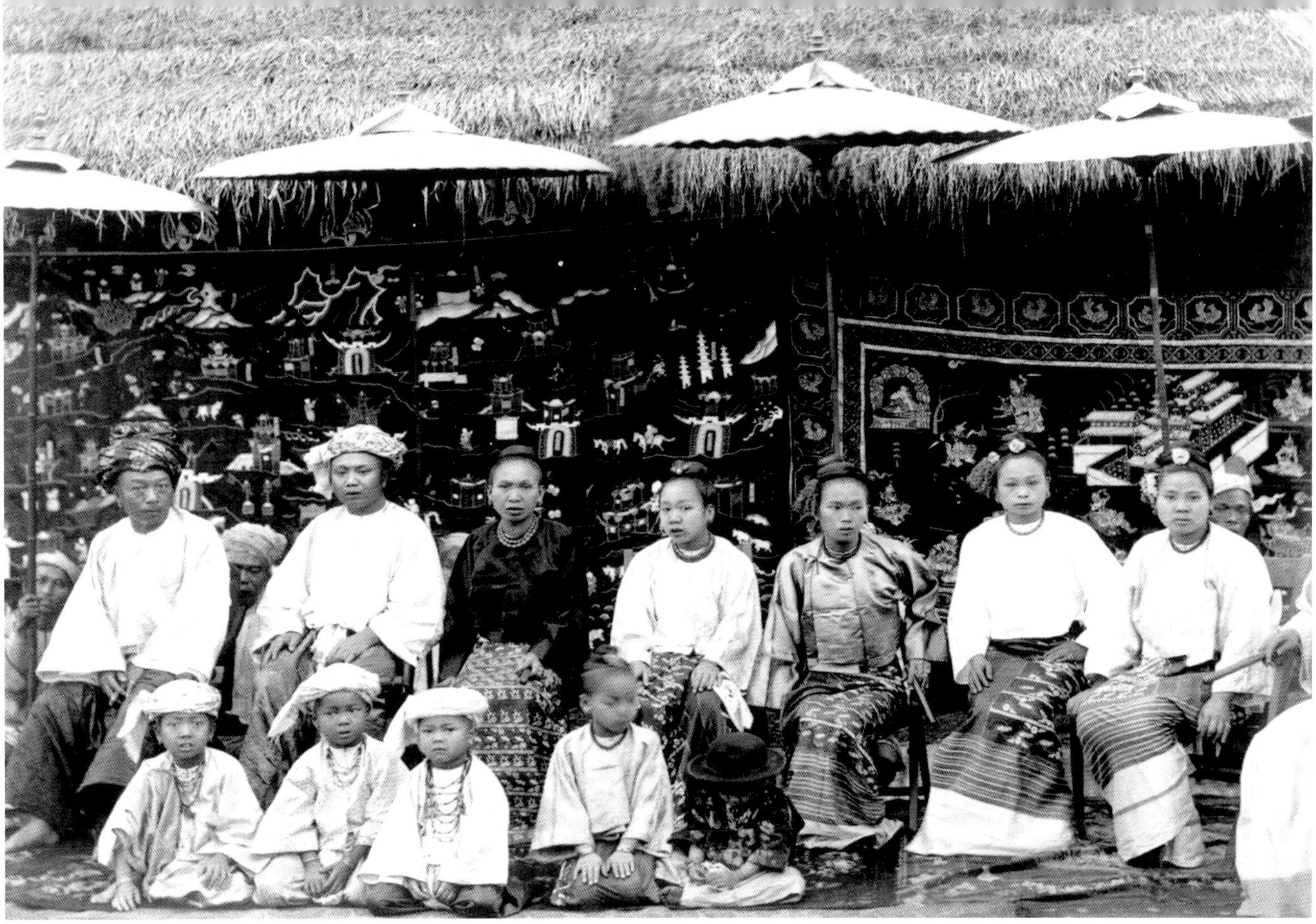

44 The *myosa* of Pangmi with his family seated in front of two embroidered hangings (*shwe chi doe*), circa 1890. *(The Oriental and India Office Collections, The British Library, London, 92/8 (37))*

From the beginning the British saw these meetings as a way of bringing lasting peace to the Shan States. In a private letter, the British envoy Sir George Scott wrote,

> *The mere fact of getting the chiefs together is most beneficial and after having met once I dare say they will be less likely to fight.*[37]

He describes football matches and military band performances that helped create an informal atmosphere at the durbars. Meanwhile in Taunggyi the capital of the Shan States, formal banquets were held while the Parliament was in session. Nel Adams, daughter of the Prince of Lawksawk wrote:

> *It was a tradition that on the last night of the Durbar [Parliamentary Session] the Commissioner would give a banquet for all the members of the Shan State Council. ...As it was one of the grandest social occasions, everyone dressed up in their best attire. The Sawbwas [princes] wore long embroidered robes over their suits, decorated with medals and silk turbans.*[38]

The late nineteenth century was a time of territorial expansion by the British and French, the British in Burma and the Shan States and the French in neighbouring Laos. Meanwhile the Chinese were making claims in the northern Shan states. The Lan Na principalities had passed under the suzerainty of Bangkok and eventually became part of the kingdom of Siam, officially renamed Thailand in 1939. All the major powers were anxious to establish permanent and mutually acceptable boundaries, and they commenced a series of surveys. The British met with a Siamese delegation in 1893 to agree the border between Keng Tung and Lan Na. The chief of the Siamese delegation arrived by elephant with his attendants. In 1894, a British team, headed by Sir George Scott, met with the French Boundary Commission led by Auguste Pavie. In 1900 they convened with the Chinese, and the land to be placed under Chinese jurisdiction was determined by the watersheds of the River Salween and River N'maika. Most of these settlements ignored the claims made by local chiefs because, it was argued, they had no proper evidence to support them. Their evidence was not accepted by surveyors from Britain, France, Siam and China, who were merely interested in gaining as much land as they could. Local land claims were based on complex tributary relation systems, on oral history and on indigenous maps that were not to scale and appeared haphazard and unprofessional in the eyes of the super powers. This was wilful ignorance as the maps in particular contained a lot of valuable detail with stupas (Buddhist monuments) as boundary markers that separated the Shan States from the Sino-Tibetan border and from India and Burma. Mountains, rivers, streams and rice fields were also marked as belonging to individual states.[39] This evidence did not impress the Boundary Commission.

The Commission also failed to take account of the traditional Tai *muong* system that involved complex tributary systems operating in even the smallest settlements, a system loosely described as "areas of influence" (see chapter one). The *muong* system had confused foreigners ever since they first penetrated the inland states. An insight into the problems facing the Commission can be seen in the case of the Prince of Muong Singh who argued that he should not give up his land to Laos under French jurisdiction because he was tributary to Siam through the court of Nan and had no tributary relations with the king of Luang Prabang. He argued that every year he sent ten horses, wax and other

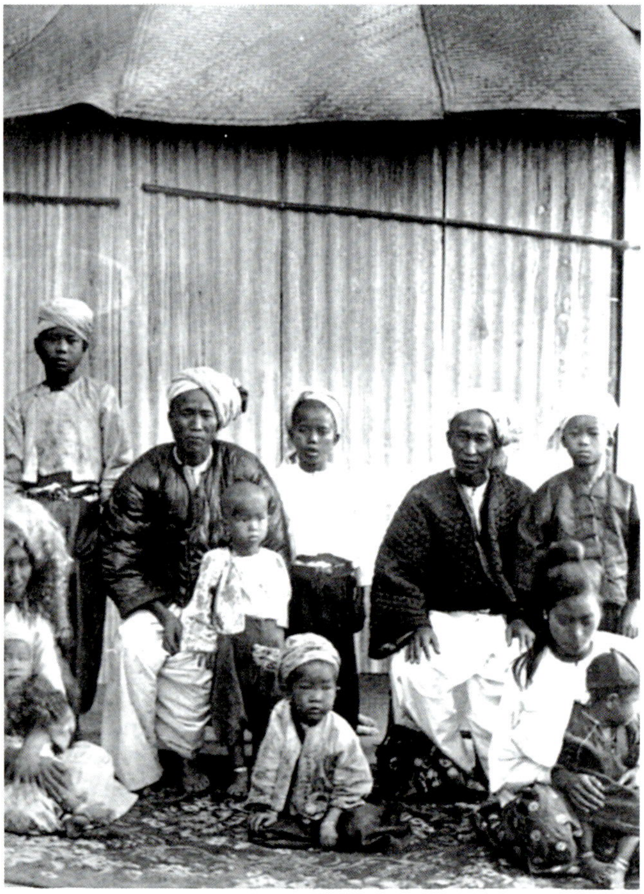

45 Officials and their families outside a durbar house in Loi Long, Shan States. The men wear glazed indigo cotton jackets. *(The Oriental and India Office Collections, The British Library, London, 92/8 (47))*

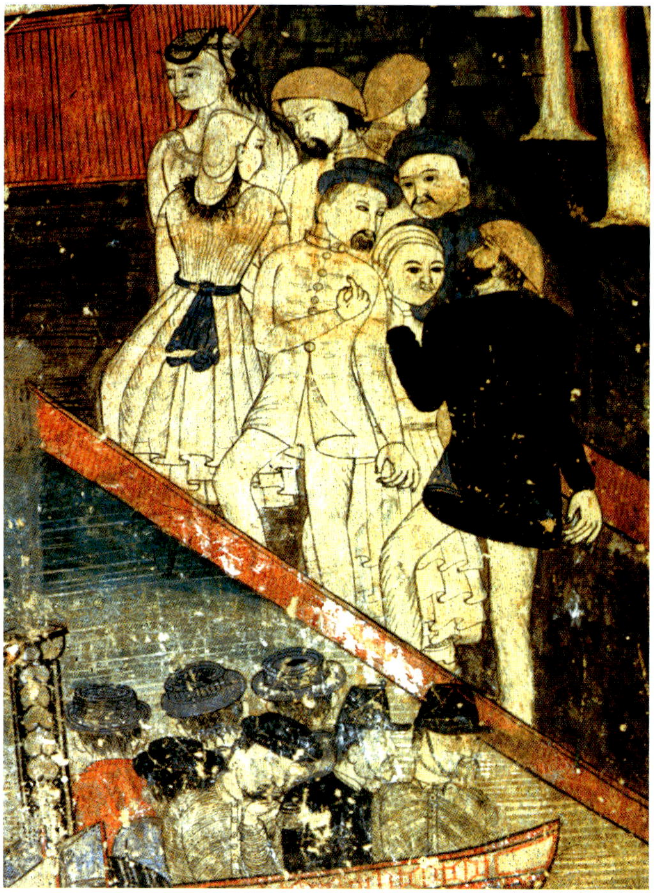

46 A mural painting of French officials and their wives. Wat Phumin, Nan, Thailand.

tributary gifts to the prince of Nan. He tried to impress this on the commissioners by appearing in Tai Lue dress with his consorts seated around him. He and most of his consorts were Tai Lue, as were many of the people of Nan. He later appeared in a Chinese dragon robe indicating that he was also tributary to China, perhaps hoping that the Chinese would recognise his claims. His pleas and his dress codes were ignored, and the Siamese and the French almost went to war over his territory. In the final judgement of the Commission, the prince lost his land on the east bank of the Mekong River and it passed to Laos under French jurisdiction. The Mekong River then became the boundary. The French-Lao border was marked on land with pillars, "except on the eastern side of the wild Wa country."[40] The Prince of Nan viewed the annexation of land from Muong Singh as his loss, and as Nan was tributary to Bangkok, King Rama V of Siam also felt aggrieved. Loss of territory became the theme of local poetry and was expressed in mural paintings produced in a Nan temple.[41] Interestingly, the Sipsong Pan Na Chronicle written in this period states that Muong Singh and other *muong* in Sipsong Pan Na were given to the French for a different and more sinister reason.

> *At the same time as the era of Chao Mom Luang, Lao was taken as a colony of the French. Xishuangbanna had to give up Muang Singh, Muang Sum Nua Sum Tai, Muang U Nua U Tai, Muang Pooka, and Muang Nam Ta to the French as well because Khun Luang Wu Yun [the ruler] surrendered these cities as payment for opium from the French.*[42]

Meanwhile the British engineer Holt Hallett argued that Shan villagers in settlements within four miles of Muong La (Semao) were tributary to Burma, not to China.[43] Of course many Shan princes had for centuries hedged their bets by paying tribute to Burma and China and the whole issue was confused even more because the Shan princes could not agree among themselves. The accepted European system of marking boundaries by watersheds and rivers suited the colonial bureaucrats in London, Paris and Peking as a tidy way of resolving the issue. The Shan states of Keng Hung and Muong Lem were transferred to China. In response to local criticism the British claimed that clear boundary markers put an end to border skirmishes that had plagued the inland states for centuries. They also stressed the success of durbars in settling land disputes between Shan rulers in the areas the British were administering. The American missionary W. C. Dodd claimed in retrospect that local people viewed border settlements, not in terms of land gained or lost, but in terms of what happened to the people. He claimed that by the early twentieth century local people said that the British ruled the Tai Khoen and the Chinese ruled the Tai Lue.[44]

As the British formalized relations with the Shan courts the princes proved their willingness to co-operate. They were given titles, regalia and privileges according to sumptuary laws operated by the court of Queen Victoria through her colonial representative the Viceroy and Governor General of India. The prince of Yawnghwe was

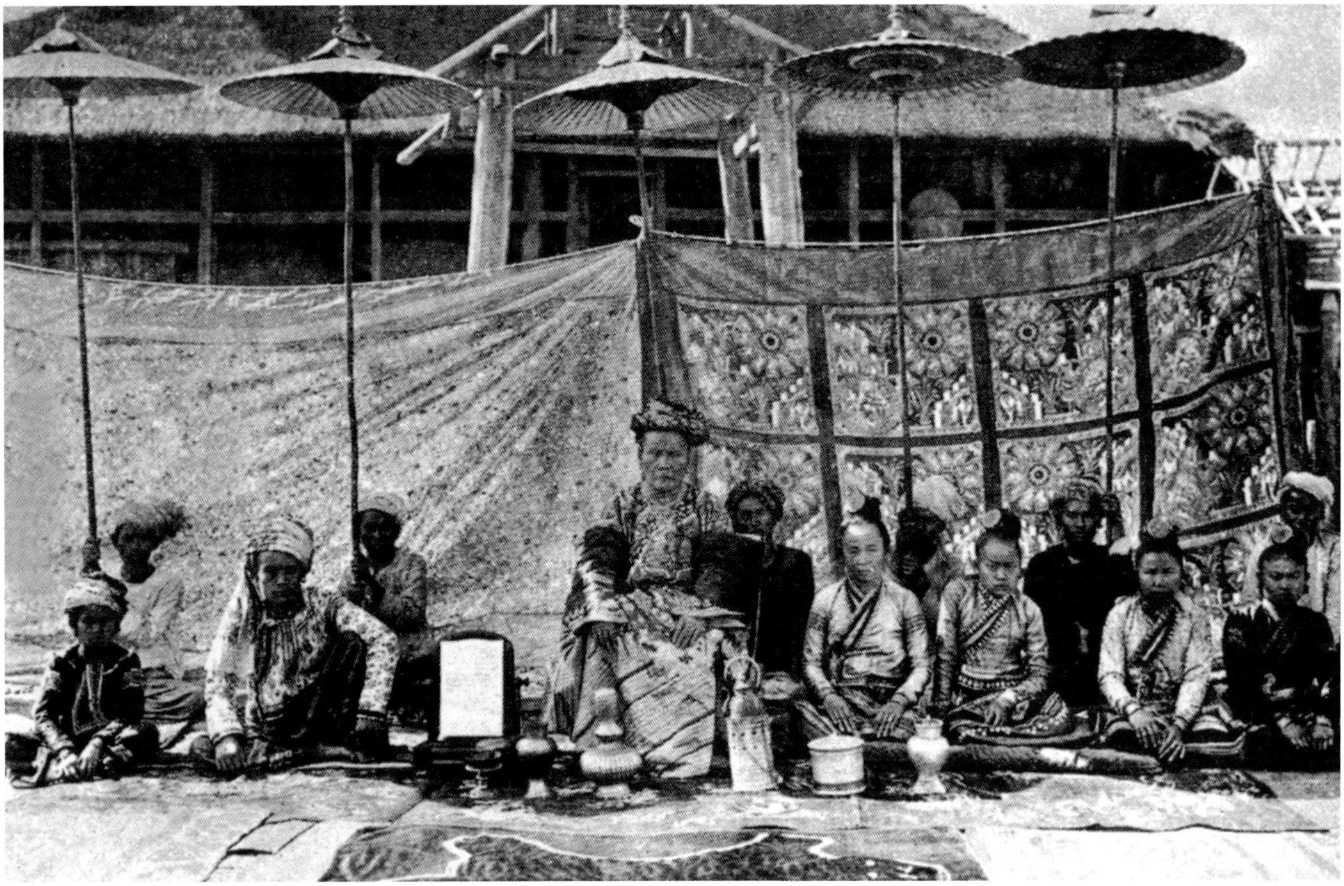

47 The prince of Muong Singh wearing Chinese robes. His consorts are dressed in Tai Lue style in Lefèvre (1898). *(White Lotus Press)*

knighted as K. C. I. E (Knight Commander of the Indian Empire), received a Delhi Durbar decoration and was entitled to a salute of nine guns. The prince of Keng Tung was granted a K. S. M (King's Service Medal) and a Delhi Durbar medal and was also permitted a salute of nine guns. The Prince of Muong Nai gained the title "Honourable" and was made a C. I. E. (Commander of the Indian Empire) and K. S. M, and was entitled to a salute of nine guns. Less powerful princes received titles and medals graded according to rank.

British reports make fascinating reading, particularly when they judge the Shan princes by Victorian notions of "civilised" society.

> *...the chiefs all have sanads or patents. They are supposed to exercise authority according to the customary laws of the Shan... Kengtung is far and away the largest, and some of the smaller ones are not much larger than an estate in England... The chiefs will want civilising before they are fit for ladies society... Moné [Prince of Muong Nai] is quite a gentleman.*[45]

In December 1903, Lord Curzon, Viceroy of India, staged a huge durbar in Delhi to mark the accession of King Edward VII following the death of Queen Victoria. Princes and senior officials from all parts of the British Empire attended. The display of exotic dress, military uniforms and caparisoned animals was the greatest visual spectacle of the age. A group of senior princes and their consorts attended as representatives of the Shan States and were photographed in exotic court dress that was a legacy of the ancient tributary systems operated from Burma and China. Displayed on the carpet at their feet were the ceremonial vessels and containers that were their regalia of office. There was no monarch to represent the Burmese because the British had exiled King Thibaw in 1885, and with his departure the Burmese court had been disbanded. At the Delhi Durbar it was the Shan princes who in their elaborate dress and regalia reflected the history and cultural affiliations that had existed before the British arrived.

In keeping with their wish to maintain existing hierarchies the British drew up a "List of Order of Precedence," published in the *Shan State Manual* of 1925. First came the *saohpa* of Keng Tung, then Hsipaw, Muong Nai, Yawnghwe and Tawngpeng. South Hsenwi and North Hsenwi were given equal status, then Muong Mit, Muong Pai, Lawksawk, Laikha, Mawkmai, Muong Pan, Muong-pawn, Manglun, Kantarawadi, Samka and Muongkung. The *myosa* were listed in order of precedence, with first the *myosa* of Nawngwawn, then Muongnawng, Muong Sit, Kehsi-Mansam, Mawnang, Loi Long, Hsatung, Wanyin, Hopong, Namkhok, Sakoi, Muongshu, Kenglun, Bawlake, Kyetbogyi, Hsamongkham, Maw and Pwela. For the chiefs (*ngwegunhmu*), Yengan was first, then came Pangtara, Pangmi, Loi-ai, Kyaukku, Loimaw, Kyone and Namtok.[46]

This order was close to existing hierarchical systems, and the domestic lives of the Shan princes were not immediately

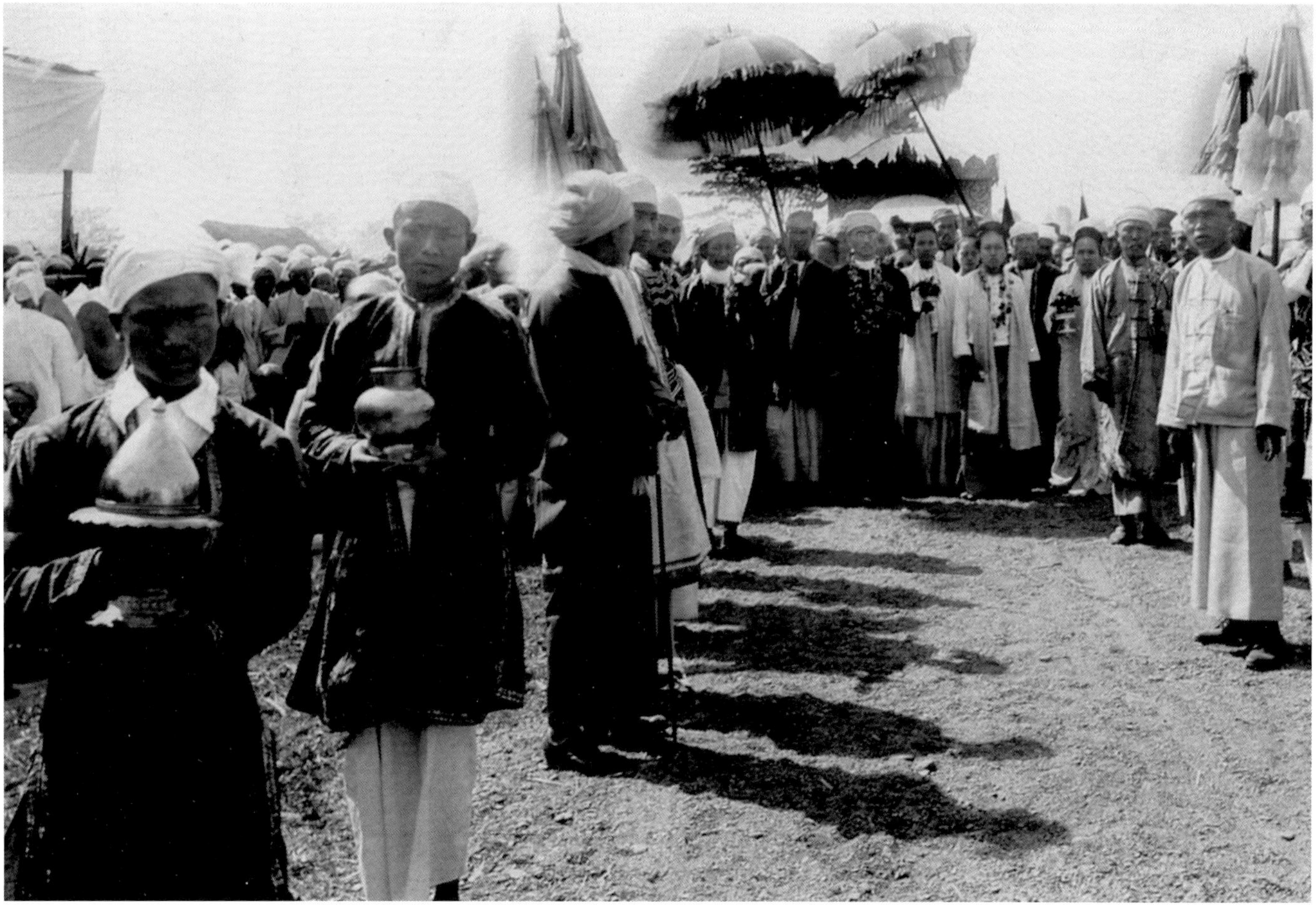

48 The ceremonial entrance of Sao Shwe Thaike, Prince of Yawnghwe, and his consorts to the city of Yawngwhe, 1927.

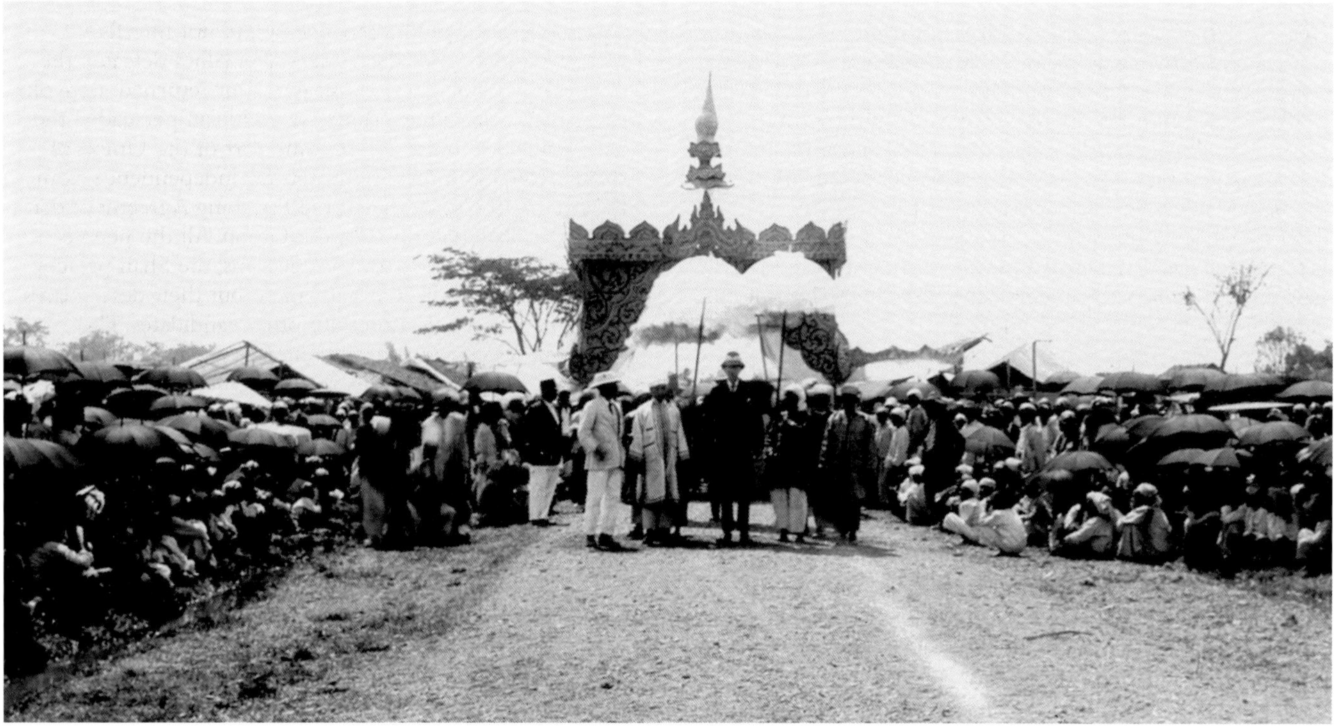

49 The British Governor is greeted by royalty and officials at the entrance to the city of Yawnghwe, 1927.

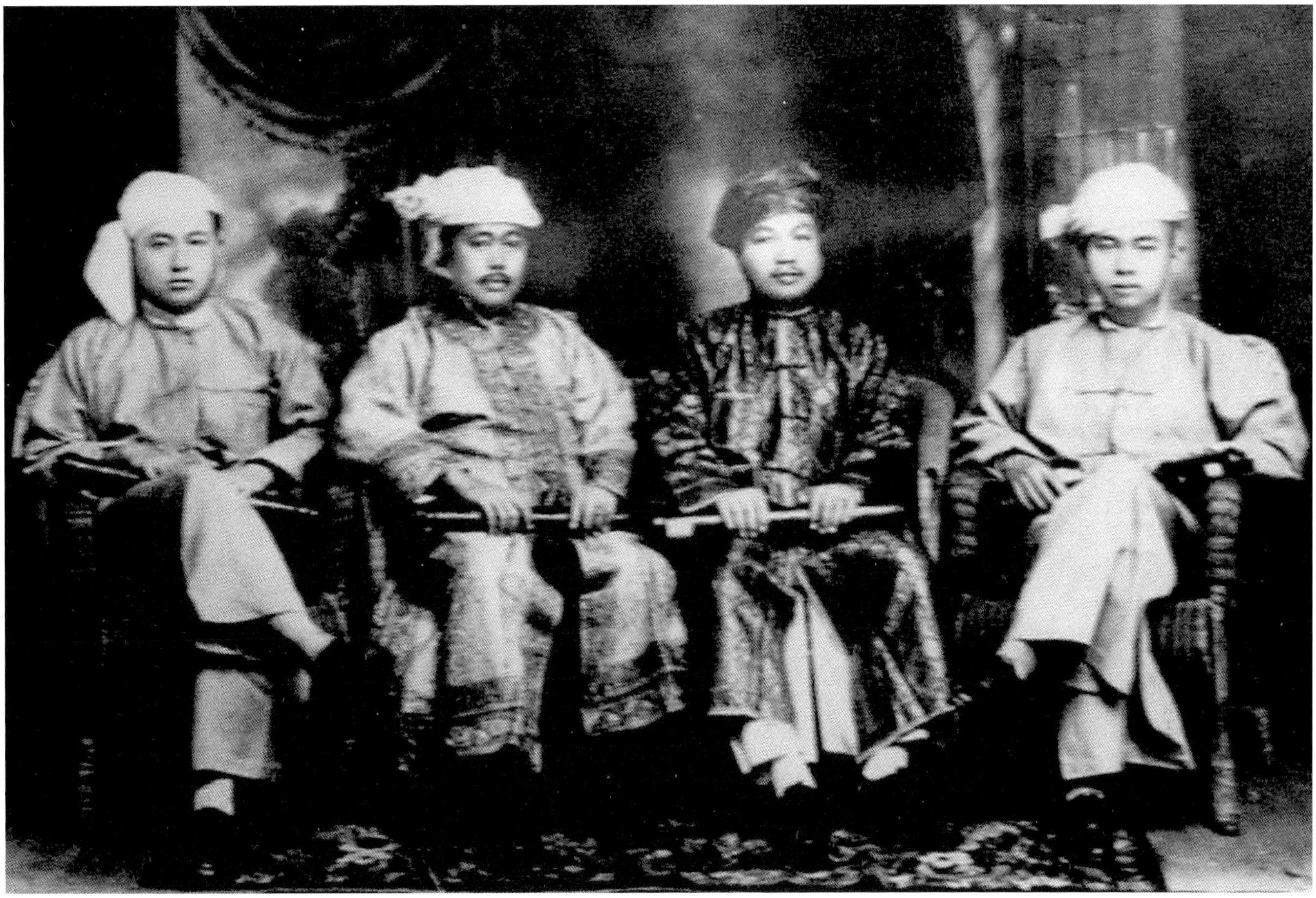

50 A group of Shan princes, left to right: Sao Hkun Kyi, *saohpa* of Hsi Hseng, Sao Kyaw, *saohpa* of Muong Nai, Sao Hkun Hsa, *saohpa* of Muongnaung and Sao San Htun, *saohpa* of Muong Pai.

affected by British presence. Slowly however, they began to replace traditional Shan palaces with buildings that were an assimilation of Shan and European colonial style, considered a "happy compromise" by Maurice Collis writing in the 1930s (see chapter five). Collis also noted that some princes built large country houses in English style. Others like the prince of Hsenwi kept their old palaces for use on ceremonial occasions with a few retainers in residence to take care of the building and grounds while they resided in new palaces built with modern amenities, including running water.

The Shan princes went to school in England, or to a British-style school established in Taunggyi in 1902, built especially for the sons of ruling families and the elite. This mirrored earlier times when the princes had been sent to the court of Ava, and later to Mandalay, to learn the ways of the Burmese. While they were in Britain, some princes attended court ceremonies and were introduced to members of the royal family. The prince of Hsipaw (born 1893) was educated at Rugby and Oxford and attended the coronation of Edward VII. Some sons and daughters of the princes married into British families as in earlier times they had intermarried with the Burmese.

The political order and stability that the British created in the Shan States collapsed in 1942 when the Japanese invaded Burma. In 1943 the Shan States came under Japanese rule although the Japanese did not interfere with the authority of the princes. The Allies defeated the Japanese in 1945 and a British governor returned. Bogyoke Aung San, a prominent Burmese politician persuaded the Shan princes to unite and become part of the Union of Burma, joining in their campaign for independence from Britain. In 1947 they signed the Panglong Agreement that made the Shan states part of the Union. All the people were to have equal rights and freedoms; the Shan princes served as life members of Parliament but their descendants were to stand for election with other candidates. The Panglong Agreement was binding for ten years. Aung San met the British Prime Minister Clement Attlee in 1947 and an agreement was signed giving the Union of Burma dominion status. Aung San did not live to see his dream of an independent country as he was assassinated on July 19 1947. The Vice President of the Union, U Nu continued with preparations for Independence celebrations that took place on the fourth of January 1948. Burma joined the United Nations but chose to leave the Commonwealth. The independent government had just been established when there was internal unrest leading to a civil uprising. The government survived but was severely weakened. New elections were held and the Shan princes took their seats in the newly established Parliament. The Prince Sao Shwe Thaike of Yaungwhe (1927-1959) became the first

President of the Union of Burma and for a period the Shan princes worked well with the government of U Nu.

However, as had happened throughout the history of the Shan States, China and Burma were competing for supremacy in the region. The Chinese Kuomintang army that had been driven out of Communist China was attempting to gain a stronghold in the northern Shan States by pushing south from their base in Yunnan. In an effort to prevent a Kuomintang invasion the Burmese army, under the leadership of General Ne Win, decided to take control and U Nu was ousted in a military coup. On March the second 1962 the army stormed the Government Building where parliament was in session and, at gunpoint arrested and imprisoned the President, the Prime Minister and his cabinet, the princes and many of their relatives. The Shan princes were in conflict with the military dictatorship and as ten years had passed since they signed the Panglong Agreement, they decided to secede.

In response General Ne Win forced the Shan rulers to relinquish their power and hereditary rights. The Burmese army ransacked Shan households and confiscated all weapons. Some princes and senior officials died in suspicious circumstances, others disappeared and those who survived were released but not allowed to return to their states and their people. As the British had deposed the King of Burma and with his deposition destroyed the culture of kingship in Burma, so the Burmans now destroyed the traditional relationship that existed between the Shan people and their rulers. Fortunately Buddhist religious institutions survived and continued to thrive although many historic Shan palaces were confiscated or destroyed and collections of court regalia and dress were dispersed. Some were eventually taken to museums or have survived in private collections. Today the descendants of Shan royalty live in Burma (Myanmar) and are scattered across the world in the USA, Thailand, Australia, Malaysia and Europe.

This chapter has charted the long history of Tai settlement in the Shan States, and drawn attention to the tradition of intermarriage between ruling families, as well as the Tai elite of other inland principalities and the treaties and marital alliances formed with powerful hill-residing families. On the wider diplomatic stage it has shown how the Shan rulers interacted with the Burmese, Siamese and Chinese and in the Colonial Era, with the British and French. All these relationships required a sophisticated level of diplomacy which the Shan princes demonstrated, although they were weakened by their inability to create and sustain a united force.

The most powerful Shan princes ruled over principalities the size of small European countries and lived in grand style. They employed skilled artisans to build and decorate their palaces and maintain the grounds. Weavers, dyers and embroiderers, goldsmiths, silversmiths and lacquer workers were commissioned to provide furnishings for the interiors, and court dress and regalia for ceremonial use. This was an indigenous tradition that mirrored local culture, although the princes also received and wore other forms of dress associated with tributary and sumptuary laws established in China, Burma, Siam and Britain.

Minor princes and rulers of outlying settlements generally kept more modest dwellings and wore moderate forms of court dress that reflected regional affiliations and ethnic loyalties. They too were allocated tributary dress and regalia, although it did not match the splendour of the items distributed at the major courts. In summary, Shan court dress, textiles and regalia relate directly to the historical and political issues summarised in this chapter and signify the importance attached to rank and ceremony at all levels of society.

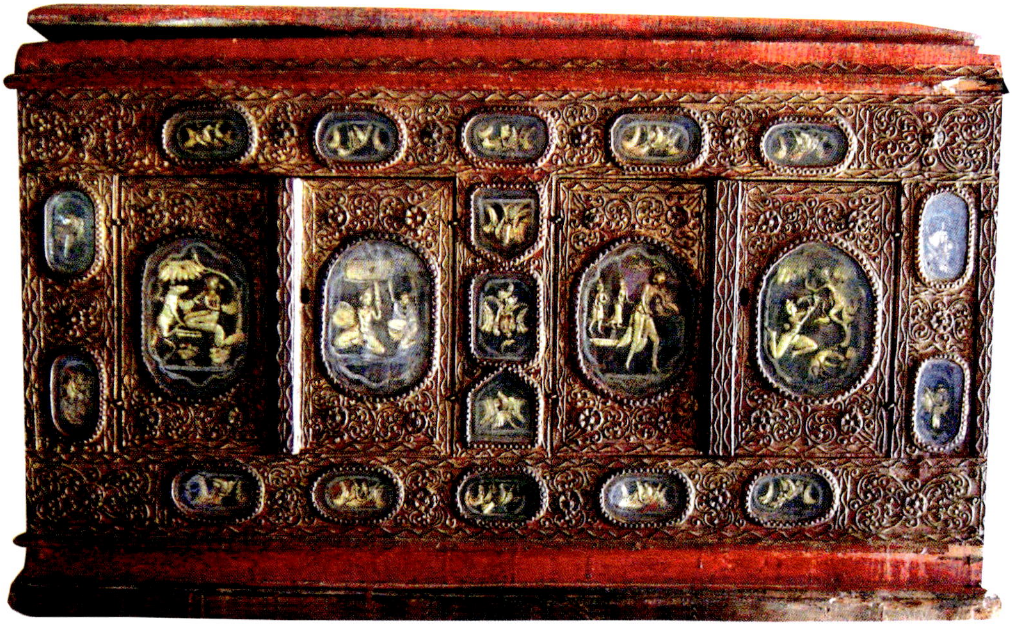

51 A lacquered, gilded and inlaid manuscript chest in the collection of the Shan Palace Museum, Yawnghwe.

Endnotes

[1] Sao Saimong Mangrai, *Padaeng Chronicle and the Jengtung Chronicle* translated, University of Michigan, Ann Arbor, 1981.
[2] In the Tavatimsa Heaven, reside the thirty-three gods.
[3] They were dressed in similar style to the depiction of the Buddha portrayed as a Shan prince.
[4] T. A. Trant, *Two Years in Ava from May1824 to May1826 by an Officer on the Staff of the Quartermaster General's Department*, London, 1827, p. 297.
[5] It is accepted that the Buddha was born in 543 BC.
[6] Authur Phayre, *History of Burma*, Susil Gupta, London, 1883, reprint, London 1967.
[7] George Scott and J. P. Hardiman, *Gazeteer of Burma and The Shan States*, Superintendent of Government Printing, Rangoon, 1900, 1901, Vol. II, pt. II, p. 3.
[8] E. H. Parker, 'The Early Laos and China', in *The China Review*, Sept-Oct. 1890.
[9] Leslie Milne and Wilbur Cochrane, *Shans at Home*, London, John Murray, 1910, reprint New York, 1973, p. 13.
[10] G. H. Luce, 'The Early Syam in Burma's History', *Journal of the Siam Society*, Nov. 1958.
[11] Phayre, 1967.
[12] D. G. E. Hall, *A History of Southeast Asia*, London, 1966, reprint 1981, p. 160.
[13] Phayre, 1967, p. 116-117.
[14] Sao Saimong Mangrai, *The Shan States and British Annexation.* Data Paper no. 57, South East Asia Program, Cornell University, Ithaca, 1965.
[15] Htin Aung, *A History of Burma*, Columbia University Press, 1967, p. 116.
[16] King Bayinnaung is credited with banning Shan funeral sacrifices in which the favourite elephant, horse and slaves of a *saohpa* were killed and buried with him.
[17] 'Report of Thao Sitthimongkhon' in Wilson, Constance, M. and Hanks, Lucien, M., *The Burma-Thailand Frontier Over Sixteen Decades: Three Descriptive Documents.* Monograph in International Studies, Southeast Asia Series, Athens, Ohio, No. 70, 1985, pp. 14-25.
[18] Maurice Collis, *Lords of the Sunset*, Faber and Faber, London 1938, reprint Bangkok, 1996.
[19] Harold Fielding-Hall, *Palace Tales*, Harper Brothers, 1900, reprint Bangkok, 1997.
[20] Many descendants of Keng Tung royalty were successful in Chiang Mai. Khamtan Sirorot became the head of frontier defences at Mae Sariang, while others became wealthy businessmen.
[21] Fielding Hall, 1997.
[22] Constance Wilson and Lucien Hanks, 'The Burma Thailand Frontier over Sixteen Decades: Three Discriptive Documents' Monograph in International Studies, Southeast Asia Series No. 70. University of Ohio, Athens, 1985.
[23] *Ibid.*
[24] Sao Saimong Mangrai, 1965.
[25] *Ibid.*, p. 269. Collis, 1996, pp. 97-99, 203-204.
[26] Captain McCleod, 'A Journal kept by Captain W. C. McCleod, 'Assistant to the Commissioner in the Tenassarim Provinces during his Mission to the Frontiers of China 1836-1837'. India and Oriental Collections, The British Library, London Parliamentary papers, Vol. 50 (1869).
[27] Francis Garnier, *Further Travels in Laos and Siam: The Mekong Exploration Commission Report 1866-1868,* Vol. 2 reprint White Lotus Press, Bangkok, 1996, pp. 52, 105-108.
[28] A viss measured 3.652 lbs.
[29] William Clifton Dodd, *The Tai Race*, 1923, reprint White Lotus Press, Bangkok, 1996.
[30] *Ibid.*
[31] Sao Saimong Mangrai, 1965, p. 110.
[32] Hildebrand, 'British Policy and the Shan States 1886-1942', Foreign Office Report F.O. 69/65: 16, Public Records Office, Kew, London.
[33] *Ibid.*
[34] They formed approximately 21,000 square miles in total.
[35] George Scott, *Burma and Beyond*, Grayson and Grayson, London 1932, p. 251.
[36] *Ibid.*
[37] Nel Adams, *My Vanished World*, Cheshire 2000, p. 32.
[38] Tin Sai Aung, 'The Tai Ethnic Settlement in the Hkamti Long Area', *Myanmar Historical Journal,* No. 5, June 2000, pp. 37-61.
[39] *Ibid.*
[40] David Wyatt, *Temple Murals as an Historical Source: The Case of Wat Phumin*, Bangkok, Nan Thai Studies Section, Faculty of Arts, Chulalongkorn University, 1993.
[41] Xishuang Banna Chronicle, trans. Tawee Sawangpanyangkoon, Bangkok, n. d.
[42] Holt Hallett, *A Thousand Miles on an Elephant in the Shan States*, Edinburgh and London: Blackwood and Sons, 1890, reprint White Lotus Press, Bangkok, 1988, p. 151.
[43] William Clifton Dodd, *The Tai Race: Elder Brother of the Chinese*, Cedar Rapids, The Torch Press, 1923, reprint White Lotus Press, Bangkok, 1996, p. 191.
[44] Scott, 1932.
[45] Scott and Hardiman, 1900.

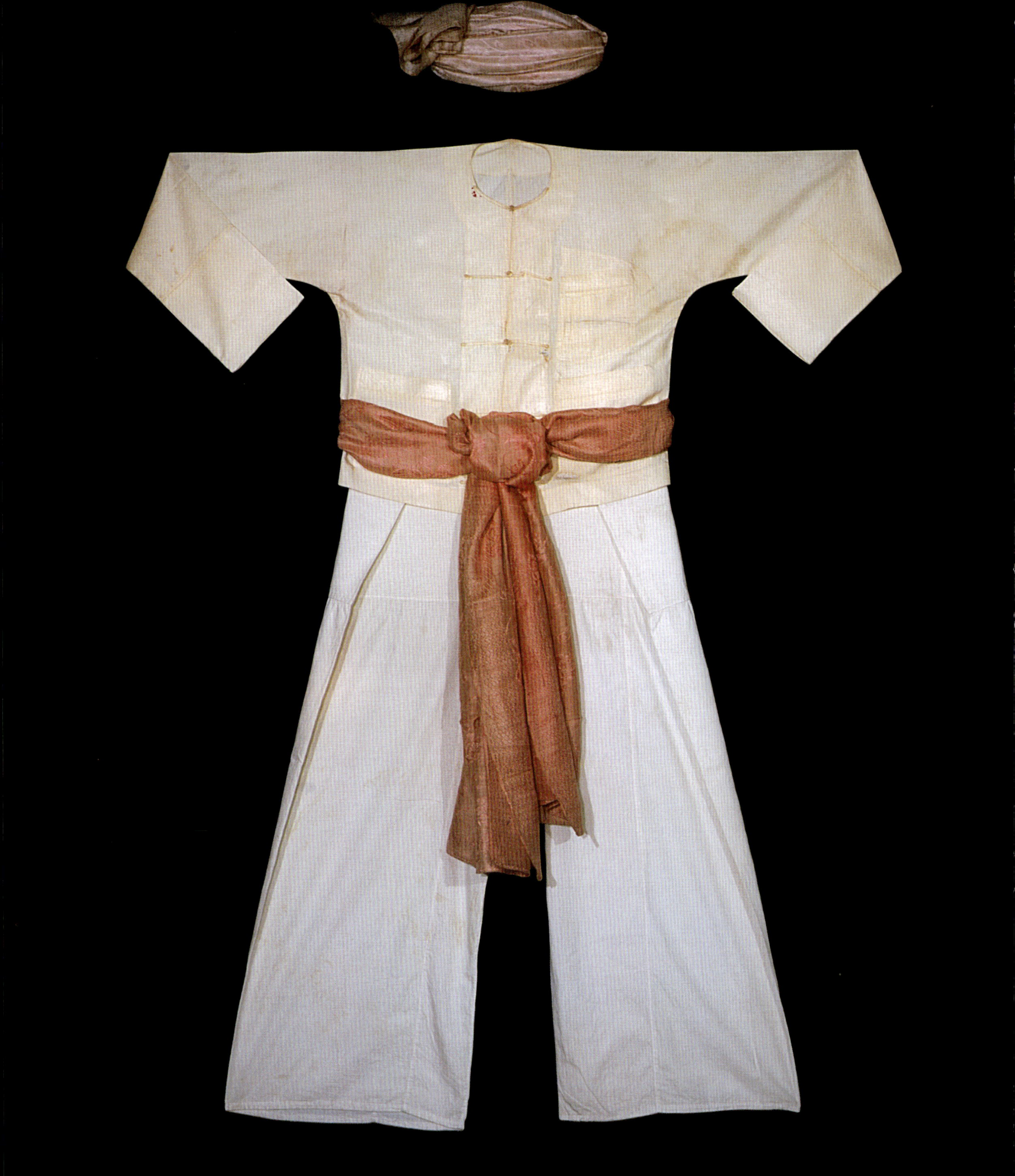

Chapter 3
Male Dress in the Shan States

This chapter examines dress and body decoration worn by villagers and the ceremonial dress of the princes, senior officials and local chiefs. This is a fascinating area of study because the complexities of local politics, ethnic identity, and international tributary relations affected the way senior men dressed. Although the finest clothing was reserved for royalty, village dress could be equally vibrant. On festive occasions men would turn out in colourful turbans, shoulder sashes and sarongs, while the ladies wore skirts woven with silk and silver and gold metal thread. Important events in family life, such as a young man's induction ceremony for the Buddhist novitiate, and the ear boring ceremony, also involved wearing one's best clothes. This chapter will include forms of male dress and body decoration particularly associated with astrology and spirit religion.

According to the Shan chronicles, when royal ancestors came down from the Tavatimsa Heaven to rule the earth, they were decked in shining robes and carried gem-studded regalia. Dress at the Shan courts reflected this mythology, and in the nineteenth century, the princes presided in gilded Audience Halls, seated on gilded thrones and wearing fabrics embroidered with gold and silver metal thread, gemstones, beetle wings and sequins that sparkled in the intense tropical light. This tradition continued through the centuries until the Shan rulers were deposed in the 1960s and their dress and regalia passed into private hands or into museum collections. For villagers, recent trade patterns and political upheaval have led to the almost total abandonment of locally produced, indigenous Tai, particularly Lue, Khoen and Tai Yai, dress in favour of cheap mass-produced Chinese textiles.[1]

In the nineteenth century Shan men were distinguished by their long hair that was twisted into a knot and worn at the side of the head, or above the forehead. It was usually wrapped with a turban cloth. It was common to see men labouring in the fields tending rice, or working around the village, wearing loose tabard-shaped vests, or indigo cotton shirts, and rectangles of cloth wrapped around the waist and hitched up between the legs. Or they wore loose-legged indigo cotton trousers (referred to as Shan trousers) fastened at the waist with a pleat and tuck and held in place with a cotton sash or belt. In the rainy season they wore coats made from palm leaves, and in the summer they covered their turbans with large floppy straw hats to protect them from the sun. On cool evenings they wrapped themselves in hand-woven cotton blankets, and when the weather got cold, wore padded and quilted jackets, the most striking made of highly glazed indigo cotton that was water proof (see fig. 45). Minor chiefs and officials also dressed in this simple way. While travelling in the Shan states in the 1860s Captain McLeod wrote,

52 (Opposite) Male court dress: turban, shirt, sash and trousers. *(Akadet Nakbunlang collection)*

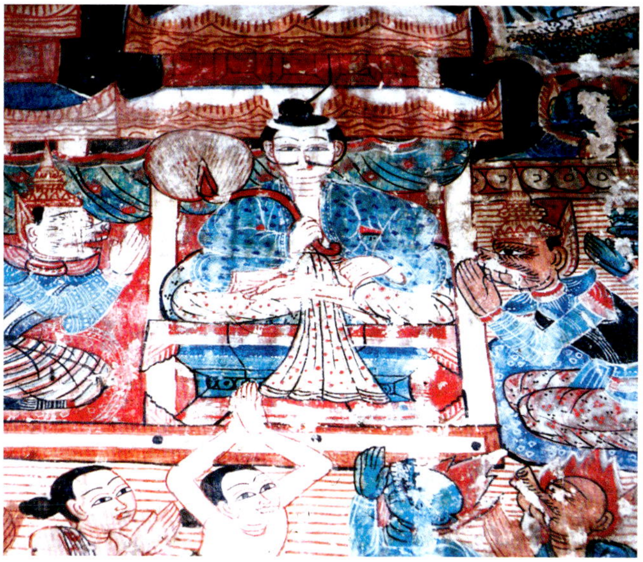

53 Mural painting of a Shan prince. Wat Pa Daet, Mae Chaem, Thailand.

> *The chiefs dress in glazed dark blue Shan jackets and wide trousers, the Chinese jacket of cloth or fur is common among them. They preserve their long hair and wear a turban like the Burmans, and in the day time when going out* [wear] *a Chinese hat. The only ornament worn by the chiefs is a gold bangle.*[2]

If one of the distinguishing features of a Shan male was his coiled, shiny hair, his turban (*gaung-baung*) was an equally important symbol of identity. Nineteenth-century mural paintings and photographs indicate a wide range of fabrics and styles. How a man wore his turban was said to reflect his personality and a great deal of care and attention went into its styling.[3] A turban cloth might be tightly wrapped around the head with the hair coil left outside, or the hair might be concealed in the pleats. Tight, neat pleats were said to imply a disciplined personality. Many men, deemed to be flamboyant, chose styles that involved a generous amount of fabric wrapped in loose pleats and tied with an elegant bow at the side, or at the back of the head, with the ends left loose to trail over the shoulders. Some men favoured a rakish angle with the pleats off-centre, while others preferred a high cone shape that made them look impressively tall. Women often prepared the more elaborate styles and used jewelled pins to keep the folds in place. Shan turban cloths were made from a range of homespun hand-woven cottons. Some were trimmed with bands of supplementary weft. The wealthy wore pastel-coloured Chinese silks and silk brocades, and Indian silk brocades.

Villagers carried their personal belongings in locally made shoulder bags. Contents might include a snack and a small knife, some betel and lime kept in small metal or

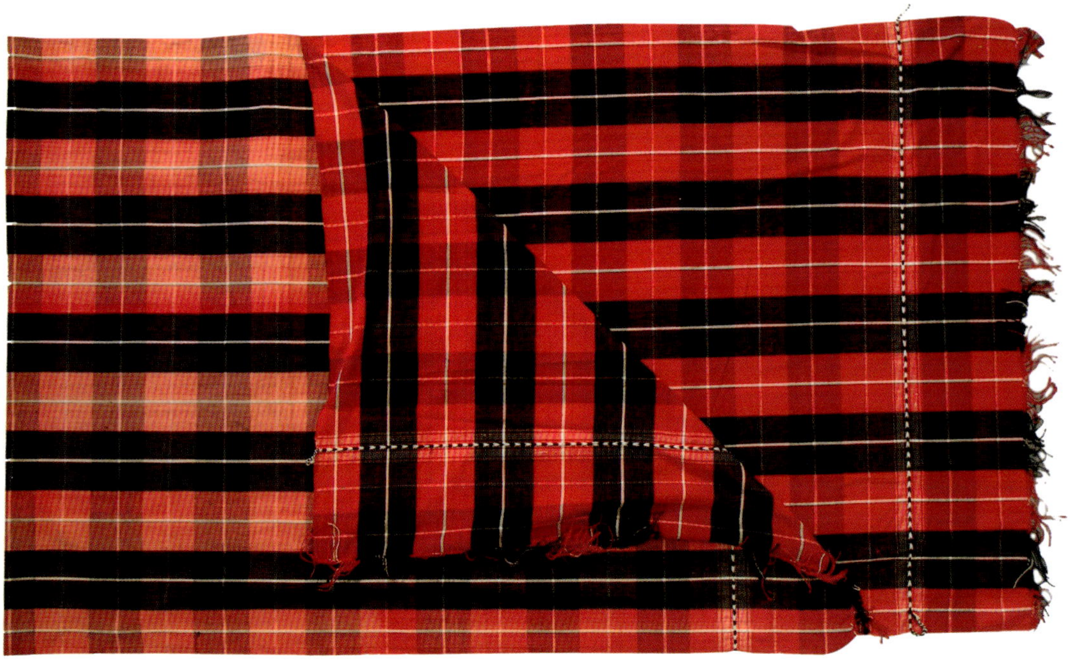

54 A cotton blanket with bands of red, black and white cotton in the warp and the same configuration of bands in the weft. Woven in plain weave. Red, black and white warp fringe.
(Denison University collection, Granville, Ohio, DU1968.174)

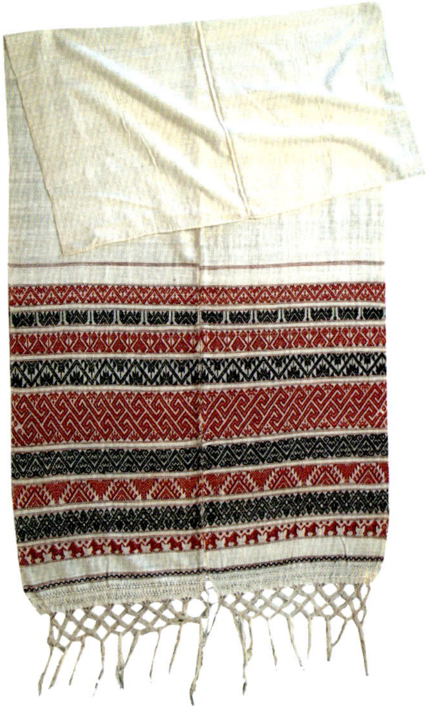

55 A bed sheet, with a hand-spun cotton warp and weft, woven in plain weave with a wide supplementary weft border. The patterns include rows of zig-zags and stylised roof spires *(hti),* water dragons *(naga)* and offering bowls with floral and leaf patterns. Two loom widths are joined along the selvage.
(Denison University collection, Granville, Ohio, DU1969.248)

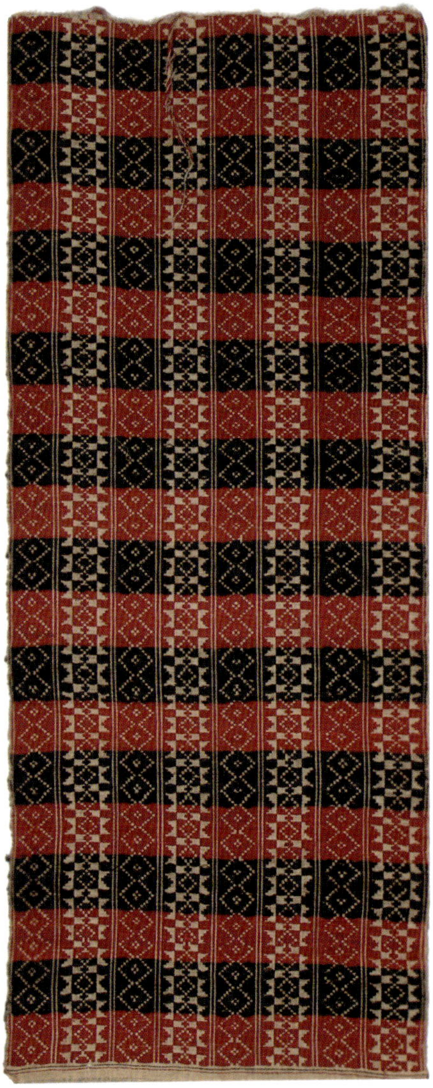

56 A blanket with a plain cotton warp and red and black striped cotton weft, and a repeat supplementary weft pattern of diamonds and stylised flowers in plain cotton.
(Denison University collection, Granville, Ohio, DU1967.51)

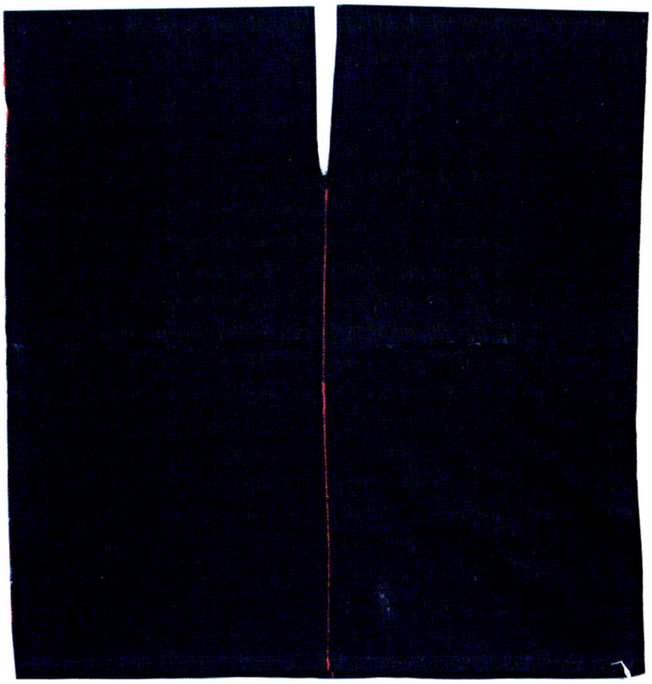

57 A sleeveless, indigo, cotton tunic woven in plain weave. It is made from two loom widths with red cotton overstitching along the selvage, and openings left for the head and arms.
(Denison University collection, Granville, Ohio, DU1967.214)

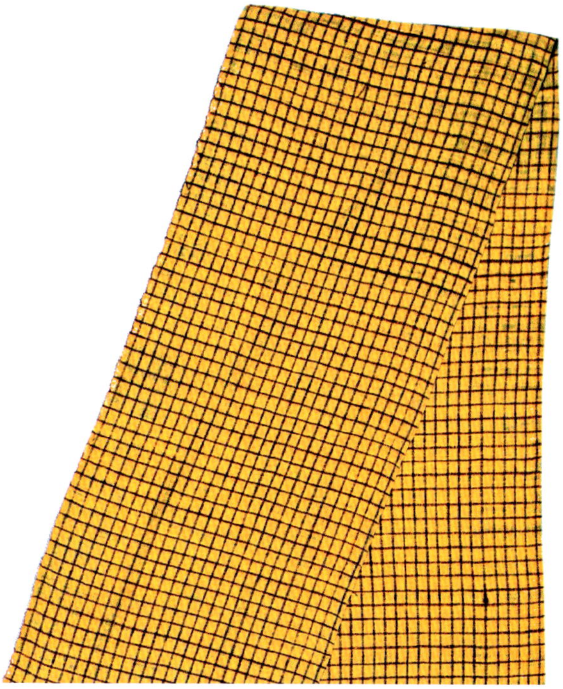

58 A narrow length of hand-spun yellow cotton, with narrow red stripes in the warp and weft, used as a turban cloth or a sash.
(Denison University collection, Granville, Ohio, DU1968.304.1)

lacquer containers, and possibly an opium pipe. Most bags were woven in cotton with bands of supplementary weft. They were waterproofed inside with plant resin. In the nineteenth century shoulder bags were a popular gift to present to missionaries. These bags were often woven with personal dedications or season's greetings, produced in English or in Shan. When princes and chiefs travelled, retainers carried their personal belongings and their regalia, which included ceremonial water vessels, betel box sets and spittoons made by local artisans. They were graded according to rank.

Nineteenth-century mural paintings and folding paper manuscripts portray Shan nobility and senior officials wearing rectangles of fabric wrapped around the body and over one shoulder (see chapter two, fig. 34). The fabric could be worn like a sarong with the excess fabric tucked in pleats in the front, or it could be wrapped around the waist and passed between the legs to create draped breeches. The Shan princes were often portrayed in fabric with wavy line patterns intended to represent the complex silk tapestry weave, that in Burmese is described as *acheik-luntaya*. This was expensive fabric and was an important symbol of prestige. Those who could not afford the necessary length to produce a complete outfit would buy one length of *acheik-luntaya* and have it sewn as a border on plain, plaid or striped silk (fig. 66). The *acheik-luntaya* panel was worn pleated in the front for maximum effect. Many chiefs wore locally woven cloth in plain, striped or plaid cotton with bands of supplementary weft in the borders. Two lengths were sewn together along the selvage so that it was wide enough to drape, tuck and pleat around the body. In the nineteenth century, the Shan princes wore loose, wide-legged trousers that, when they sat down, often looked like skirts. In the late nineteenth century, there was a fashion among the upper classes for trousers with tight cuffs at the ankles, probably copied from those worn by Indian princes.

There were several types of shirt worn by the Shan. The simplest was two lengths of cotton (often dyed with indigo) joined at the selvedge with the seams left open at the armholes. There was an indigenous style with a fitted bodice and tight sleeves. The bodice flared for a few inches below the waist and fastened in the front or at the side with fabric ties or with buttons and fabric loops. The other was a Chinese style with a straight, loose body, a mandarin collar and long loose sleeves. It fastened in the front with fabric knots, buttons made of silver coins or other metals, or mother-of pearl passed through fabric loops. The Shan elite wore shirts made of Chinese silks and silk brocades, and in the nineteenth century, of Indian silk that was available in the main markets. In cool weather, a lightly padded cotton or silk jacket was worn over the shirt, and in the cold season, a thickly padded jacket or a long coat, sometimes lined with fur.

In the nineteenth century, the British colonial officer, Sir George Scott, and later in the early twentieth century, Colonel James Green, took photographs during their extensive travels in the Shan States. Many princes were photographed at their palaces, while they were on tour, or at political meetings and at social events organised by the British colonial administration. In the 1870s, the French explorer, Louis de Carné, led an expeditionary force to the Shan States and took with him the artist Delaporte who made sketches during audiences held at court, which were later reproduced as etchings. The professional photographer, Philip Klier, established a studio in Rangoon in the 1870s and photographed Shan royalty. These images provide

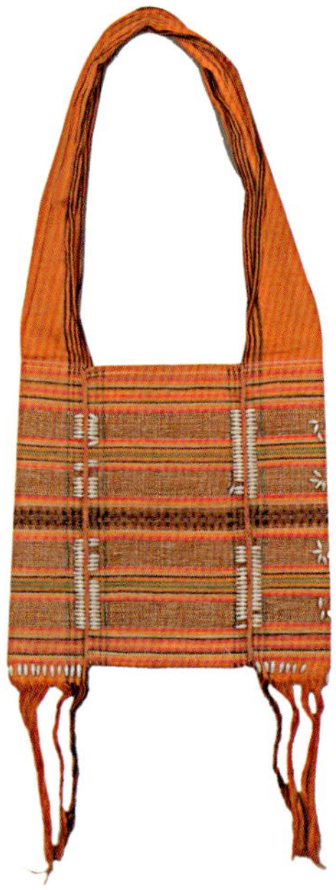

59 A shoulder bag with a tan cotton warp and a black warp stripe. The weft is tan cotton with a supplementary weft of pink, yellow, purple, green and black cotton, and silver metal thread. It is decorated with "Job's tears." The shoulder strap is woven in plain weave. The warp fringe is tan cotton with a black cotton stripe. *(Denison University collection, Granville, Ohio, DU1970.24)*

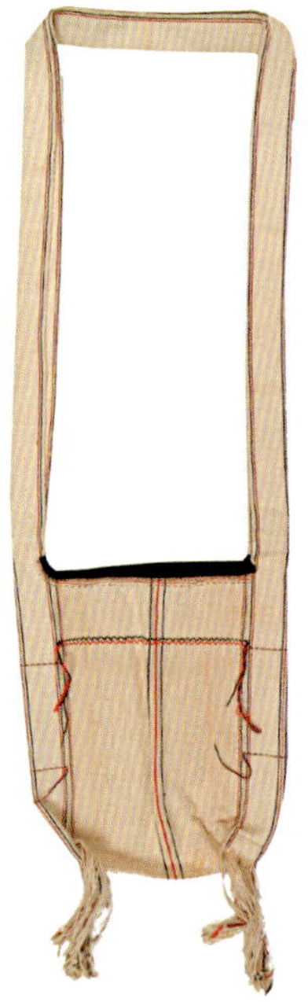

60 A shoulder bag of hand-spun cotton woven in a warp-faced plain weave. The warp has black stripes and the weft has a narrow band of black and red cotton supplementary weft with the end threads left loose as decoration. The bag is trimmed with a strip of mill cotton braid. *(Denison University collection, Granville, Ohio, DU1968.283)*

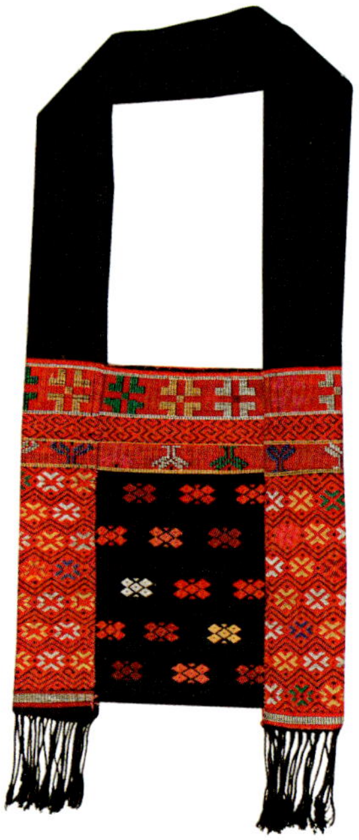

61 A shoulder bag with a black cotton warp and weft, and a supplementary weft of sets of repeat crosses in white, yellow, pink and tan cotton. The side panels have red, white yellow, and green supplementary weft in zig-zag and floral patterns. The shoulder strap is black cotton woven in plain weave. *(Denison University collection, Granville, Ohio, DU1968.178)*

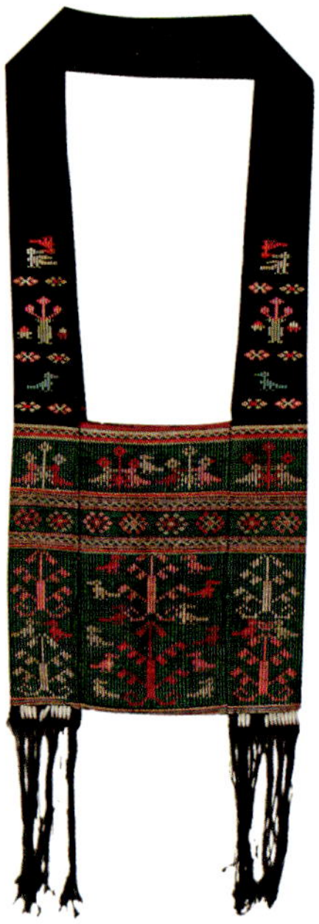

62 A shoulder bag with a black cotton warp and weft, and a supplementary silk weft with a complex pattern of multicoloured trees and birds. There is a central row of repeat floral patterns, weft stripes and zig-zag patterns. The bag opening is bordered by rows of stripes and zig-zag patterns. The shoulder strap is black cotton woven in plain weave with a supplementary weft of trees, birds and floral patterns. The black cotton warp fringe has a row of Job's tears set in the top. *(Denison University Collection, Granville, Ohio, DU1969.9)*

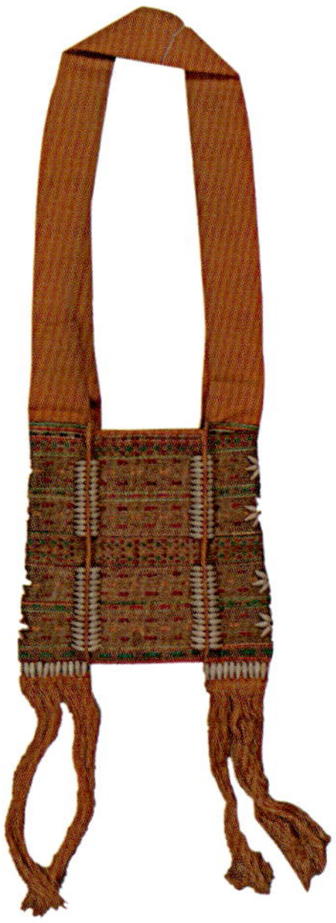

63 A shoulder bag with a tan cotton warp and weft, and a supplementary weft of gold metal thread and cerise, tan and turquoise silk, decorated with Job's tears arranged in double rows and in floral shapes. The shoulder strap is tan cotton woven in plain weave. The warp fringe is tan cotton. *(Denison University collection, Granville, Ohio, DU1979.9)*

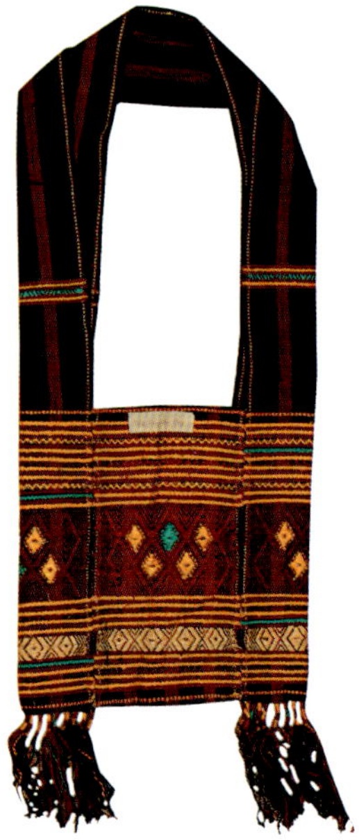

64 A Wa shoulder bag with bands of red and black cotton in the warp, woven in warp-faced plain weave. The weft-faced supplementary weft includes rows of yellow, orange and turquoise stripes and a band of yellow silk diamonds. There are yellow and turquoise cotton diamonds stitched in the central panel. *(Denison University collection, Granville, Ohio, DU1968.7)*

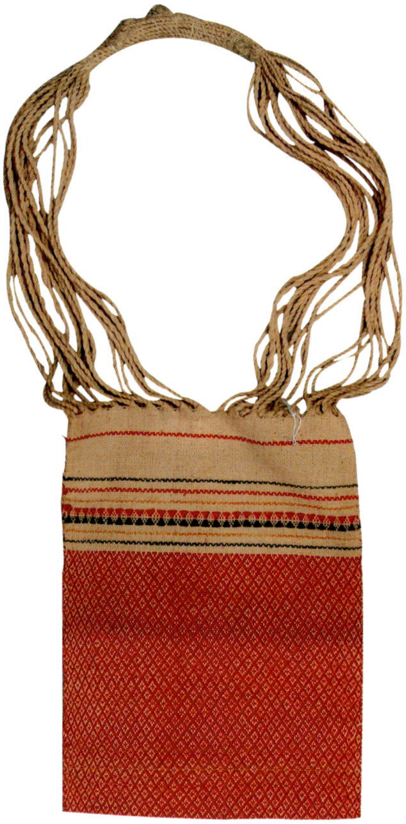

65 A shoulder bag of natural hand-spun cotton with a red cotton supplementary weft of repeat diamonds. The top border is natural cotton with a supplementary weft of yellow, green, red and black cotton. The unusual shoulder strap is formed from a long warp fringe that has been plaited and bound together at the ends.
(Denison University collection, Granville, Ohio, DU1967.158.1)

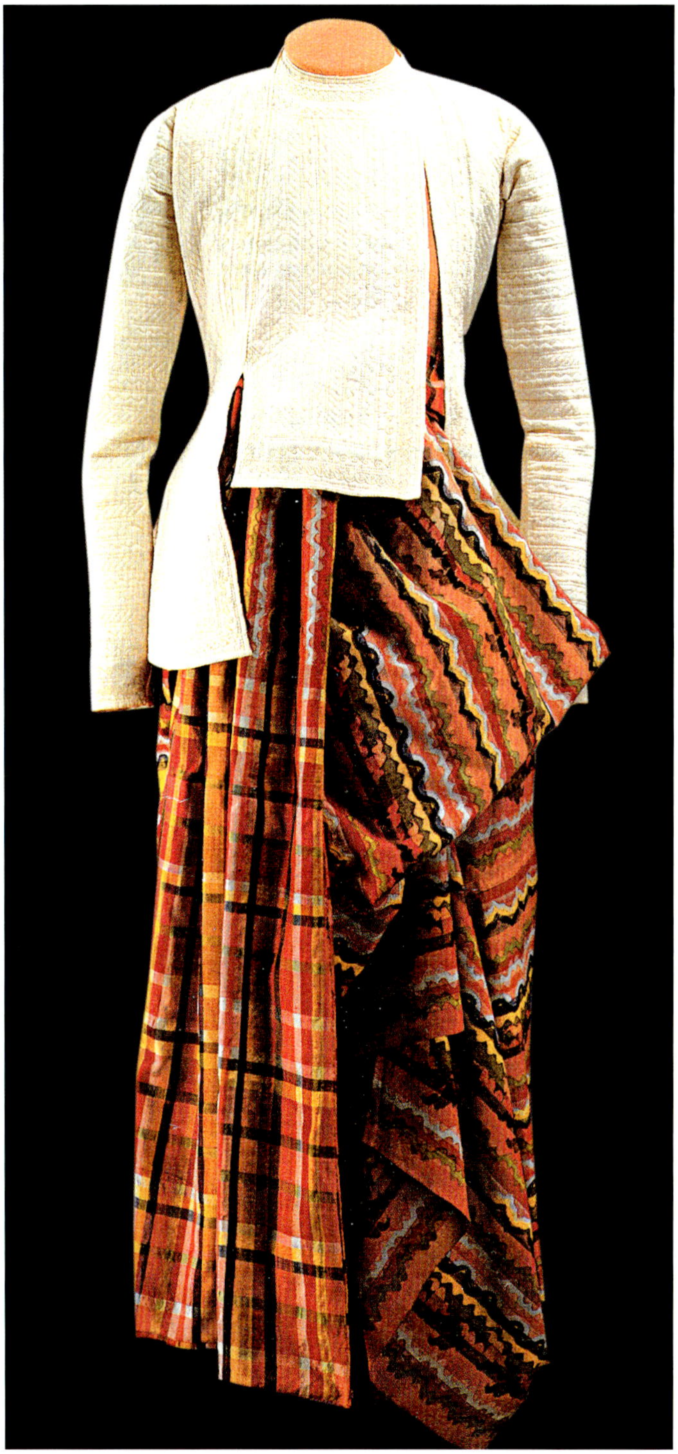

66 Male dress in Burmese style, sometimes worn by the Shan elite. A lower silk garment *(pah soe)* with a *luntaya* border, and a quilted cotton jacket *(ein gyi).*
(The Victoria and Albert Museum, accession no. 0798 (IS) and 5631 (IS))

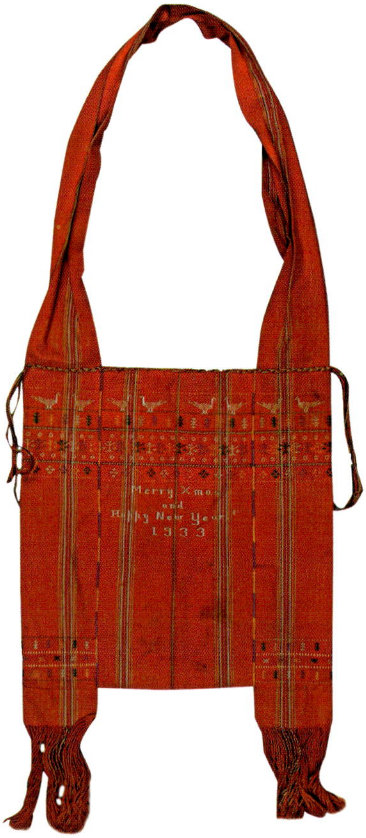

67 A cotton shoulder bag presented to the American missionary Ms Marshall, to mark a Christian holiday in 1933. Woven in pink/tan cotton it has the name "Mama Marshall" woven in supplementary weft in cream silk on the front, and "Merry Christmas and Happy New Year" on the back. There is a supplementary weft of birds and flowers woven in yellow, lilac and green silk.
(Denison University collection, Granville, Ohio, DU1970.22)

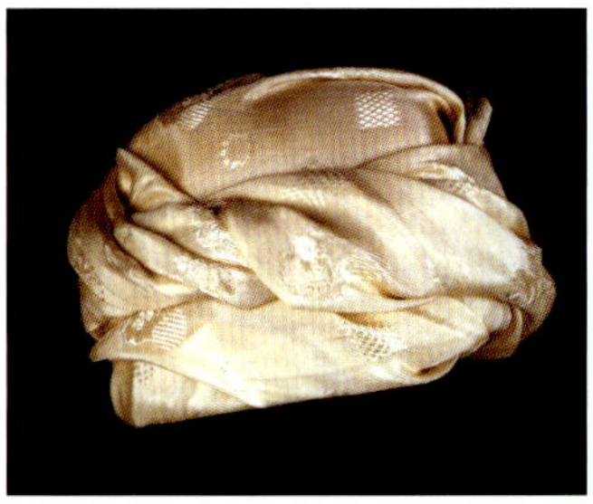

68 A Shan turban of Chinese brocaded silk.
(Akadet Nakbunlung collection)

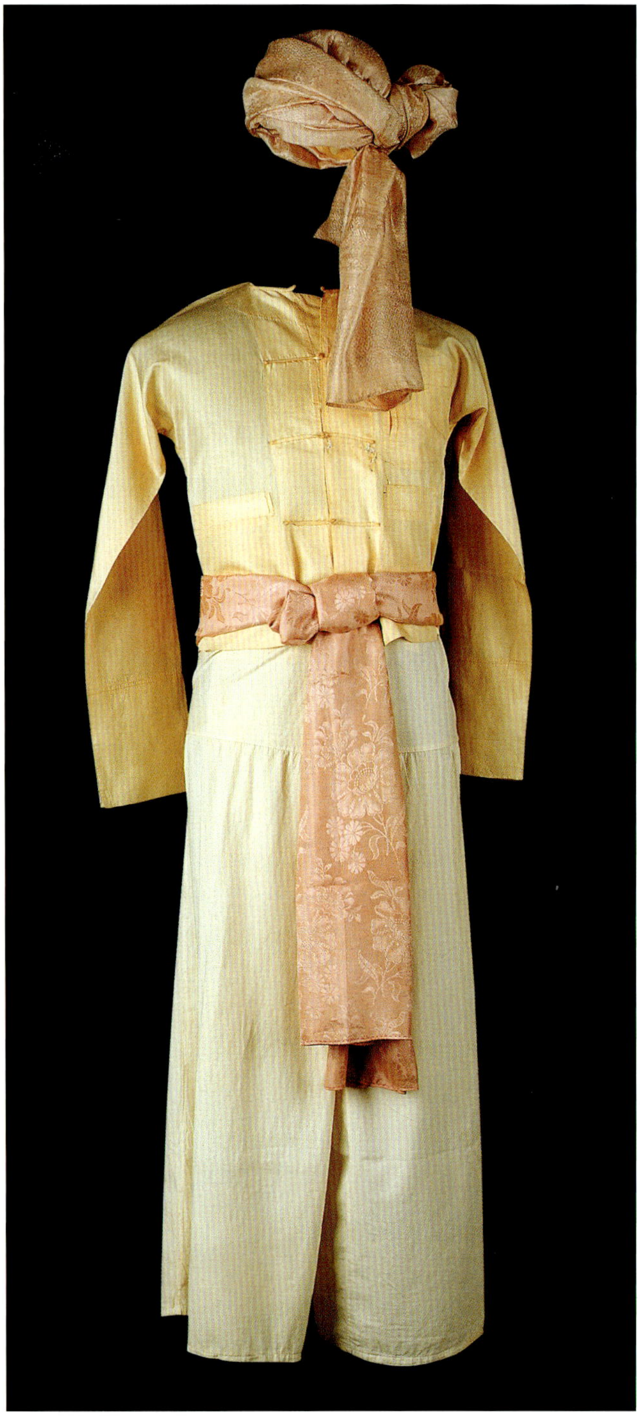

69 Shan dress. A long-sleeved, front-fastening Chinese silk shirt and loose-legged silk trousers secured with a silk sash at the waist.
(Akadet Nakbunlung collection)

important information about the variety of dress and textiles worn throughout the Shan States at this time.

Sir George Scott photographed Hkun Hsang Awn of the state of Tawng Peng. He was a powerful Palaung chief who had been appointed in 1877 under the patronage of King Mindon of Burma.[4] In the photograph he is seated in the open air with his consorts and family around him. His ability to maintain a number of consorts was an automatic symbol of wealth and status, enhanced by an impressive display of regalia in the foreground of the photograph. He wears a patterned turban tied with a generous bow at the side of his head and a long coat with a fur collar and trimmed sleeves.[5] Loose-legged Shan trousers are just visible below the coat. He is smoking a silver pipe.

Scott also photographed a *myosa* of Tawng Peng. This is probably Hkun Hkam Chok, a leader who Scott described as "a nominal Buddhist."[6] He is seated with his ministers between the teak pillars that support the floor of his large house. The staircase leading up to the house can be seen to the left of the photograph. The *myosa* wears a turban cloth with the pleats arranged on the right side of his head, completely covering his hair. The bow is tied at the back of his neck. He wears a plain undershirt and a long-sleeved, front-opening jacket fastened with button knots. He also wears a pair of loose-legged Shan trousers. The three ministers to his left wear turbans, thickly padded glazed indigo cotton jackets and Shan trousers. The two standing behind him wear turbans, side-fastening shirts with shaped bodices, and loose-legged trousers secured with cotton waist sashes. Because the clothing is similar, the seating arrangement and body language indicate who is the senior person in the group.

In the 1920s Colonel Green photographed the prince of Putao, Hkamti Long, seated with his senior consort and children in front of a thatched dwelling that probably formed part of his compound (fig. 72).[7] The prince was Kachin and he ruled over a population of Kachin, Shan and other, scattered hill groups.[8] In the photograph he is wearing a neat turban that frames his face and hides his hair. He has a mid-calf length tunic with long sleeves worn with a pair of loose-legged Shan trousers. A large silk umbrella with a gilded spire (*hti*) at the apex is held over him. The outfit worn by his wife is described in Chapter four. A pottery water vessel with a metal drinking cup, a tray, and a metal spittoon are displayed on the carpet at his feet. These were the regalia that denoted his authority.

Scott photographed *myosa* Sawlawi of Kantarawadi who was the senior *myosa* of the five states of Karenni (see fig. 73 and map). He is seated at a table on an open veranda, surrounded by his consorts and attendants. A large embroidered hanging (*shwe chi doe*) is displayed in the background. The *myosa* wears a loosely folded conical-shaped turban and an ankle-length coat trimmed with ribbons at the neck, front facings and sleeves. His water vessels and silver cups, his lacquer betel box, spittoon and other ceremonial containers are displayed on the table and at his feet. His attendants wear turbans and shirts and jackets. The jackets are in Shan and Chinese style. One of the men is holding a folded umbrella with a gilded spire (*hti*). As a senior *myosa* Sawlawi was invited by the British to attend the Delhi Durbar of 1903, where he was granted the title *saohpa*. He was photographed with the other princes who attended.

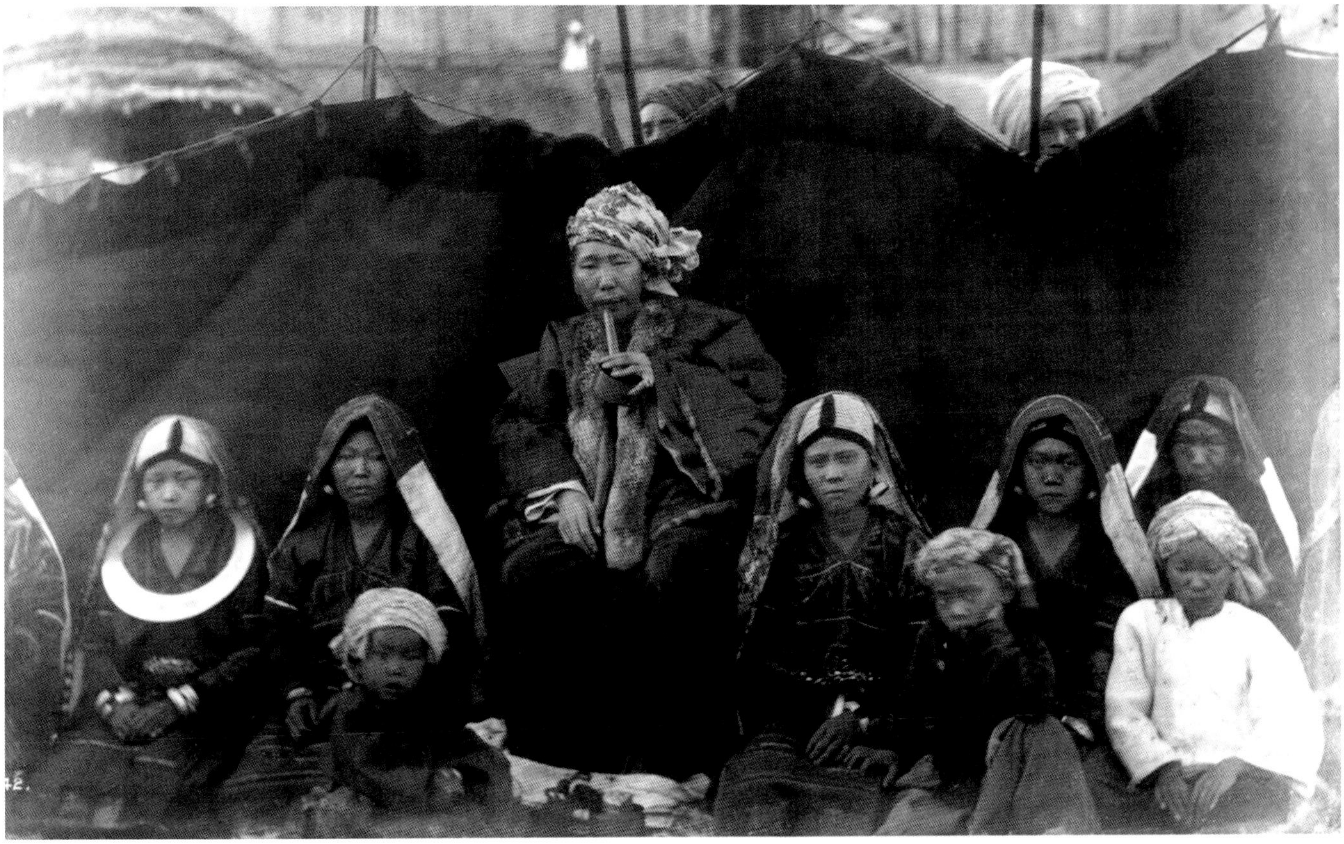

70 The Palaung *saohpa* Hkun Hsang Awn of Tawng Peng with his consorts and children.
(The Oriental and India Office Collections, The British Library, London, 92/2 (50))

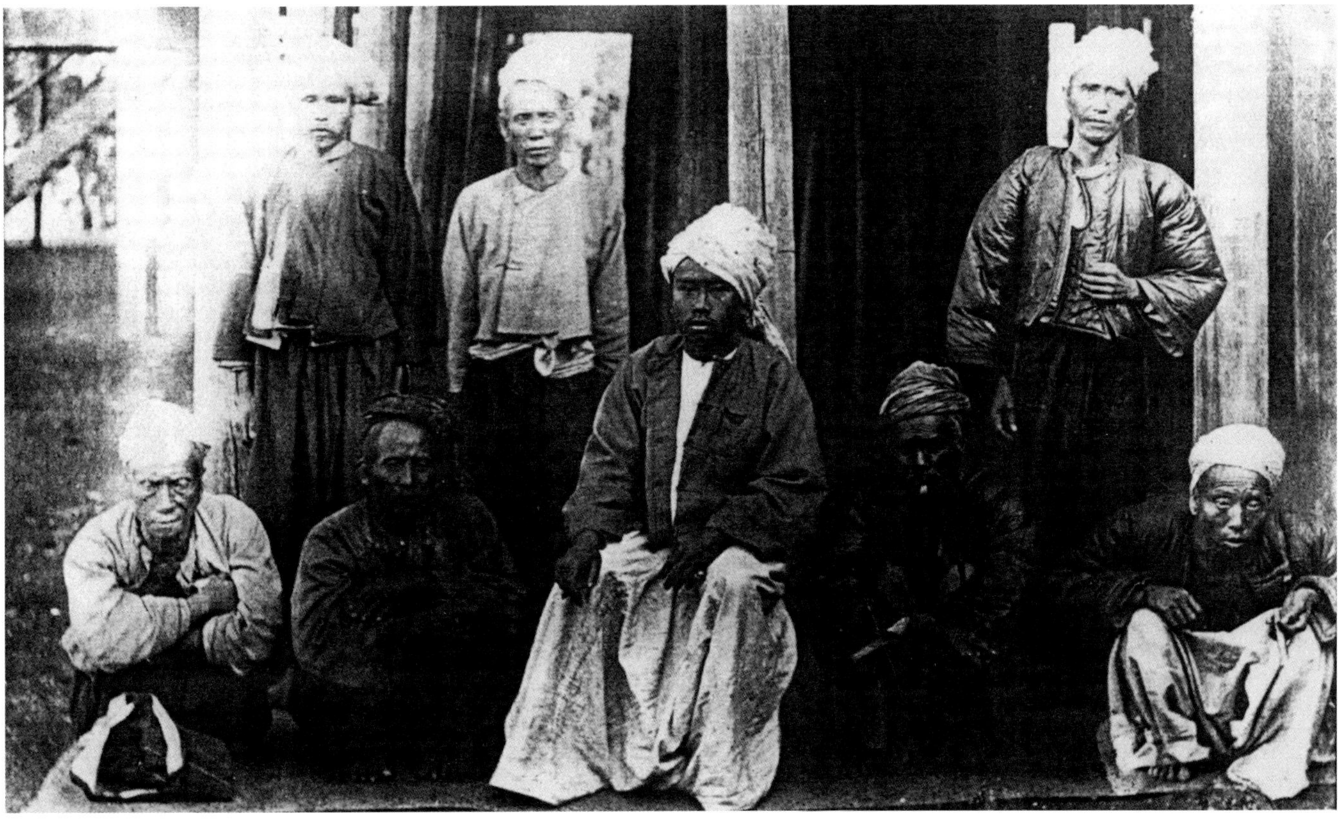

71 The *myosa* of Tawng Peng and his officials.
(The Oriental and India Office Collections, The British Library, London, 92/8 (51))

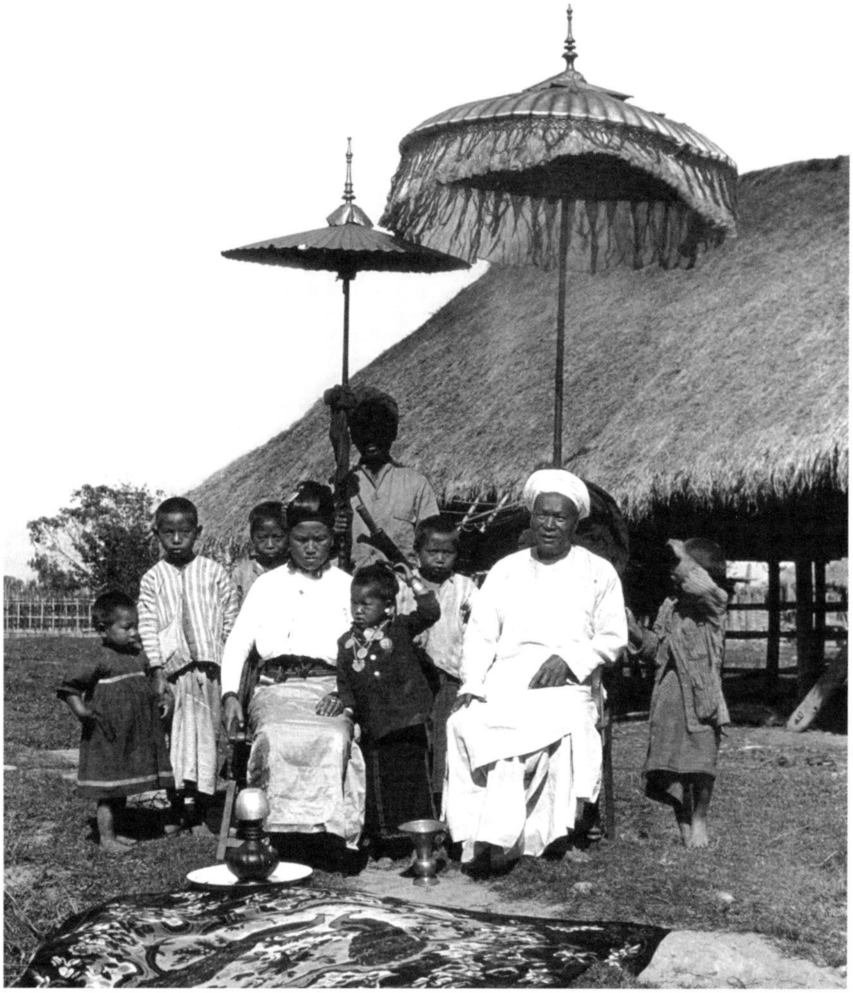

72 The *saohpa* of Putao, Khamti Long, with his family.
(The Green Centre for World Art at The Royal Pavilion Art Gallery and Museums, Brighton)

74 (Opposite left) Sir Sao Che, prince of Hsipaw (1872-1928), The Shan Palace Museum, Yawnghwe.

75 (Opposite right) A brocaded silk coat worn by a Shan prince. Sao Hkam Hip Hpa.
(The Green Centre for World Art at The Royal Pavilion Art Gallery and Museums, Brighton)

73 The ruler of Karenni, his family and attendants at the China-Burma Border Commission of 1899.
(The Oriental and India Office Collections, The British Library, London, 92/6 (11))

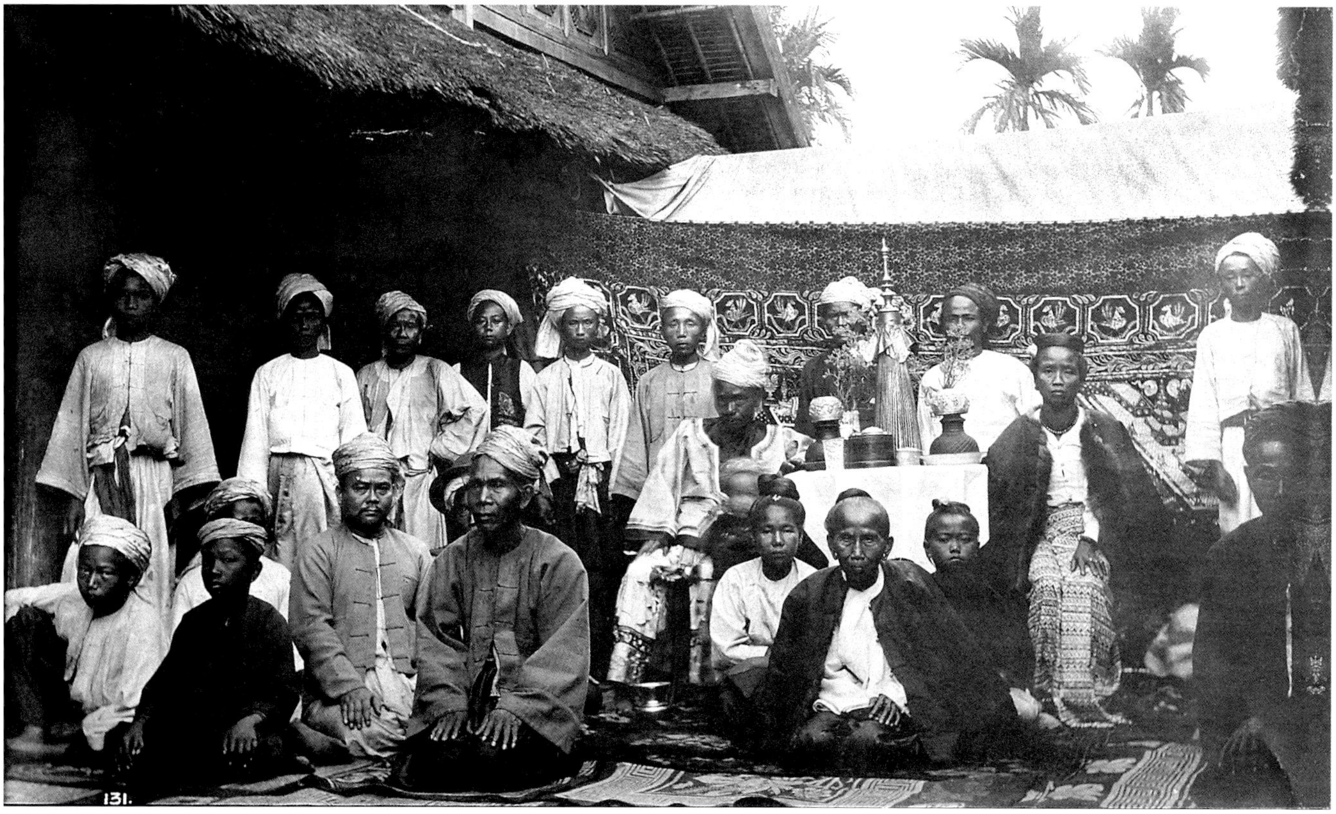

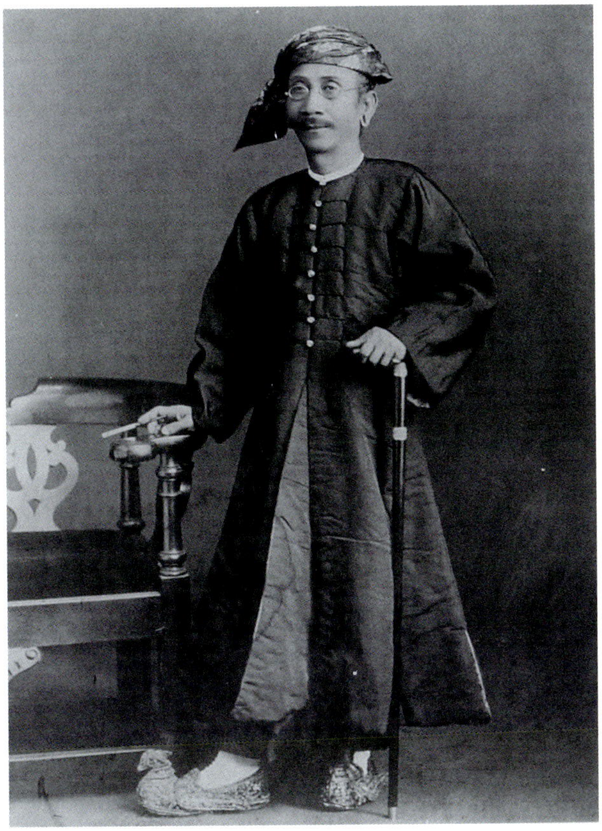

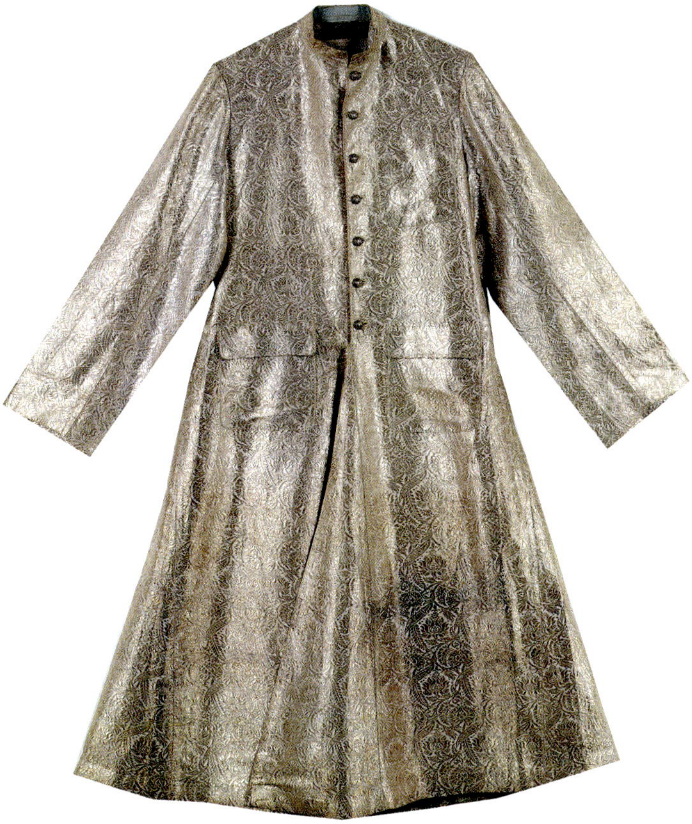

Sir Sao Che, *saohpa* of Hsipaw (1872-1928), was photographed in a plain version of a Shan court coat. It has a round neck, a fitted bodice and flares slightly from waist to hem. There are long loose sleeves. The fabric is dark-coloured silk with a lighter silk lining and a thick interlining. The coat fastens at the front with eight mother-of-pearl buttons and silk button loops. The prince wears narrow-legged trousers in Indian style and a pair of leather slippers in the shape of a mythical bird (*hintha chay nin*) couched with silver and gold metal thread, beetle wings, cut glass and sequins.[9] He is standing by a carved European-style chair leaning on an elegant cane walking stick with a cigarette in a holder in his right hand. He wears a small patterned turban cloth, tied in a bow on the side of his head, and his ears are pierced with large boreholes, usually plugged with gold cylinders or rolls of jade.

Prince Shwe Thaike of Yawnghwe was photographed in 1937 with his consort, Princess Sao Hearn Kham, on their wedding day (see fig. 130). The prince is wearing a tightly wrapped turban with a jewelled turban pin. His silk coat has a round neck and long sleeves. He wears Shan trousers, socks and shoes.

The artist Delaporte sketched the Prince of Muong You during an audience granted to members of the French expedition (see fig. 40). The prince is wearing a patterned turban, a round-necked shirt, trimmed at the neck and sleeves with beetle wings, and a pair of short trousers that cover his knees. He is lying on a couch beneath a canopy and is leaning on a triangular shaped pillow. The account of this audience, recorded by De Carné, suggests that the prince had an extensive wardrobe. De Carné also gives an excellent description of his earplugs.

> *In the corner of this hall, under an ornamented canopy, the king was lazily seated on cushions of silk embroidered with gold. He wore a turban, elegantly arranged with a woman's hand, its ample folds entirely covering the head and hiding the hair. His costume was composed of a vest and trousers of green satin, with gold ornaments. In his ears he wore large gold cylinders in the lobes, set off one end with diamonds, and with emeralds at the other. They were a present from the King of Ava... A narrow window near the throne was so arranged that the sun's rays made the king's dress sparkle like the wings of a glittering beetle. All the most precious vases in the palace were grouped near their owner and the attendants brought each of us a large box in embossed silver, containing all the materials for the preparation of a betel quid... We saw him five times and always in a different costume.*[10]

From formal photographs taken at court and on state occasions it is evident that the indigenous dress of the senior Shan princes consisted of a turban, a silk coat and loose-legged Shan trousers. This may have replaced an earlier form of dress that consisted of a length of silk worn like a toga, as illustrated in temple mural paintings. The princes were subject to fashion; for example, some princes chose to wear Indian-style tight-legged trousers instead of Shan trousers. The princes also wore jewellery, particularly earplugs and jewelled pins in their turbans. On ceremonial occasions certain senior princes and chiefs from other ethnic groups, including the Karen and Palaung, wore silk turbans, silk coats and trousers in Shan court style. When they participated in tribute ceremonies associated with Burma and China, the princes wore other forms of dress.

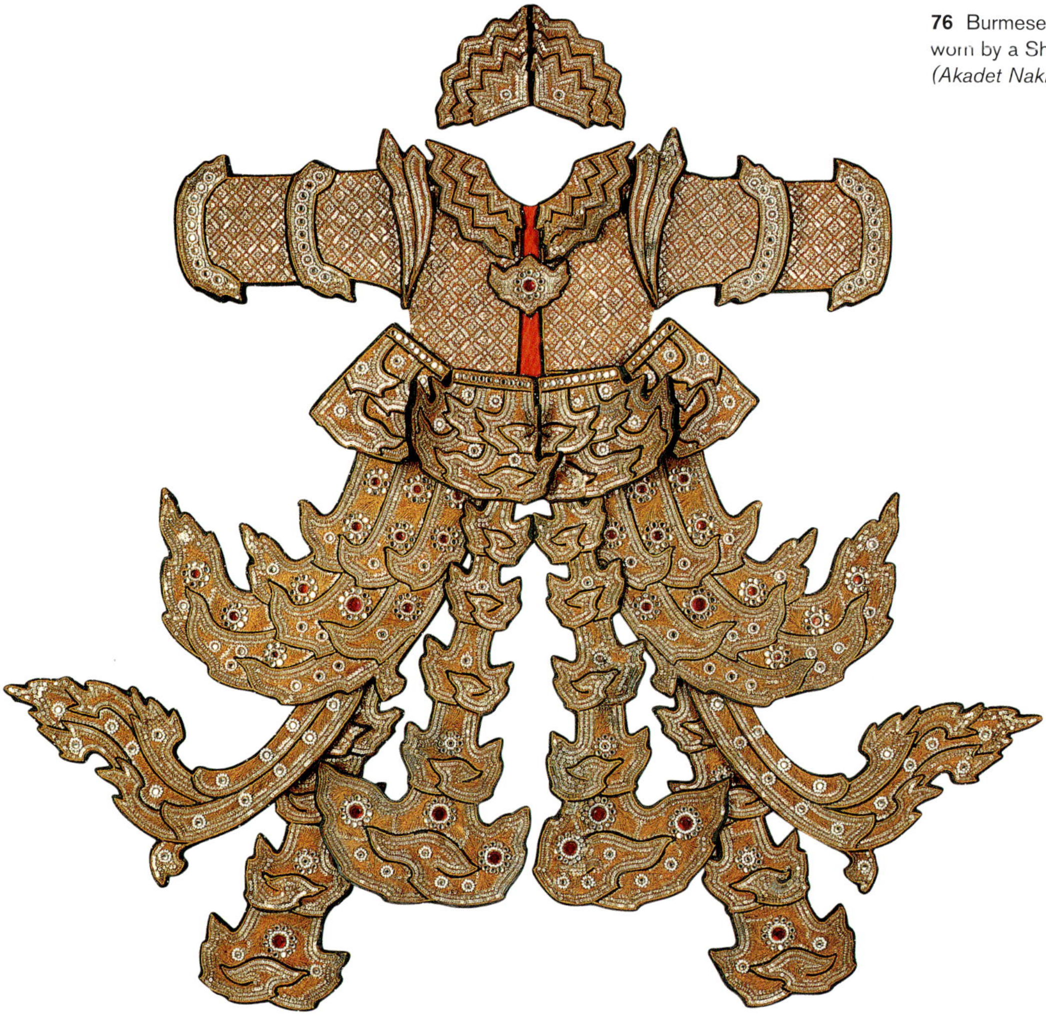

76 Burmese tribute dress worn by a Shan prince. *(Akadet Nakbunlung collection)*

Burmese Dress for the Shan Princes

The Shan princes who paid tribute to Burma were allocated court dress and regalia according to Burmese sumptuary law, an ancient hierarchical system that controlled expenditure on all aspects of court ceremonies. The lord chamberlain (*akyok-won*) administered the system. Every item was prescribed. He also supervised the display of the regalia of the king of Burma, set according to a special treatise (*shwe bon nidan*). The Burmese kings granted gifts of dress, textiles and regalia to those who cooperated with them, particularly in times of war. In the sixteenth century, King Bayinnaung of Pegu demanded conscripts for his military campaigns. According to Phayre, the prince of Keng Tung provided five thousand troops. He was amply rewarded with bolts of silk, gold cloth, gilded furniture, and animal trappings.[11]

The senior Shan princes journeyed to the Burmese court to pay respect (*kadaw*) to the king. *Kadaw* ceremonies took place three times a year, and the Shan princes attended at the end of Buddhist Lent. If a prince was ill, then a senior member of his family represented him. It was the custom for a newly crowned king to move his court to a fresh site. In the eighteenth century *kadaw* ceremonies took place in the palace of Amarapura, then the court moved to Ava and during the reign of King Mindon (ruled 1853-1878) to Mandalay. After his death King Thibaw kept the court at Mandalay until 1885.

Burmese artists recorded the elaborate ritual when the tributary princes gathered to pay tribute to the king. In manuscripts, the king is portrayed with his consorts and attendants seated in pavilions before rows of Burmese ministers, court officials, regional governors and the Shan princes, all wearing the robes and regalia assigned to them according to sumptuary law. In terms of precedence, the Shan princes were seated behind the senior Burmese princes.

> *The princes of the royal blood, ministers, Shan sawbwa [saohpa and chao fa], governors of provinces and officials with their wives, all in gala dress, took their places to the right and left of the throne, according to rank. Each brought a tributary gift. When the king entered with his entourage, all those assembled prostrated in front of the monarch. The presents were carried in and displayed.*[12]

The king of Burma, referred to as 'Lord of Life and Great and Just King' was at the pinnacle of the tribute system and when he entered the audience hall, he and his chief consort produced an amazing spectacle that dazzled those assembled. In 1795 the British envoy, Major Michael Symes, described a ceremony at the court of King Bodawpaya (ruled 1782-1819) in Amarapura. The king wore a gold costume that resembled a suit of armour with wings on each shoulder, estimated to weighed at least fifty pounds. The king's conical crown and regalia were made of solid gold encrusted with precious stones. According to Symes the grandeur and

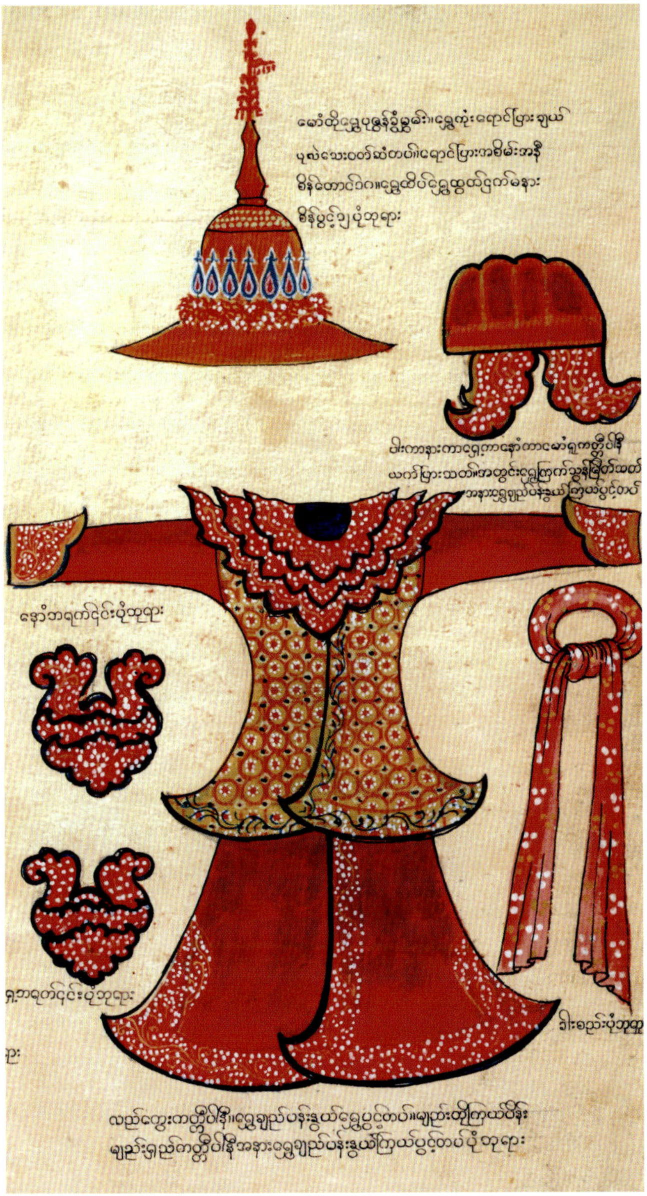

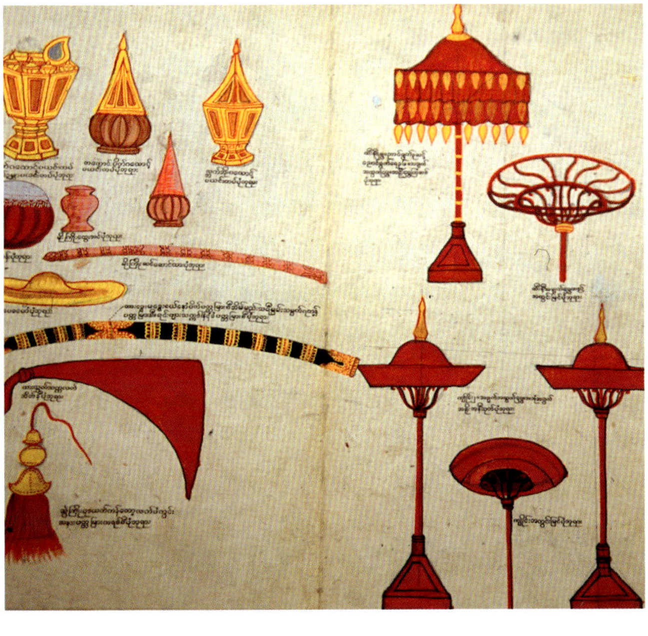

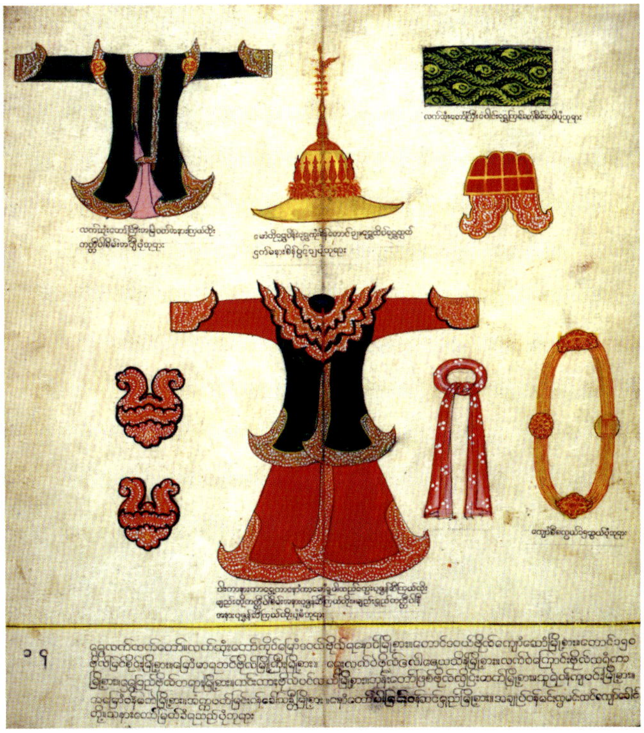

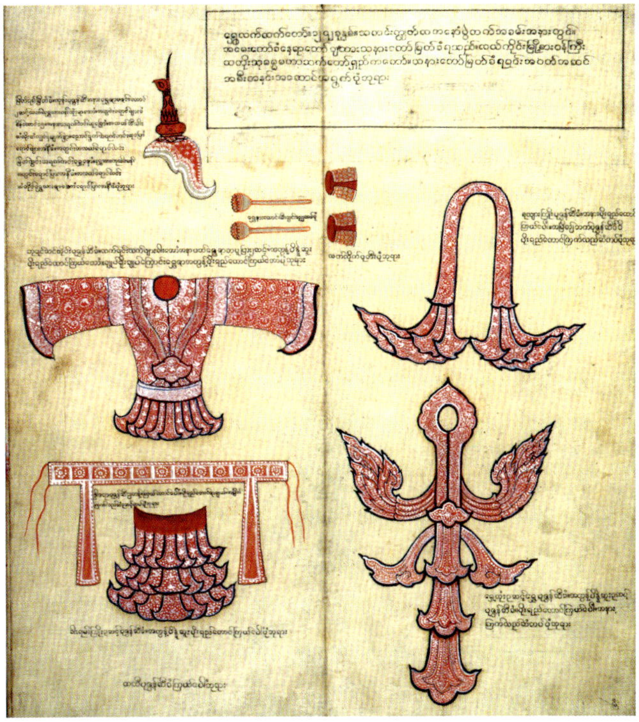

77-81 Pages from a Burmese court manuscript illustrating various forms of military and civil tribute dress.
(Victoria and Albert Museum, London, IM 320-1924)

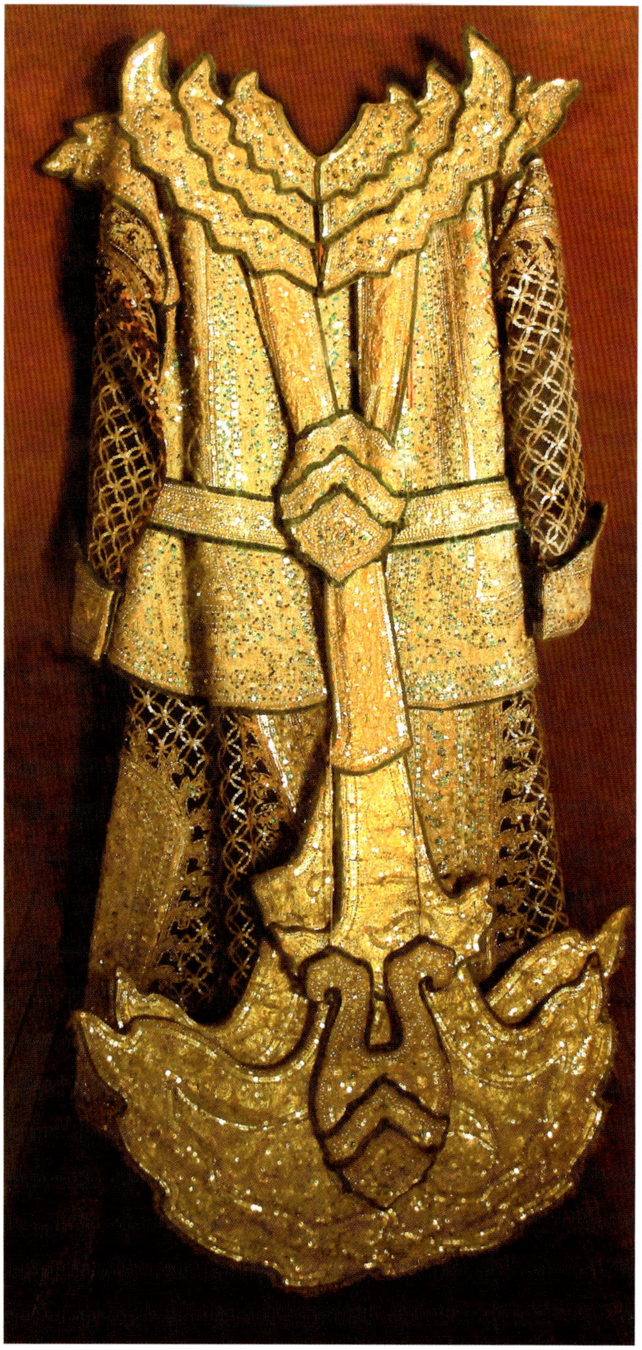

82 Burmese tribute dress in the collections of the Shan Palace Museum, Yawnghwe.

nobility of the spectre sent shivers down his spine.[13] A similar display mesmerized Major Trant, a British officer granted an audience at the court of King Bagyidaw (ruled 1819-1837) successor to King Bodawpaya. Trant was summoned to Ava to witness the signing of a peace treaty with the British following the First Burmese War (1824-1826). His stunned reaction to the arrival of the king, his chief queen and their attendants, captures the magic of the spectacle.

> *Its first appearance was splendid; it seemed like a moving mass of gold; which, by reflecting the rays of the sun, prevented us at first from distinctly seeing of what it was composed; but as it slowly advanced, we gradually could perceive, under a canopy of gilt umbrellas…two figures dressed in the most gorgeous and extraordinary manner: they were covered with gold ornaments and embroidery, and behind them were fourteen others habited in a similar mode…there was something so unexpected in the sudden appearance of this brilliant procession…my mind involuntarily recurred to those tales of fiction related of the East, and I could almost have fancied myself an inhabitant of Faery-land…*[14]

The correct dress and regalia for those attending court ceremonies was documented in hand-painted folding manuscripts (*parabaik*). Robes, accessories, jewellery and the type of fabrics and trimmings permitted to each level of the hierarchy were illustrated in colour. The manuscripts also feature ceremonial umbrellas, betel sets, water vessels, tea containers and the type of palanquins, boats and animal trappings permissible when travelling. Sir George Scott described the rigorous ranking system as it related to the Shan.

> *…almost every article of use, as well as ornament, particularly in their dress, indicates the rank of the owner; the shape of the betel box…his ear-rings, cap of ceremony…even the metal of which his spitting pot and drinking cup are made…all are indicative of the gradations of society.*[15]

The most senior Shan princes were entitled to the same style of uniform and regalia as allocated to Burmese regional governors. There were two sets of dress, one military and one civil.

The military dress consisted of a close fitting cap (*mauk-you*) with a stiff neck shield and earflaps lined on the inside with cotton, and covered on the outside with silk velvet couched with gold and silver sequins, gold metal wire and silk braid. The cap was worn under a stiff dome-shaped hat (*muk-toe*) with a wide brim. A row of gilded metal lotus petals circled the crown that tapered to a finial. The two-tiered military robe (*myin-she*) had a bodice that flared below the waist. It was made of brocaded silk or velvet trimmed on the front edge, hem and sleeves with gold brocade and tinsel cloth. A stiff collar, like a ruff (*leh-kwe gwe*) was worn over the robe. It was made from three reinforced scalloped tiers of velvet, embroidered with gold thread and appliquéd with silver sequins, gold wire, mother-of-pearl beads and cut glass. A set of shoulder epaulettes, worn just below the edge of the collar, and a large waist buckle were decorated in a similar fashion. On some outfits embroidered detachable sleeve cuffs replaced scalloped epaulettes. A long embroidered sash, used as a belt on loose-legged Shan trousers or to secure a sarong, completed the outfit.

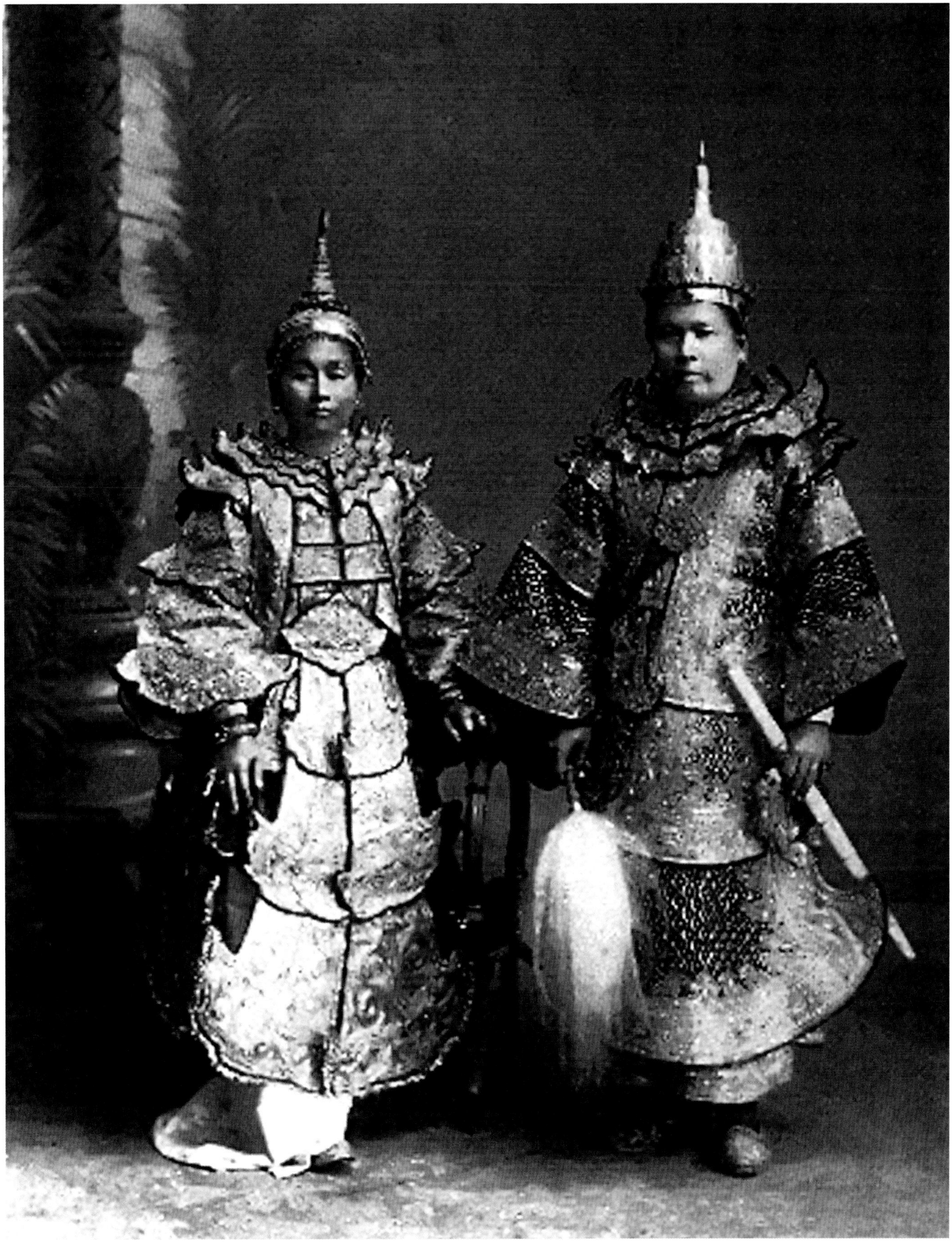

83 The prince of Yawnghwe with the *mahadevi* photographed in Burmese tribute dress at the studio of the photographer P. Klier, Rangoon, circa 1900. *(Permission of Nel Adams. (Sao Noan Oo))*

Civil court dress consisted of a stiff helmet with a curved crown circled by gilded metal lotus petals and flowers. It was covered in velvet and trimmed with tinsel cloth. A long-sleeved velvet robe was trimmed with gold brocade on the neck, front edges, hem and sleeves. It was worn with an embroidered silk scarf (*sulyar*), a set of gold trumpet-shaped earplugs (*nadaug*) and a set of gold chains with repoussé bosses (*tsaloe*). The set of golden chains (*tsaloe*) was one of the most important elements in the Burmese ranking system. Issued as "The Order of the Golden *Tsaloe*," this was an honour dating back to the Ava Period (1287-1539).[17] As head of the Order, the king of Burma was entitled to two gold *tsaloe* worn over his right and left shoulders and crossed diagonally over his chest. Each *tsaloe* had twenty-four chains with nine repoussé bosses on each. The bosses were decorated with royal seals that in the nineteenth century included a peacock, symbol of the Konbaung Dynasty; a lion, the royal beast; a rabbit, sign of the moon; a hare, symbol of the sun and a serpent (*naga*) representing fertility and protection.[18] The Burmese heir-apparent was permitted one *tsaloe* with twenty-one chains; the princes of the blood were entitled to twelve to eighteen chains; and other members of the royal family were granted up to fifteen. High-ranking army officers and senior Shan princes were entitled to twelve to eighteen chains. Government officials, clerks and legal advisers were permitted three chains. The kings of Burma exercised a degree of discretion in the distribution of *tsaloe*, granting extra chains to those whom they wished to honour. For his loyalty to Burma, King Bodhpaya (ruled 1782-1819) awarded Prince Mahakhanan of Keng Tung two *tsaloe* with fifteen chains on each. The King also conferred the award on foreign dignitaries. Major Burney, the first English resident at the court of Ava was a recipient, and in 1871 King Mindon granted Edward, Prince of Wales a *tsaloe* with twelve chains.

Under the complex ranking system the senior Shan princes were entitled to a prescribed number of silk umbrellas with gilded lotus-shaped trimmings and gilded spires (*hti*). They were also entitled to use gilded betel sets and spittoons, ornate pickled tea containers, gold water vessels, ivory-handled flywhisks and swords with embossed and repoussé hilts. These were displayed at court ceremonies. Sumptuary laws also dictated the type of sedan chairs (*htan-sin*), palanquins (*yin*) and elephant howdahs they were allowed to use for travel.

In the late nineteenth century Shan princes commissioned portraits from professional artists and photographers who had established studios in the major cities. The prince of Yawnghwe and the *mahadevi* were photographed in Rangoon in the studio of Philip Klier who worked in Moulmein and Rangoon from the 1870s (see fig. 83). The prince is wearing a form of Burmese civil court dress. His tight-fitting dome-shaped helmet is tiered and has a gilded spire. His coat is couched with gold metal thread, silver and mother-of pearl sequins, and beetle wings. Wide bands of tinsel cloth (*pazun-zi*) form the border on the front facings and sleeves. The tiered and scalloped apron has panels of velvet embroidered with gold metal thread, silver and mother-of pearl sequins, and cut glass, and is edged with wide bands of tinsel cloth. It is reinforced at the back with cotton and bamboo. A three-tiered scalloped collar and a set of scalloped epaulettes, couched with gold metal thread, silver sequins, pearl beads and cut glass, and trimmed with velvet, are overlaid on the neck and shoulders. Just visible below the hemline of the coat are a pair of trousers with embroidered cuffs. The prince wears a pair of embroidered slippers and he holds a yak tail whisk in his right hand and an embossed sword and scabbard in his left. A *tsaloe* with a large repoussé boss is displayed prominently over his coat. Although it is not possible to count the number of chains in this photograph, according to sumptuary law he was entitled to twelve rows. This form of court dress, generally associated with *kadaw* ceremonies, was worn until the reign of King Thibaw. They were then held on an irregular basis in Mong Nai, but lacked the strict protocol enforced at the Burmese court.

In 1885 the British forced King Thibaw into exile. The Burmese court was disbanded, and in 1890 the British stripped the Great Audience Hall in Mandalay. The king's robes of state, his regalia, and the manuscripts that illustrated the rules of sumptuary law, were shipped to England.[19] Under the Burmese system, the Shan princes who flouted sumptuary laws were subject to severe penalties, but after 1890 they themselves administered a Shan system of hierarchy. Some Burmese artisans who had worked for the king of Burma were persuaded to resettle at the Shan courts, where they produced regalia and other fine objects in the Mandalay court style.

Although Burmese sumptuary laws were no longer observed, the tribute system and sumptuary laws were adapted to suit a British hierarchical system. With their colonial government well established in India, the British were experts at re-ordering societies to fit an imperial system with the British monarch at the apex.[20] British officials were sent to the Shan States to meet the princes and chiefs and to demand an oath of allegiance to Queen Victoria. When they took the oath they were issued with letters of appointment. The British formalized relations by distributing titles and regalia according to sumptuary laws operated by the court of Queen Victoria through the office of her colonial representative, the Viceroy and Governor General of India. This included gun salutes. The number of guns permissible provides a measure of how the new system worked in the Shan States and throughout the British Empire. The Queen Empress Victoria was entitled to twenty-one guns, British governors to seventeen. African kings, Indian princes, Malay rajahs and Shan princes were all granted salutes according to a universal ranking system, intended to draw together all royalty and officials throughout the Empire.

The first Shan prince to swear allegiance to Queen Victoria was the Prince of Hsipaw, who as a mark of honour was greeted with a cavalry escort and an eleven-gun salute. When he swore allegiance Sao Maung, Prince of Yawnghwe, was given the title K. C. I. E (Knight Commander in The Most Eminent Order of the Indian Empire), K. S. M (King's Service Medal), and was entitled to a salute of nine guns. The prince of Keng Tung was granted a K. S. M. and the Prince of Muong Nai gained the title 'Honourable,' was made a C. I. E. (Companion in The Most Eminent Order of the Indian Empire) and K. S. M, and was entitled to a nine-gun salute. The prince of Lawksawk was decorated on three occasions, with the K. S. M., D. S. O. (Distinguished Service Order) and C. I. E., and the prince of Muong Pawn was granted a K. S. M. Some *myosa* were promoted to the rank of *saohpa* and received titles and medals accordingly.

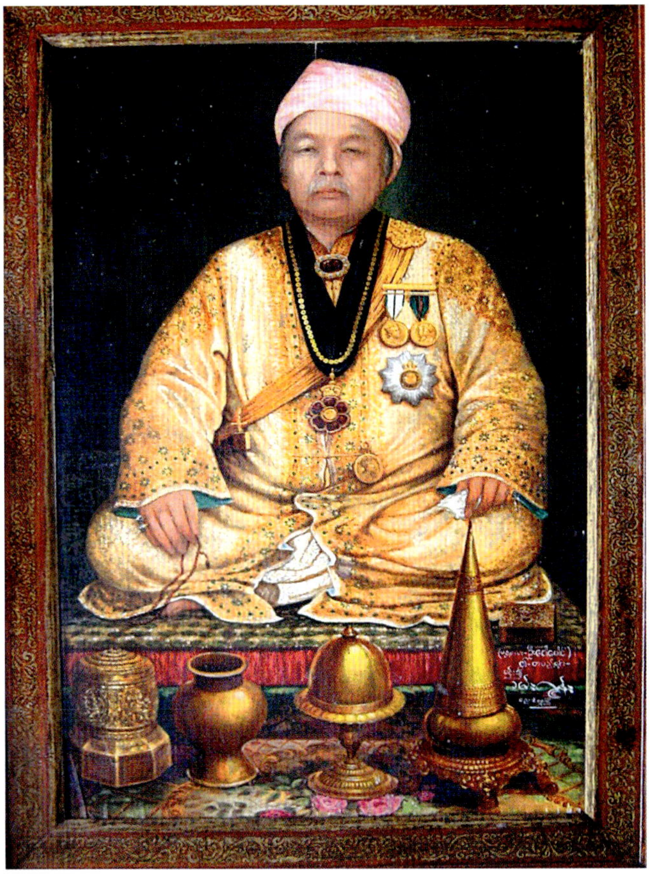

84 A portrait of Prince Sao Maung of Yawnghwe, K. C. I. E., K. S. M. (ruled 1897-1926), Shan Palace Museum, Yawnghwe.

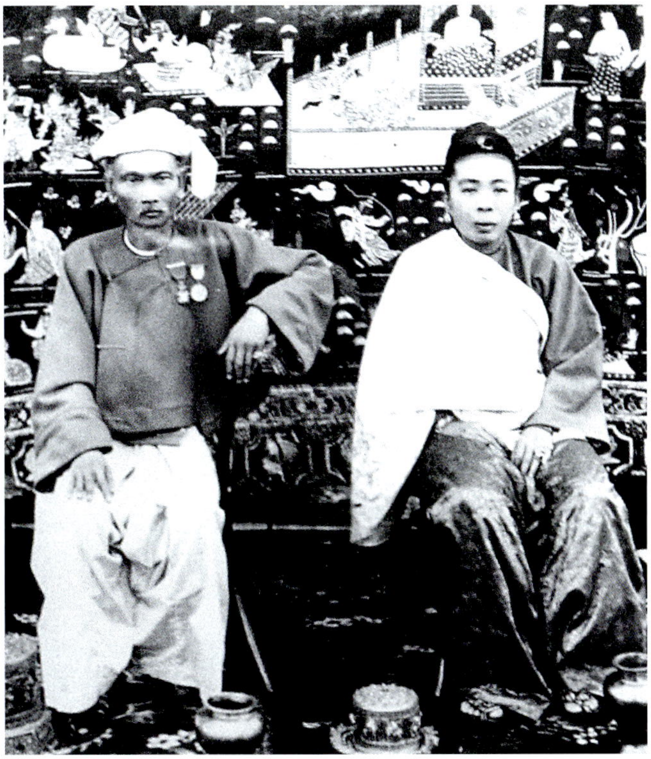

85 The *saopha* Sao Kyaw Hse of Muong Nai with the *mahadevi*. He wears the C. I. E. and K. S. M. medals awarded to him by the British, Shan Palace Museum, Yawngwhe.

The Shan elite accepted Imperial honours and awards and the British kept most of the Shan hierarchical system intact. According to the Shan State Manual of 1925 (Appendix II), the Order of Precedence under British rule was first the prince of Keng Tung followed by the prince of Hsipaw and then Muong Nai, Yawnghwe and Tawng Peng. They were all entitled to a salute of nine guns. The princes of South Hsenwi and North Hsenwi were deemed to be of equal rank. They were followed by the prince of Muong Mit, then Muong Pai, Lawksawk, Laikha, Mawkmai, Muong Pan, Muong Pawn, Manglon, Kantarawadi, Samka and Muongkung The order of seniority for the *myosa* was first Nawngwawn, followed by Muong Nawng, Muong Sit, Kehsi-Mansam, Mawnang, Tawng Peng (Loi Long), Hsahtung, Wanyin, Hopong, Namkhôk, Sakoi, Muonghsu, Keng Lon, Bawlake, Kyetbogyi, Hsamongkham, Maw and Pwela. The primacy of the *ngwegunhmu* (chiefs) was first Yengan, then Pangtara, Pangmi, Loi-ai, Kyaukku, Loimaw, Kyone and Namtok.

Many chiefs who were decorated by the British had their portraits painted or were photographed wearing their Burmese and British decorations. Prince Sao Maung of Yawnghwe (ruled 1897-1927) is shown sitting cross-legged on a raised platform, wearing a pink turban cloth and a yellow silk robe embroidered with gold and silver metal wire, gold and silver sequins, and beetle wings. The sleeves are lined with turquoise silk. A Burmese golden *tsaloe* with a large repoussé boss, passes across his left shoulder and he wears a Burmese medal, set with rubies on a black ribbon around his neck. Pinned on the left side of his coat are the British orders of K. C. I. E., K. S. M. and a Delhi Durbar medal. A gold ceremonial tea container (*lahpet-o*) and betel nut set (*kun-kwet*) are displayed on the floor in front of him.

Prince Sao Kyaw Hse of Muong Nai was photographed wearing his C. I. E. and K. S. M. medals. Ceremonial vessels and an embossed betel box, are displayed in front of him. The prince of Lawksawk wore his medals when he attended the Shan State Council in Taunggyi and at other local ceremonies.[21] Sir George Scott noted that whenever the Prince of Yawnghwe received guests he wore his medals and was proud that he had been one of the first princes to be invested. The British honours system, as administered in the colonies, was subject to lofty comments in some quarters. Lord Elgin, Governor-General of Canada, exclaimed,

> *In the colonies, premiers and chief justices, fight for stars and ribbons like little boys for toys, and scream at us if we stop them.*[22]

Elgin was wrong if he thought the Shan princes were easily seduced by honours. If British policies went against the best interests of their people, they could be stubborn and uncooperative.

For their part, the British paid great attention to installation ceremonies held throughout the Empire, and the colonial system reached its zenith in India with the organisation of major durbars in 1877, 1903 and 1911. The Delhi Durbar of 1903 was a splendid occasion organised by Lord Curzon, Viceroy of India and presided over by the Duke of Connaught, son of Queen Victoria. The British viewed the princes of the Empire as "native aristocracy" and encouraged them to appear in the splendour of indigenous court dress. Describing the Shan contingent at the Durbar, Sir George Scott wrote:

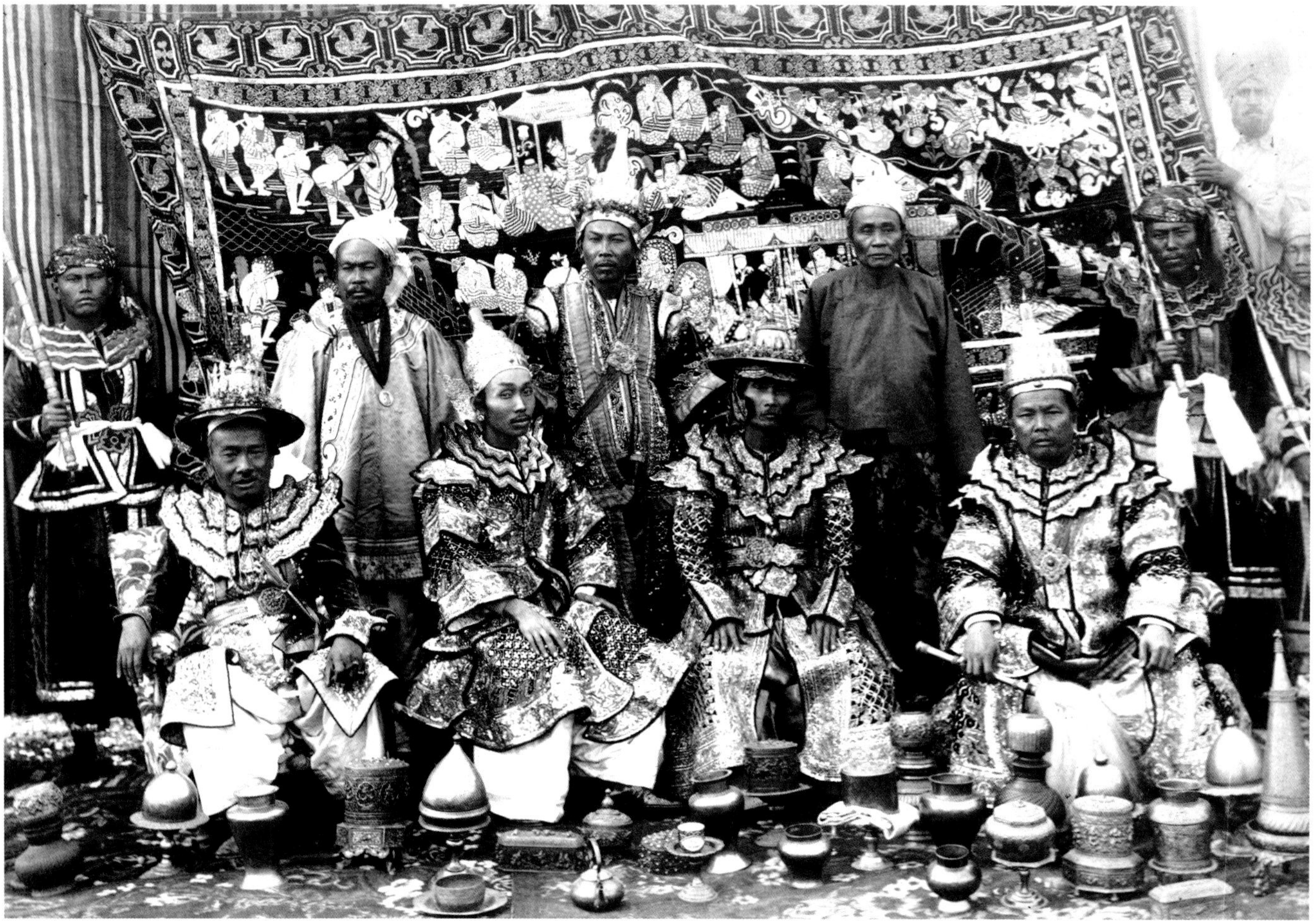

86 The Shan princes at the Delhi Durbar (also called the Accession Durbar) of 1903. Front row left to right: *Saohpa* of Muong Pawn, Keng Tung, Muong Nai and Yawnghwe. Back row left to right: *myosa* of Hsamuongkham, *Saohpa* of Hsenwi, and *Myosa* of Kantarawadi. *(The Oriental and India Office Collections, The British Library, London, 99 (45))*

> *They were all dressed in their magnificent state dresses, coats with tiers of collars superimposed one on the other, double sleeves...heavily encrusted with gold. On his head he* [the prince of Yawnghwe] *wore the state crown.*[23]

The exotic dress, military uniforms and caparisoned animals were a spectacular sight and the pageantry was carefully staged. Fig. 87 shows a photograph of the rehearsal for the Delhi Durbar of 1903. An elephant, ridden by a uniformed mahout, is decked in a gilded and embroidered leather head-cloth and ornate saddlecloth strapped with a gilded and lacquered wooden howdah. A group of attendants wear patterned turbans, silk coats and loose-legged trousers. Behind them march Shan guards bearing swords and wearing large straw hats, shirts, jackets and loose-legged Shan trousers. A single attendant, dressed in a turban and an ankle-length coat with a stiff scalloped collar like a ruff, marches directly in front of the elephant. A group of Indian soldiers stand watching the rehearsal. The illustrated book, produced as an official record of the Durbar, notes that the Shan princes were "well noticeable."[24]

The British arranged for photographs to be taken of all the princes who attended the Durbar of 1903. The Shan contingent posed in the open with an embroidered and appliquéd cloth hanging (*shwe chi doe*) as a backdrop. In the front row, and in the centre back row, the princes wear the helmets, robes and embossed chains (*tsaloe*) issued to them under Burmese sumptuary law. Prince Hkun Hti of Muong Pawn (far left, front row) and the Prince Hkun Kyi of Muong Nai (second right, front row) wear Burmese military court dress of the rank of a Secretary of State. It consists of a close-fitting cap worn under a gold helmet with twelve gold leaves and flowers around the brim. A three-tiered scalloped collar and a velvet robe trimmed with gold brocade and gilt embroidery are also part of the outfit.

Prince Kawn Kiaw Intaling of Keng Tung (second left, front row), the Prince Sao Maung of Yawnghwe (first right, front row) and the Prince of Hsenwi (centre, back row) wear forms of Burmese civil court dress. The princes of Keng Tung and Yawnghwe wear tiered and scalloped cloud collars and embroidered robes trimmed with gold brocade and tinsel cloth. The prince of Hsenwi wears an elaborate silk coat trimmed with tinsel cloth. In the second row on the left, the *myosa* Muong Po of Hsamongkham wears a form of Chinese tributary dress with a turban and silk robe. He has a medal on a ribbon round his neck. The prince of Kantarawadi, Karenni States, wears a turban, a silk shirt and an *ikat* sarong in Inlay Lake style. The guards standing on each side are dressed in turbans, tiered and scalloped collars, silk coats and trousers trimmed with tinsel cloth. Displayed on the carpet are many items of regalia, including water vessels, betel nut sets, tea containers, bowls and dishes.

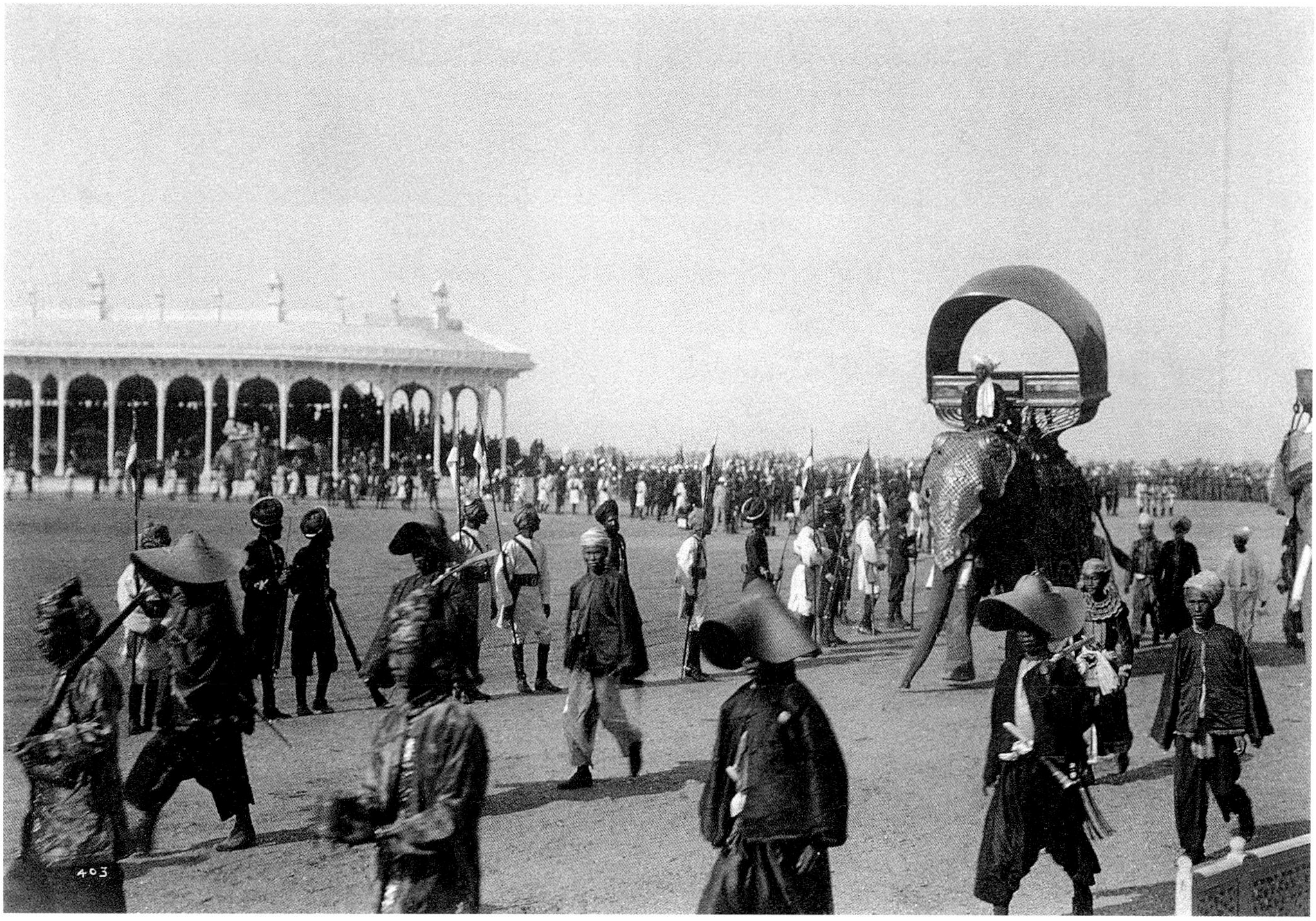

87 Dress rehearsal for the Delhi Durbar of 1903.
(The Oriental and India Office Collections, The British Library, London, 430/12 (35))

At the time of the Delhi Durbar of 1903, the king of Burma had been living in exile for over eighteen years, and it was the Shan princes who reflected in their elaborate tribute dress and regalia the political history and tributary relations that had existed with Burma. The *myosa* Muong Po in a Chinese robe signalled ancient tributary relations with China. A certain mystery surrounds the outfit worn by prince of Kantarawadi, Karenni State, who in 1899 had been photographed by Sir George Scott wearing an elaborate Shan court coat (see fig. 73), a more impressive outfit than the shirt and sarong seen in this photograph.

In Victorian, and later in Edwardian Britain, the photographs taken at the durbars captured the vision of the Empire as a powerful and unified force, with the exotic and mysterious Orient as an important component. The British widened the scope of pageantry by inviting the senior princes of the Empire to London where they attended court ceremonies and were introduced to members of the British royal family. At the coronation of Edward VII the prince of Hsipaw joined the procession of dignitaries, all clad in court robes, ribbons, medals and sashes. This coronation parade was intended as a spectacle to match the splendour and colour of an Indian durbar. Members of the Shan royal family continued to attend court ceremonies in Britain, including the wedding of Princess Elizabeth in 1947 (see fig. 161).

Although the great Indian durbars have attracted the most attention, colourful ceremonial processions, admittedly on a smaller scale, were always part of Shan court life. Processions through the main thoroughfares formed part of annual Buddhist ceremonies and rites associated with ancestor spirits. The princes also went on tour to be seen by their subjects, and to acquaint themselves with local politics. The royal family processed when there were important weddings and funerals. The princes wore indigenous Shan dress, and in some instances a mix of Shan and Burmese or Shan and Chinese dress. Writing in the early twentieth century, the American missionary William Clifton Dodd attended a state procession in Keng Tung, and the hat he describes was probably part of Burmese civil court dress.

> *The Chao Fa* [prince] *of Kengtung, the Khun* [Khoen] *chief, rides a very richly caparisoned elephant. His state robes are entirely of cloth of gold, and his pagoda-like coronet or tiara is also covered with gold.*[25]

In 1921, the daughter of the prince of Keng Tung, Princess Sao Ven Kiao married Prince Sao Hkun Hsa of Lawksawk, and the bridegroom wore Burmese civil court dress, similar to that worn by his father-in-law at the 1903 Delhi Durbar (see fig. 89). His close-fitting cap with earflaps can be seen under a tiered and gilded helmet. He wears a coat trimmed with tinsel cloth and embroidered with gold metal wire, sequins, semi-precious stones and beetle wings, and a three-tiered scalloped collar. He wears a set of chains

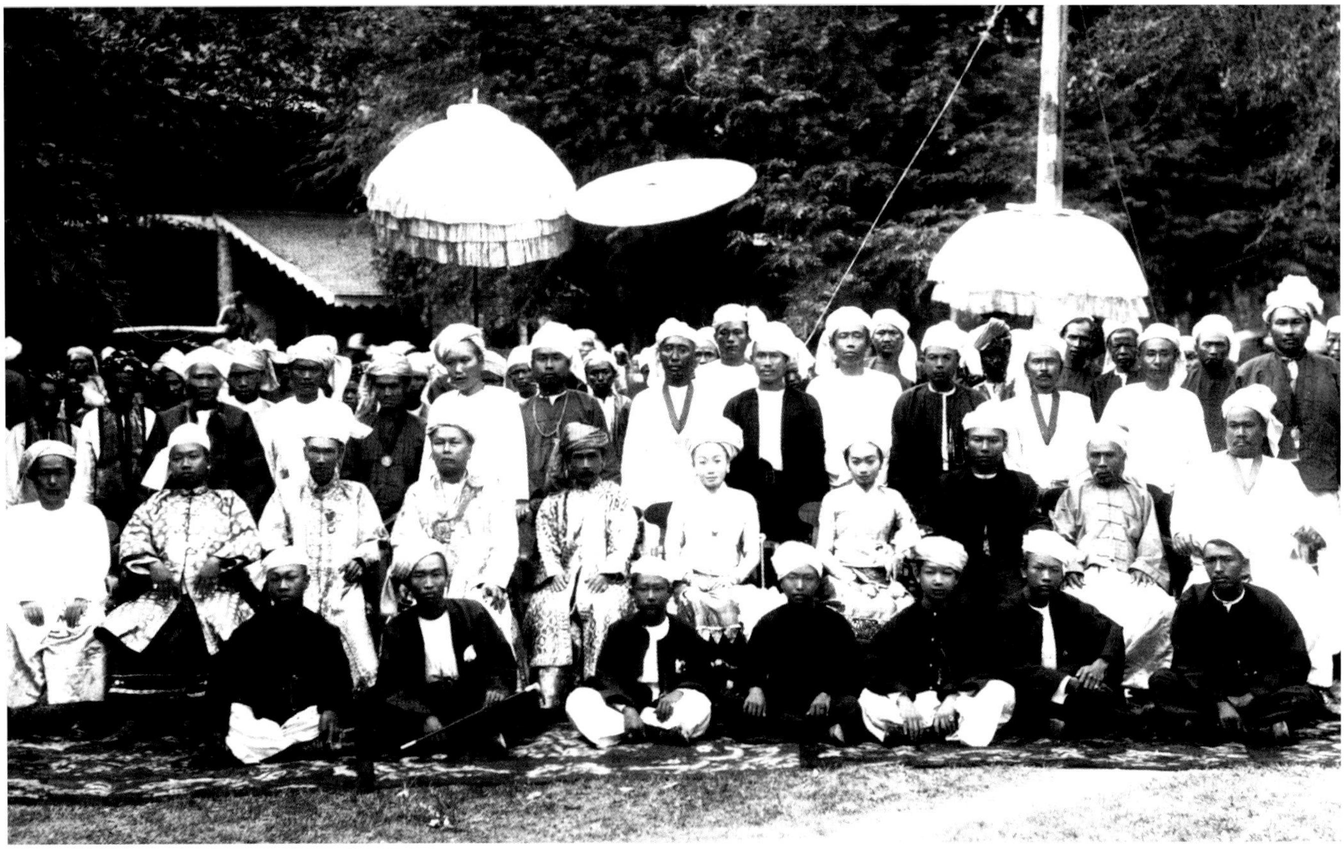

88 Princes, princesses and chiefs of the Northeast Division of the Southern Shan States at a durbar held in 1909. *(The Oriental and India Office Collections, The British Library, London, 163/1 (166))*

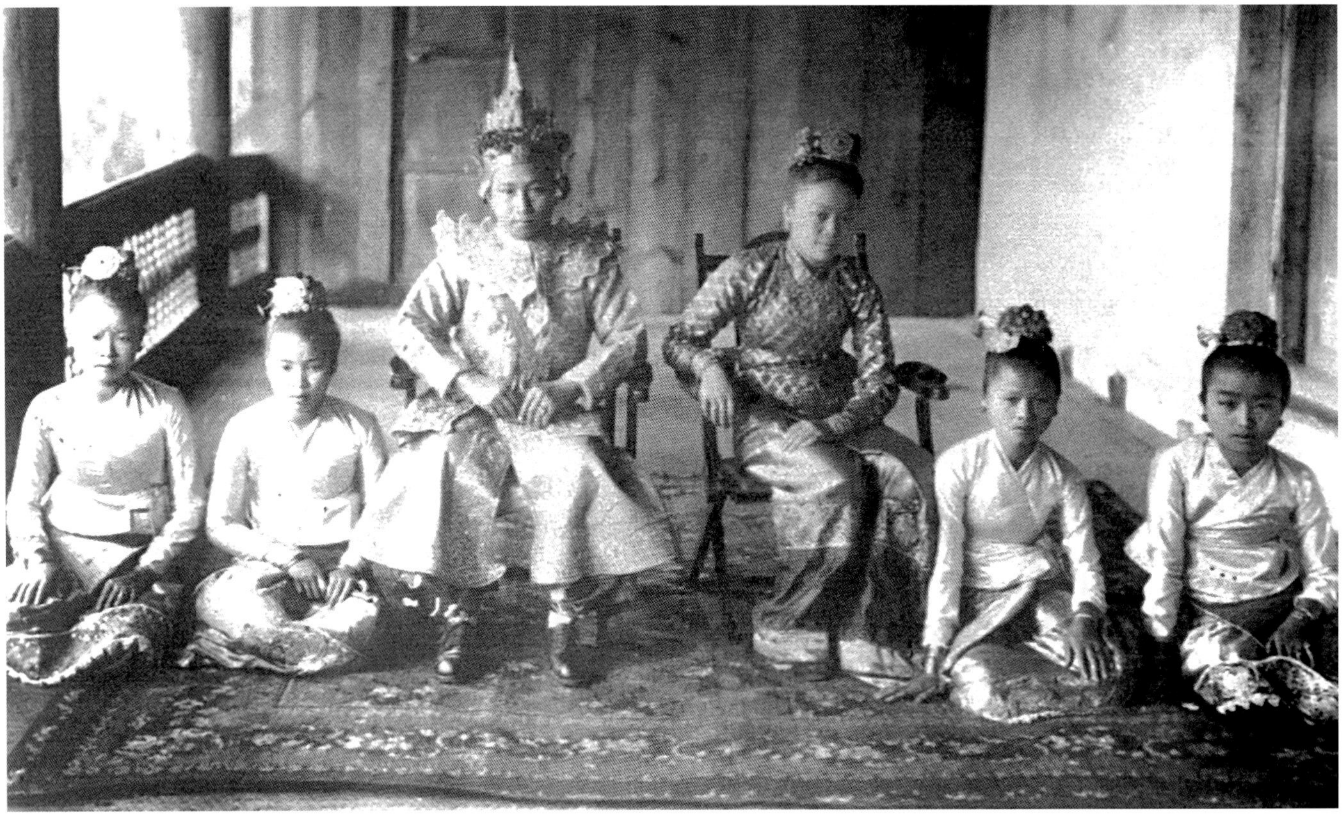

89 Prince Sao Hkun Hsa of Lawksawk and Princess Sao Ven Kiao of Keng Tung photographed with bridesmaid attendants on their wedding day in 1921. *(Permission of Nel Adams (Sao Noan Oo))*

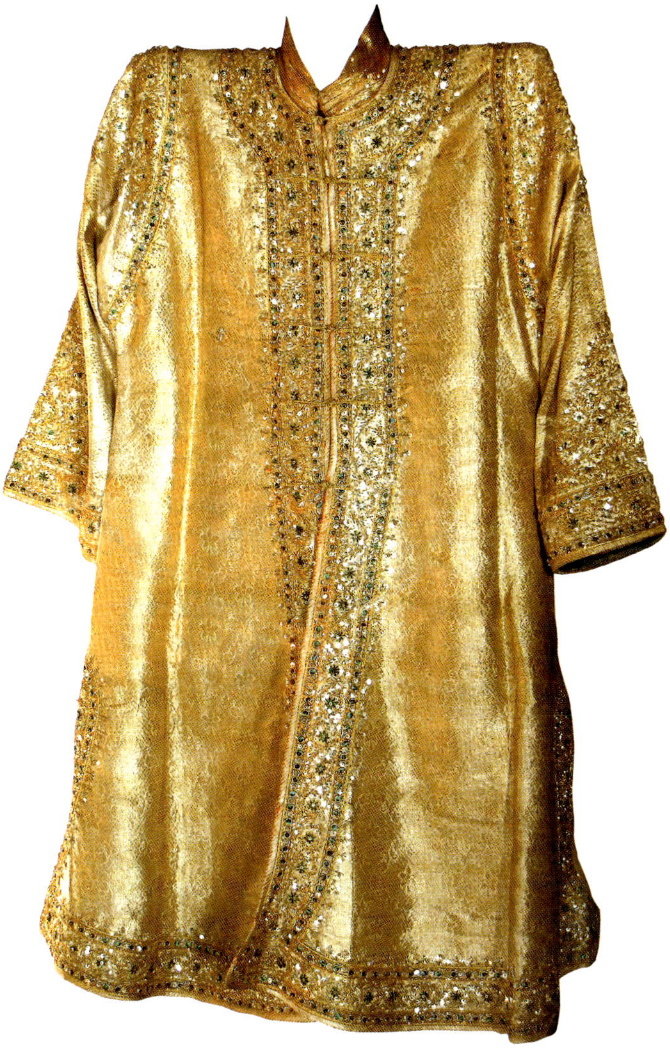

90 A Shan court coat. Shan Palace Museum, Yawnghwe.

91 Detail of the side vent on a Shan court coat. *(Paothong Tongchua collection)*

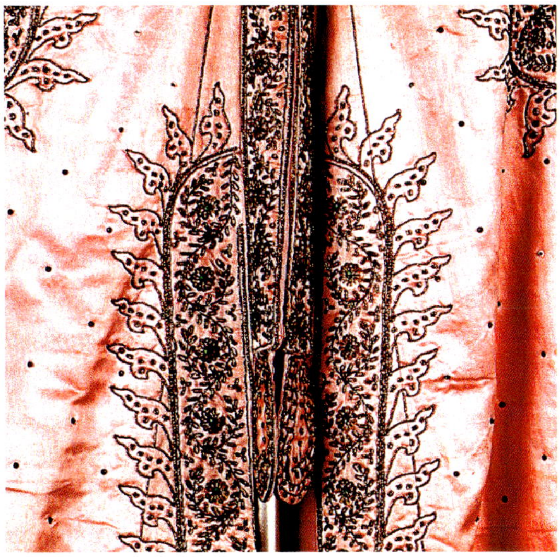

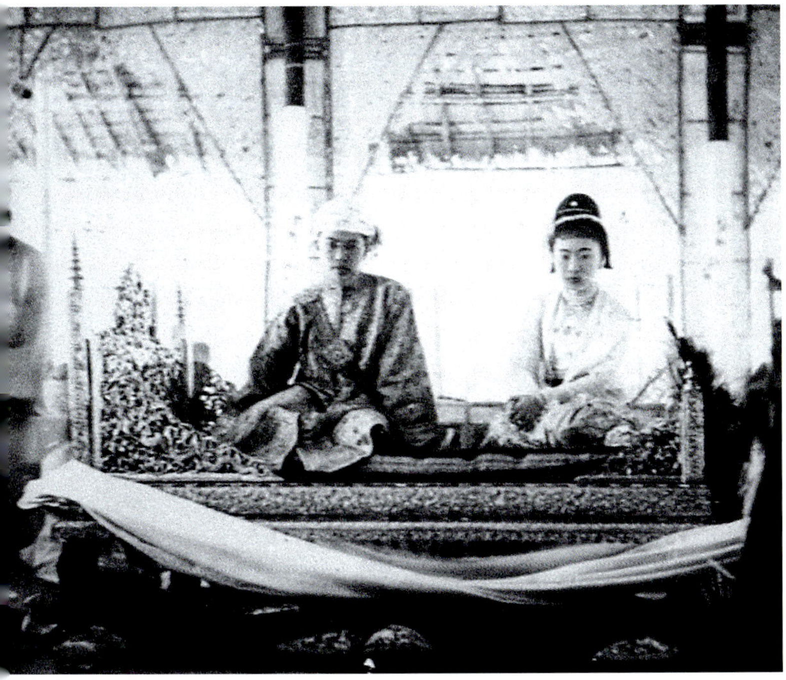

92 The *saohpa* Sao Num of Laikha with his consort, Princess Sao Shwe Bin, 1933. *(Private collection)*

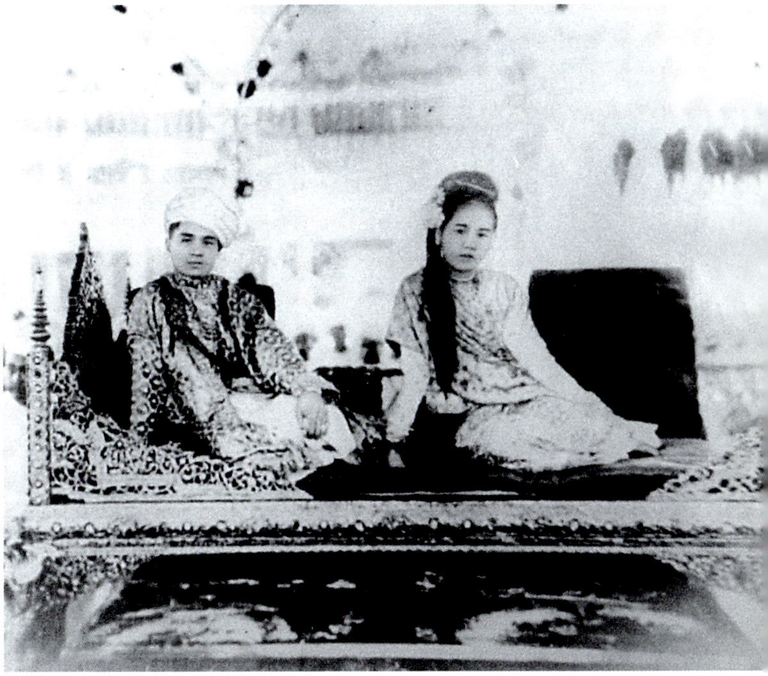

93 The *saohpa* Sao Hsei Houn of Muong Yai and the *mahadevi* Sao Nyunt Kyi, 1939. *(Private collection)*

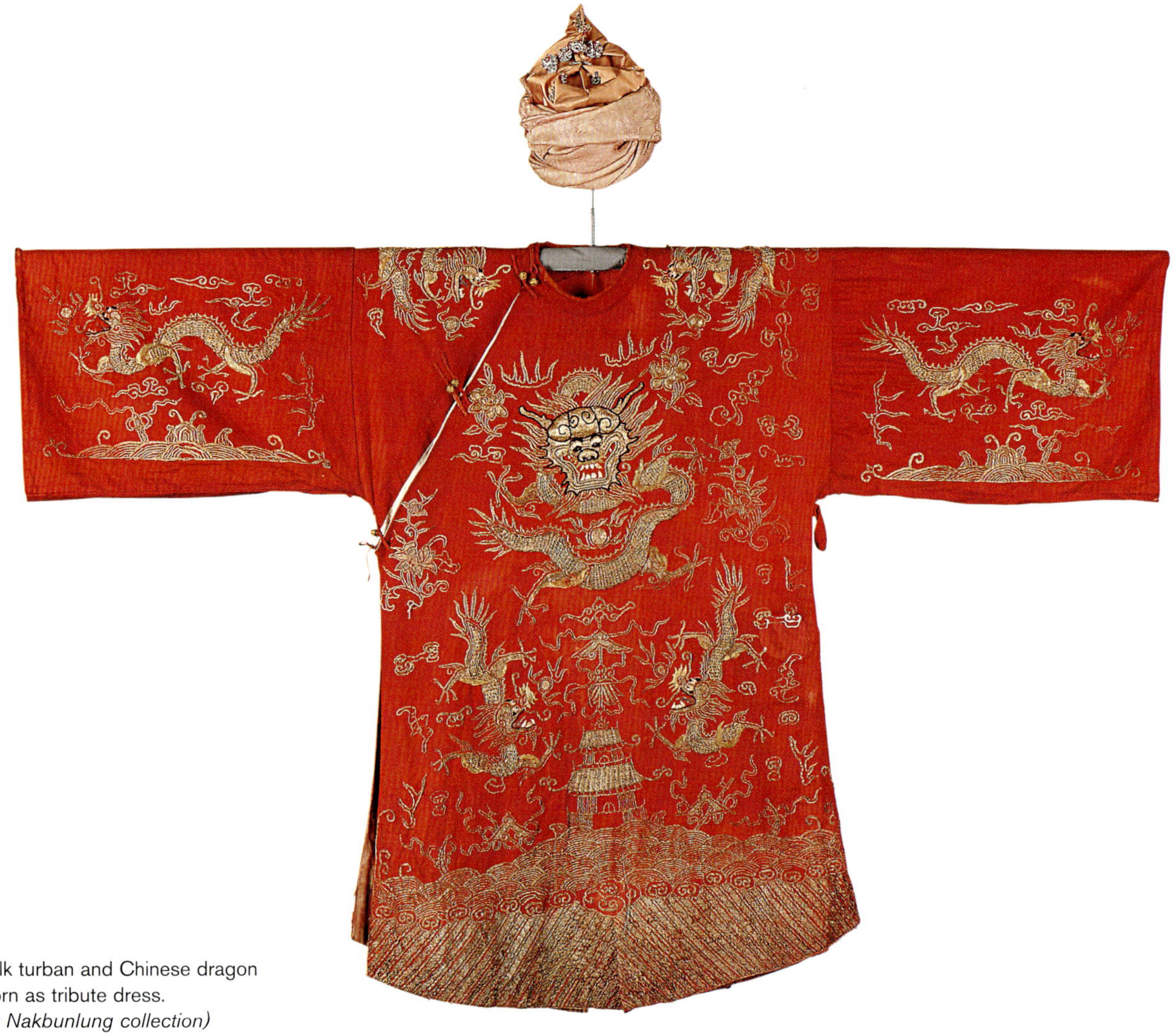

94 A silk turban and Chinese dragon robe worn as tribute dress. *(Akadet Nakbunlung collection)*

(*tsaloe*) with a large repoussé boss over his right shoulder. His European-style lace-up shoes are a break with local tradition.

Although there are photographs of the princes wearing Burmese court dress, it was Shan court dress that was worn for state banquets held in Taunggyi, where the Shan State Council met during British rule. In 1909 Scott photographed the chiefs of the North East subdivision of the Southern Shan States when they attended a durbar (see fig. 88). Seated in the centre row are the senior male princes and princesses who can be identified by their elaborate dress. They wear turbans wrapped in several styles and Princess Tip Htila (fifth from right) has created the most dramatic effect in comparison with the men seated around her. The prince seated on the end to her right wears a neat turban tied at the side of his head and a silk coat with a repeat roundel pattern. Next to him sit two princes wearing tightly wrapped turbans and mid-calf length silk coats trimmed with embroidery. The prince next to Tip Htila is her son-in-law who wears a brocade coat with a geometric pattern. The other princes and chiefs in the photograph wear turbans and Chinese style jackets. Several display medals pinned on their robes or worn on ribbons around their necks. The silk coats seen in this photograph were trimmed at the neck, front facings, pockets and hem with tinsel cloth, braid and gold metal wire, gold and silver sequins, mother-of pearl sequins and beetle wings. In the nineteenth century, fabrics and trimmings could be purchased from itinerant Chinese merchants who made regular visits to the Shan courts. The royal families employed tailors to make up the fabric and needlewomen to add the trimmings. The princes wore this form of dress after independence from Britain in 1948 until 1962 when General Ne Win of Burma dissolved the Shan State Council and abolished the hereditary system of authority that had existed for hundreds of years.

Chinese Dress for the Shan

China operated a tribute system in the Shan States, primarily in the Sipsong Pan Na region, although at various times in history the Chinese had tried to extend their authority further south (see chapter two). This led to conflict with the Burmese and with powerful local rulers. The complexity of this situation can often be interpreted through dress and regalia.

The Chinese records contain accounts of tributary ceremonies in the eighth century AD when princes from the Shan States expressed obeisance by prostrating themselves facing north towards Peking.[26] The records also contain colourful descriptions of the princes who wore tiger skins and were accompanied by attendants carrying cloth banners, fans and umbrellas made of kingfisher feathers. The Chinese expressed admiration for the jewellery worn by the Shan princesses, particularly their pearls, fine jade and amber. Although they took tribute from the Shan, the Chinese did not invite the princes to the Peking court to *kadaw* to the

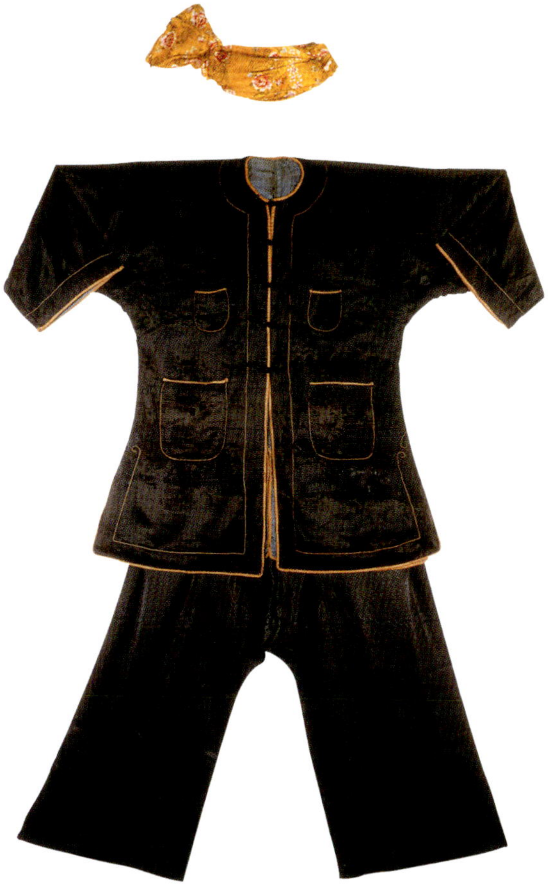

95 "Mandarin" dress, worn by attendants at the Shan courts of Sipsong Pan Na.
(Akadet Nakbunlung collection)

emperor. They were not permitted to enter Peking, the Forbidden City, and were granted travel permits only as far as the southern city of Muong Meng (Puer) in Yunnan Province. Chinese tribute and tribute exchange gifts were managed through the office of the governor of Yunnan, acting under orders from Peking.

The princes sent to the emperor, via the governor of Yunnan, gold and silver tribute trees, pack animals, rice, forest products and hand woven textiles, and in the nineteenth century, sixty-five and a half viss (10.7 kilograms) of silver, donated according to the individual wealth of the princes. It is recorded that the *saohpa* of Muong Long paid ten viss (1.656 kilograms).[27] Captain McLeod was told that the princes of the minor states each sent to the emperor a gold cup weighing 2.5 ticals, silk cloth decorated with gold and silver thread, plain silk cloth, a pair of shoes, a cake of salt, a viss of tea, a viss of candles covered with gold leaf, a viss of candles covered with silver leaf and candles decorated with gold and silver flowers.[28]

In return for tribute the Chinese sent robes, bales of silk, hats and metal seals. The robes were embroidered with dragons, stylised clouds and mountains rising from water. They were worked in multi-coloured silks and couched with gold and silver metal wire. The hats were finely woven bamboo covered with silk, and with a silk lining, and decorated with coral and jade for the senior princes, or with coloured glass and gold and silver metal sequins for those lower down the hierarchy. The seals were thin sheets of gold or silver plate stamped with Chinese characters.[29]

The ruler of Keng Hung, Sipsong Pan Na, wore Chinese dress on ceremonial occasions, although according to McLeod a mix of Shan and Chinese dress was otherwise common.

> *The chief's dress, on particular occasions, is entirely Chinese, the upper garment of silk, worked and ornamented with various figures and devices in gold and silk, reaching the ground, with a conical light hat with the button of rank on it... The hair being permitted to grow long behind, is plaited into a tail. At other times they are habited in a mixture of Chinese and Shan dresses; sometimes wearing turbans (with the hair confined under it) of blue cloth with a fringe of gold thread at the end, which goes around the head two or three times They wear shoes on all occasions, but avoid treading on a carpet with them on.*[30]

The prince of Keng Hung presented McLeod with a Chinese dragon robe, a bamboo hat and a metal plate stamped with Chinese characters. The prince insisted that he wear the outfit for the court to see, and according to McLeod they were satisfied with his appearance.[31]

There was a strong Chinese presence in the region, particularly Chinese merchants and artisans who were married to Shan women. Some were seasonal labourers who arrived to seek employment in the dry season and departed in the monsoon (see chapter seven). There were officials dressed in Chinese dress serving at court, although it is not clear whether they were from the mainland or from Yunnan. When he arrived at the court of Muong Nai, the British officer Richardson was met by a secretary who was dressed in a heavy fur-lined Chinese silk jacket. Richardson soon discovered that this was official dress for government officers in that region.[32]

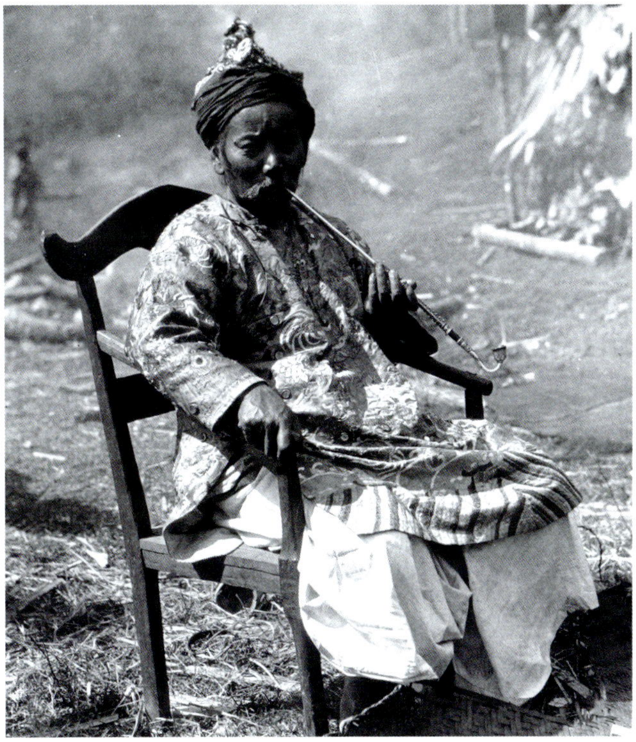

96 Chief *(duwa)* Nga Lang La wearing a silk turban topped with semi-precious stones and pearls, a Chinese dragon robe and loose-legged Shan trousers. His territory bordered Putao. *(The Green Centre for World Art at The Royal Pavilion Art Gallery and Museums, Brighton, 0166)*

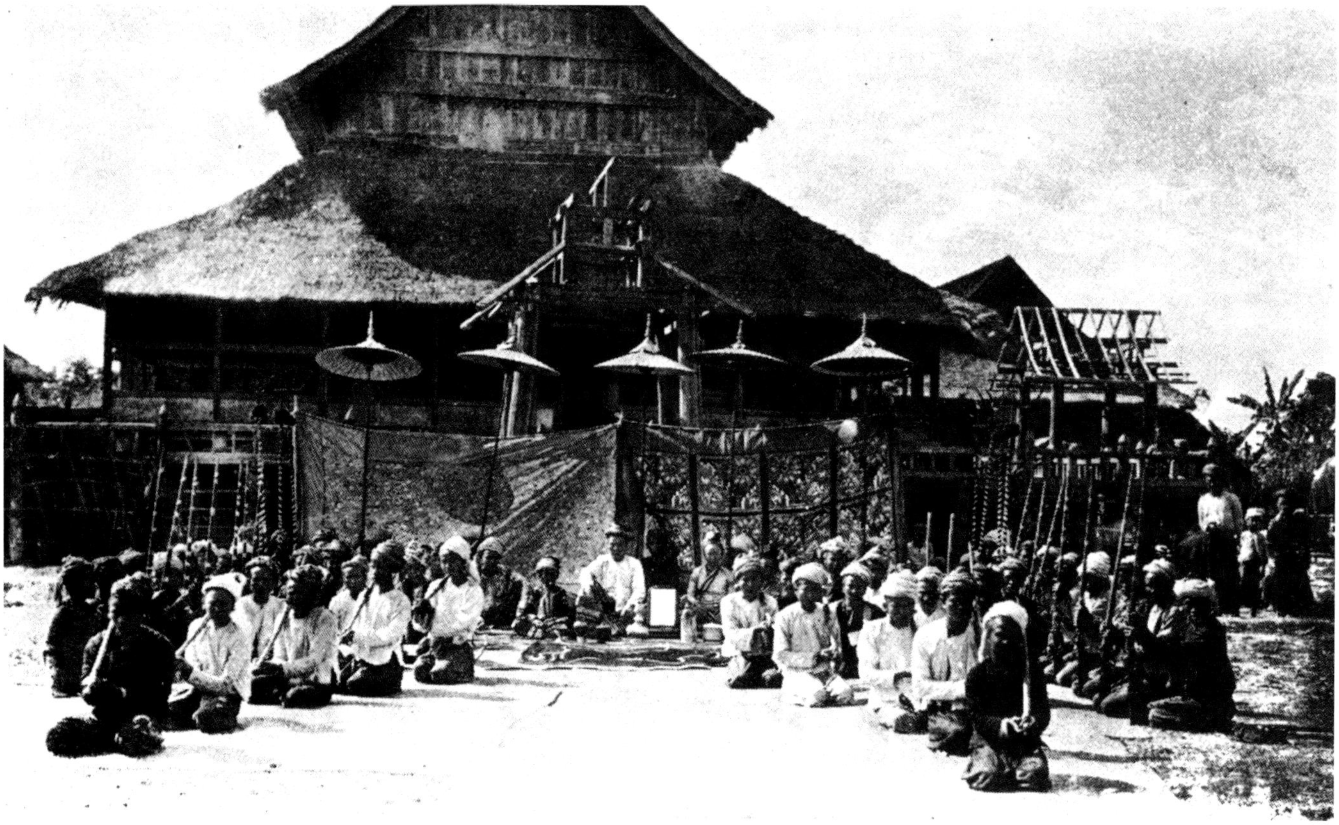

97 The prince of Muong Singh with his family and attendants, photographed in what was described as 'open durbar'. Survey of India Offices, Calcutta, 1899. *(White Lotus Press)*

The French explorer Francis Garnier identified Chinese dress and furnishings, when in 1867 he called on the prince of Keng Hung.

> *His majesty provisionally lived in a poor bamboo house of very ramshackle appearance. The reception hall had been hastily adorned with Chinese carpets...to give an idea of the higher power of the sovereign. After a rather long wait, the king appeared, the assembly bowed, the horns sounded and four small blunderbusses were fired. We saw a young man of nineteen to twenty years of age...he was wearing a big Chinese hat adorned with bells and dressed in a red silk tunic with a green undergarment and a pair of white trousers. In his hand he had a sabre with a sculptured ivory handle.*[33]

Louis de Carné accompanied Garnier to meet the prince and he described the prince's dress slightly differently, stressing a mix of Burmese and Chinese style. He acknowledged the Chinese hat with bells but included a scalloped tiered collar and a set of gold chains (*tsaloe*) "so much sought after by Burmese nobles" that had been sent to him by the king of Burma "as a mark of honour."[34] De Carné does not say how many rows of chains the prince was wearing, a factor that would have identified his status in relation to Burma.

De Carné later attended a session of the Council of Keng Hung and on this occasion he identified the dress as almost entirely Burmese. The *pah-soe* "in Burmese colours" was probably a Burmese *acheik luntaya* tapestry-weave fabric.

> *The principal functionaries, to the number of twelve, were ranged on each side of the prime minister who was enthroned on a bedside carpet. They were attired with turbans, white vests, and wide trousers, or else in white calico dressing-gowns, with a great langouti* [pah-soe] *in Burmese colours, girt around the waist and brought over the shoulders. To the left of the prime-minister was seated the Burman mandarin; a place to the right, ordinarily occupied by the Chinese mandarin, was vacant...*[35]

As the French explorers progressed further north towards Semao they witnessed some unpleasant Chinese practices, including foot binding. They saw a number of Chinese women hobbling on mutilated feet that had been bound since childhood, a custom never practised by the Shan. When they reached the city of Semao, they were granted an audience with the governor of Yunnan. Garnier wrote an account of this meeting.

> *We entered the inner keep of the city by a double arched door...we were halted in the second court: the governor had not yet come. A few moments later a chair* [borne by] *eight porters came in with the noise of crackers: a man of sixty years dressed in the official costume of a Chinese mandarin stepped down. A fur cappa magna was displayed on his silk robe and a lump of coral towered on his hat. We were dealing, or so we thought, with an official of the red insignia, i.e. belonging to one of the four highest grades of the Chinese hierarchy.*[36]

Garnier expresses some doubt about the true rank of this governor. He surmises that most of those in authority in the region were local people who promoted themselves to the Chinese rank of mandarin without central authority.

Semao was probably the northernmost point where there were Tai Lue, Tai Khoen and Tai Shan communities. Further north were territories that had belonged to the Shan, but were, in the nineteenth century, under the authority of China. In the late nineteenth century, Sipsong Pan Na with its Tai Lue, Tai Khoen and Tai Shan culture and its complex Burmese and Chinese tributary system, was considered by the major European powers as an important buffer zone. This included the territory of Prince Soulinor of Muong Singh who was Tai Lue. He dressed in Tai Lue style and was photographed with his consorts, family and attendants. Lefèvre who had visited Soulinor in 1895, wrote:

> *He is dressed in a magnificent jacket in blue silk, quilted, buttoned on the side and with a pair of trousers with silver embroidery on emerald silk. The multicoloured stripes of the Lu* [Tai Lue] *people are replaced by a large strip of embroidery with enamelled metal spangles. On his head there is the traditional large turban of the Lu and on his feet sandals the tip of which terminates in a point that is turned back on the foot.*[37]

His son also dressed in Tai Lue style. Lefèvre wrote:

> *I had the pleasant surprise to see coming to meet me, the oldest son of the Prince of Muong Sing, surrounded by the whole cortege of sabre-bearers and umbrella carriers. He himself was dazzling, in his national dress, in which embroidered and striped satin alternated with the silk of his wide trousers, his elegant vest and multicoloured turban. Everything, up to the gilded umbrellas shading his very dazzlingly harnessed horse, recalled the Oriental luxury of the small court of Xieng Hong.*[38]

On other occasions Prince Soulinor wore a Chinese dragon robe, signalling tributary relations with China (see fig. 47). Interestingly, his wives, photographed with him, always appeared in Tai Lue dress. Soulinor tried to use dress to protect his land, an issue explained in chapter two.

Rulers of other ethnic groups were also issued with Chinese dragon robes and hats, including the Kachin chief (*duwa*), Nga Lang La, whose lands were close to the border with China (see fig. 96). He was photographed wearing a cone-shaped hat inset with coloured glass, pearls and sequins and held in place with a turban cloth. His Chinese silk robe is embroidered with dragons and stylised clouds and waves inset with circles of semi-precious stones and coloured glass. Visible below his robe is a pair of loose-legged Shan trousers, and he is smoking an elegant silver opium pipe.

Body Decoration

Politics, ethnicity and hierarchy were the major factors that affected male dress and regalia worn in the Shan States. Another important element was body decoration. In the 1870s, Louis de Carné had been granted an audience with the prince of Muong Li, a Shan state tributary to Keng Tung, and he made the following observation.

> *At last he* [the Prince of Muong Li] *presented himself in great pomp, dressed in striped yellow and black silk* [trousers]*…a large white calico dressing gown reaching below his knees, half hiding his thin calves which were tattooed all over; and a turban of green silk on his head.*[39]

In the 1880s the German explorer Carl Bock had also discovered that the princes were tattooed and he noted in neighbouring Lan Na that they retained their own tattoo artists.[40] It is probable that most princes were tattooed, although often on only small, concealed areas of their bodies.[41]

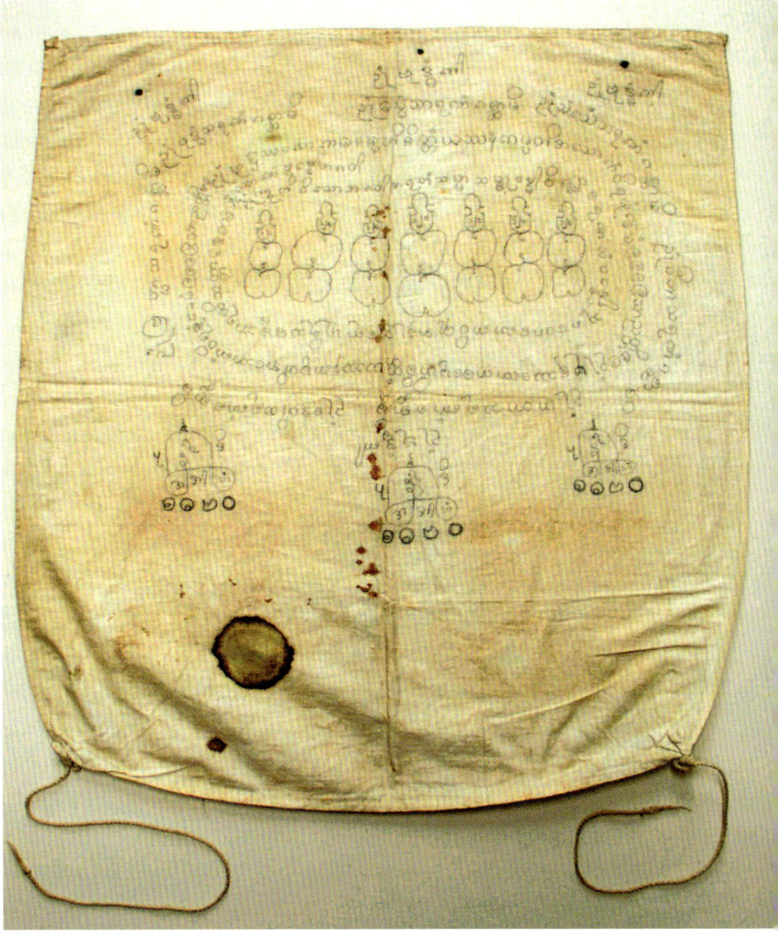

98 A cotton cloth drawn with stylised figures, mystical diagrams and symbols arranged in magic formulae *(ingwet)*. *(Collections of the Ashmolean Museum, Oxford, 1968:103)*

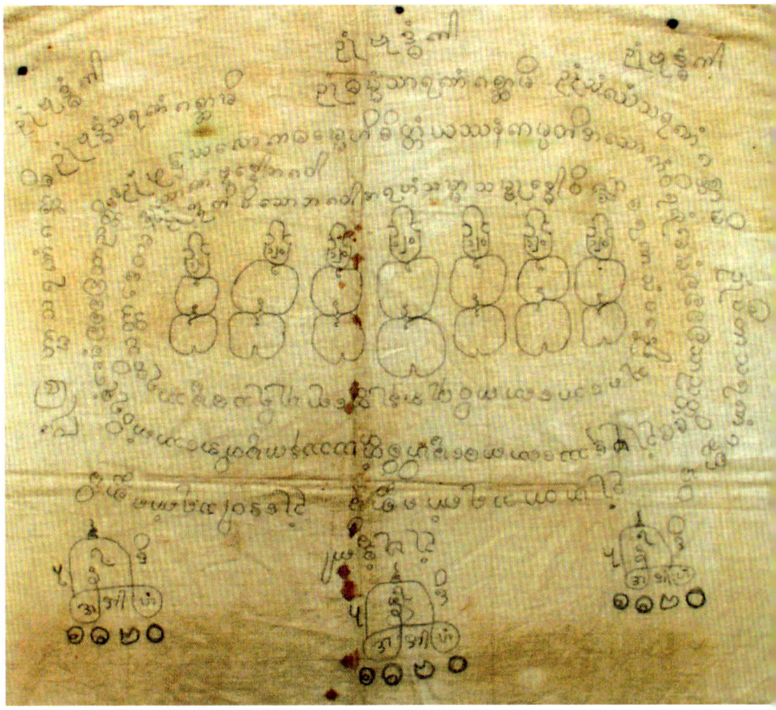

99 Detail of fig. 98.

The most striking tattoos covered the legs from thigh to ankle, the choice of the prince of Muong Line described above. Others were tattooed from the thigh to the knee, also common among the princes of Lan Na and Luang Prabang, or they were tattooed in isolated areas, such as the top of the thigh or on the upper arm or on the shoulders. Those who were extensively tattooed could make an impressive display by wearing their sarongs (*pah-soe*) folded, twisted and tucked up high between the thighs so that most of the leg and thigh were visible. Some men had their stomachs and buttocks tattooed, and in the case of some charismatic spirit doctors, their whole bodies, a process that took several weeks.

Considered as a symbol of manhood among all classes, young men were considered "unripe" or "not cooked" and certainly not ready for marriage until they had been tattooed. The process was usually carried out while they were in their teens.[42] It was believed that tattoos gained potency in proportion to the pain endured in the process, and it took several days to complete a set of leg tattoos (*shan baung-bi*). The tattoo artist (*hyasa*) first drew the patterns freehand with a brush or imprinted them with a tattoo stamp. Using a special needle with longitudinal grooves to hold the pigment. He pricked the designs below the surface of the skin. Border patterns were applied with a sharp serrated plate resembling a comb. The recipe for pigment included burnt animal fat, soot or lamp-black mixed with the bile from a pig, a bear or a bull, with water added to achieve the correct consistency.[43] Opium was administered to ease the pain inflicted during the tattooing process. Not all men endured the suffering, and some gave up before the process was finished.

Tattoo designs were recorded in manuscripts inscribed on palm leaf, and drawn on paper made from mulberry bark. Some have survived on individual sheets of Shan paper. The designs included legendary humans (particularly a cannibal king called Bawdithada), mythical beasts and monsters. The tiger (*singha*), the dragon (*naga*), the monkey god Hanuman and other animals and birds were also popular. Men selected some animals in the belief that their natural instincts could be transferred through the tattoo image. Soldiers and professional thieves had a preference for tigers because they believed they would gain the strength and speed of a tiger.[44] The monkey Hanuman was thought to bring longevity, while cats were associated with stealth. Men tattooed with an image of Bawdithada resisted bullets, sword cuts and beatings and were said to become outstanding athletes.

Tattoo designs also included complex grids and mystical diagrams drawn with squares and circles containing numbers, letters and symbols (*yantra*). These were arranged in special magic formulae (*ingwet*) intended primarily as a form of protection. Numbers often represented stars, suns and planets or mythical gods and goddesses, and were selected according to the horoscope of the person for whom the magic was created. The mystical diagrams were in some instances incorporated with *nat* figures, demons and animals that were thought to enhance the power of the tattoo and were particularly sought by soldiers and others exposed to high risk. When the tattoos were completed, a spirit doctor (*shaman*) interpreted the contents of the circles and squares and recited them as magical incantations (*gatha*).[45]

Some Shan men believed they could increase their personal levels of protection by having their chests, shoulders and arms tattooed with red pigment concocted from vermilion dye mixed with animal fat. Although dramatic in appearance, tattoos of red pigment were less permanent than black. Red pigment tattoos were usually restricted to talismanic symbols and mystical symbolic diagrams. A particularly strong magical formula tattooed on the back could render a person invulnerable to sword and bullet wounds. Spirit doctors were responsible for creating

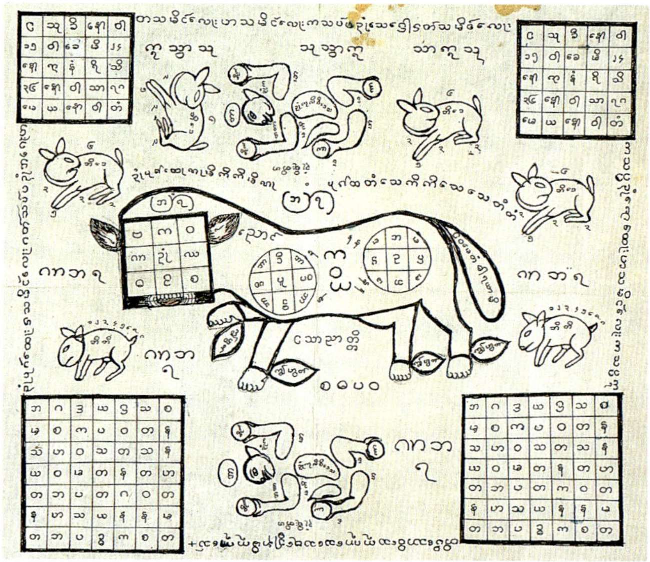

100 Paper scroll printed with mythical animals and magic formulae. Such scrolls were often burnt then dissolved in water and drunk as part of induction ceremonies for an apprentice shaman. *(Fowler Museum of Cultural History, University of Los Angeles, X86.2747)*

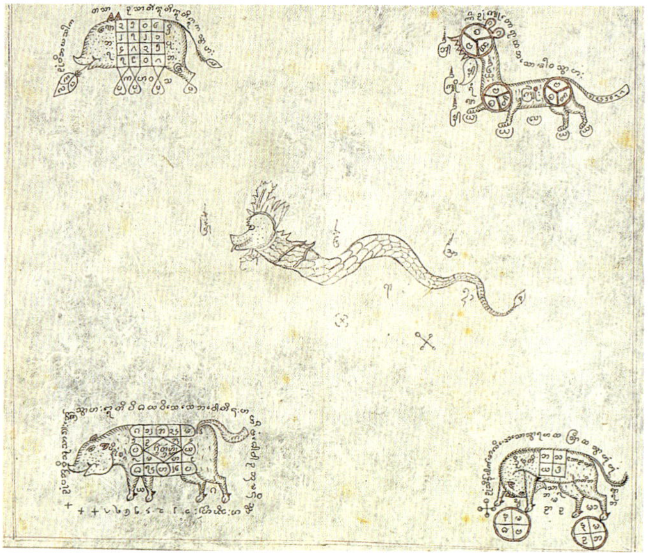

101 Paper scroll printed with mythical animals and magic formulae. *(Fowler Museum of Cultural History, University of Los Angeles, X86.2748)*

102 (Opposite) The cannibal king Bawdithada, mythical animals and magic formulae on a cotton vest. *(The Oriental and India Office Collections, The British Library, London, Or 15085)*

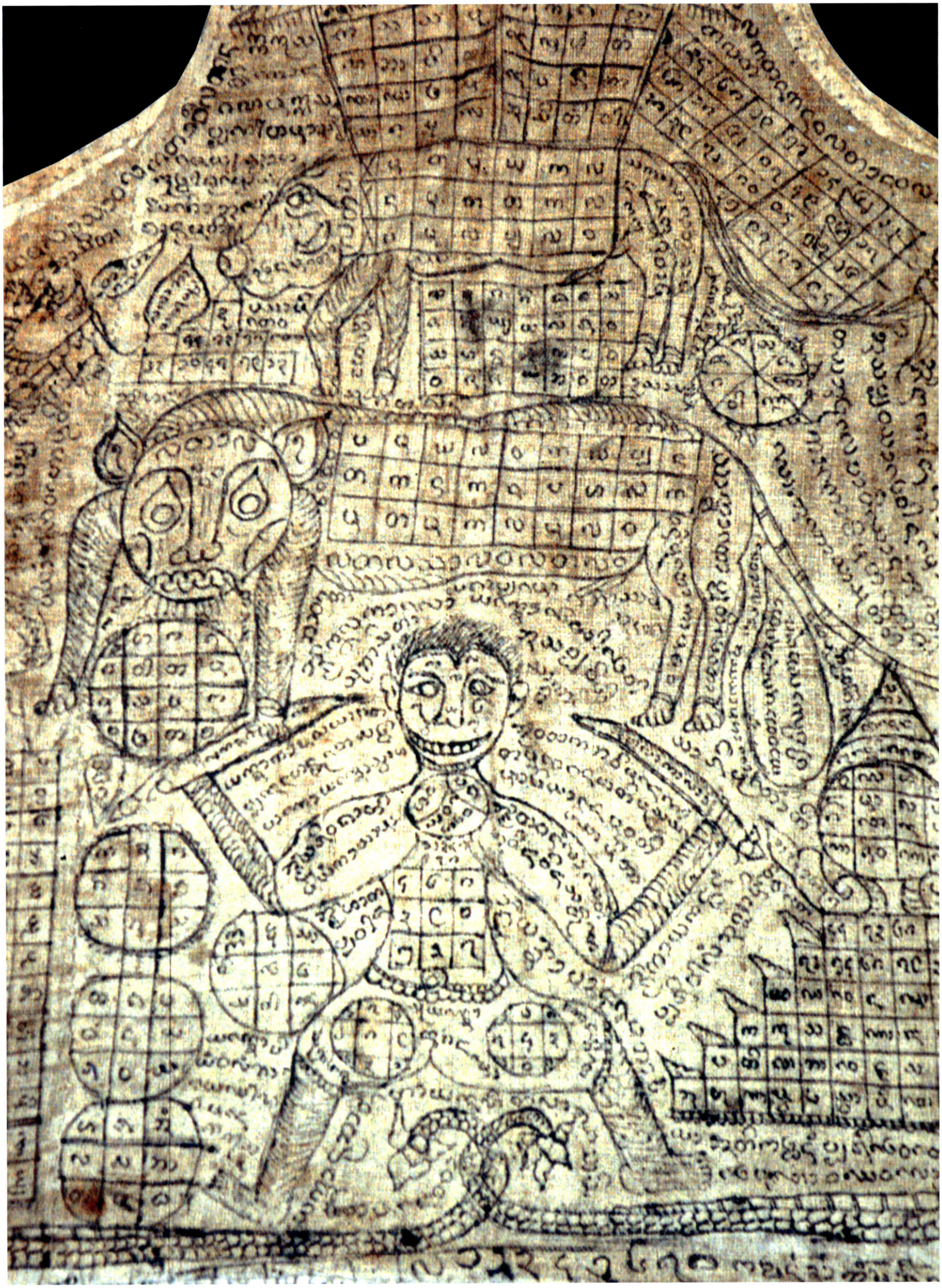

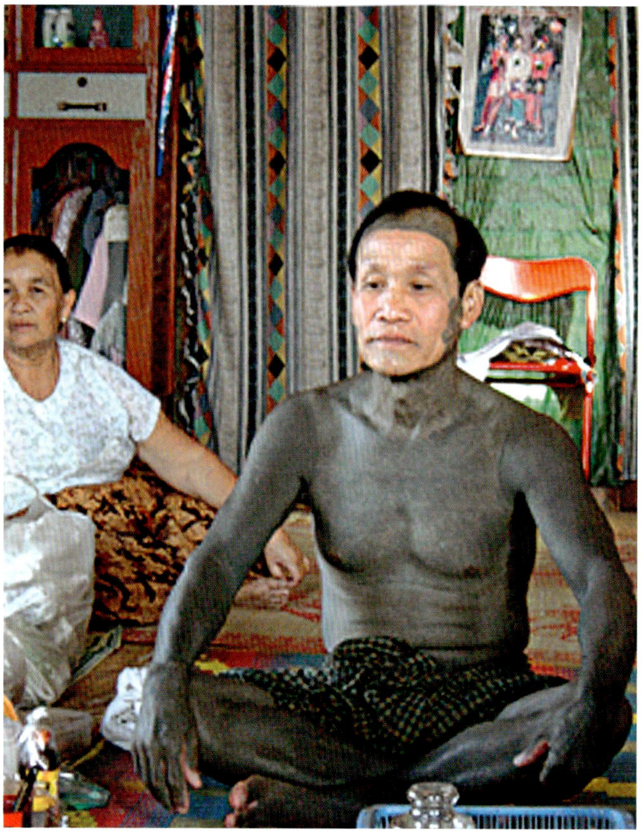

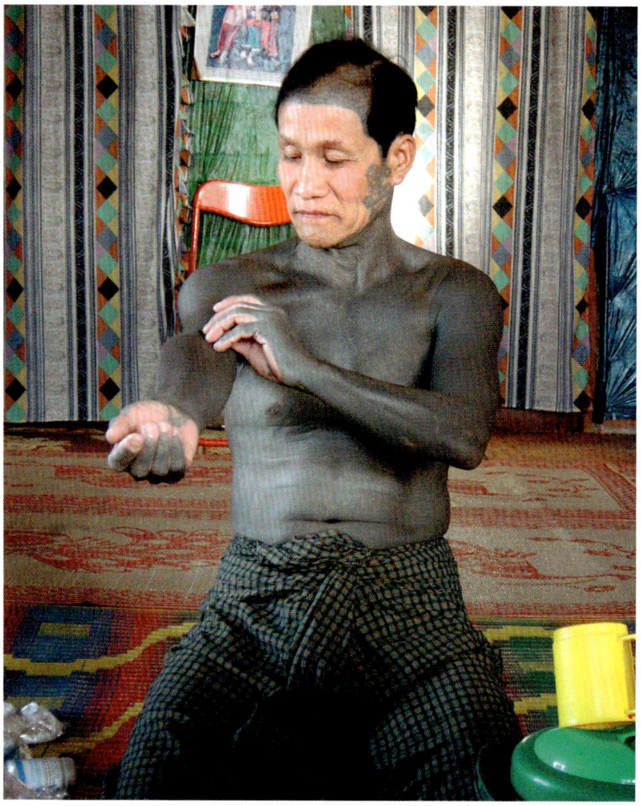

103 A shaman, who was tattooed by thirty-two tattoo artists, preparing for a ceremony. Shan States, 2004.

104 Demonstrating that sharp objects cannot penetrate his tattooed skin. Shan States, 2004.

the magic symbols, incantations and formulae, and they passed their skills down from one generation to the next. Induction in the arts involved an apprenticeship with the study of meditation and mysticism, carried out by recognised masters. The apprentice was given reference books with diagrams and texts that were written in indigenous scripts and in Burmese. Interestingly Shan script was considered particularly powerful and was used on *yantra* cloths in Sipsong Pan Na, the Shan states and Luang Prabang.[46] When a candidate was considered competent he prepared for the induction ceremony by fasting and might be expected to drink water in which the ashes of *ingwet* scrolls had been dissolved. When he began to practice, he kept his books and other important ritual paraphernalia on a special altar in the spirit doctor's house. Clients could consult him in his house, or he might be requested to attend them at home.

Spirit doctors gave out magical prescriptions on Shan paper, printed on wood or incised on metal in the form of amulets. They selected the iconography and copied or traced it from their reference books, creating formulae to meet the needs of individual clients. Images that were used frequently were carved on small wooden blocks and printed. They were usually produced in black ink, although some were then coloured. A *yantra* representing the stars, the suns, planets and mythical gods and goddesses was punched on thin ribbons of metal that could be carried in a small pouch or in a metal container attached to a necklace or bracelet.[47] It was formulated according to the horoscope of the individual for whom the magic was intended. In many cases, a Buddhist monk considered to have special powers would be asked to bless such objects, and many Shan did not believe them to be effective without a blessing.

The type of magical iconography described above was also reproduced on cotton cloth, either drawn freehand with a stylus or printed with a wooden block. Black pigment was the most common medium, although red and yellow pigments were also used. Men took their turbans, waist sashes, cotton jackets and vests to be covered with images that would ensure their personal protection, particularly when they were embarking on a dangerous journey or going to war.[48] Cotton cloths were also printed with magic formulae intended to deter malignant spirits from entering the home.

Other charms for invulnerability involved using precious stones, such as rubies, balls of mercury, iron or orpiment, or fine gold wires or small gold and silver discs that were inserted into incisions in the skin. The British surveyor Holt Hallett wrote,

> *It is not at all uncommon to meet a Shan with several knobs on his chest, concealing the talismans that he has inserted as charms to render him proof against bullet and sword.*[50]

Many men chose to wear amulets around their necks on a chain or in a small pouch.[51] Some were engraved with a fish, a monkey, a crab and a peacock, animals whose form the Buddha had assumed in previous lives before taking the appearance of a man. These animals were imbued with intelligence and wisdom and wearing their representations endowed a person with their attributes. Some charms were incised with mystical numbers and symbols. They were hung on cord worn around the waist, the upper arm, the neck and around each ear. The spirit doctor who created them put them through a special test, and if they passed, they also provided protection from bullet wounds and cuts from swords. Some shaman created magic potions that men drank before going into battle, and for added protection they mixed ash with creams and oils that were smeared on the body.[52]

Although the creation of magical formulae was the work of shaman priests, it is significant that Buddhist priests were willing to add their blessings. This was acceptable because the Yuan sect of Buddhism as practiced in the Shan States, acknowledged that there were monks with magical powers.[53]

Male court dress, as worn by Shan rulers, can be linked to local political and ethnic affiliations and to a wider network of tributary relations with China and Burma, the main competitors for authority in the region for most of the nineteenth century. In states where both major powers held influence, the Shan rulers wore a combination of Burmese and Chinese dress. Others, like the prince of Muong Singh, wore ethnic dress, and on some occasions Chinese tribute dress. Tribute dress is a marker of how, at a particular moment in time, the Shan princes and chiefs reacted to political authority. After the overthrow of the Burmese monarchy, the British introduced their own form of tributary dress, although it was generally sashes and medals that could be worn on existing court dress. At village level, most men dressed in cotton work clothes, reserving best dress for religious and festive occasions. This might, although not always, communicate ethnic identity. Body decoration was an important element of Shan dress, expressed in tattoos and charms inserted under the skin, in cotton textiles and clothing printed with magical formulae, and in metal charms worn on the body. In some cases they were not considered potent unless blessed by a Buddhist monk.

Endnotes

1 This is in contrast to north Thailand (Lan Na) where there has been a revival of beautiful hand-woven indigenous dress, worn on festive occasions.

2 Parliamentary Papers, V/4/session, 1868/1869, Vol. 46, p. 617, India Office Collection, The British Library, London.

3 Sylvia Fraser Lu, *Burmese Crafts Past and Present*, Kuala Lumpur 1994, p. 262.

4 Loi Long was the Shan name and Taung Baing was the Burmese name, which the British altered to Tawng Peng.

5 George Scott noted that Tawng Peng had been ruled by Palaung and Karen chiefs.

6 George Scott, *Burma: A Handbook of Practical Information*, 1906, reprint Orchid Press, Bangkok, 1999.

7 Putao was situated in the state of Hkamti Long to the west of Yunnan Province, China.

8 Scott, 1999, p. 497.

9 Sequined leather shoes were worn by some princes and by novice monks at initiation rites.

10 Louis de Carné, *Voyage en Indo-Chine et dans l'Empire Chinois*, 1872, Dentu Ed., Paris. reprint White Lotus, 2000, pp. 198.

11 Arthur Phayre, *History of Burma*, Susil Gupta, London, 1883.

12 George Scott and J. P. Hardiman, *Gazeteer of Upper Burma and The Shan States*, Superintendent of Government Printing, Rangoon, 1900, 1901, Vol. II, pt. I, p. 85.

13 Michale Symes, *An Account of an Embassy to the Kingdom of Ava sent by the Governor-General of India in the year 1795,* London, 1800, reprint, Madras, 1995.

14 T. A. Trant, *Two Years in Ava (1824-1826)*, London, 1827, p. 297

15 Shway Yoe (George Scott), *The Burman, His Life and Notions,* Macmillan, London 1882, reprint New York, 1963, p. 310.

16 Although it was a secular award, the *tsaloe* has been linked to the sacred thread *(upavita)* worn by Brahmins in India.

17 Fraser-Lu, Sylvia, 1994, p. 169.

18 In 1948 the Lion Throne was returned to Burma, and in 1964 part of the royal regalia was also sent back. They are now on display in the National Museum, Yangon.

19 P. J. Marshall, 'Empire and Authority in the Late Eighteenth Century', in *Journal of Imperial and Commonwealth History*, Vol. XV, 1987, p. 105.

20 Nel Adams, *My Vanished World*, Horseshoe Publications, Cheshire, England, 2000.

21 Quoted in Cannadine, David, *Ornamentalism*, Oxford University Press, New York, 2001, p. 88.

22 George Scott, *Burma and Beyond*, London: Grayson and Grayson, 1932, p. 59.

23 *Coronation Durbar Illustrated*, Wieleand Klein, Madras, 1903.

24 William Clifton Dodd, *The Tai Race: Elder Brother of the Chinese*, The Torch Press, Cedar Rapids, 1923, reprint White Lotus Press, Bangkok, 1996, p. 201.

25 Leslie Milne and Wilbur Cochrane, *Shans at Home*, John Murray, London, 1910, reprinted New York, 1970, p. 13.

26 McCleod, quoted in Grabowsky and Turton, *The Gold and Silver Road of Trade and Friendship*, Silkworm Books, Chiang Mai, 2003, p. 394.

27 A tical was one hundred viss (1600 grams).

28 Verity Wilson, *Chinese Dress*, Victoria and Albert Museum, London, 1986.

29 McLeod, in Grabowsky and Turton, 2003, p. 392.

30 *Ibid* p. 395.

31 Richardon, quoted in Grabowsky and Turton, 2003, p. 490.

32 Francis Garnier, *Further Travels in Laos and in Yunnan: The Mekong Exploration Commission Report (1866-1868),* Vol. 2 (trans. W. Tips), White Lotus Press, Bangkok, 1996, p 90.

33 de Carné, 2000, p. 208.

34 *Ibid* p. 206-207.

35 Garnier, 1996, p. 107.

36 E. Lefèvre, *Travels in Laos*, (trans. by W. Tips), White Lotus Press, Bangkok, 1995, p. 70.

37 Pierre Lefevre-Pontalis, *Travels in Upper Laos and on the Borders of Yunnan and Burma*, (trans. by W. Tips), White Lotus Press, Bangkok, 2000, p. 296.

38 de Carné, 2000, p. 180.

39 Carl Bock, *Temples and Elephants, Travels in Siam 1881-1882,* Oxford University Press, 1884, reprint Oxford University Press, 1986, p. 171.

40 Oral communication, Sao Hkam Hpa of Hsenwi, April 2005.

41 Interestingly, they were also considered immature ('uncooked') if they had not served as a novice monk.

42 Bock, 1986.

43 Scott and Hardiman, *Gazeteer of Upper Burma and The Shan States*, Vol. II, Superintendent of Government Printing, Rangoon, 1900, 1901, p. 79-83.

44 *Gatha* is the Pali word for magical chanting.

45 Oral communication with monks in Keng Tung, November 2004.

46 Milford E. Spiro, *Burmese Supernaturalism*, Prentice-Hall, New Jersey, 1976, pp. 35-39.

47 The Liverpool Museum has an amulet in this form coiled inside a protective strip of leather (access. no. 56.26.279) See S. Conway, *Silken Threads Lacquer Thrones,* 2004, p. 84.

48 Milne and Cochrane, 1910, pp. 66-67. Le May 1926 reprint 1986, pp. 120-121.

49 Holt Hallett, *A Thousand Miles on an Elephant in the Shan States*, 1890, reprint 1988, Bangkok.

50 Milne and Cochrane, 1910, pp. 66-67, Le May 1986, pp. 120-121, Hallett, 1898, p. 138.

51 Scott and Hardiman, Vol. II pt. 1, pp. 79-83.

52 Charles Keyes, 1971, 'Buddhism and National Integration in Thailand, in *Visakha Puja*, B. E. 1514, Bangkok, pp. 22-34.

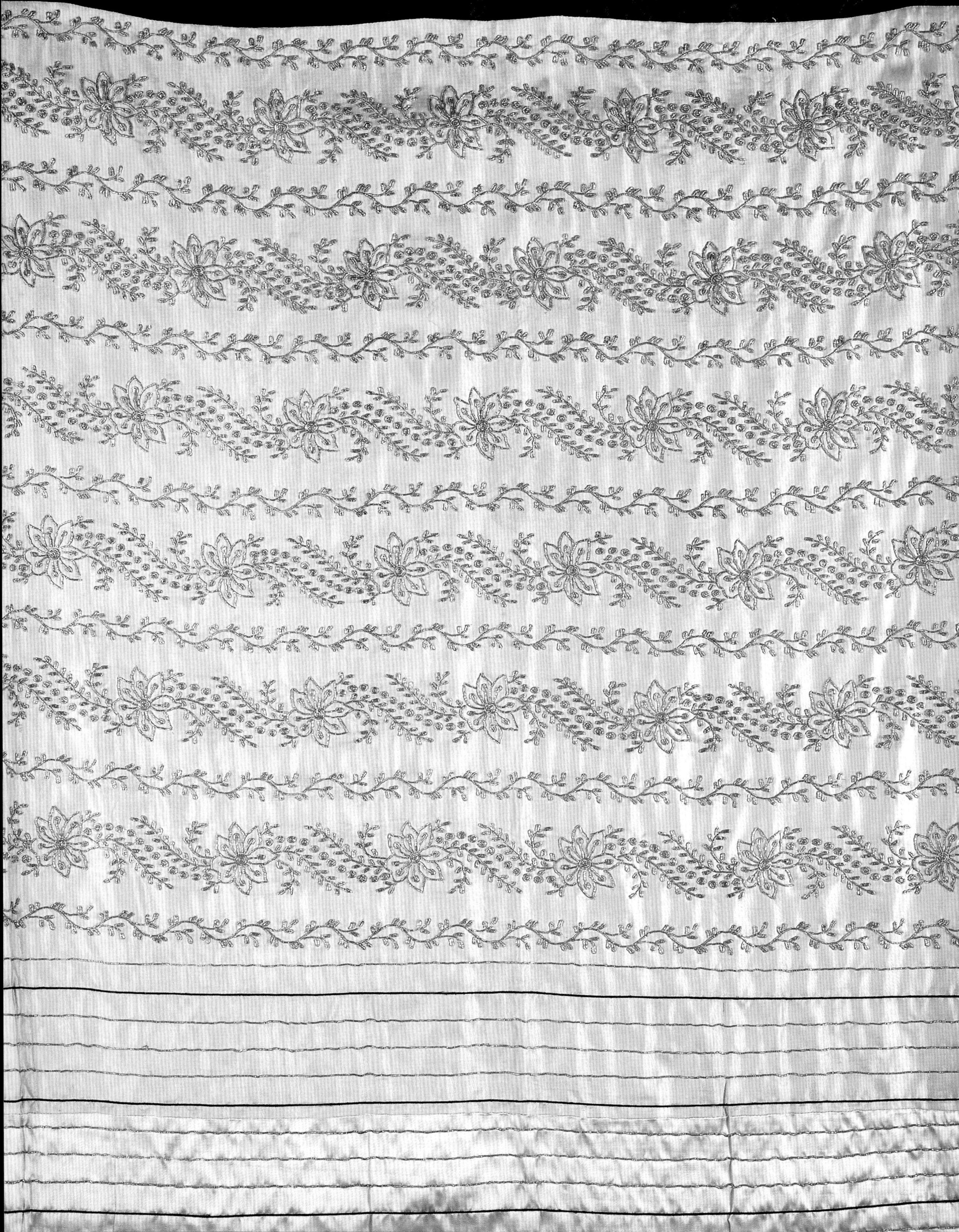

Chapter 4
Female Dress in the Shan States

This chapter examines female dress worn by the consorts of the rulers and chiefs and village women in the Shan States from the second half of the nineteenth century to the 1930s. The chapter includes women from the northern states of Hkamti Long and Muong Baw that border Assam and China, from Keng Tung that shares boundaries with China, western Laos and Lan Na (north Thailand), and from the state of Yawnghwe that borders Burma.

The term associated with female dress in inland Southeast Asia is "traditional," meaning in this context that the way women dressed was linked to a particular ethnic group or homeland and had been worn in that style for an extended, although undefined period. The ethnic groups who are the main focus of this chapter are the valley dwelling Tai Khoen, Tai Lue, Tai Yai and Tai Neua of the Shan States, although there are also descriptions of other groups including the Karen, the Kachin, the Palaung and the Wa.

Another term frequently used to describe women's dress in Southeast Asia is "correct". What is meant by this term is clearly illustrated in the photograph of Tai and Kachin women taken in the 1930s by the British military officer Colonel James Green. The Kachin women are wearing turbans, heavy silver jewellery, cotton knee-length skirts, cloth leggings and rattan leg rings. They are easily distinguished from the Tai urban women in the photograph with their sleek oiled hair, delicate silk blouses and ankle-length skirts. What each group is wearing in this photograph was viewed as "correct" dress for two distinct ethnic groups in a particular place and at a time when there were accepted perceptions of hill tribe "primitiveness" and lowland "civilised" societies. The contrast between the dress of hill and valley dwellers, very obvious in this photograph, was not always so easy to identify, as is evident in other photographs reproduced in this book.

One example is a set of clothes collected by Max and Bertha Ferrars at the end of the nineteenth century and described by them as belonging to a Shan woman (see fig. 107).[1] The shape, fabric and trim on the blouse and the style of the shoulder bag, decorated with Job's tears, are generally attributed to hill dwellers, whereas the accompanying ankle-length skirt with its horizontal stripes and patterned hem border (*teen jok*) is in lowland Tai style. The interesting question is how these items of clothing came together as a set. In the valleys and hills of the Shan States, dress was frequently varied to suit all manner of circumstances. Many hill dwellers wore distinctive knee-length skirts, cloth leggings and rattan leg rings like the ones seen in Green's photograph. They were perfectly adapted for climbing steep hills while protecting the legs from thorny plants and insects, particularly leeches. This protection was not needed if a group migrated to lower altitudes or settled in the valleys. The women either lengthened the warp prepared for weaving skirts, or they wove two lengths of fabric and sewed them together along the selvedge to create a longer skirt that reached to mid-calf or to the ankles, thus coming closer in style to the dress worn by women in valley communities. The weavers did not necessarily alter the patterns they produced, or change the dye colours. However, if they no longer cultivated, dyed and spun cotton and bought the yarn ready-processed in the market for weaving, the skirts they produced in this way came to be known among the hill people as "plain dweller's skirts."[2]

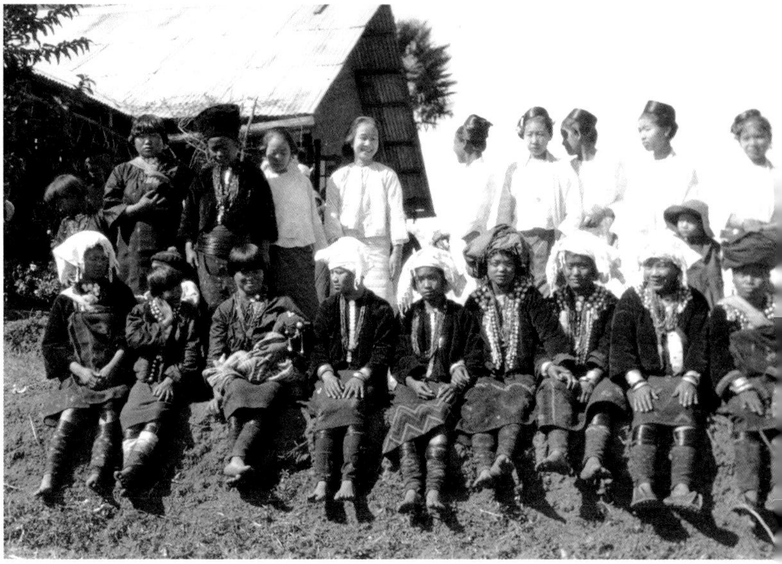

106 A photograph of Shan women (standing) and Kachin women (mainly seated) illustrating the difference between valley and hill dress. *(The Green Centre for World Art at The Royal Pavilion Art Gallery and Museums, Brighton, 1253)*

Migration is an important theme running through the history of dress in inland Southeast Asia and most people did not move by choice. Epidemics of smallpox and tropical fever could decimate whole communities, and those who were able-bodied fled from affected areas, often to settle among people of a different ethnic group. Valley dwelling farmers were captured, transported and resettled in foreign lands. In wartime, whole villages were taken and resettled in the state of a victorious ruler. In the eighteenth and nineteenth centuries large numbers of Tai Khoen, Tai Lue and Tai Yai suffered as a result of this type of intervention. When these groups, frequently identified by a distinct form of dress worn by women, came to live in close proximity, there was a degree of assimilation in terms of weaving patterns and dress styles. There were exceptions; some communities who were resettled near main trade routes were able to buy from itinerant merchants the same type of materials as they used in their original homelands, therefore maintaining "traditional" dress.[3]

105 (Opposite) A woman's yellow silk skirt embroidered with silver metal thread.

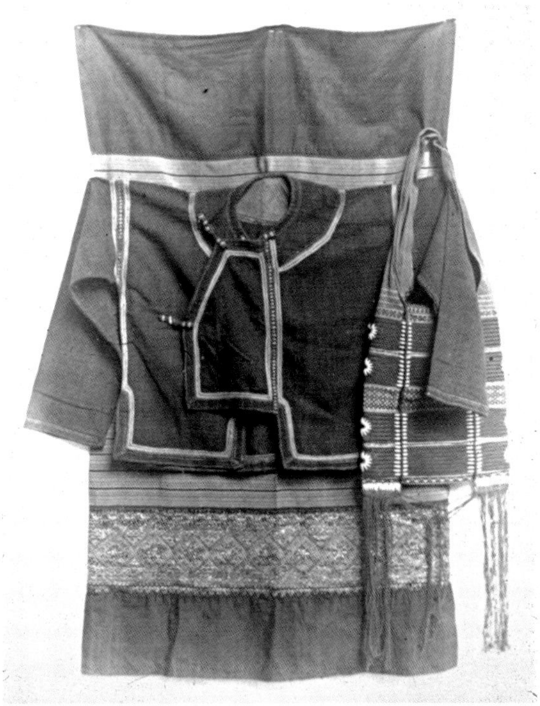

107 A hill tribe jacket and shoulder bag with a Tai Yuan (Lan Na) skirt, from the book *Burma* by Ferrars and Ferrars, 1901.

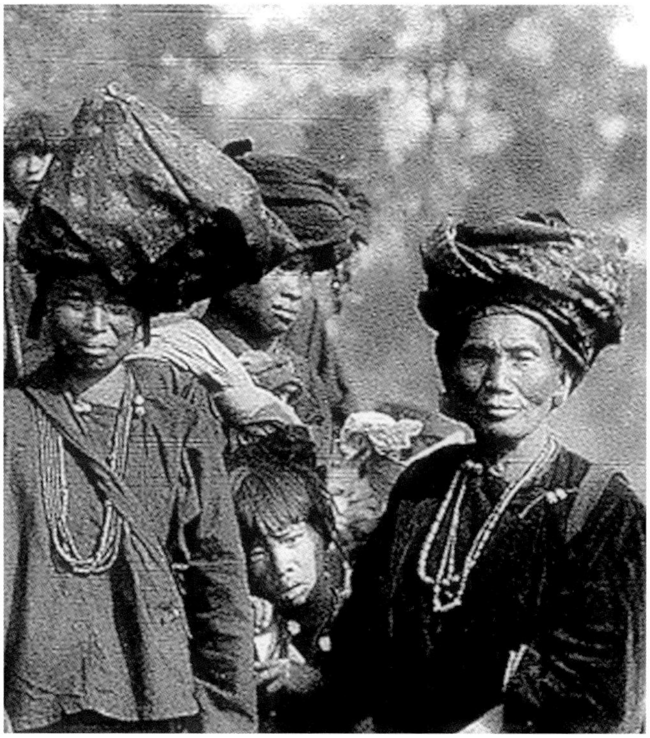

108 Kachin women wearing voluminous turbans. *(The Green Centre for World Art at The Royal Pavilion Art Gallery and Museums, Brighton, 0250)*

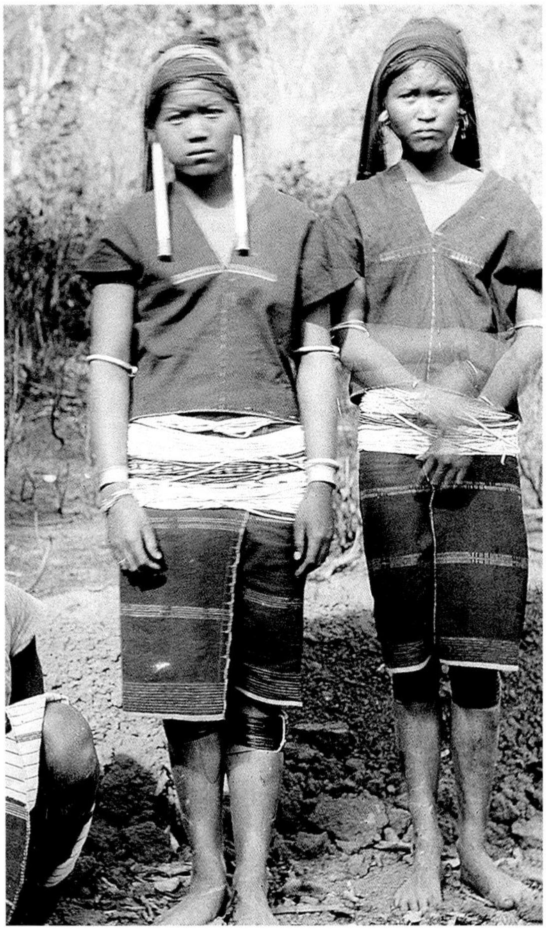

109 Wa women posing in tunics *(hse),* wrapped skirts and bamboo rings. They are carrying cloth shoulder bags with the straps across their foreheads. *(White Lotus Press)*

Adapting to new surroundings was a strong incentive for modifying dress, but personal preference and fashion were at times important factors. In the 1920s, some Kachin women took a fancy to voluminous turbans that replaced their more modest head coverings.[4] Hill-dwelling women who visited lowland markets returned home with skirts in lowland style and wore them as best dress, probably the reason why the clothes collected by Max and Bertha Ferrars ended up together. Many elite Karen and Kachin women wore Shan-style blouses made of Chinese silk or satin to replace hand-spun cotton tunics (*hse*). Traders sold the same type of Chinese and Burmese embroidery to wealthy Shan women who used it to trim their skirts and jackets, and to the wives of hill chiefs who embellished the hoods of their capes. Writing in the early twentieth century, the Roman Catholic missionary Charles Gilhodes claimed that many women in the Shan States wore Burmese, Chinese and European textiles when it suited them.[5] Although this is an exaggeration, it does reinforce the idea of versatility in dress codes.

There was also an interchange of weaving patterns between groups. Tai weavers in the northern Shan States, for example in Hsenwi, create continuous supplementary weft patterns in their turbans and ankle-length skirts that are also produced by Karen and Kachin weavers in their skirts, although not necessarily to a similar scale. Wa, Karen, Kachin and Tai women living in lowland communities wore cotton skirts for everyday with rows of horizontal ikat stripes and plied yarns. The arrangement and scale of the patterns is an indication of who wore the skirt. For example, the knee-length skirts worn by the two Wa women in the photograph have narrow bands of ikat and plied yarns, whereas the Karen skirt has six wide bands of ikat in the centre and four narrow bands evenly spaced above and below the centre. Weavers using back, strap looms tended to introduce ikat and plied yarns in the warp, whereas if a frame loom was used, the patterns were more likely to be inserted in the weft.

Many claims are made about the origin of weaving patterns. Young claimed that Wa women "borrowed" patterns from Karen weavers.[6] In a contradictory assertion Tai and Karen weavers are said to have copied Wa patterns.[7] As these groups had been bartering yarn, cloth and dyes for many centuries, it is difficult to authenticate claims of original ownership. There are some items, particularly sarongs, cotton blankets, and cotton bed sheets, that have plaid and striped patterns, and are produced by hill dwellers and lowlanders throughout inland Southeast Asia (see figs. 54 and 58).

There are interesting issues of class and ethnicity associated with women's dress. In the nineteenth century, wealthy Tai Khoen and Tai Lue women in Keng Tung wore similar silk turbans, blouses and silk skirts. This was described as "ordinary" court dress because royalty dressed in a similar way.[8] However when they were in ceremonial court dress, distinctions between the two groups were obvious. The consorts of the Shan princes and chiefs were bound to forms of "traditional" or "correct" dress on ceremonial occasions. They were polygamous, and marital alliances were negotiated between elite Shan States families, and, in the wider political arena, with sons and daughters of powerful hill chiefs, particularly Wa, Karen and Kachin.[9] Marriages were also arranged with elite families in Sipsong Pan Na, Luang Prabang (western Laos), Lan Na (north Thailand), Yunnan and also with Burma. On public occasions the consorts were seen in the "correct" dress of their homelands as a way of demonstrating the extent of a ruler's political influence. Nineteenth-century drawings, etchings and photographs provide evidence of these dynastic displays. There are also written accounts. William Dodd commented on the dress of Princess Nang Wen Tip who was a Tai Khoen princess married to the Tai Lue prince of Keng Hung.

> *Chow Nang Wen Tip, the Chow Fa's* [Prince's] *older sister, was married to the Chow Fa of Chiengrung* [Keng Hung]. *She made her home in the Lü* [Lue] *country but retained her Kün* [Khoen] *dress.*[10]

The princesses wore indigenous dress on important occasions in their home courts. The wealthiest dressed in silk interwoven with gold and silver metal thread and trimmed with gold and silver sequins, semi-precious stones, beetle wings and mother-of-pearl beads. The cost of this clothing can be assessed by the fact that a court lady would pay thirty times the price of a village woman's cotton skirt for a thin band of silk embroidery to trim her hem.[11] However, when they were not in the public eye most women at court wore a simpler form of dress in silk that resembled which worn by village women. The line between rich and poor, and high and low status was not subject to formal regulation in the countryside, so there was room for flexibility. The wives and daughters of minor rulers and officials, powerful village leaders and wealthy farmers usually owned at least one costume trimmed with imported materials, such as Chinese and Burmese silk, embroidery, velvet, metal and mother-of pearl buttons and silver and gold metal thread, purchased from itinerant merchants. As will be evident in the photographs reproduced in this chapter, some members of the elite in the smallest Shan states wore Burmese silk *acheik-luntaya* (see figs. 73 and 132). In years when there was a good harvest even poor village women could afford to buy some silk yarn, if they were not able to produce it

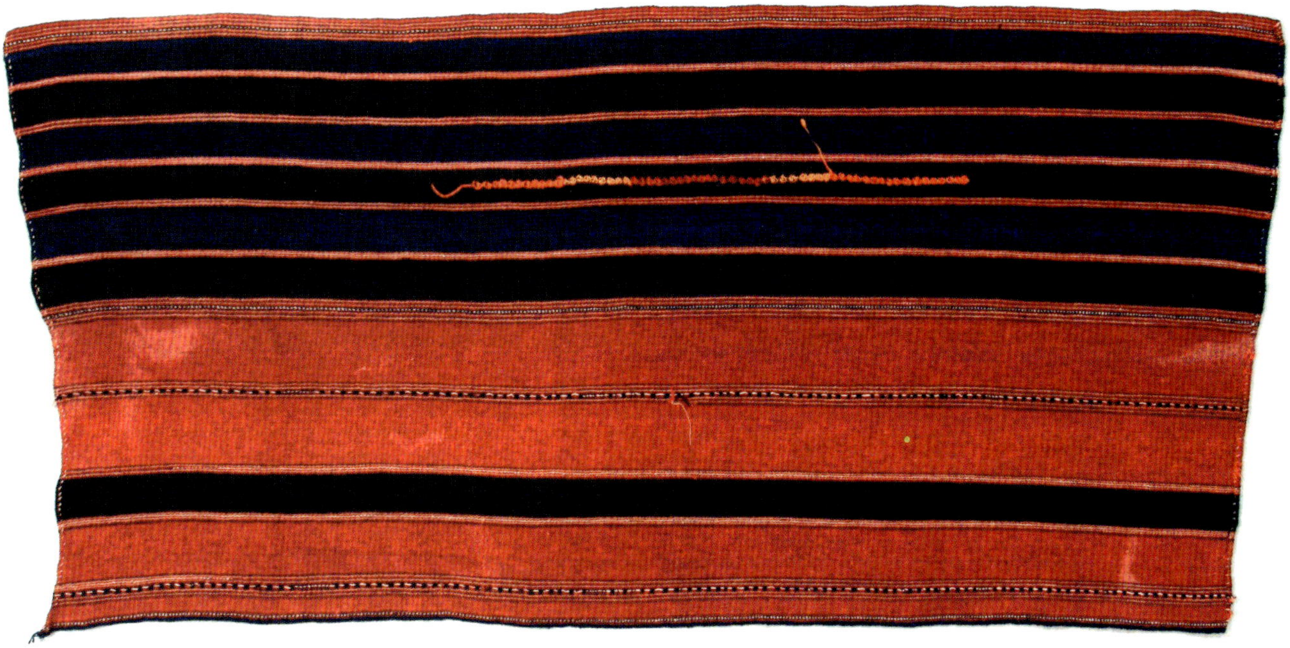

110 A rectangular cotton skirt worn by a Wa woman. It has a warp of blue, blue-black and red cotton stripes of varying widths, interspersed with lines of plain cotton, and single rows of red and plain cotton, plied together before weaving. The skirt is woven in a warp-faced plain weave. There is a horizontal line of white cotton couched with a row of black cross-stitch in the upper portion of the skirt, and a row of embroidery knots in pink, yellow and red cotton in the lower section. *(Denison University collection, Granville, Ohio, DU1968.6)*

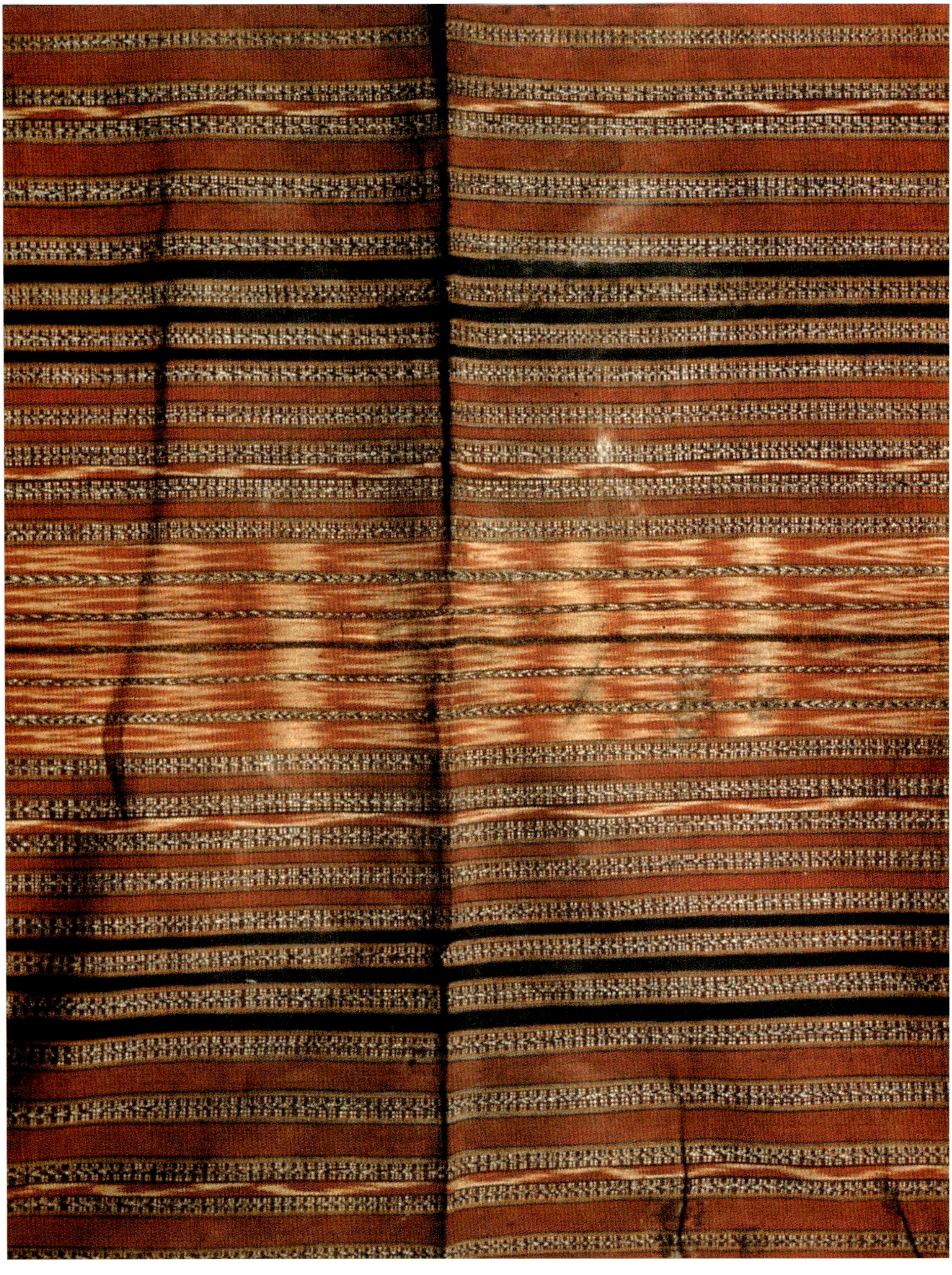

111 A striped cotton Karen skirt with bands of ikat, late nineteenth century. *(Private collection)*

themselves, and possibly a little gold and silver metal thread and strips of embroidery to decorate their best skirts.

Although ethnic identity was a major issue in how women dressed, for senior Shan royalty sumptuary laws were also an important factor. China, Burma, Lan Na and Siam had for hundreds of years sent dress, textiles and regalia as part of tributary exchange gifts. There are references to princesses in states tributary to China, wearing robes "in the Chinese style," probably a reference to dragon robes.[12] There are also photographs of Shan princesses who accompanied the princes to the court of Burma to pay tribute. They wear Burmese court dress allocated to them according to sumptuary laws (see fig. 149).

There are other codes relating to female dress that are associated with Buddhist and spirit religion beliefs. Buddhist lore recognises the head as the most sacred part of the body and the feet as the most polluting. Women's skirts and petticoats were made with a distinct waistband that could not be confused with the hem border that is always at risk of being polluted by mud and dust on the feet.[13] The Karen, Kachin and Wa who practiced spirit religion were not affected by this convention and wore skirts with balanced patterns that did not differentiate between waist and hem. Many who held Buddhist beliefs (George Young used the term 'animistic-Buddhist' to describe them) and those who converted to Buddhism changed the construction of their skirts so that there were distinct waistbands and hems.[14] Women's skirts and undergarments were also seen as potential polluters of men and great care was taken to ensure that they did not come into contact with a man's head.

There were other items of dress that crossed ethnic and class lines. Some Shan princesses wore heavy silver necklaces, earplugs and bracelets usually referred to as "hill tribe" jewellery. Hill residing women and valley dwellers, including members of the elite, had their ears pierced when they were children; small wooden plugs were inserted and replaced over time with bigger plugs until the holes were large enough to insert cylinders of gold, silver or plugs of jade or semi-precious stones. In other states, the jewellery was closer to the designs worn by Burmese women, and there are many photographs showing princesses wearing gold and silver filigree earrings, necklaces and bracelets inset with precious stones. This fashion extended to the hills. The missionary A. Gilhodes described the Kachin taste for pearls, although indigenous silver jewellery was also worn,

> *Lords and rich people wear round their necks a string of precious pearls of a yellow colour. On grand occasions they exhibit a small complete toilet requisite, which hangs on a button of their vest, and consists in tooth picks, ear cleaners, pincers to pull out hair, etc and, of course everything in silver...*[15]

Putao, Hkamti Long

Hkamti Long (Land Of Gold) was one of the northern most Shan States. Interestingly, Sir George Scott judged that the people were prosperous by the silver jewellery worn by the children, and the silver coins used as buttons on their shirts and blouses.[16]

In the 1930s, Colonel Green took a series of photographs of the royal family of Putao, the capital of Hkamti Long. In his photograph of the chief consort

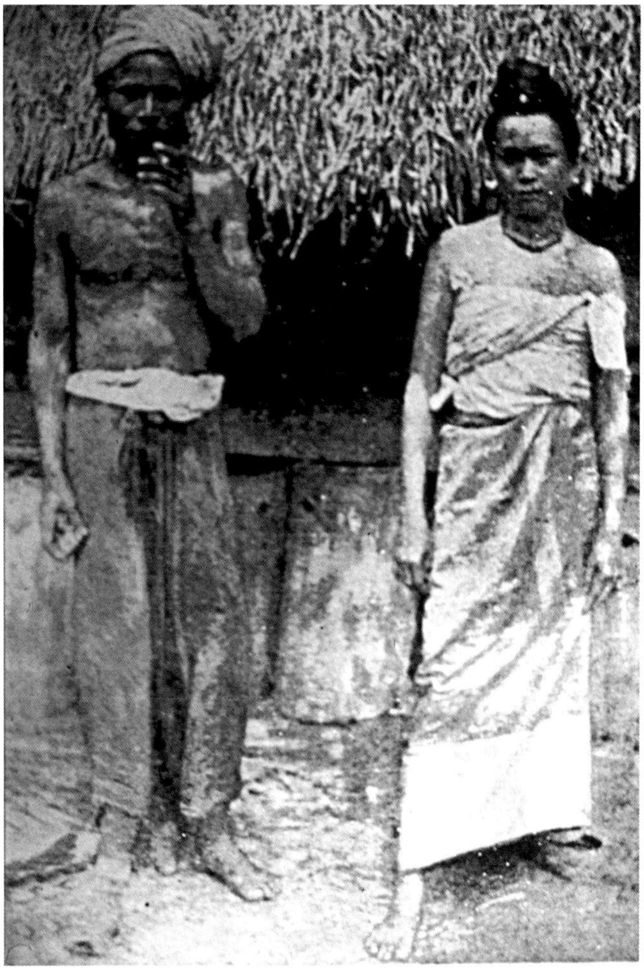

112 A Shan couple outside their house. Milne and Cochrane, 1910.

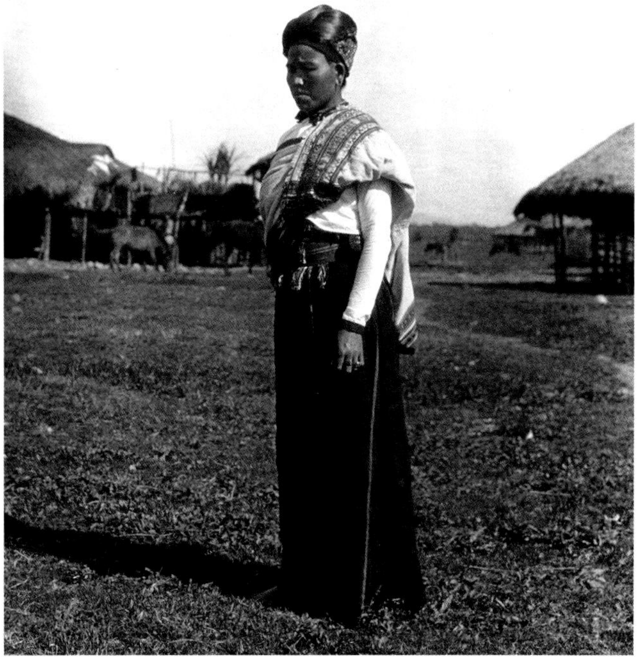

113 The Queen of Putao, Hkamti Long, circa 1926.
(The Green Centre for World Art at The Royal Pavilion Art Gallery and Museums, Brighton, 0124)

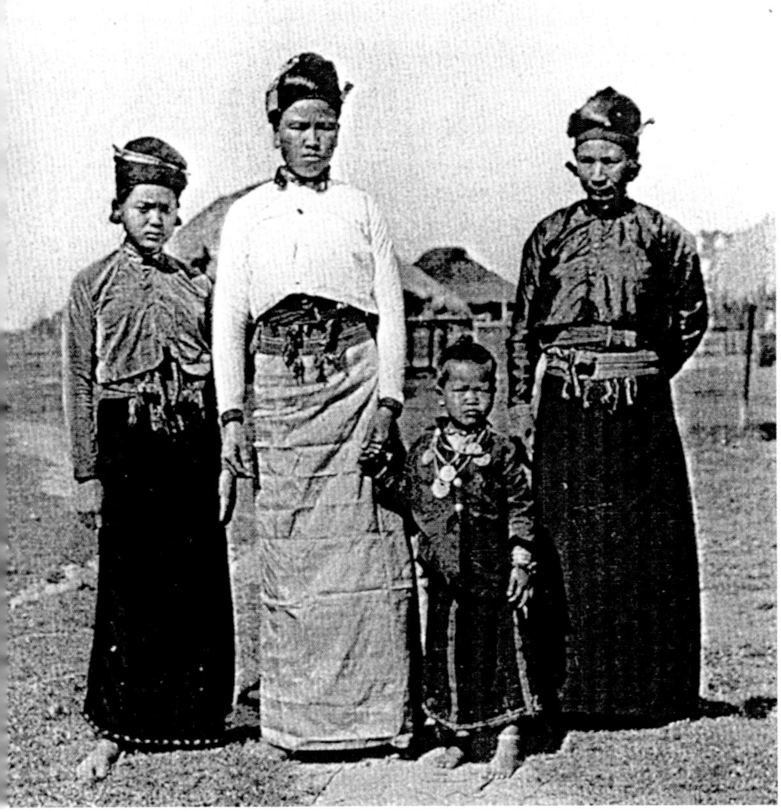

114 The Queen of Putao, Hkamti Long and family.
(The Green Centre for World Art at The Royal Pavilion Art Gallery and Museums, Brighton, 0125)

(described by Green as the Queen of Putao), she is wearing her oiled hair in a topknot secured with a turban cloth and fastened with disc-shaped silver pins. Her earlobes have large holes, bored so that circular plugs of silver or semi-precious stones could be inserted. Her long-sleeved blouse is trimmed with darker fabric at the neck and cuffs and her ankle-length tubular silk skirt has simple vertical stripes. She wears a striped and fringed waist sash and a shoulder sash with a wide band of supplementary weft. Green also photographed her with the *saohpa* and their children (fig. 72). An attendant holds a gilded umbrella over her. In a third photograph (above) she is posing with members of the family who are wearing turbans, long-sleeved blouses in satin and velvet, fringed waist sashes and ankle-length skirts. They have large circular plugs of metal inserted in their ears and wear turbans secured with pins. The British explorer, F. Kingdom Ward, wrote of this form of dress:

> *They are very dainty in tight skirts of dark blue cloth relieved with a few stripes of red or brown, reaching to the bare ankles, and close-fitting short-sleeved jackets...their clothes are always tight fitting, and the trick of edging the trim sleeves of their dark coloured jacket with brighter red...draws attention to just those points. Often a white wrap with coloured stripes at each end is flung loosely across the breast and over the shoulder.*[17]

Although the women in the photographs are wearing blouses, most Khamti Shan women in the villages did not. They pulled the waistbands of their skirts up under their armpits so that their breasts were covered.

Hsenwi

Hsenwi was a large and prosperous state to the southeast of Hkamti Long. In the nineteenth century, following British annexation, it was divided into North and South Hsenwi, each with its own head of state. The inhabitants were primarily Shan (Tai Yai and Tai Neua) with a minority population of Kachin and Wa, and there was intermarriage among the elite of these groups. A great variety of Chinese yarns, fabrics and trimmings were available in Hsenwi because of its close proximity to China, and Yunannese traders were regular visitors at court. Textiles were also imported from Burma and Inlay Lake.

Hsenwi ladies dressed their long hair with perfumed coconut oil and twisted it into coils decorated with gold and silver combs, chains and pins, and fresh flowers. When they were outdoors, they wore turbans in black or indigo cotton with borders of plain, brightly-coloured silks. These were interspersed with stripes of silver metal thread and distinctive bands of supplementary weft in diamond, zig-zag, swastika and chevron patterns, worked in multicoloured silks and silver and gold metal thread. Interestingly, Kachin weavers used similar supplementary weft patterns to decorate their skirts and shoulder bags. There were many Kachin communities living in Hsenwi, and this is typical of pattern sharing between hill and valley dwellers. Turban cloths were also made from narrow lengths of Chinese silk and Chinese silk brocade. Some were printed or brocaded with small floral and leaf patterns. Particularly distinctive were the silk turban cloths made in the villages around Inlay Lake, where weavers produced intricate patterns that combined narrow bands of weft ikat, tapestry weave, and supplementary weft set between rows of plain silk interspersed with rows of plied yarns. The Hsenwi elite wore blouses made of Chinese silk, glazed cotton and Indian printed cotton. Lightweight silk chiffon and cotton lawn were worn in the hot season. If the fabric was semi-transparent or sheer, a camisole was worn underneath (see fig. 122). In the cool season, a lined silk or satin jacket with long sleeves was worn over the blouse, and in the winter, quilted jackets with extra cotton padding or a fur lining were worn. Jackets and blouses were fastened with fabric button knots or with buttons made of metal-, mother-of pearl, glass or gold or silver coins. Some were stamped with the head of Queen Victoria, and later with those of Edward VII and George V. The buttons were fastened in Chinese style through fabric loops. Some blouses tied at the side with ribbons.

The ankle-length tubular skirts worn in Hsenwi had cotton waistbands and central panels of black cotton or black velvet, stitched with bands of appliqué, with hem borders of plain black cotton or velvet. The central panels of appliqué, applied in vertical bands with a horizontal border at the lower edge, were usually extremely colourful. Some of the fabric was woven locally and some was imported (see fig. 120). The locally woven fabric included bands of supplementary weft in multi-coloured cotton and silk yarn interwoven with silver and gold metal thread in geometric patterns; these were similar to the patterns woven by the Kachin, as described earlier. There were also bands of imported Chinese embroidery in floral and leaf patterns, worked in multi-coloured floss silk and couched with silver and mother-of-pearl sequins and gold and silver metal wire. Some skirts were appliquéd with off-cuts of pastel-coloured Chinese silk brocades and silk prints normally used for

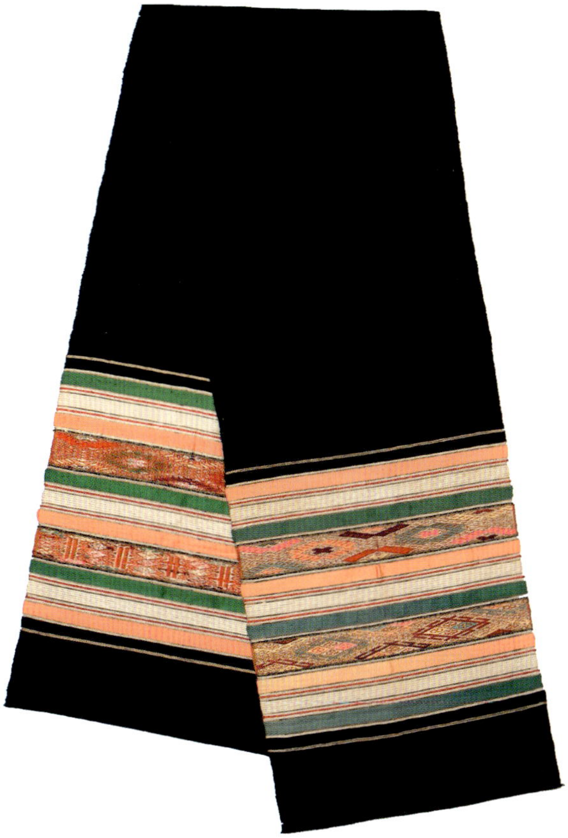

115 A turban with a black cotton warp and weft in plain weave with matching end borders of weft stripes in ivory, pink, tan and green silk that are set between rows of grey and red silk and gold and silver metal thread. There are two bands of supplementary weft in geometric patterns woven in cream, yellow, pale blue, green, cerise, purple, maroon and black silk and gold metal thread.
(Denison University collection, Granville, Ohio, DU1967.52)

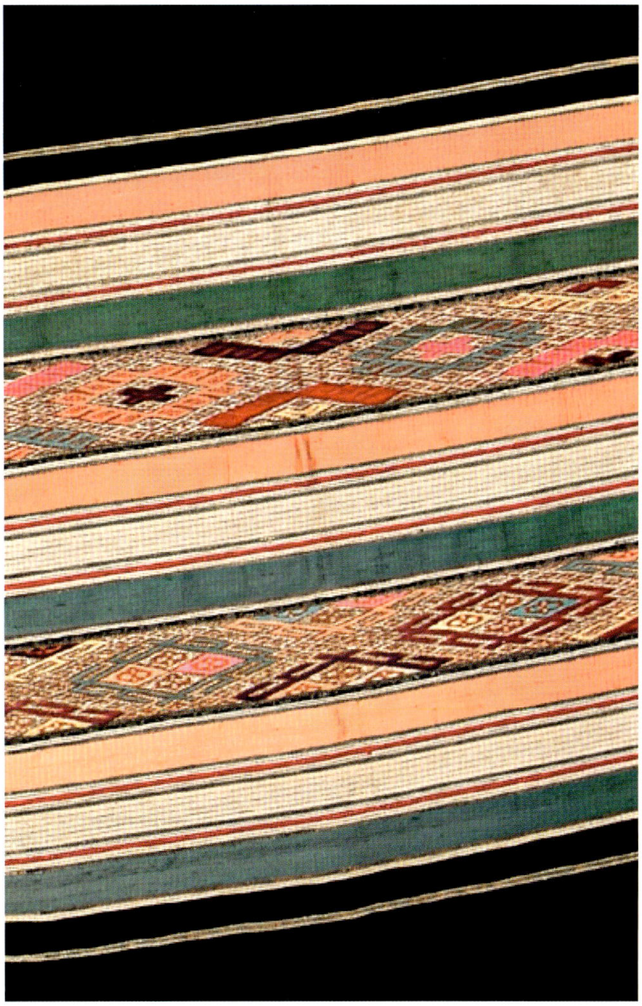

116 Detail of fig. 115.

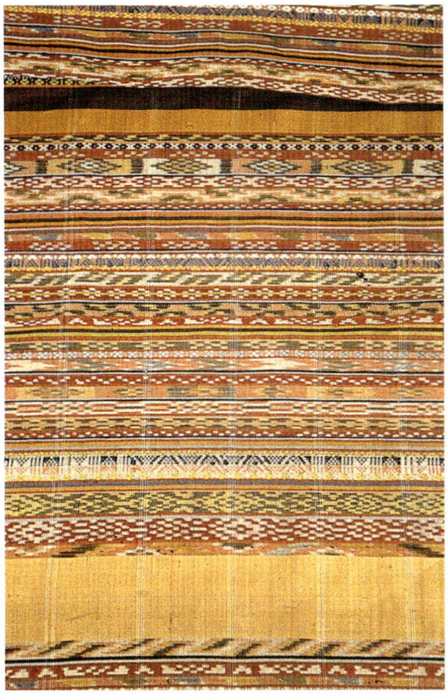

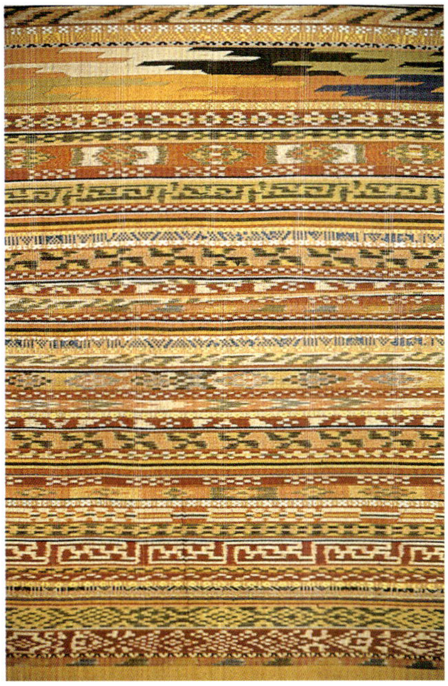

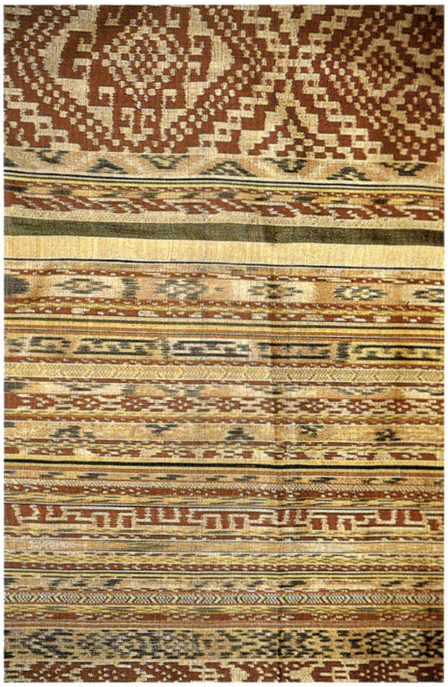

117-119 Silk turban cloths incorporating a range of weaving techniques including supplementary weft, ikat, plied yarns and tapestry weave. *(Private collection)*

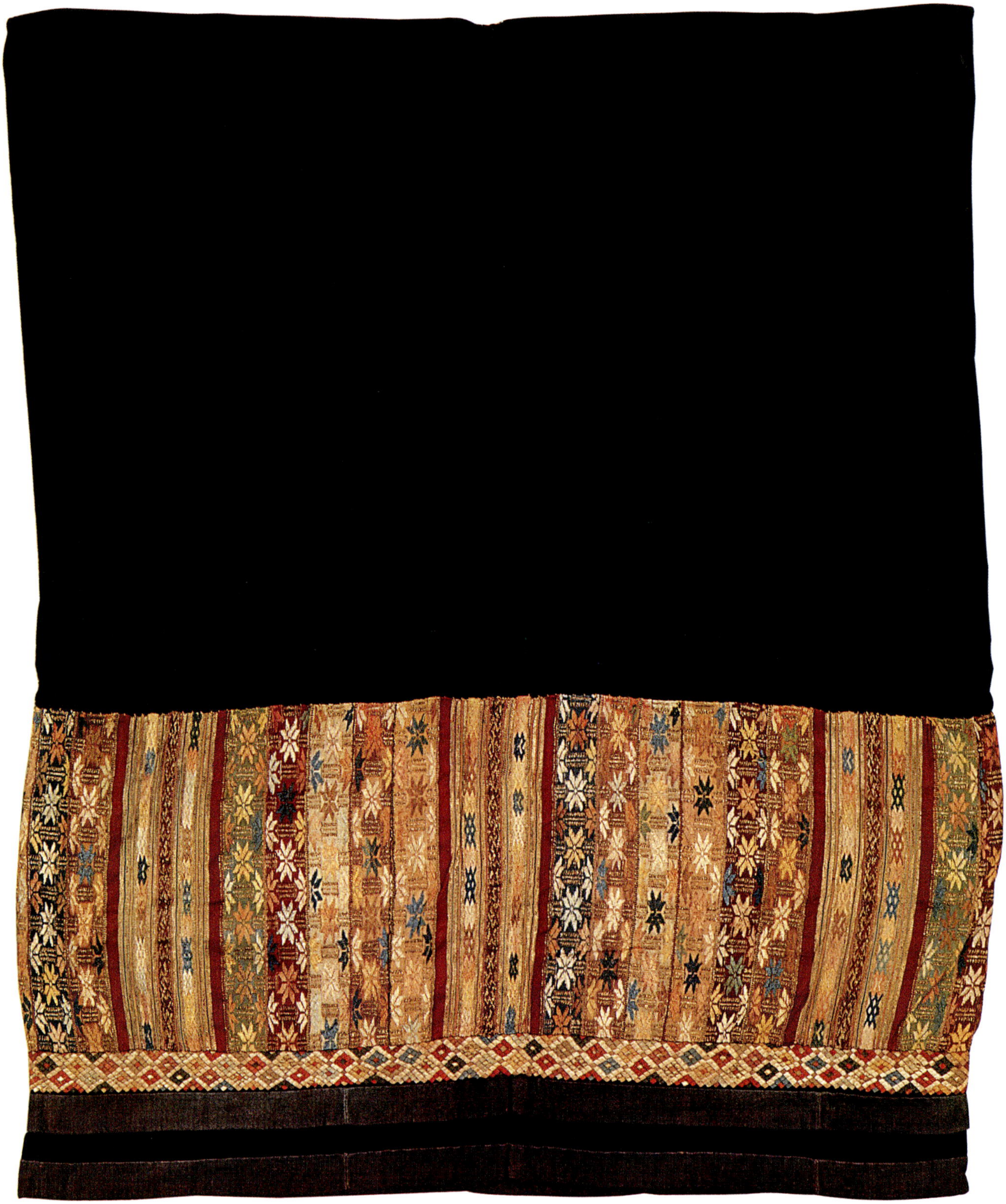

120 A woman's ankle-length skirt with strips of appliqué applied in vertical bands. *(Private collection)*

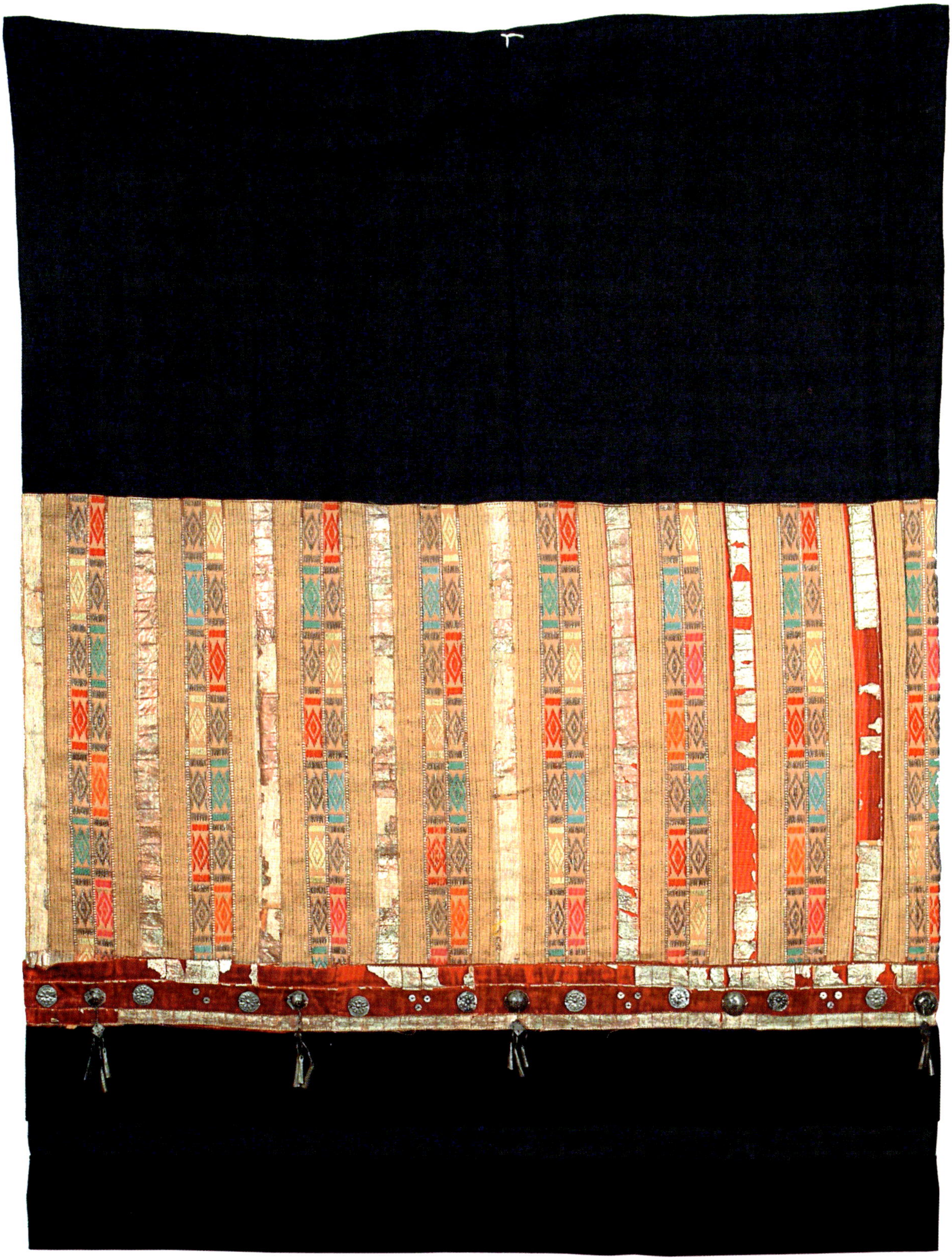

121 A Shan skirt of indigo cotton, woven in a diamond twill pattern. The central panel has a tan silk warp and weft with single vertical lines of silver and copper metal thread interspersed with wide vertical bands of supplementary weft in diamond patterns of yellow, orange, red, turquoise and cerise silk and rows of silver metal thread. There are vertical bands of appliquéd leather covered with strips of beaten silver and copper. The lower horizontal border is burnt sienna velvet which is partly covered with strips of silver foil. There are attachments of silver sequins, flat metal sequins, and dome-shaped sequins with metal cone-shaped attachments. The lower hem is a band of indigo cotton in diamond twill weave, set between two bands of black cotton velvet. *(Denison University collection, Granville, Ohio, DU1974.4)*

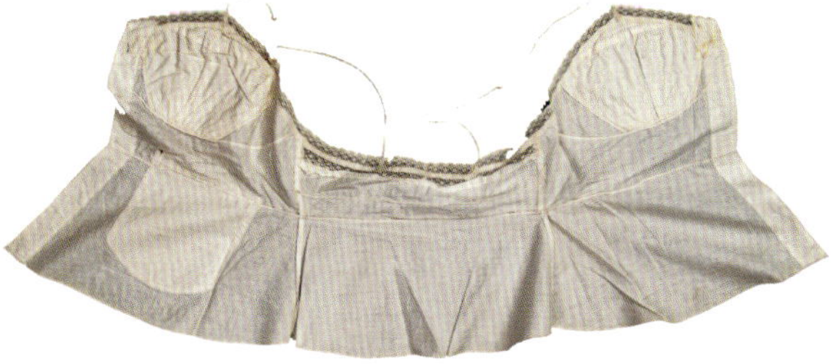

122 A fitted camisole worn under a transparent blouse. The breast cups are machine stitched. There is a pocket inset on the right front and the trimming is imported machine lace.
(Denison University collection, Granville, Ohio, DU1968.27)

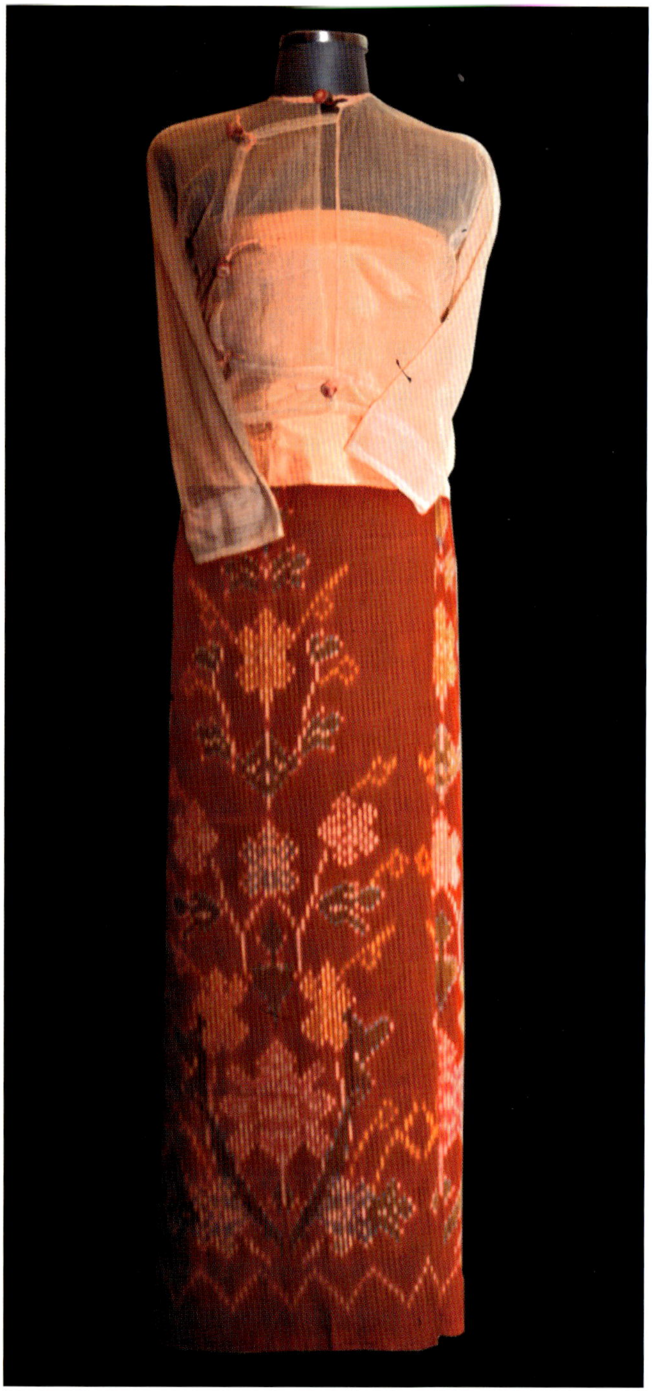

123 A silk chiffon blouse, a matching camisole and an ikat silk skirt from the Inlay Lake region woven in twill.
(Paothong Tongchua collection)

turban cloths. Others included plain strips of indigo cotton or red, locally dyed and woven, cotton. Imported crimson and green velvet, lengths of narrow satin ribbons, tinsel cloth and bands of gilded goatskin were also used (see fig. 121). Silver sequins shaped like flowers and tiered flat discs were sometimes added to the hem band. The fabrics used for these skirts were selected and arranged to create harmony in colour and pattern.

Some women in Hsenwi wore silk skirt lengths woven in ikat designs, produced by weavers in the villages around Inlay Lake. The silk weft yarn was tie dyed into floral and leaf patterns and geometric designs and was woven in bands between stripes of plain coloured silk. The weavers produced the patterns in balanced plain weave or in twill that created a ribbed diagonal effect. The skirts described above were worn by ladies at court and by many women on festive occasions; but for everyday village women wore skirts with plain cotton waistbands, with rows of horizontal stripes in the central panels and with plain cotton hems. These skirts were reproduced in a style worn by Wa and Karen women who traded with valley dwellers, and by Tai Yuan women in neighbouring Lan Na. When produced in silk yarn, this simple style was also worn by members of the royal family as everyday wear (see fig. 142).

The range of imported fabrics available in Hsenwi increased, when towards the end of the nineteenth century, European department stores opened in Rangoon and smaller stores in Taunggyi, the administrative capital of the Shan States. Firms like Whiteway, Laidlow and Co. Ltd. and Rowe and Co. catered to the elite and to the growing numbers of British colonial officers, administrators and traders, and their families, who settled in Burma and the Shan States. The stores imported European, Chinese and Indian textiles, including the latest designs in machine printed silks, velvets and cottons, chiffon, lace and broderie anglaise and novelty fabrics that reflected Art Nouveau and Art Deco styles. The Hsenwi royal family, particularly the younger generation of fashionable women, bought these new designs, although traditionalists continued to buy from Chinese merchants who for centuries had provided the palaces with dress, textiles and trimmings.

It was fashionable in the late nineteenth and early twentieth centuries to wear ankle-length skirts that were hand-embroidered, usually with flowers and leaves, worked in silk and silver and gold metal thread, sequins and beads. In some cases the skirts were layered. A plain opaque fabric, usually silk, was used as the underskirt and the overskirt was made of lace, veiling or chiffon, embellished with silk flowers, butterflies and leaves or couched with gold and silver metal wire, gold and silver sequins, mother-of-pearl sequins and glass bugle beads (see fig. 125). The overskirts were embroidered by hand, but in the 1920s machine embroidery was carried by itinerant merchants and was available in major market towns. It was purchased by the yard. Some overskirts and blouses were trimmed with lace made by local women who were taught by female missionaries. Machine-made lace was also imported at about the same time as machine embroidery.

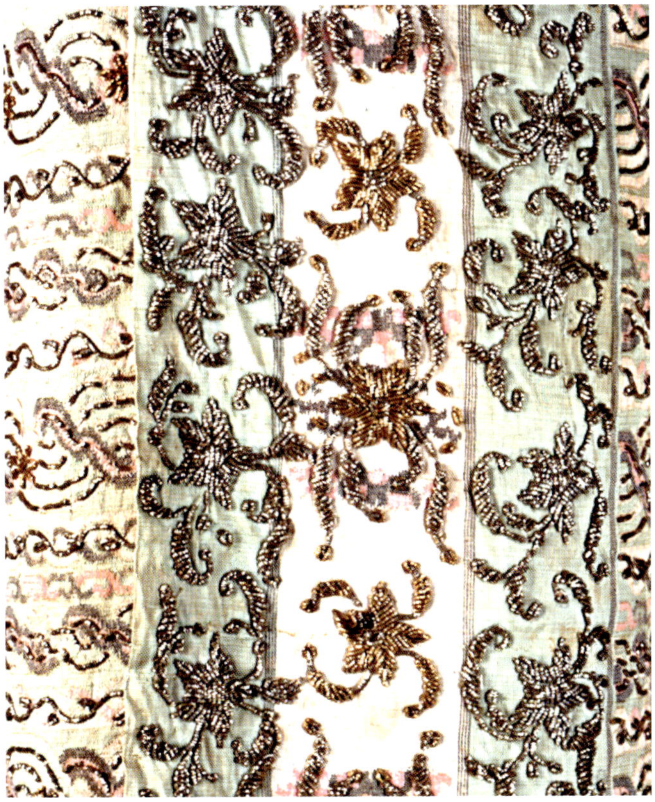

124 Detail of silver and gold metal thread in floral patterns couched on the side panel of a woman's skirt. *(Private collection)*

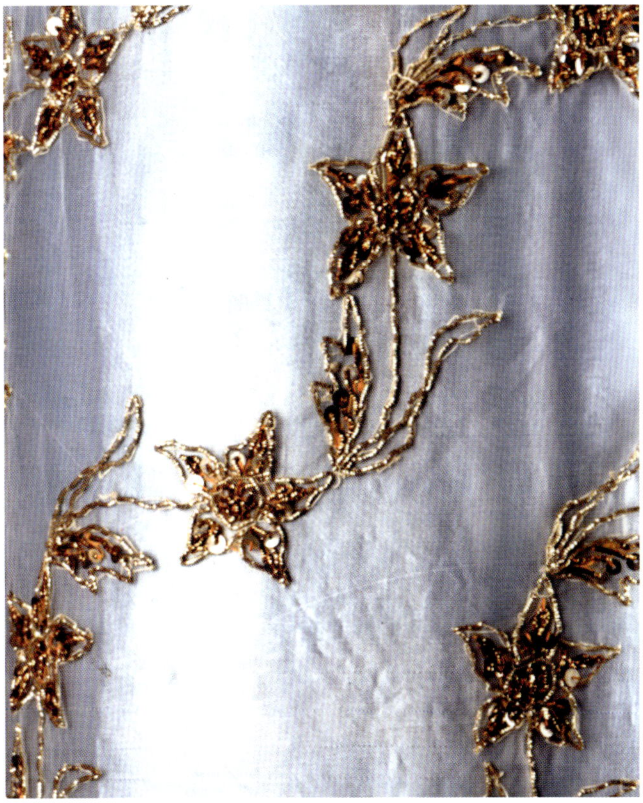

125 Art Nouveau style embroidery with flowers and leaves in silver and gold metal wire couched in a diagonal pattern on transparent silk (see fig. 129). *(Private collection)*

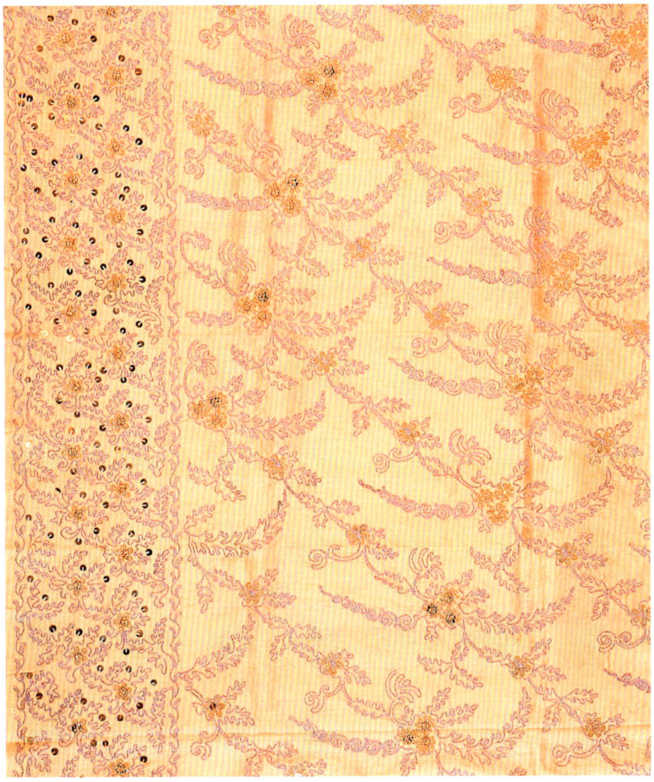

126 Detail of couched silver and gold metal wire in repeat floral and leaf patterns.

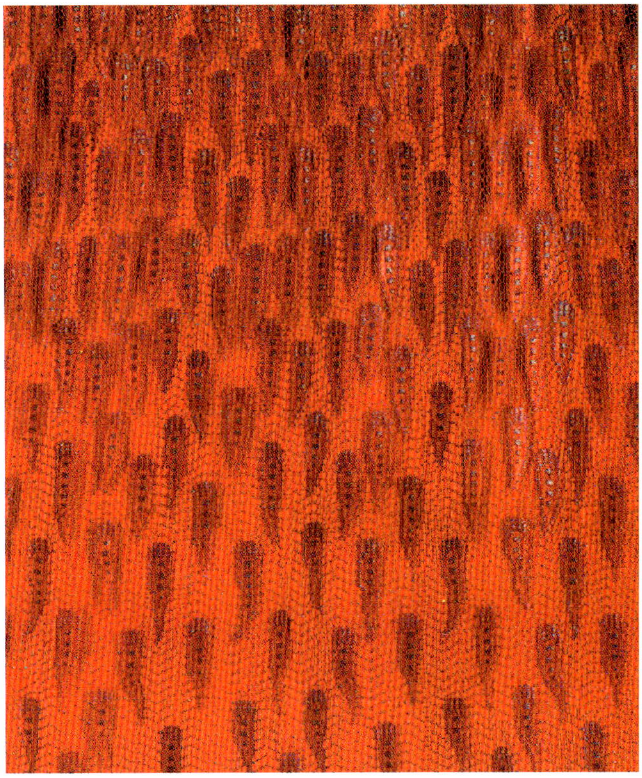

127 A skirt with a silk underskirt and an overskirt of imported machine lace with gilded teardrops in Art Deco style.
(The Green Centre for World Art at The Royal Pavilion Art Gallery and Museums, Brighton, WA507049, donated by Eleanor Gaudoin)

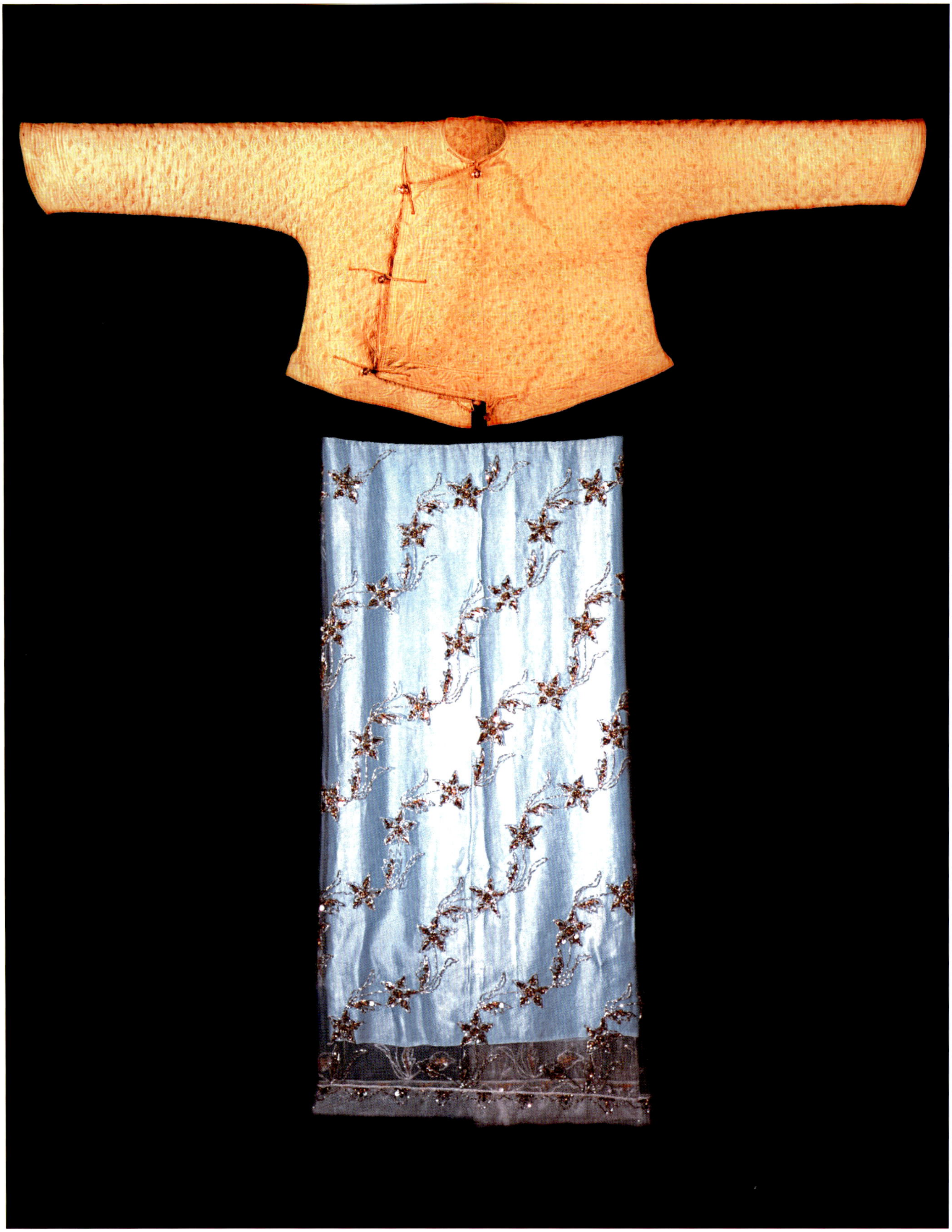

128 A side-fastening cotton jacket finely quilted with silk stitching and an Art Nouveau style skirt. *(Private collection)*

Tawng Peng

The state of Tawng Peng was situated to the west of Hsenwi and had a majority Palaung population with smaller Kachin and Tai settlements. In the late nineteenth century, the ruler was photographed with his consorts who were Palaung and Tai women (see fig. 70). The Palaung consorts in the photograph wear a distinctive form of headdress composed of a tight fitting cap, stitched with silver metal wire that covers the hair, and a hooded cape. Writing in the early twentieth century, Leslie Milne said the hoods were about fifty-two inches in length and about a yard wide and fell loosely over the shoulders and back.[18] They were made of remnants of local and imported material, including plain and printed Chinese silk brocades used as turban cloths by the Shan, off-cuts of hand-spun cotton and strips of red cotton flannel (see fig. 129). The strips were sewn together and strengthened with decorative overstitching and embroidery. The resulting patchwork designs were trimmed with strips of brightly coloured velvet and braid. The overall patterns were, according to Leslie Milne, intended to represent the skin of a dragon (*naga*).[19]

Some of the more elaborate hoods had panels of *shwe chi doe* embroidery sewn in the centre and on the back panel of the cape section. The *shwe chi doe* was worked with gold metal wire, silver wire, cut glass, silver and gold sequins, and mother-of-pearl beads. When European fabrics, such as printed and voided yellow and green velvet and machine-printed silks, became available in local markets, they were added to an already extensive range of off-cuts. The hoods are lined with plain cotton. The earliest samples were hand sewn but later samples were machine stitched. The Palaung women in the photograph also wear tunics (*ka pro*) with V-shaped necks. The sleeves that cover the forearms are not attached to the tunic and can be removed when the women are working. They wear skirts with horizontal stripes, and according to Milne, the width and colour of the stripes related to clan affiliation.[20] The women also wear large metal earplugs and silver bracelets, and one consort in the photograph wears a large flat collar of silver. The consort seated on the ground to the left of the *saohpa* wears a turban cloth tied at the side of her head, a long-sleeved blouse and an ankle length skirt, in Shan style.

Hsipaw

The state of Hsipaw, to the south west of Hsenwi had a majority Shan population and was ruled by a *saohpa*. The court photograph (circa 1900), from the Museum of the Shan, Yawnghwe, portrays the senior consort of *saohpa* Sao Ohn Kya (1893-1938). The *mahadevi* wears her hair in a coil decorated with chains and pins, and is also adorned with a necklace, earrings and bracelets (see fig. 131). Her breast cloth (*yin-zi*) is made from a flat panel of cotton, silk or velvet that is wrapped over the bosom and tucked at the side. It is worn under a long-sleeved fitted jacket (*ein-gyi*) in a light fabric, probably silk or cotton lawn and is left open at the front to display the pattern on the breast cloth. She

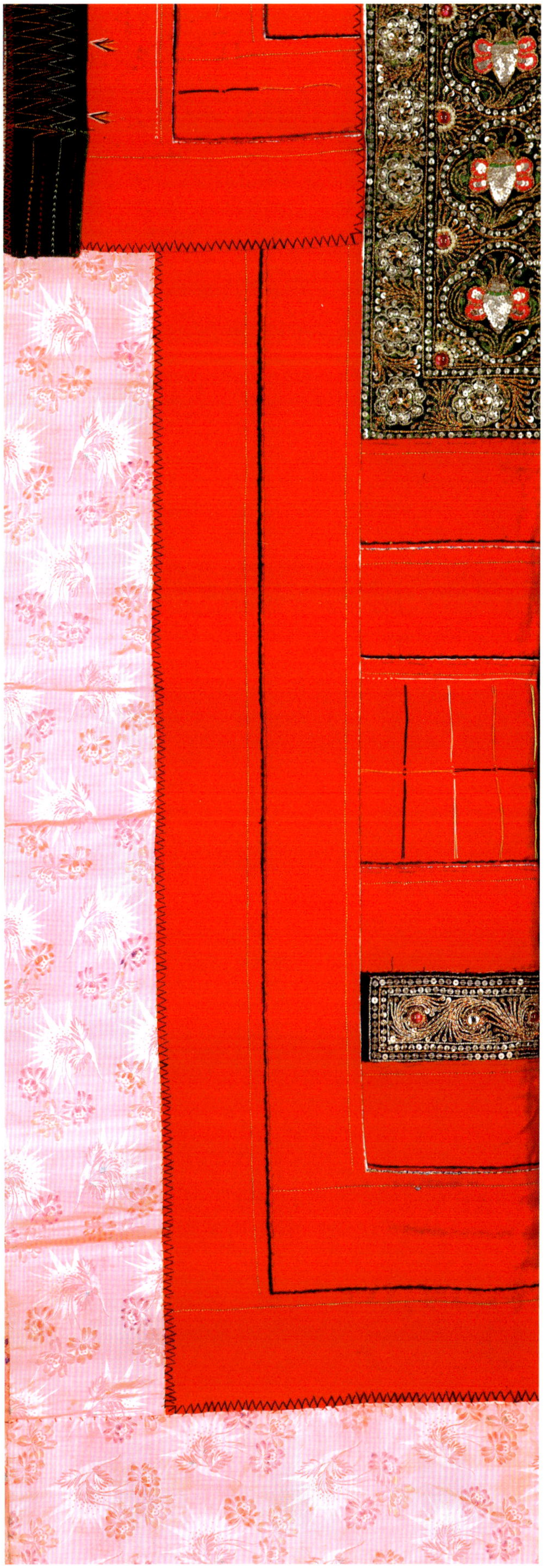

129 A Palaung hood, late nineteenth century. Panels of red flannel, Chinese printed and brocaded silk, dark green silk and *shwe chi doe* embroidery appliquéd on an undyed cotton backing.
(The Green Centre for World Art at The Royal Pavilion Art Gallery and Museums, Brighton, WA508619.1)

has a light printed sash draped over her left shoulder. Her rectangular skirt (*hta-mein*) wraps around the body and is secured at the waist with a tuck. There is no side seam so that it opens at the front to reveal the lower leg and forms a short train at the back when she walks. The waistband, not visible in the photograph, was probably made of cotton and the central panel is couched with gold and silver wire, sequins and beads. This type of skirt was worn on many state occasions. Small sprigs of flowers were couched in repeat patterns on the main panel that might also include rows of wave-pattern stitching resembling tapestry-weave (*luntaya*). The end borders along the selvage were couched with floral and leaf patterns and might include the mythical *hamsa* bird. The hem border was plain silk, or embroidered with horizontal stripes in running stitch and couched with silver and gold metal thread. Princess Sao Hearn Kham was photographed in a similar skirt on the day of her wedding to *saopha* Sao Shwe Thaike of Yawngwhe.

Pangmi (Pinhmi)

Pangmi was a tiny state of twenty-nine square miles in the southern Shan States. It was ruled by a chief (*ngwegunhmu*) who was described by Sir George Scott as a Danu, a person of mixed Tai and Burmese parentage. The chief was a practising Buddhist. Photographed in the 1890s, he and his consorts are seated under gilded umbrellas (see fig. 44). The consorts wear their long, oiled hair in top-knots decorated with combs, flowers and pins. Their loose-fitting, round-necked, long-sleeved blouses are enhanced with chain necklaces. Their ankle-length skirts are in Burmese style with central panels of embroidery or tapestry weave (*acheik luntaya*) and rows of horizontal stripes, and silk hem borders. The lady on the far right wears a plain silk ankle-length skirt. Although it was a small state, the quality of the clothing, particularly the imported Burmese silks, suggests it was prosperous.

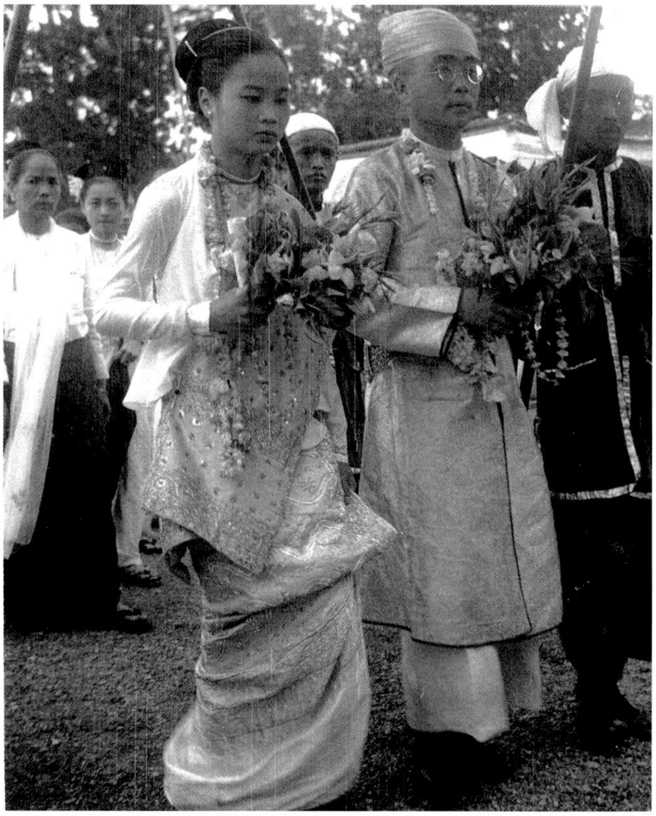

130 Prince Sao Shwe Thaike and Princess Sao Hearn Kham on their wedding day in 1937. *(Permission of Sao Hkam Hip Hpa)*

131 Sao Ohn Kya and the *mahadevi*, Shan Palace Museum, Yawnghwe.

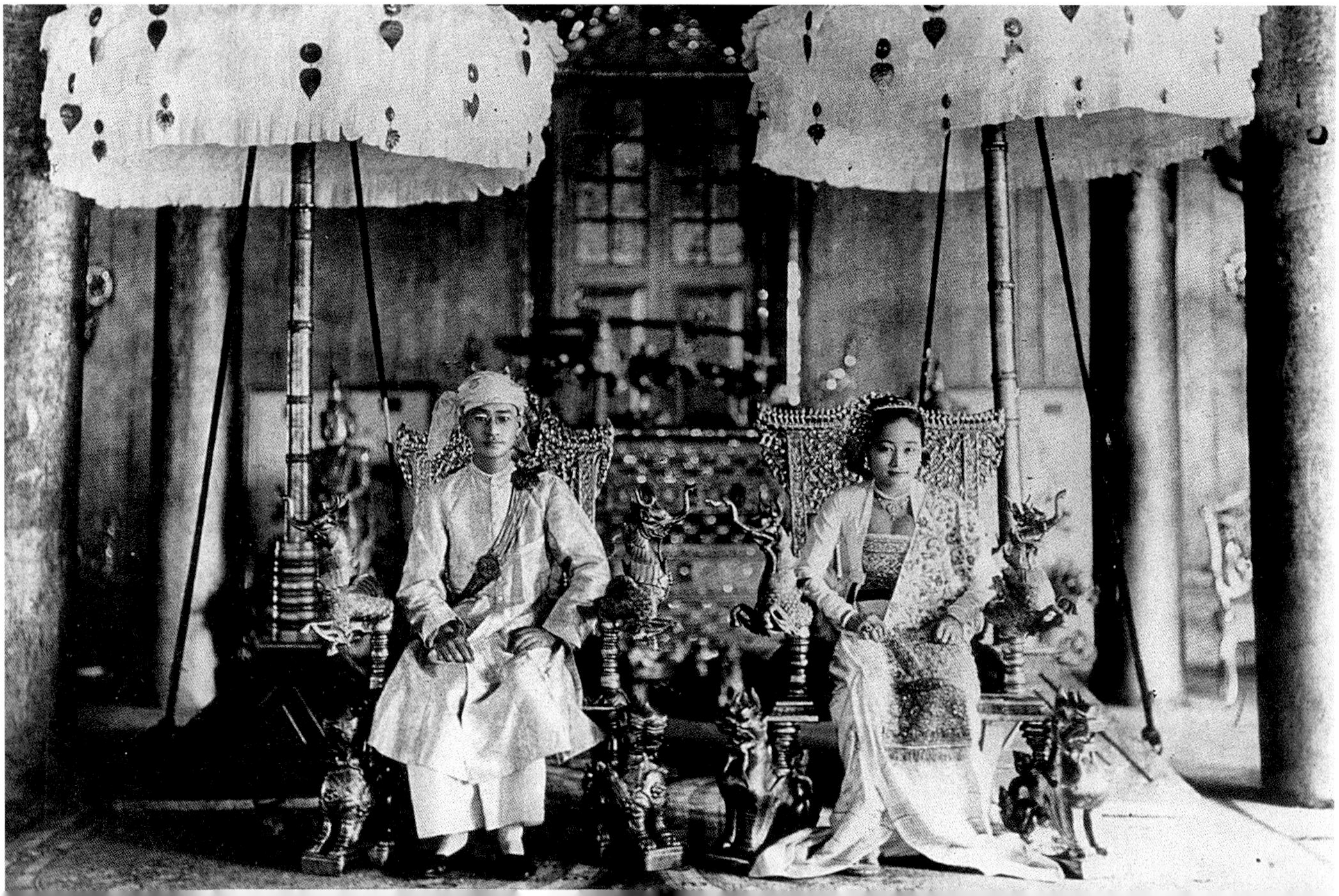

Muong Pawn

Muong Pawn was a state to the southeast of Hsipaw. It was strategically important because the main route to the Salween River passed through the city. The population was mainly Tai and Palaung. In the late nineteenth century, the state was ruled by *saohpa* Hkun Hti who was photographed with his consorts, other relatives and his baby son and heir.[21] The ladies seated to his left have their long hair in topknots decorated with pins and combs. Their round-necked blouses have long loose sleeves. One lady wears an ankle length skirt in plain silk, and the other a skirt with rows of horizontal stripes in the centre and a plain hem border. She also wears a light rectangular shawl. The consort sitting to the right of Hkun Hti wears a skirt with vertical stripes interspersed with geometric patterns, probably supplementary weft, in a design generally associated with Tai Neua and Tai Lao weavers. The woman to her right wears a loosely tied turban, a long-sleeved blouse and a plain silk skirt. There are two women seated on the floor wearing long-sleeved blouses, shawls and ankle-length skirts, probably plain silk.

Karenni

Karenni was a set of five states to the far south of the Shan States on the border with Burma and Lan Na. Some inhabitants were referred to as Kayah or Red Karen because of the red dye used for women's clothing. Scott photographed the ruler and consorts of one of the Karenni states but he did not identify it by name. The ruler in the photograph is probably Hkun Nan of Kantarawadi who attended the Delhi Durbar of 1903 (see fig. 134). He is standing in the back row with one of his consorts and a group of his children. Other consorts and family members are seated on a small mat in front of him. The consorts seated in the centre are wearing Karen dress with striped hoods and horizontally striped cotton skirts secured with sashes at the waist. They have rows of rattan rings above their ankles. They wear silver hoops in their ears and silver bracelets and necklaces hung with silver coins. The women seated around them are dressed in Shan style, their hair in topknots, with long-sleeved silk blouses, silk sashes and ankle-length skirts with simple horizontal stripes.

132 The *saohpa* Hkun Hti of Muong Pawn with his consorts and baby son, circa 1890. *(The Oriental and India Office Collections, The British Library, London, 92/2(12))*

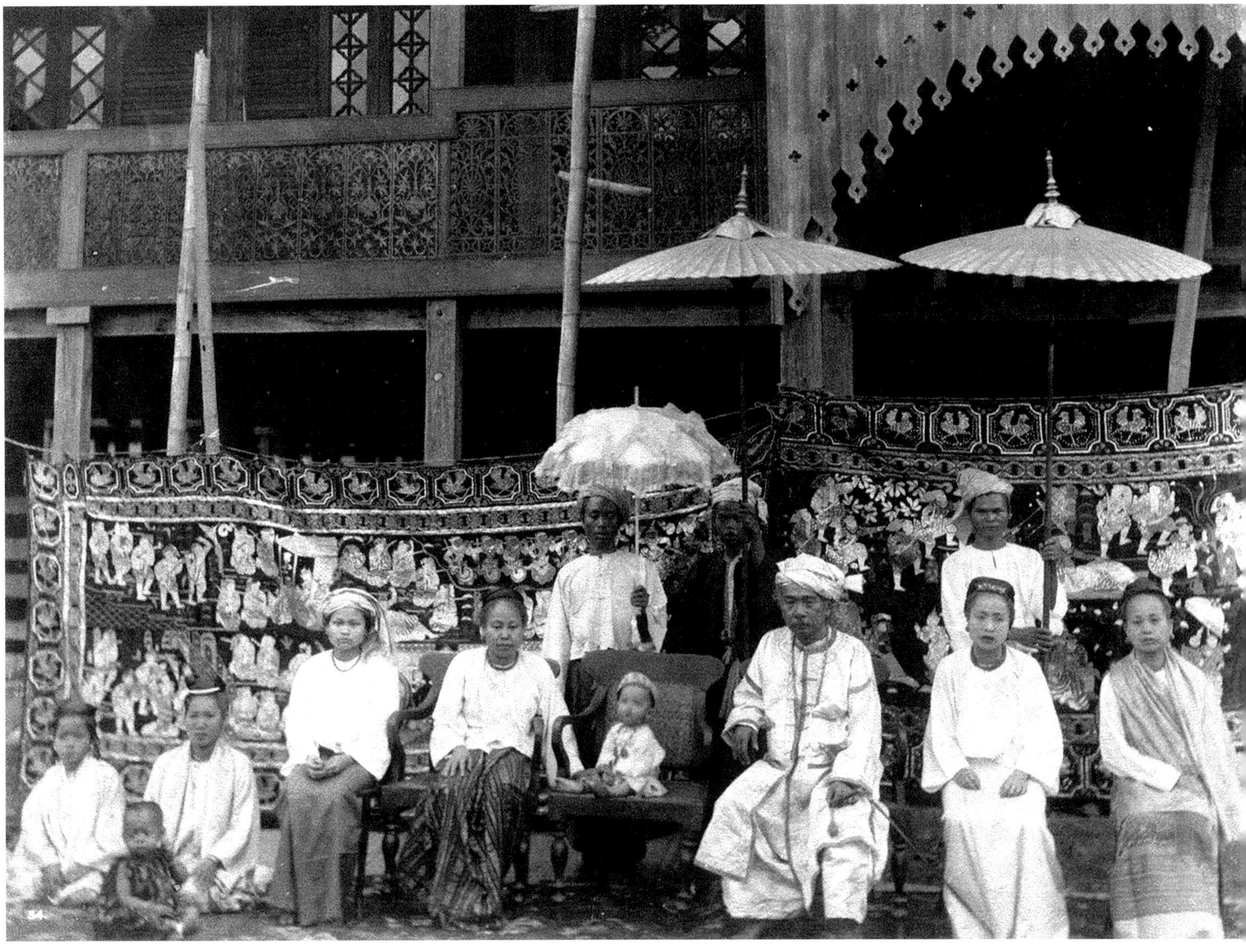

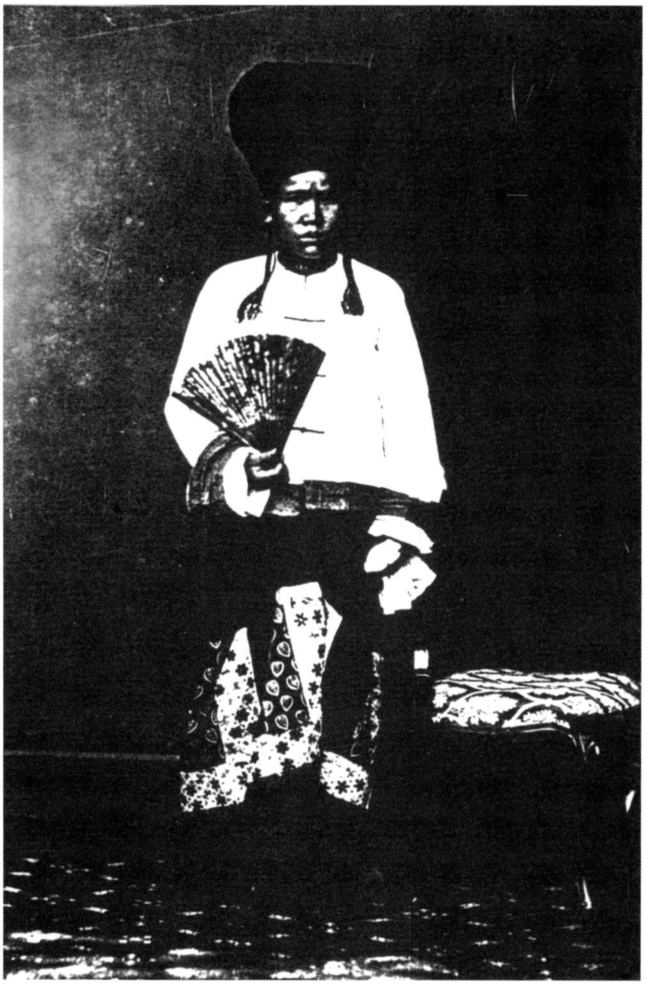

133 The Queen of Eastern Karenni posing in a photographic studio, circa 1870. *(The Oriental and India Office Collections, The British Library, London, 335/1(201))*

134 The ruler of Karenni, probably Hkun Nan of Kantarawadi, circa 1900. *(White Lotus Press)*

An earlier photograph from the 1870s is labelled "Queen of Eastern Karenni," is probably a senior consort, or the mother of *saohpa* Hkun Nan. Looking uncomfortable in this posed studio portrait she wears a high turban, a light-coloured Chinese style blouse with a mandarin collar, and a darker trim on the sleeve cuffs, fastened with fabric loops and button knots. She wears an ankle length skirt appliquéd with horizontal strips of printed fabric, similar to the skirts worn by the Tai women of Hsenwi. She holds a Chinese fan and stands by a European chair. Her clothing suggests that she was Tai rather than Karen, although like other women of the royal family, she may have worn Shan clothing on official occasions.

Yawnghwe

Called Nyaung Shwe by the Shan and Yawnghwe by the Burmese and British, this state adjoins Inlay Lake. It was ruled by a *saohpa* with a population of Tai, Karen, Burmese and Intha ("Sons of the Lake"), who are said to have migrated to the Inlay Lake area from Tavoy and Tenarassim in the twelfth century.[22] According to Sir George Scott this photograph of the *saohpa* (fig. 137), the *mahadevi* and their children was taken at a durbar he organised in 1890. The *mahadevi* has her hair swept up in a topknot decorated with pins and flowers. She wears a long-sleeved side-fastening blouse and a rectangular ankle-length silk skirt with Burmese *acheik-luntaya* pattern. It is wrapped and tucked around the waist and is slightly open at the front to reveal her ankles. Her daughters are similarly dressed. A set of regalia, including ceremonial vessels and betel sets, are displayed on the rug in front of them.

In the 1920s, Sao Nang Ya, *mahadevi* of Yawnghwe sat for a portrait in the luxurious setting of the Yaungwhe palace. The princess is seated on a raised platform spread with a gold embroidered floor cover, and there is a tasselled velvet curtain in the background. She wears a black breast cloth (*yin-zi*), or the black waistband of her skirt has been drawn up and tucked under her armpits to cover her breasts. It is almost totally concealed by the heavy sash, embroidered and

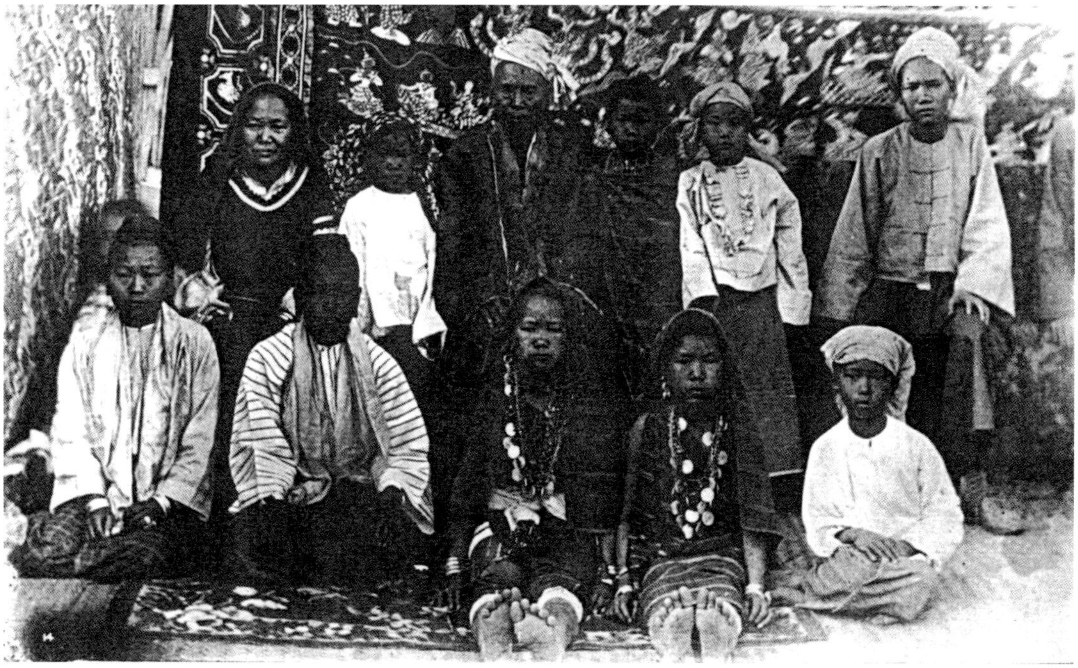

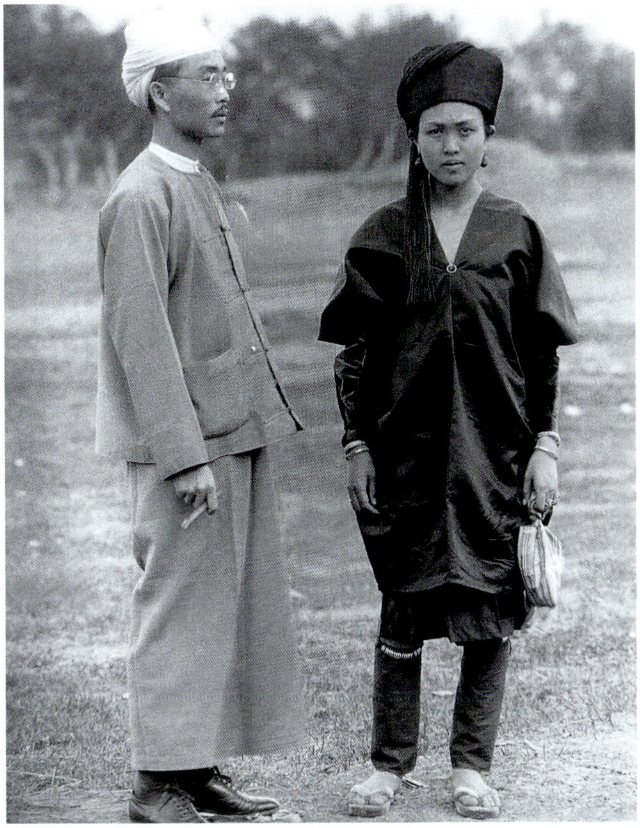

135 Sao Shwe Thaike with one of his consorts in Palaung dress. *(The Green Centre for World Art at The Royal Pavilion Art Gallery and Museums, Brighton, 1472)*

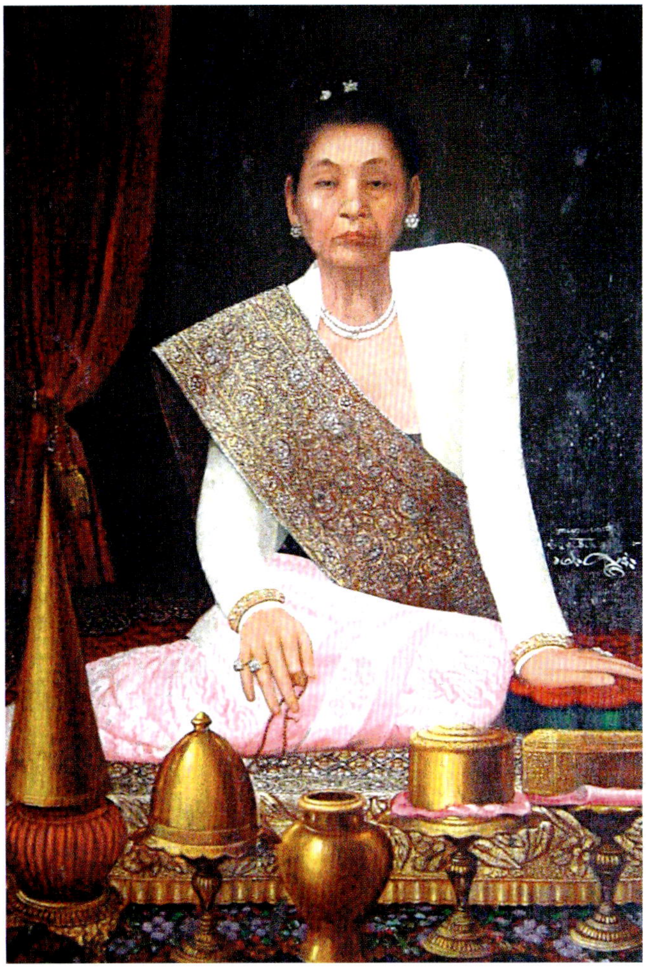

136 Sao Nang Ya, *mahadevi* of Yawnghwe, Shan Palace Museum, Yawnghwe.

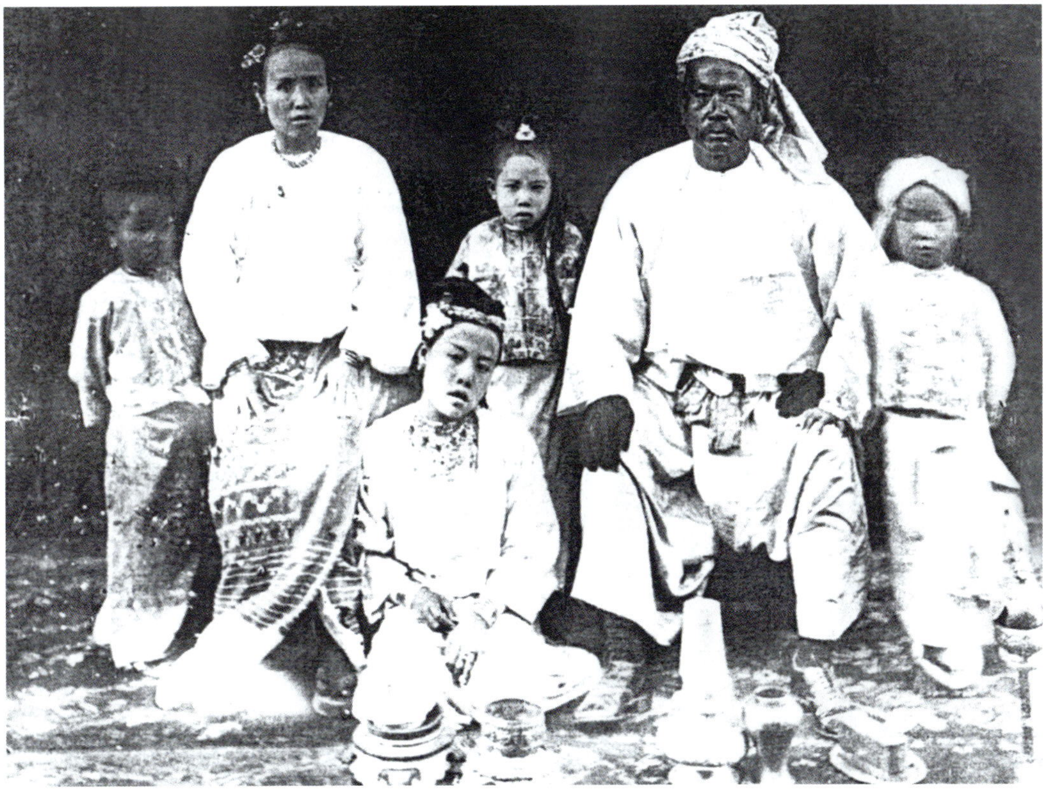

137 A *saohpa* and his family seated in front of a *tawmaw*, circa 1890. *(The Oriental and India Office Collections, The British Library, London, 92/4 (72))*

couched with gold and silver metal thread, pearls and beetle wings which is worn over her right shoulder. Her long-sleeved fitted jacket (*ein-gyi*) is open at the front and was probably made of a light silk fabric. Her skirt has a central panel of *acheik-luntaya* in pink and white silk and silver and gold metal thread. It is similar to the skirt she wore in the photograph. Her double-strand pearl necklace, diamond earrings and finger rings, her gold bracelets and diamond hairpins, and the golden regalia displayed in front of her are a symbol of her high status as the wife of a senior Shan prince. Like other wealthy women of the time, she has changed from large cylindrical earplugs to dainty European style earrings.

In the 1930s, *saohpa* Sao Shwe Thaike of Yawnghwe and his consort *mahadevi* Sao Nang Yi were photographed with their eldest son Sao Hsi Hseng Hpa at the palace of Yawnghwe[23] (see chapter two fig. 36). The *mahadevi* has her hair fastened in a coil, decorated with pins and combs. She wears a necklace, bracelets and finger rings. Her long-sleeved silk blouse is worn under a light rectangular shawl of chiffon or gauze. Her ankle-length skirt is printed and embroidered with flowers and leaves in the style fashionable in the 1930s. Her slippers are couched with gold and silver wire and silver sequins.

Colonel Green took a series of informal photographs of *saohpa* Sao Shwe Thaike standing out of doors with his consorts[24] (see fig. 135). The consorts pose in Shan or in Palaung dress. Members of the royal family were photographed in hill clothing, and it was not an unusual occurrence, although today it is usually described as "dressing up." However, at the time the photograph was taken, this was a significant gesture. The Palaung were a sub-group of the Karen, a major poli-tical force in the region. Their raids frequently threatened the stability of Yawnghwe.[25] Treaties and marital alliances between Shan royalty and powerful Karen families were part of the political bargaining process for maintaining peace. The princess was probably wearing Palaung dress as a placatory gesture to the Karen. In other instances, members of the royal family, who were of mixed Tai and hill tribe parentage, or were related in some other way to a leading hill dwelling family, chose on certain occasions to appear in hill dress. Later, when ethnic purity became a political issue, hill and valley inter-relationships were no longer expressed publicly.

Keng Tung

Keng Tung was the largest of the Shan States and was ruled by a Tai Khoen prince. In the nineteenth century, the majority of the population was Tai Khoen, but there were also large settlements of Tai Lue. One of the most striking photographs of a Tai Khoen princess was taken in a photographer's studio in 1902. It captures Princess Tip Htila, sister of the prince of Keng Tung, standing in front of a painted backdrop, her right hand resting on a European-style chair. Her hair is worn in a topknot dressed with flowers and combs. She wears a printed silk blouse with a fitted basque-shaped bodice and long tight sleeves. The most striking part of her dress is the ankle-length skirt (*sin mai kam*) that has a side seam, in contrast to Burmese-style skirts that were flat rectangles and wrapped around the body. The waistband of the skirt in the photograph is tucked and pleated and hidden under an elaborate silver repoussé belt with a large silver clasp. The central panel of her skirt has horizontal bands of gold and silver metal thread woven in supplementary weft, interspersed with rows of silk. The hem border consists of a wide band of embroidery in repeat floral and leaf patterns, worked in Chinese floss-silk and couched with silver and gold metal wire and silver and gold sequins. These are set above a wide band of Chinese satin, decorated with raised silver sequins. Ribbons of Chinese silk brocade, silk velvet and tinsel cloth, and more rows of raised silver sequins, provide a border on the lower hem.[26]

Although not visible in the photograph, a cotton petticoat with a hem sewn with silk ribbons and sequins was usually worn underneath. These beautiful skirts greatly impressed foreign visitors to Keng Tung who described how they shimmered and sparkled in the tropical light. Some foreigners commented on the huge cost. Dodd noted that that each gold flower and leaf in the band of embroidery in the hem cost one rupee, more than a days' wages for most labourers.[27]

Tai Khoen court dress was also worn at the wedding of Princess Sao Ven Kiao of Keng Tung to *saohpa* Sao Hkun Hsa of Lawksawk in 1921 (see chapter three, fig. 89). In the wedding photographs the princess and her attendants wear their hair in coils and pleats fastened with elaborate hairpins, silver link chains and flowers. The hairpins have flat front and back circular discs described as "faces." The discs are about three and a half inches in diameter and incised with flowers and leaf tendril designs.[28] The attendants wear

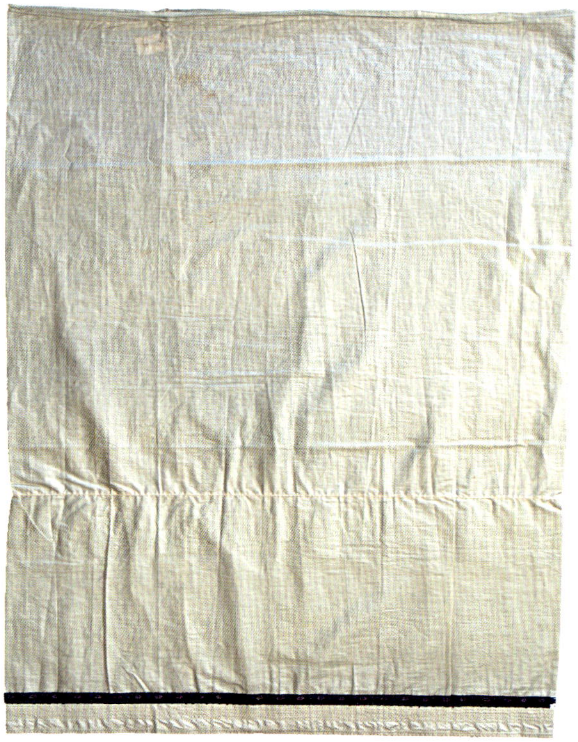

138 An ankle-length glazed cotton petticoat with a narrow band of Chinese silk brocade in purple and lilac.
(Denison University collection, Granville, Ohio, DU1973.76)

139 (Opposite) Princess Tip Htila, sister of the prince of Keng Tung photographed in 1902.
(The Oriental and India Office Collections, The British Library, London, 430/78 (75))

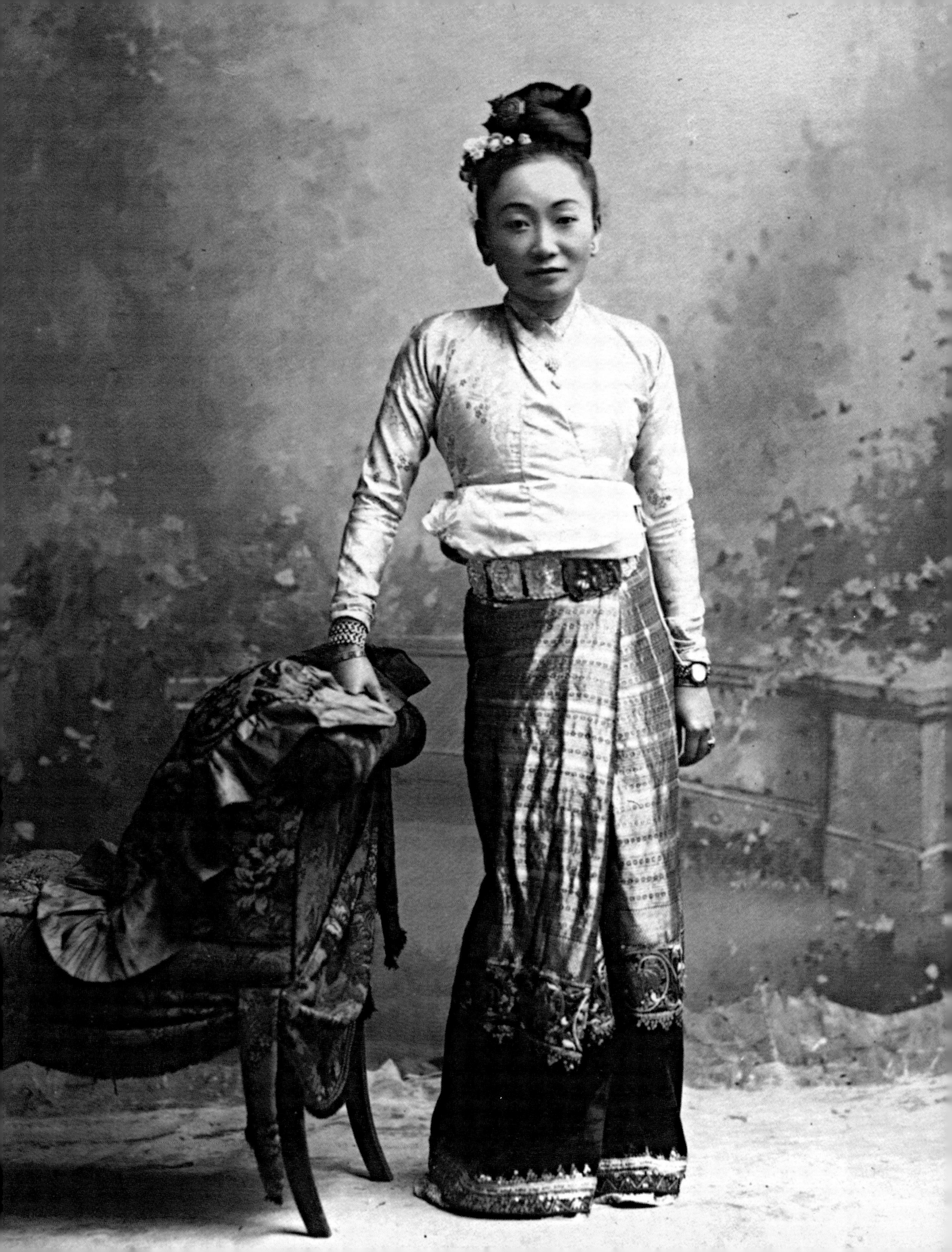

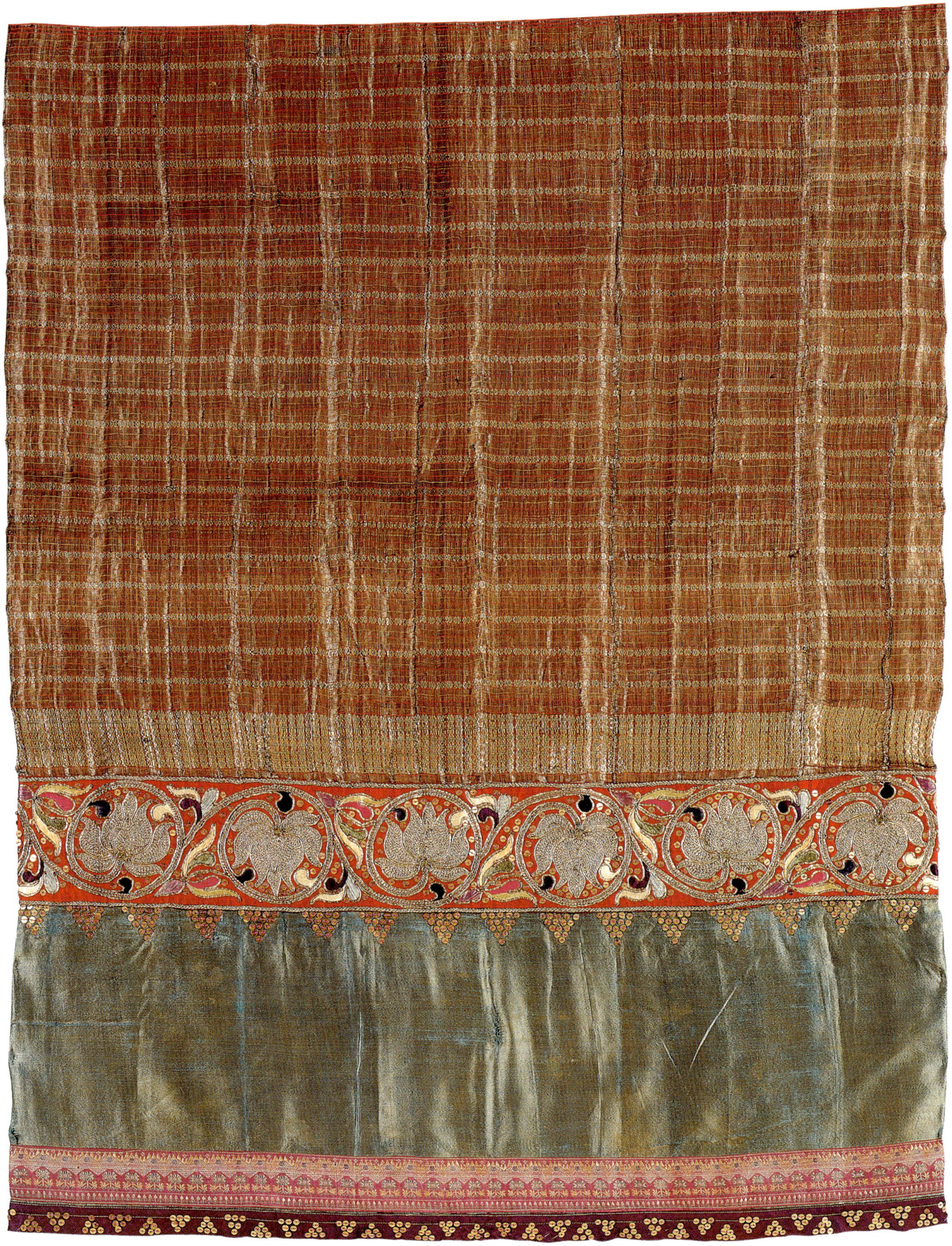

140 A Tai Khoen skirt woven with gold and silver metal thread and with bands of Chinese floss silk embroidery, Chinese satin, silver sequins and brocaded silk. *(Private collection)*

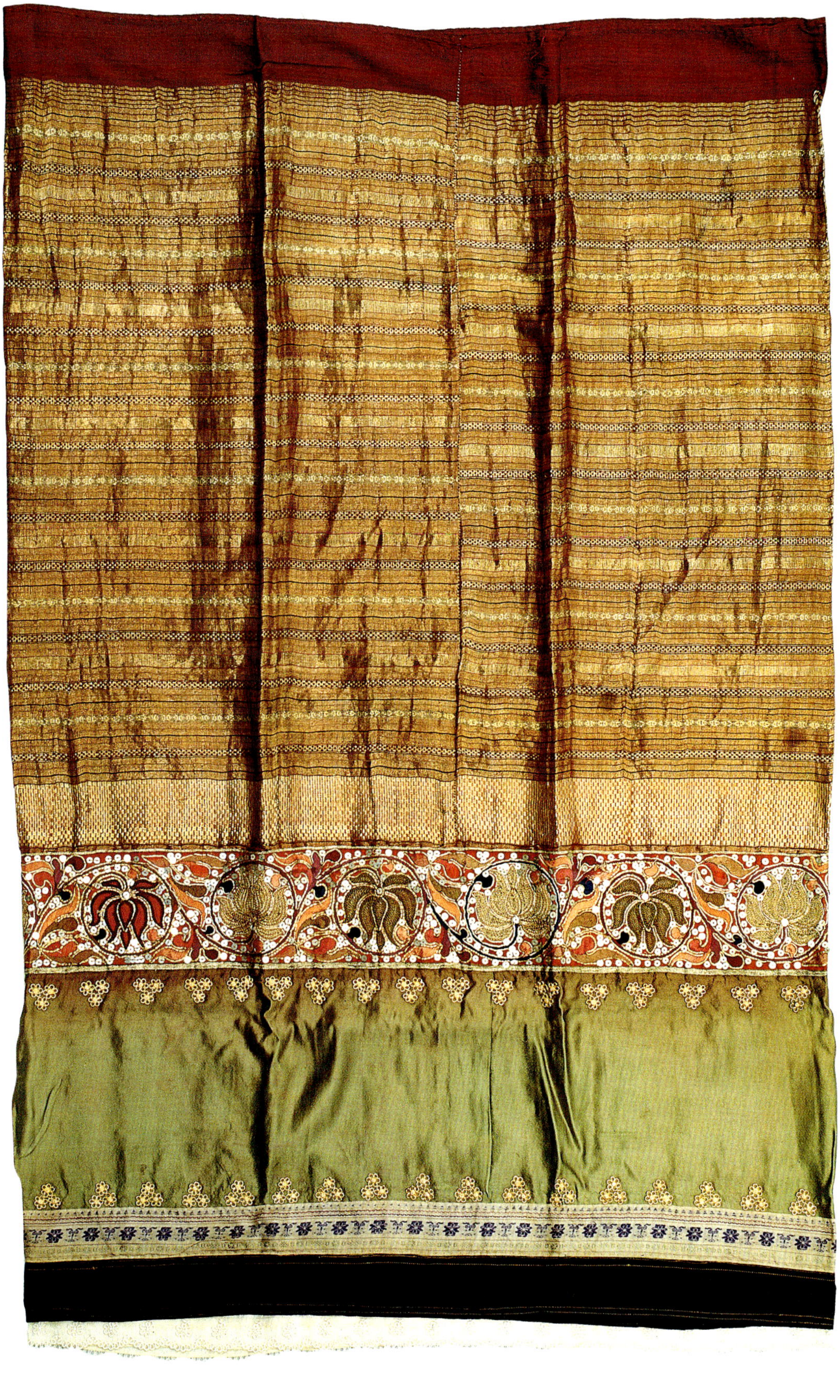

141 A Tai Khoen skirt with similar patterns to fig. 140.
(Private collection)

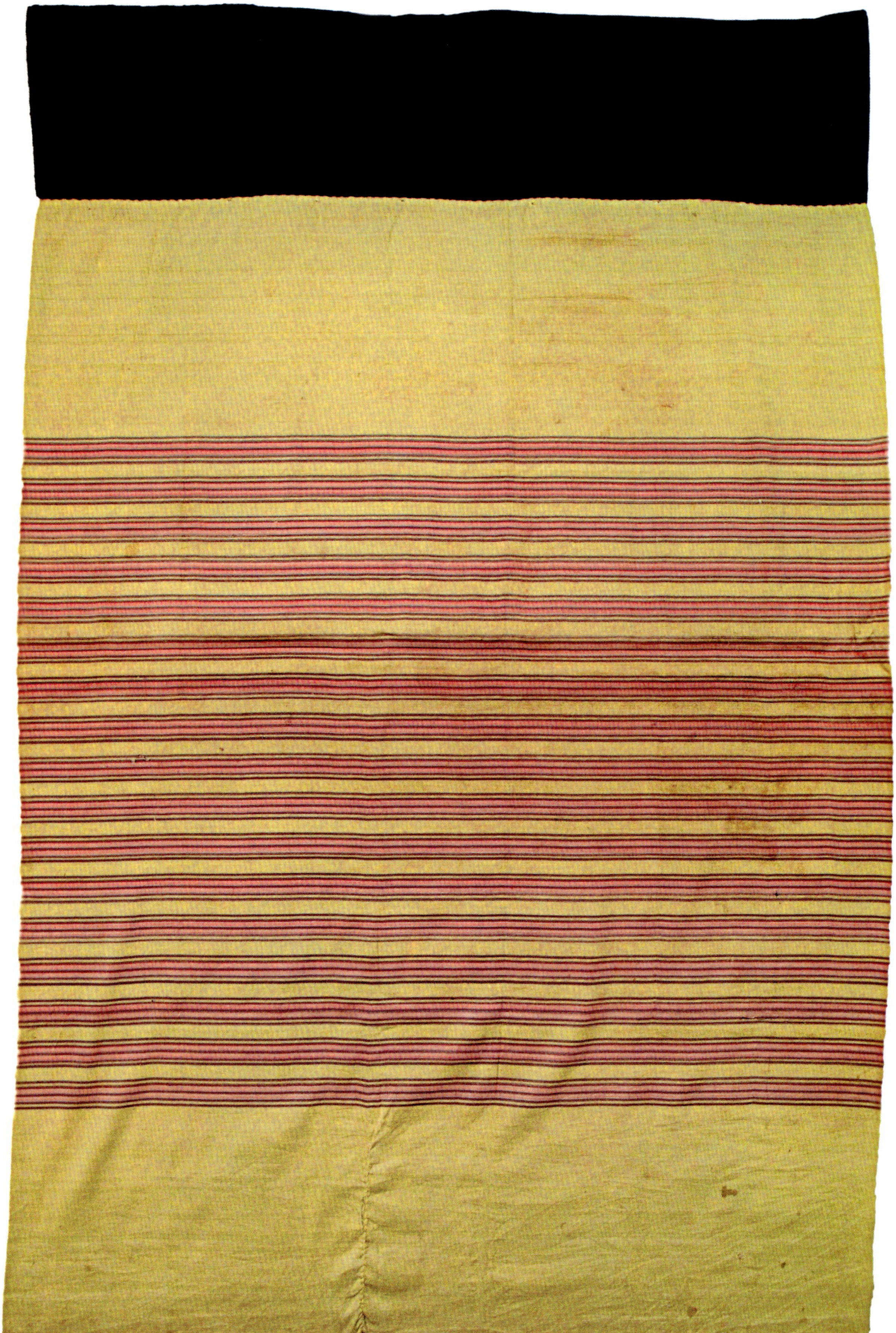

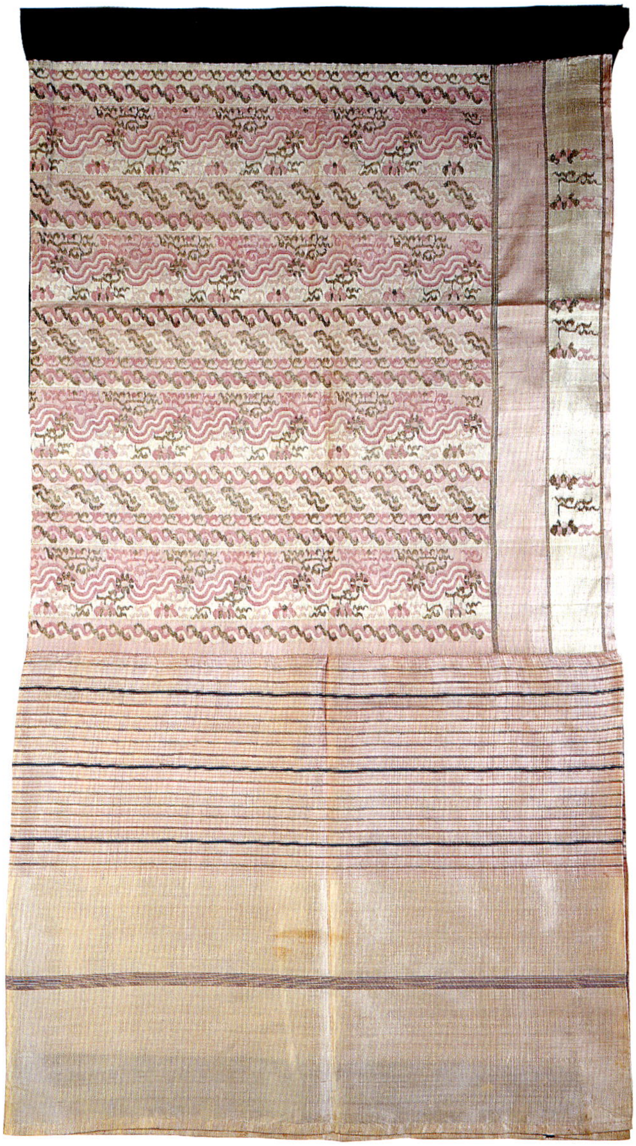

143 An ankle-length skirt with *acheik-luntanya* pattern in the central panel, woven in pink silk. *(Private collection)*

142 (Opposite) A silk skirt with a cotton waist band and horizontal stripes in the centre panel. This type of silk skirt was worn by wealthy Tai women for everyday wear.
(Denison University collection, Granville, Ohio, DUXX121)

long-sleeved blouses (*seua pat*) made of Chinese silk or satin with fitted sleeves. The bodices are cut in a basque-shape that flares below the waist and crosses over at the front to fasten at the side with ribbons. Princess Sao Ven Kiao has chosen a blouse of silk brocade in a diamond pattern, cut in the same style as her attendants. All the ladies wear Tai Khoen skirts similar to the one worn by Princess Tip Htila. Expensive and relatively delicate skirts like the ones described above were kept for ceremonial occasions and much simpler skirts were worn for everyday. Described as "ordinary" court dress they had a cotton waistband, a central panel of silk woven in horizontal stripes, plain silk or satin, and a hem border of a wide band of plain green satin or silk brocade. Some decoration might be added to the hem, for example rows of silver and mother-of-pearl sequins, although this was relatively simple decoration in comparison with formal court dress.

There was an even plainer form of Tai Khoen skirt with a cotton waistband, a silk central panel with horizontal stripes interspersed with rows of plied yarns, and a plain silk hem band. This style was similar to the cotton skirts worn by many Tai village women in the Shan States and in neighbouring Lan Na where they were referred to as *sin mai*.

Although Tai Khoen ladies were well known for their beautifully dressed hair, when they were out of doors they wore turbans made of delicate pastel-coloured Chinese silk, often printed with tiny floral patterns. Some women like Princess Tip Htila, who was a woman of great character and flair, chose to wear large turbans in a flamboyant style. They were often folded slightly to one side of the head giving a jaunty look (see chapter seven). In the cool season, Keng Tung women wore long-sleeved jackets (*sua kop long daeng*) with a basque-shaped bodice that flared below the waist and crossed over at the front to fasten at the side with fabric ties. Made of Chinese silk and silk brocade, cotton and velvet, they were quilted and lined with flannel and, in the cold season, with fur.

The Tai Lue in Keng Tung

The large Tai Lue population in Keng Tung included some elite families who intermarried with Tai Khoen royalty. In terms of cut, Tai Lue female dress in Keng Tung was similar to Tai Khoen, as both groups wore long-sleeved blouses (*seua pat*) with a basque-shaped bodice that crossed over in the front and an ankle length skirt sewn into a tube. They also wore flat discs of silver in their hair. However Tai Lue dress was distinctive because they used multi-coloured satin ribbons, appliqué, silver sequins and embroidery for trimmings on their blouses and the hem borders of their skirts. They were particularly fond of light blue satin ribbons bought from itinerant Chinese merchants.[29] In winter they wore quilted jackets (*sua kop long daeng*) made of heavy weight silk, silk brocade or black velvet, lined with cotton or red flannel and cut in similar style to their blouses. The front and neck edges were trimmed with strips of Chinese brocade, satin ribbons and couched gold wire set with silver sequins, coloured glass and beetle wings. Some Tai Lue wore ankle-length tubular skirts with a cotton waistband and central panel of plain horizontal stripes alternating with bands of continuous supplementary weft woven in cotton, silk and silver and gold metal thread. Tai Lue skirts might include bands of ikat and bands of tapestry weave, the latter described as a "running water" pattern. If the bands on the

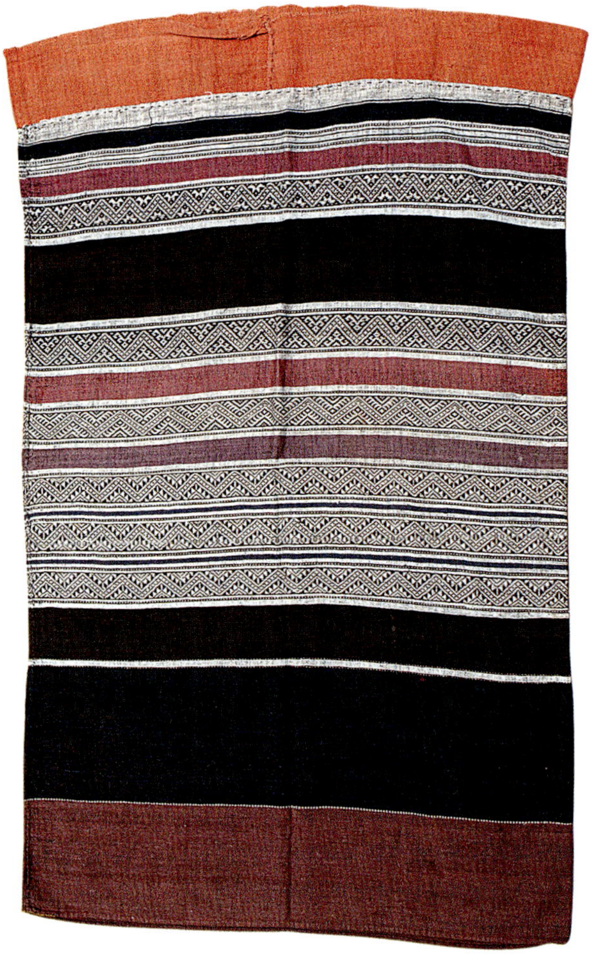

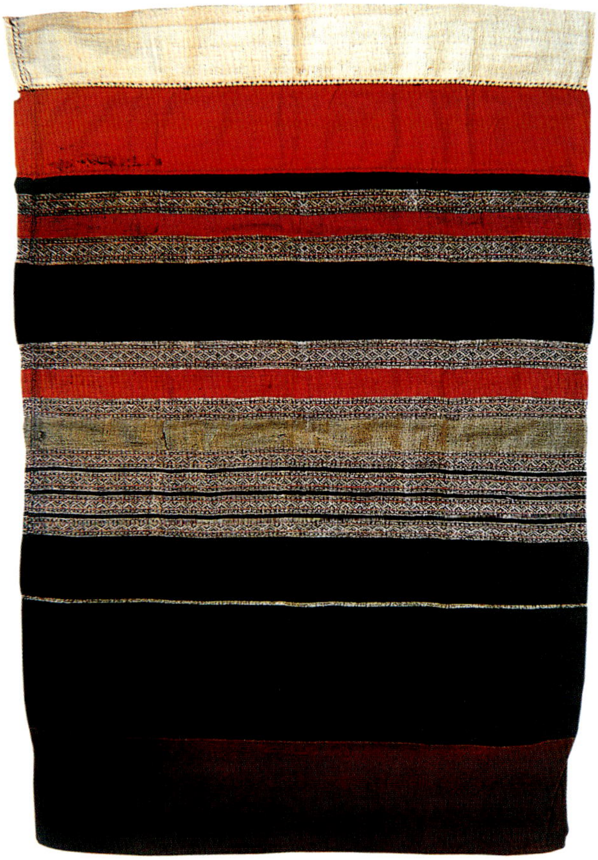

144-145 Tai Lue ankle-length skirts. *(Duangjit Thaveesri collection)*

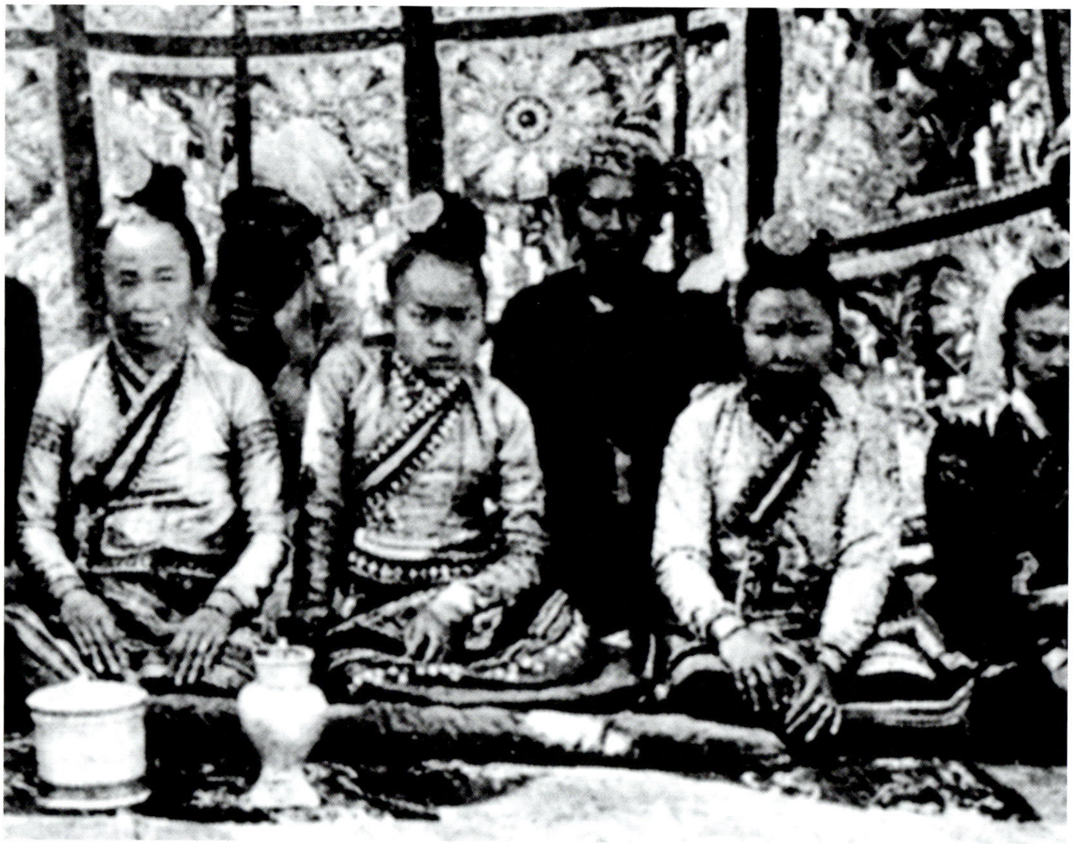

146 A group of Tai Lue women photographed at a durbar. Survey of India Offices, Calcutta, 1899. Published in Scott and Hardiman (1900, 1901).

skirt were evenly spaced they were called *sin pong* and, if irregularly spaced, *sin man*.[30] There was either a plain border or it was trimmed with bands of ribbon and embroidery on the lower hem.

In the 1890s, the British engineer Holt Hallett had described what he considered to be a typical Tai Lue skirt with horizontal red stripes interwoven with gold metal thread alternating with black, blue and red stripes.[31] Dodd wrote a similar description of a Tai Lue skirt adding that a band of green silk was worn at the hem.[32] This reference to a green silk hem, also worn by Tai Khoen, suggests an assimilation of Tai Lue and Tai Khoen designs.

Muong Singh

The principality of Muong Singh was due east of Keng Tung and across the Mekong River in what was considered, by Europeans in the nineteenth century, as a buffer zone. Its population was made up of Tai Lue, Tai Neua and hill dwelling groups. The *saohpa* who was Tai Lue was photographed on several occasions with his consorts and attendants, dressed in Tai Lue style. In some photographs, the consorts are wearing turbans made of hand spun indigo or black cotton with patterned end borders, similar to the designs worn by women in Hsenwi. In other photographs, they wear their hair in topknots fastened with combs and pins topped with flat silver discs, similar to those worn by the Tai Khoen.[33] Their long-sleeved blouses (*seua pat*) were made of Chinese silk or satin with a basque-shaped bodice that flared below the waist, crossed over at the front and tied at the side with ribbons. Silk ribbons, strips of brocade and rows of sequins were used as trimmings.[34] They wear ankle-length tubular skirts with central panels of horizontal stripes.

The horizontal bands of their skirts can be identified in figures 147 and 148. In figure 148 they wear their hair in topknots with large disc-shaped hair decorations. They have earplugs of silver, wide silver bracelets and silver girdles with repoussé bosses and clasps. Their long-sleeved satin blouses are trimmed with ribbons and rows of silver sequins arranged in geometric patterns. The ankle-length skirts have horizontal stripes of varying widths in the central panel and ribbons and brocade are added to the hems. The American missionary Reverend Clifton Dodd gave an excellent description of Tai Lue dress and the use made of the implements hanging from their girdles.

> *The skirt of many colors is striped horizontally with a ten or twelve inch border of bright green and a display of four or five inches of a white underskirt trimmed with folds of colored cloth. The waist* [blouse] *of dark homespun, in two colors in a shot effect, or of foreign goods in delicate tints, is made surplice style with a short tight waist and very long tight sleeves. It is always trimmed with bright colored folds beautifully hand stitched, with a gay imported trimming of flowered silk. The turban is black with a band of black and gold across the front. This turban is essentially Lü* [Lue]. *So are their ornaments, round armlets of silver covering half the arm either above or below the elbow and large gold or silver hair ornaments are stuck into the heavy coil of black hair on top of the head. But the most striking thing about a Lü debutante's costume is the girdle, large heavy medallions of beaten silver fastened together with silver chains with a chatelaine at one side of silver chains with picks and probes and other toilet implements.*[35]

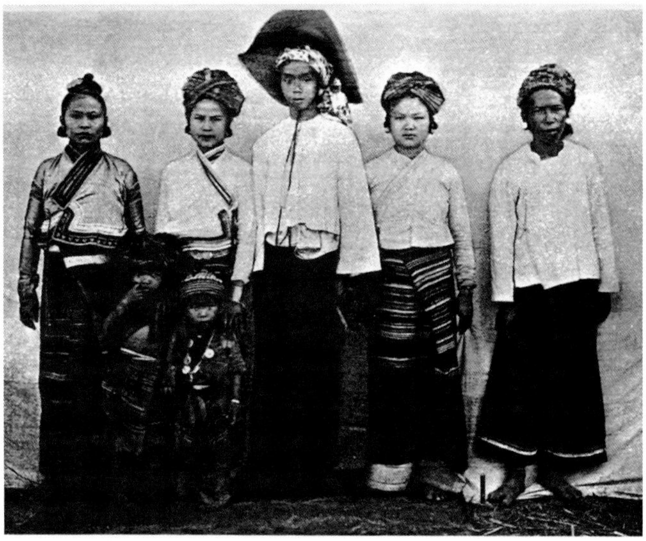

147 A Tai Lue family. Milne and Cochrane, 1910.

Keng Hung (Chieng Rung)

Keng Hung, capital of Sipsong Pan Na, was situated due north of Keng Tung and was ruled by a Tai Lue prince. In the nineteenth century, Keng Hung was also considered to be a buffer zone. The ruler paid tribute to China and Burma, although Chinese culture was recognised as a stronger force in local society. In the 1830s, Captain McLeod visited the *mahadevi* of Keng Hung, who was Regent at the time of his visit. He noted

> *They too were richly, though to me fantastically dressed, in a mixture of Shan and Chinese costumes; their attendants were dressed in the same style.*[36]

McLeod saw their dress as similar in many ways to what he had seen in Keng Tung. He thought that on great occasions of state they dressed in Chinese style, implying that they wore Chinese robes.

Muong Baw

The Tai Neua, called Chinese Shan by the British, were a majority population in Muong Khwan, Muong Kung Ma and Muong Baw in Sipsong Pan Na and their communities extended into northern Laos. When he travelled in the region, Dodd described their dress.

> *The dress of the Tai Nüa* [Neua] *women is in marked contrast to that of their Tai neighbours the Lü* [Lue] *and Kühn* [Khoen]. *Dress and turban are of dark blue or black, the surplice waist* [blouse] *with just a narrow edge of white is tucked under the waist and the somber effect is sometimes relieved by a belt or narrow girdle of bright red. The skirt has a thread of white running through it in a rather indistinct pattern, making a grey effect, with a stripe which runs vertically instead of horizontally as in the gay skirts of their Tai cousins. Their distinctive ornaments are a heavy bracelet of silver filigree three or four inches wide, and large silver rings in floral patterns sometimes extending from the second to third joint of the finger, with a narrow band overlapping inside which can be opened when it is taken off. They also have large plain silver earrings.*[37]

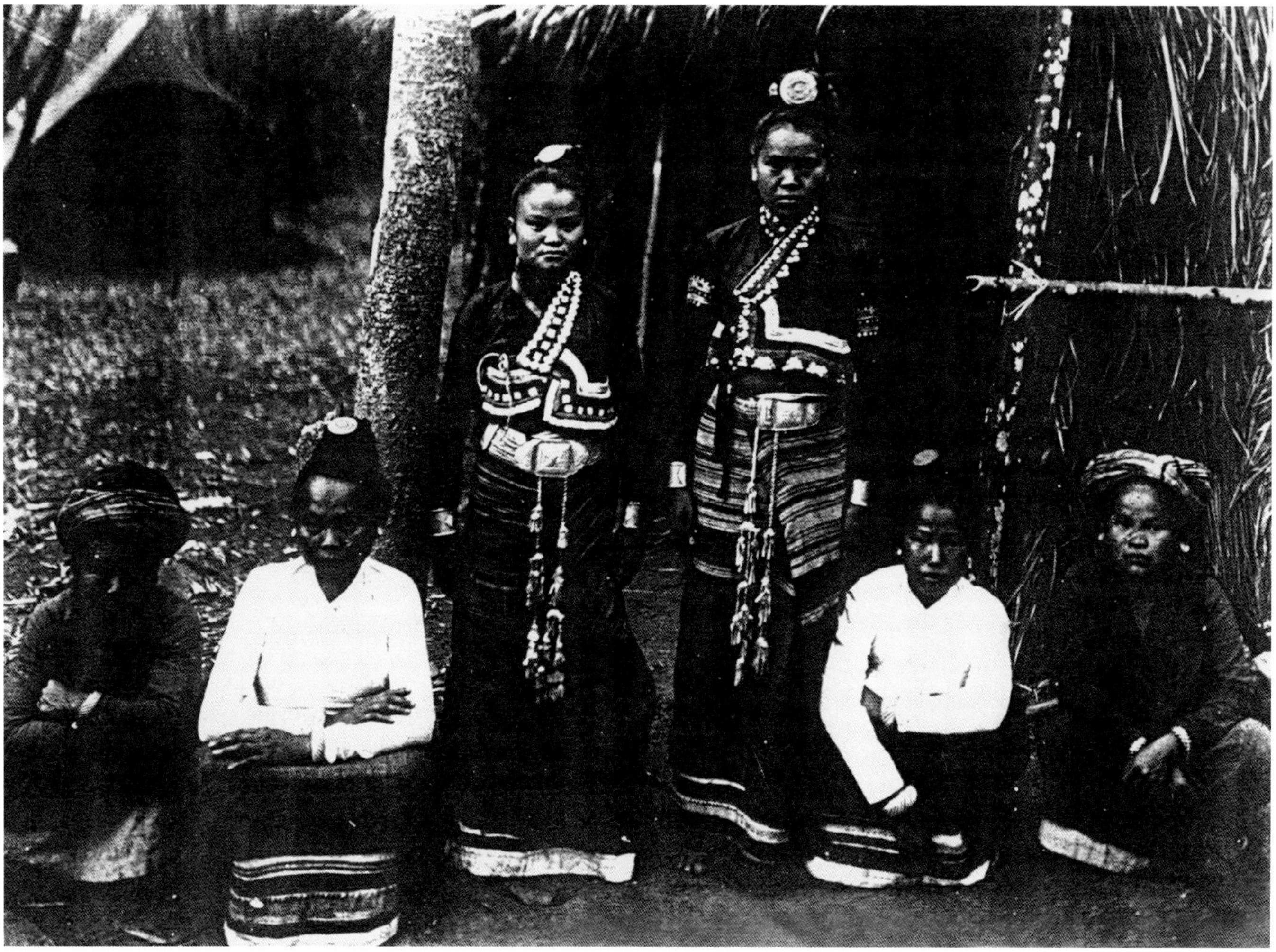

148 Tai Lue women with ornate silver girdles. *(White Lotus Press)*

It is interesting that Dodd acknowledged that horizontally striped skirts were associated with the Tai Lao, the Tai Neua and the Khamti Shan in contrast to the horizontal stripes of the Tai Lue and Tai Khoen.

Although Dodd described the everyday skirt as "sombre," the skirts of the Tai Neua could be colourful. Ankle-length skirts with cotton waistbands and central panels of black cotton or black velvet were stitched with vertical bands of appliqué and a horizontal band at the lower edge, a similar style to those worn by the women of Hsenwi. Panels of supplementary weft in multi-coloured silk and cotton, and silver and gold metal thread, bands of Chinese embroidery in floral and leaf patterns, off-cuts of pastel-coloured Chinese silk brocades and silk prints, strips of plain cotton, crimson and green velvet, lengths of satin ribbon and tinsel cloth were used for the appliqué.

When a group of Tai Neua ladies from the royal family of Muong Baw visited Dodd while he was staying in Keng Tung, he concluded that the dress of royalty was more colourful.

> *They came mounted on ponies, the ladies wearing the most gorgeous skirts of striped silk in all colors of the rainbow.*[38]

To the north of Sipsong Pan Na on the southern and western borders of Yunnan, the Tai lived mainly in the rural areas, and in the nineteenth century, the Chinese were in control of the cities. The Chinese had built over the remains of Shan settlements. Interestingly, Chinese cultural dominance included dress codes, and Dodd claimed that Shan women were being coerced into Chinese dress.

> *These excellent Shans were troubled in mind by a proclamation just issued by the Governor General Ts'en, ordering them, or rather their wives and daughters, the Chinese dress. They were of the opinion that everyone should be allowed to follow his own religion, theirs was that women should dress in tunics and skirts, and not in sacks and trousers.*[39]

In the late nineteenth century, this area was viewed as the final outreach of Tai culture, although recent historical studies have reassessed the extent of Tai settlement in the region.[40]

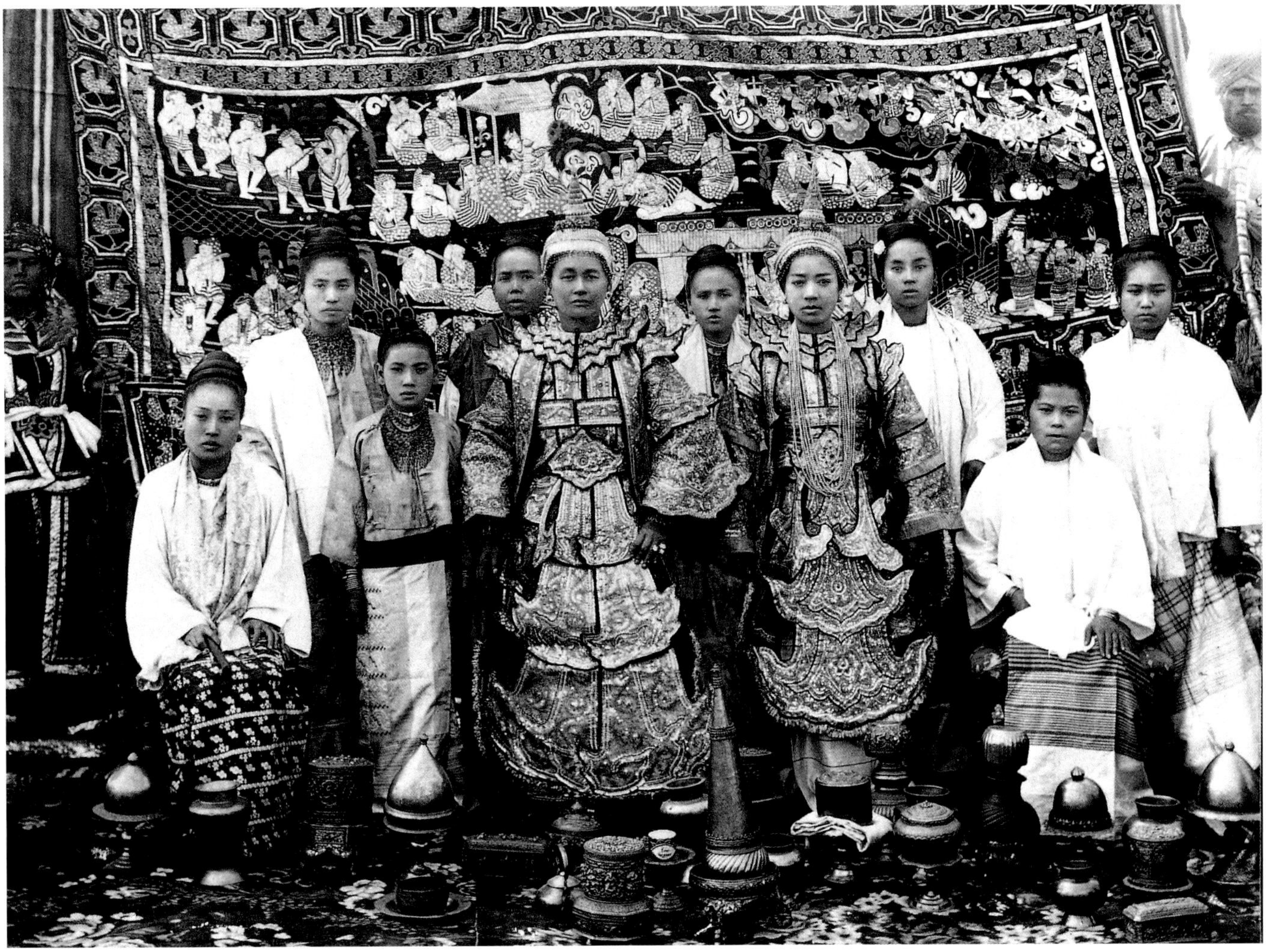

149 Shan princesses photographed at the Delhi Durbar of 1903. *(The Oriental and India Office Collections, The British Library, London, 430/78 (74))*

Burmese Tributary dress

The senior princesses of the Shan States accompanied the princes when they went to pay respect (*kadaw*) to the king of Burma. They were given the same rank as wives of Burmese governors and were issued with dress, jewellery and regalia through the office of the Burmese court chamberlain. They were allocated according to sumptuary laws. The senior princesses were entitled to a headdress (*sibon*) shaped like a helmet and decorated with gold tinsel, filigree lace and beetle wings, and surmounted by a gilt finial. The blouse (*du-yin-daing*) had a stiff bodice of reinforced tinsel cloth, with circles of mother-of-pearl beads, silver and gold sequins and coloured glass, trimmed with narrow bands of green velvet, and lined throughout with cotton. The sleeves were detachable and made in two or three separate sections that slotted together. A detachable "cloud collar," worn like a stiff ruff, was constructed from three reinforced scalloped tiers of tinsel cloth embroidered with gold thread and appliquéd with silver sequins and coloured glass, and trimmed with green velvet. The outfit also included a pair of shoulder epaulettes constructed and embroidered like the cloud collar. A scalloped belt and clasp with silver sequins, pearl beads and coloured glass, trimmed with green velvet was worn at the waist. An ankle-length, wrap-over silk skirt (*hta-mein*) of Burmese *acheik-luntaya* fabric acted as the underskirt for sets of stiffened flat attachments supported on bamboo frames.

Each attachment consisted of scalloped tiers made from reinforced tinsel cloth with a cotton lining, the surface couched with silver and gold sequins, beetle wings, pearl beads and coloured glass, and was trimmed with green velvet. The number of attachments varied with each costume but there was an apron (*hka-yan-kyo*) and at least one set (*yin hlwan*) of side panels. These were attached at the waist. The other type fitted around the neck and over the shoulders (*she-hpo-thong-hsin*) to hang down in two sash-like panels at the front. They were cut with tiered scallops. A pair of leather slippers couched with sequins and gold metal wire completed the outfit.

When King Thibaw of Burma was sent into exile by the British in 1885, these ornate costumes were no longer needed for defunct *kadaw* ceremonies in Mandalay. They were however kept in store at the Shan palaces and brought out for important ceremonies. Two Shan princesses were photographed in Burmese tributary dress at the Delhi Durbar of 1903. Sir George Scott described outfits worn by the consorts of the prince of Yawnghwe, probably the two ladies in the centre of the photograph (fig. 149).

> *His wives...were also there wearing the peculiar tabard skirts of the old nobility, a sort of series of wings folded over from each side, also heavily encrusted with gold.*[41]

In the photograph the Shan princesses pose in front of the same cloth hanging (*shwe chi doe*) as was used to photograph the princes. The two senior princesses are wearing gold filigree headdresses shaped like helmets, surmounted with tiered gilt spires. Their gold jackets (*du-yin thin-daing*) are embroidered with sequins and gold and silver metal thread, and have tiered sleeves trimmed with embroidered scallops and bands of velvet. Their jackets are overlaid with tiered and scalloped collars and scalloped epaulettes. The princess on the left of the photograph is wearing flat scalloped panels of embroidery (*she-hpo-thong-hsin*). The panels pass around the neck so that the scallops hang down in two matching sections at the front. The princess on the right has one scalloped panel worn like an apron with two side panels. Diamond-shaped scalloped clasps help keep the panels in place. Beneath the attachments, they are wearing ankle-length wrapped skirts (*hta-mein*). The other ladies in the photograph have their hair coiled in topknots and wear long-sleeved blouses under light shawls and ankle length skirts with silk panels of *acheik-luntaya* or horizontal stripes and plaids. The ceremonial vessels, tea chests, betel nut boxes, display stands and covers that had been photographed with the princes are also seen in this photograph.

After Burma gained independence from Britain, the first President of Burma was the prince of Yawnghwe. His consort, Princess Sao Hearn Kham, *mahadevi* of Yawnghwe and First Lady of democratic Burma attended many state functions and dressed in a mix of Shan and Burmese style. This tradition continued until the 1960s when the Shan royal family disappeared or were forced into exile (see chapter two).

This chapter shows the range of fabrics and the style of dress worn by women in the Shan States in the late nineteenth and early twentieth centuries and reveals the wide range of indigenous and imported fabrics available to hill and valley dwellers. It demonstrates the relationship between dress and ethnicity and dress and politics, and the difference between "ordinary" and "court" dress. It also shows how attempts to suppress indigenous dress codes, particularly by the Chinese, were resented and seen as an infringement of personal liberty. When the British annexed the Shan States, they encouraged the wearing of indigenous Shan court dress and tributary dress, as part of the grand Imperial spectacle. The relationships between hill and valley peoples were openly expressed in dress codes, but were later denied when issues of ethnic purity were politicised.

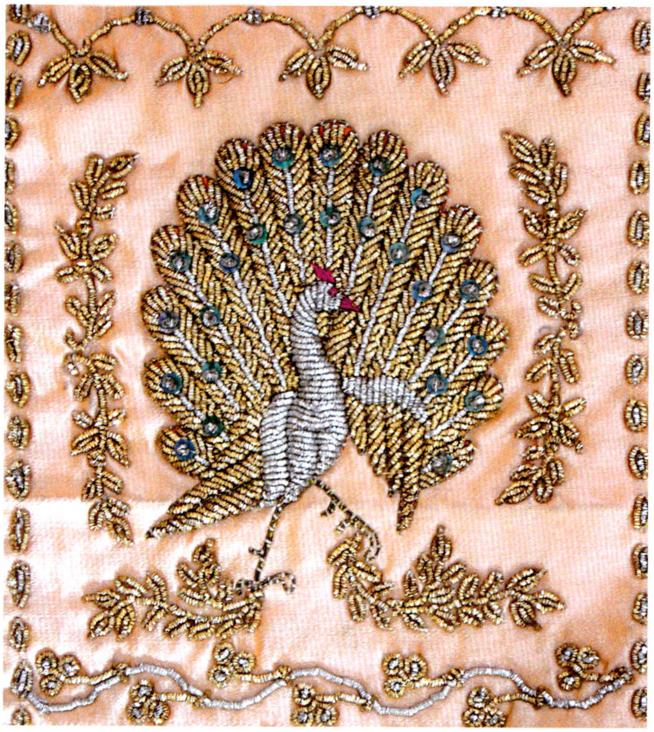

150 Detail of fig 152.

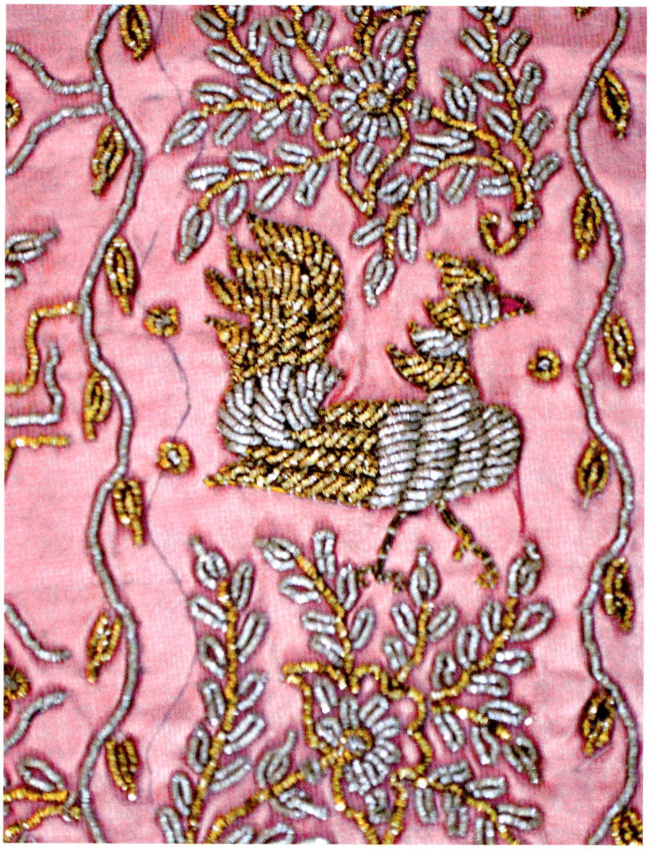

151 Detail of silver and gold metal wire couched on a skirt belonging to Sao Thu Zanda. *(Private collection)*

152 (Opposite) The sash (*hpa wai*) worn by Sao Thu Zanda, Nang Kyemmong of Hsenwi on her wedding day in 1924. *(Private collection)*

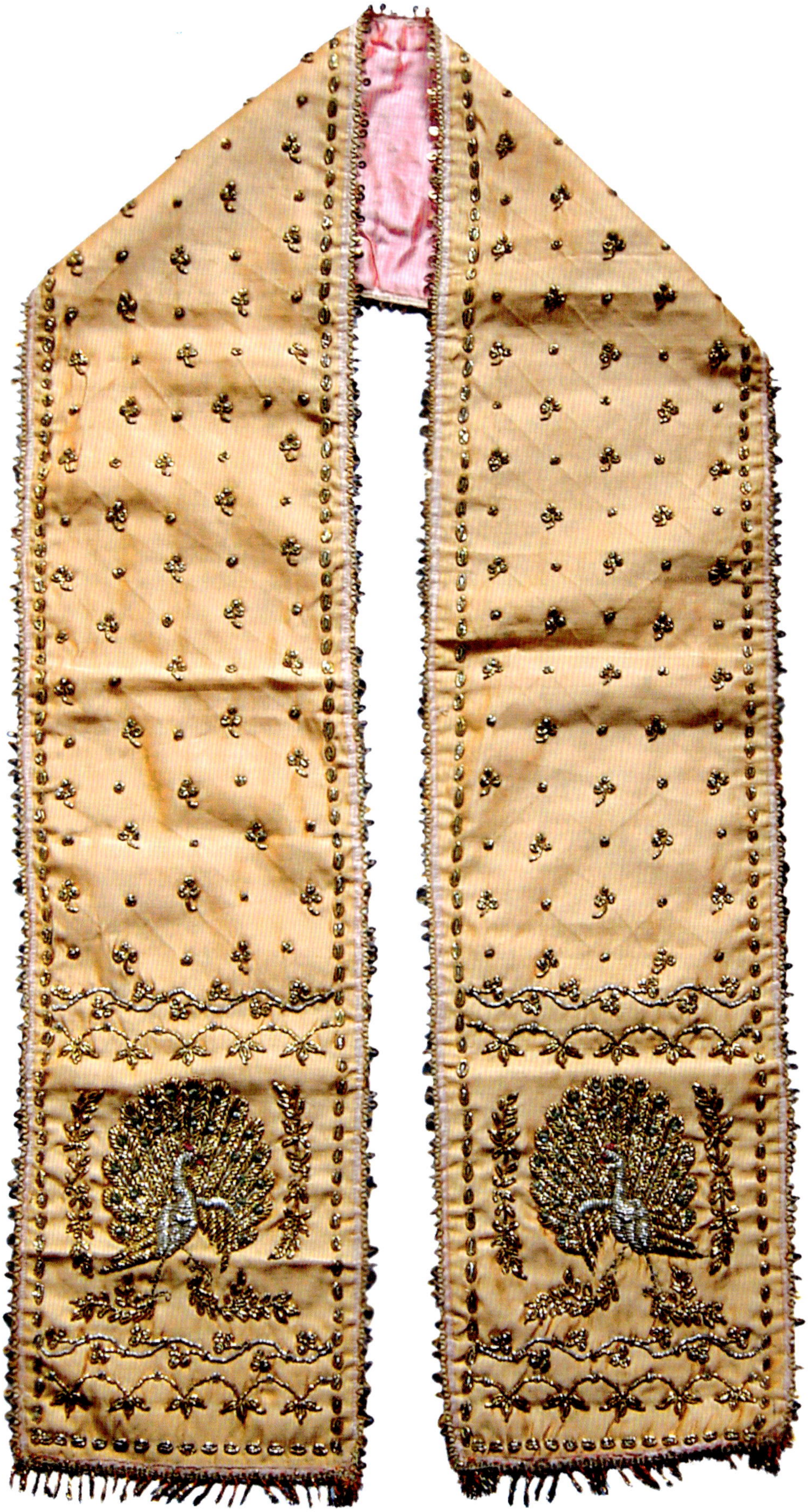

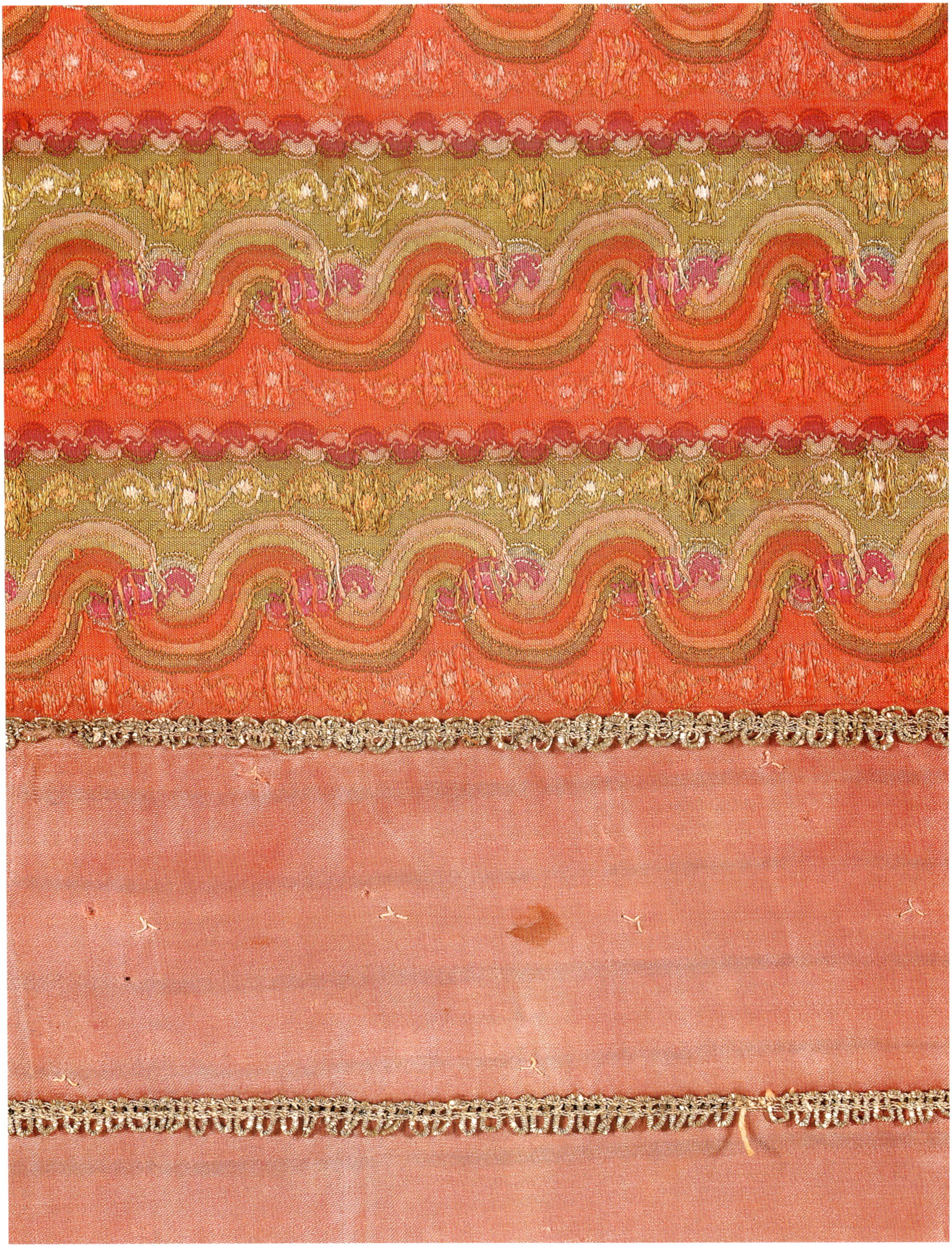

153 Woman's ankle-length skirt with *acheik-luntaya* in the central panel and a silk hem border with silver thread. *(Private collection)*

154-56 (Opposite) A selection of *acheik-luntaya* panels from women's ankle-length skirts. *(Private collection)*

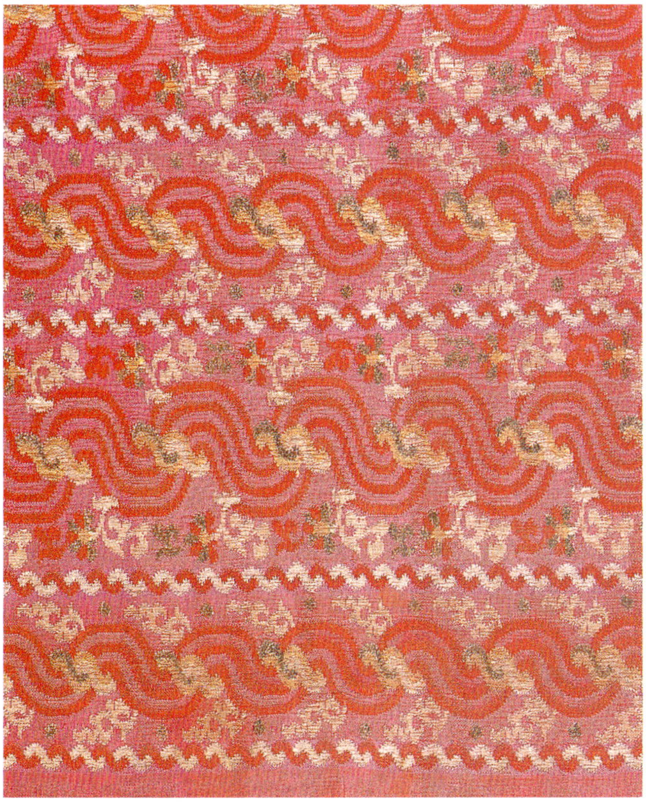

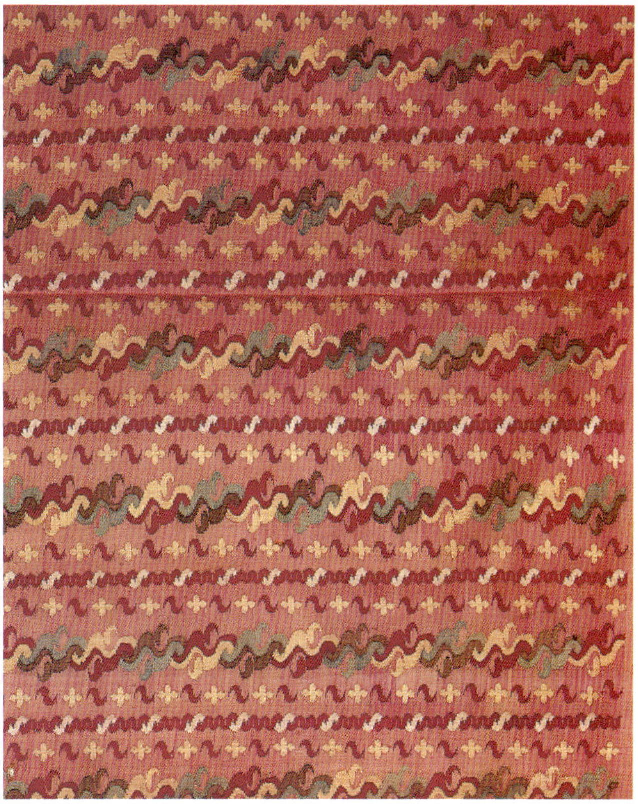

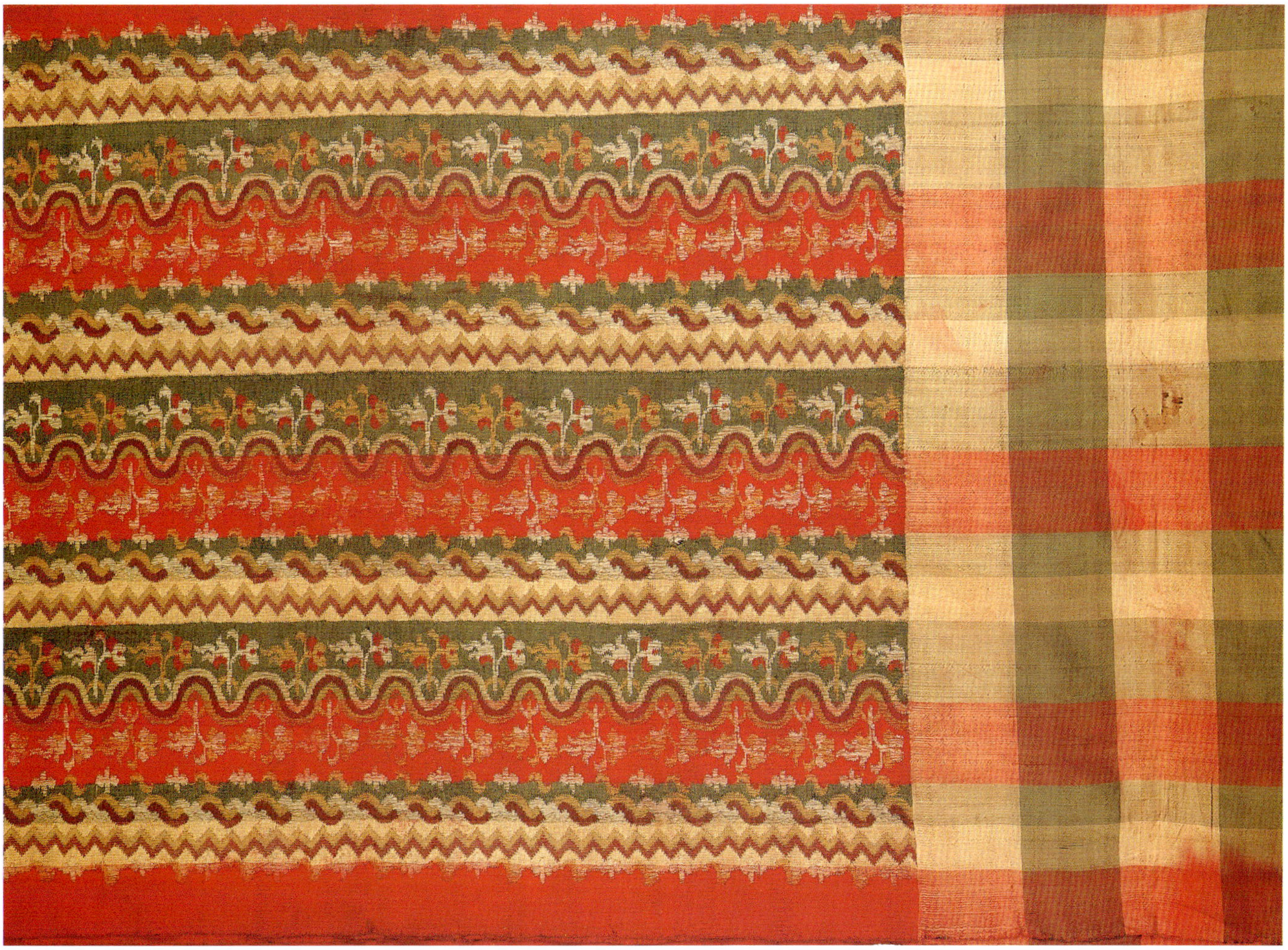

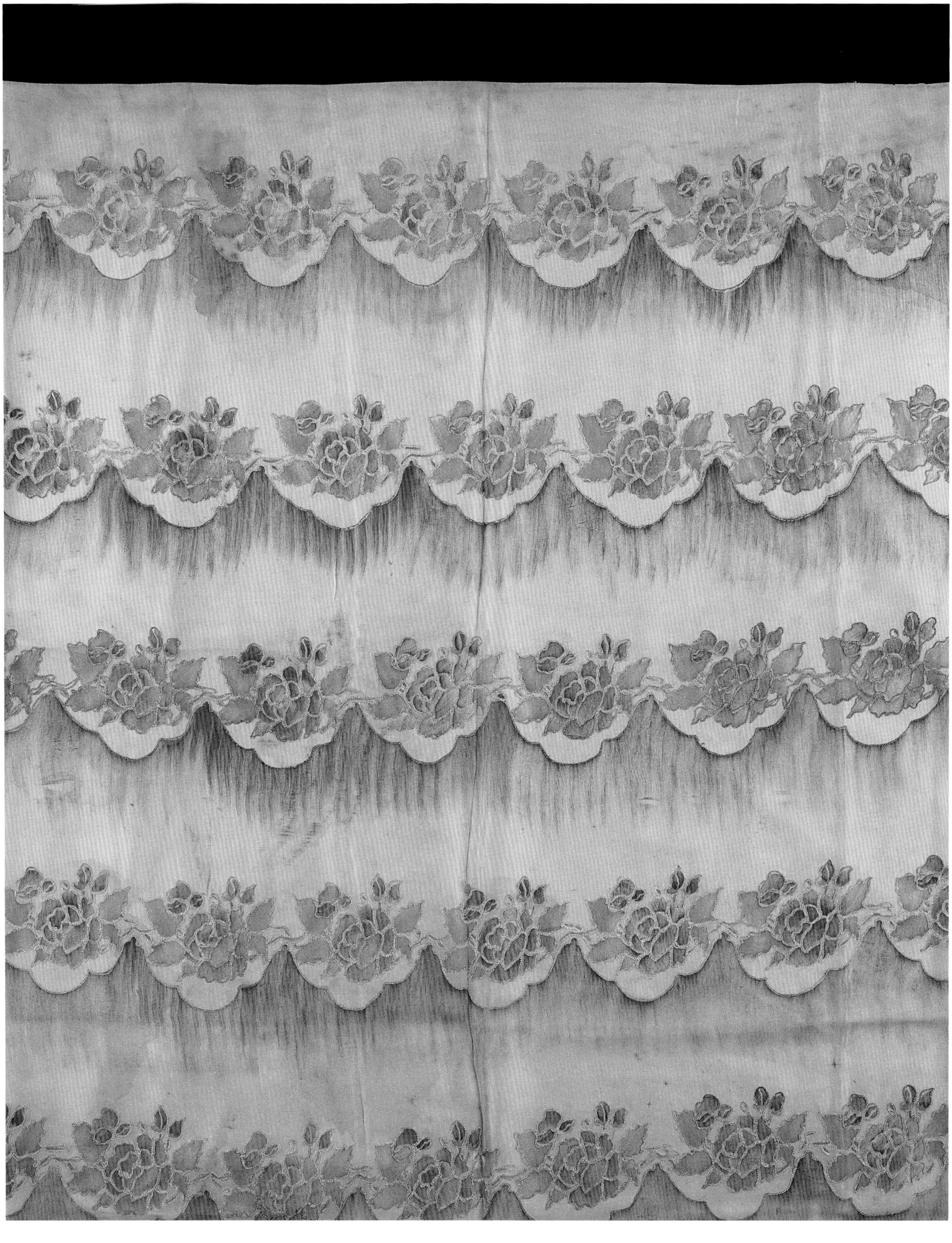

157 An unusual woman's ankle-length skirt emulating *acheik-luntaya* weaving patterns, painted silk with embroidery. *(Private collection)*

158 (Opposite) Woman's ankle-length skirt with an embroidered central panel couched with silver and gold metal wire and mother-of-pearl sequins. *(Private collection)*

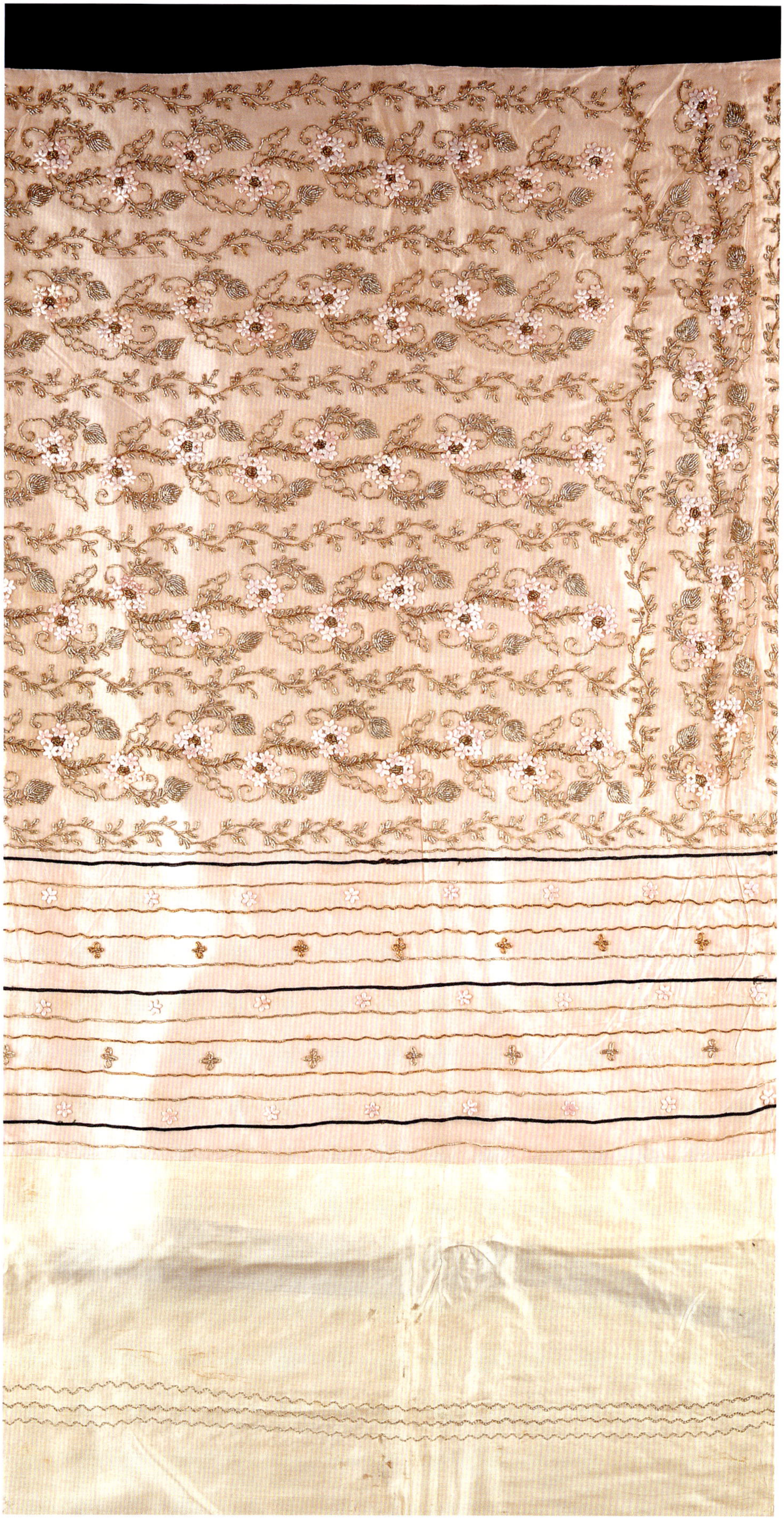

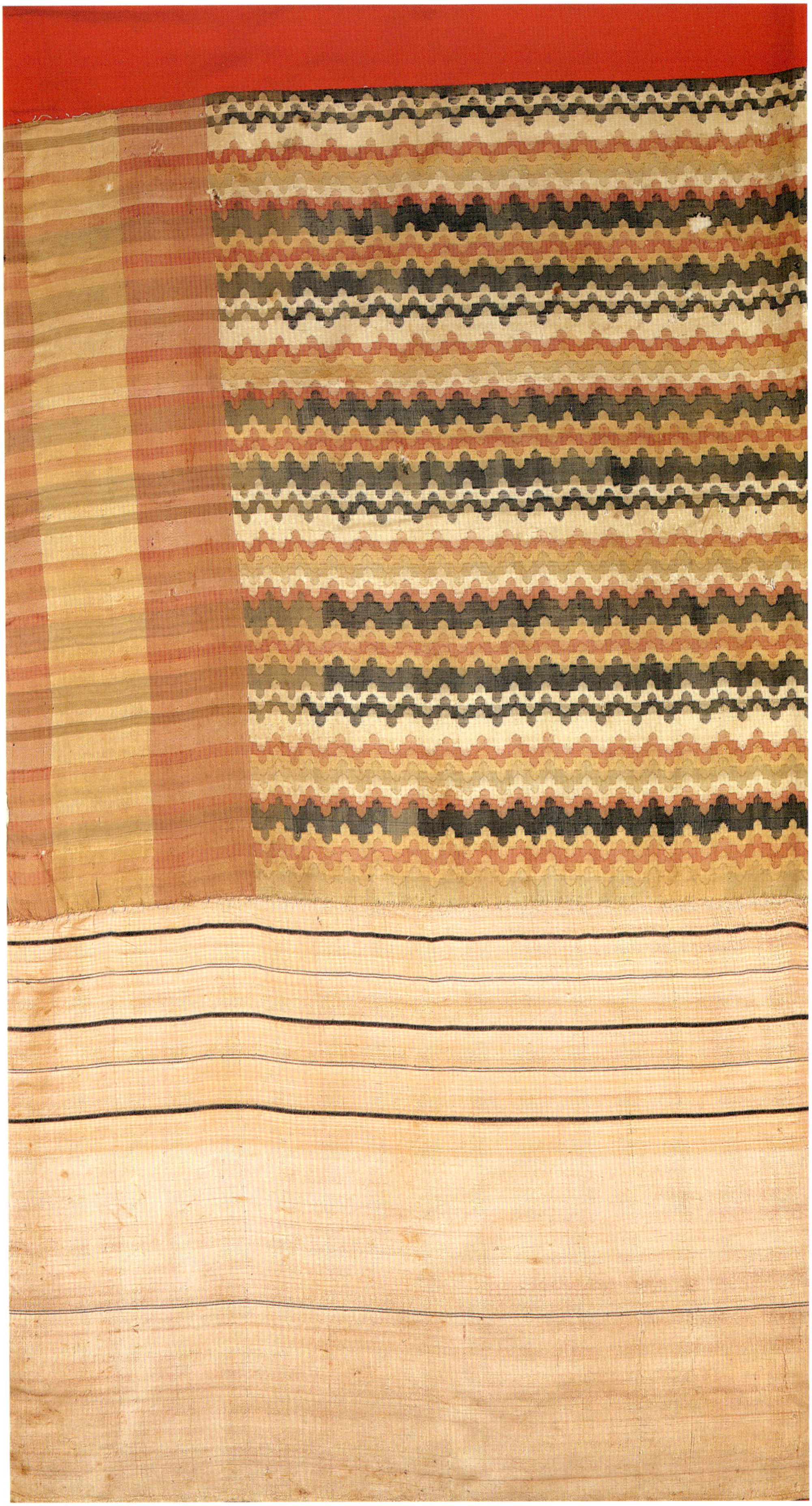

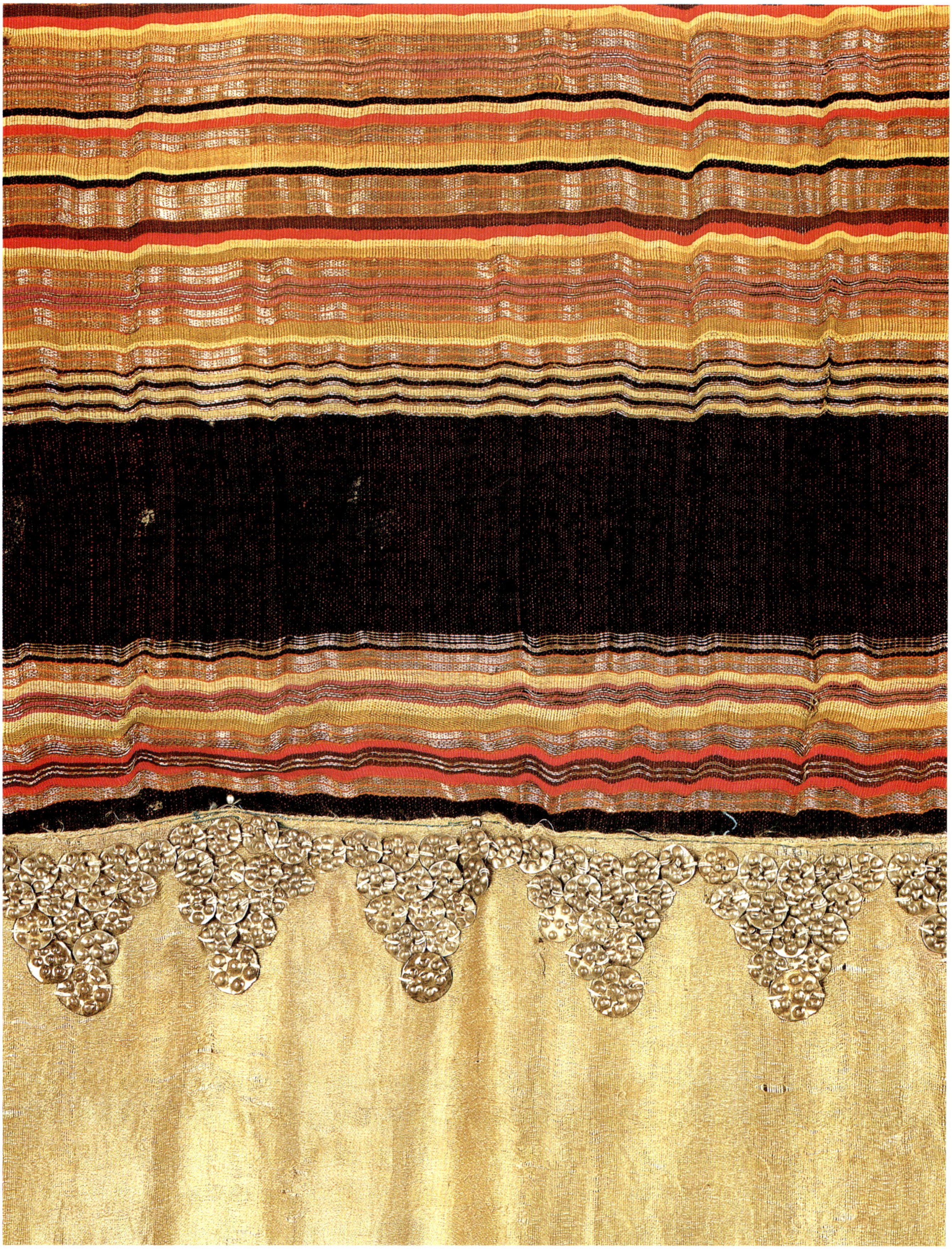

159 (Opposite) Woman's ankle-length skirt with an *acheik-luntaya* pattern in the central panel. *(Private collection)*

160 Detail of a Tai Khoen woman's ankle-length skirt woven with gold and silver thread and couched with silver sequins. *(Private collection)*

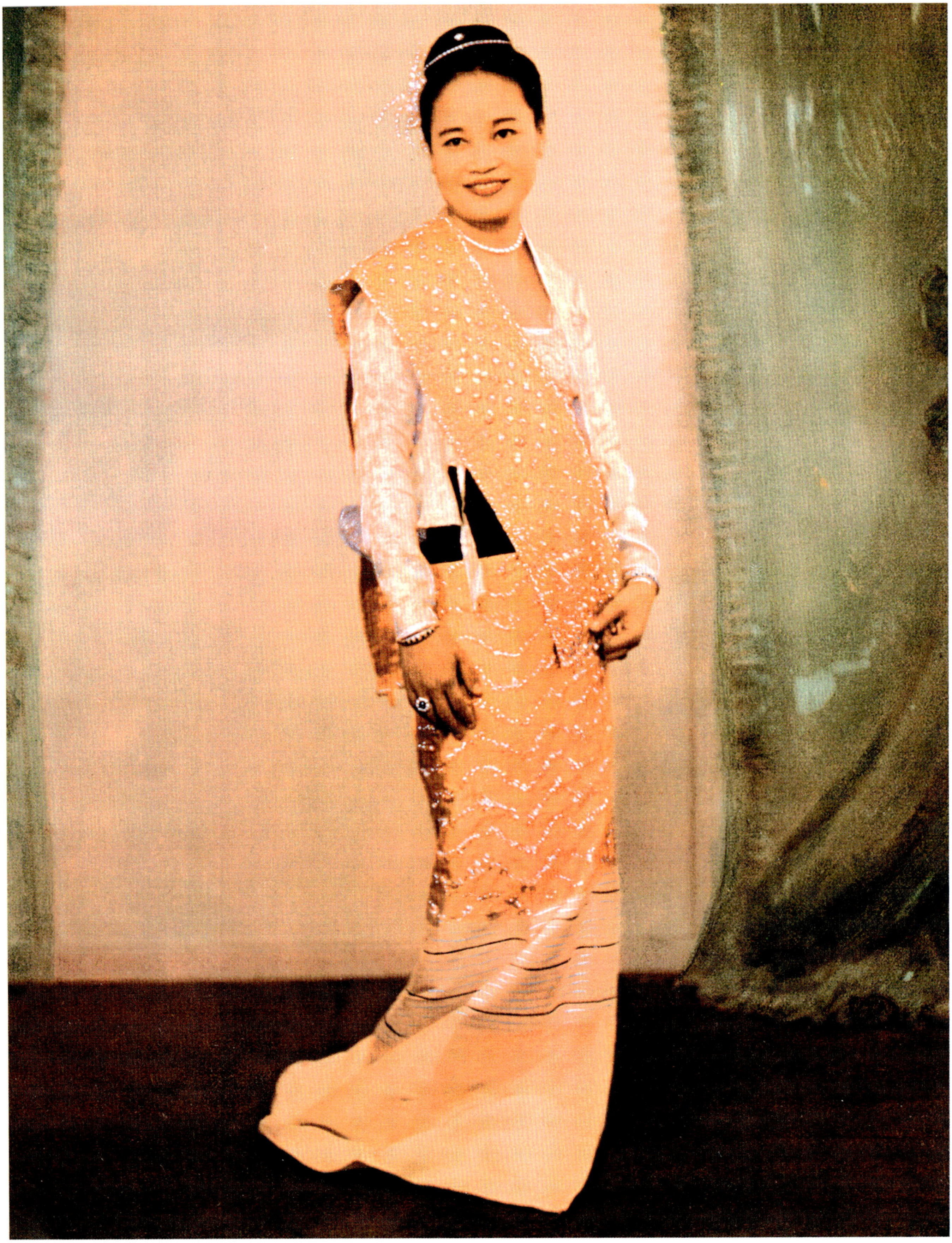

161 Princess Sao Nang Hearn Kham of Hsenwi, married to Sao Shwe Thaike of Yawnghwe, first president of Burma, photographed at the wedding of Princess Elizabeth and Prince Philip in London in 1947. *(Private collection)*

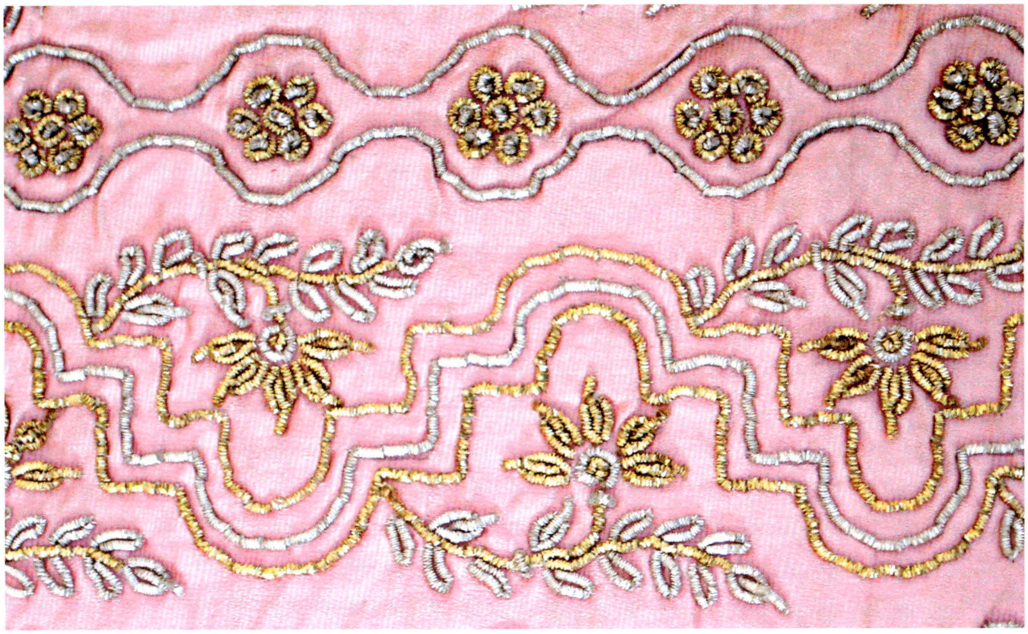

162 Detail of silver and gold metal wire couched on the skirt belonging to Sao Thu Zanda. *(Private collection)*

Endnotes

1 Max Ferrars and Bertha Ferrars, *Burma*, Sampson Low, Marston and Co., London and New York 1901, reprint Ava Press. Bangkok 1996.
2 Paul Lewis and Elaine Lewis, *Peoples of the Golden Triangle*, Thames and Hudson, London, 1984.
3 Susan Conway, *Silken Threads Lacquer Thrones*, River Books, Bangkok, 2000.
4 Carl Bock, *Temples and Elephants, Travels in Siam 1881-1882*, Oxford University Press, reprint. 1986, p. 327
5 Mandy Sadan, *"The Kachin Photographs: a documentary record of contact"* in E. Dell (ed.), *Burma: Frontier Photographs*, Merrell, London and The Green Centre for World Art, Brighton, 2000, p. 72.
6 Charles Gilhodes, *The Kachins*, 1922, reprint White Lotus Press, Bangkok, 1996.
7 George Young, *The Hill Tribes of Northern Thailand*, Bangkok, The Siam Society, 1962.
8 S. Prangwattanakun and P. Cheesman, *Lan Na Texiles Yuan Lue Lao*, Center for the Promotion of Arts and Culture, Chiang Mai University, 1987, p. 67.
9 William Clifton Dodd, *The Tai Race: Elder Brother of the Chinese,* The Torch Press, Cedar Rapids, 1923, reprint White Lotus Press, Bangkok, 1996, p. 201.
10 At times in history when Tai "purity" became a political issue, the history of inter-marriage was suppressed.
11 Dodd, 1996, p. 201.
12 Bock, 1986, pp. 324-326.
13 McCleod, quoted in V. Grabowsky and A. Turton, *The Gold and Silver Road of Trade and Friendship*, Silkworm Books, Chiang Mai, 2003, p. 393.
14 Interviews with Ba Sangda Bansiddhi, Chom Ton, 1983, Akadet Nakbunlung, Chiang Mai, 1983; Princess Vilai na Keng Tung, Chiang Mai, 1996.
15 Young, 1962, p. 55.
16 Gilhodes, 1996, p. 112.
17 George Scott, *Burma: A Handbook of Practical Information*, 1906, reprint Orchid Press, Bangkok, 1999.
18 Kingdom-Ward, *In Farthest Burma: The Record of an Arduous Journey of Exploration and Research Through the Unknown Frontier Territory of Burma and Tibet*, London, 1921.
19 Leslie Milne, *The Home of an Eastern Clan*, Oxford 1924, reprint White Lotus Press, Bangkok, 2004, p. 212.
20 *Ibid,* p. 213.
21 Leslie Milne and Wilbur Cochrane, *Shans at Home*, John Murray, London, 1910, reprinted New York, 1970.
22 He was a Buddhist and had received the K. S .M. (King's Service Medal) from the British. He attended the Delhi Durbar of 1903.
23 McCleod, quoted in V. Grabowsky and A. Turton, 2003, p. 188.
24 Sao Shwe Thaike became the first president of Burma after Independence in 1948.
25 The *saohpa* had four consorts who were sisters.
26 Richardson, quoted in V. Grabowsky and A. Turton, 2003, p. 505 and pp. 522-32.
27 Informants state that the sequins were made in Keng Tung (interviews with Khun Duangjit Thaveesri and Khun Akadet Nakbunlung, 1983).
28 Dodd, 1996, p. 201.
29 From the footnotes of *The Padaeng and Jengtung Chronicle*, (trans. Sao Saimong Mangrai), Center for South and Southeast Asian Studies, University of Michigan, 1981, p. 288.
30 Michael Moerman, "Chiangkham's Trade in the "Old Days", in G. Skinner and A. Thomas Kirsch (eds.) *Change and Persistence in Thai Society: Essays in Honor of Lauriston Sharp*, Ithaca, Cornell University, 1975.
31 Prangwattanakun and Cheesman, 1987.
32 Holt Hallett, *A Thousand Miles on an Elephant in the Shan States*, Edinburgh and London: Blackwood and Sons, 1890, reprint White Lotus Press, Bangkok, 1988.
33 Dodd, 1996.
34 Lefévre-Pontalis, *Mission Pavie Indo-Chine, 1879-1895*, Paris, Ernst Leroux, 1902, reprinted as *Travels in Upper Laos and on the Borders of Yunnan and Burma* (trans. W. Tips), White Lotus Press, Bangkok, 2000, p. 303.
35 Moerman (1975) recorded that Tai Lue women were particularly fond of light blue ribbon, brought by Yunnanese traders, which they used to decorate their jackets.
36 Dodd, 1996, p. 183.
37 McCleod, quoted in V. Grabowsky and A. Turton, 2003, p. 385.
38 *Ibid*, p. 172.
39 Dodd, 1996, p. 176.
40 *Ibid,* pp. 158-159.
41 Zhu Liangwen, *The Dai*, D. D. Books, Bangkok, 1992.
42 George Scott, *Burma and Beyond,* Grayson and Grayson, London, 1932, p. 59.

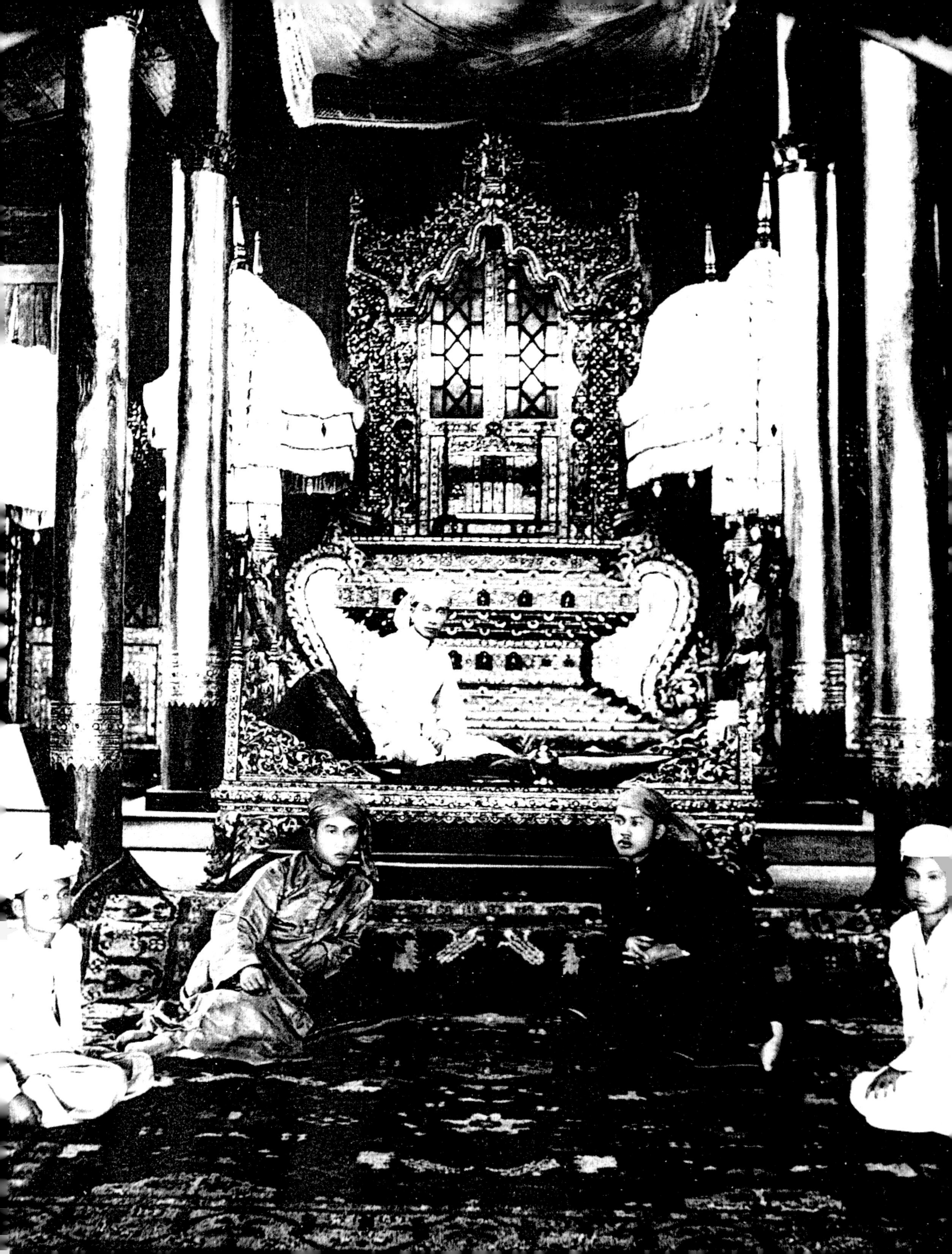

Chapter 5
Princes and Palaces

According to Theravada Buddhist cosmology, a Shan prince is a being on the way to Enlightenment (*bodhisattva*). He resides in a royal palace (*haw*) which has been built as a symbolic celestial mountain and is situated in the "sacred centre" of a Shan city. On ceremonial occasions, he should be seated on a gilded throne under a canopy and wear a tiered crown that together symbolise cosmological and protective forces.[1] When building a palace he should seek the advice of an astrologer to identify an auspicious site and calculate a propitious day for work to begin. In reparation for trees felled for the building, he should ensure that the guardian spirits (*phii*) of the forest are appeased with offerings, and he should make merit by presenting gifts to a monastery. Throughout history, donations have included Buddha images, small shrines, temple furniture and monk's robes. The men who felled the trees were also expected to make a contribution. The painted and gilded wooden shrine in the collection of Chiang Mai Museum, Thailand is one example. On the day a site for a palace was to be levelled, the guardian spirits who occupied the land in the immediate vicinity were appeased. The prince sponsored Buddhist services of blessing and further offerings were made to the spirits to mark important stages in the building process.

A palace was built under the supervision of a master carpenter. The Shan princes could draw on their subjects for corvée labour, although as workers were in short supply, itinerant labourers were often hired. They were given food and lodgings while the building was in progress. Skilled artisans were often paid in silver. A palace was constructed on teak posts (*Tectona grandis)* with a base of kiln-baked brick or stone. A raised ground floor was a common device, allowing air to circulate beneath the floor and preventing the building from flooding in the monsoon season. A skeleton post and lintel structure was assembled, and then the roof, floors, and wall partitions were added using well-seasoned teak. A multi-tiered gilded roof (*pyatthat*), terminating in a finial, was assembled over the space reserved for the audience hall. At certain times in history, the kings of Burma imposed architectural and design restrictions on Shan palaces, administered according to sumptuary laws. This included dictating the number of tiers permissible on the roof of an audience hall. During the reign of King Mindon (1857-1885), the prince of Hkamti Long was entitled to two tiers while the prince of Muong Nai, to whom King Mindon was related by marriage, was entitled to five tiers.[2]

The palace apartments had covered wooden balconies and terraces leading from the main rooms. In the hot season they provided a shady place to sit. A grand staircase with a covered canopy led up to the door of the main entrance that was used by senior members of the royal family and important visitors. Others entered the palace by a side entrance. The audience hall and the apartments of the prince and his senior consort were built at a slightly higher elevation than the quarters reserved for minor consorts. Sao

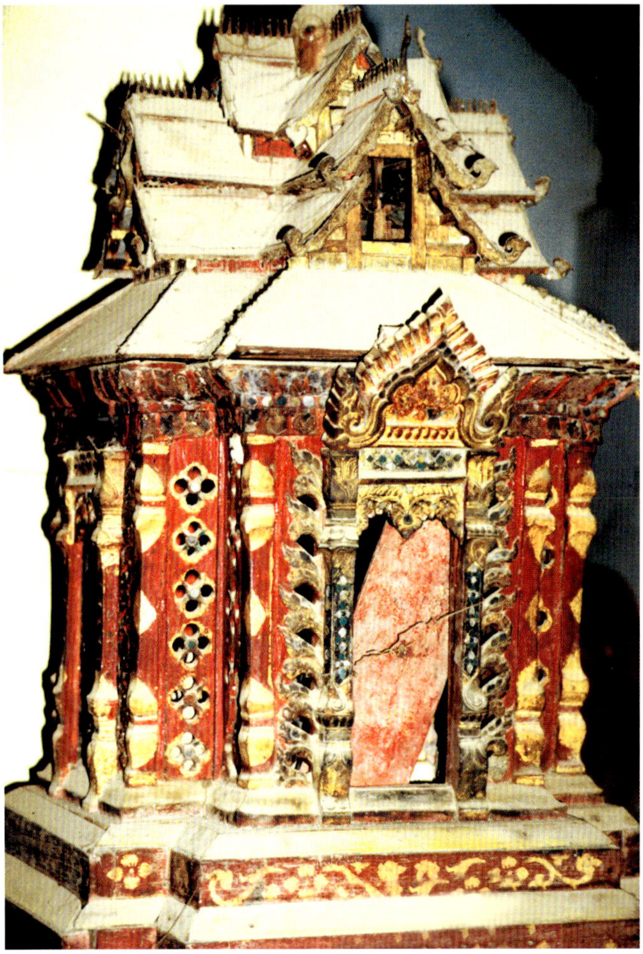

164 A painted and gilded wooden shrine donated to a temple by a Shan family. *(Chiang Mai National Museum)*

Noan Oo (Nel Adams) described the living quarters of her grandfather, Prince Sao Hkun Suik of Keng Tung (ruled 1900-1943),

> *On either side of the reception room were about a dozen or so guest rooms, while directly behind was grandfather's private sitting room. He had two bedrooms for himself, a cool room for summer and a warm room for winter and three other bedrooms for three of his wives.*[3]

If the palace could not accommodate all the consorts, they might be housed in another building in the palace grounds.

Finely carved wooden barge boards, lintels, doors, window frames, shutters and balustrades were usually produced in sections in a workshop and assembled later on site. They were carved in two or three dimensions with

163 (Opposite) Prince Sao Hom Hpa of Hsenwi seated on a couch with the heir presumptive, Sao Yape Hpa (right), and the heir apparent, Sao Hman Hpa (left) seated on the floor. Two younger brothers, Sao Pyem Hpa and Sao Kyan Hpa, are seated at each side.

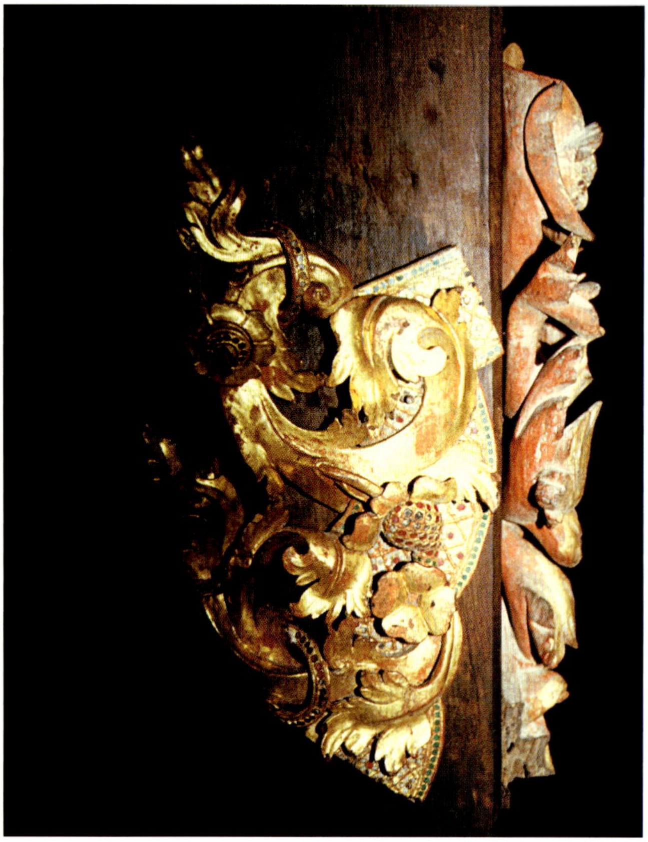

165 Painted and gilded wooden carving on a teak pillar in a Shan palace.

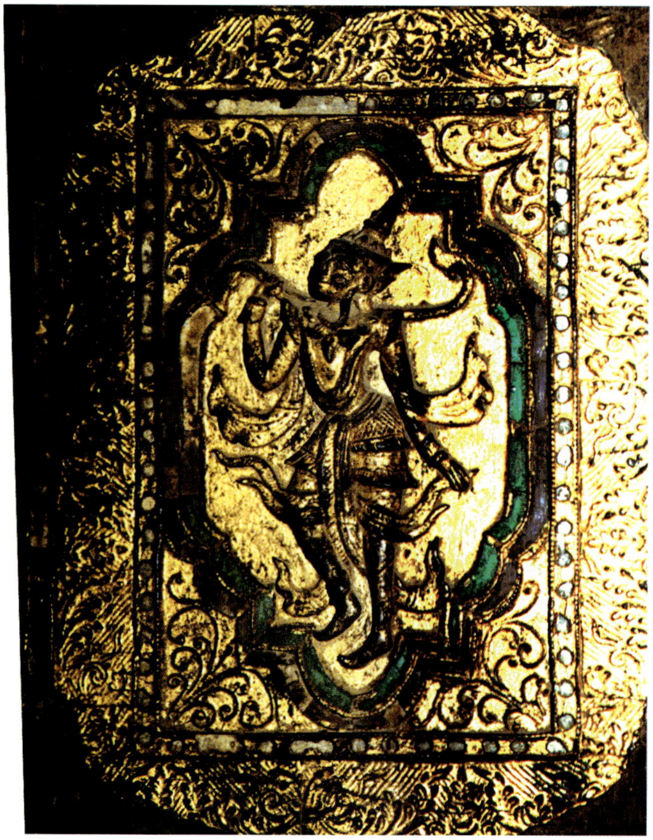

166 A two-dimensional lacquer guardian figure set in a lacquer frame with gilded floral and leaf patterns. Shan Palace Museum, Yawnghwe.

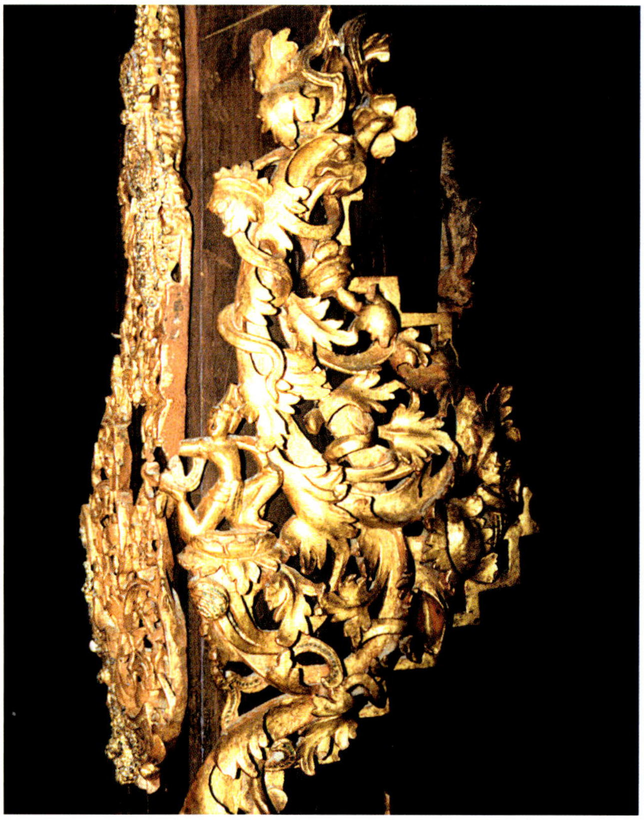

167 Detail of a painted and gilded wood carving in the Shan Palace Museum, Yawnghwe.

twisting plant and floral designs, flame patterns, characters from Buddhist mythology, Shan spirits and mythological animals and birds. Smaller carvings with similar imagery were attached to interior pillars, door frames and walls. Some were lacquered, painted and gilded. The Keng Tung Chronicle provides lavish descriptions of a palace built according to sumptuary laws in operation during the reign of King Bodawhpaya of Burma (ruled 1782-1819). The palace had twelve main rooms, described as "pavilions," and their walls were painted with cinnabar. The central audience hall had a tiered roof that was totally gilded and was decorated with carved and gilded barge boards. The interior walls, pillars and beams of the audience hall were painted and stencilled with gold and decorated with carved and gilded *hamsa* birds. Small gilded bells with strikers shaped like the leaves of a bodhi tree were suspended from the carvings on the roof eaves.[4]

The photograph of the exterior of the palace of Hsenwi shows an impressive building with a tiered spire over the audience hall in the middle of the building and another tiered spire over the entrance hall. The roofs have carved wooden barge boards and thick teak pillars act as visible supports.[5] The exterior of the palace of the prince of Muong Pawn can be seen in a photograph taken of him and his family, circa 1890 (see fig. 132). The group is seated in front of the palace and the tall wooden pillars that support the raised floor can be seen in the background. The balcony balustrade is carved with panels of stylised flowers, leaves and tendrils in repeat patterns. The windows are inset with panes of glass cut in diamonds and triangles. A curved

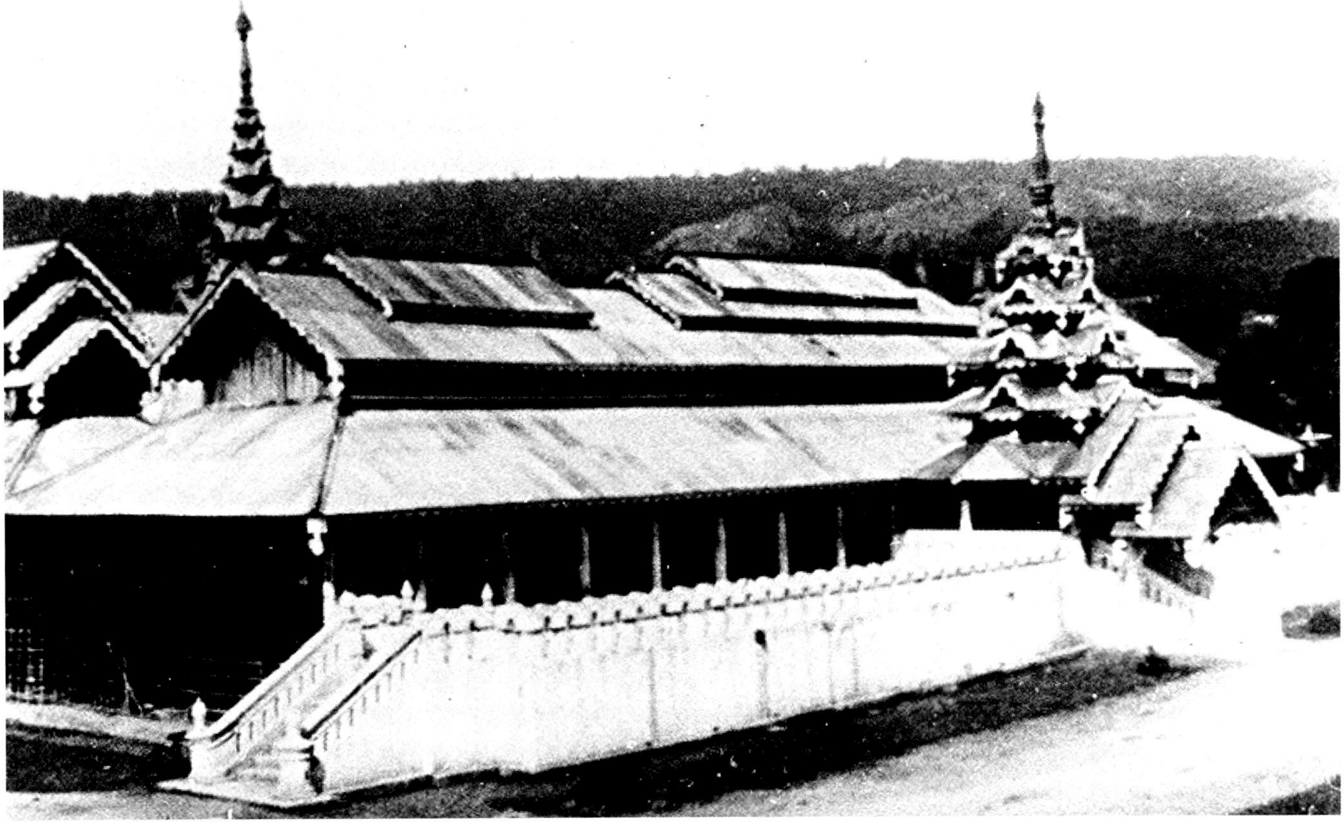

168 The palace of Hsenwi, destroyed during Allied bombing in 1945.

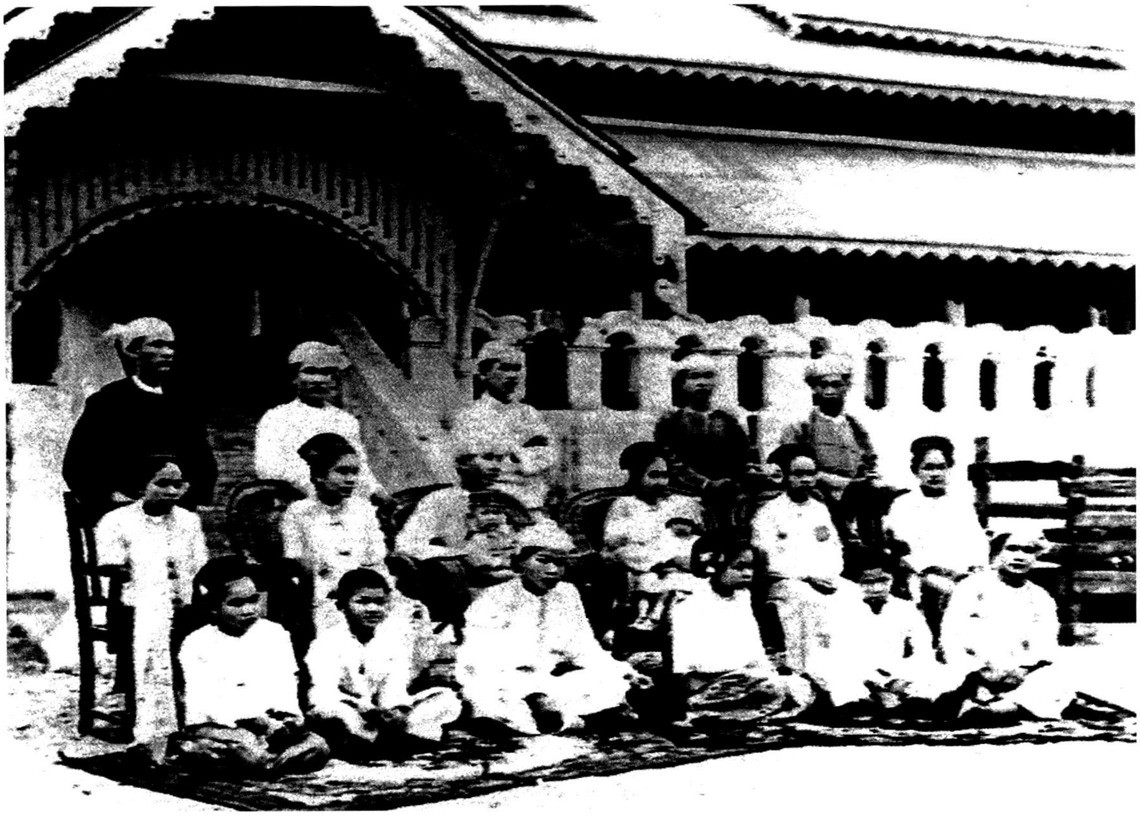

169 The royal family of Hsenwi, photographed in 1928 outside the palace shown above.

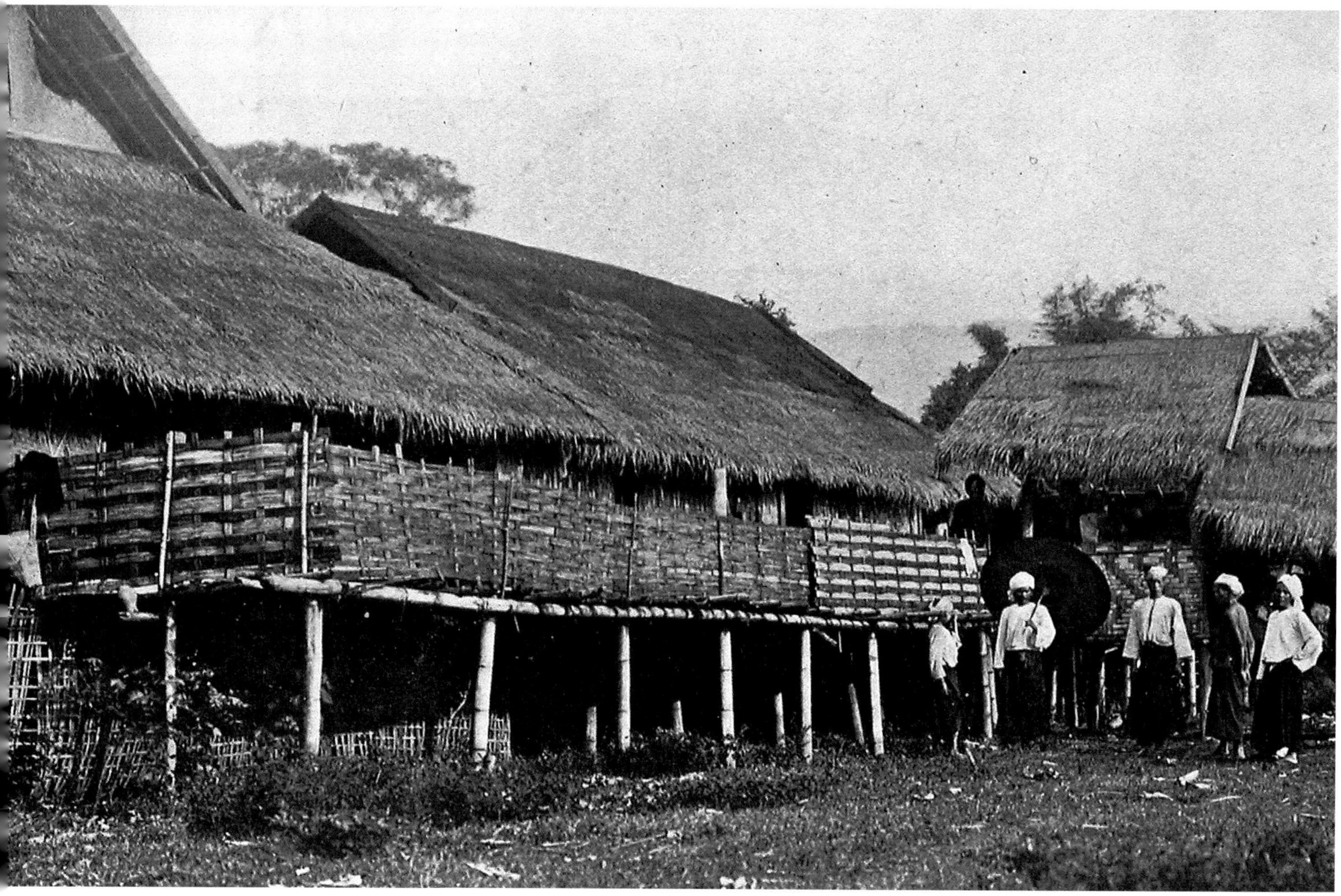

170 A Shan bamboo palace on teak pilings, Milne and Cochrane, 1910.

wooden porch with repeat geometric designs and a pendant-shaped border provides a cover for the entrance. A photograph of the royal family of Hsenwi, taken in 1928, also shows the front elevation with a carved wooden porch and stairs leading up to the entrance, and carved bargeboards and finials on the main roof (see fig. 169).

The grounds included accommodation for servants, and there were a number of outbuildings and storerooms. Most palaces had extensive grounds with flower and vegetable gardens, a fruit orchard, and other trees including a bodhi tree (*Ficus religiosa*). A wall, built of kiln-baked bricks and mud or of stone, surrounded the compound. Those entering were expected to observe rules of obeisance that included dismounting from their horses and elephants, folding their umbrellas, and before entering the palace building, removing their shoes.

Most palace retainers were not housed in the compound but lived close enough so that they could be summoned by the sound of drumbeat. Figure 171 shows a large drum, now in the Shan Palace Museum, Yawnghwe. According to local legend, it is one of a set of three made by a group of hill tribe artisans and were carved from one large tree. The sample in the museum is covered in animal hide, lacquered, painted and gilded. In the nineteenth century, the sound of drumbeat was a common form of local communication. The French explorer Francis Garnier described, how while he was travelling with the French Exploration Commission in the 1860s, a headman had summoned their replacement porters by sounding a large village drum.[6]

The princes also kept some retainers who lived in outlying villages. The village of Ho Ko, a few miles from the city of Keng Tung, was the site of the royal stables and the place where the grooms lived. Villagers recall New Year ceremonies in the time of the last prince of Keng Tung, when their fathers groomed elephants and horses ready to be caparisoned for ceremonial processions.[7]

Although Shan palaces shared essential design features, the size of the buildings and the number varied considerably. In the late nineteenth century, the prince of Yawnghwe maintained a large retinue with well over one hundred guards and sentries. He owned three elephants and five hundred horses and employed eight stablemen and grooms. His entourage included umbrella bearers, stewards and pages. In his administration there were three *myosa*, three ministers, two revenue officers, four deputy ministers, a judicial clerk, eight other clerks, a collector of fines, a finance officer and a jailer. There were sixty boatmen to row the prince around Inlay Lake in his golden barge in the shape of a mythical bird (*hintha*). The prince of Keng Tung kept a similarly large household. He also maintained a troupe of dancers, musicians and puppeteers. The English writer Maurice Collis attended a dance performance at the

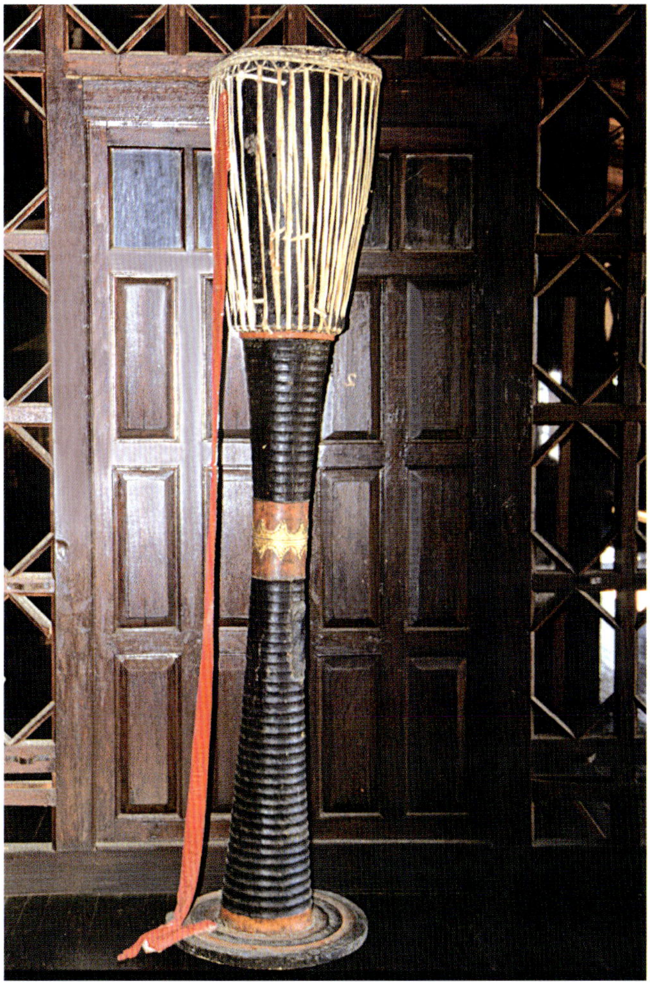

171 A lacquered drum in the Shan Palace Museum, Yawnghwe.

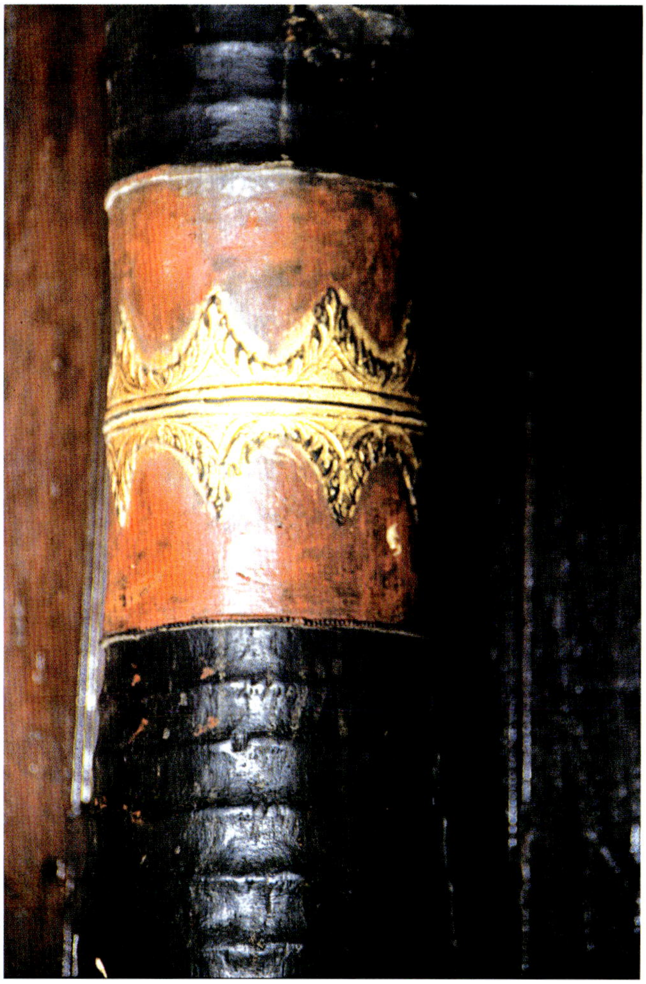

172 Lacquered leather detail on the drum.

palace of Keng Tung, staged to mark the end of Buddhist Lent.

> *The dancing began, animal dancing, for the dancers were wearing animal masks of birds, dragons, horses, and serpents. An old music was played and the animals began to strut and caper and glide. They were rejoicing at the end of Lent... But from time out of mind there has been animal dancing in the Shan States at the close of Lent and the Sawbwa carried on the custom in order to give colour to his party and to indulge his subjects...*[8]

Prince Hom Hpa of Hsenwi also sponsored singers and musicians to perform at court. Collis described their songs as oriental poems with musical phrases like a long procession, as if the Buddha's life was a scroll painting. Five musicians made up the group who performed while he was visiting.

> *I looked closely at the singer. She was a small woman, dressed in a pale skirt and a black jacket, worn over a white one... In her right hand she had two silver cymbals, shaped like bells and delicately held, the one between forefinger and thumb and the other between little and middle finger. These she tinkled together in her flexible palm as she sang, while with a stick which she held in her left hand she struck at intervals a stout piece of bamboo which lay in front of her on the floor... Behind the singer were the four musicians. The first played on a harp shaped like a boat with a high prow... The second musician had a patya before him, an oblong, carved box in which bamboo keys were set in a scale and emitted a staccato note when he struck them with little wooden mallets. The third musician had a violin and the fourth a flute.*[9]

Rulers like the princes of Keng Tung, Yawnghwe and Hsenwi lived in some splendour but there were many minor princes who occupied buildings with thatched roofs, bamboo and matting walls and with bamboo palings as boundary fences. In the 1890s, Prince Henri d'Orleans visited the wood, bamboo and thatch palace of the prince of Hkamti Long in a remote part of the northern Shan States. D'Orleans noted that the palace was slightly larger than the dwellings around it and was marked as a royal residence by the roof which had two tiers. Carved wooden dragons (*naga*) marked the position of the audience hall. A thin bamboo partition separated this important ceremonial chamber from the other rooms. The audience hall had thick teak columns and ceiling beams that were painted and stencilled with animal figures. Brightly coloured cotton textiles were used as curtains and wall hangings.[10]

Many Shan palaces have been destroyed over the last forty years. However, the palace of Yawnghwe has been converted into a museum and those visiting can get a sense of the past from the enduring beauty of the interior. Filtered tropical light reflects off the polished teak floors and catches

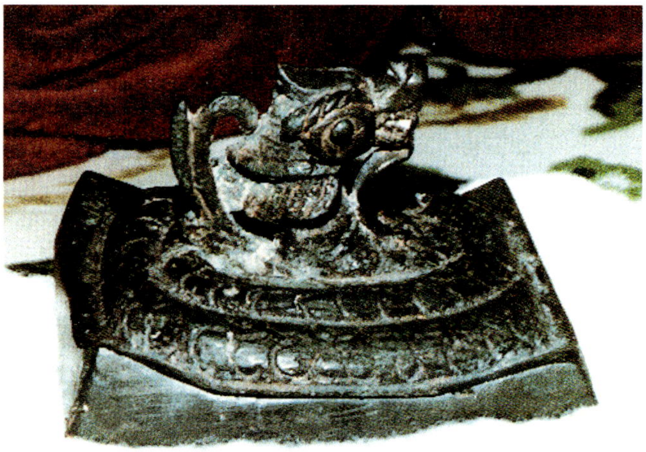

173 The handle of the seal of the prince of Hsenwi in the shape of a dragon. *(Private collection)*

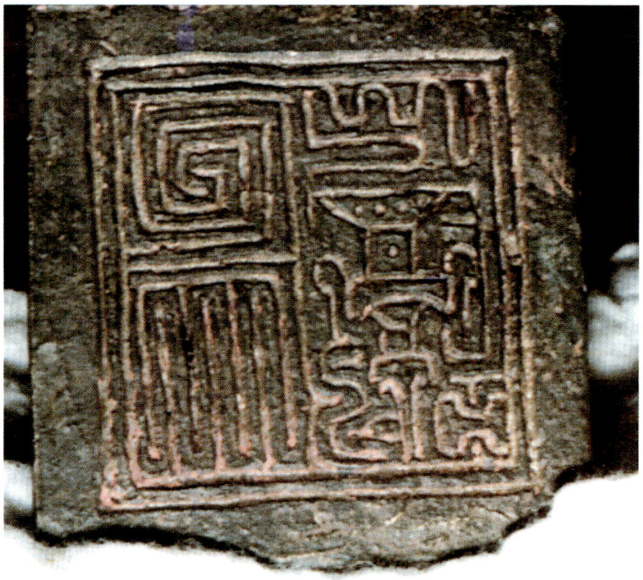

174 The pictorial inscription on the seal of the prince of Hsenwi. *(Private collection)*

the detail on wooden ceilings, pillars and walls that are gilded, painted and stencilled with gold and cinnabar. Finely carved guardian figures, mythical animals and birds, plants and flowers add to the faded grandeur. Many are lacquered and gilded, and inlaid with mother-of-pearl, semi-precious stones and coloured glass.

In the nineteenth century, the audience hall was viewed as the sacred centre of the palace. Minor princes and chiefs and senior officials were received there at the time of Buddhist New Year, when they swore allegiance to the senior prince. It was also at the hub of fiscal discussions. Tribute payments and taxes were negotiated there, and tribute exchange gifts presented. In times of war, the palace was at the core of operations, and in peacetime was a centre for diplomacy. The Shan rulers had for centuries maintained a sophisticated level of communication between principalities and with the major regional powers, China, Burma and Siam. Political and diplomatic emissaries were regular visitors and the exchange of letters between courts provides evidence of high levels of literacy and linguistic skill among the elite.[11]

It was the custom that all official correspondence be marked with an official seal. The princes owned two seals, one for personal correspondence and the other for bureaucratic use.[12] The personal seal of the prince of Muong Nai was about four inches high with an ivory handle in the shape of a pagoda. It was incised with a hare (symbol of the moon) surrounded by raised lettering that proclaimed he was ruler of Muong Nai and the neighbouring state of Kengtawng.[13] The personal seal of the Prince of Hsenwi, now the property of his descendants, has a handle in the shape of a Shan dragon. The inscription is pictorial with three distinct areas. Half the seal represents a pagoda-like structure, one quarter a crenellated pattern and the other a parallel zig-zag shape. These elements imitate the form of official Chinese seals although the iconography on the handle is an indigenous design.[14]

The Shan princes who were tributary to Burma received seals in the form of thin sheets of gold incised with the Royal Deeds of Grant. If a prince was sovereign over more than one state, he was granted additional sheets. The princes who paid tribute to China were issued with gold or silver plates stamped with Chinese script. The Wa chiefs, who lived in outlying districts, were granted incised silver plates that recognised their claims to land, and were some awarded Letters of Appointment (*sanad*) written in ink on parchment and sent from the Colonial Office in Calcutta.[15]

Official envoys and guests who visited the Shan courts were met with a degree of civility appropriate to their rank. Guest quarters in the larger palace compounds accommodated royal relatives, diplomats and friends from neighbouring states. Rooms could be separated into individual sleeping areas by hanging curtains as screens and servants prepared kapok-filled mattresses that were stored concertina-fashion during the day and set out on mats with bed linen at night. Until the end of the nineteenth century Shan palaces were built of wood or of bamboo and thatch. During the Colonial Era, building and carving techniques were adapted to incorporate advances in technology, particularly the use of precision tools. The British established a policy of forest conservation and imposed taxes on timber that made building in wood expensive. Brick, cement and plaster began to replace wood as the main construction materials. Maurice Collis noted that by the 1930s there were several types of Shan palace in existence. He described a "pure" [Shan] wooden style, a type where European elements had crept in, a fanciful "Shanesque" castle style and a modern style, built like an English country house.[16]

The American missionary William Clifton Dodd noted in 1905 that the old wooden palace of Keng Tung had been torn down and a brick building erected in its place, built by "Indiamen, of Indian architecture."[17] While it was under construction the prince lived in a temporary bamboo house. The new palace was built in a fusion of Indian and European design. The turrets, domes, towers and arched windows, and the official flag pole set in formal flower beds, was in a style favoured by architects of the Gothic Revival in India. Private palaces throughout the British Empire reflected a similar vision of imperial society as integrated, respected, time-honoured and hierarchical.[18] Meanwhile more modest colonial buildings were constructed in the

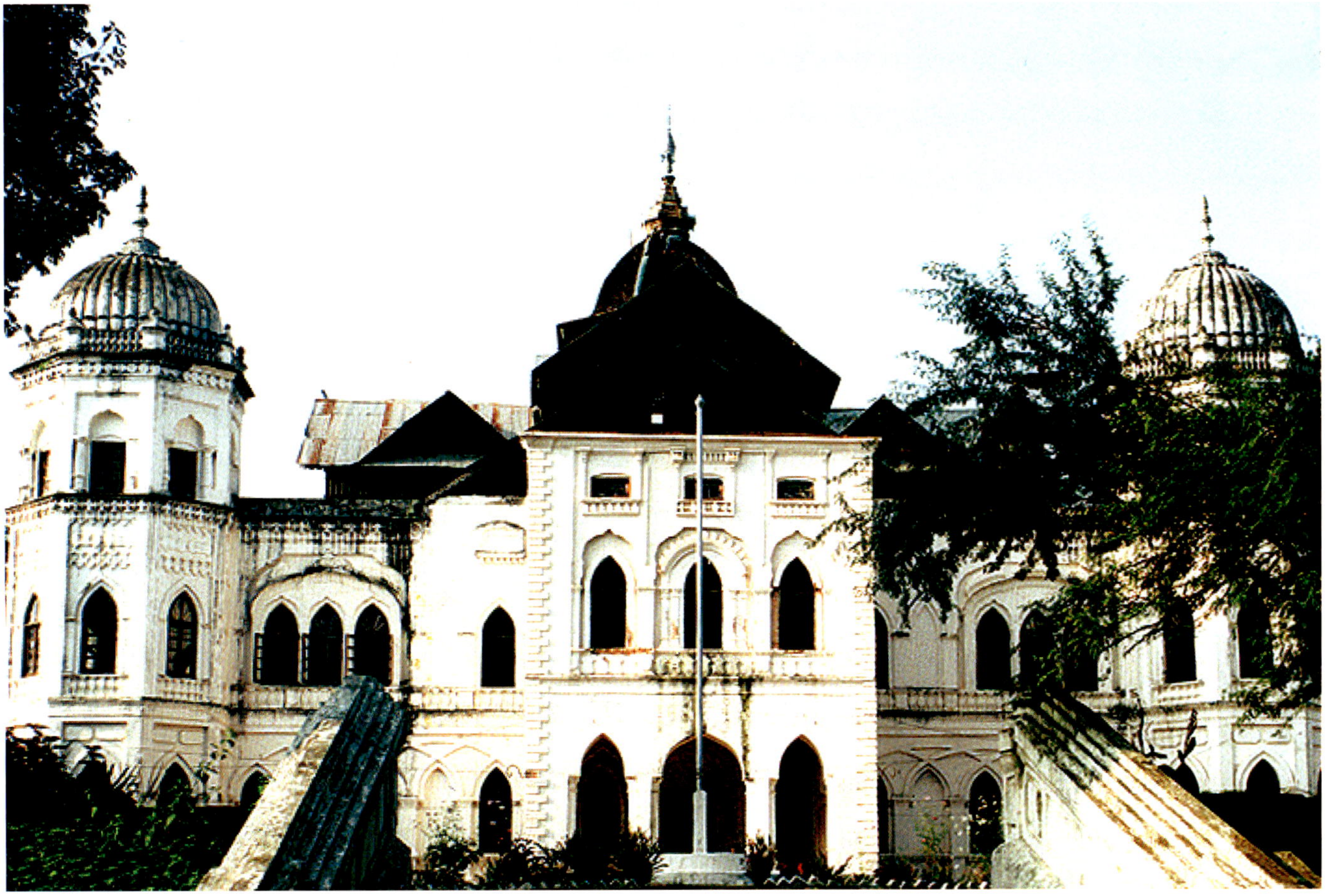

175 The royal palace of Keng Tung, destroyed on November 9th, 1991.

British administrative centre established in Taunggyi at the beginning of the twentieth century. Prince Sao Houn Hpa and his officials and tax collectors are seated in front of this practical form of colonial architecture. The brick building has a long veranda fronted with the ubiquitous colonnades (see fig. 11).

The annexation of Burma by the British and the exile of the king in the late nineteenth century brought an end to Burmese sumptuary laws and the Shan princes were no longer restricted in their choice of decoration and embellishment to their new buildings. The wealthy, with no connection to royalty, were also free to build large "palaces" without limitation beyond cost.

Some princes preferred to live in the old court style and stayed in their wooden palaces without the advantages of modern plumbing and bathroom facilities that were becoming fashionable with the younger generation. Visiting the palace of Laikha in the late 1920s, Maurice Collis wrote,

> *The Haw* [palace] *itself was a very old-fashioned building of wood and mat, a rambling place with the audience hall upstairs, the quaintest palace, like a fairy story. A rickety stairway led up to the hall...*[19]

Many princes moved to new buildings but maintained the old palaces, taking particular care of the audience halls that continued to be used on ceremonial occasions. Although Indo-European style affected architecture in the late nineteenth century, the process was not one-way. British administrators adopted Shan *tawmaw*, temporary buildings that were used to accommodate guests attending durbars and Buddhist religious festivals (see fig. 43). A circular bamboo frame was erected on wooden posts with a steep roof frame that was thatched and a bamboo or wooden planked floor was laid above ground level. The exterior walls were of bamboo and woven matting and a veranda might be added to create extra space. The interior could be divided with bamboo screens or curtains depending on the number of guests it was intended to house. For major assemblies and festivals, a number of *tawmaw* were assembled to provide sleeping accommodation, meeting halls, kitchens and a building for entertainment that might include theatre, puppet shows or Shan boxing.

A *tawmaw* intended for ritual use often had wall hangings and curtains hung at intervals from the frame in place of bamboo and matting walls. The curtains could be tied back so that visitors could observe the rituals. When privacy was needed, the curtains were drawn. Maurice Collis described a funeral ceremony in the state of Muong Mit that involved the construction of a number of *tawmaw*.

> *I first noticed an elaborately roofed house of bamboo; then over to the right I saw a circular building of the same materials which made me think of a Mongol's tent, some chieftain's yurt from the steppes of Tartary. My companion told me that this was the Ti-pyu-Yon or Hall of the White Umbrellas, in which the body of the sawbwa* [prince] *lay in state... The guest*

houses or tawmaw were along the a section of the circumference, forming a crescent on the northern side.[20]

Later when he was shown his accommodation in a *tawmaw* Collis wrote,

> *You reached the little verandah by a short flight of steps. Inside was a sitting room and two bedrooms, sufficiently furnished and fitted with electric light. The floor was of split bamboo, very springy under the feet. There was a ceiling of white cotton cloth… The house, being just built had the clean smell of fresh wood. It was a house that would last without repairs for two years, and had probably cost ten pounds… We were staying for three nights. On our departure it would be taken down and the materials sold… The Shans are lucky people to have bamboo and a climate which together make it pleasant to live in a ten pound house.*[23]

British administrators frequently used *tawmaw* when they were travelling to remote areas to meet with the Shan rulers and their officials. Sir George Scott took many photographs of these buildings, used when he was on tour. They were more comfortable than tents and when they were no longer needed they could be dismantled and the building materials sold locally.

The use of wooden audience halls for major events, including the Oath of Allegiance Ceremony continued well into the twentieth century, long after the princes had moved to modern buildings. Recalling the tribute ceremonies held at the court of Keng Tung, Nel Adams (Sao Noan Oo) has written:

> *Grandfather would preside here* [in the Audience Hall] *twice a year when district headmen came to pay tribute… The eastern corner of the room was reserved for shrines of Buddha and figures of angels where fresh food, water and flowers were offered as a thanksgiving.*[24]

On such occasions the senior prince was seated on a gilded couch placed under a canopy with courtiers and family in attendance. The canopy, symbol of protective forces, was built with a bamboo or wooden frame. Stretched over it was a panel of plain or printed silk with a decorative flounce or fringed border. At floor level, the sacred space around the gilded couch was marked by a set of turned railings, gilded and painted with cinnabar. There are written accounts, drawings and photographs of encounters with foreigners that took place in this setting. When Captain McLeod entered the presence of the prince of Keng Tung, he wrote,

> *The Prince of Keng Tung was reclining on a low gilt couch that had been placed in front of the throne and in attendance were a group of guards holding swords in gilt scabbards. The prince's two eldest sons were seated on the ground to his right and senior officers were ranked in lines on each side.*[23]

In 1867 the prince of Muong You granted an audience to members of the French Mekong Exploration Commission who were accompanied by the French artist Louis Delaporte. He sketched the meeting held in the audience hall and portrayed the prince reclining on a couch leaning against embroidered triangle-shaped cushions, with a large rectangular canopy suspended over his head. The French delegation sat on a large rug on the floor in front of the prince (see chapter two, fig. 40).

The Shan Palace Museum, Yawnghwe has a gilded couch, circa 1860, in its collection, and it is labelled as belonging to the Prince of Yawngwhe. It has a rectangular frame carved with repeat floral and leaf patterns that are gilded and inlaid with mica and coloured glass. A rectangular wooden rim, painted with cinnabar and gold, provides a frame for the mattress. The headboard is carved and gilded and the pedestal feet take the form of arched dragons (*naga*).

176 Exterior of the Shan Palace Museum, Yawnghwe, formerly the royal palace.

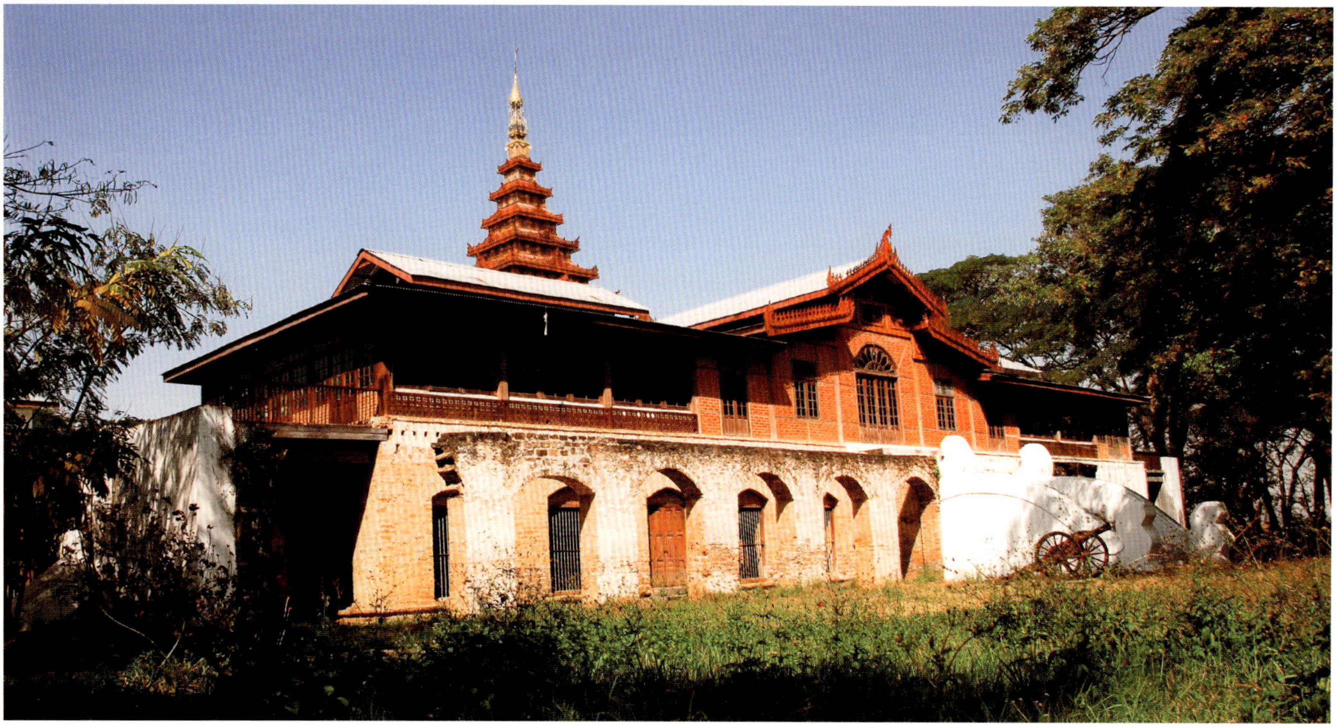

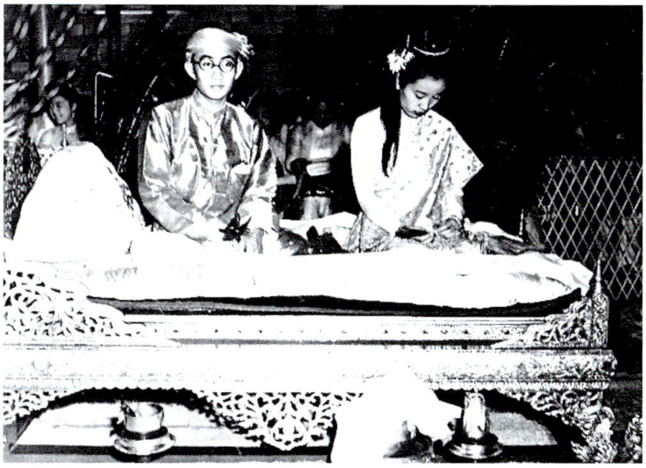

177 The wedding of Prince Sao Hsi Hseng Hpa of Yawnghwe, son of Sao Shwe Thaike, to Princess Sao Shwe Ong of Hsenwi, 1948.

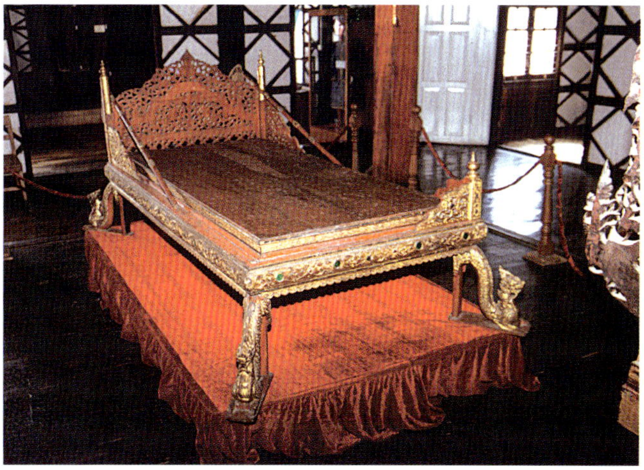

178 A couch used by the prince of Muong Yai, northern Shan States, circa 1900.

An official photograph taken in the audience hall of the prince of Hsenwi shows Sao Hom Hpa Long seated on an ornate couch under a large canopy suspended from the ceiling (see fig. 163). He is leaning against a triangular cushion. Behind him is the magnificent pedestal throne of Hsenwi, which is set in front of a pair of gilded latticework doors with an ornate carved and gilded portal. Seated at the feet of the prince are his sons, Prince Yape Hpa Long to his right and Prince Hman Hpa Kyemong to the left. His two younger sons, Prince Pyem Hpa and Prince Kyan Hpa, are seated to the side. White silk umbrellas with tiered flounces are visible between gilded, stencilled and inlaid teak pillars. An eye-catching feature of many audience halls was a large pedestal throne that on ceremonial occasions was placed behind the gilded couch. In the nineteenth century, King Bagyidaw (1819-1837) had ruled that senior Shan princes were allowed to display, but not sit on the pedestal thrones in their audience halls. The designs were modelled on a Burmese throne, referred to as a "Lion Throne." It was a tall pedestal, shaped like an hourglass, with a wide wooden base and tiered layers that narrowed gradually to the centre and then widened out to form a platform. The hourglass shape was intended as a representation of two triangles, one symbolising fire and the other signifying water, that together expressed the role of the king as Lord of Destruction (fire) and Lord of Creation (water).[24] Each tier of the pedestal was carved and gilded with floral, leaf and flame motifs and inset with mother-of-pearl, semi-precious stones and cut glass. The platform was also gilded. The pedestal stood in front of a pair of raised iron latticework doors that were gilded and set with rectangular and diamond shaped glass panels. A gilded wooden portal, carved with mythological animals and guardian figures, set amid scallops, scrolls and floral and leaf patterns, framed the doors. They were raised above ground level so that they opened at the level of the platform. On ceremonial occasions the king of Burma ascended a concealed staircase at the back. He entered onto the platform and was seated on silk cushions and leant for support on stiff triangular or square-shaped pillows, embroidered with silver and gold metal thread.

When the British explorer Captain McLeod visited the palace of Keng Tung in 1837, he saw a copy of the Burmese Lion Throne in the audience hall and described it as "in Ava

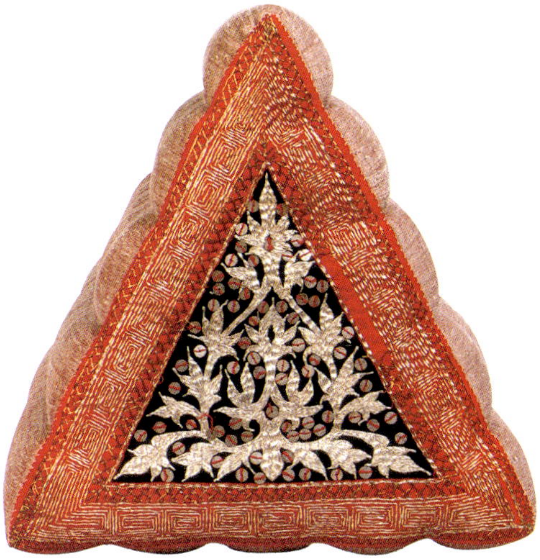

179 A triangular shaped cushion used as armrests. (Collection of Khun Duangjit Thaveesri, Chiang Mai)

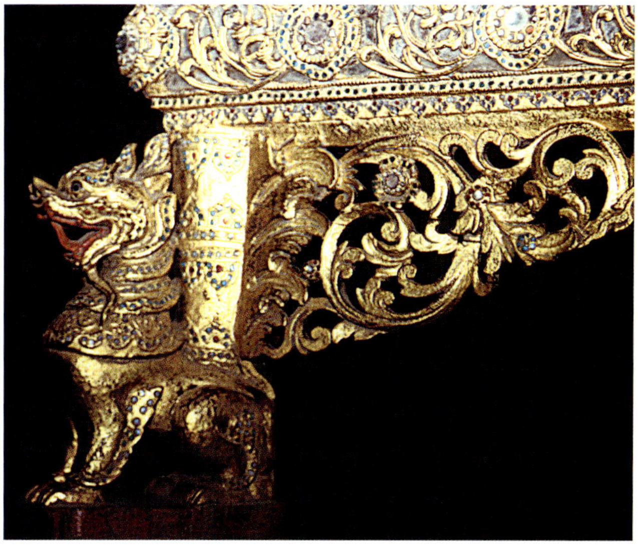

180 The lion foot of a gilded couch. Shan Palace Museum, Yawnghwe.

style." It was standing in the corner behind a set of turned railings.[25] During the reign of King Mindon (1853-1878) who moved his court to Mandalay, Lion Thrones listed as gifts to senior Shan princes were described as "in Mandalay style." They were issued in accordance with sumptuary laws.

Although there was a Burmese edict preventing the Shan princes from sitting on a Lion Throne, evidence suggests that it was occasionally ignored. The prince of Hsenwi took Maurice Collis to see the throne in his audience hall and showed him the concealed steps at the back leading up to the latticework doors through which he said he passed to sit on the platform.[26] Interestingly a senior consort might occasionally have joined the prince, although this was not normal etiquette.[27] Writing of the situation in the state of Muong Mit, Maurice Collis stated:

> *There are certain state occasions when, dressed in crown and royal robes and wearing the regalia, he sits there with his Mahadevi. One of these occasions is called a Kadaw-pwé or the Ceremony of Obeisance, when the state officials and the smaller country lords, such as Myosas and Hengs, assemble in the hall… The throne room* [audience hall] *had…six gilded pillars and the throne sparkled with coloured glass.*[28]

The throne described by Collis as "sparkling with coloured glass" was produced by Shan artisans and is similar to the throne of the prince of Keng Tung, now on display at the Museum of the Shan Chiefs in Yawnghwe. It has a wide base inset with rectangles of opaque white glass, and the tiers above are set with multi-coloured glass cut in geometric shapes and arranged in repeat patterns. The middle tiers have narrow bands of multi-coloured and opaque glass in floral patterns set between rectangular bands of opaque glass. The tier immediately below the platform has multi-coloured glass and opaque glass arranged in floral and curling leaf patterns. This type of inlay was also used to decorate pillars and altars in the Shan monasteries, for religious furniture such as monk's chairs and pulpits and for smaller items such as fan holders and stands for Buddha images. Although the days of producing regalia for royalty are long gone, artisans continue to make beautiful objects for the monasteries (see chapter seven).

In the late nineteenth century, some Shan princes and their consorts were photographed while seated on gilded chairs. Writing in 1904, William Clifton Dodd described an Oath of Allegiance Ceremony he attended in the audience hall of the palace of Keng Tung. The Prince was wearing his state robes and was seated on a high-backed chair which, according to Dodd, had been passed down through generations of rulers.[29] This was probably the chair described in the Keng Tung Chronicle as:

> *four cubits high, gilded and decorated with gems; two deva images each shouldering a sword were at the foot…*[30]

181 A gilded royal throne in the Shan Palace Museum, Yawnghwe.

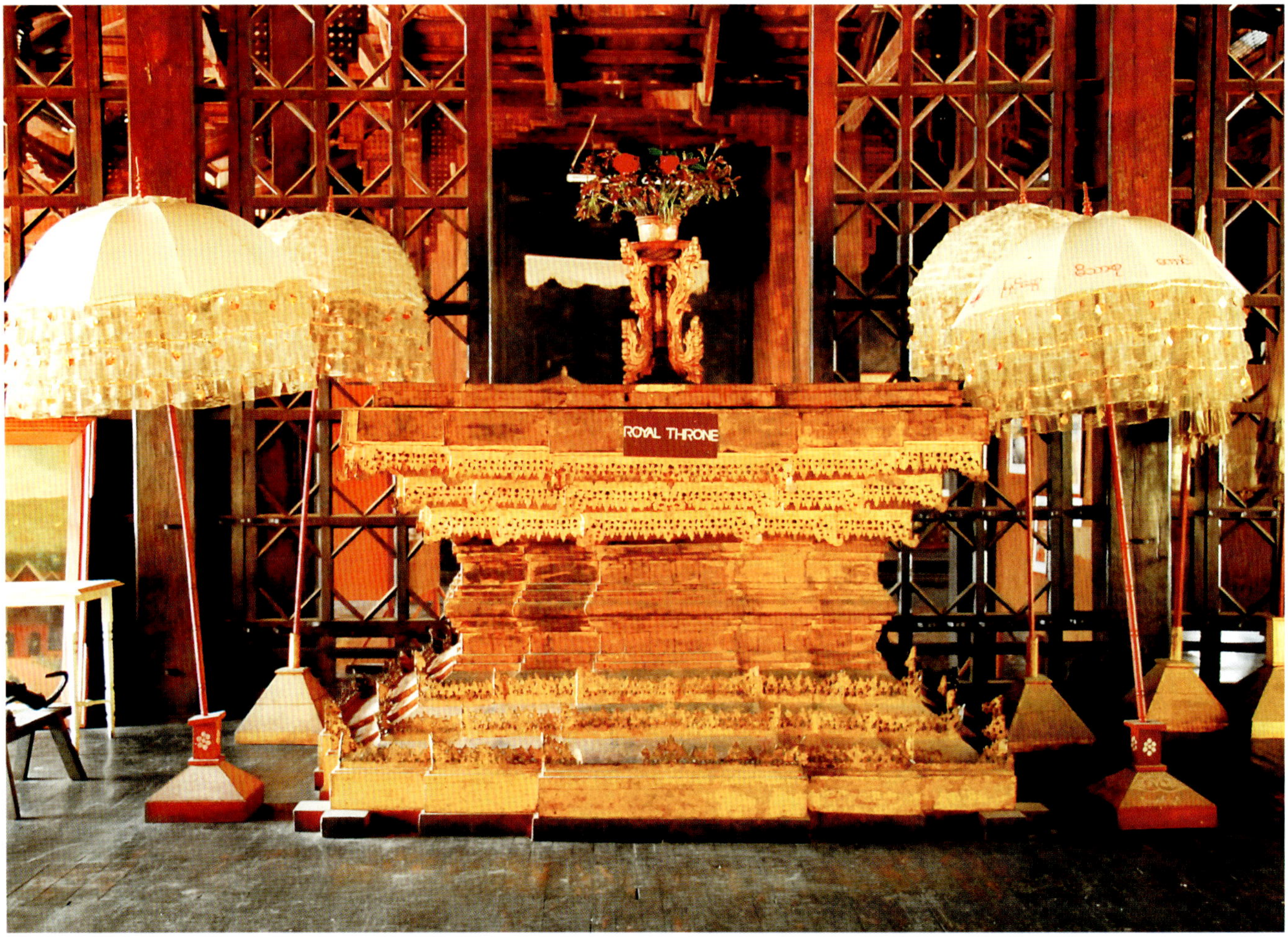

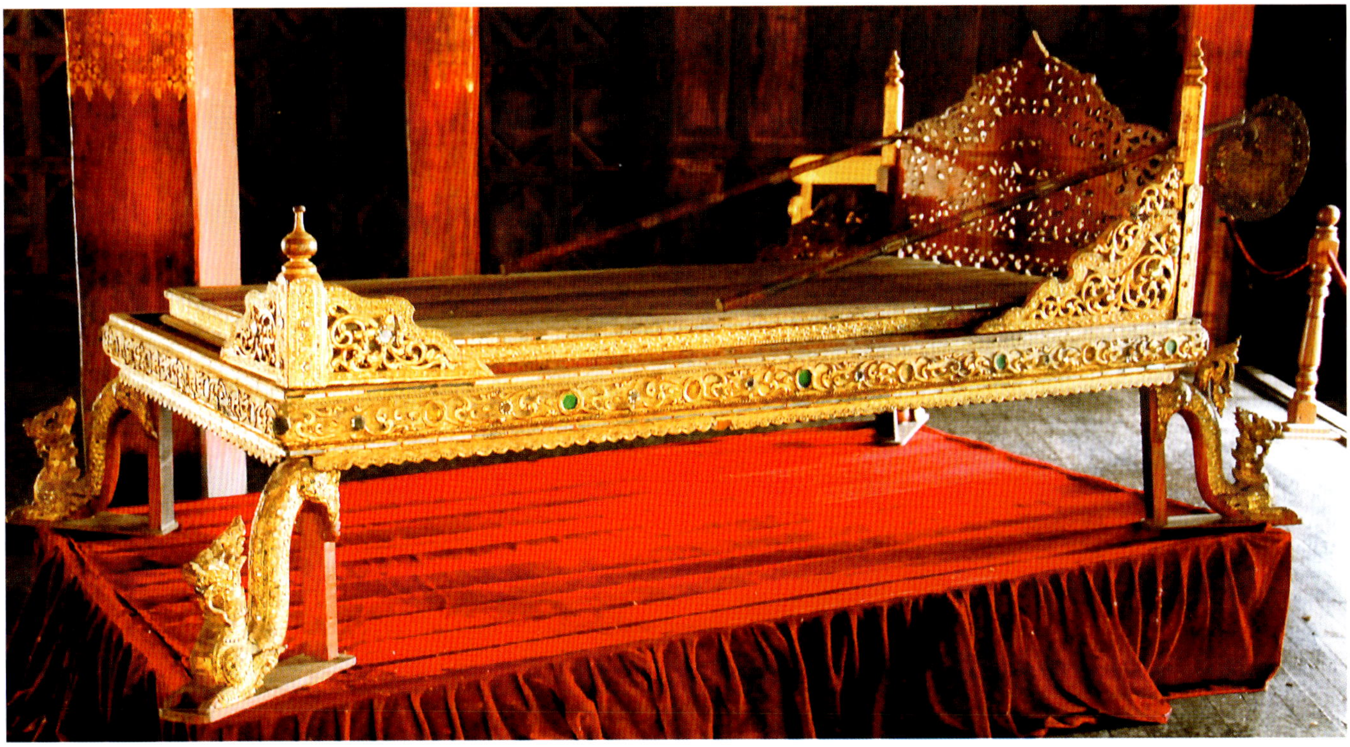

182 A gilded couch inlaid with coloured glass, Shan Palace Museum, Yawnghwe.

Prince Sao Ohn Kya (1893-1938) and his chief consort *mahadevi* Sao Thunandar (see chapter four, fig. 131) were photographed while seated on similar gilded chairs, the backs carved with *deva* figures and elaborate scrolls. The armrests are in the form of *makara*, mythological creatures with the heads of elephants and the bodies of scaled dragons. According to local mythology, the *makara* were emissaries between earth and the realm of the gods, and at the time of death accompanied the soul on its flight to Tavatimsa Heaven.[31] The front legs of the chairs are supported on lions (*singha*) symbols of strength. They are positioned in front of a Lion Throne.

The gilded chairs in this photograph are similar to those on display at the Shan Palace Museum, Yawnghwe. One sample is dated as early twentieth century and is described as the property of the former prince of Muong Yai. It has a high back carved with a peacock in the centre of a lotus medallion. The latter is set among delicate leaf and flame scrolls with side rows of winged celestial beings (*deva*), their hands joined in prayer. This delicate carving is set above heavy bands of scrolling and inter-locking flame patterns. The side wings are carved with tiered guardian figures supported by stylised trees, branches and leaves. Floral and leaf tendrils have been carved around the edge of the seat and on the armrest supports. The armrests are carved with scaled and winged dragons with curling tails (*makara*). The front legs are supported on gilded lions exposing sharp teeth through gaping jaws, and the sturdy back legs are plain gilded wood. The carving on the back, and on the armrests is light and full of movement, in contrast to the heavy carving on the legs. Lacquer mixed with cinnabar, applied to the seat, provides a rich, red contrast to the gilding.

The museum has a second gilded chair. The back is carved with a panel of floral, scroll and leaf designs set above rows of turned railings. A square panel of velvet acts as a backrest. The armrests are carved with winged and scaled *makara*, their sinuous legs thrusting forwards as if in flight, and their thin elongated bodies supported by short back legs. Elephants with large tusks hold up the front chair legs and the back legs are animals with fish heads and claw feet. The seat of the throne is covered in silk velvet. Interestingly, the National Museum in Yangon owns a similar carved and gilded chair that is described as the property of a Palaung *saohpa*, probably Hkun Hsang of Tawng Peng who was appointed in 1877, under the patronage of King Mindon of Burma.

Those granted audiences with the Shan princes often describe the sumptuous regalia they saw displayed in the audience halls. Francis Garnier, member of the French Mekong Exploration Commission wrote of his meeting with the prince of Muong You:

> *He was a young man of twenty-six with a distinguished face and infinitely gracious in manner... At his feet were the insignia of his rank, i.e. his sabres and richly chiselled golden vases.*[32]

The artist Delaporte included the regalia of the prince of Muong You in a drawing he made of this encounter. The prince is seated amid a set of ceremonial vessels. A Buddha image and some manuscripts, and an assortment of vessels and containers are arranged on the shelves above his head. Ceremonial swords and spears are displayed on racks near two folded umbrellas and large elephant tusks are arranged on the floor (see chapter two, fig. 40). Weaponry was often dispayed in the audience hall and Henri d'Orleans described some trophy flint and matchlocks he saw arranged in patterns on the walls of the palace of Hkamti Long. Maurice Collis noticed the difference between modern weaponry in practical use in the Shan States in the

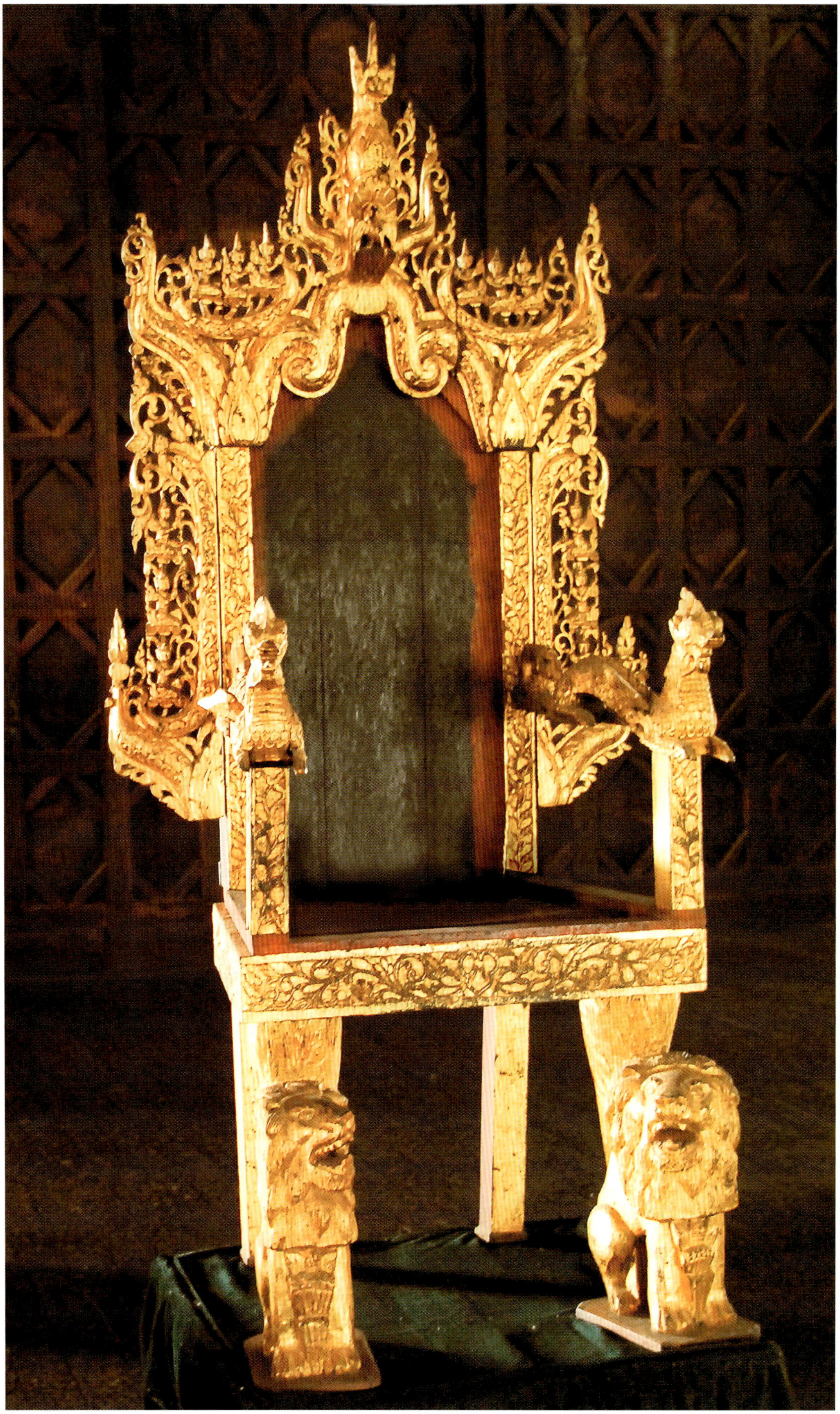

183 A Shan royal throne of carved and gilded wood. Shan Palace Museum, Yawnghwe.

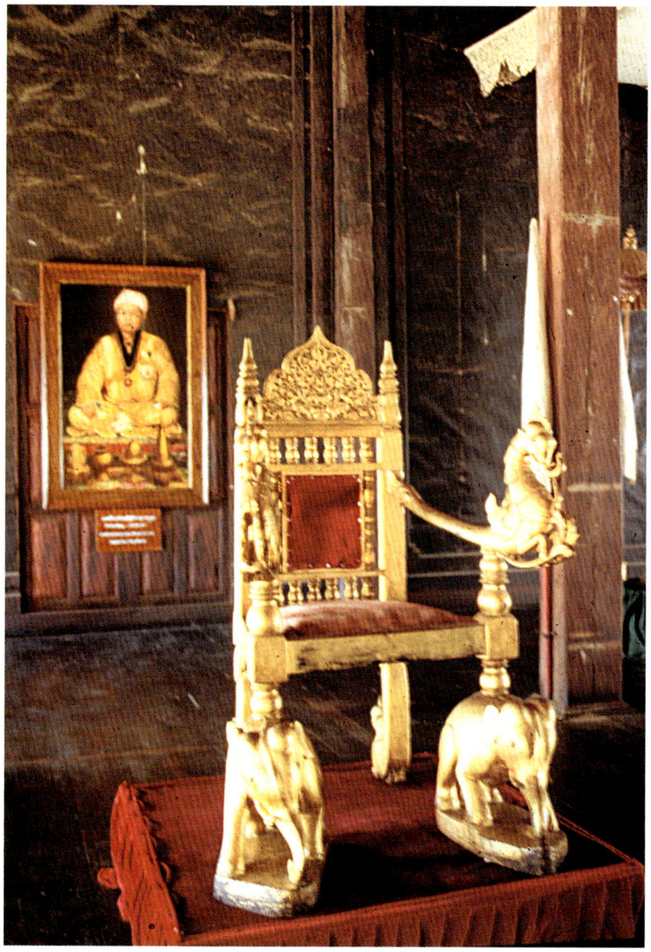

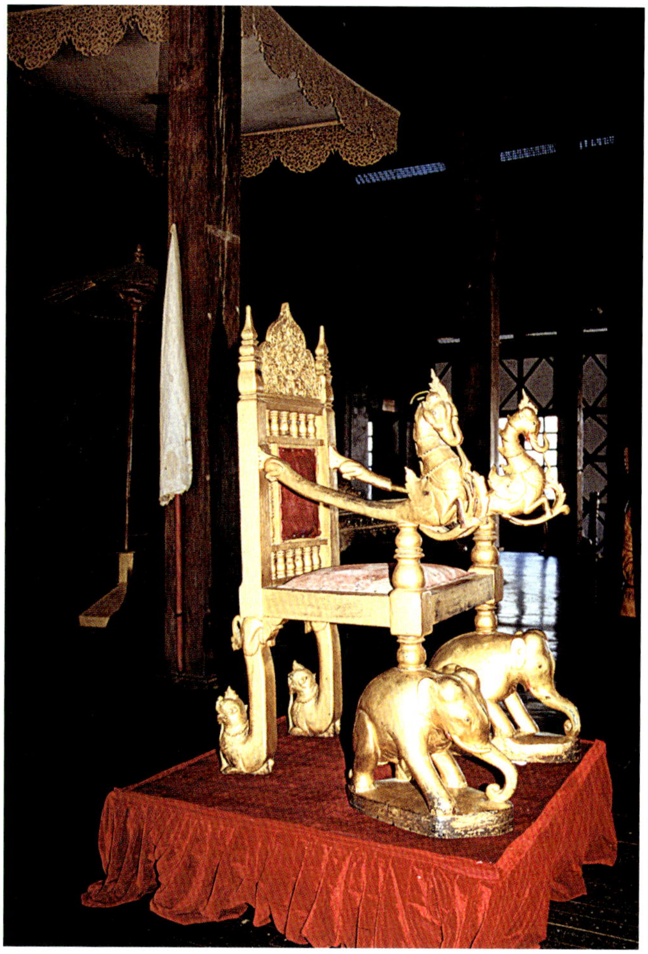

184 and **185** Two views of a carved and gilded wooden throne. Shan Palace Museum, Yawnghwe.

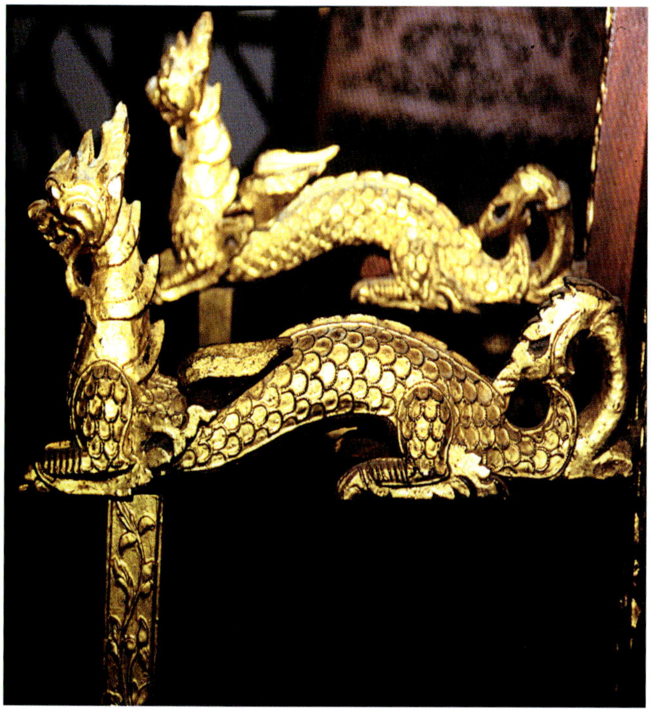

186 The arm rests of the throne in fig. 183.

early twentieth century and the swords and muskets kept for ceremonial occasions.

> *Round the sides of the hall were elephant tusks and gongs, gilded spears and halberds of the guard for use in royal procession, for the guard is now armed with rifles and revolvers. Ceremonial swords had embossed silver and ivory handles and the blades were made of plain or embossed silver or of iron. The silver scabbards were embossed with repoussé work and embellished with inlay of semi precious stones and mother-of-pearl.*[33]

Ceremonial umbrellas with gilded handles were allocated according to sumptuary laws. Prince Mahakhanan of Keng Tung (1781-1857) received from King Bodawhpaya of Burma (1782-1819), and later from his heir King Bagyidaw (1819-1837), four white umbrellas with gold handles and ferrules. The silk shades were decorated with pendants shaped like the leaves of a bodhi tree and each umbrella had a three-tiered fringe.[34] Although sumptuary laws helped to ensure that Burmese rules of hierarchy were observed at the Shan courts, they were abolished following the exile of King Thibaw. The Shan resorted to their own ranking system. Prince Ohn Kya (1893-1938) of Hsipaw and his *mahadevi* Sao Thunandar (see fig. 131) displayed two impressive silk umbrellas with gilded handles. The prince of Hsenwi displayed four. The shades were tiered and fringed and festooned with metal bodhi tree motifs. The prince of Putao (see fig. 72 chapter three), who was lower in the established hierarchy, was entitled to a plain silk umbrella with a gilded handle, while his senior consort merited a

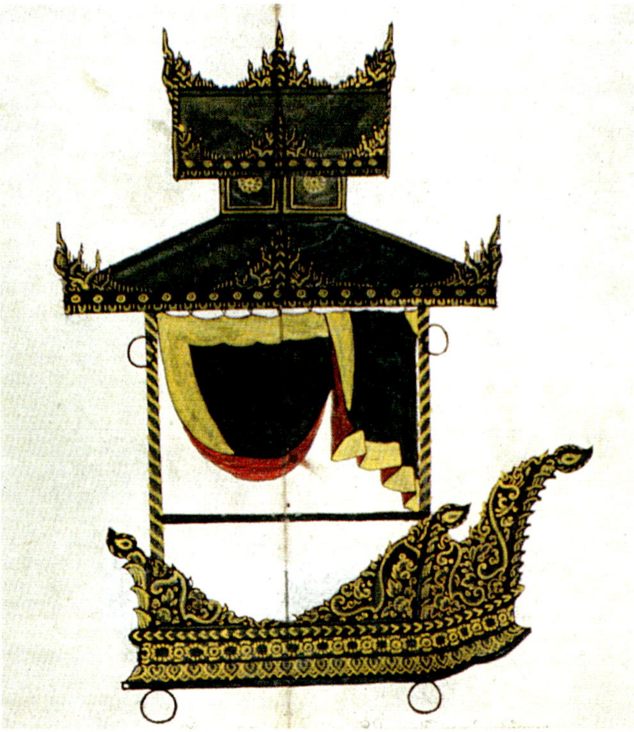

187 A roofed palanquin illustrated in a manuscript documenting sumptuary laws. *(Victoria and Albert Museum, access. No. IM 320-1924)*

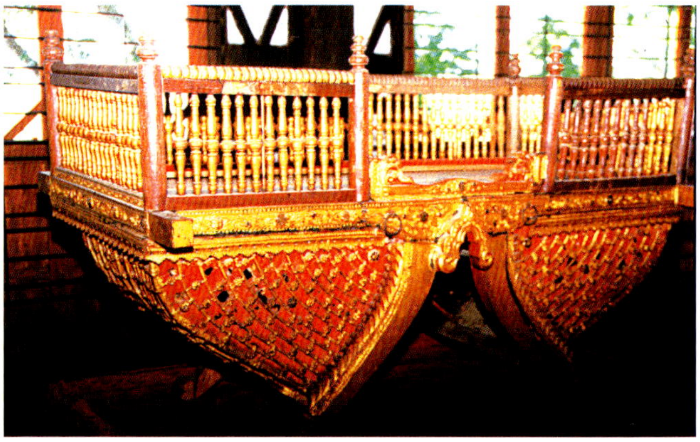

188 A lacquered and gilded Shan howdah. Shan Palace Museum, Yawnghwe.

gilded paper umbrella. Some administrators (*myosa*) were photographed with up to six gilded umbrellas. As a senior ruler, Prince Hom Hpa of Hsenwi (1902-1963) was entitled to four silk, and ten gold umbrellas. When they were open and on display in the palace, the large silk umbrellas were placed in painted and gilded wooden stands, some carved with guardian figures or mythological animals.

When a Shan prince led a procession out of doors, the umbrellas were always carried by attendants. If he was riding in an elephant howdah, the umbrellas were fitted with extra long handles. For rites performed during the period of Buddhist Lent, the number of umbrellas was reduced and the designs were kept simple. When the prince of Keng Tung lead the annual Lenten bathing ritual, held at hot sulphur springs outside the city, only one satin umbrella was held over him in the procession. He spent five days in retreat and on the journey back to the city he was dressed in white robes and accompanied by the same satin umbrella. However, when he reached the main city gate of Keng Tung, the procession halted, and he changed into state robes and entered the town with his full allocation of tiered silk umbrellas. The missionary William Dodd witnessed the return of the prince.

> *The Chow Fa of Keng Tung the Khun* [Tai Khoen] *chief rides a very richly caparisoned elephant. His state robes are entirely cloth of gold, and his pagoda-like coronet or tiara is also covered in gold...*[35]

Describing a similar ceremony at the end of Lent in Hsipaw, Sir George Scott wrote:

> *The state has an annual festival when the sawbwa, his son and family ride in state on elephants with his officials processing in front. The prince financed a display of fireworks which he attended surrounded by the palace guard and his umbrella carriers and displaying his regalia of office, including betel boxes, spittoons and water vessels.*[36]

When the Shan rulers travelled abroad, to the court of Burma, or in British times to Calcutta and Delhi, state robes and regalia were packed and taken with them. In audiences with the king at the Burmese court, the princes were seated in strict order of precedence with their regalia displayed in front of them.

At the Delhi Durbar, organised by the British in 1903, the embossed and repoussé silver betel boxes, silver spittoons, food containers and stands, ceremonial offering bowls and water vessels, clay pots and lacquer bowls were included in the formal photographs of the Shan princes and princesses (see fig. 86). At the Durbar, the princes also took part in a brilliantly staged procession, riding in gilded elephant howdahs with attendants walking in front carrying the state regalia.

The howdah of the *saohpa* of Yawnghwe (circa 1890s) is on display in the Shan Palace Museum, Yawnghwe, and is typical of the style produced in the nineteenth century. It has a wooden frame with turned gilded railings around the wooden seat. The base is lacquered, gilded and inset with semi-precious stones and coloured glass. The elephants were also fitted with elaborate animal trappings that included lacquered and gilded leather head-covers set with pearls, rubies and semi-precious stones. On less grand occasions, the princes used ponies or, as Maurice Collis noted, they travelled, like the *myosa* of Muong Hsu, in a palanquin pulled by bullocks.[37] Some were designed with poles that could be carried by male porters. According to the Keng Tung Chronicle, King Bodawpaya of Burma (1782-1819) established specifications for palanquins and animal trappings.[38] A Hsenwi manuscript relating to sumptuary laws includes an illustration of the type of covered palanquin permitted to the Shan princes. It has a dome-shaped roof and carved wooden panels on the base. There are curtains draped over the frame that could be drawn to provide privacy.

When the princes lived in the old Shan palaces, most items of regalia were kept on permanent display in the audience halls. When they moved to more modern buildings, the regalia were either left in place with retainers keeping guard, or stored for safekeeping. Maurice Collis watched in the audience hall of the prince of Keng Tung while a group of retainers unpacked boxes of regalia in

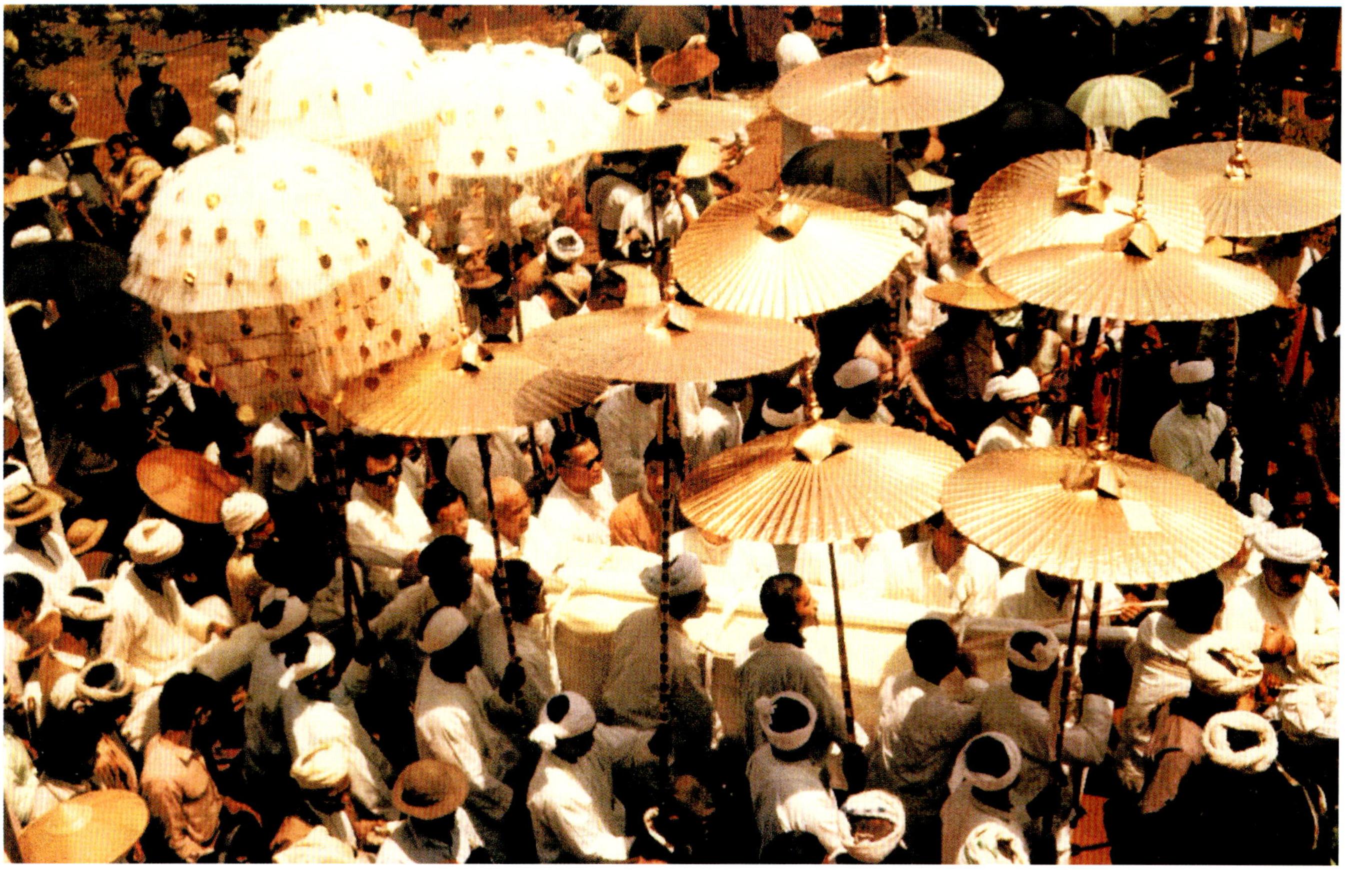

preparation for an Oath of Allegiance Ceremony. His account describes objects that had been passed down from generation to generation, including coronation robes, hats, gold slippers, swords and yak-tail whisks that can be identified in the photographs of the period.

> *We went to a room off the Hall of Audience, where they were being unpacked from boxes. The keeper and his assistants laid them out on carpets and explained to me the various pieces. I saw the Crown of Victory, the Victorious Sword, the Yak-tail whisk, the White Umbrella and the Golden Slippers… There were also a number of objects connected with state ceremonies, gold betel boxes, many swords with carved ivory handles and gold scabbards, caparisons and bells for horses and elephants, banners embroidered with dragons and magic circles, gilt umbrellas like mandarins' hats, a great jewelled belt and a pair of massive ear-rings. The coronation robes were also shown. The collection was of great interest. It recalled that the sawbwas* [saohpa] *of Kengtung* [Keng Tung] *were in practice kings as late as the nineteenth century, when, indeed they repulsed with their own troops three Siamese invasions…*[39]

The Shan princes commissioned indigenous artisans to produce and repair their regalia. They imported some precious raw materials, but a gold mine was in operation until 1850 in the Shan state of Hsamonghkham (Hsaimong) and silver was mined in Mawson and in Muong Lem. Metalworkers obtained some silver by melting down coins for recasting. The silver regalia of the prince of Hsenwi is displayed in the Burmese Gallery of the Green Centre of World Art, the Royal Pavilion Art Gallery and Museums, Brighton. The set consists of a silver chain of office (*tsaloe*), an embossed silver sword with an ivory handle, a silver scabbard, an embossed silver pipe, a set of repoussé silver

189 The funeral of Prince Hom Hpa of Hsenwi in 1963. Four silk umbrellas and ten gold umbrellas were held over the casket.

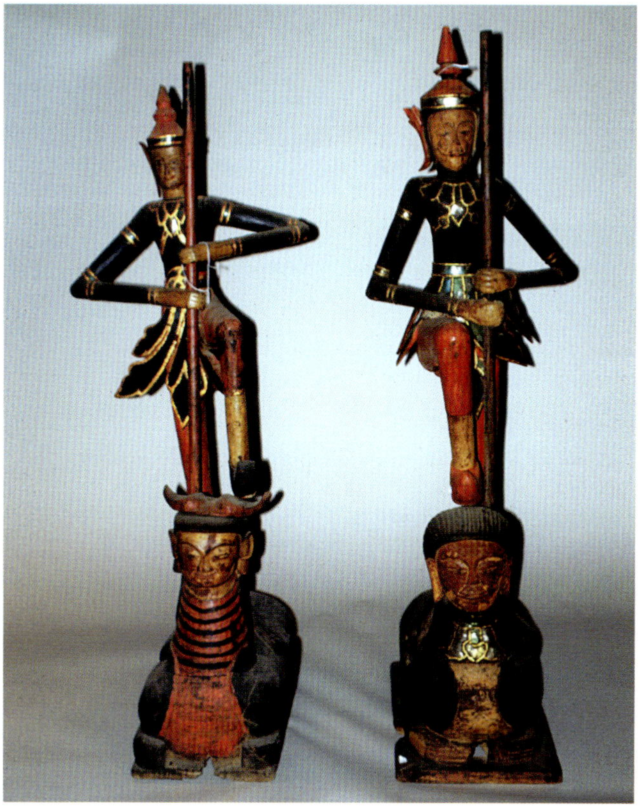

190 Umbrella holders in carved and painted wood. *(Private collection)*

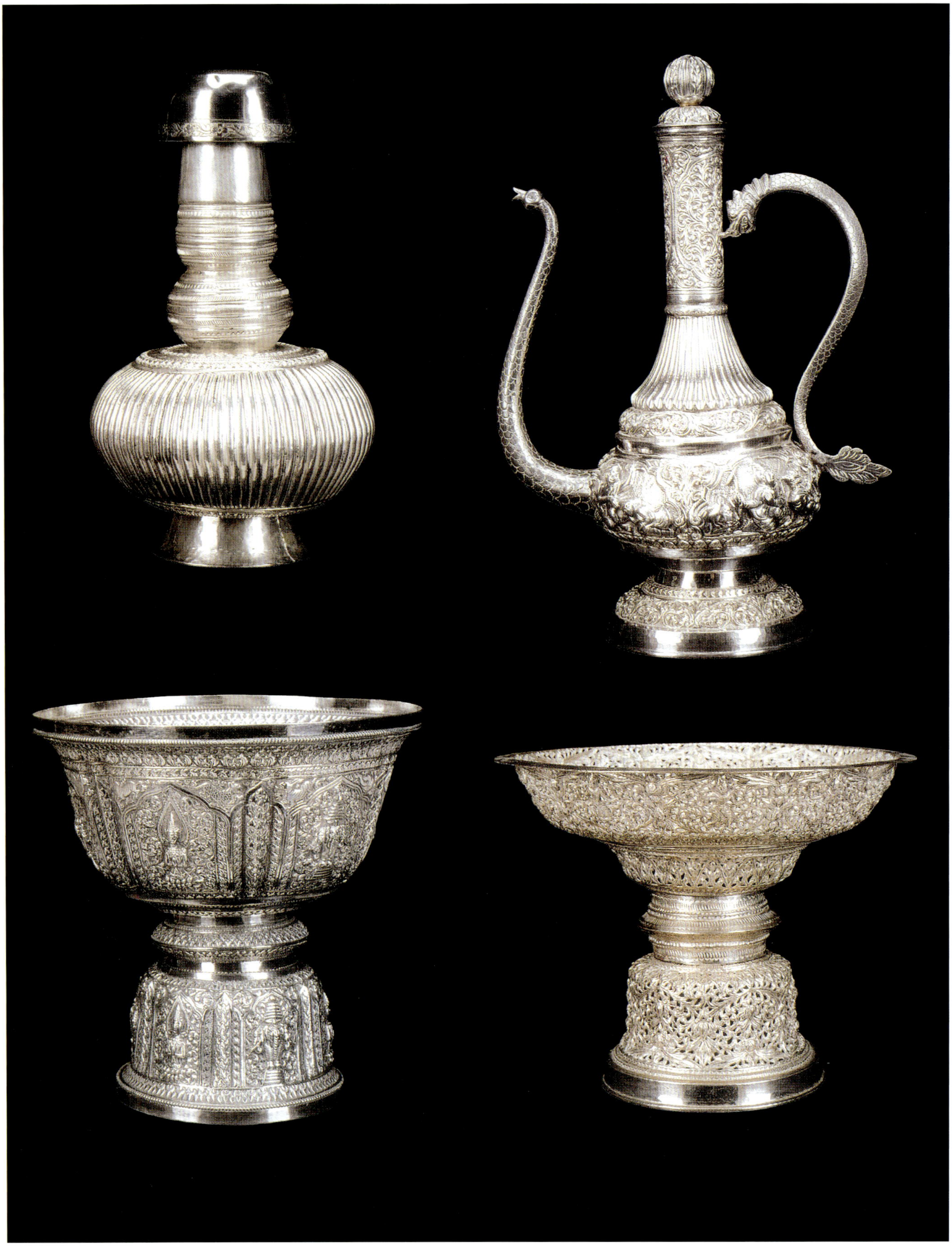

191 A set of ceremonial silver objects, probably made by silversmiths in Keng Tung. *(Private collection)*

containers, a silver spoon and an elaborate silver repoussé water bottle, a betel box set and the seal of the prince of Hsenwi.

Some items of Shan regalia were made of lacquer. Keng Tung, Muong Nai and Laikha were well-known centres of manufacture (see chapter six). The princes sent silver and lacquer ware as part of tribute payment and gifts to foreign dignitaries. They included trays, dishes, stem bowls and covers for food, rice containers, offering vessels, gift boxes, and betel boxes.

The Shan Palace Museum, Yawnghwe has a collection of Shan regalia that includes an elaborate food container with dragons (*naga*) supporting the base. The cover is dome-shaped and tapers to a spire at the pinnacle (see fig. 193). It is lacquered, gilded and inlaid with semi-precious stones, mother-of-pearl and coloured glass. The moulded lacquer decoration is in floral and leaf patterns. The collection also includes a lacquered and gilded woven-bamboo stand for a mirror and several gilded and lacquered manuscript chests.

The Shan princes also received regalia as part of the tribute exchange system. They were considered as important symbols of status and the Shan Chronicles include lists of the gifts given by foreign kings and princes. The Keng Tung Chronicle records,

> *Prince Mahakhanan* [of Keng Tung] *received as gifts from the King of Burma, a twelve-cornered gold pedestal tray and dishes studded with gems, a gold pedestal tray studded with gems, a pedestal tray studded with gems for pickled tea and a gold spittoon. He also received two twelve-cornered gold bowls studded with gems, a gold crown, a double-edged sword with a gold handle and a sheath studded with gems, a pair of gold sandals, a pair of fifteen strand sash-chains and swords wrapped in black velvet. The four white umbrellas had gold ferrules and decorative bodhi tree leaf motifs as pendants on the three-tiered fringe. There were four gilded umbrellas, four gilded palm-leaf fans, a gilded carriage, gilded rattan canes, four bull elephants, two cow elephants, two elephant head-cloths of gold threaded net, gold tassels for elephant trappings, a gilded drum-shaped chair. There was one red drum, a set of wind instruments and two Burmese oboes.*[41]

Gifts were also exchanged at the time of coronations, royal weddings and funerals. When the funeral ceremony of Prince Mahakhanan took place in Keng Tung, the king of Burma sent three pounds of gold bullion, a gold drinking cover, red and white sandalwood, a gold chain, a gold belt and rings, four glass bottles of perfume and twelve bolts of Benares cloth. He also donated sets of robes and utensils for the monks of Keng Tung. The prince of Muong Laem sent a horse, a silver bowl and silver bullion. The state of Keng Hung, Sipsong Pan Na contributed silver bullion, a horse, a silver bowl, a bolt of brocade, a ceremonial offering set and a silver pedestal tray. The Shan Chronicles record that Jenghaeng was at war with neighbouring states and could only afford a small amount of silver and ceremonial offering bowls. In the circumstances, the chronicles say, the gift was deemed acceptable. In return the prince of Keng Tung was obliged to provide exchange gifts to those who attended the funeral. The Burmese contingent who came from Ava and from the Burmese military station in Muong Nai, were presented with swords with silver sheaths, some woollen fabric, plaited and lacquered betel boxes, silver bullion and a food allowance for the journey home. The family of prince

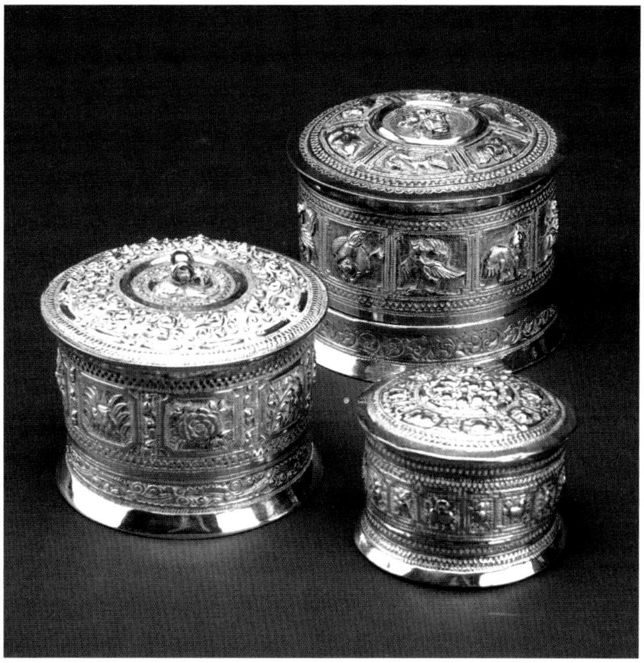

192 Silver betel boxes formed part of the Shan princes' regalia. *(Elephant House Collection)*

Mahakhanan distributed Benares silk and lacquered bamboo betel boxes to other dignitaries who attended the funeral rites.

As a senior Shan ruler the prince of Keng Tung sent substantial gifts when new princes in other states were anointed. The prince of Muong Laem received an elephant, a silver pedestal tray, a gold betel box, a plaited betel box and silver bullion. The prince of Keng Tung did not go personally to Muong Laem but sent court officials to present the gifts. When the prince of Keng Hung was anointed, the prince of Keng Tung sent a silver pedestal tray, a gold ceremonial vessel and a sword with a silver sheath.

The pageantry that accompanied all princely ceremonies continued well into the twentieth century, and is perhaps best captured in English by Maurice Collis who attended the funeral of the Prince of Muong Mit.

> *At the time of the funeral the princes who had come from Yawnghwe, Tawng Peng and Mong Pawn joined the Crown Prince of Mong Mit to pay their final respect to the deceased. The four, dressed in white mounted the dais and knelt by the coffin and paid their last respects. They descended and the princesses took their place, led by the new mahadevi and her medaw (mother-in-law). The four princes and four younger members of the royal family lifted the coffin from the catafalque and carried it from the Hall of White Umbrellas. Eight attendants bearing white umbrellas walked beside them. The procession was led by three elephants and by footmen dressed in the Mong Mit state livery of long red coats and hats. They bore the prince's insignia and gilded spears. There was a band of musicians playing what was described as "Music of Heaven" with Shan pipes, gongs and string instruments. A full moon rose as the procession made its way to the pyre. The eight princes circumambulated the pyre three times with attendants carrying the white umbrellas high in the air. They were shaped like lotus blossoms with handles of red lacquer and gold. A group of monks watched as the coffin was placed on the funeral*

pyre. The next day, the residuary bones were collected and placed in an earthen pot and enclosed in a gold casket wrapped in yellow velvet. The procession to the mausoleum involved a group of female attendants carrying trays with lacquer betel boxes, jars and tobacco. They were followed by men carrying regalia and dressed in crimson coats and tall spiked hats. Behind them came three elephants, the centre animal bearing an official seated in a howdah holding the casket containing the bones. A white umbrella was held over him and six attendants with white umbrellas walked at the side. A mahout dressed in a black velvet coat directed the elephant. At the back of the procession walked the eldest son of the deceased Prince of Mong Mit and the British Commissioner in a black mourning coat and grey hat. The casket was placed in a niche in the mausoleum.[42]

All the Shan princes maintained family mausoleums and the site in Keng Tung is behind a brick and cement wall in the centre of the city, close to the city spirit shrine. The last major Shan state funeral to take place in Hsenwi followed the death of Prince Hom Hpa, *saohpa* of Hsenwi (1902-1963). His embalmed body lay in state for one month and although the Burmese army imposed restrictions on travel, an enormous number of his subjects came to pay their last respects. On the day of his funeral, four white silk umbrellas festooned with golden bodhi leaves, and ten gold umbrellas, denoting the highest rank of royalty, were carried over the casket that was draped in white cloth. It was placed on a float formed in the shape of a mythical *hintha* bird covered with a metal, silvered roof with multiple tiers and spires. The central spire was gilded. Floral tributes were placed around the casket (see figs 196-99). The procession made its way from Lashio, capital of the Northern Shan states, to the state capital of Hsenwi where the family burial ground is situated, a distance of about thirty-two miles. Banner bearers, dressed in white, formed up to accompany the casket. The procession stopped many times on the long journey so that villagers could pay their last respects. When the cavalcade finally arrived at the family mausoleum, the casket was received by the monks and taken to the tomb where prayers were said and offerings made. Sao Yip Hpa, the eldest son of the *saohpa,* had returned from exile for the funeral, and he led the final ceremony of respect. The tomb was then sealed. Monasteries throughout the state of Hsenwi, and in other states held simultaneous ceremonies for the soul of the *saohpa.* Since that funeral there have been no Shan royal ceremonies permitted by the Burmese military government.

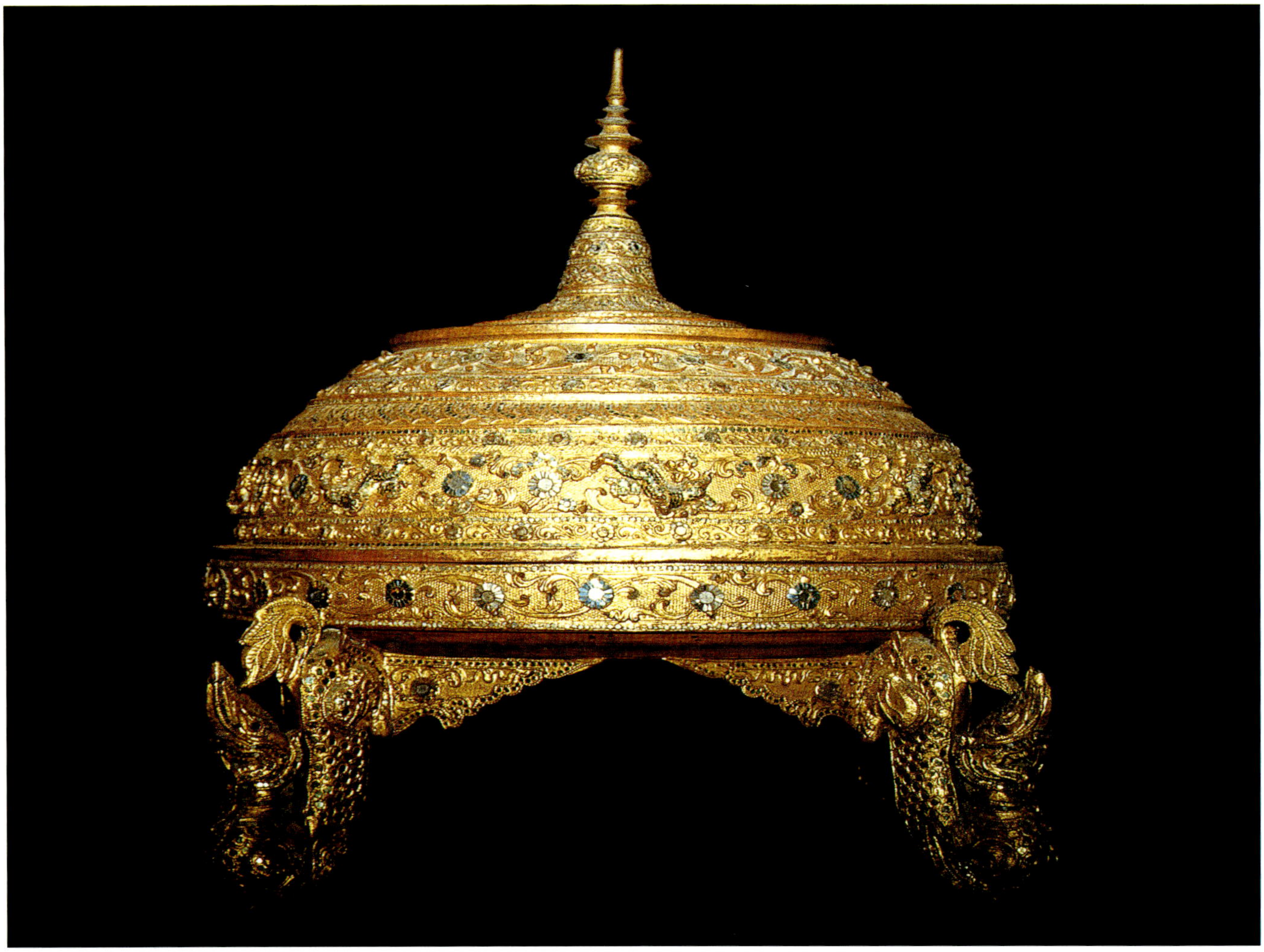

193 A lacquered and gilded food cover. Shan Palace Museum, Yawnghwe.

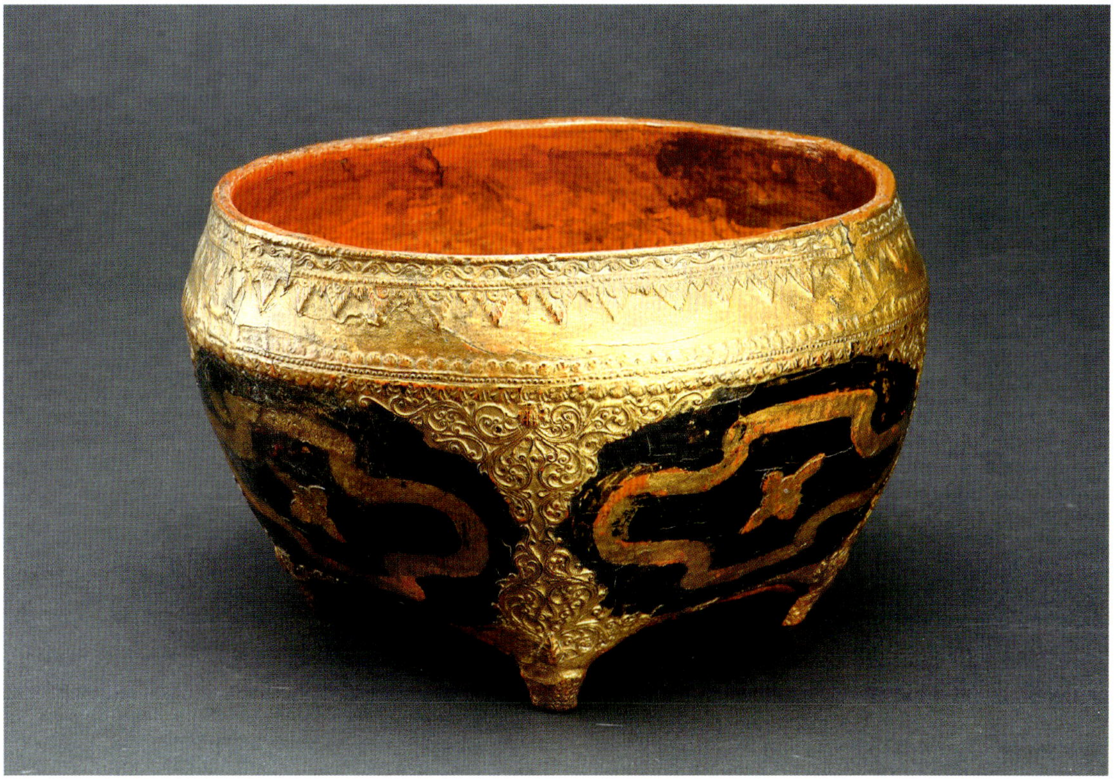

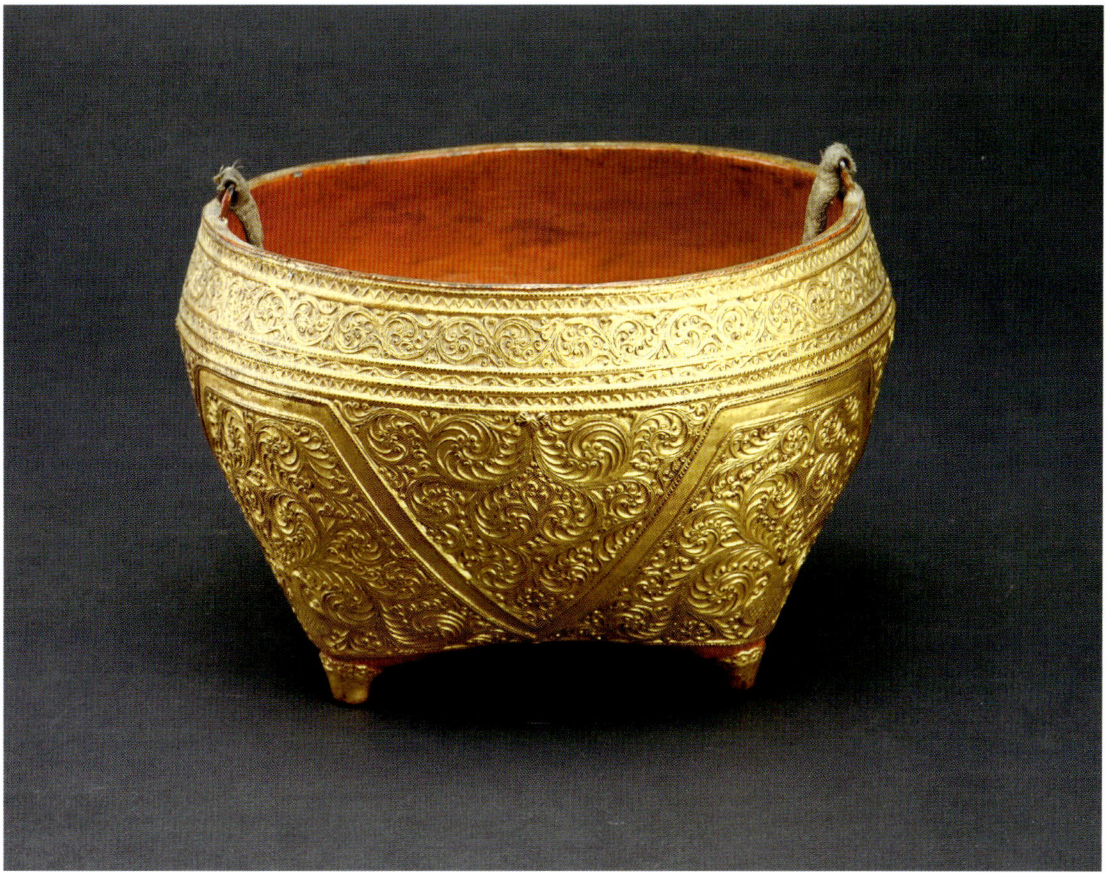

194-95 Two lacquered and gilded bowls, Shan States. *(Elephant House collection)*

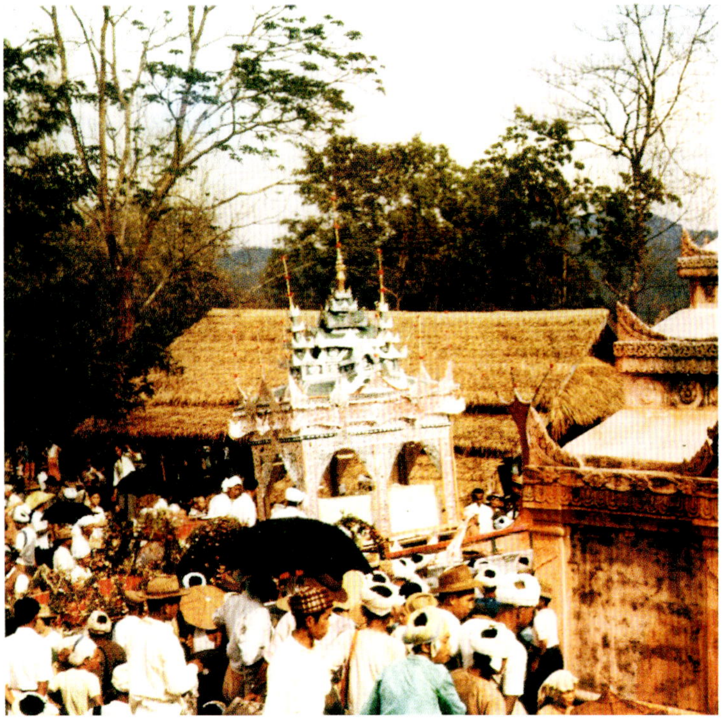

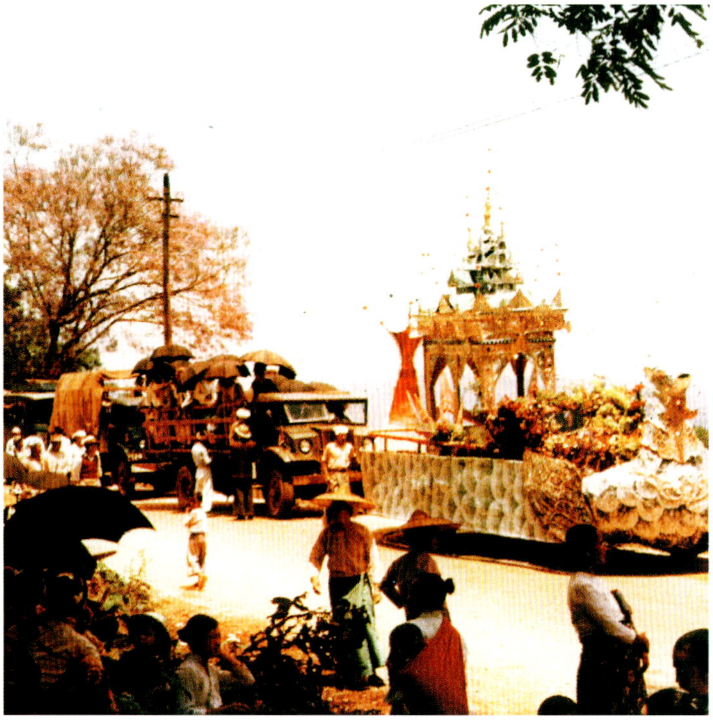

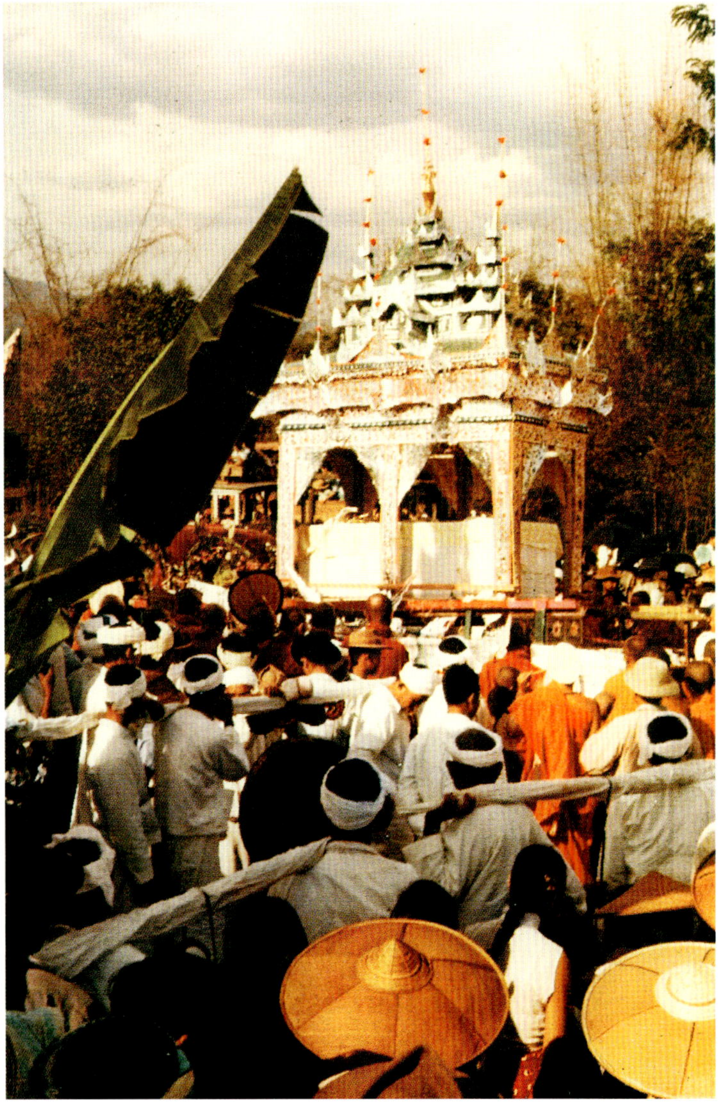

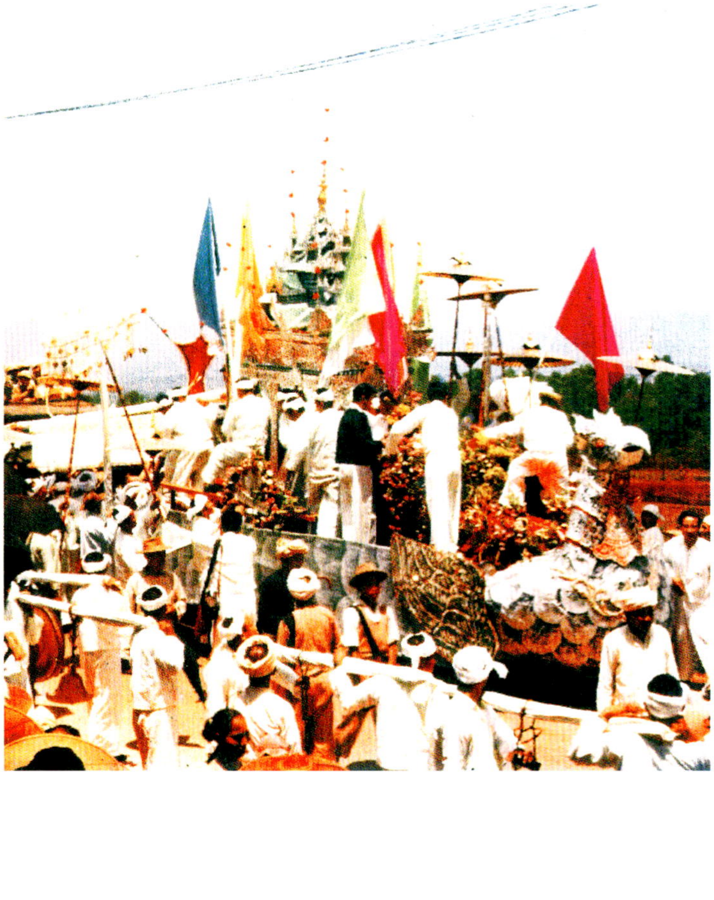

196-99 The funeral of Prince Sao Hom Hpa, Prince of Hsenwi, 1963. The photographs include the procession of the *shwe hintha* (mythical golden bird) bearing the casket, the procession thronged by villagers, the casket being received by Buddhist monks, and the arrival at the family burial ground. Monasteries throughout the Shan States held simultaneous services for the soul of the prince.

Endnotes

1 R. Heine-Geldern, 'Conceptions of State and Kingship', *Southeast Asia Far Eastern Quarterly*, Vol. II, 1942.
2 Sao Saimong Mangrai, 'Shan States and the British Annexation', data paper no. 57, Southeast Asia Program, Dept. Asian Studies, Cornell, 1965, p. 75.
3 Nel Adams, *My Vanished World*, Cheshire, 2000, p. 16.
4 Sao Saimong Mangrai, *The Padaeng Chronicle and the Jengtung Chronicle Translated*, The University of Michigan, Center for South and Southeast Asian Studies, Ann Arbor, Michigan, 1981.
5 The palace was bombed by the Allies in 1945.
6 Francis Garnier, *Further Travels in Laos and in Yunnan: The Mekong Exploration Commission Report (1866-1868)*, Vol. 2, reprint (trans. by W. Tips), White Lotus Press, Bangkok, 1996, p. 80.
7 Interview with Lung Ji Nom and Ba Kong Kham, Ho Ko village, Keng Tung, November 2004.
8 Patricia Elliott, *The White Umbrella,* Post Books, Bangkok, 1999, p. 43.
9 Maurice Collis, *Lords of the Sunset*, 1938, reprint Ava House, 1996, p. 272.
10 *Ibid.* pp. 200-201.
11 Henri d'Orleans, *From Tonkin to India by the Sources of the Irawadi*, 1895, quoted in W. Dodd *The Tai Race*, Torch Press, 1923, reprint. White Lotus Bangkok, 1996, pp. 220-222.
12 Constance Wilson, and Lucien Hanks, 'The Burma-Thailand Frontier Over Sixteen Decades: Three Descriptive Documents,' Monograph in International Studies, Southeast Asia Series, No. 70, University of Ohio, 1985, p. 12; Mangrai, 1981, p. 289, note 82.
13 Oral communication, Sao Hkam Hip Hpa, May 2005.
14 George Scott, *Burma and Beyond*, Grayson and Grayson, London, 1932, p. 245.
15 Letter to Lisa Maddigan, Brighton Museum, from Annabel Gallop, Curator Southeast Asia Dept., The British Library, March 22, 2000.
16 Scott, 1932, p. 240.
17 Collins, 1996.
18 W. C. Dodd, *The Tai Race*, Torch Press, 1923, reprint. White Lotus, Bangkok 1996, p. 204.
19 David Cannadine, *Ornamentalism*, Oxford, 2001.
20 Collis, 1996.
21 *Ibid*, p. 178.
22 *Ibid*, p. 180.
23 Nel Adams, 2000, p. 16.
24 McCleod quoted in Mangrai, 1965, pp. 60-61.
25 Collis, pp. 203-204.
26 McCleod quoted in V. Grabowsky and A. Turton, *The Gold and Silver Road of Trade and Friendship*, Silkworm Books, Chiang Mai, 2003, p. 344.
27 Collis, 1996, pp. 151-252.
28 Oral communication, Keng Tung, 2004.
29 Collis, p. 204.
30 Dodd, 1996, p. 203.
31 Mangrai, 1981.
32 'The Abbot's Cremation and the Hatsadiling' in Newsletter, the National Museum Volunteers, Bangkok, No. 10, October 2004, pp. 19-22.
33 Garnier, 1996, pp. 75-76.
34 D' Orleans, Henri, *From Tonkin to India by the Sources of the Irawadi,* London, 1895.
35 Collis, 1996, p. 204.
36 Mangrai, 1981.
37 Dodd, 1996, p. 201.
38 Scott, 1932, p. 261.
39 Collis, 1996, p. 145.
40 Mangrai, 1981, p. 289, note 82.
41 Collis, 1996, pp. 277-278.
42 The fifteen strand sash chain was a *tsaloe* (see chapter three).
43 Mangrai, 1981, pp. 259-260.
44 Collis, 1996, pp. 187-190.

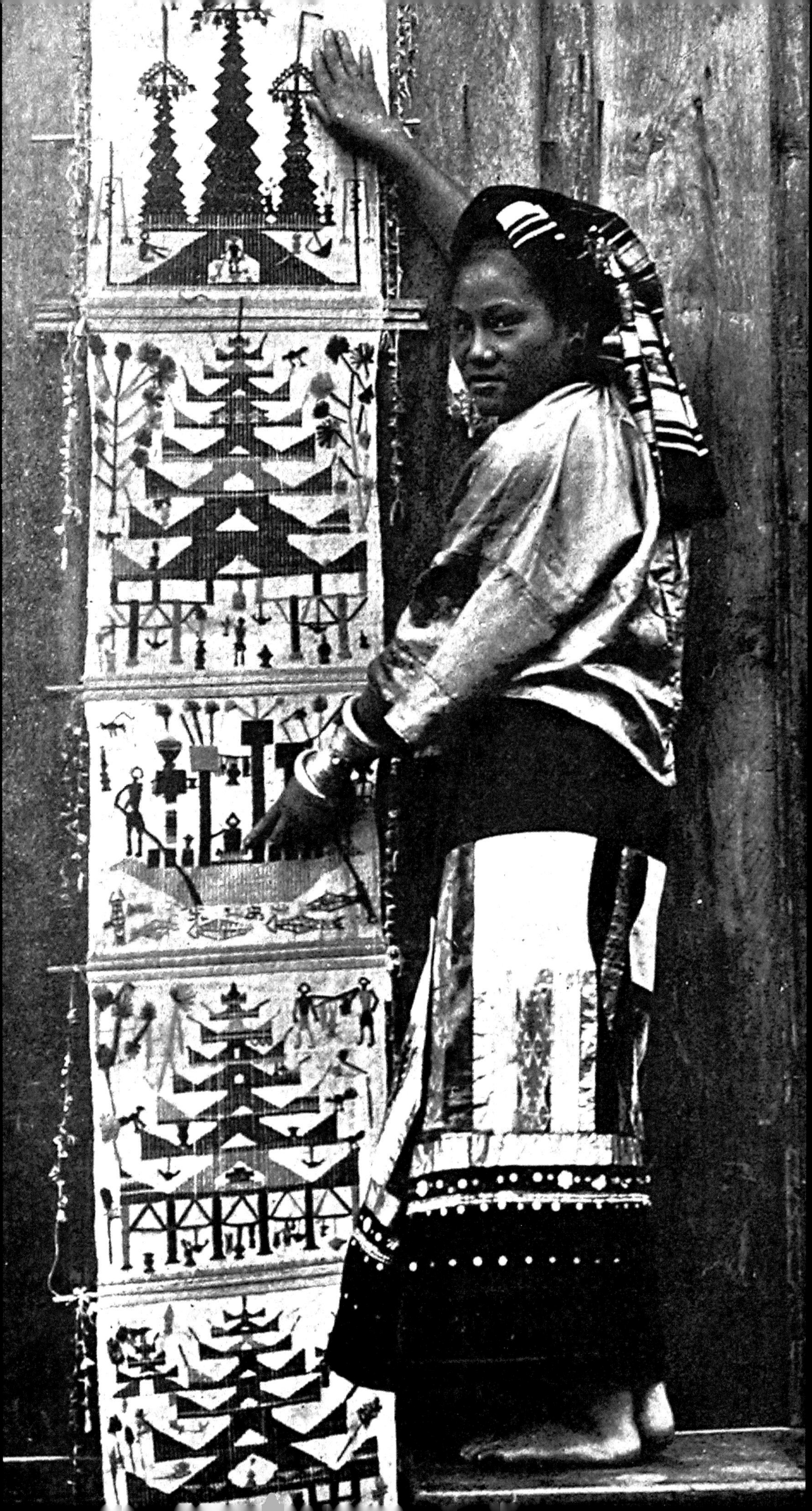

Chapter 6
Shan Arts and Crafts

When they first arrived in inland Southeast Asia, foreigners were quick to recognise the skill of Shan artisans, but their reputation as makers of fine arts and crafts was already legendary among their neighbours. The beautiful objects they produced can be found in museum collections throughout the world, although they are often wrongly labelled as Burmese because there is little understanding of the contribution of non-Burmans to the arts and crafts of this part of inland Southeast Asia. More recently there has been some attention given to Shan arts and crafts, and publications have drawn attention to lacquer ware and textiles in particular.[1] The translation of Tai chronicles into English has enabled scholars to chart the ethnic origin and occupations of artisans working in the Shan States, their movements from one inland principality to another, and development from principality to major kingdom.[2]

The Chiang Mai Chronicle records that, in the thirteenth century, King Mengrai of Lan Na (1259-1317) petitioned the king of Ava for skilled men to work in his expanding kingdom. Mengrai distributed the workers throughout Lan Na, and according to the chronicle, some were settled in Keng Tung where Mengrai's son was installed as senior prince.[3] The tables were turned in the nineteenth century when King Mindon of Burma (ruled 1853-1878) moved his capital from Amarapura to Mandalay. With skilled labour still in short supply, he sent demands to the Shan princes for a supply of labourers and artisans to work on his building programme. Some stayed on to settle permanently in Mandalay.

Artisans were the pawns in princely negotiations and they were treated as part of the spoils of war. In the nineteenth century following the defeat of the Burmese by the Siamese, the powerful Prince Kawila of Chiang Mai (ruled 1781-1825) ordered the seizure of silversmiths, wood carvers, lacquer makers, tanners and potters from the Shan States. They were forcibly marched to Chiang Mai, and from there some were taken to other Lan Na cities where they were settled in special areas set aside for artisans. Some of their descendants continue to live and work in the neighbourhoods where their ancestors were resettled.[4] According to local residents, the city of Keng Tung has not recovered to this day. The lack of silversmiths was cited as an example.[5] The chronicles and temple manuscripts that provide information about artisan resettlement list men, so that although women artisans were also taken captive their movements are not recorded. From oral history, we know that their numbers included weavers, dyers, spinners and embroiderers.[6]

In the late nineteenth century, the British drove King Thibaw of Burma (ruled 1878-1885) into exile causing the collapse of the court and the abandonment of hundreds of skilled workers who were sponsored by the king. Some found work in the construction and repair of monastic buildings, while others worked for the newly emerging elite, including British colonial and military officers and their families. Some musicians, actors, dancers, wood carvers, metal workers, weavers and embroiderers, moved to the Shan States where they found patronage among the Shan princes. Some were the descendants of those who had been moved to Mandalay during the time of King Mindon. Although this influx increased the number of artists and artisans, the Shan rulers still suffered skill shortages. Migrants came from Sipsong Pan Na, Yunnan and western Laos. Many were seasonal workers, although some married local women and settled. The American missionary William Clifton Dodd wrote of Keng Tung in 1897,

> *....the butcher, the baker and the candlestick maker was each a Tai Nüa* [Tai Neua]. *Does the Sawbwa* [saohpa] *or Chief wish to erect a new court house? The contract for all the work is let to Tai Nüa men. They fell and haul the timbers. They quarry and haul the foundation stones. If they do not burn all the tiles and brick, they at least haul them. And they are the carpenters and masons who do all the building work. Tai Nüa build all the monasteries, and the houses of the nobility.*[7]

Artisans were employed at the Shan courts and to work for monastic communities. Wood carvers, gilders and painters, lacquer makers and metal workers enhanced the exteriors

200 A Shan girl displaying a temple banner with images of Buddhist temples, stupas *(kong moo)* and a boat with men rowing, Milne and Cochrane, 1910.

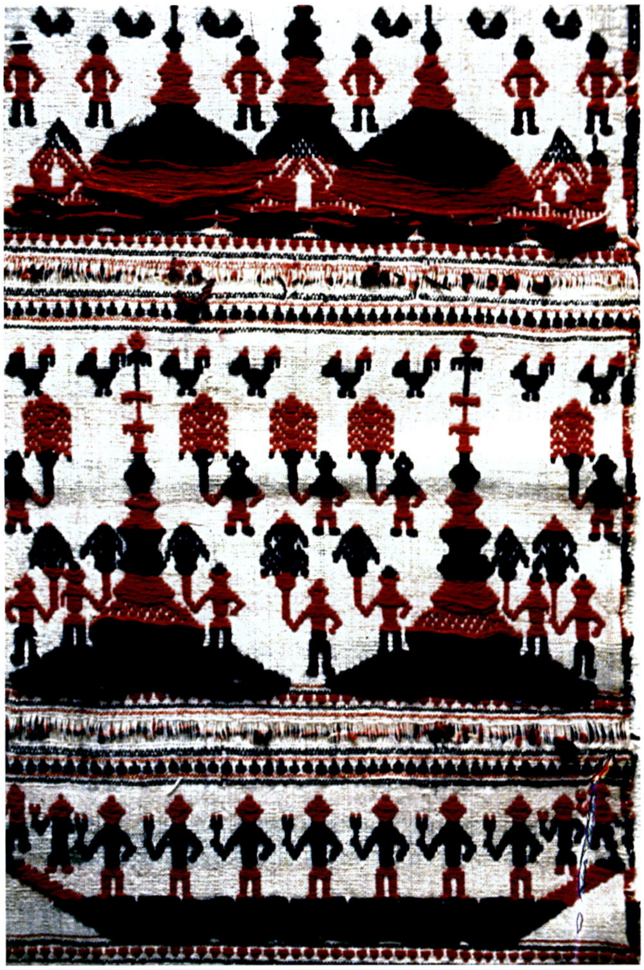

201 Detail of a cotton banner with a plain cotton warp and weft and a supplementary weft of stupas *(kong moo),* men, birds and boats. *(Private collection)*

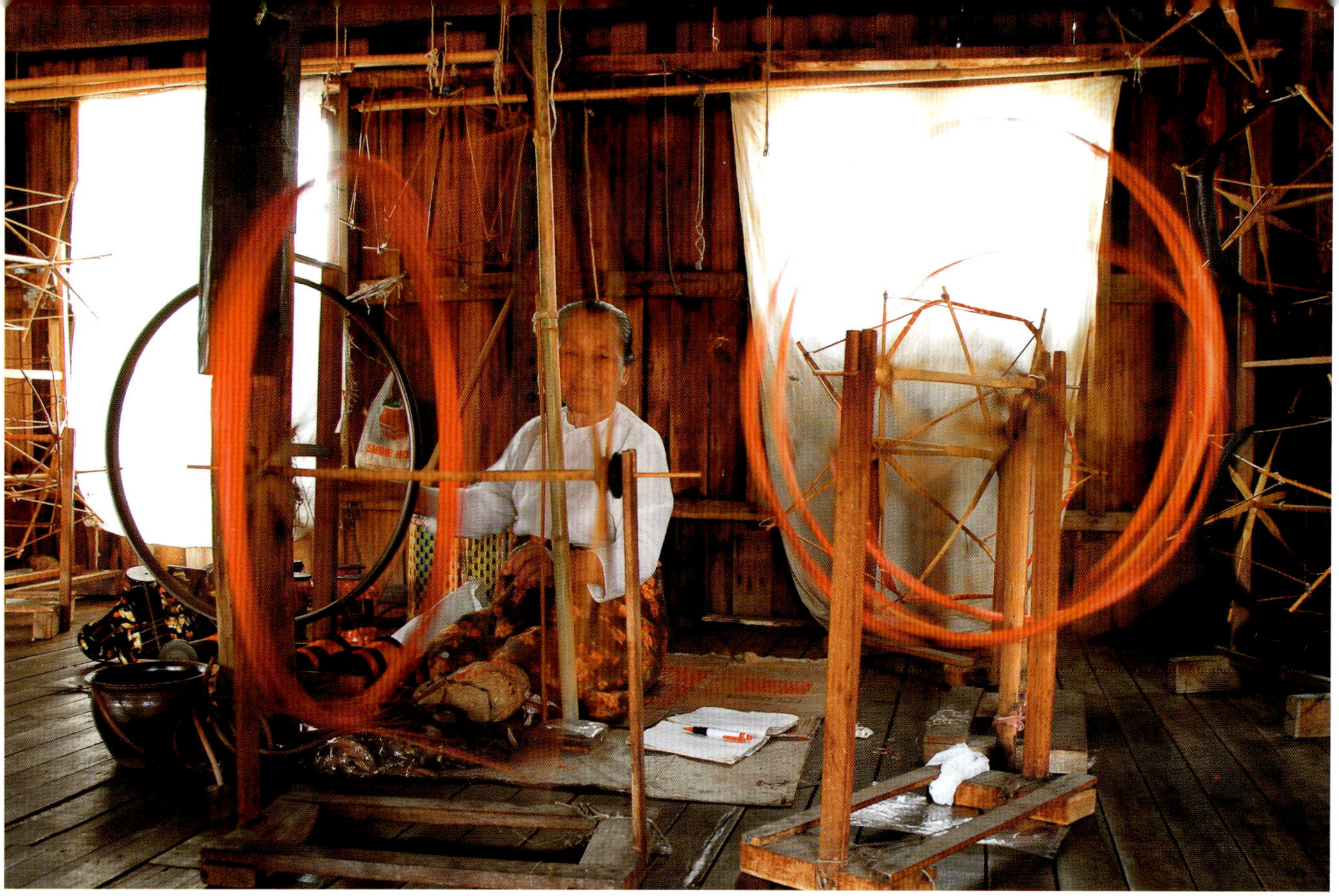

202 Woman reeling silk, Inlay Lake.

and interiors of temples and palaces. Others worked on small precious items such as gold and silver regalia and jewellery. At the village level, there were men and women making goods for everyday use. Today cheap, mass-produced objects have replaced many items previously made by hand, but there are still craft workshops in operation in the Shan States and some of their work is illustrated in this chapter.

Most artisans operated in small workshops with assistants and apprentices. They were connected through family networks and their skills were passed down from one generation to the next. There was no caste system, so they could move from one occupation to another if they developed the necessary skills. However, there were some trades that were spurned by Buddhists, particularly tanning and shoe making that tended to be Chinese and Indian occupations.

Those who worked in the service of the Shan princes were paid in rice, measured by weight, per month, while the most highly skilled were paid in silver.[8] In the outlying districts, minor princes and chiefs relied on village workshops for everyday items and commissioned specialised work from artisans working in the major states. The wood carvers of Muong Nai, the metal workers of Ngwe-Daung and the lacquer workers of Laikha, Muong Nai and Keng Tung were among those who supplied items to the minor courts.

Artisans did not work in isolation and they often came together on major projects. The Keng Tung Chronicle describes the coffin, funeral chariot and cremation site prepared for Prince Mahakhanan of Keng Tung (1781-1857).[9] A team of carpenters, wood carvers and painters built the coffin and funeral chariot. It was inset with tiers of gemstones, and the lid was gilded and carved with gem-studded floral designs. Four male guardian figures (*devaputta*) and four female figures (*deva*), carved in wood, were placed at the corners. The tiered plinth was inlaid with gemstones and mother-of-pearl. Wooden *hamsa* birds were carved on the funeral chariot, and the tiered canopy (*prasad*) was gilded. At the cremation site a team of workmen erected a border of fencing posts that were topped with gilded lotus buds wrapped in red cloth woven by local women. A potter provided clay water pots to be placed at the foot of the fencing posts. A twentieth-century version of the funeral carriage described here can be seen in chapter five (see fig. 187-189). It was made for the funeral of Prince Hom Hpa of Hsenwi (1902-1963).

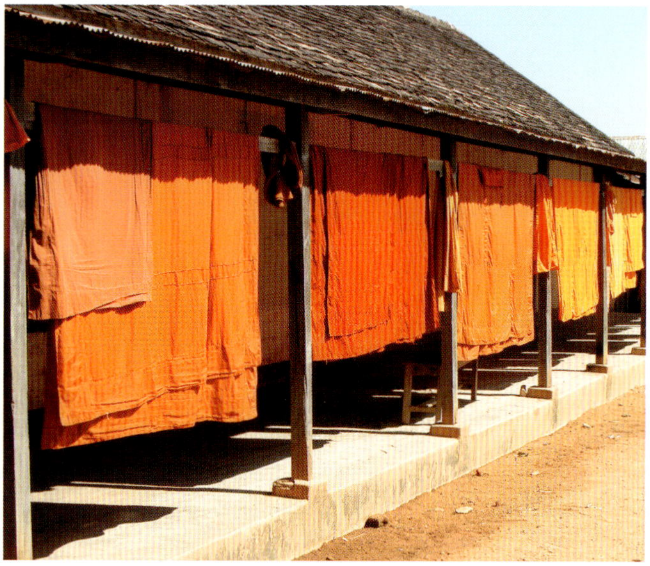

203 Monk's robes drying in the sun in a monastery compound, Keng Tung.

Spinning, Weaving and Dyeing

Almost all women learnt the arts of spinning, weaving and dyeing from an early age. These skills were passed down from generation to generation. Many female members of the royal family also learnt to weave and to embroider, and they and their attendants made some of the clothing worn at court. Until recent times, when cheap mass-produced textiles have swamped the market, production in the villages was linked to the annual cycle of rice cultivation that still forms the basis of the economy.[10] At the start of the monsoon season the waterlogged fields are planted with rice seedlings, and cotton is sown at that time. The rice ripens at the end of the monsoon season, and from November to January the harvest is gathered in. Once the rice crop is safely stored in the village granaries, women turn to a more prolonged period of processing and dyeing yarn and preparing warp and weft for weaving.

Cotton bolls are picked by hand and laid on mats in the sun to dry. The dried bolls are ginned to remove the seeds and then cleaned. To make the cotton fluffy like cotton wool, the bolls are bowed in a basket with a device shaped like a hunting bow. The bowstring is plucked rapidly to vibrate against the fibres. The fluffy cotton tufts are rolled around a wooden dowel to produce elongated cigar-size strands that are rotated and twisted on a spindle to produce a continuous thread. The spun yarn is reeled onto bamboo frames and wound into skeins ready for dyeing. In contrast to cotton production, sericulture was rarely practised. This was the case in the nineteenth century, when Captain McLeod wrote,

> *Silkworms are reared here but not in any large numbers, the silk being merely for home consumption.*[11]

Most silk yarn was imported from China. It is said that the Shan elite favoured hand-reeled Laotian and Khmer silk with its smooth rounded texture and dull sheen that was distinct in character from Chinese silk.[12] It was hard to come by and today is produced commercially on a small scale.

Until the importation of aniline dyes at the end of the nineteenth century, dyes and mordants were harvested locally and from the forest. Some dyes were cultivated in home gardens. Scott and Hardiman drew up a list of seventy-four dye plants in use until the end of the nineteenth century[13] (see page 195).

Cheap imported textiles began to enter the market at the end of the nineteenth century, although they did not impede local production, as most villagers considered indigenous cotton textiles to be more durable than imports. Sir George Scott noted the vibrancy of local production.

> *All but the poorest people own a loom, and everyday clothes are usually of home manufacture though all sorts of cheap British and Indian stuffs are imported. Sometimes gold and silver threads are woven into the women's holiday skirts until they are stiff and glistening. Blankets, bags and towels are all locally made and are strong and durable.*[14]

The lowland Tai throughout inland Southeast Asia use a wooden frame loom about two metres long by one and a half metres wide, referred to as a Burmese Frame Loom.[15] They are usually set up in the space under the raised floor of the house and are built by village carpenters using tongue and groove joints and wooden pins so that they can be quickly assembled after the rice harvest, and just as easily

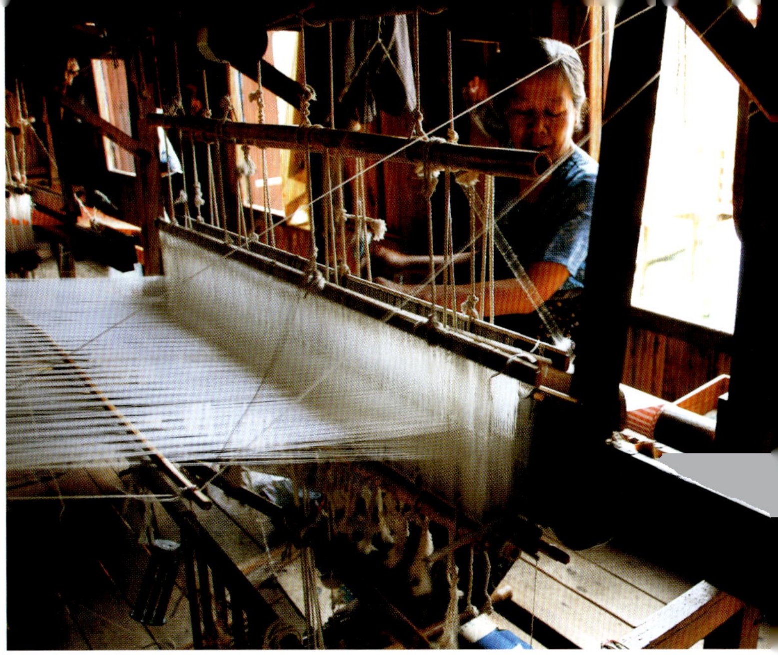

204 Weaving silk, Inlay Lake.

dismantled at the times in the year when space is needed for drying agricultural products and raising small farm animals. The beat of clacking looms greets those who visit villages in the weaving season after the rice has been harvested.

To prepare a warp, skeins of yarn are transferred from reels onto a warping frame with a group cross to help keep the threads separated. The number of times the warp passes around the warping frame dictates the width of the finished cloth. The length of the warp is generally between four to nine metres and may be prepared in the weaver's compound, or if space is at a premium, in a village lane. To prepare the weft, the yarn is wound from skeins onto reels by means of a wooden reeling device. It is then rewound onto bobbins to fit the shuttles required for a particular type of weave.

The purpose of a loom frame is to provide tension for a warp. To create a space in the warp so that the weft can be interlaced involves the use of a shedding device of cotton heddles. For complex weaves the number of heddle shafts may be up to sixteen. The warp is also passed through a reed comb made from palm wood held in a wooden frame called a beater. Weavers often store sets of heddle shafts and beaters set in a range of patterns together, with the end threads of a previous warp running through them. The weaver can select the set she wants and tie the new warp to the end-threads left from the previous warp. This ingenious short cut saves completely re-threading the heddles and reed every time a new warp is prepared.

When the warp is threaded and the heddle shaft and beater are attached to the loom frame, the end warp farthest from the weaver is passed across the top of the loom frame, over the supporting beam to be tied on the beam above her head. The near end is attached to the cloth or breast beam. The weaver sits on a bench in front of the breast beam. The back beam is set higher than the front beam to produce a good shed. The weaver passes the weft through the shed with the aid of a wooden shuttle that may vary in length from twenty-five to fifty-five centimetres, depending on the complexity of the weaving pattern and the thickness of the yarn. Shuttles are carved in narrow curved shapes and planed to a smooth surface that passes easily through the shed. After each line of weft, called a pick, is inserted, the weaver "beats in" with the beater.

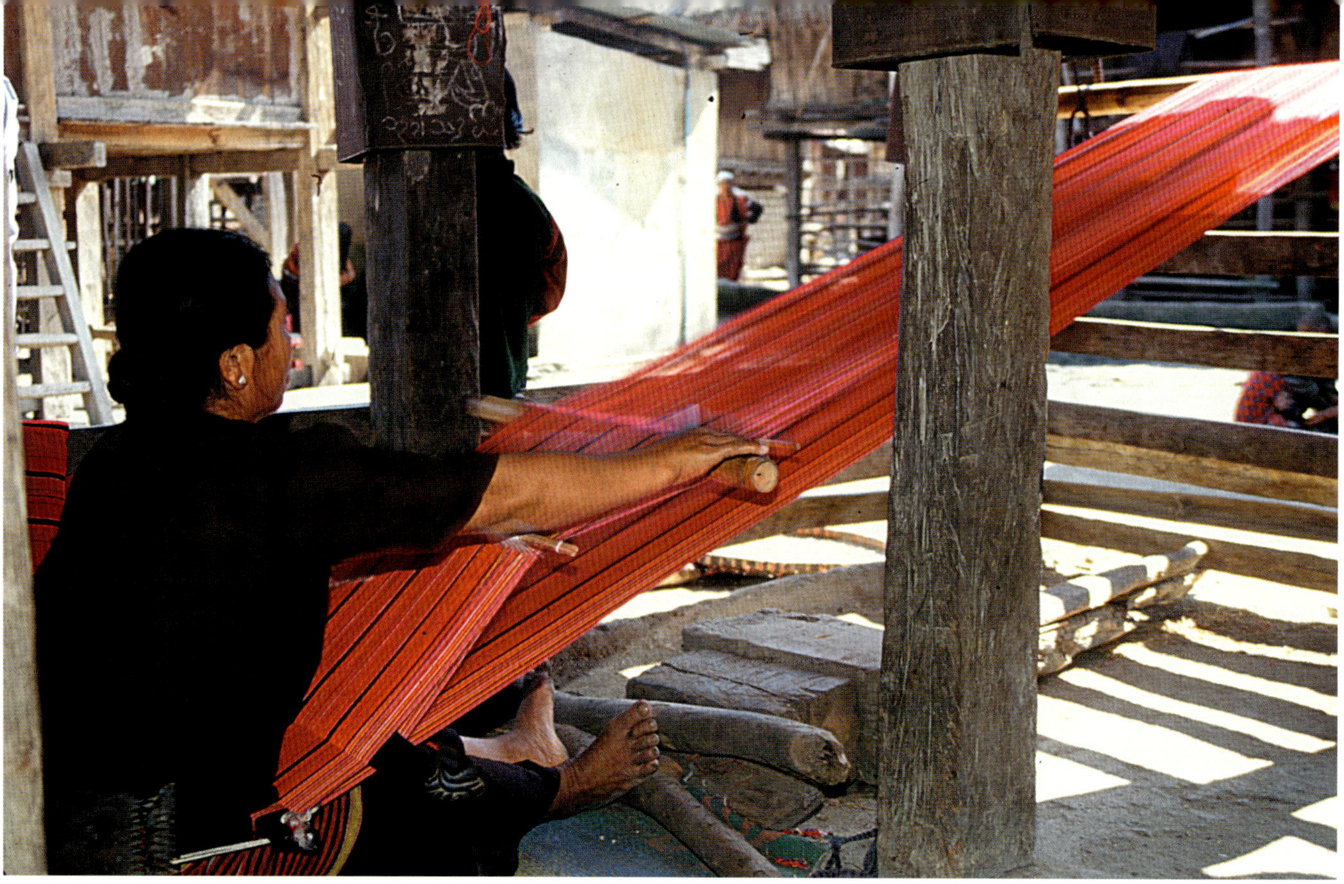

205 A Palaung weaver using a back strap loom. Baan Pao Palaung, Keng Tung.

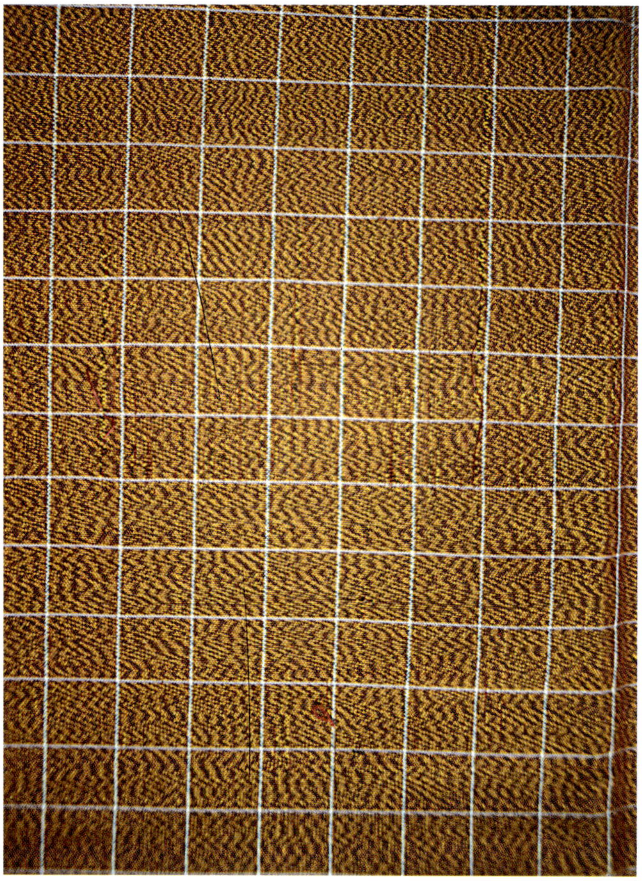

206 A man's check silk sarong woven with plied yarns in the warp and weft.

All Shan weaving equipment is simple and practical, but many pieces illustrate the skill and creative ability of the male wood carvers. Some loom frames have turned railings and patterned corner pieces. Shaft pulleys are produced in the form of animals and birds, particularly elephants, horses, mythical birds (*hintha*) and half-bird and half-human figures (*kinnari*).

The palm wood for the reed in the beater is a precision tool made with a variety of gauges. For fine silk thread, a narrow gauge is needed, for thick cotton a wide gauge. With frequent use, palm reeds develop a smooth patina and produce an excellent beat. The wooden frame of the beater is carved with floral and leaf patterns and curving end-scrolls, and some wooden shuttles have simple designs around the bobbin holder.

In the commercial sector that now dominates the handloom industry, weavers use a modified frame loom. The warp is rolled onto a circular beam with a ratchet device so that it can be moved evenly forward. There is a similar device at the front of the loom onto which the newly woven cloth is revolved. Wider cloth can be woven in this way. A flying shuttle operated by pulling on a cord, speeds up the weaving process. Although these looms are ubiquitous, the majority of textiles illustrated in this book were produced at a time when the traditional Burmese frame loom was in use.

Communities in the hills, including the Kachin, Palaung and Karen use back strap looms.[16] As there is no rigid frame, the warp beam can be attached to two upright posts anywhere in the house and the weaver sits on the floor. The loom has a warp beam, a breast beam attached to a back strap, a heddle, a reed, a shed stick, a beater and several laze rods. The warp is wrapped continuously round the warp beam and the breast beam and the laze rods help keep the warp straight and free from tangles. The creation of the shed is effected by shed stick and heddle.

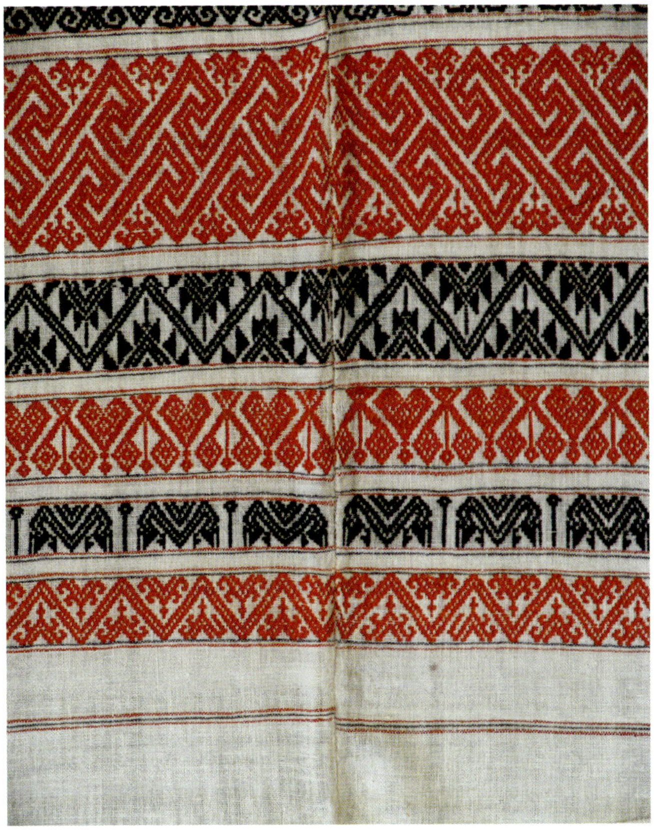

207 Detail of the hem border of a bed sheet with a hand-spun cotton warp and weft and a supplementary weft, woven in two lengths and joined at the selvedge.

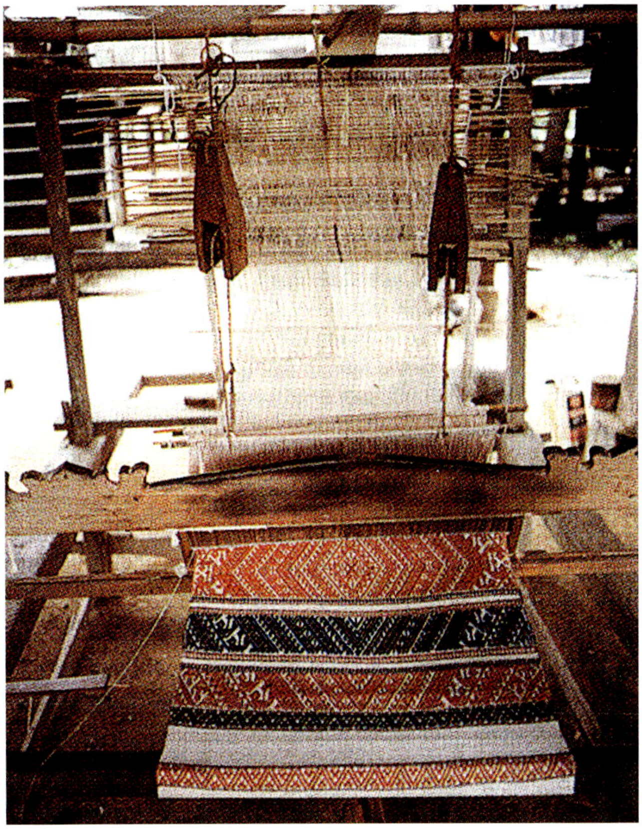

208 A loom threaded with a string heddle system. The pattern in the strings reflects the pattern on the woven cloth.

The width of cloth produced on Burmese frame looms and on back strap looms is relatively narrow, so that for items, such as blankets and sheets, two widths are matched and sewn together along the selvedge. For ankle length skirts, the waistbands and central panels are produced in separate sections. Narrow items such as turbans and shoulder sashes are produced in one piece.

Plain weave produced on a frame loom requires two heddle shafts and two attached treadles. The weft passes over and under each warp thread, then under and over on the following line. Although the term "plain weave" implies a simple technique, it can be manipulated to create amazing variations in colour and design. To make colour and shade variants, the warp and weft are of different colours, a technique referred to as "shot." This is most effective if woven in silk. Different coloured yarns can be twisted together (plied) to create a shaded or speckled effect, often referred to locally as "squirrel's tail." This technique may be used in isolated rows, as in Tai, Wa and Karen skirts, or the entire warp and weft can be worked with plied yarns. This is often used for the muted fabrics worn by elderly women and men.

Stripes of different colours and varying widths can be prepared in the warp or woven in the weft. If warp and weft are both striped, the result is a plaid pattern. The yarn may be woven in a dense weave with many threads per centimetre or an open weave with far less threads. If the warp and weft are the same ply and equally spaced, the resulting cloth is described as "balanced plain weave." If the number of warp threads per centimetre is more than the number of weft threads, the cloth is described as warp faced. If the number of weft threads per centimetre is more than the warp threads, the cloth is weft faced. Balanced plain weave is used for monk's robes and male sarongs. Lengths of cotton woven in plain weave were often dyed with indigo and cut to make loose-legged trousers, usually called "Shan pants," and work shirts and shoulder bags.

Twill or float weave involves the warp or weft threads skipping or floating over one or two threads before being interwoven. When the float is patterned into a diagonal, it is referred to as twill weave. Twill weave is identified by the ratio of threads passing over and under the warp. The common ratios are 1/2, 1/3 and 1/4. Float weave patterns may involve the use of two shafts for a plain weave binding, and in addition, the warp is threaded through an extra set of shafts which are lifted in sequence to create a float weave pattern resembling a simple geometric damask. The weavers also use a 1/2 twill for weaving ikat patterns, thus adding a diagonal effect to the design.

Supplementary weft patterns are woven into plain weave or into a variety of twill patterns requiring up to eight heddles. One of the oldest methods involves hand picking the pattern row by row using a wooden sword to create a shed for the insertion of a supplementary weft between rows of plain weave. Or, a pre-determined shed-selection process is used in which shed sticks or supplementary string heddles inserted in the warp accelerate and simplify the weaving process. Shed sticks are commonly used to produce a single image or a row of images, for example dragons (*naga*), boats, human figures and temple monuments (see fig. 212). If a mirror image is required the shed sticks are

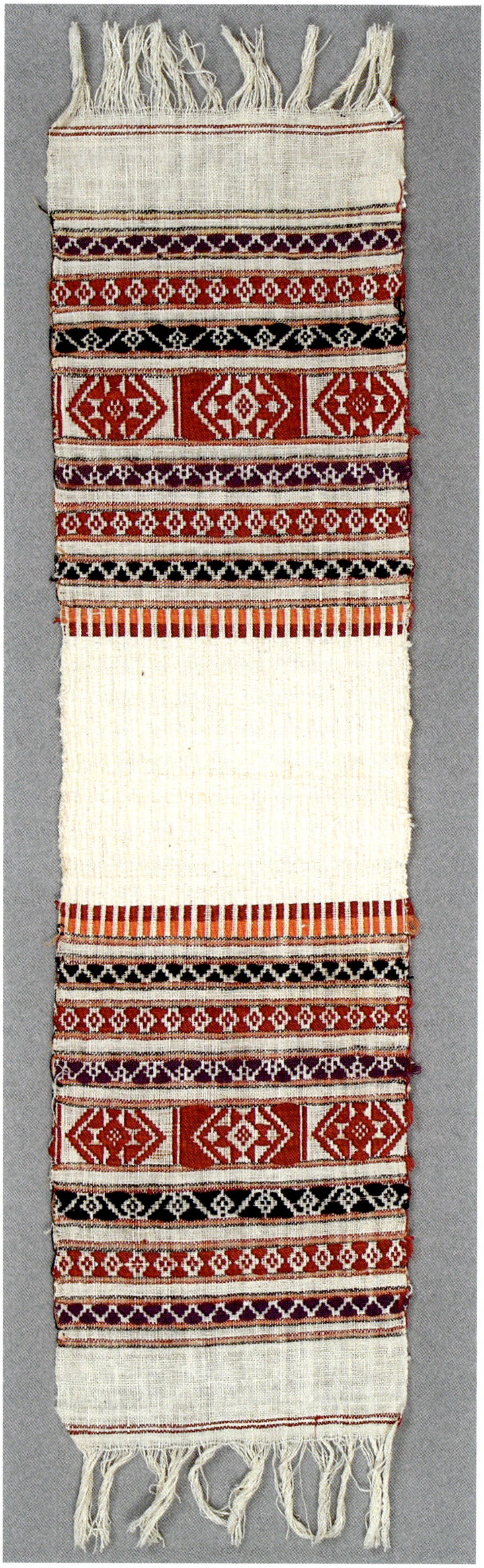

209 A man's shoulder cloth *(hpa hoi).* Plain cotton warp and weft with a supplementary weft of stylised flowers and geometric patterns. *(Private collection)*

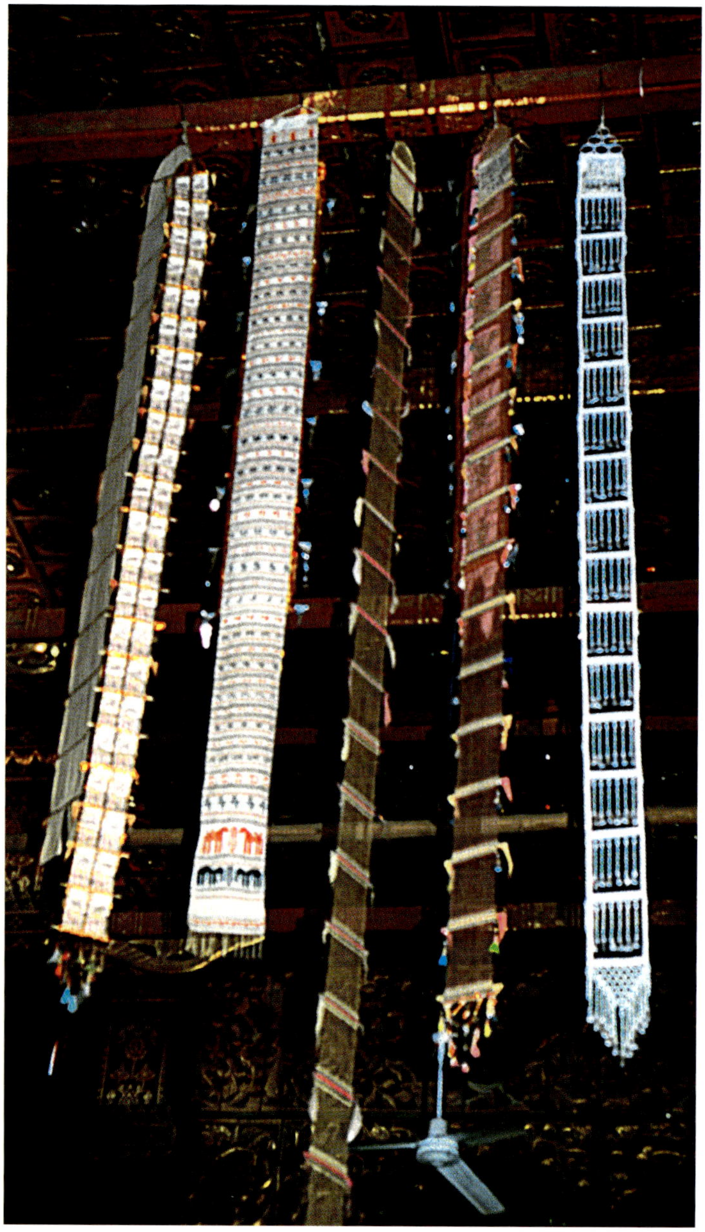

210 Woven cotton and plaited bamboo banners *(hpa tung)* hanging in the interior of Wat Chieng In, Keng Tung.

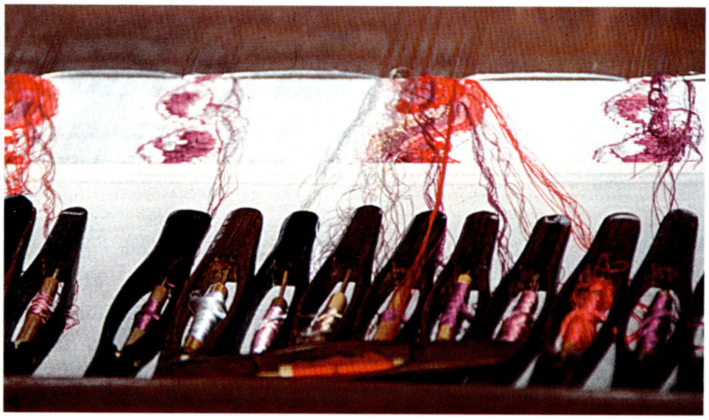

211 A set of small shuttles being used to weave silk *acheik luntaya,* a complex form of tapestry weave.

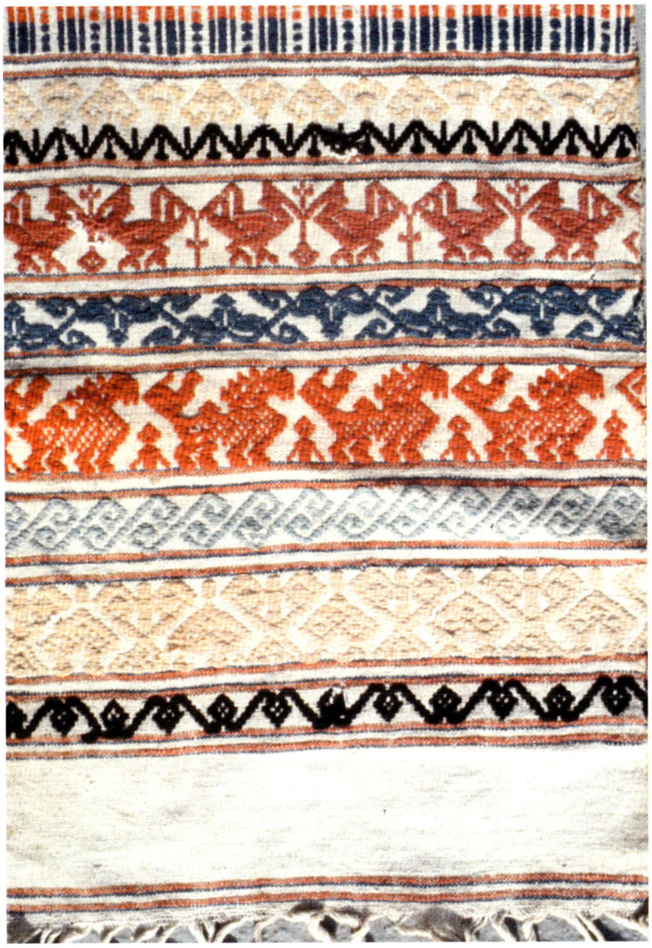

212 Detail of a man's shoulder cloth *(hpa hoi).* Plain cotton warp and weft with a supplementary weft of birds, dragons and geometric patterns. *(Private collection)*

inserted sequentially until the middle of the pattern and then they are inserted in reverse order. Floral and geometric patterns are woven in this way, as seen on the borders of men's shoulder cloths, sashes, bed sheets and pillows.

The technique of using a sequence of shed sticks to pre-select the pattern of a supplementary weft can be incorporated in a complex heddle system. Here the sticks are interwoven in a string harness set at right angles to the warp and tensioned between upper and lower beams set on the loom frame. The intersection of the ground weave is controlled by two shafts which the weaver activates by treadles. If the loom frame is small and the string harness close enough to the weaver, she may undertake the procedure on her own. To set up the loom, the pattern to be woven is first picked row by row into the vertical string harness using bamboo shed sticks. The strings of the harness are connected to individual warp threads by string loops. To operate the system, the weaver moves the first shed stick down towards the warp. A wooden sword is inserted into the shed created by the lowered stick; the sword is flipped on its side and drawn forward towards the cross to allow insertion of a supplementary weft yarn. While the shed stick remains in the harness above the warp, another stick is inserted into the harness below the warp in the same shed. The upper shed stick can then be removed. The weaver then inserts one row of plain weave. To continue the pattern the next shed stick in the harness is lowered towards the warp and the whole process is repeated. When only one stick is left in the upper part of the harness, the process is reversed and the sticks pass in sequence from below to above the warp. The process continues with the shed sticks passing in sequence above and below the warp until the required pattern sets have been completed. Like heddle shafts and beaters, string heddle harnesses systems may be kept threaded and stored for future use.

The most refined supplementary weft system involves introducing discontinuous supplementary weft yarns into a ground weave. The weaver usually works on the reverse side, using her fingers or a small pick. The discontinuous weft consists of multi-coloured silk and gold and silver

213 Silk *luntaya* fabric for a woman's skirt. *(Private collection)*

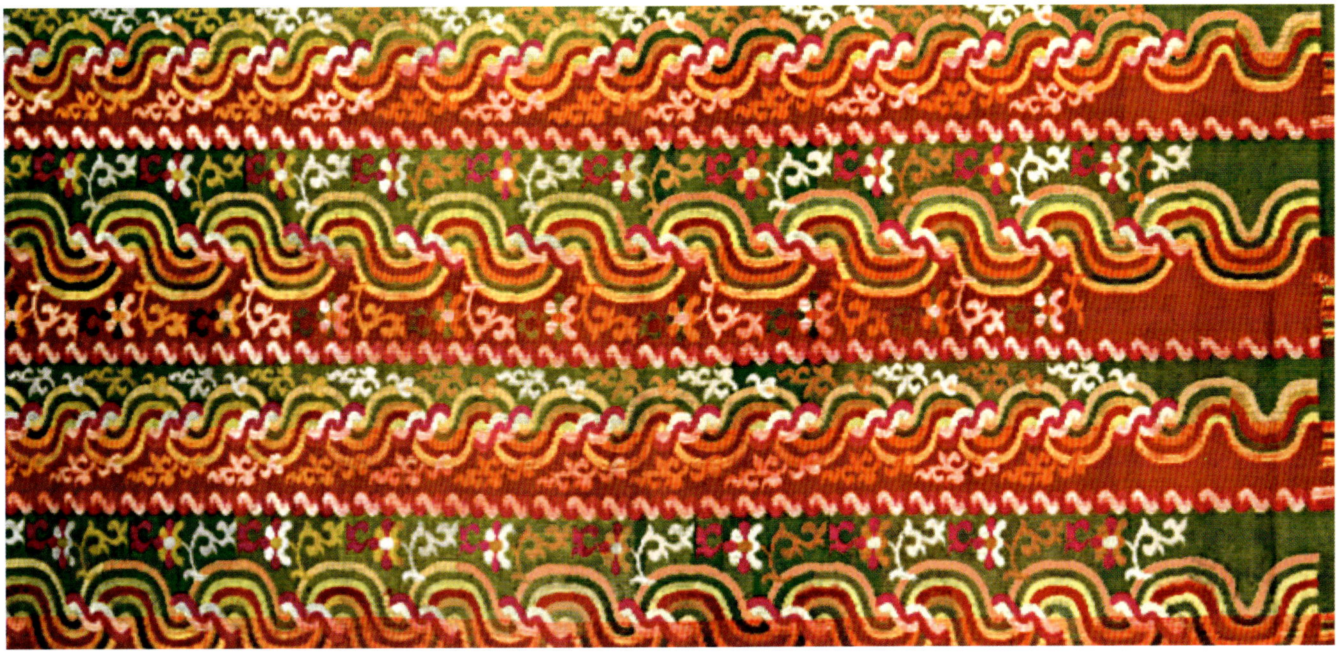

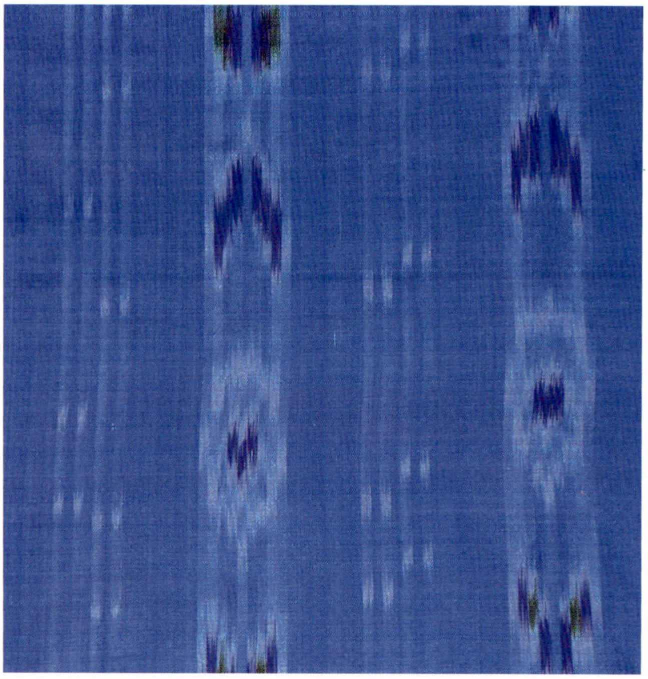

214 Silk ikat fabric. This type of design, woven in plain weave or in a simple twill weave, was produced in the villages around Inlay Lake.

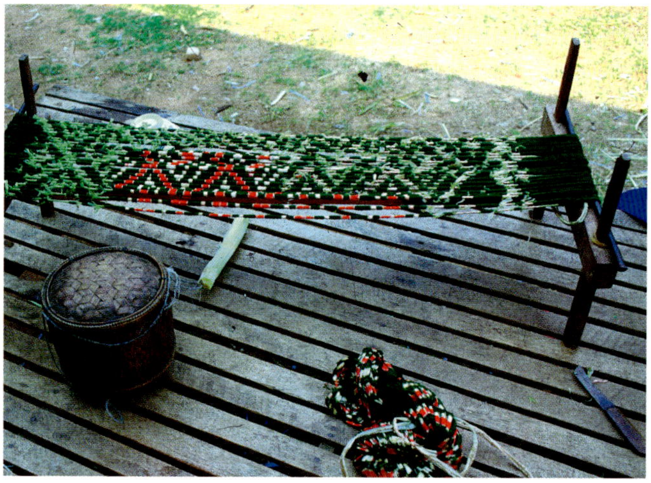

215 Silk weft being tied and dyed on a wooden frame. The frame has been set to the width of a woman's skirt.

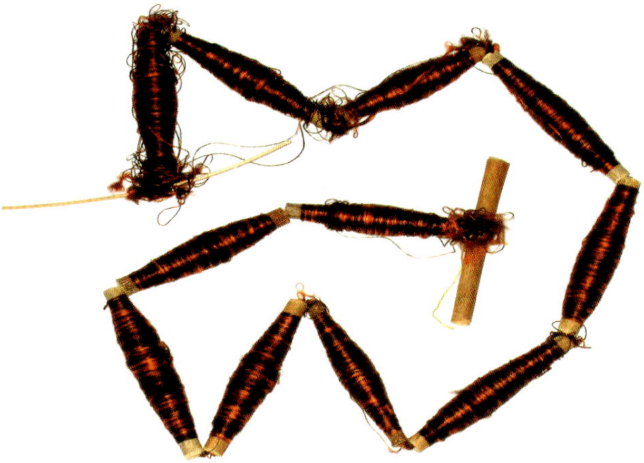

216 Spools of silk ikat yarn. The spools are kept in sequence on a length of twine. The weaver takes the spools one by one from the twine to weave the pattern.

metal yarns. The patterns are so fine and intricate that it can take up to six weeks to produce a band about fifteen to eighteen centimetres in length. Balanced plain weave usually provides the ground weave for this type of supplementary weft.

Tapestry weave is a plain weave of discontinuous weft. The weaver keeps a quantity of small shuttles in front of her and weaves isolated motifs of contrasting colours that together form the cloth structure. This technique is used for women's skirts, for turban cloths and shoulder bags.

A more complex tapestry weave is known as *acheik luntaya*. It involves the use of between one hundred and two hundred small shuttles. The weaver works with the wrong side of the cloth facing her. Multi-coloured silks and silver and gold metal thread are worked in patterns of undulating horizontal bands (*acheik*) that twist and intertwine with flowers, leaves and vines. The inspiration for the bands comes from nature and natural forces like the form of ripples on water, lightening strikes, the silhouette of mountains and the shape of clouds. This type of weaving was time-consuming and required extremely skilled weavers. Although they may have worked at the Shan courts, most accounts suggest this fabric was imported from Burma. *Acheik luntaya* was worn by many upper class women in the Shan States, as illustrated in the formal photographs reproduced in this book.

Ikat is a technique that involves tying and dyeing the warp or the weft yarns in predetermined patterns before weaving. The yarn is tensioned backwards and forwards on a measured wooden frame. To produce a pattern of more than two colours, the yarn is tied and dyed, then retied and re-dyed or has extra ties added for each colour. Impregnation of the principle colours takes place in a dye bath, but small amounts of dye may be added with a brush. When the dyeing process is completed, the patterned yarn is untied and wound onto a frame ready for reeling. The bobbins are kept in sequence by stringing them on a length of twine (see fig. 216). The most common use for ikat was for women's skirts (see fig. 214). If the ikat pattern is prepared in the warp, a warp-faced plain weave will reveal the pattern more clearly. If the ikat pattern is prepared in the weft, a weft-faced plain weave is effective. In some cases weavers use 1/2 twill so that the ikat pattern takes on a diagonal appearance. Although many textiles are produced using one or two weaving techniques, there are many beautiful hand-woven fabrics that combine at least three. For the silk turban cloths illustrated in chapter four figs. 117-19 the weaver has combined rows of ikat in geometric patterns, lines of plied yarns, bands of supplementary weft and bands of tapestry weave.

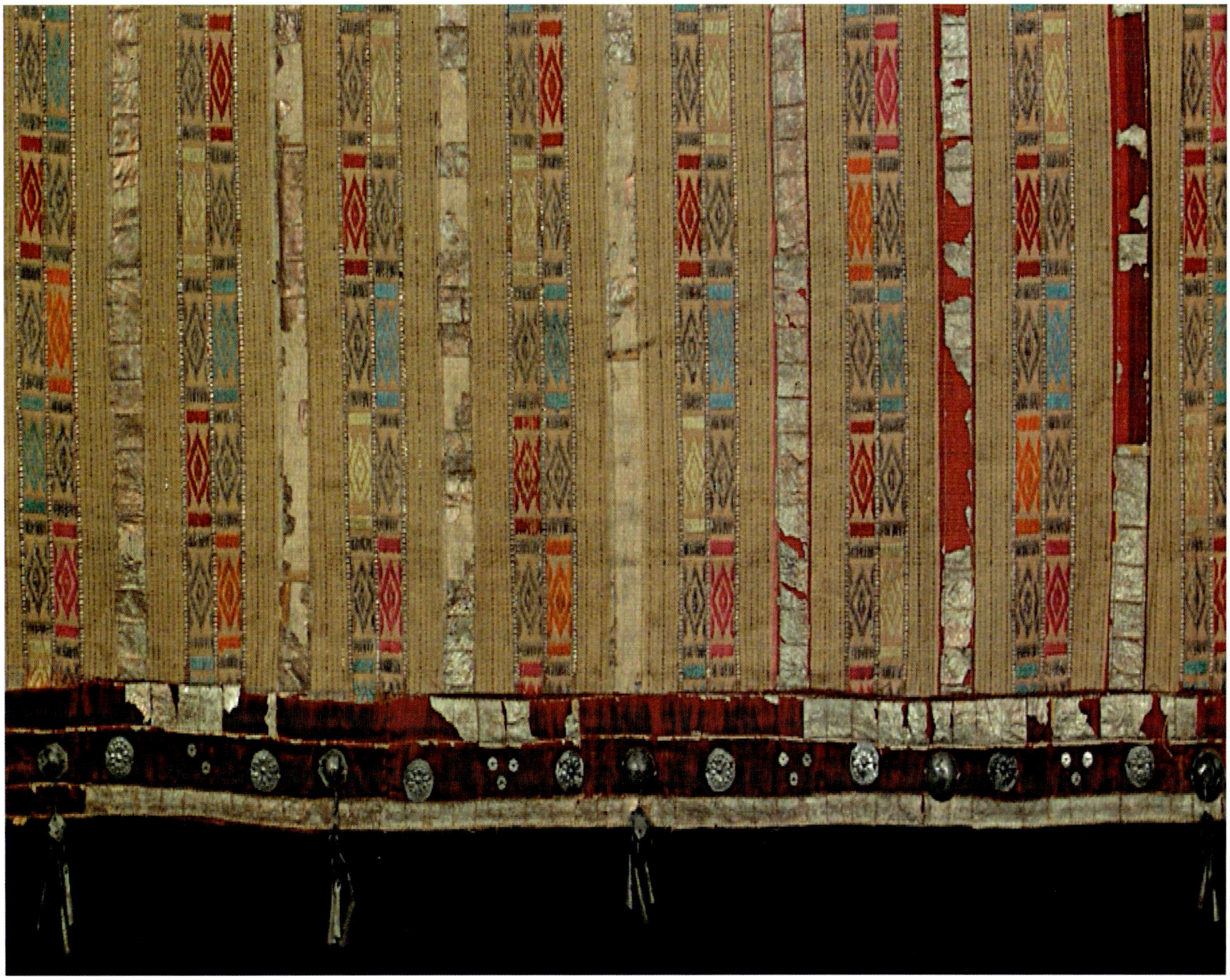

217 Detail of the central panel of a Shan skirt appliquéd with strips of leather covered with beaten silver and copper, and bands of supplementary weft. The lower border is burnt sienna velvet partly covered with strips of silver foil. There are attachments of silver sequins, flat metal sequins, and dome-shaped sequins with metal cone-shaped attachments. *(Denison University collection, Granville, Ohio, DU1974.4)*

Appliqué

Appliqué is a technique that involves sewing pieces of one fabric onto another so that the colours and shapes form a harmonious pattern. Strips of hand-woven cottons with supplementary weft patterns of multi-coloured silks and cottons, and gold and silver metal thread are combined with brightly coloured pieces of plain silk and silk brocade, panels of Chinese floss silk embroidery, narrow lengths of gilded leather, and silk ribbons. Many of the fabrics are remnants from turban cloths and blouses and other garments that can be identified in this book, whereas the ribbons, gilded leather and bands of embroidery were purchased by length. Appliqué provides an instant record of the types of fabrics and trimmings available at any given time. Local fabrics and Chinese silks were probably the most enduring, but in the nineteenth century machine-made Indian and European silks and cottons, voided velvets and red cotton flannel were available in the Shan State markets. The combination of indigenous and imported fabrics created appliqué that was unique to this region.

Once the fabrics were arranged and stitched on the backing, they were finished with decorative hand stitching, intended to protect the edges from fraying. Interlaced herringbone, satin stitch and buttonhole stitch were common. Silver and mother-of-pearl sequins and metal pendants were added to some designs. The introduction of sewing machines at the end of the nineteenth century meant machine stitching often replaced hand finishing. In the northern Shan States, appliqué provided decoration for the central panel of women's ankle-length skirts. Black cotton and velvet formed the backing and the hem border. Appliqué was also used on the skirts worn by Tai Khoen women. Bands of Chinese floss silk embroidery and ribbons of silk brocade and tinsel cloth were appliquéd to a cotton or velvet backing. Tai Lue women used appliqué for the bodices and sleeves of their blouses and jackets and similar fabrics and trimmings were used to embellish the hem borders of their skirts. Palaung women appliquéd their distinctive hooded capes. Chinese silk and silk brocades, and panels of embroidery were common, but when imported fabrics became available, they used European and Indian fabrics, including machine-voided cotton velvet, machine-printed Indian silks and off-cuts of red flannel.

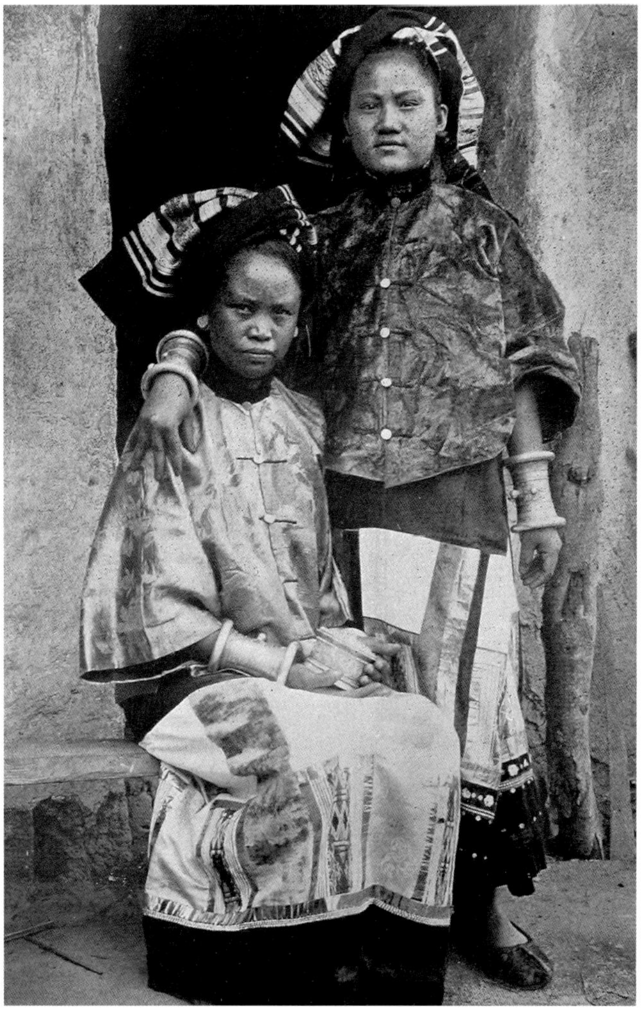

218 Shan women wearing woven turbans, Chinese silk jackets and appliqué skirts, Milne and Cochrane, 1910.

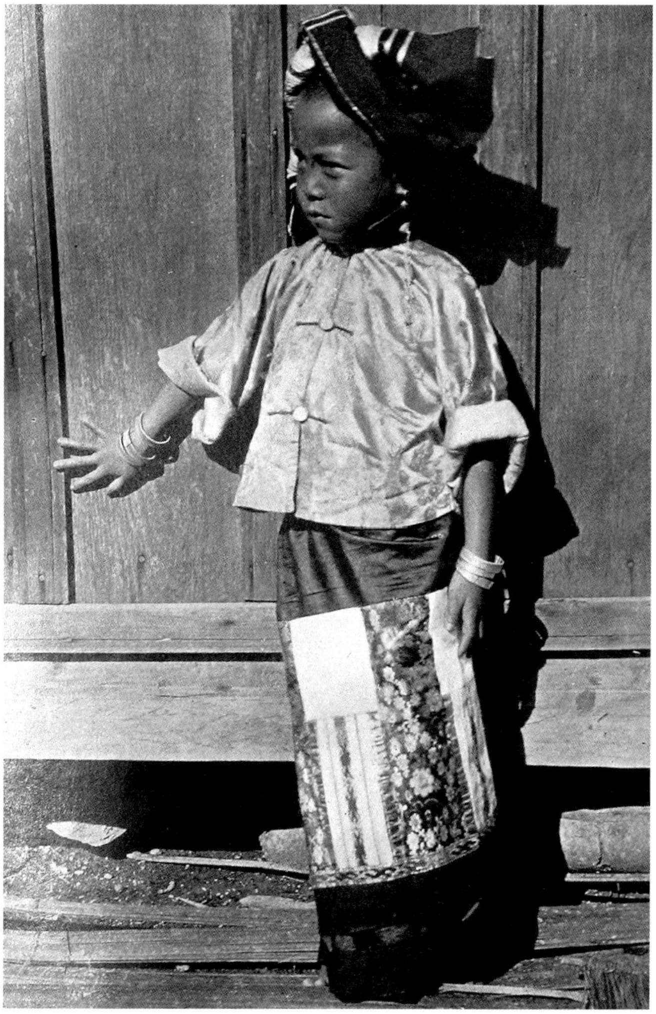

219 A Shan girl in a woven turban, Chinese silk jacket and appliquéd skirt, Milne and Cochrane, 1910.

Embroidery

Couching involves sewing down threads laid on the surface of a fabric in a predetermined design. Several cotton strands are twisted together to create a thread strong enough to hold metallic gold and silver thread *in situ*. This method is favoured because the metal thread does not have to be pulled through what is usually delicate silk fabric. It is also economically preferable as expensive gold and silver thread is not wasted on the back of the cloth.

This was a technique used to decorate women's blouses, sashes and ankle-length skirts, and court coats worn by the Shan princes. The designs included curled tendril and leaf patterns, flowers and the mythical *hintha* bird. In the most skilful work, gold and silver metal thread was cleverly used to create a shaded, two-dimensional effect. Although most designs were indigenous, this technique was adapted in the 1920s and 1930s to create Art Nouveau and Art Deco designs, particularly for women's ankle length skirts. Silver and gold metal thread, beads and sequins were couched on layers of semi-transparent or transparent chiffon, cotton gauze and fine silk and veiling. These textiles were then made into an overskirt worn with a plain silk underskirt. Another fashion in this period was for women's ankle length skirts to be embroidered with chain stitch, running stitch, feather-stitch, satin stitch and French knots, worked in multi-coloured silks, and embellished with sequins and bugle beads. This type of embroidery was also used to trim jackets, blouses and silk sashes.

When they attended the Burmese court to *kadaw* to the king, the senior Shan princes and their consorts wore special court dress issued according to sumptuary laws. Their garments were couched with gold thread and stitched with thousands of gold and silver sequins enhanced with beetle wings, pearls and semi-precious stones sewn so densely that none of the backing cloth was visible. Although these garments were extremely heavy, the use of thin gold and silver foil wrapped around a cotton or silk core, made them lighter than if solid gold and silver wire were used. The sequins were stitched in groups to form geometric, floral and leaf patterns, or they were laid in lines to create borders. Gem stones and pearls were arranged in clusters or placed individually to form centrepieces for floral designs. The embroiderers had terms to describe these designs. Stitching sequins in clusters was "spraying with stars" or "spreading flowers," while stitching them in overlapping lines was called "fish scales" or "*naga* skin." Triangular arrangements were known as "cooking tripod."[17] Some names like "circle of pearls" and "cluster of gems" are self-evident.

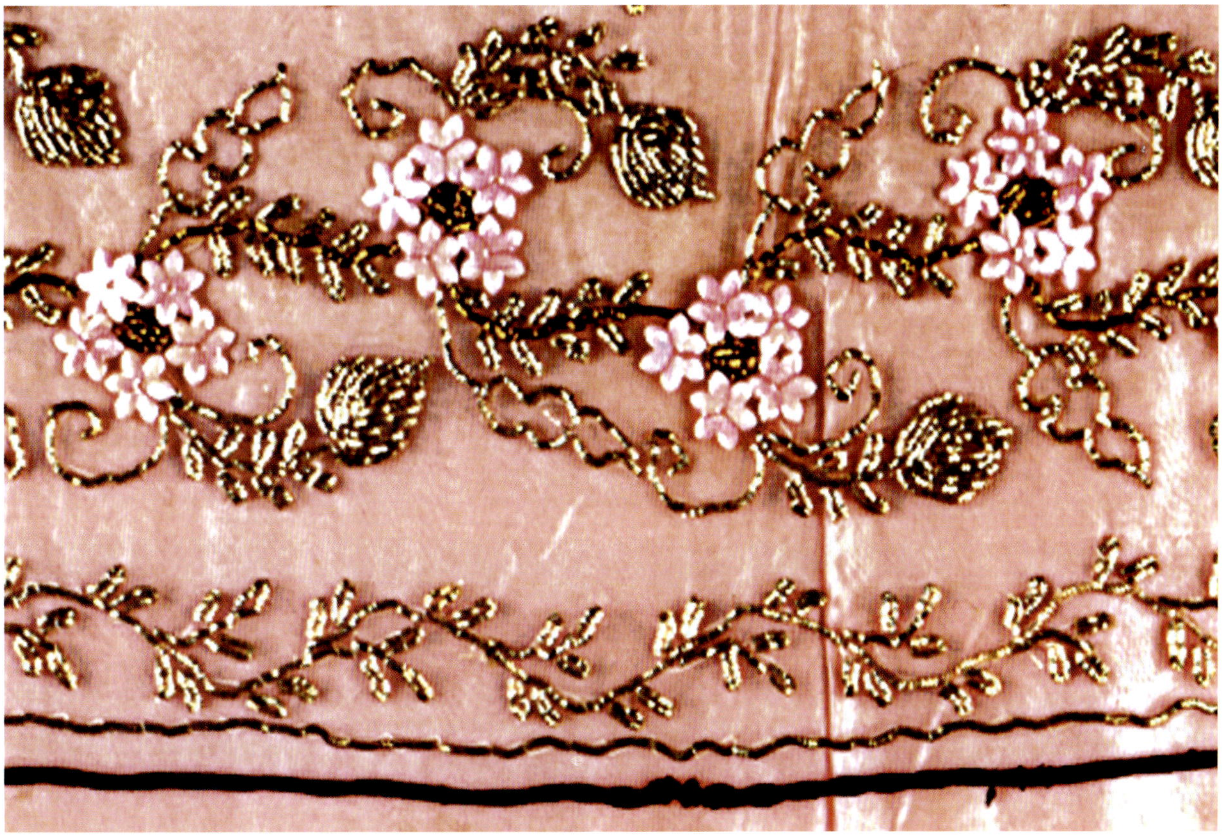

220 Detail of women's ankle-length skirts, couched with gold and silver wire, mother-of pearl and silver sequins. *(Private collection)*

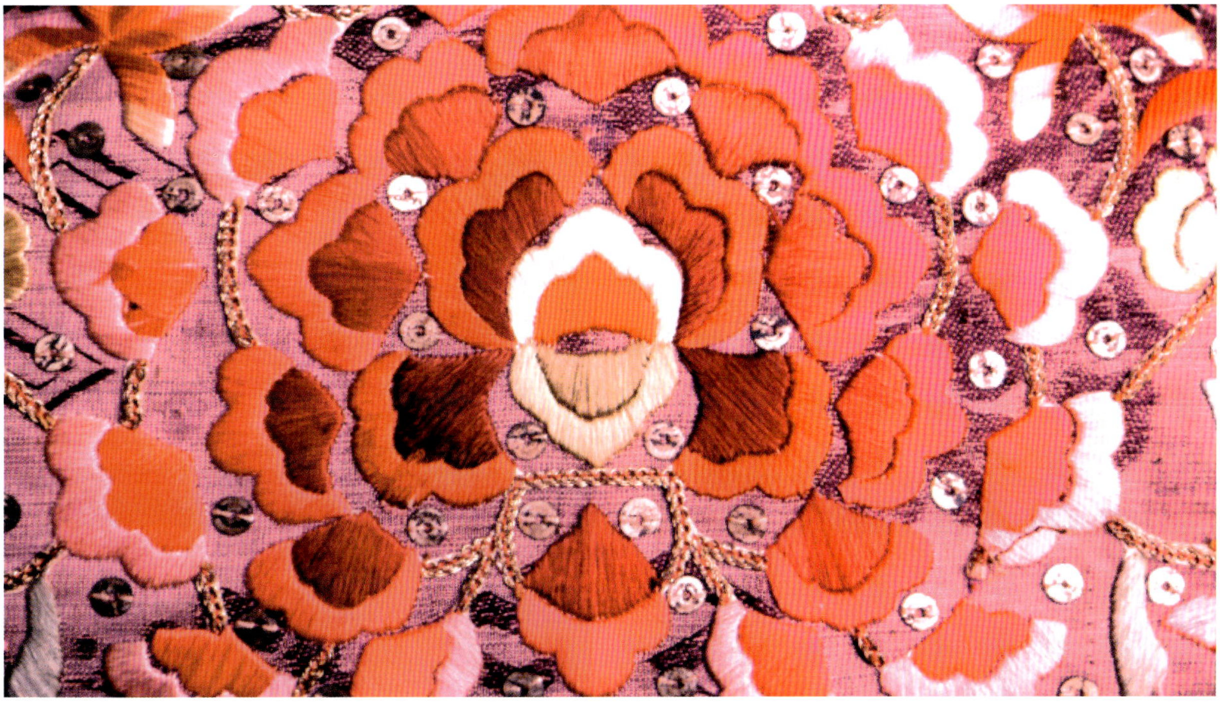

221 Detail of a cushion embroidered with Chinese silk thread and sequins. *(Private collection)*

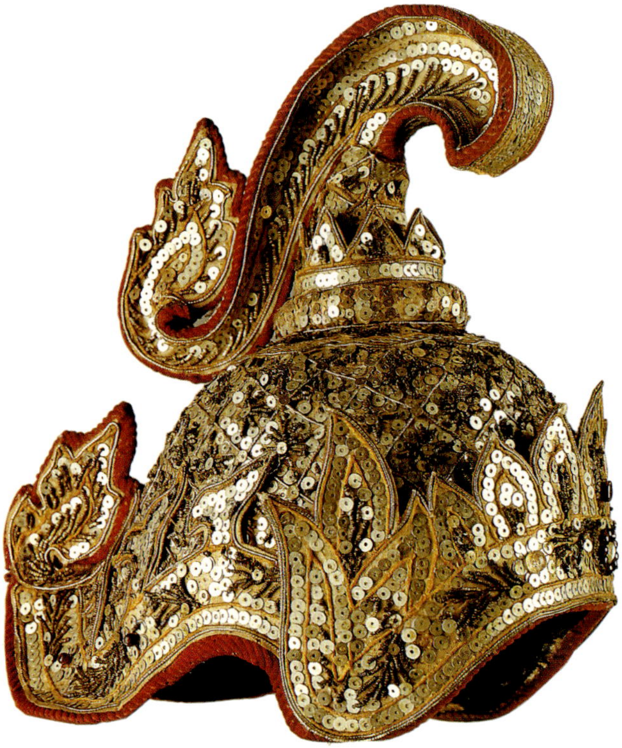

222 A headdress decorated with *shwe chi doe* embroidery, worn by a young man in the initiation ceremony for the monkhood.

Similar designs were used on crowns and headdresses. A stiff pâpier-maché helmet shape was covered with a cotton base and over-sewn with tinsel cloth and velvet to form a backing for gold and silver metal thread, pearls, sequins and semi-precious stones. Leather saddles, harnesses, floor covers, shoes, cushions and coffin covers were decorated in a similar fashion.

In the Shan States appliqué and couching techniques were combined to create wall hangings, curtains and smaller items such as cushions. They were also used as backdrops for live performances and puppet shows. Described by European and Burmese scholars as *shwe chi doe* or *kalaga*, the designs feature scenes from the Buddhist Jataka stories and Shan history and mythology, lunar calendars, signs of the zodiac and stylised landscapes.[18] The most elaborate *shwe chi doe* were produced by groups of skilled female embroiderers working under royal patronage. Nineteenth-century hangings were highly embellished with gold and silver metal thread, silver and gold sequins, tinsel cloth, mother-of-pearl sequins, semi-precious stones, coloured beads and coloured glass.[19] Sumptuary laws controlled their production and distribution.[20] Making a large hanging was a complicated process. An artist marked out the plan on a backing cloth, indicating where all the main characters and scenes were to be placed. The figures, background elements, and border designs were prepared individually by a number of skilled female embroiderers. They used an assortment of fabrics and stitched them to a cotton backing cloth, stretched on an

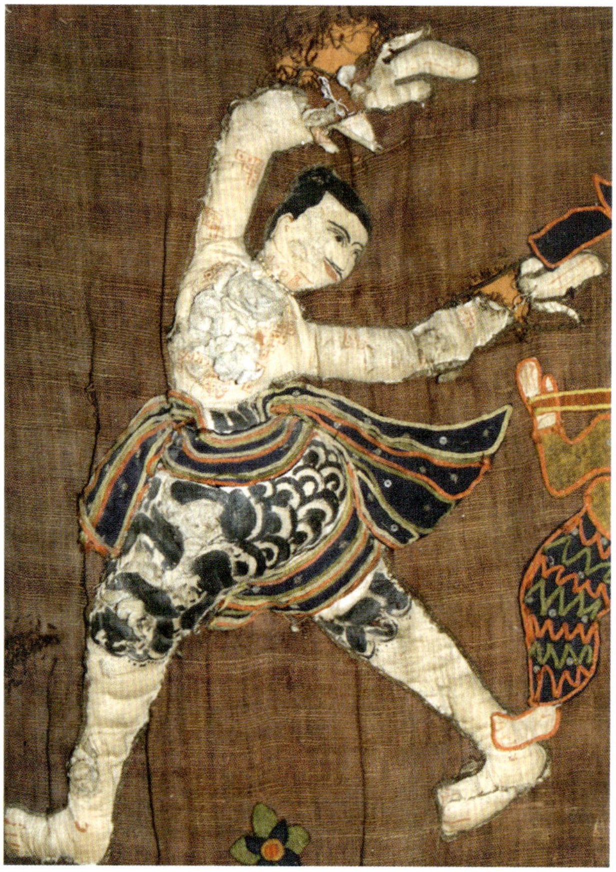

223 Detail of appliqué on a wall hanging. The damaged surface reveals the cotton used to stuff the figure. *(Private collection)*

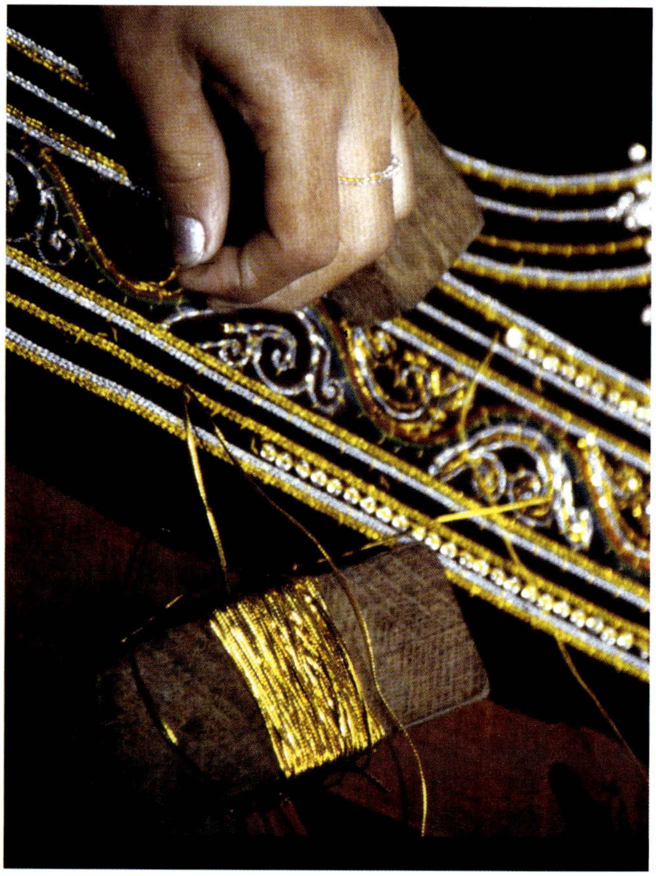

224 Couching gold metal wire.

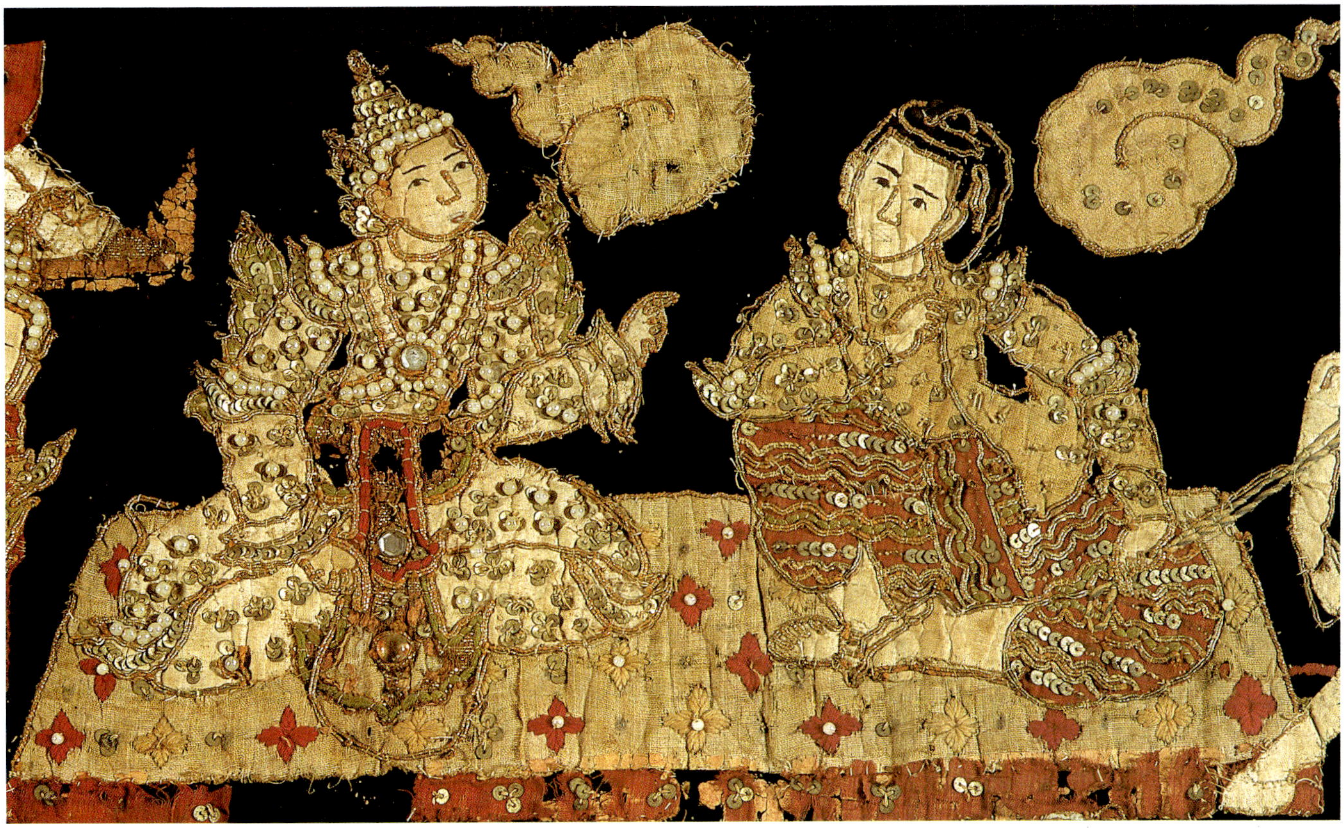

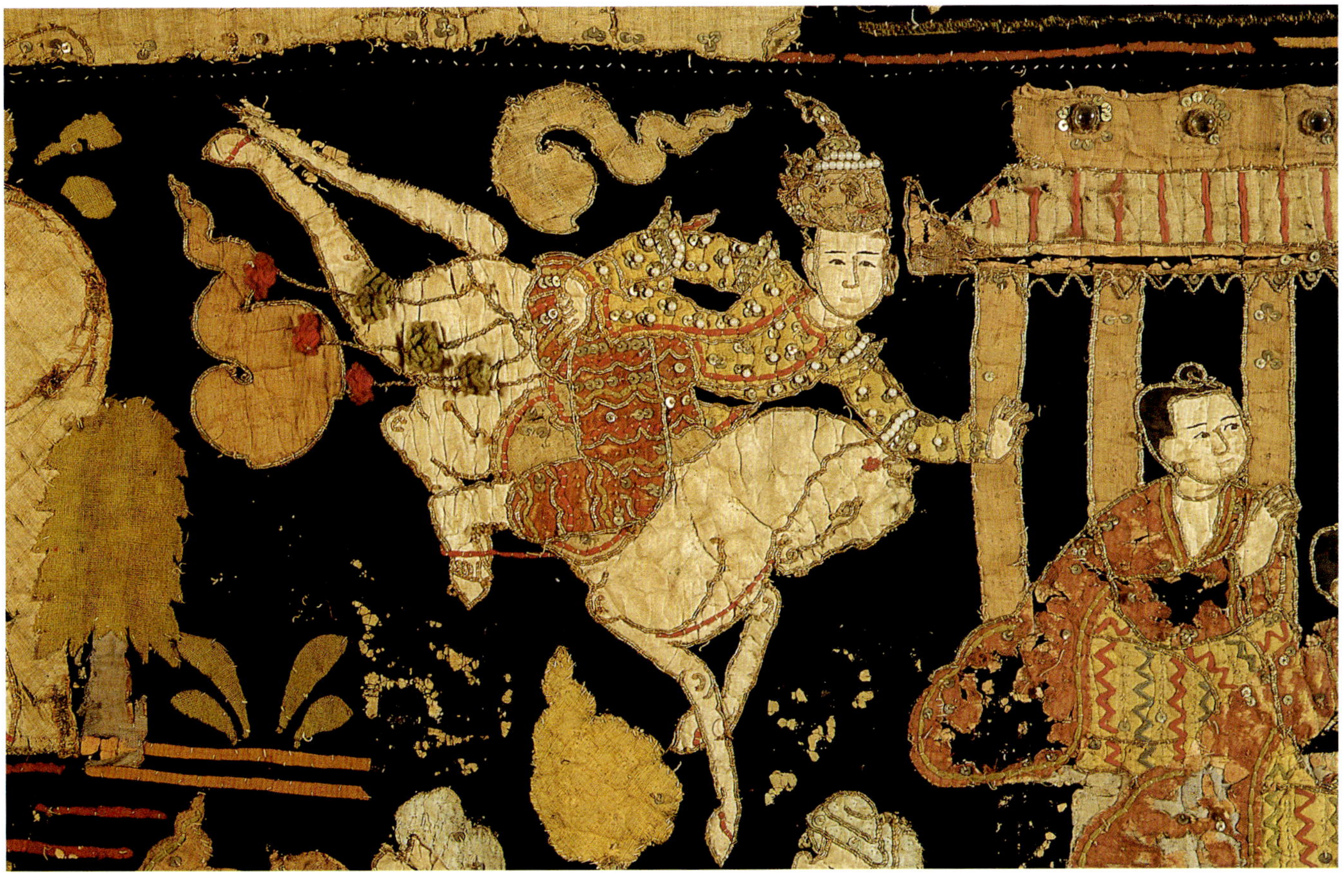

225 and **226** Details from a large hanging of *shwe chi doe* embroidery. The theme is the Life of the Buddha. *(Private collection)*

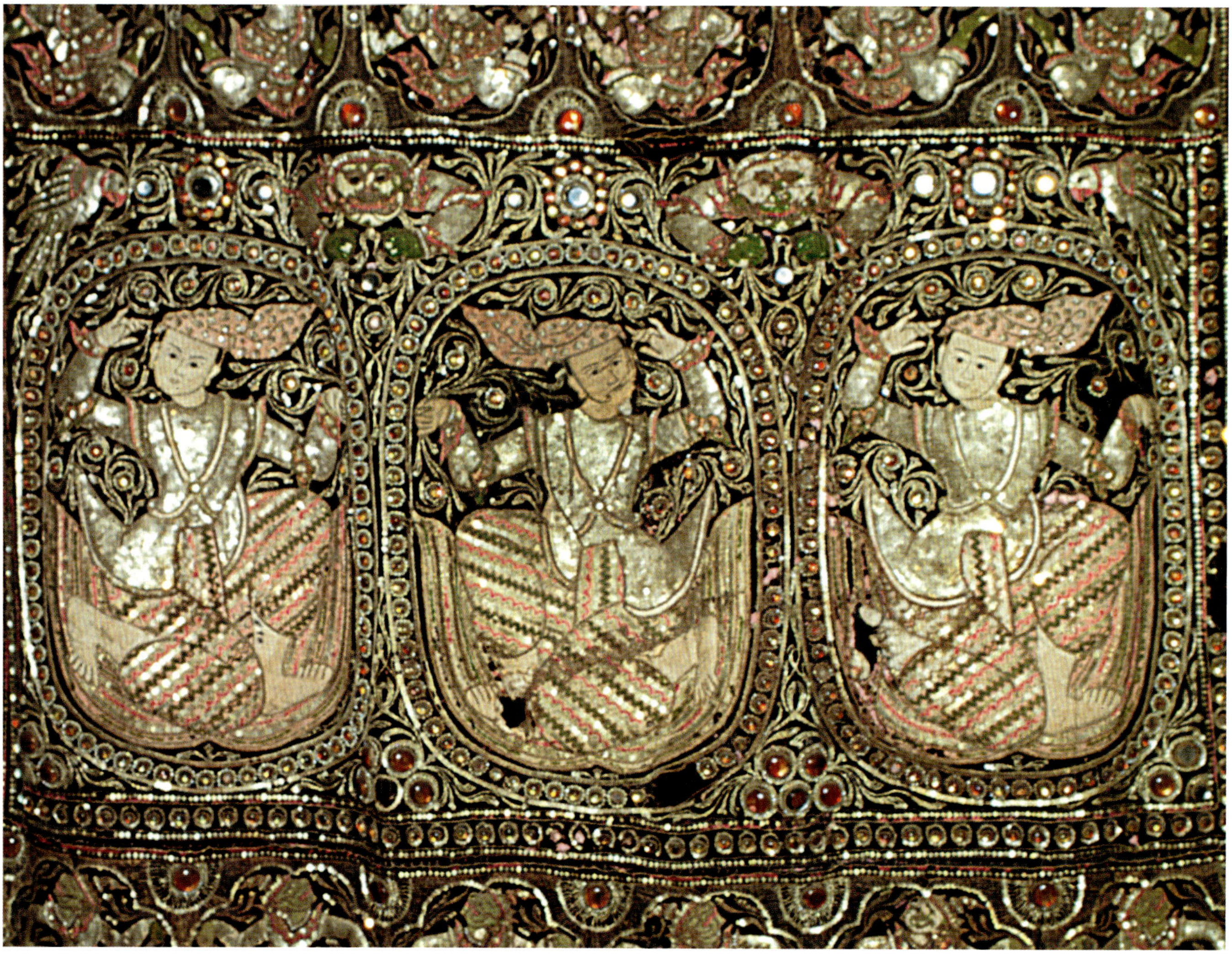

227 Detail of a *shwe chi doe* embroidery. *(Private collection)*

embroidery frame. The finest detail in the designs, for example the faces, were drawn with ink and covered in simple embroidery stitches, or they were cut from minute scraps of fabric. Trimmings of ribbons and sequins and couched gold and silver metal thread were laid over the fabrics. Some figures were padded with cotton to add a three-dimensional effect. When a design was finished, it was taken off the embroidery frame and stitched in place on the main backing cloth. When all the pieces were in place, final embellishments were added. The backing cloth provides a contrast to the brightly coloured appliqué fabrics and couched gold and silver thread. If a very large hanging was made, it was reinforced with an extra layer of cotton backing. A rod is passed through the top hem, or threaded through hooks attached to the top of the hanging so that it can be suspended from a wall or secured between wooden posts.

On ceremonial occasions, members of the Shan royal families posed in front of these impressive hangings. The Shan princes and princesses were similarly photographed at the Delhi Durbar of 1903 (see chapter three, fig. 86 and chapter four fig. 149). From these photographs and the style, content and type of fabrics used, it is possible to estimate a date when the hanging was made. In the photograph of the *myosa* of Pangmi and his family, there are two cloths in the background that are stylistically different (see chapter two fig. 47). The hanging on the right side of the photograph is similar in theme, design and content to other Shan *shwe chi doe* but that on the left is a Chinese landscape with mountains, rocks and pagodas.

Quilting

Quilting involves stitching a layer of cotton padding between two layers of fabric. The patterns are created with running stitches that are worked through all three layers. This technique was used to make blouses and jackets for the cool season. The fabrics were silk and cotton. If white or cream was used, the stitching was worked in a slightly darker or lighter shade to create interesting tonal contrasts. Silk stitching on cotton fabric also achieves subtle textural contrasts. The stitches were worked in geometric repeats or in simple floral and leaf patterns, with a border design on the front openings, the hem, the collar and sleeve cuffs.

229 A quilted cotton jacket with silk stitching in geometric patterns. *(Private collection)*

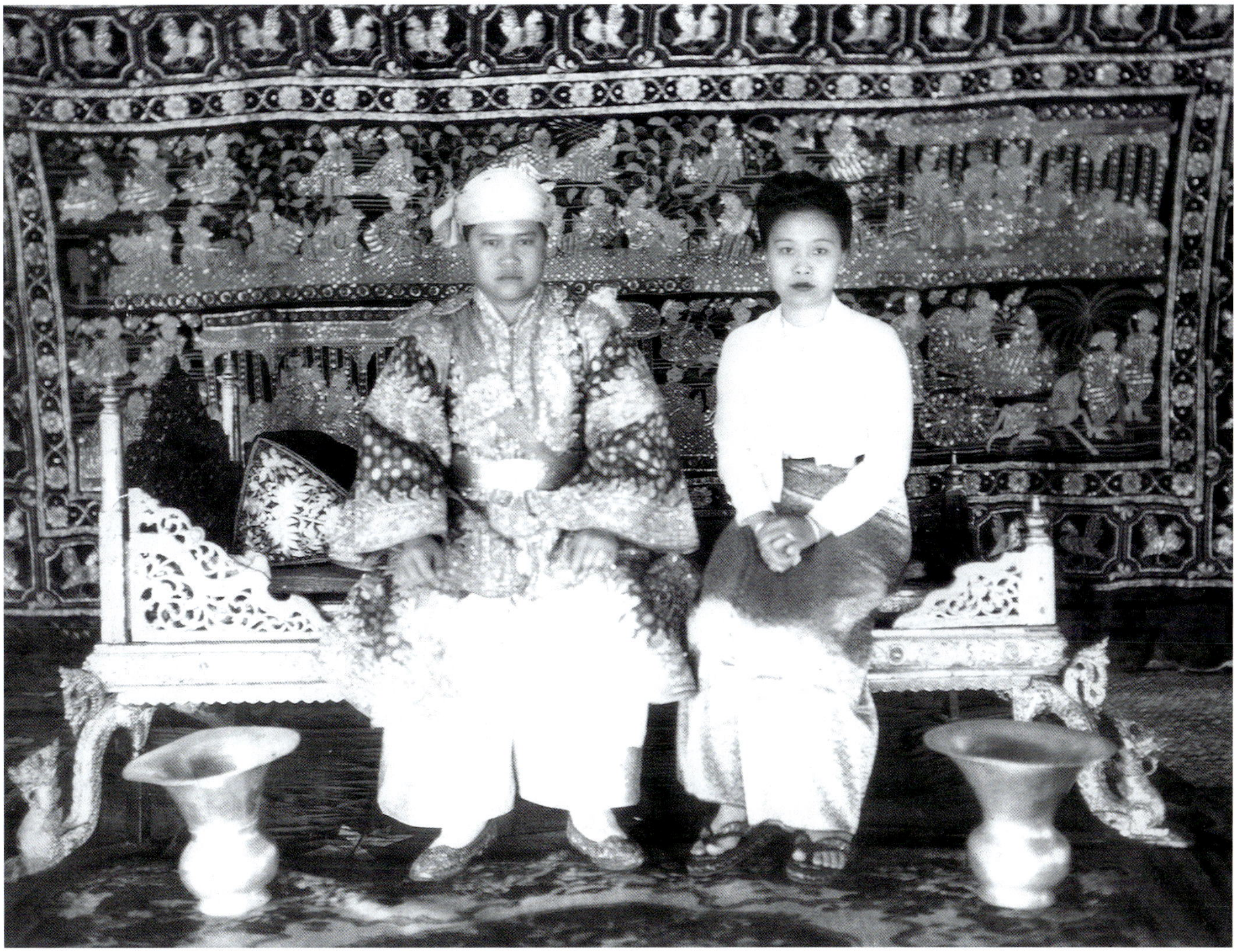

228 A photograph of Sao Hso Hom of South Hsenwi (Muong Yai) and Sao Nyunt Kyi of Lawksawk seated in front of a *shwe chi doe* hanging. They were ready to receive local officials and village chiefs who had come to pay tribute. *(Permission of Nel Adams (Sao Noan Oo))*

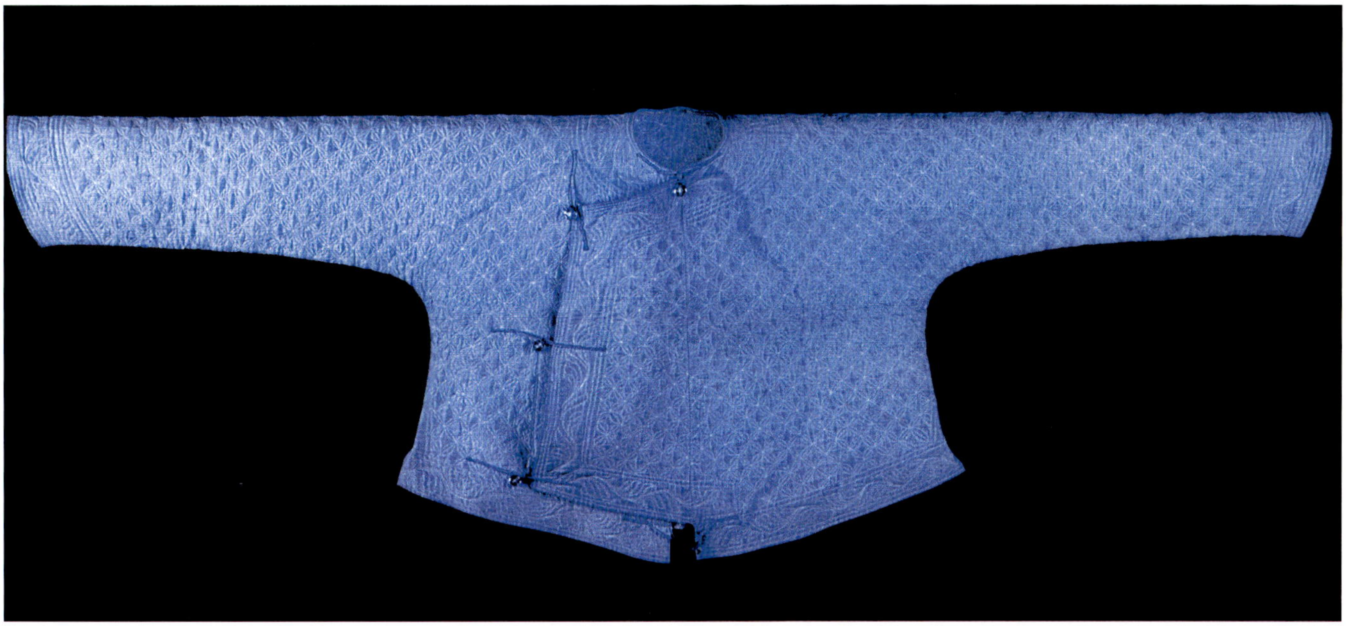

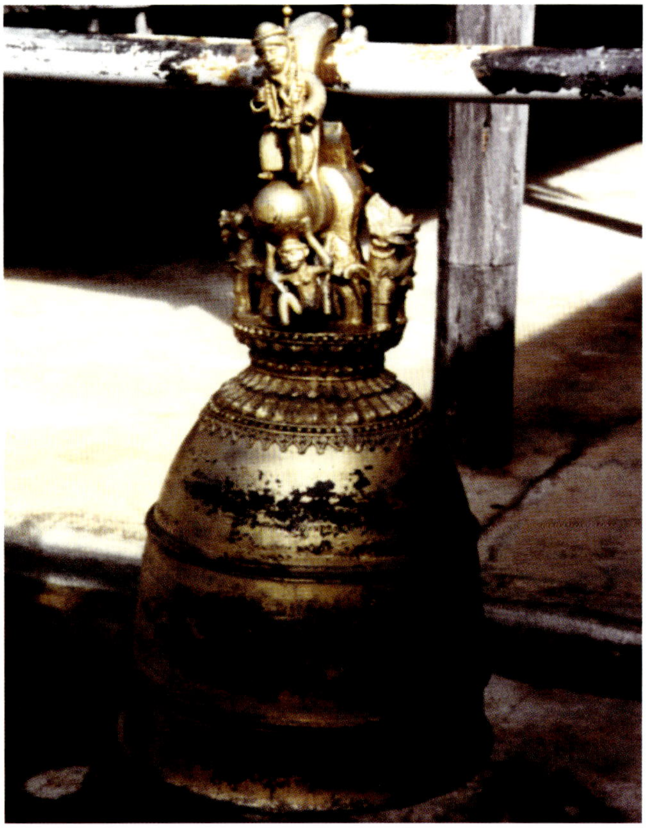

230 Bronze bell at Wat Maha Kaew.

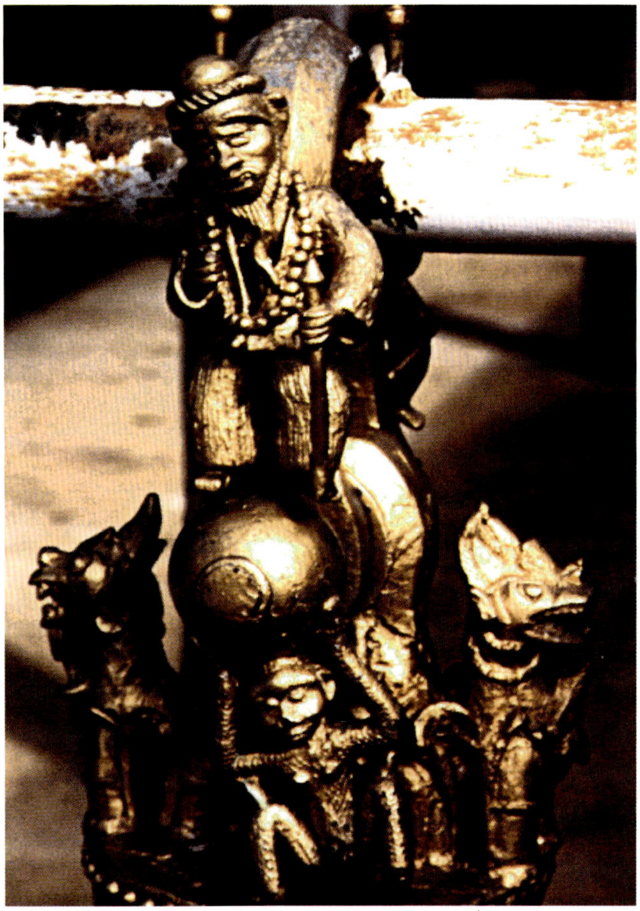

231 The handle of the bronze bell shown above.

Metalwork

The Shan were famous for the quality and tone of their bronze bells. Many, still in use today, are ancient, like the bell at Wat Maha Kaew, a monastery on the outskirts of Keng Tung. The monks claim it has been in continuous use for over five hundred years, and it produces a rich, mellow tone.[21] The bell-making process involves the lost-wax technique. First a bell-shaped clay core mould is made and left to dry. It is then coated with a layer of soft wax to which a little oil has been added. Fine details are etched in the wax and moulded pieces of wax are added if a surface relief pattern is intended. Great care is taken because the design of the bell depends on the skilful way the wax is crafted. When this stage is completed, the wax is coated with a clay slip. An outer shell of coarse clay is built up, layer upon layer, until it is thick enough to support the molten metal during the casting process. A number of thin, hollow rods are inserted through the layers of clay and wax to give support. At the time of casting, the clay mould is heated, and the wax liquefies and runs out through the rods. Molten bronze is poured in to replace it. Care is taken to ensure there are no air pockets. The metal is left to cool, after which the outer mould is carefully removed, along with the support rods. Then the inner clay core is chipped away. Any rough surfaces are removed with a cold chisel, and the bell is smoothed with a file. Bells with the best sound are cast from bronze made of four parts copper and two parts tin.[22] Silver, donated by the Buddhist faithful, is often added to the melting pot.

The casting of Buddha images is treated as a special assignment and due deference is shown at all stages of production. The lost-wax technique is the method used. If the proposed image is large, it is cast in sections and soldered together, or secured with brass pins. Great care is taken on the detail applied to the wax mould, particularly for the features, the hair, the hands and feet and the folds of the robe. When the image is removed from the cast, it is smoothed with a chisel, rubbed with sandpaper and steel wool and polished with oil. The whole process can take many weeks.

The Shan also produced excellent silverware and Keng Tung and Laikha were particularly well known for the high quality of their products.[23] Sir George Scott described the tools and raw materials used by the silversmiths.

> *The silver worker's whole stock-in-trade is not very great. He has some anvils of bronze and iron, and some punches of the same materials, a few clay crucibles, and a bamboo blast, a blow pipe, solder and flux, wire plate and beading plate, aquafortis and mercury, and a few hammers of different sizes.*[24]

With these simple tools, Shan artisans produced the finest engraving, repoussé and inlay work for ceremonial vessels, dishes, betel boxes and swords and scabbards.[25] Their skill and finesse is evident in the silverware displayed in Shan court photographs.

Scott claimed silversmiths never kept bullion in stock and that it was supplied by customers in the form of rupees which were melted down. However, there were productive silver mines in the northern Shan States, particularly at Bawdwin. The silver was over ninety-five per cent pure and was favoured by artisans because it was light and flexible to work with.[26] In 1918, output from Shan silver mines was recorded as one hundred and twenty-five thousand ounces, valued at over five thousand pounds sterling.

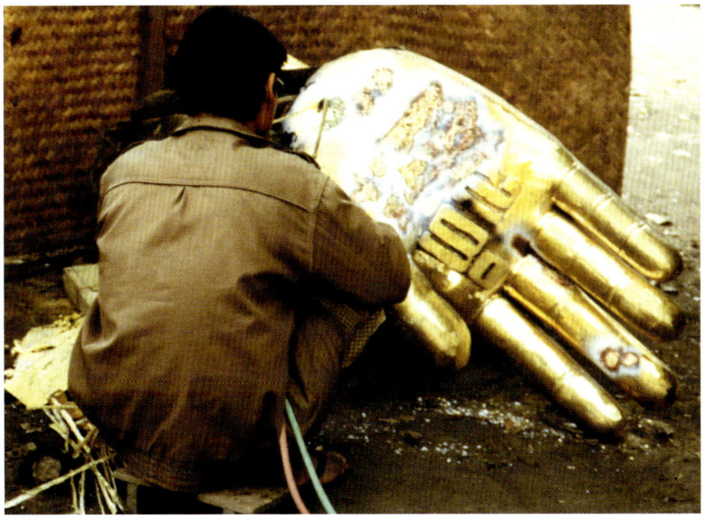

232 A metalworker preparing a hand to form part of a large Buddha image.

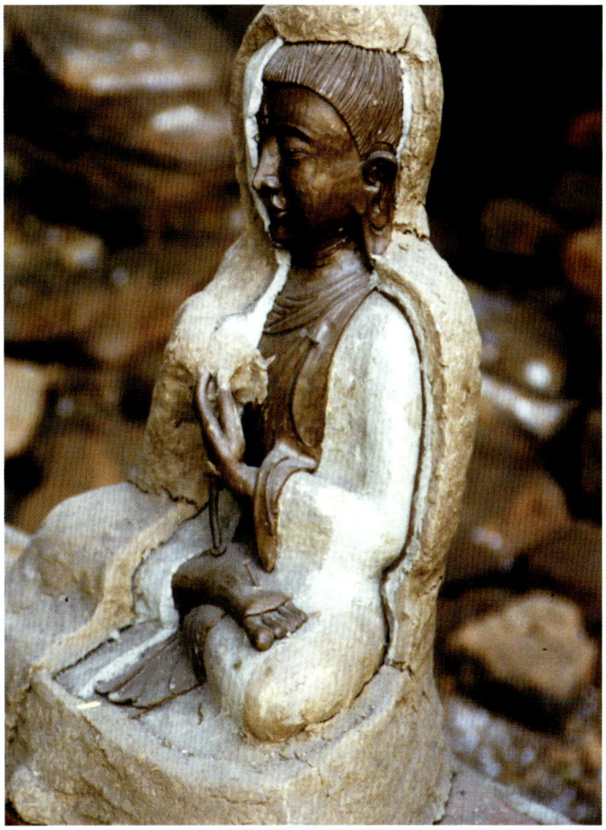

233 A Buddha image emerges from the casting process. The outer layer of coarse clay and the inner layer of clay slip are clearly visible.

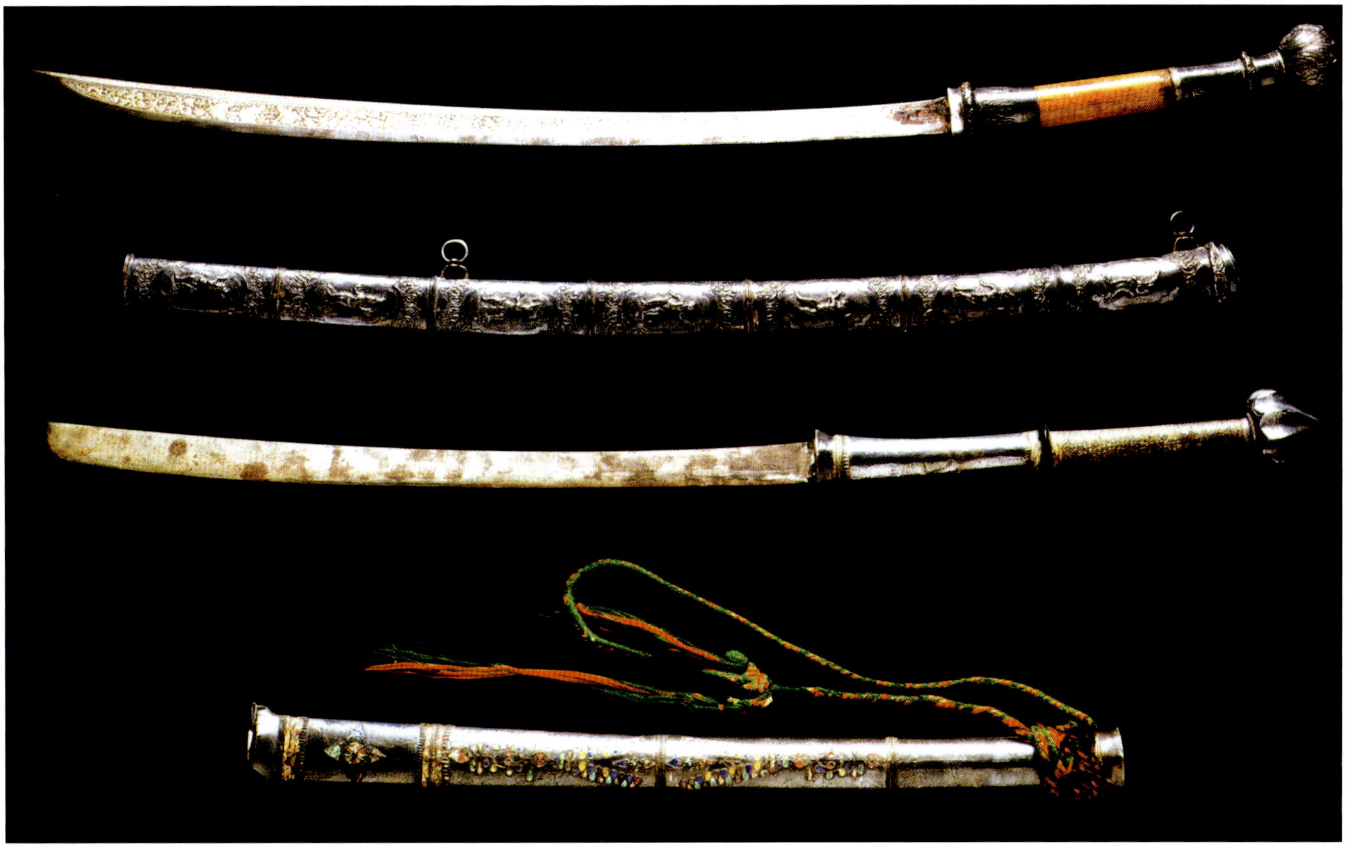

234 Top: A Shan sword and scabbard made of embossed and repoussé silver. The sword has an ivory handle.
Below: Shan sword with an iron blade and silver handle, and a scabbard inlaid with semi-precious stones. *(Private collection)*

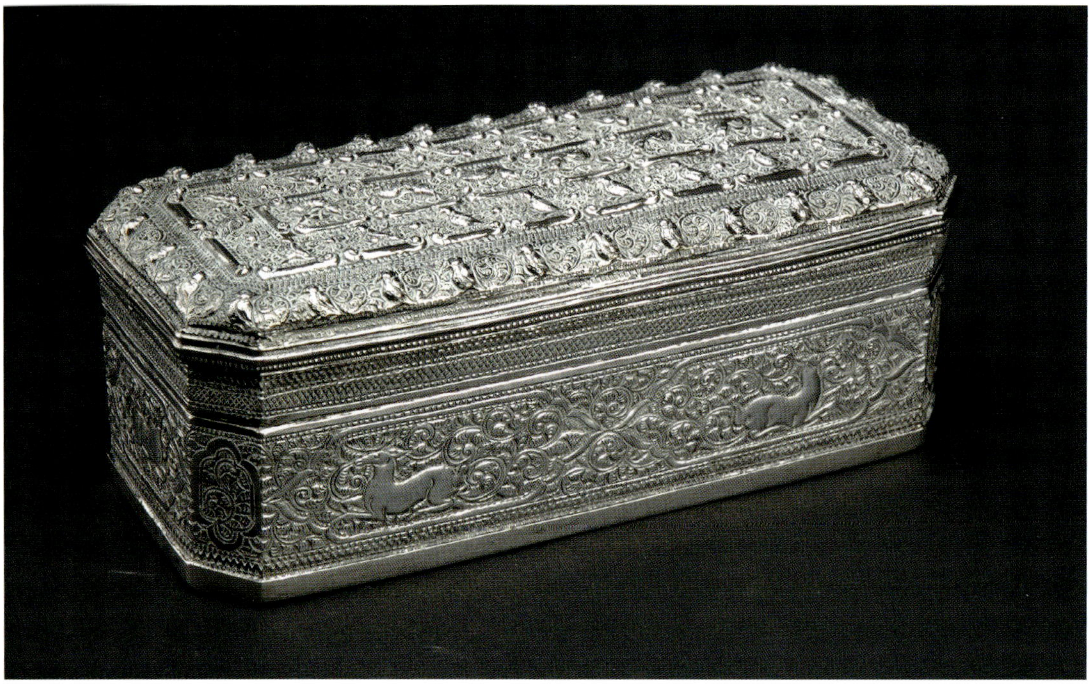

235 Silver repoussé box. *(Elephant House collection)*

The repoussé technique involves carefully punching a design into relief on the surface. The designs are first marked in charcoal and etched with an engraver. The best repoussé is the work of masters who can create fine details and a sense of movement in the flora and fauna, which were popular subjects.

The Shan also produced fine jewellery. The silver mines of Baw-dwin have already been mentioned and gold was panned in the rivers although amounts were small. Muong Mit was rich in rubies, garnets and spinelles, and jade and amber were mined in Singkaling Hkamti. Amber came from a valley north of Myitkyina. The most important ruby and sapphire mining district was Mogok. Many mines were owned by, or leased to, members of the Shan royal family.

Shan jewellery was mainly worn in the form of ear cylinders, chains, filigree pendants, brooches, bracelets, and hair ornaments. The elite had their jewellery set with rubies, sapphires, garnets and spinelles. They also wore jade and amber as necklaces and earplugs. The distinctive Shan topknot was held in place with silver pins, combs and chains. A love of jewellery was found at every level of society. Carl Bock claimed that there were one or two artisans working in every major village, filling orders for silver earrings, bangles, bracelets and hairpins.[27]

Diamonds and emeralds were imported from India and pearls were from Sri Lanka or Mergui in Burma. From the late nineteenth century, pearl necklaces, gold and diamond ear studs set with rubies, and diamond hair ornaments were set in European style. The photograph of Sao Nang Ya of Yawnghwe (see chapter four, fig. 136) shows the type of jewellery worn by the upper classes at that time. Imported items were often incorporated with locally mined gemstones. When he called on the *mahadevi* of Laikha, Maurice Collis wrote,

> *Round her neck she had a string of heavy pearls, under which hung huge tassels of rubies. ...In the knot of hair coiled over the nape of her neck was a diamond comb.*[28]

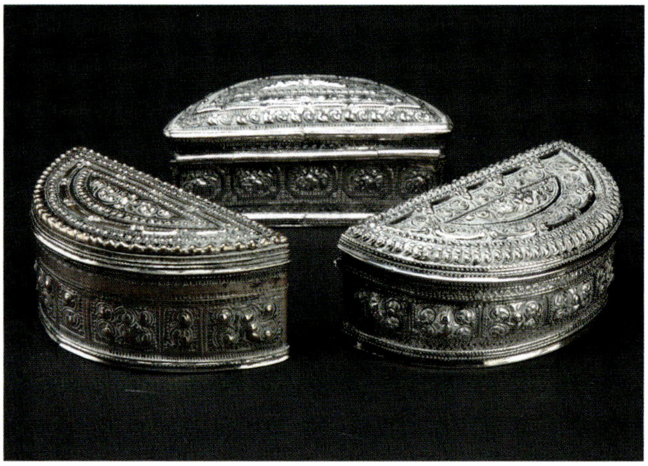

236 Shan silver boxes. *(Elephant House collection)*

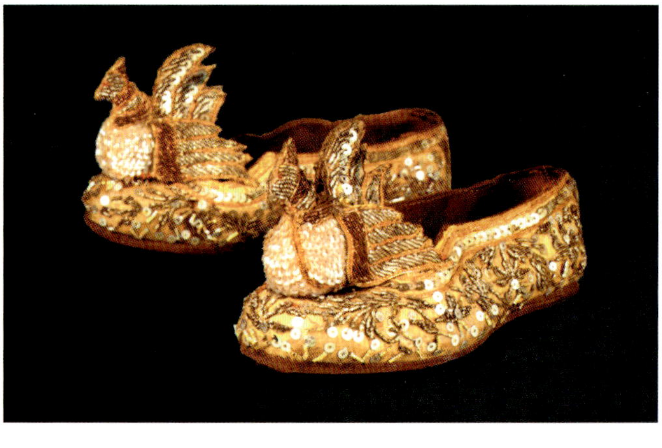

237 A pair of shoes in the shape of a *hintha* bird, couched with gold wire and sequins.

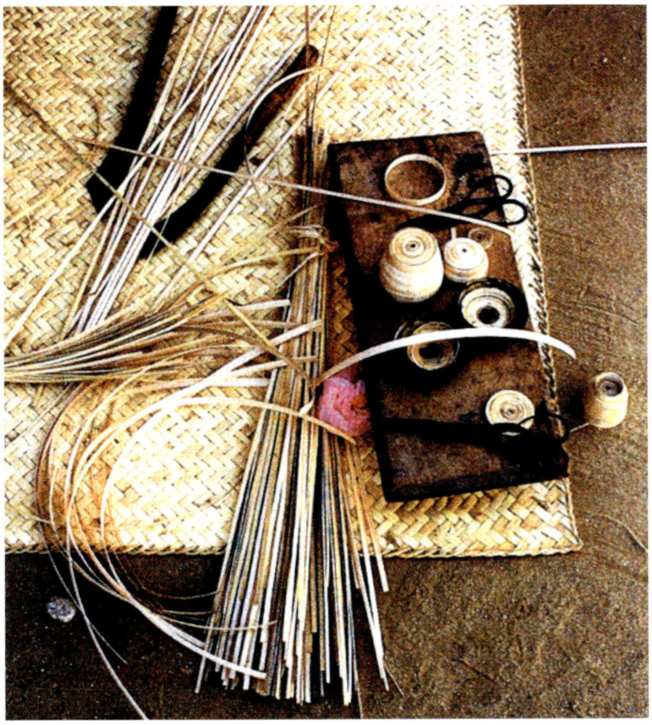

238 Narrow strips of bamboo and tools used to construct the coiled and plaited bamboo foundation for lacquer, from *Burma and the Art of Lacquer*, Isaacs, R. and Blurton, T. R., 2000, p. 32.

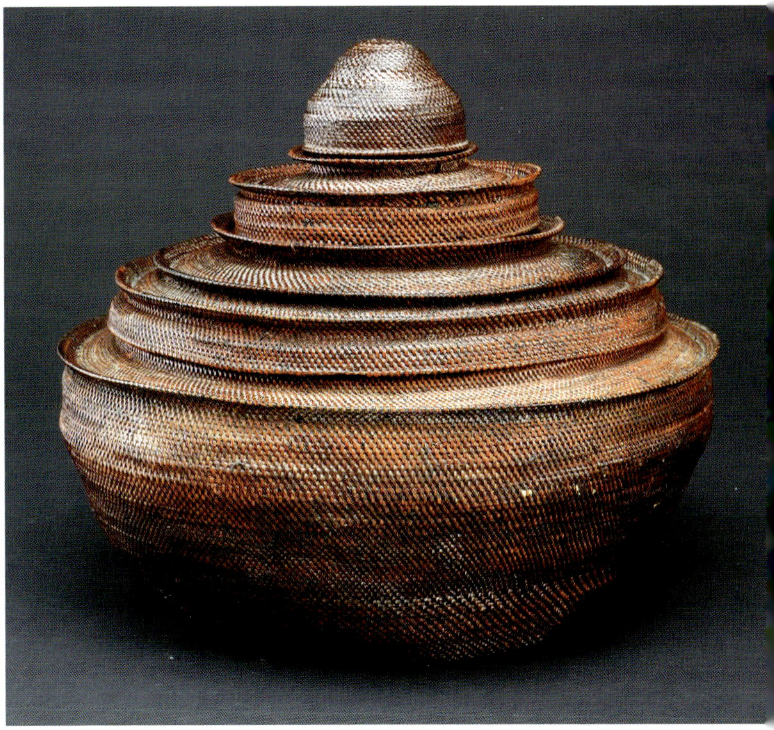

239 Set of lightly lacquered bamboo baskets. *(Elephant House collection)*

When the British occupied the Shan States, they commissioned local artisans to create a range of items in silver that demonstrated the customs of the British Raj. Card and menu holders, napkin rings, elaborate table centre pieces, salt and pepper shakers and salvers set the tone for their formal dinner parties. Elegant teapots, sugar bowls, spoons and jugs were produced for afternoon tea and card boxes for bridge parties.[29]

Shoes

Shoes for everyday were made of buffalo and bullock hides. Some were backless or a leather sole was fitted with a thong. Shoes for ceremonial use were couched with silver and gold metal thread and silver and gold sequins. The *hintha* bird was a decoration used on royal shoes, as can be seen in the photograph of Sir Sao Che of Hsipaw (see chapter three, fig. 74). Brightly coloured fabric shoes with leather soles were decorated with floss-silk embroidery and metal sequins.

Lacquer

Artisans in the Shan States were famous for high quality lacquer that in the nineteenth century was produced in Laikha, Mong Nai and Keng Tung, and in workshops around Inlay Lake, particularly in the district near the Hpaung-taw U pagoda.[30] Henry Burney, Resident of the East India Company at the Court of Ava wrote in 1832,

> *The first and by far the best articles are brought from the Shan countries... The Shan ware may be distinguished by the lightness and elegance of the manufactures, and the superior brilliancy of the varnish and colours.*[31]

Lacquer is produced from the resin of the tree *gluta usitata* that grows profusely in the Shan States. It is harvested by scoring the bark of the tree from which the sap runs, a technique similar to rubber tapping. The resin can be used to waterproof and heatproof the surface of bamboo, wood and leather.

The construction of lacquer objects involves a foundation of coiled or plaited bamboo, or bamboo and horsehair for the smallest containers. This basic shape may be dipped in diluted lacquer that strengthens and waterproofs it without concealing the plaited patterns. Or, part of the object may be lacquered, usually the base and stem, so that a portion of the plaited bamboo is exposed. Finely woven lacquered bamboo, and gilded containers produced in this way, are listed with other gifts presented by Shan royalty to the princes and chiefs throughout inland Southeast Asia.

In terms of surface decoration, the Shan produced relief-moulded lacquer (*thayo*), inlay (*hmanzi shwei-cha*), incised lacquer (*yun*) gilded lacquer (*shwe zawa*) and dry lacquer (*man hpaya*). If the object is to be completely lacquered, it is coated on the inside with a paste (*thayo*) made of lacquer sap and ash or lacquer sap and fine clay. The *thayo* fills the tiny spaces between the plaiting, and produces a smooth surface. The vessel is then left for a week in a dark, damp store to dry. The exterior is coated again in the same way and left to dry. This process continues until the lacquer paste has penetrated the plaiting and a surface has been achieved that can be smoothed evenly on a lathe. Next, a finer lacquer paste is made from lacquer sap and the ash of cow bones or of rice straw. It is applied with the fingers and requires great skill and dexterity to create a smooth patina. This is again dried and finally the lacquer surface is smoothed. Further

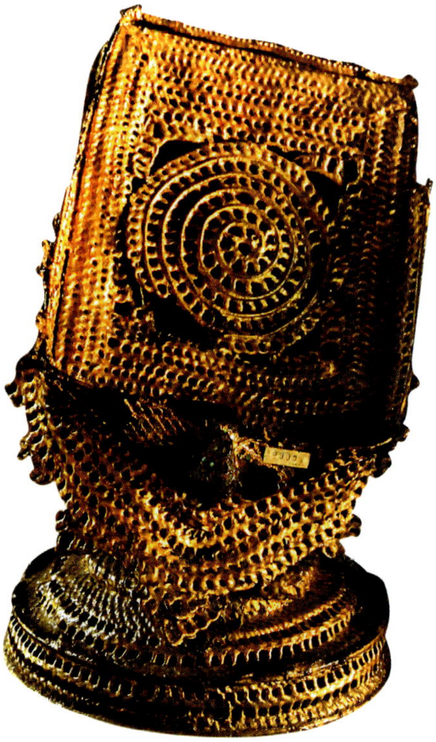

240 A lacquered and gilded bamboo mirror and stand. Shan Palace Museum, Yawnghwe.

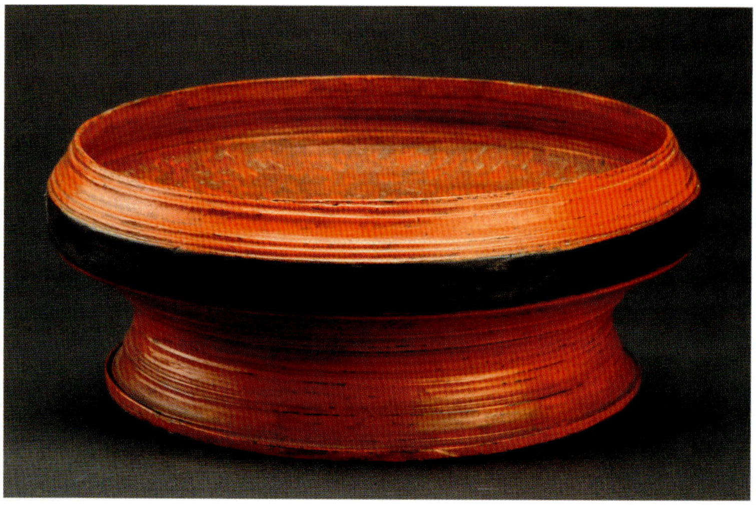

241 A lacquered bamboo pedestal tray. *(Elephant House collection)*

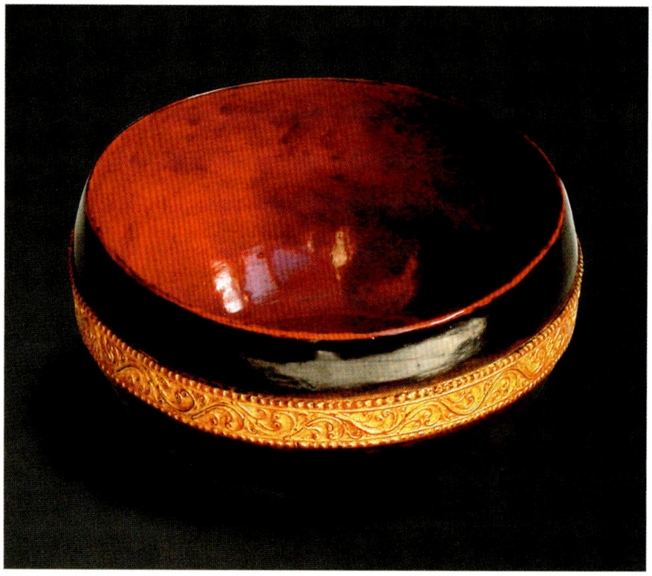

242 A lacquered and gilded bowl. *(Private collection)*

applications of plain lacquer sap help build the sheen that is the hallmark of high quality. If the final colour is to be other than black, pigment is added to the lacquer sap and applied by hand on top of the black lacquer. Red made from cinnabar and yellow from orpiment were common applications. This coating is also polished.

Relief-moulded lacquer involves preparing a fine lacquer and ash paste (*thayo*) that is rolled into long threads and applied to a smooth, lacquer-coated surface to form raised decoration. The artisan coils and twists the threads on the surface to create floral and leaf patterns and swirling geometric designs. Larger designs featuring excerpts from Buddhist mythology, human figures, mythical animals and birds, are produced in moulds that are filled with a thick lacquer paste. When dry they are turned out and lacquered, possibly gilded, and glued to the surface of the object. This mould technique was also used to create two-dimensional decoration on the interior wall panels and wooden pillars of temples and palaces. The most expensive form of relief-moulded lacquer is inlaid with semi-precious stones, coloured glass and mother-of-pearl. Each piece is coated with lacquer on the back and embedded in the design. *Thayo* is used to fill gaps. This surface may be given a covering of gold leaf, using thinned lacquer as glue. When the glue is dry, the surface is washed and the gold leaf comes away from the glass and stones and any other areas where the glue was not applied. The loose gold leaf is carefully saved for re-use. The elaborate food container on display in the Shan Palace Museum, Yawnghwe, (fig. 185) and the monk's preaching chair in Wat Na Phe Chaung, Inlay Lake (page 6), are fine examples of this technique.

Lacquer can be engraved using a tool that creates a groove in the smooth lacquer surface. The incisions are cleaned of any debris and filled with a mixture of lacquer and a colouring agent that adheres to the incised design. The article is left to dry and then polished with paddy husk on a lathe. Extra engraving lines and other colours can be added and the process repeated. Red, green, yellow and orange are the most common colours. When the process is finished, the surface is left to dry and then coated with neem (*Azadirachta indica*) resin.

The gilded lacquer technique involves using a neem resin glue mixed with a colouring agent. This is applied with a fine brush to a black lacquer surface to create the designs. Thin sheets of gold leaf are laid over the glued area. When the glue is dry the excess gold leaf is wiped off the unglued surfaces and kept for recycling. Another method involves using a water-soluble solution of yellow orpiment to paint the areas that will resist the gold leaf. Glue is applied to the remaining area and is covered in gold leaf. The object is left to allow the gum to dry. It is then washed to remove the resist paste and any excess gold leaf. This technique was used to decorate small items such as bowls and dishes.

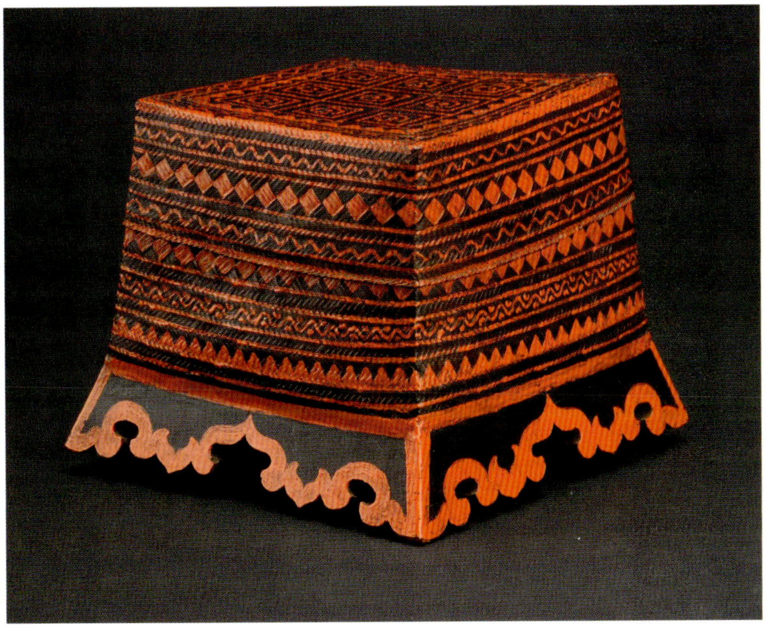

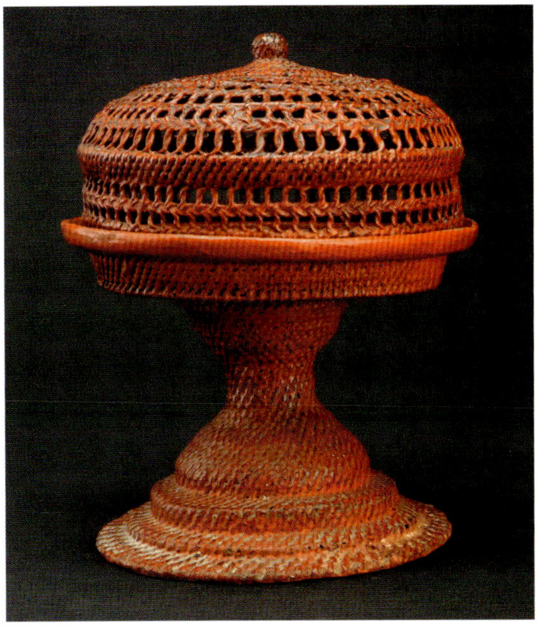

243 A lacquered bamboo woven box. *(Elephant House collection)*

244 A lacquered food container with lid. *(Elephant House collection)*

245 A large lacquered and gilded bowl on a pedestal. *(Elephant House collection)*

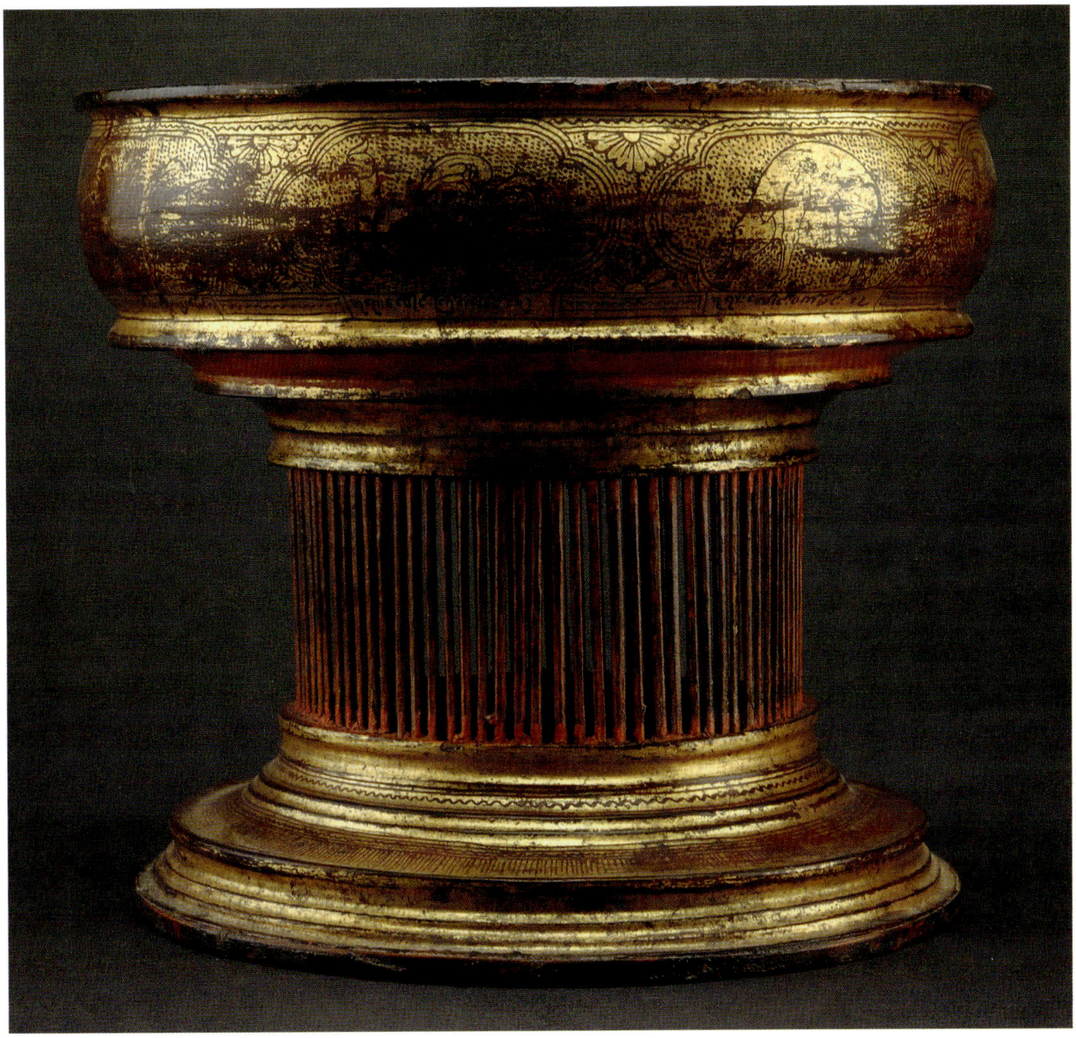

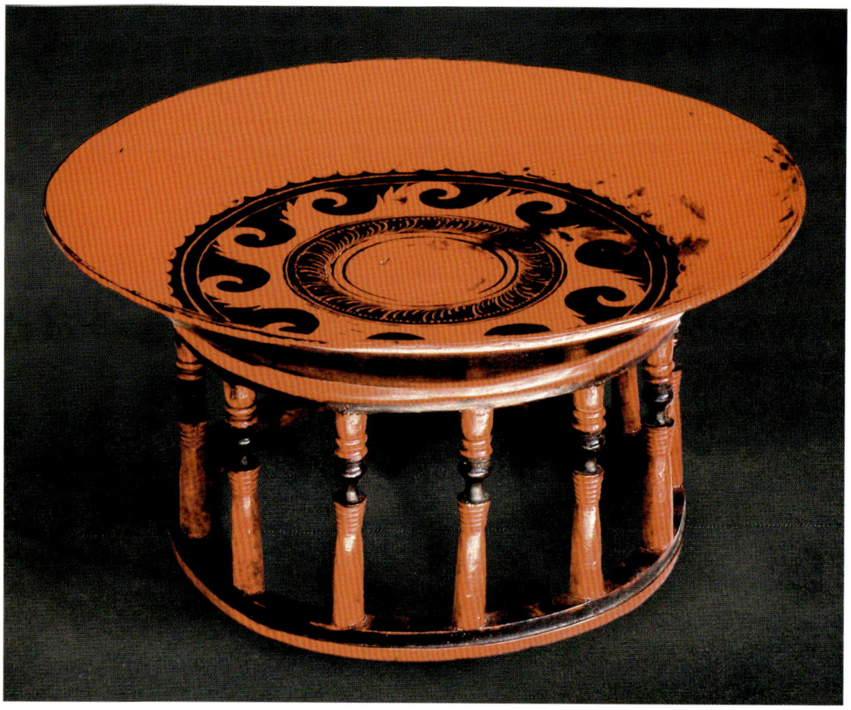

246-49 Three lacquered offering trays and a flat tray with typical Shan-style decoration in black and red.
(Private collection)

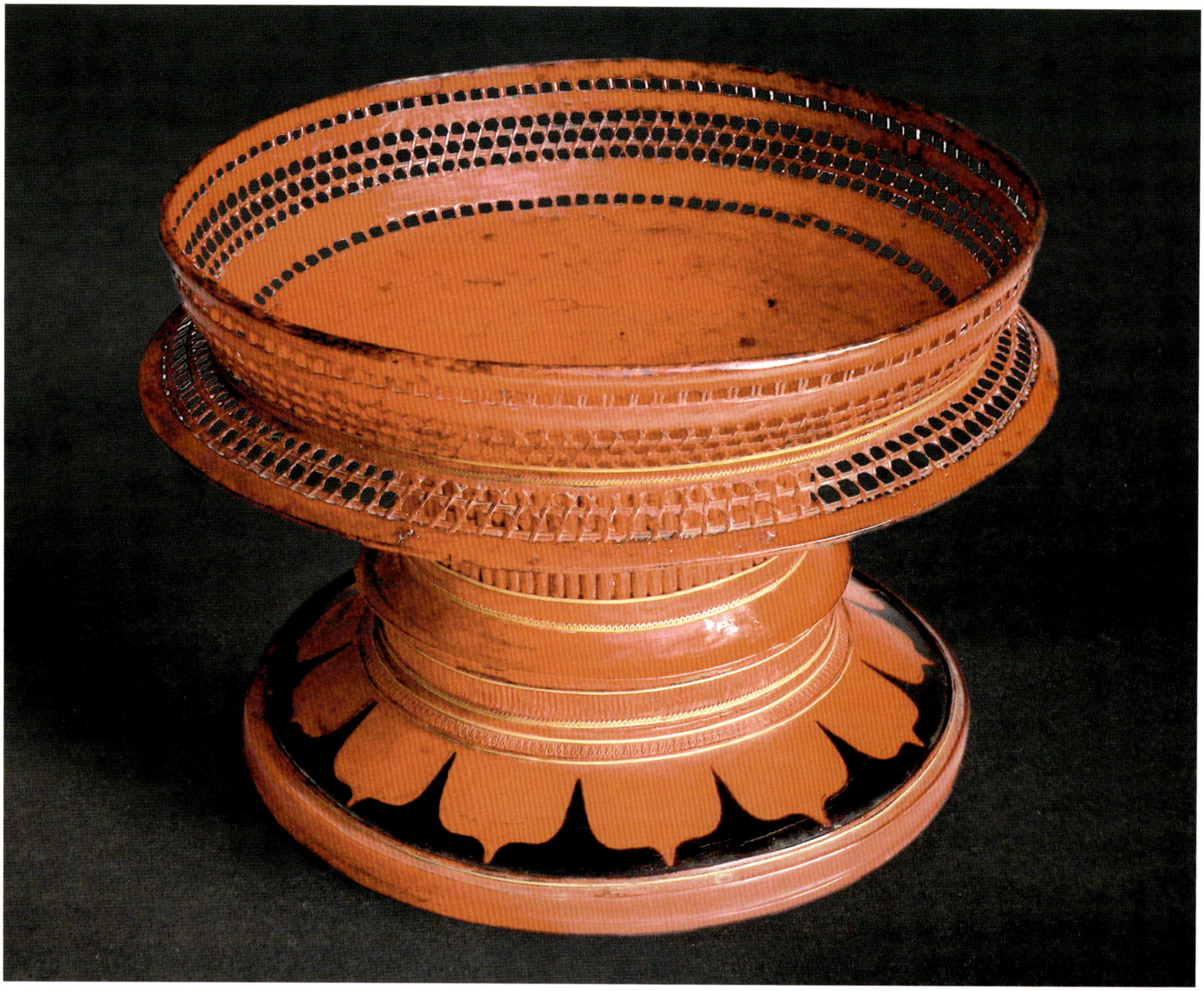

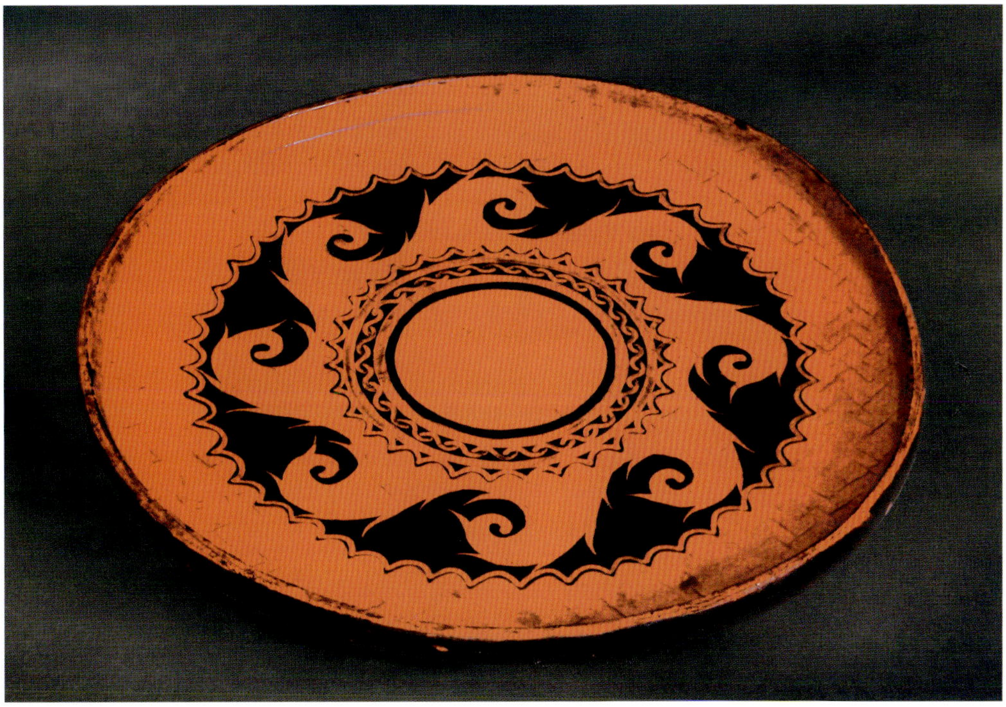

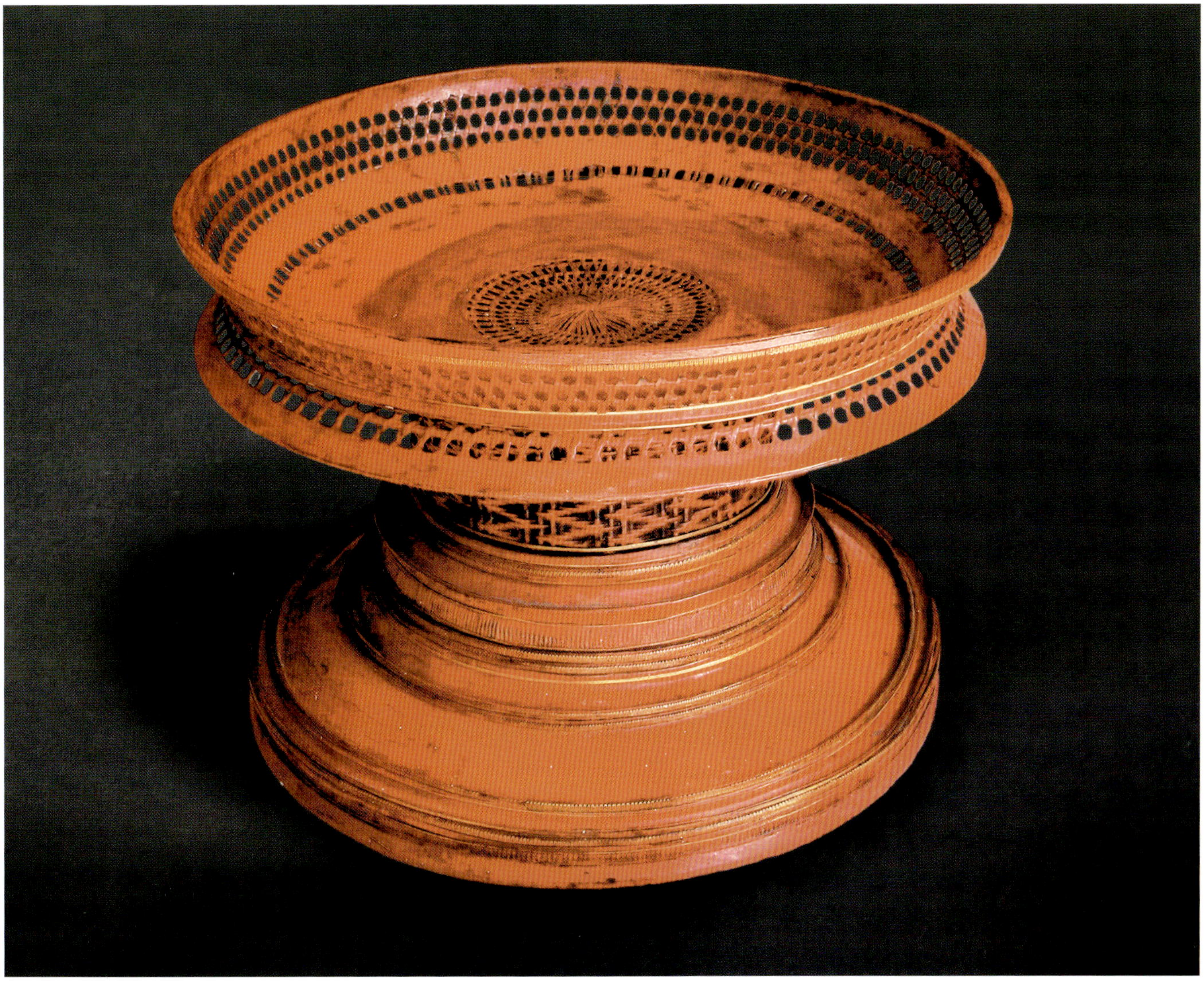

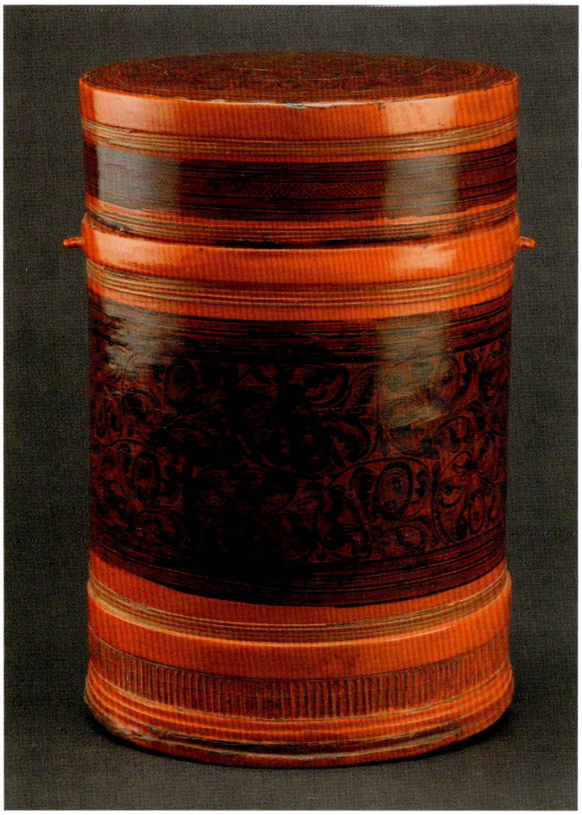

250-52 Red and black lacquer with a variety of floral motifs.
(Elephant House collection)

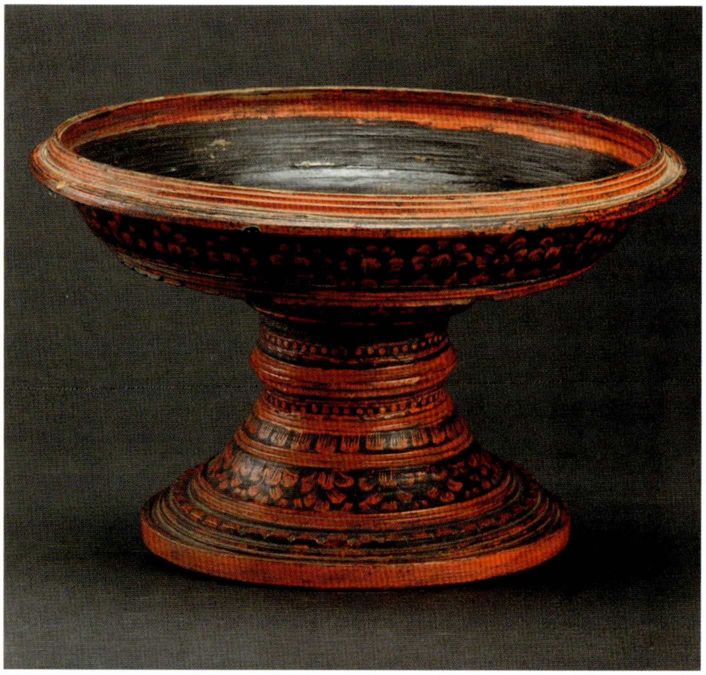

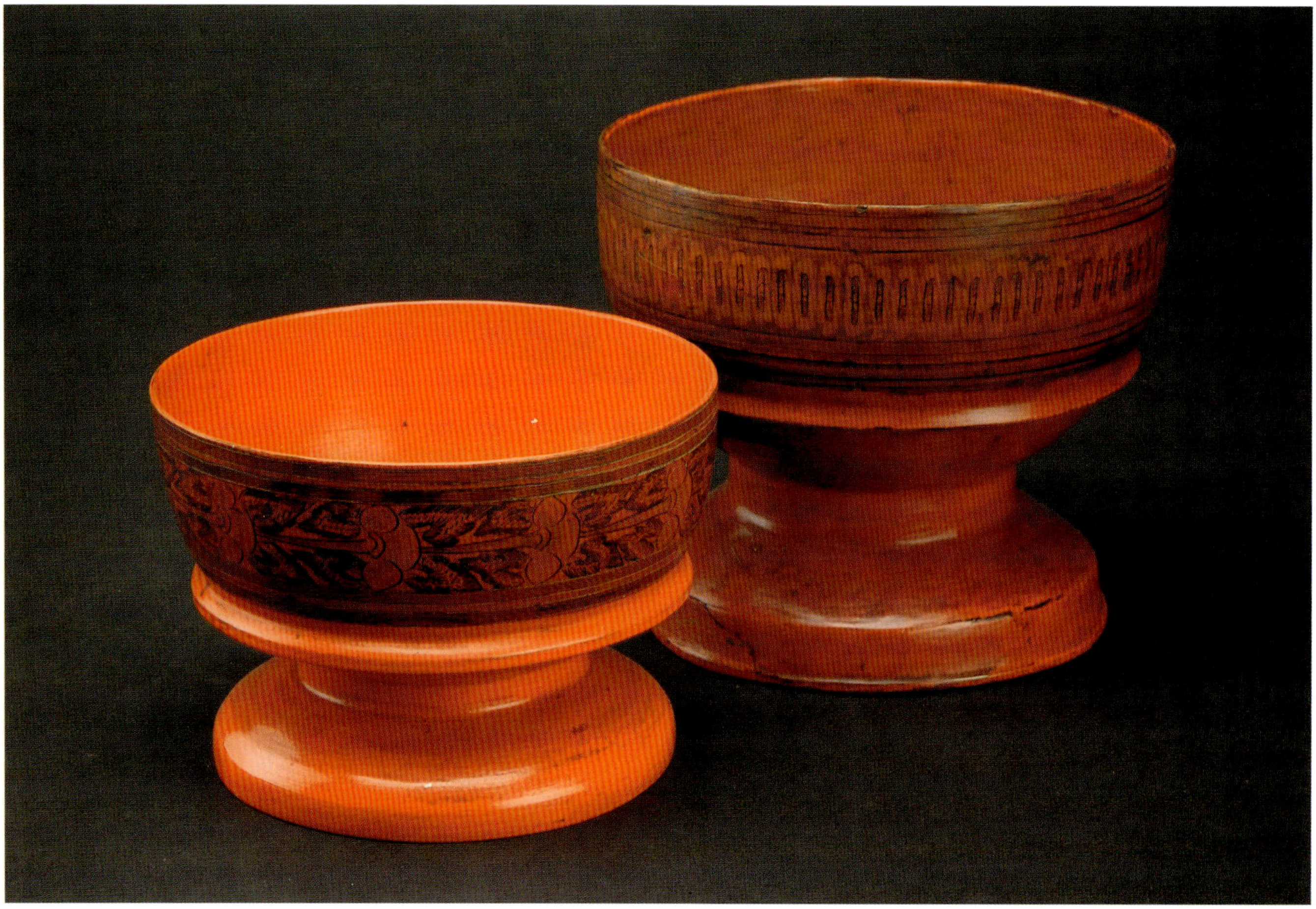

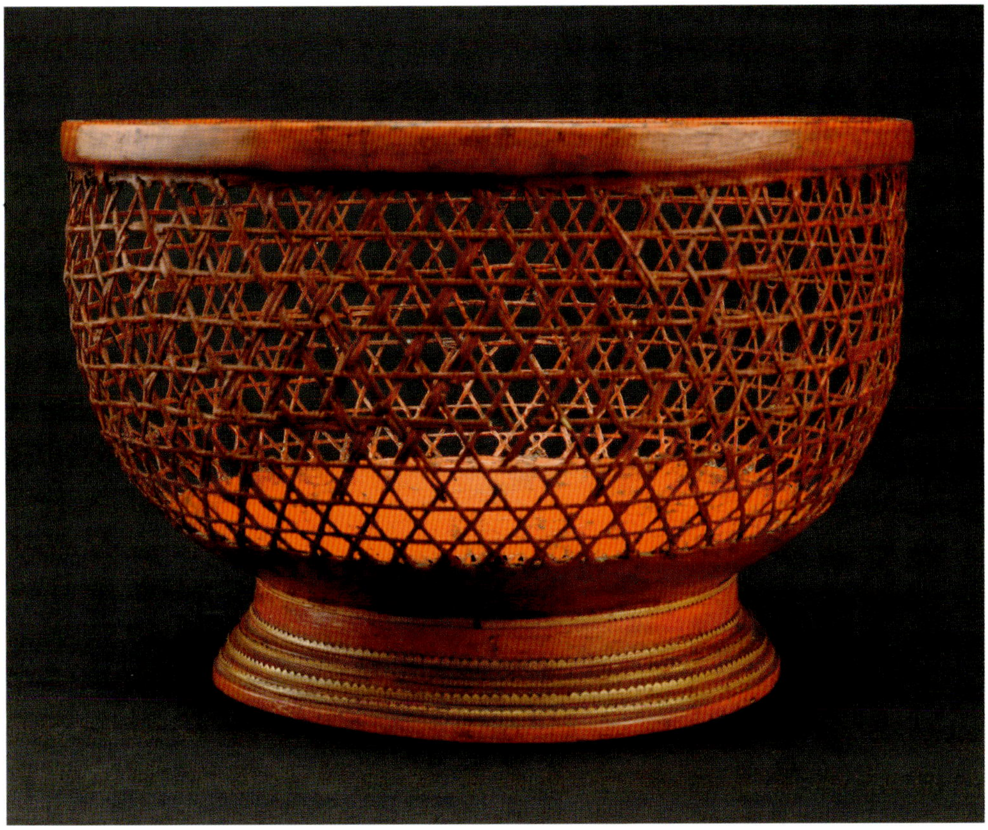

253. Open work lacquer bowl, Inlay Lake. *(Elephant House collection)*

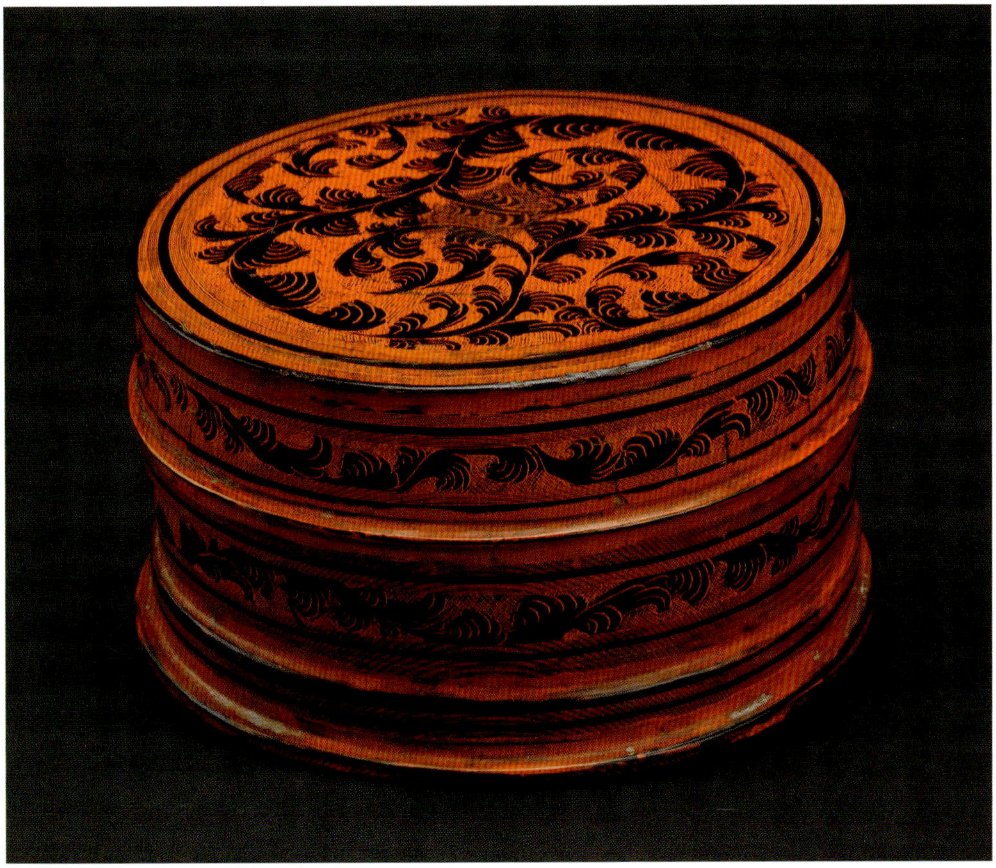

254 Black and red lacquer box, Inlay Lake. *(Elephant House collection)*

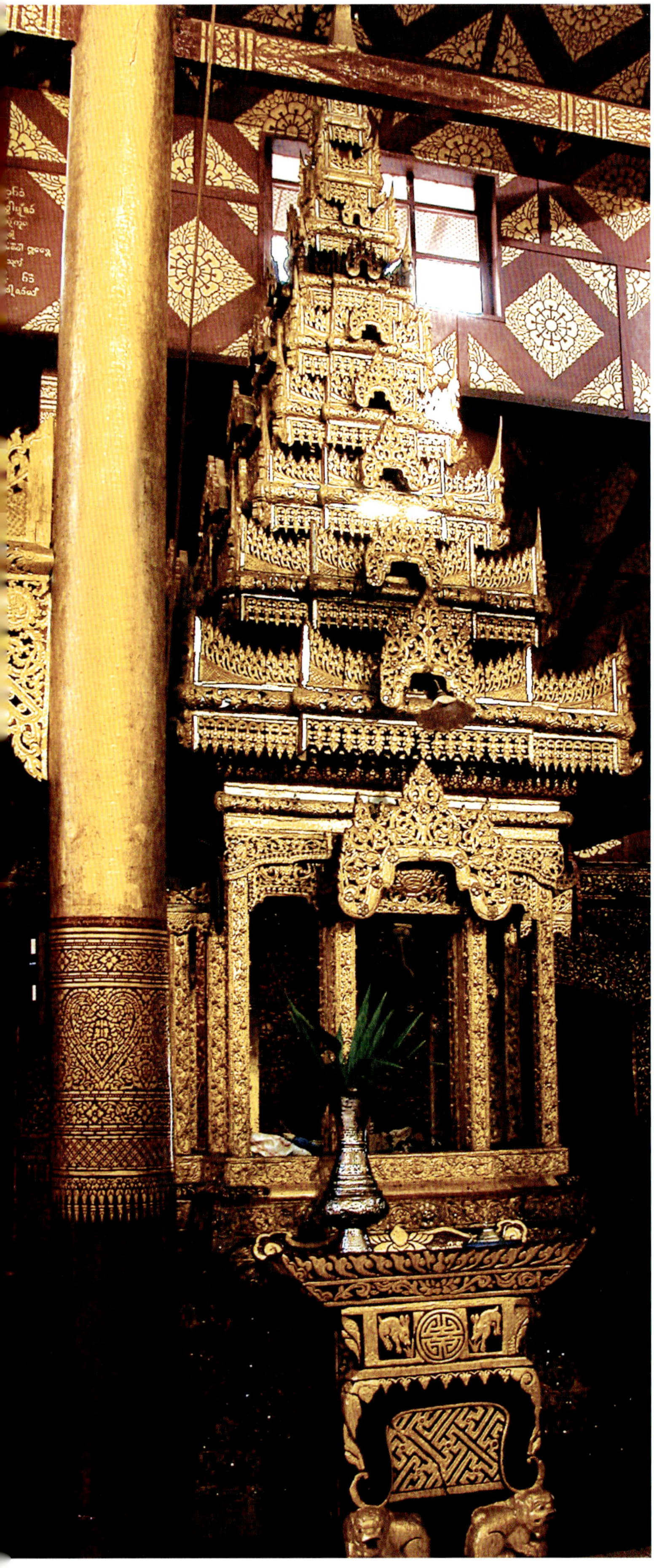

Lacquer was also used in the process of stenciling and painting temple and palace interiors. Cinnabar-red lacquer or black lacquer provided the ground. An artist cut a set of stencils, laid them on the surface and applied a coat of lacquer glue with a brush. A layer of gold paint, or gold leaf was added. This method was used to create silhouettes of Buddha images, guardian figures and scenes from Buddhist mythology.

The dry lacquer technique is used to create Buddha images. A rough form of the image is made of clay and coated with layers of lacquer mixed with ash and sawdust. The head, hair, features, hands and folds of the robe are etched in the lacquer with a small knife and a stylus. When the lacquer is thoroughly dry, the clay core is removed by washing. This may involve cutting parts of the image. If this is necessary, the openings are then sealed with further coats of lacquer. The image is given several extra coats of lacquer and the features are refined. A final smoothing is given with a stone lubricated with sesame oil.[32]

Inlay

The Shan also produced objects, such as pedestal thrones and Buddha stands, that were primarily decorated with coloured glass. This technique involves using thin sheets of plain and coloured glass with a mercury-treated backing. They are cut into pre-determined shapes to form a pattern. The shapes are arranged in groups and laid out to achieve the correct alignment. A skilled cutter can create curving lines, as well as straight-edged pieces, that when laid in patterns produce the most elegant floral and leaf motifs. The most outstanding designs can be seen in monastery buildings. They include delicate floral repeat patterns inset in red and gold lacquered ceilings, teak pillars and walls. Equally as striking, but on a smaller scale, are religious objects such as manuscript stands and fans, plinths for Buddha images and small stupas displayed in the monasteries (see chapter one, fig. 18). In modern designs the glass pieces are set close together to create a mirror effect. Lacquer was the traditional adhesive used to set the glass, but powder glue mixed with gloss paint is a more recent innovation. In the nineteenth century the main source of coloured glass was China, but today it is also imported from Europe.[33]

255 Elaborately carved and gilded structure for a Buddha image.

256 The gilded and inlaid doorway of a temple in Keng Tung.

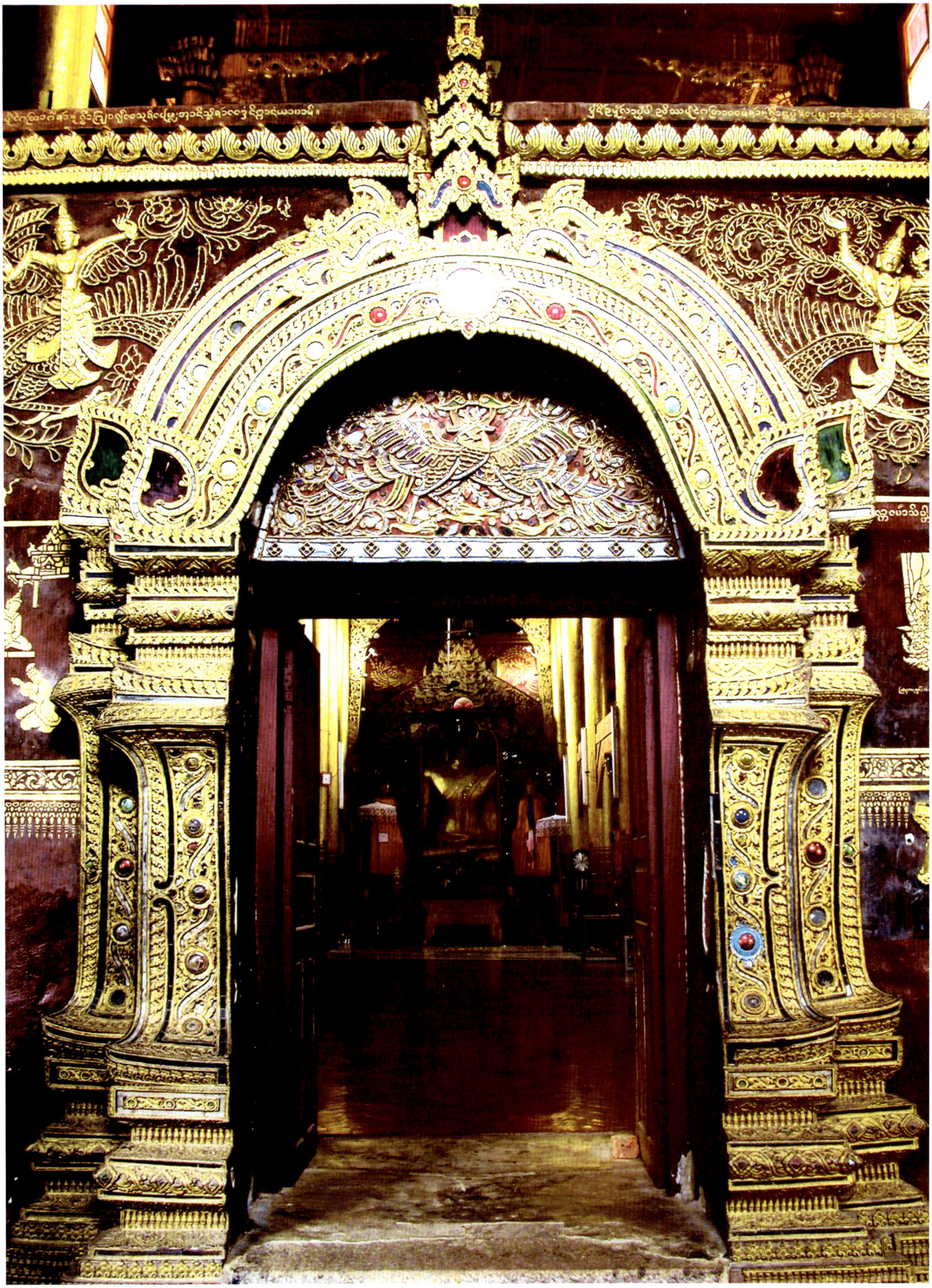

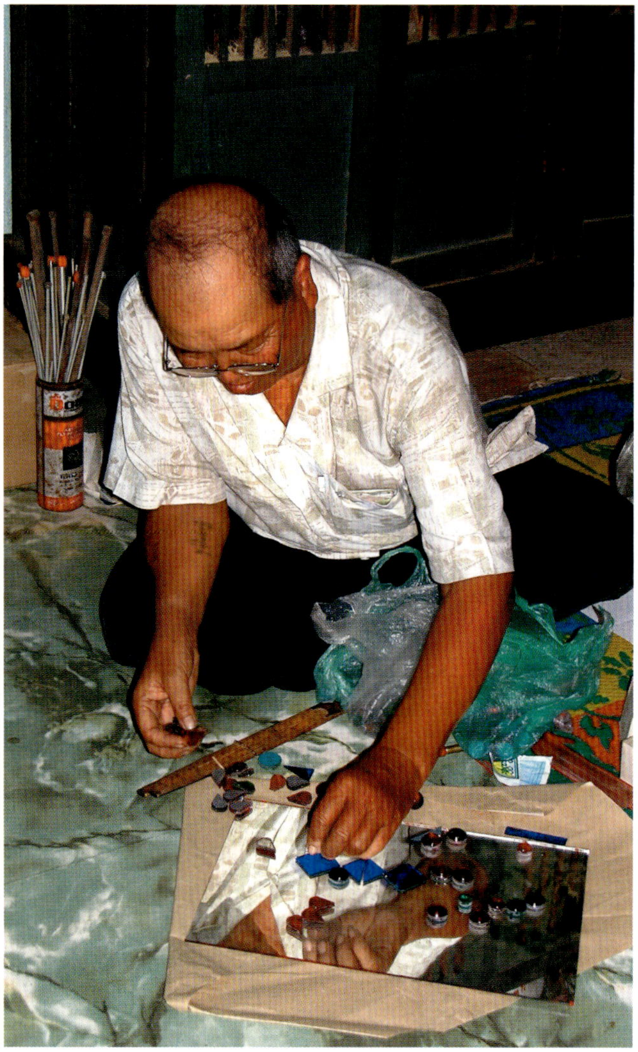

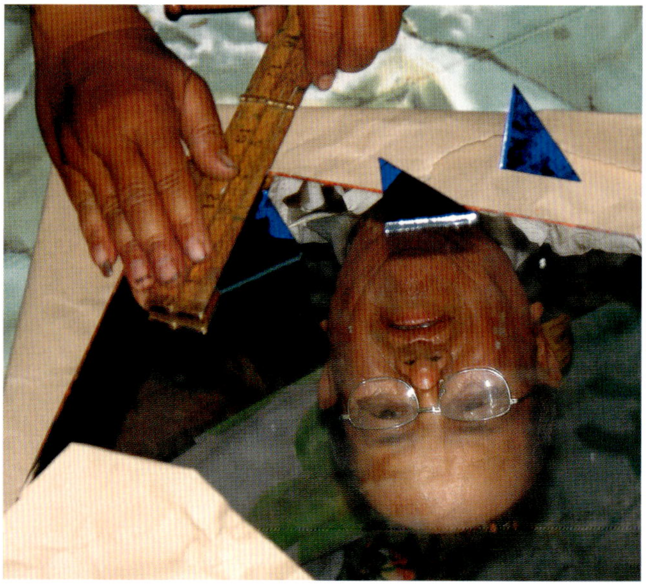

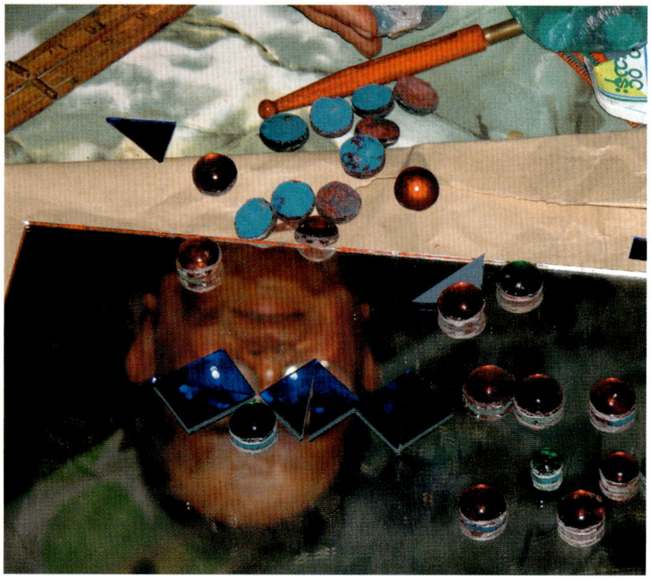

257-61 The craftsman Lung Saw Jing from Yang La village cutting pieces of coloured glass and mica to form patterns for inlay, Keng Tung, 2004.

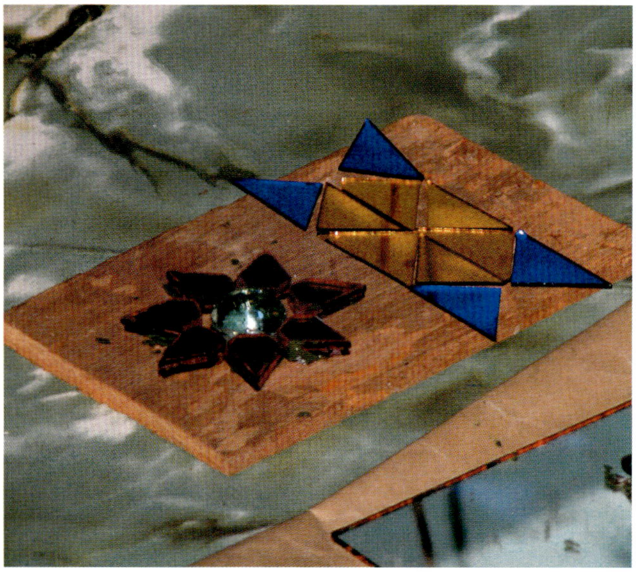

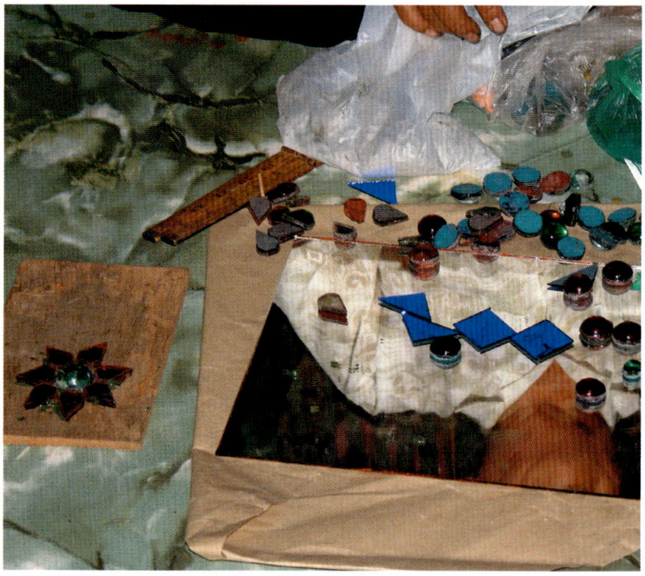

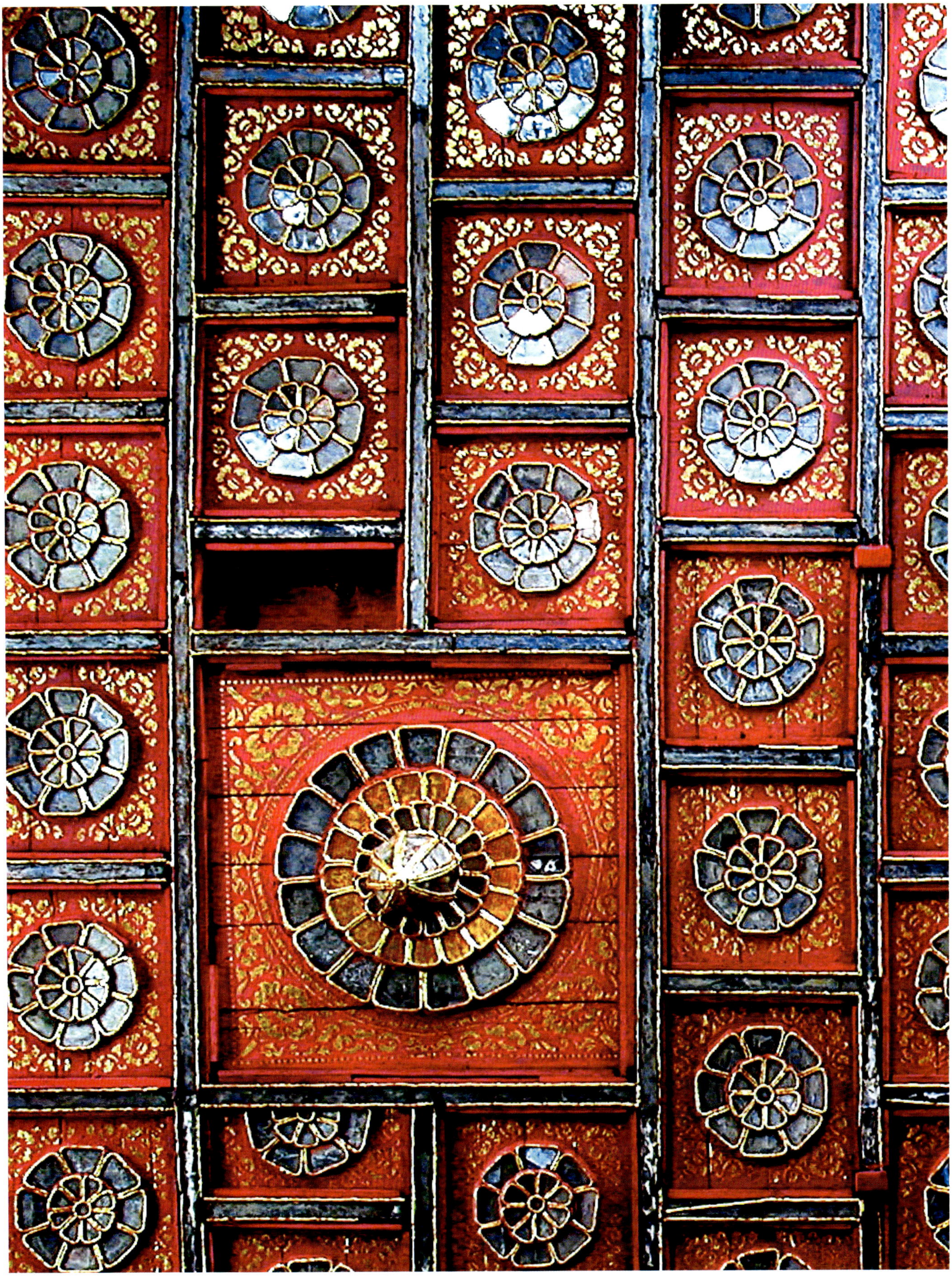

262 The lacquer and inlay ceiling of a temple, Keng Tung.

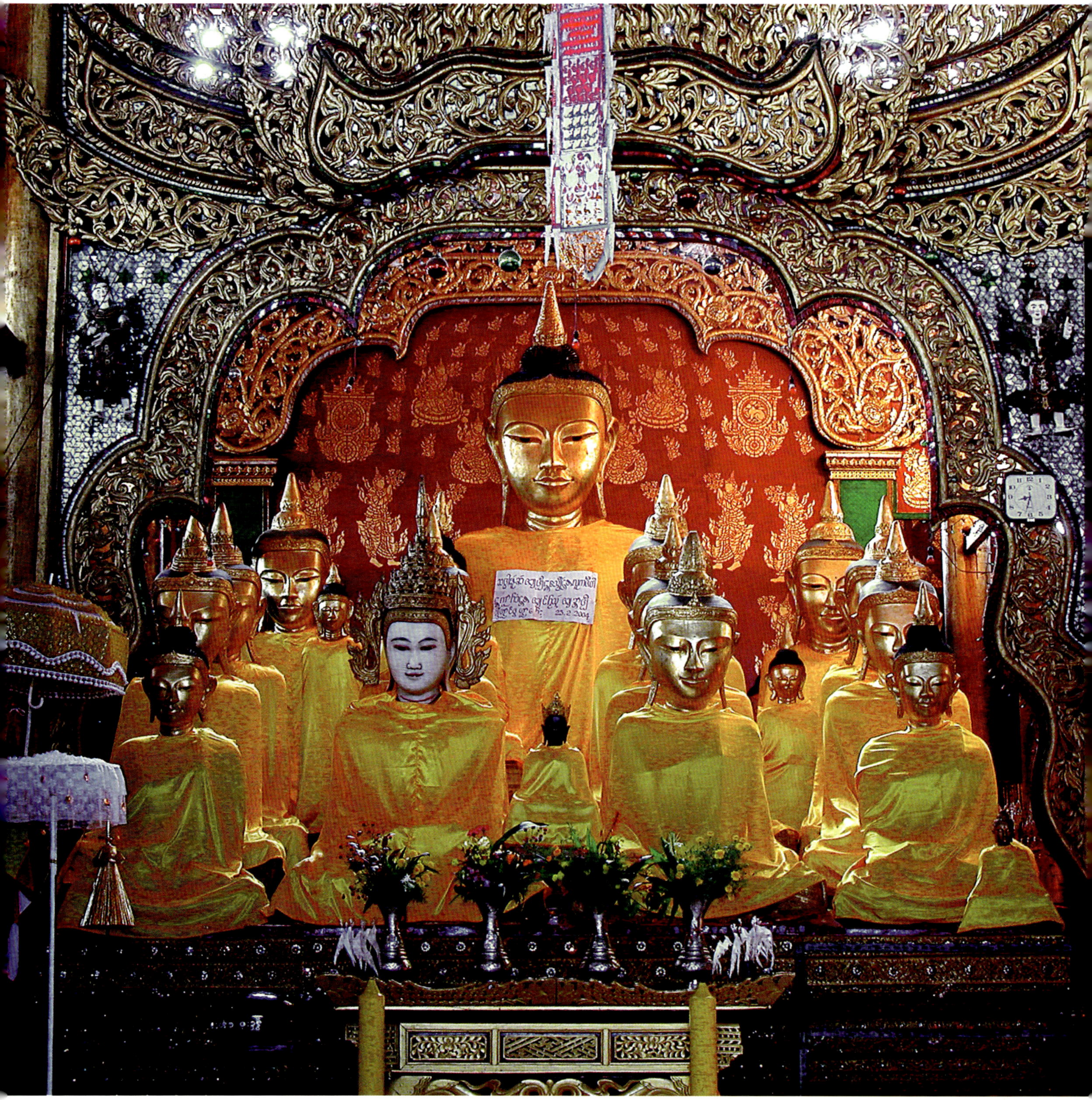

263 and **264** (Opposite above) Shan altars typically have a conglomeration of Buddha images, with elaborately carved and gilded surrounds and bases, Keng Tung.

265 and **266** (Opposite) Two gilded and inlaid stupas *(kong moo),* Wat Zom Khum, the one on the left is reputed to date from the thirteenth century.

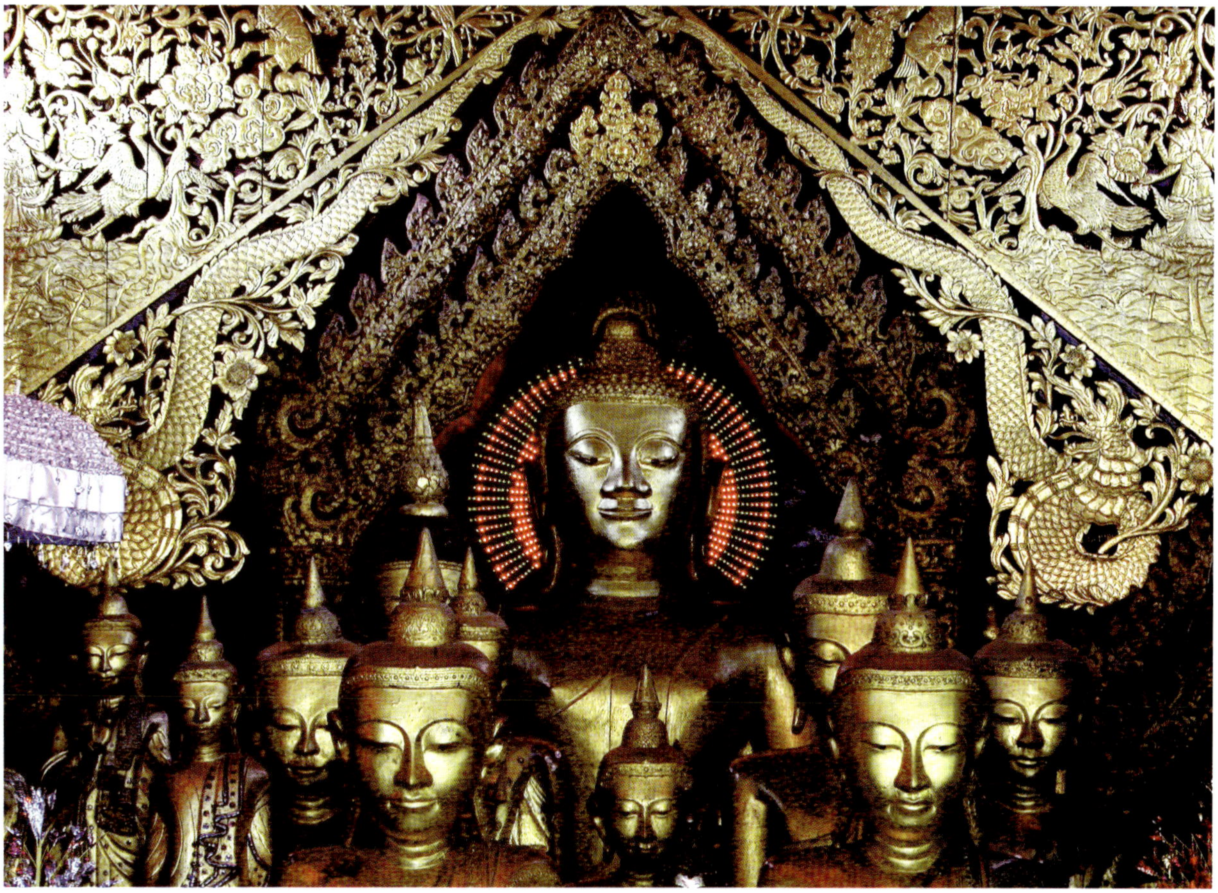

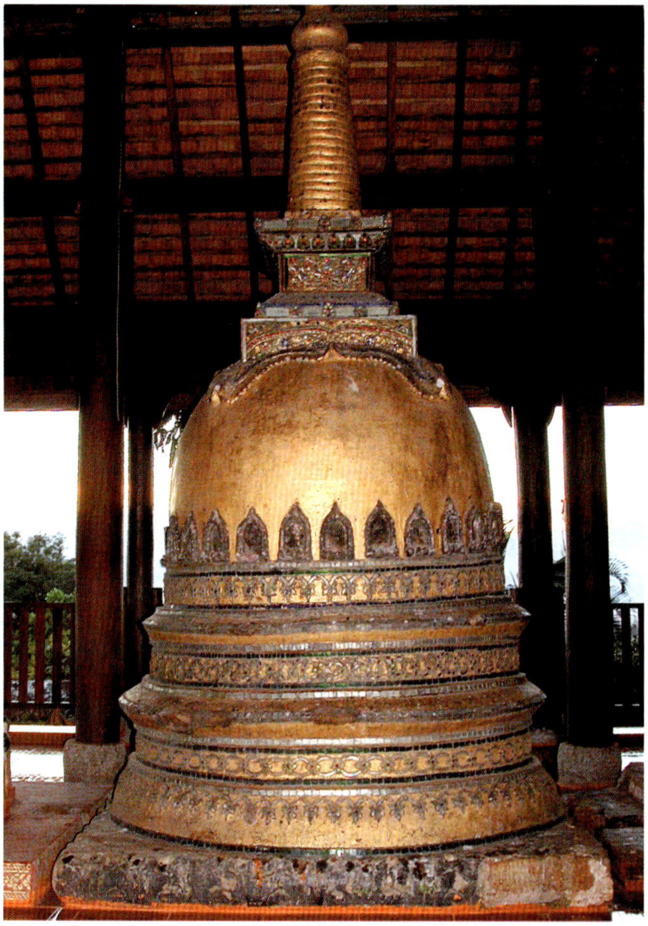

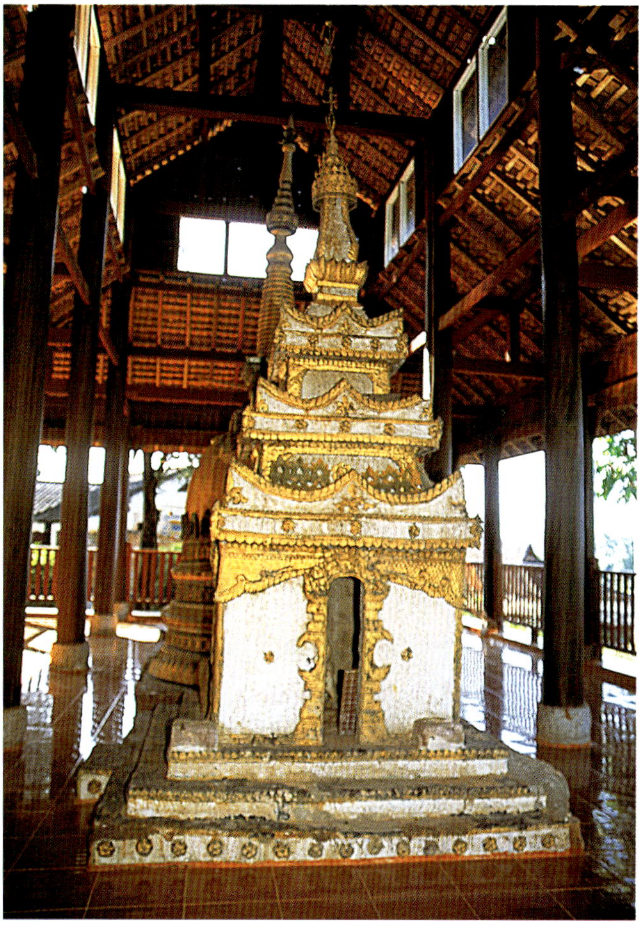

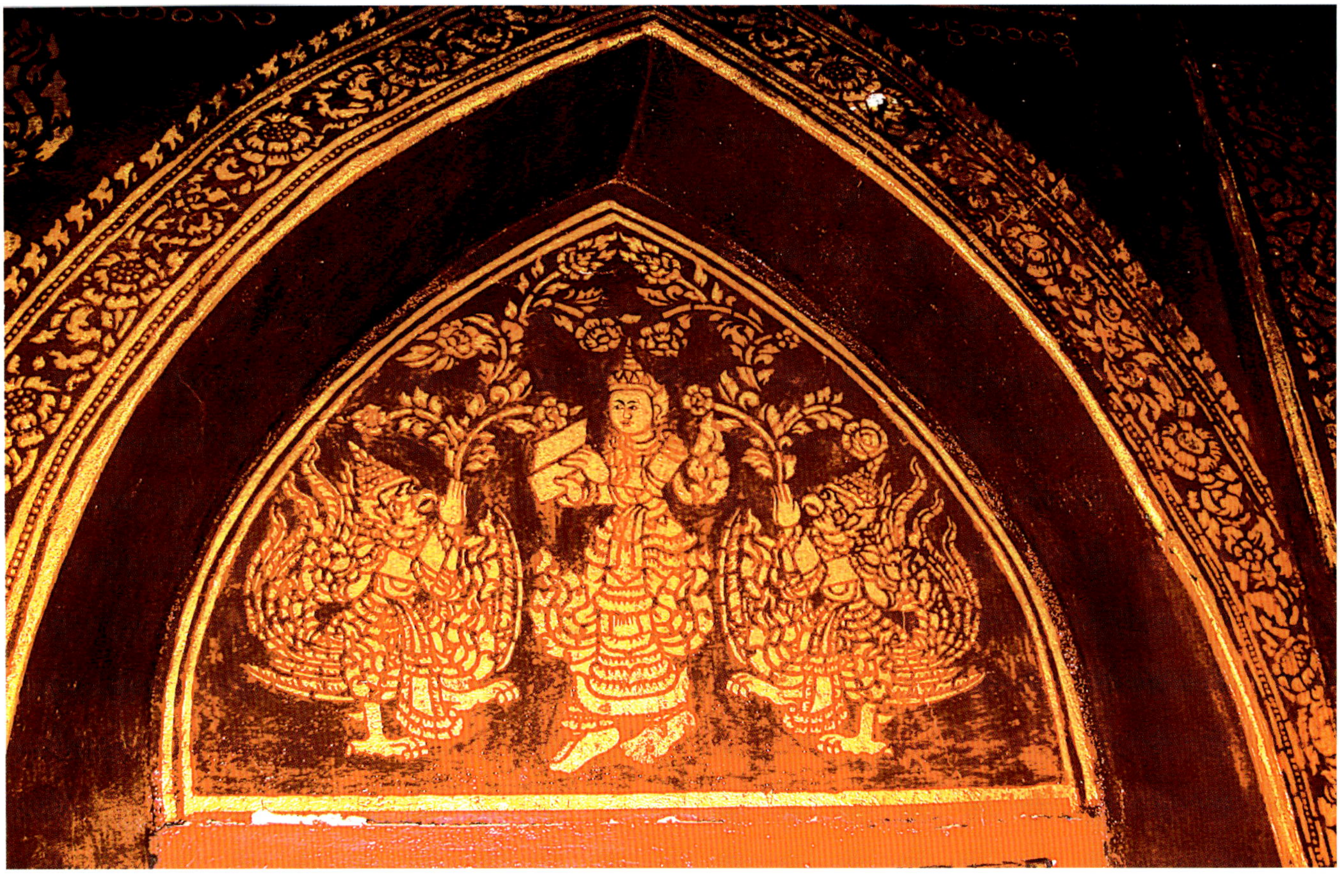

267-269 Gilded stencilling is an important part of the Shan decorative tradition, used to portray *Jataka* tales and local legends. Photographs taken in Keng Tung.

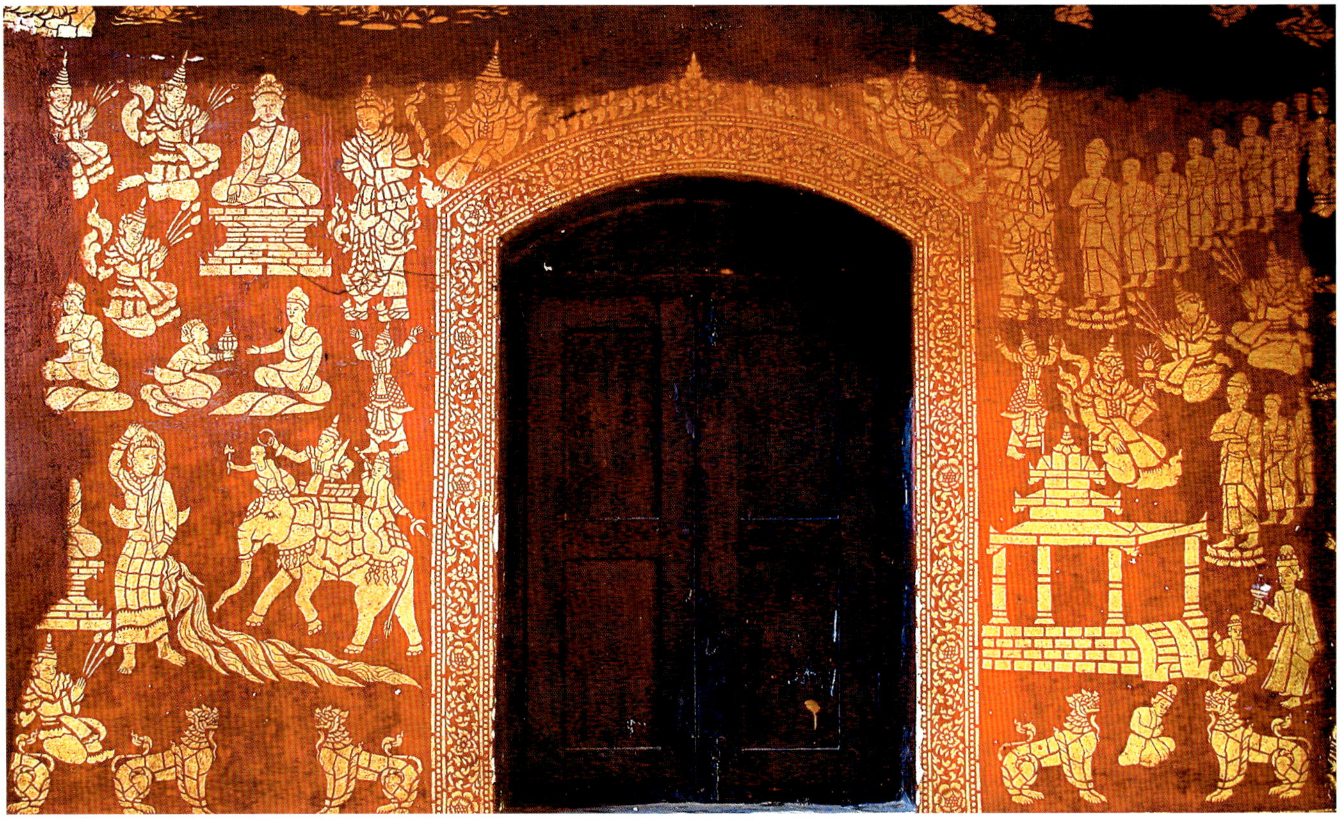

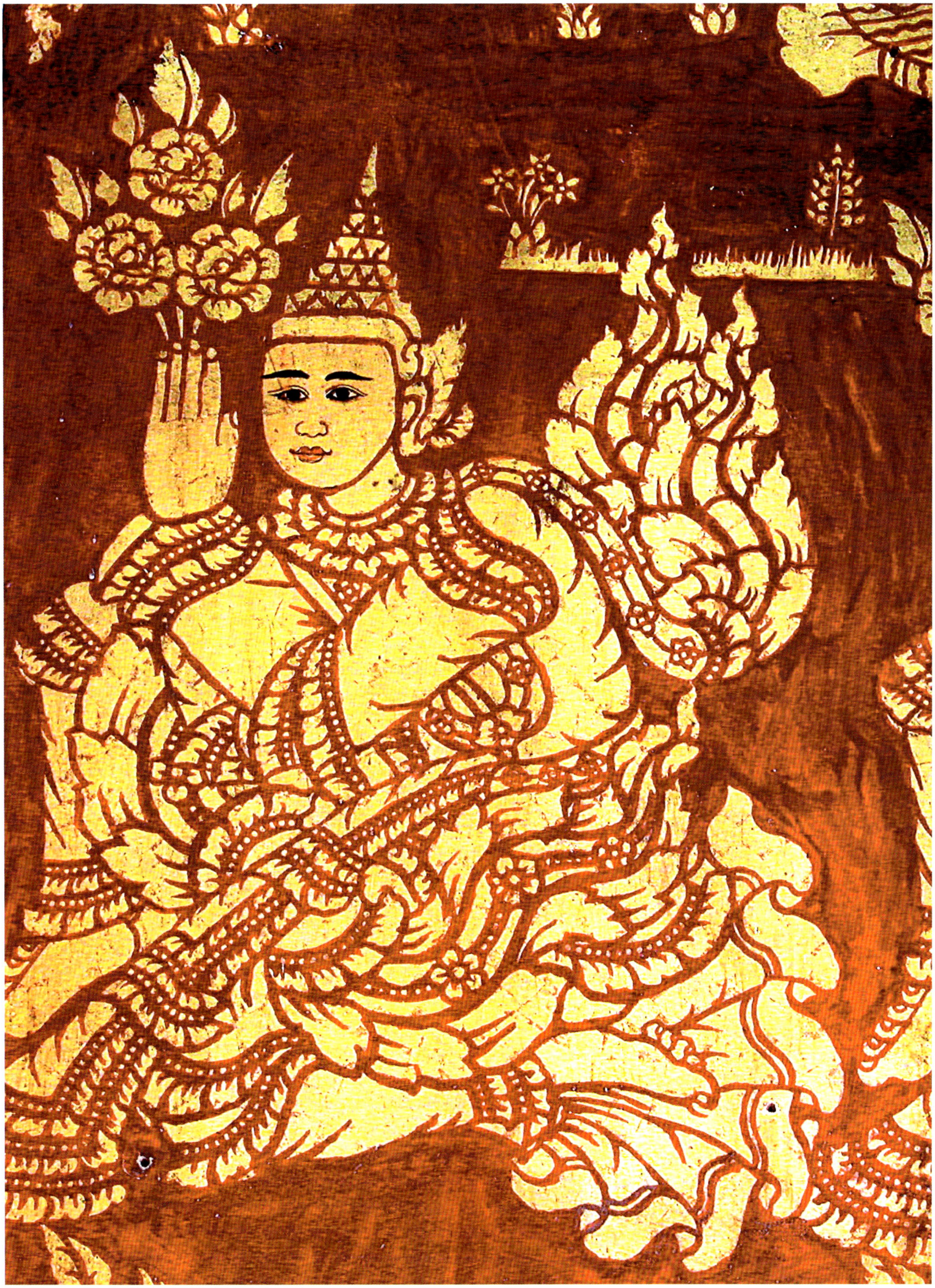

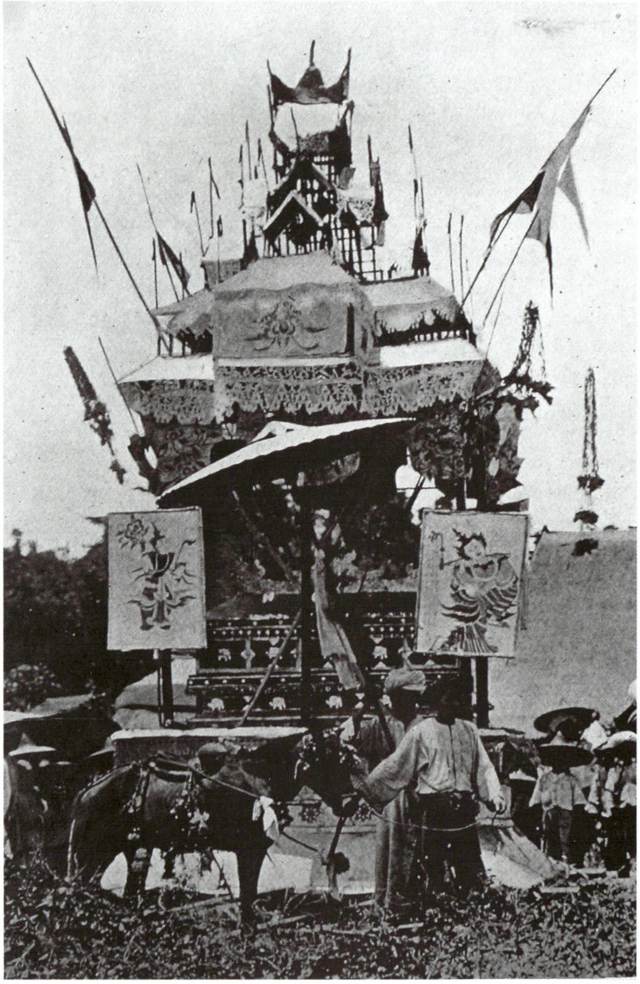

270 A Shan funeral procession. The casket and carriage are decorated with flags, painted banners and paper cut-out decorations. Milne and Cochrane, 1910.

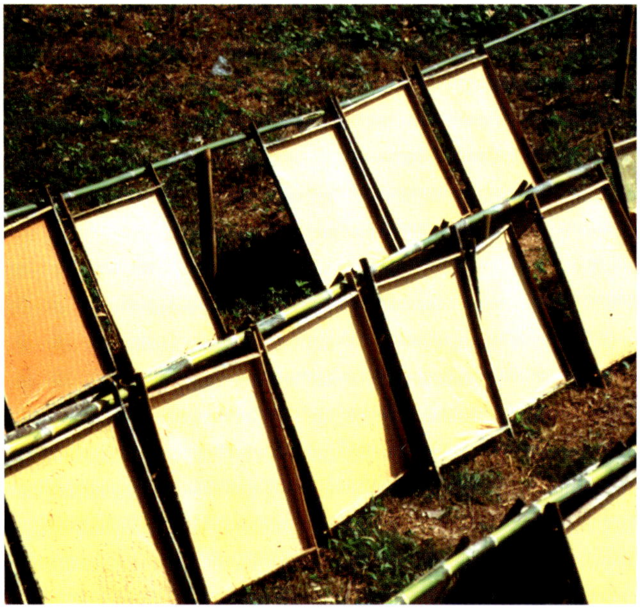

271 Sheets of Shan mulberry paper drying on frames.

Palm Leaf and Paper Manuscripts

Two types of manuscripts are produced in the Shan States, palm leaf and mulberry paper. Palm leaves (*broussonetiia papyrifera*) are cut into long rectangular strips, boiled to remove the sap, and dried first in the shade and then in the sun. They are collected, trimmed and sorted into bundles of twelve leaves. They are presented to the monks as gifts for merit making or given to a local scribe, if a secular commission is to be undertaken. The surface is prepared for writing by smoothing and polishing each leaf. Parallel lines are drawn to act as guidelines for the scribe who uses a stylus to engrave the letters and illustrations. When the engraving is complete the leaves are rubbed with ink paste made from gum and charcoal to fill the grooves. The excess is wiped off the surface. If the script fades over time, the grooves can be refilled with ink paste. When the scribe has finished a set of leaves, they are stacked in order and numbered. The number of leaves in a complete set varies from twenty-five to about one hundred. Holes are bored through each set so that twine can be threaded through to hold them together. The end panels are made of wood that is lacquered or painted with cinnabar. The finest manuscript covers were lacquered, gilded and inlaid.

For paper manuscripts, the inner bark of the mulberry tree (*corpha umbraculifera*) was used. The bark is shredded and pulped by boiling it in water and then pounding with a wooden mallet to break down the fibres. When it reaches a smooth porridge-like texture, it is spread on frames stretched with cotton and left to dry in the sun. When dry, it can be peeled off the frame, trimmed to a rectangular shape, sized and polished. The paper is folded concertina-style. Black ink is used for the script and to outline the illustrations that are filled in with a range of colours made from mineral and earth pigments imported from China in powder form. The binder is a tree gum and the illustrations are often enhanced with gold leaf. The manuscript covers are made from sheets of paper glued together and sized and painted, or wood that is lacquered and gilded.

Shan palm leaf and mulberry paper manuscripts are beautiful objects, but their importance lies in the content of the script and the illustrations that provide a unique insight into Shan interpretations of Theravada Buddhism, cosmology, local history and legends. They are also prized because they are written in Yuan, Khoen and Lue script, derived originally from Mon, and considered by the Tai people to be a special gift from the Buddha. Another important contribution to Shan cultural heritage comes in the form of hand-drawn, painted and printed maps, produced on mulberry paper and on cotton that is sized and polished. The maps provide glimpses of the political, economic and social environment of the Shan States. They are written in Shan and Burmese, and illustrated in local style (see chapter one, figs. 3, 4, 5).

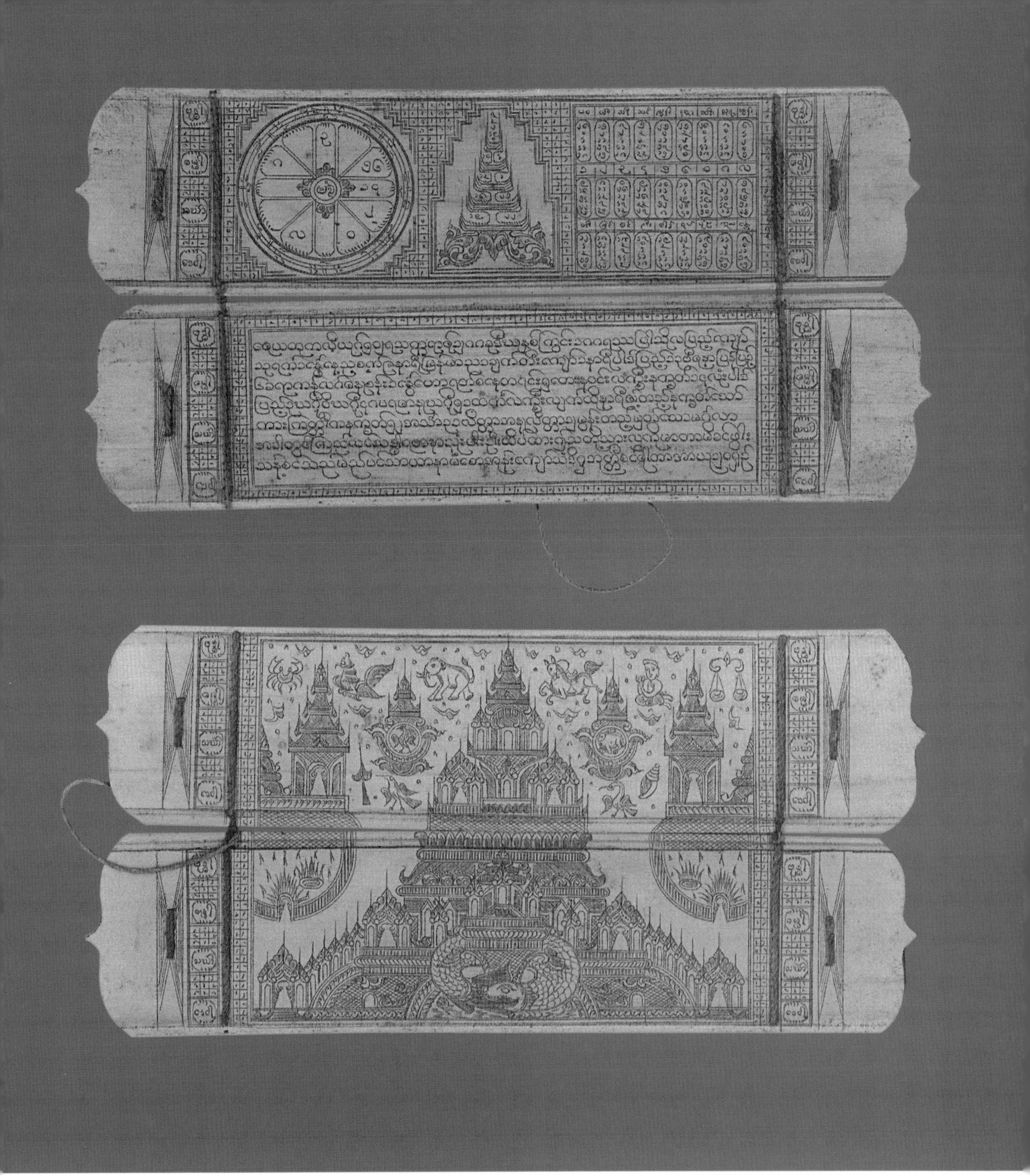

272-273 The birth horoscope of Sao Hkam Hip Hpa of Hsenwi, incised on palm leaf.
(The Green Centre for World Art at The Royal Pavilion Art Gallery and Museums, Brighton)

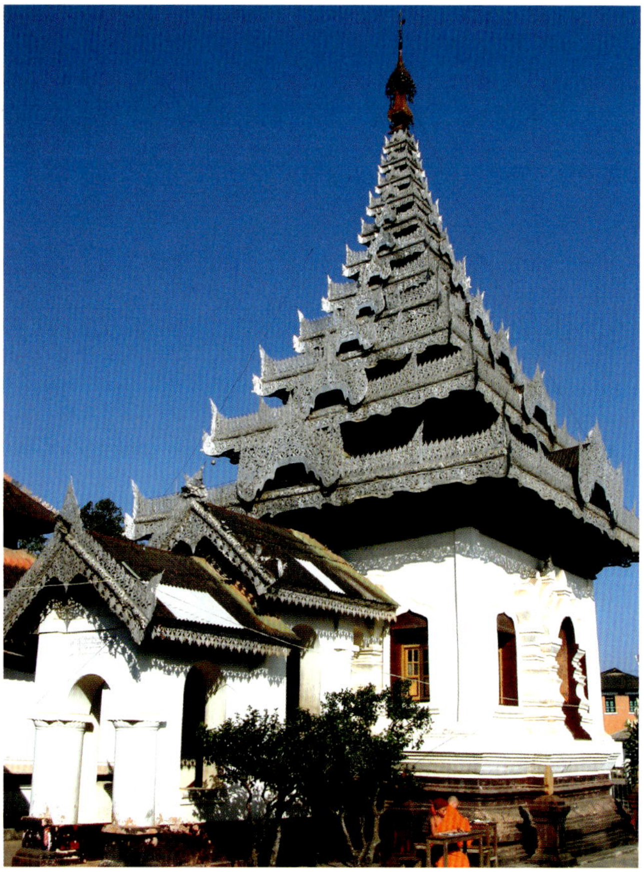

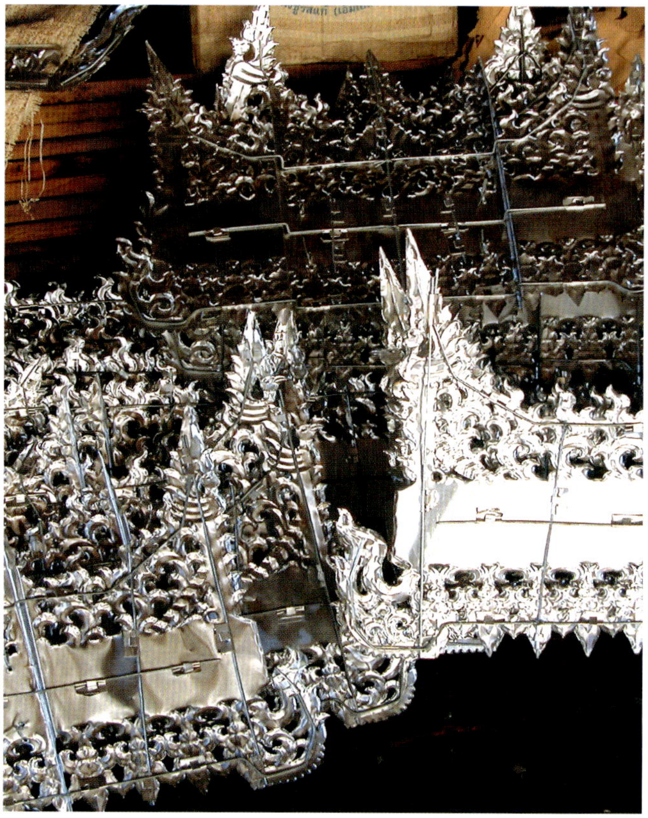

275 Sheets of aluminium cut into shape for roof decoration.

274 A Shan Buddhist ordination hall with sheet metal ornamentation on the tiered roof and entrance porch.

276 A workshop in Keng Tung with men cutting sheets of aluminium into ornamental strips.

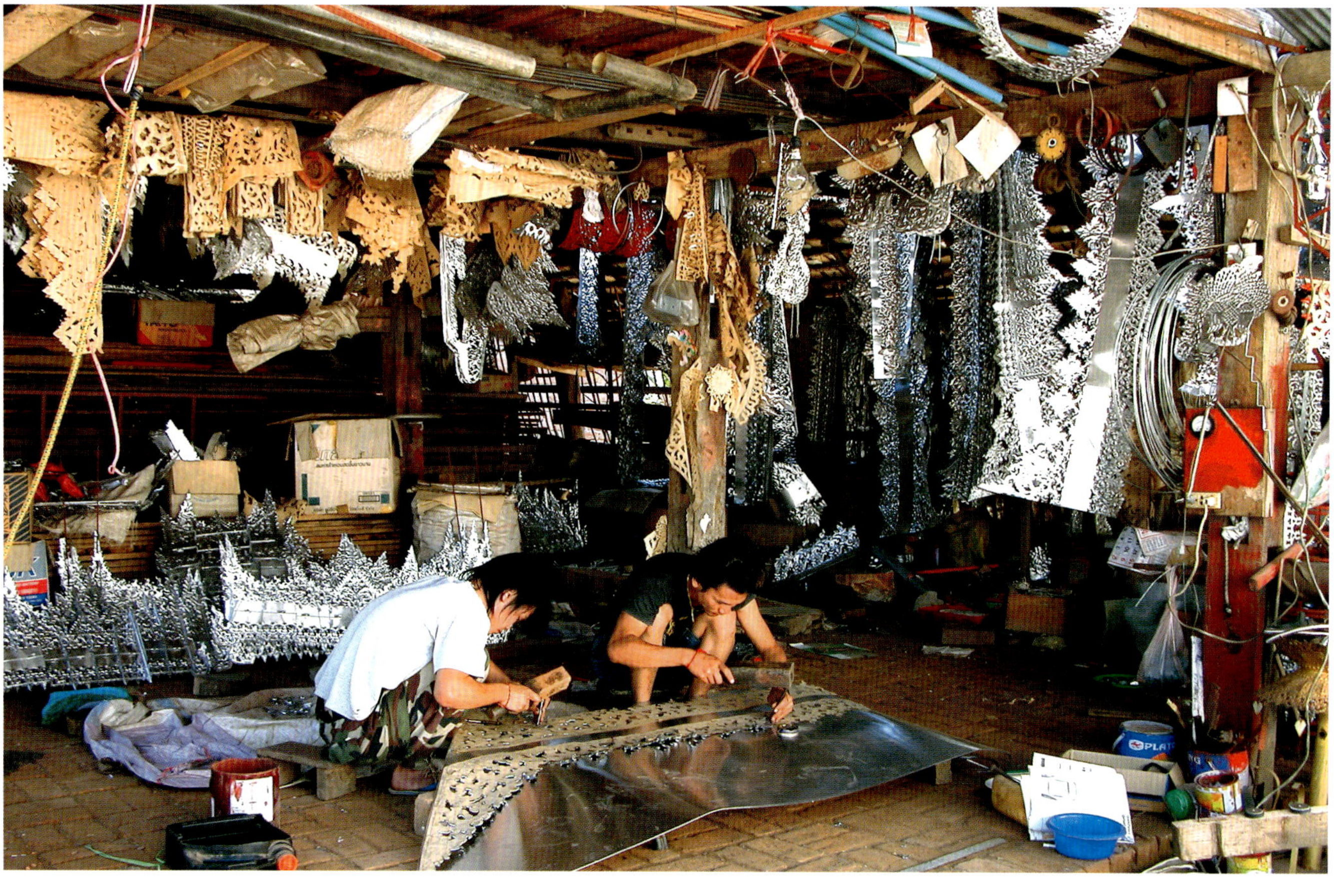

Umbrellas

Umbrellas were an important symbol of status in the Shan States and were issued according to sumptuary laws. Royal umbrellas were made of silk or waterproofed paper. Silk umbrellas were fringed and hung with gilded bodhi tree leaves. The wooden handles were gilded. They were placed in carved wooden stands that were lacquered and gilded. Umbrellas for the less senior princes were made of layers of mulberry paper that was waterproofed with lacquer and gilded. Some were given a silk lining. The ribs of the frame were made of bamboo, the hub of wood and the handle of turned wood that was lacquered and gilded. Most umbrellas had a spire (*hti*) of lacquered wood or gilded metal.

Sheet Metal Ornamentation

It is claimed that in the late nineteenth century gilded and silvered wire and sheet metal began to be used as an alternative to wood carving on religious buildings.[34] When used for bargeboard and lintel decoration, the designs are traced onto thin sheets of brass, iron, copper or tin using a template. The outline is cut with metal shears and the design punched out using a metal punch and a wooden hammer. Designs intended as roof spires (*hti*) are made from sheet metal cut into flowers, buds and leaves and soldered with curved wire for stems. The finished products were gilded or silvered. Today aluminium sheeting and aluminium wire are in common use.

Pottery

Pottery is not an exclusively male occupation and there are potteries in almost all the main towns and in large settlements. Clay is collected from special sites and transported to the potter's workshop where it is pounded and mixed with sand and water. The strongest pots are coiled and smoothed by hand. Water vessels, cooking pots, garden pots and other items for domestic use are produced in this way. Drinking vessels and alms bowls are made for the monks. The pots are fired in kilns or in pits excavated underground. Most Shan pottery comes in simple, elegant shapes and is left plain or impressed with geometric patterns.

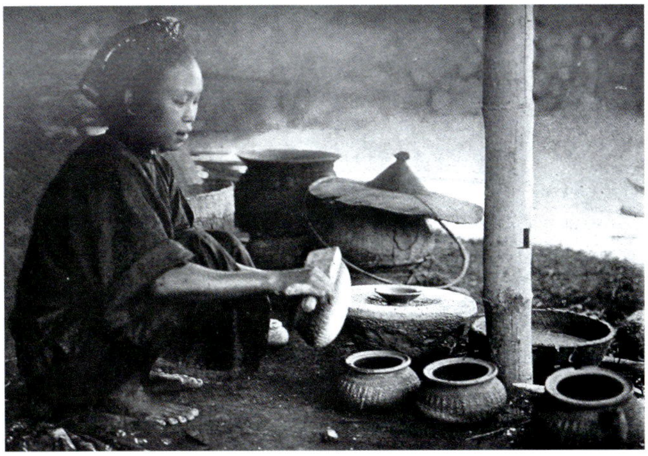

277 A woman potter in the Shan States. Milne and Cochrane, 1910 .

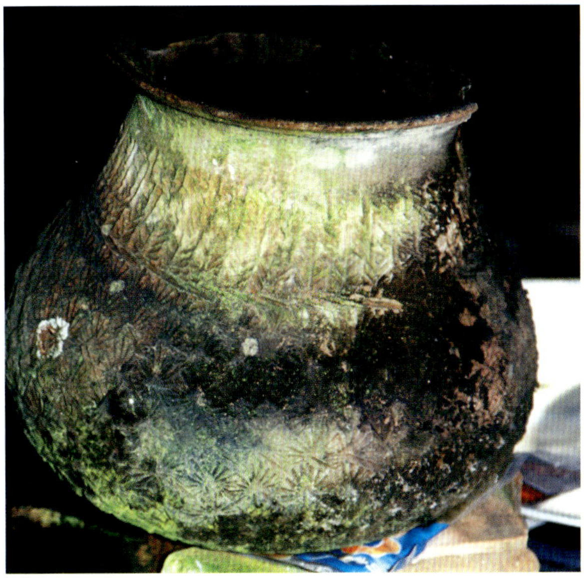

278 Kitchen water pot with surface decoration. Baan Ho Ko, Keng Tung.

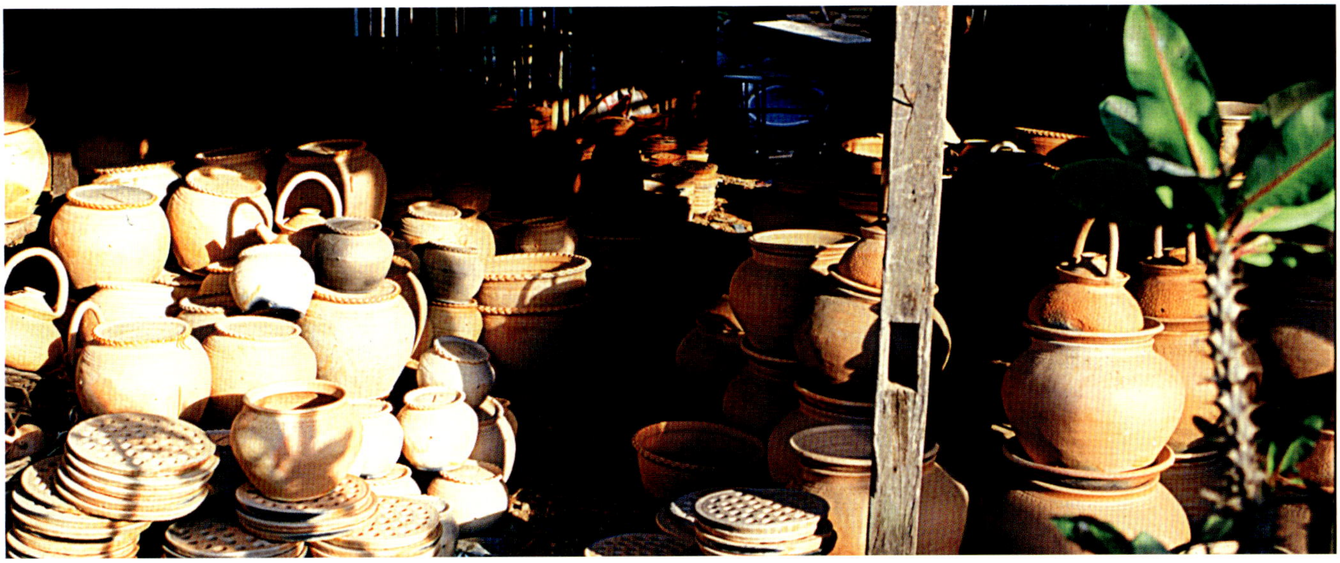

279 Pottery on sale in Keng Tung, November 2004.

The pots made on a wheel are porous unless glazed. In the nineteenth century, the glazes were made from the slag from lead mines that produces a yellow colour, or sulphate of copper mixed with iron slag and rice-water to create a green glaze.[35] A salt glaze was used for jars to store oil. The potters also produced black pots that were burnished and decorated and used as water vessels and spittoons by members of the Shan royal family. This type of pot can be identified in photographs of Shan court regalia, and are usually displayed with a silver drinking cup.

Basketry

The Shan make baskets, hats and mats to use in the fields and in their homes. Panels of bamboo matting, often woven in bold geometric designs, form the outer walls of their houses. Once in situ, they are varnished or oiled, creating a patina that highlights the woven patterns. Similar woven panels are used as room dividers. Large woven mats are laid out in the fields at harvest time to form a threshing floor and are used in the compound of the house to dry farm produce. Woven bamboo, daubed with a mixture of mud and straw, formed the base and walls of the family rice store (see chapter one, fig. 31). Bamboo baskets of cane, reed or split bamboo were used as fish traps and as containers to carry the catch from the field. Produced in a plaited half circle, they make good pens for chickens, and in an oblong shape they can contain pigs on their way to market. Baskets are also used for transporting rice and other agricultural products and are essential in the preparation of food. Special pannier baskets were made for transporting goods on trade caravans that traveled throughout the Shan States. Floor mats woven for royalty were appliquéd with panels of silk or cotton and couched with gold and silver metal thread and sequins.

This chapter has described a wide range of high quality products made in the Shan States. Today the markets are flooded with cheap mass-produced Chinese goods and the number of working artisans, particularly those making textiles, has markedly declined. Many are keeping their workshops running but cannot afford high-quality raw materials. There are notable exceptions. A few artisans continue to produce beautiful objects, particularly as gifts to the monasteries, a way of making merit in a deeply religious society. Others take special orders, for example lacquer props for the Thai film industry and lacquer ware for the Thai interior decorating market. Illegal logging keeps the woodcarving industry in business. Some artisans produce for the tourist trade although consumers in this market are rarely willing to pay for high quality products.

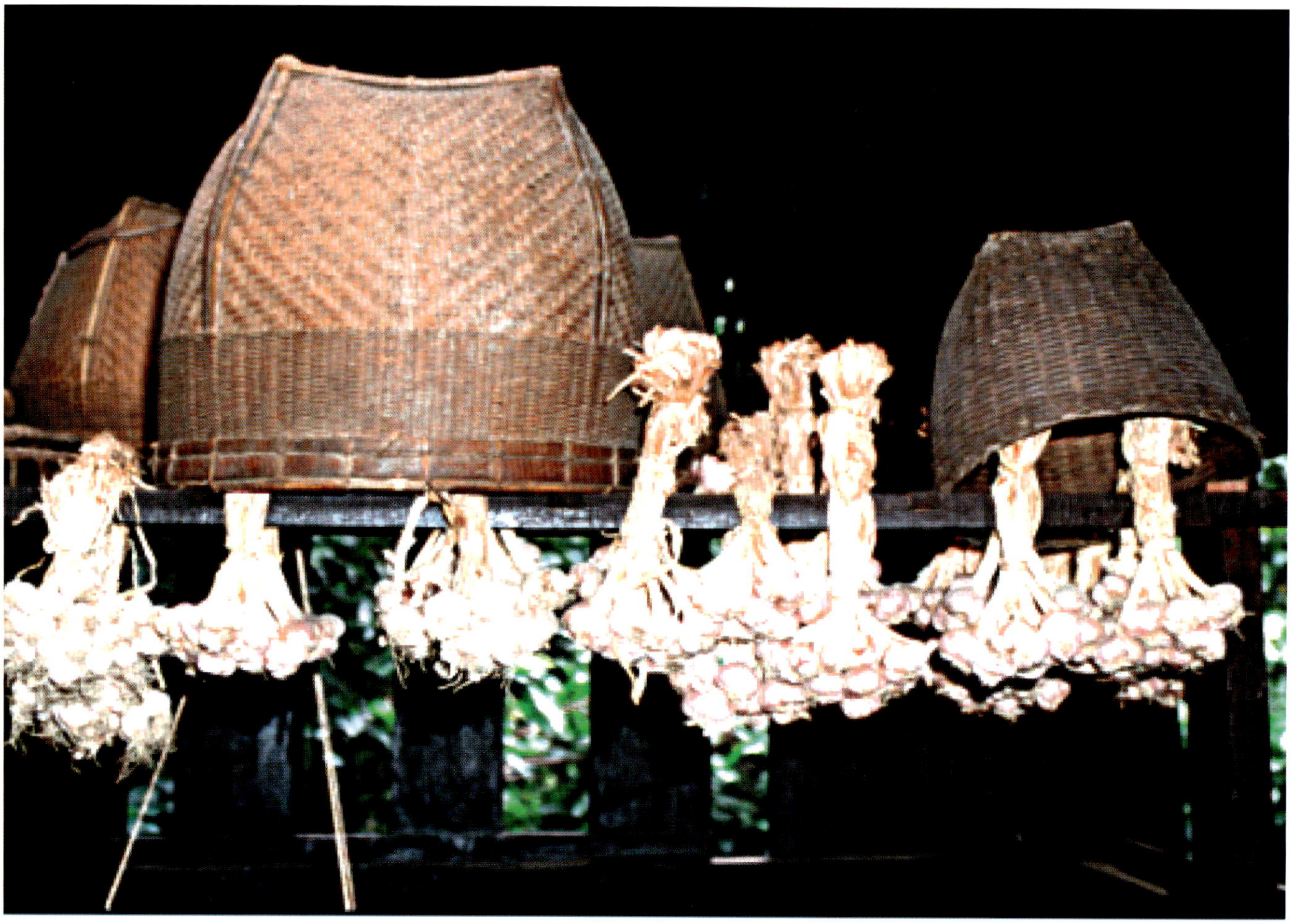

280 A collection of baskets for the kitchen.

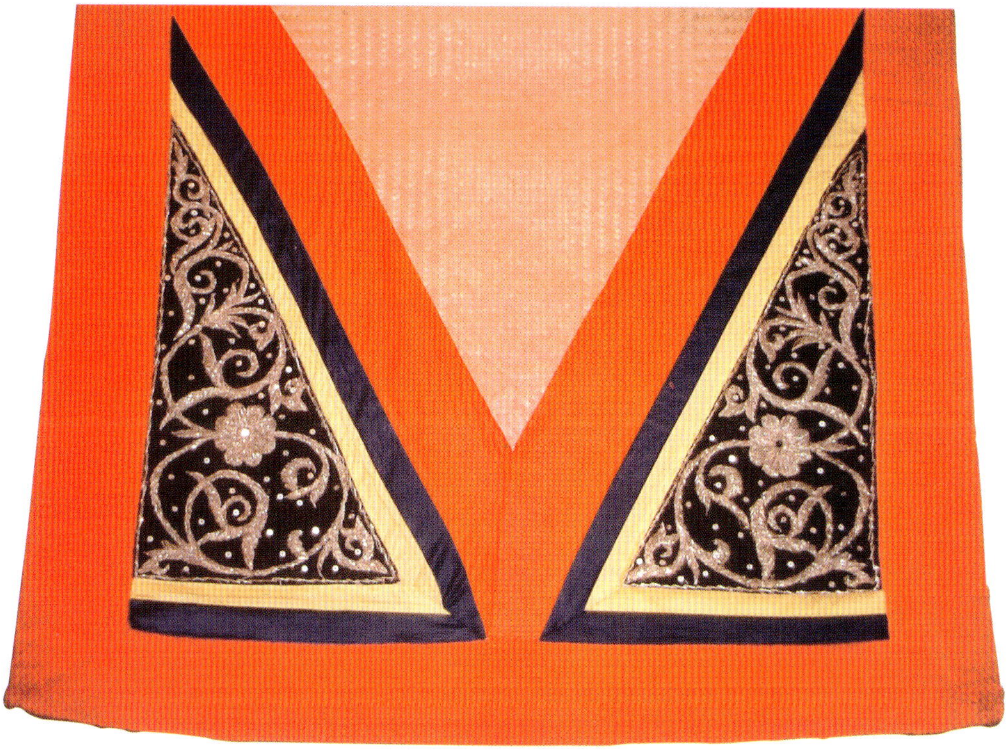

281 A bamboo mat with end borders of cotton couched with metal wire and sequins. *(Private collection)*

Endnotes

[1] Noel Singer, 'Jengtung Lacquerware', *Arts of Asia*, Vol. 21, no. 5, September-October, 1991, V. Di Crocco, 'Arts and Crafts: Shan Lacquerware' in K. Inglis (ed.), *Myanamar Style, Art, Architecture and Design of Burma*, Bangkok, 1998, pp. 170-171.

[2] Volker Grabowsky, in *Fifth International Conference on Thai Studies*, School of Oriental and African Studies, London, 1993.

[3] D. Wyatt and W. Aroonrut, *The Chiang Mai Chronicles,* Chiang Mai, 1995, pp.37-38.

[4] The silversmiths in the Wulai Road area of Chiang Mai, are descendants of captives from Keng Tung.

[5] The people of Keng Tung commented particularly on the exodus of silversmiths. Oral communication, Keng Tung, December, 2004.

[6] Interviews with weavers in Keng Tung, November 2004, and Chiang Mai, May 1994.

[7] W. C. Dodd, *The Tai Race: Elder Brother of the Chinese*, The Torch Press, Cedar Rapids 1923, reprinted White Lotus Press, Bangkok, 1996, p. 172.

[8] Tin Myaing Thein, *Old and New Tapestries of Mandalay*, Oxford University Press, 2000.

[9] Sao Saimong Mangrai, *The Padaeng Chronicle and the Jengtung Chronicle Translated*, Center for South and Southeast Asian Studies, University of Michigan, 1981, p. 263.

[10] According to oral history, there were times when men helped with processing. This included wartime when there was a premium on cloth production (oral communication, Chiang Mai and Nan, 1985).

[11] Captain McLeod's Journal, 4th January 1837 as quoted in V. Grabowsky and A. Turton, *The Gold and Silver Road of Trade and Friendship*, Silkworm Books, Chiang Mai, 2003.

[12] Oral communication, Chiang Mai, 1994.

[13] George Scott, *Gazetteer of Upper Burma and the Shan States*, Rangoon, 1901, Vol. II pt. 1, pp. 363-399.

[14] George Scott, *Burma and Beyond*, Grayson and Grayson, London 1932, p. 258.

[15] Ling Roth, *Studies in Primitive Looms*, Bankfield Museum, Halifax, 1918.

[16] Those who settled in the valleys adapted to frame looms.

[17] Tin Myaing Thein, 2000.

[18] The portrayal of landscape and architecture, and the representation of humans and animals can be linked stylistically to 18th and 19th century Tai temple mural paintings.

[19] Tin Myaing Thein, 2000.

[20] Scott, 1932, p. 360.

[21] Oral communication, the monks of Wat Maha Kaew, Keng Tung, November 2004.

[22] M. Ferrars and B. Ferrars, *Burma*, London 1900, reprint. Bangkok, 1996, pp.103-104.

[23] Tai Lue craftsmanship was particularly valued.

[24] George Scott, *Burma: A Handbook of Practical Information*, London, 1906, reprint Orchid Press, Bangkok, 1999, pp. 358-359.

[25] The Wa supplied iron ore, extracted from the hills, to make sword blades.

[26] Sylvia Fraser-Lu, *Burmese Crafts: Past and Present*, Oxford University Press, Kuala Lumbur, 1994, p. 175.

[27] Carl Bock, *Temples and Elephants*, London 1884, reprint Oxford University Press, 1986, p. 152.

[28] Maurice Collis, *Lords of the Sunset*, London, 1938, reprint Ava, Press, Bangkok, 1996, p. 113.

[29] Liverpool Museum has an excellent collection of Shan silver, produced during the Colonial Era.

[30] Fraser-Lu, 1994.

[31] Quoted in Ralph Isaacs and Richard T. Blurton, *Burma and the Art of Lacquer*, Bangkok, 2000, p. 27.

[32] Sylvia Fraser Lu, *Burmese Lacquerware*, Tamarind Press, Bangkok, 1996

[33] Oral communication, Lung Saw Jing, Yang La, November 2004.

[34] Fraser-Lu, 1994.

[35] Scott, 1932 pp. 278-280.

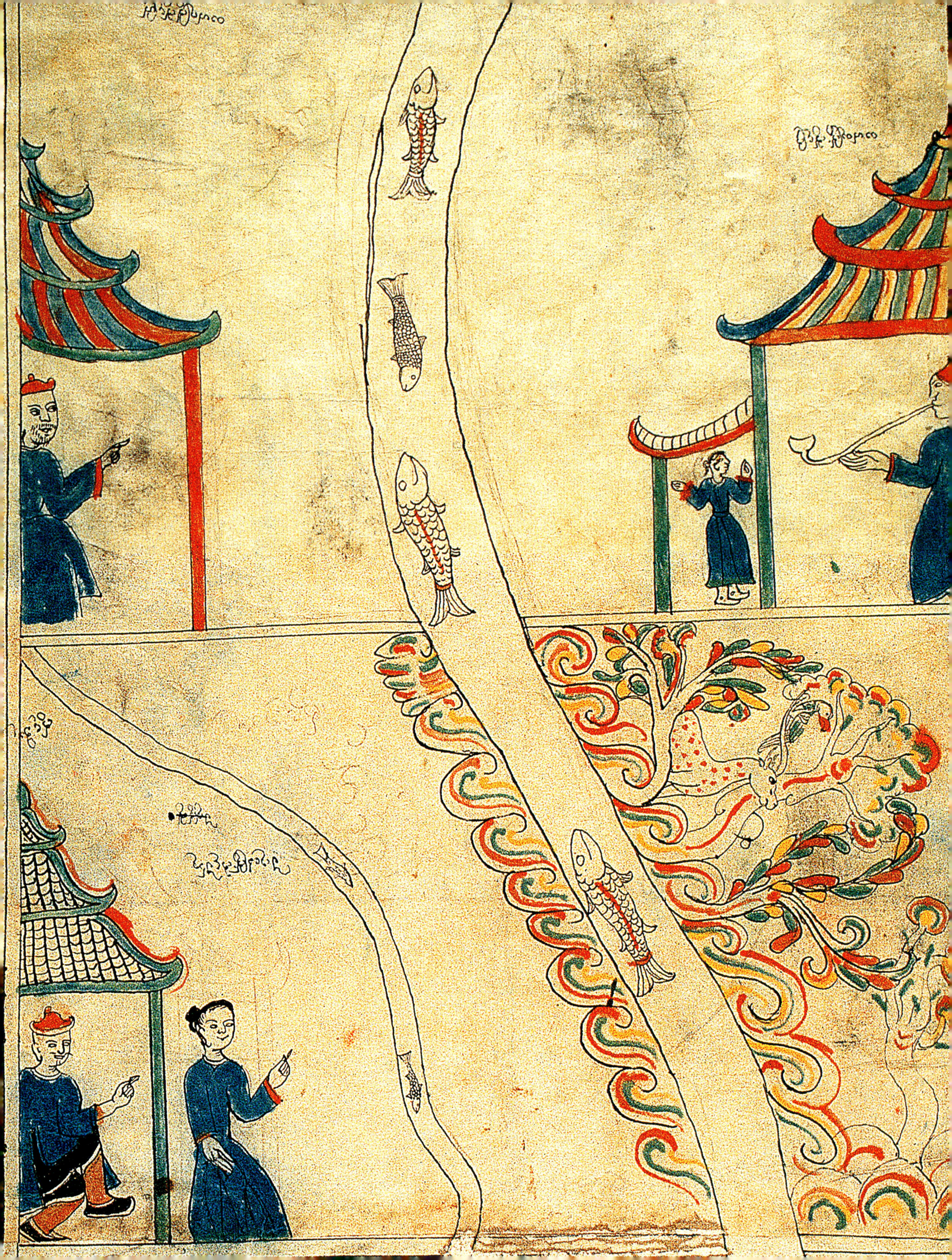

Chapter 7
Trade

The Shan States were a major hub for trade with a wide range of goods from China, Burma and India being transported to the major cities and large settlements. In the nineteenth century European imports were added to the list. The Shan traded their goods with Burma and China and with their inland neighbours in Lan Na and Laos. Because the Shan States were landlocked, goods were carried overland and on navigable rivers. Ponies, mules, and oxen were the chief pack animals and elephants were used to carry heavy loads although they were the slowest form of transportation. They could not be used on the higher mountain passes because suitable forage was not available. Porters conveyed cargoes on more accessible paths, working from one relay point to the next where a new team took over.[1] The British officer Captain McLeod provided an excellent description of how the packs were carried.

> *The load is carried on the back, a rope running under the bottom of the pack, and fastened to a* [flat piece of wood] *on the neck, to which it is fitted, and is supported by both shoulders; a rope is passed around the forehead and the upper part of the pack, this balances it and prevents it falling backwards.*[2]

Trade routes were hazardous as caravans were vulnerable to plunder by marauding gangs, often described as "dacoits." Merchants relied heavily on local informants in assessing whether they could risk setting out from one staging post to the next. Hill dwelling people were hired to defend the mountain passes but they were unreliable and sometimes raided the caravans they were supposed to protect. There were delays if the caravan paths were not regularly cleared, and in the rainy season many were impassable. The character and behaviour of some of the merchants was also cause for concern. McLeod claimed that Burmese merchants from the port of Moulmein had a reputation for bullying and cheating the Shan rulers.[3]

Political interference was another frustration. In the early nineteenth century the princes of Lan Na, under pressure from Siam, refused permission for traders to pass through their territory on the way to Keng Tung. A group of Chinese merchants, who met McLeod south of Chiang Mai, bitterly complained that the Keng Tung road was closed against their convoys, a situation they blamed on "the excessive jealousy of the Siamese towards the Burmans."[4] The British were affected by this policy as the Chiang Mai authorities pressured the Shan not to deal with them either. Meanwhile the Chinese were suspicious of all Burmese traders who entered the states of Sipsong Pan Na that were under their patronage. It is a tribute to those operating the caravans that they were able to function at all.

Accepted currency used for trade transactions in the Shan States included gold leaf and Burmese and Chinese silver, measured by weight. King Mindon of Burma (ruled 1853-1878) introduced silver coins during his reign but they were not universally accepted, and weighed silver and gold leaf remained in circulation, joined by the Indian rupee. Many deals did not involve currency as goods were bartered. Nevertheless silver coins, particularly with the head of a monarch, were in great demand for buttons. Queen Victoria, her son and grandson appear on many Shan blouse and shirt buttons. Indian silver rupees were also melted down mostly to make jewellery.

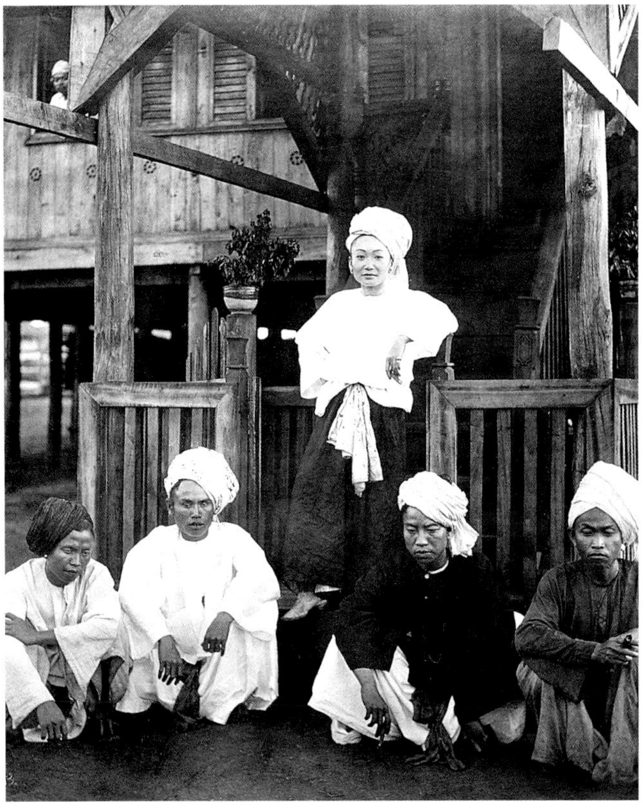

283 Princess Tip Htila, sister of the Prince of Keng Tung, with a group of her muleteers, circa 1900.
(The Oriental and India Collections, The British Library, London, BL 92/3 (66))

Items transported from one principality to another were subject to taxes imposed by the Shan rulers. Some foreign merchants operated as their business partners and could negotiate in local markets. Many members of the royal family invested in animal caravans, including some enterprising women. Princess Tip Htila, sister of Prince Intaleng of Keng Tung (1874-1935) often travelled with her muleteers, riding the lead animal and armed with a rifle. She dealt in many goods, including elephants. Chao Nang Waen Tip, consort of the Prince of Keng Hung, engaged in forestry and received a concession to haul teak logs felled by the Bombay-Burmah Company.[6] Princess Ubonwanna in neighbouring Chiang Mai was also involved in logging.

At village level women were the main traders. Rising before dawn they made their way to the regularly scheduled village or town markets where they sold rice, fish, vegetables, fruit, tobacco, flowers, wax and betel (fig. 287). Some booths sold local Shan delicacies and snacks. There were specialist stalls selling thin sheets of gold leaf to place on Buddha images, and votive offerings for the temples. Shan

282 (Opposite) Detail of a hand-drawn and painted map. The Chinese houses are inhabited by men and women in Shan and Tai style dress. The map probably represents a Shan state in Sipsong Pan Na.
(The Oriental and India Office Collection, The British Library, London, Or 3478E)

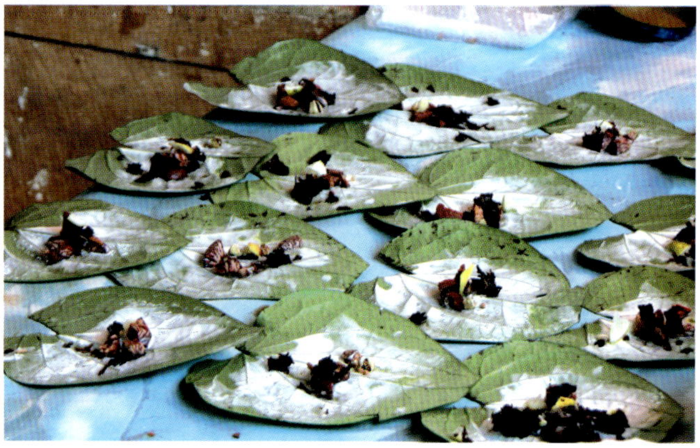

284 Betel leaves with preparations of areca palm nut, tobacco and white lime, on sale in a market, Keng Tung, 2004.

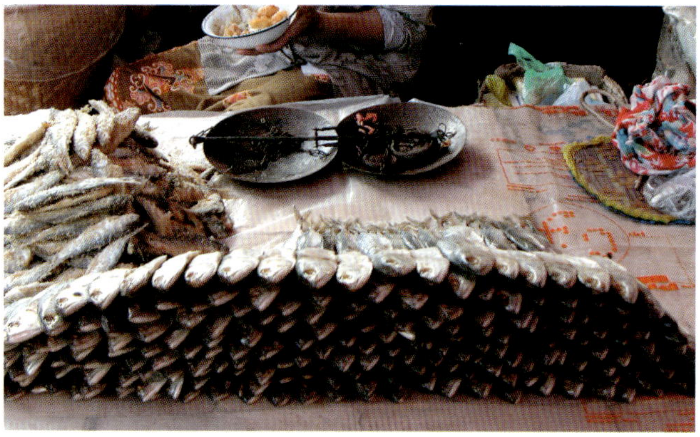

285 A market stall selling dried fish, Keng Tung, 2004.

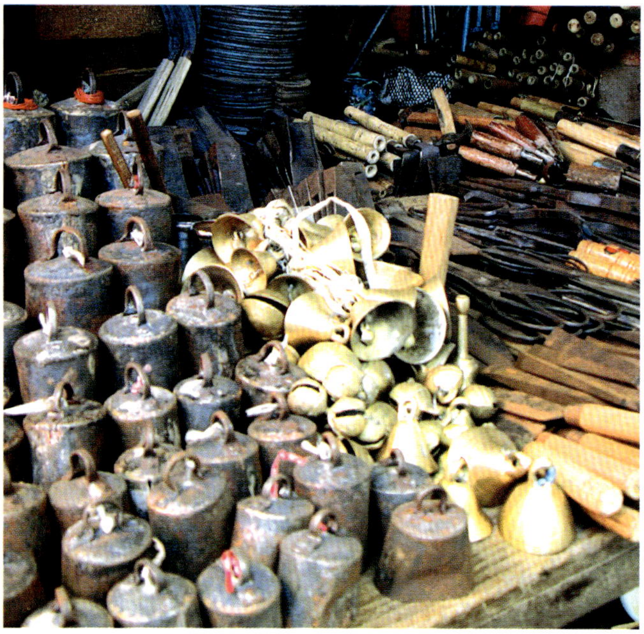

286 A market stall displaying cowbells, knives and utensils, made by the Wa, Keng Tung, 2004.

lacquer ware and pottery, and locally-woven textiles, were also available. At the end of the day the women packed up their panniers with any remaining goods and walked home.

The marketplace in Shan villages is a large open space with irregular lines of narrow unpaved paths or passages, bordered by little booths-used as shops-with thatched roofs supported by poles. There are no counters. Everything is procurable that the place affords. Rice, curries, meats etc are cooked and sold, and of which everybody appears to partake.[7]

Although women were the main participants in local markets, some village men were involved in long distance trade. Travelling with oxen, they carried rice, tobacco, sugar, fermented tea and betel. This was only possible if there was another man in the family to stay in the village and take care of the fields. Those men who did the trading came home for the rice-planting season and again at harvest time. There were some villagers who could never travel for any length of time because they were subject to demands for field labour, made by Shan rulers.

Hill dwellers were also involved in trade. The Wa bartered iron ore which they mined and smelted on primitive forges. Their knives, cowbells, and other small metal ware items were brought down from the hills to be traded. The Wa also dealt in cattle and raw cotton. McLeod claimed that in the state of Keng Tung, most of their cotton was sold to Chinese merchants. He also noted that the Wa cultivated indigo which they processed and traded in the form of a paste.[8] Interestingly on one of his tours, Sir George Scott encountered a group of Wa villagers carrying woven cotton from the town of Keng Tung back to their villages where they told him they would dye it red. He said they excelled at this particular skill and the finished red cotton was bartered with Shan villagers.[9] The Wa, and many other hill dwellers also traded in shoulder bags decorated with silk thread, coloured wool, Job's tears and other dried seeds. They made popular as gifts. The Wa living in the hills close to the Chinese border in Sipsong Pan Na extracted small amounts of gold found in river beds which they bartered for cattle, silver, betel and salt.

The Karen traded agricultural produce including corn, vegetables, betel, honey and wax. They also dealt in elephants, and cattle. They raided vulnerable villages for slaves. Captive men, women and children were sold to Tai and Indian slave traders.[10] Some hill dwellers grew poppies for opium, a trade that was taxed by Shan rulers. Because of the steepness of the terrain where hill dwellers farmed, and the lack of good paths for oxen and ponies, they transported their goods by porter and by elephant on the lower slopes.

On the international, the trans-regional and the inter-state routes the Ho (Haw), Shan, Burmese and Indians were the main traders. The Ho were Chinese Muslims domiciled in Yunnan who operated on a route from Dali (Tali) to Puer (Muong Meng) to Semao (Muong La) to Keng Hung and on to Keng Tung. When they were permitted to do so, they travelled on to Chiang Mai, a journey of fifteen days. From Chiang Mai they either went back to Dali or south to the port of Moulmein in Burma. The journey to Moulmein took about four weeks. Some Ho traders did not travel as far as Burma and were able to make two round trips between the Shan States and Dali each season.

All long-distance trade required a high level of investment. Ho caravans consisted of between fifty and one hundred mules and ponies, up to ten men to care for them

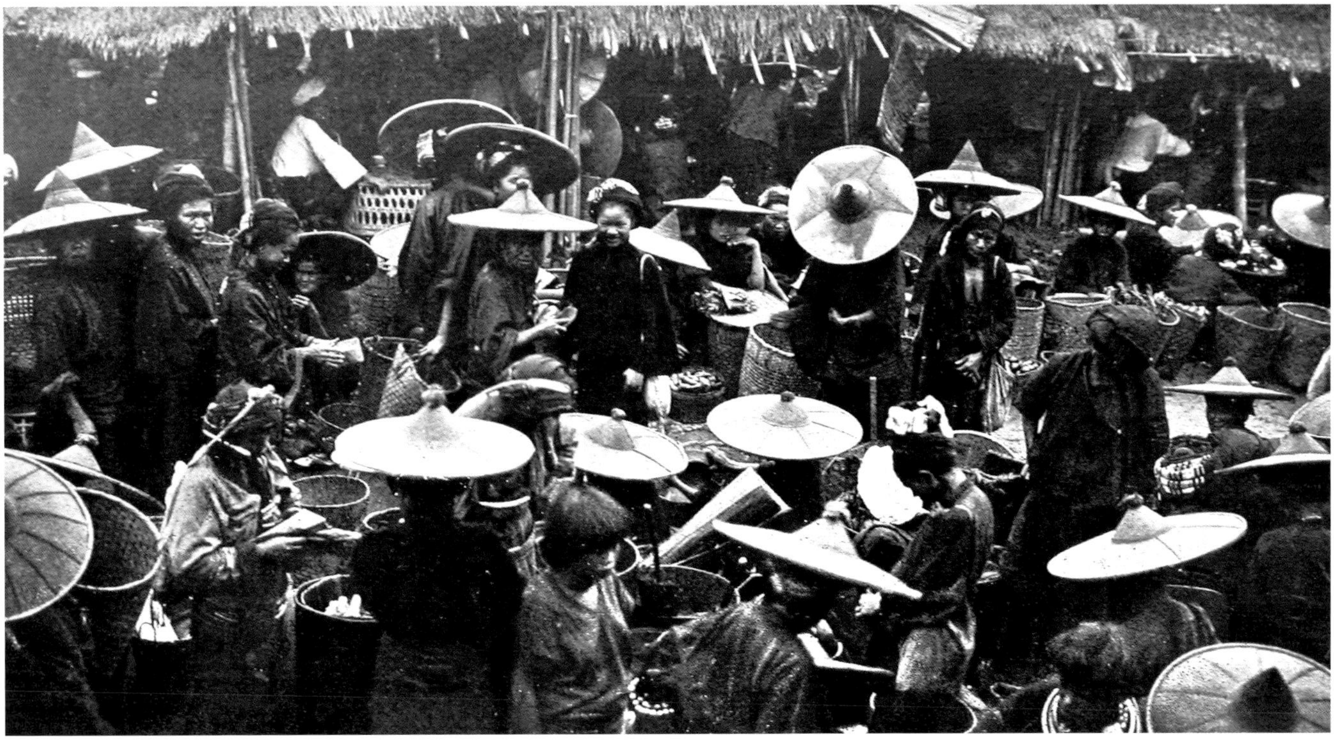

287 A Shan market with Shan and hill tribe women selling their wares. Milne and Chochrane, 1910.

and to guard the cargo, and an overseer to take charge of it all.[11] There were so many Ho caravans passing regularly through Keng Tung that Ho agents were settled in the city. The Prince of Keng Tung sold them some land as a site for a mosque and today a more recent building stands in its place (fig. 288). Not all the traders from China were Muslim and Chinese temples were also built and maintained by their communities (fig. 291).

The Tai involved in long distance trade were mainly Tai Yai, Tai Lue and Tai Khoen, generally referred to in the trade records as Shan. Their caravans crossed from Keng Tung, to Laikha, to Muong Nai and Mawkmai and to Chiang Mai and other cities in Lan Na, when the political climate was favourable. Some went from Laikha to Muong Pan then on to Muong Nai in November and December (the dry season). Many travelled on to Martaban and Moulmein arriving there in January, February or March. They returned home in April and May. The Shan called at all large settlements and were prepared to open their packs to those who approached them while they camped. Holt Hallett described a typical Shan caravan.

> *A party of Shans wearing blue trousers and jackets and great straw hats atop of the silk handkerchiefs which were twined round their top knots. All the oxen wore nose- bags of rattan cane, to prevent them from browsing by the way; and the leaders wore a mask in front of their faces, fancifully worked with cowrie shells, and topped by a beautiful peacock's tail.*[12]

Porters also carried goods on these routes.

> *They carry produce and wares between the emporiums of Burma and the land-locked areas of their own and contiguous territories..... The carriers' kit is of the lightest; each man has his rice supply in a cloth roll tied about his waist. The goods are carried by men or by pack-bullocks.*[13]

Burmese traders generally did business in the southern Shan States. Their caravans travelled from Tenasserim and carried a variety of Burmese and Indian goods and a few European items. Some Burmese traders bought Shan ponies and cattle which they took south to sell in Moulmein.

Indian traders dealt in textiles, gems and slaves. Slave trading was profitable because skilled workers and manual labourers were always in short supply in the Shan States. Some captives ended up as servants in the palaces of the princes. McLeod wrote:

> *I regret much to find that some of the natives of India now residing here have turned their attention to the degrading speculation in slaves ...The price varies from two to seven bullocks...*[14]

E. A. Blundell, British Commissioner in the Tenasserim Provinces was also aware of slave trading, noting that it was organised by Shan and Karen dealers. He wrote to McLeod:

> *It is feared that some of the natives of India who proceed to the Shan States in trading excursions are occasionally engaged in the traffic of slaves that takes place between the Shans and the Red Karens.*[15]

Maurice Collis, who visited the Shan states in the 1930s, met a gang of Indian gem traders in the state of Muong Mit. The royal family told him that such traders were regular visitors to the Shan courts.

> *We returned to the camp and entered the prince's tawmaw. Some Indian jewel merchants had arrived from Mogok, the ruby mines, and desired permission to display their wares before the Mahadevi. Soon there were boxes of gems strewn on the floor...*[16]

British traders, latecomers by local standards, were interested in generally expanding Southeast Asian inland trade and were particularly focussed on the prospect of a railway. The Shan States were subject to numerous British expeditions, sent from Lower Burma, beginning in the 1820s. In 1860 the President of the Manchester Chamber of Commerce wrote to Lord Palmerston:

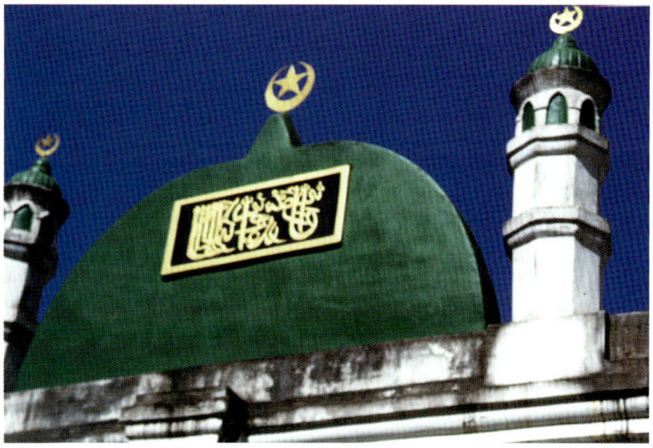

288 The roof of a mosque, built by Chinese Muslim (Ho) traders in Keng Tung. The Prince of Keng Tung donated the land on which the building stands.

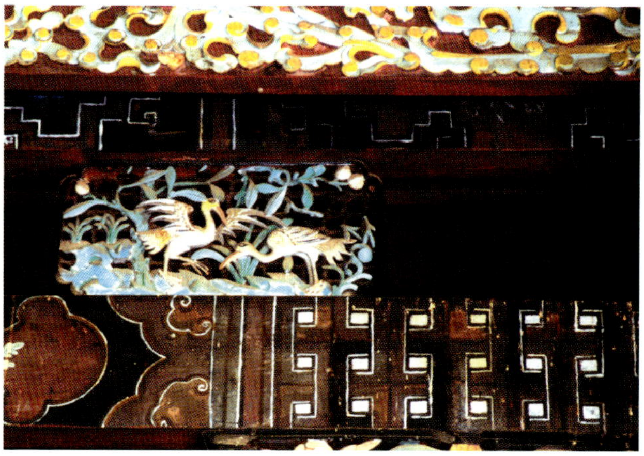

289 Detail of gilded wood carving on a Chinese temple built in 1773 by Chinese merchants. It is situated in a weaving village. The nearby town of Amarapura was built ten years later. The Chinese have a long history of trading silk with the weavers in this area.

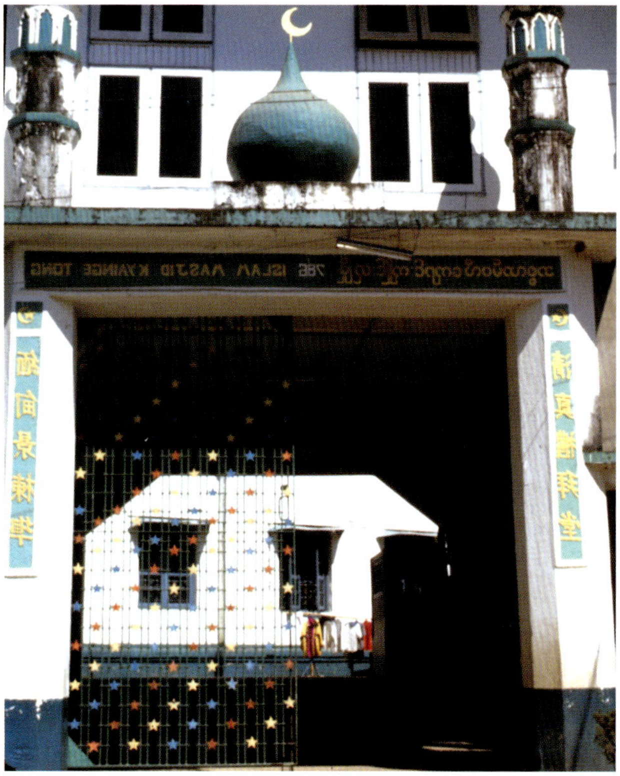

290 The front entrance to the Chinese mosque in Keng Tung.

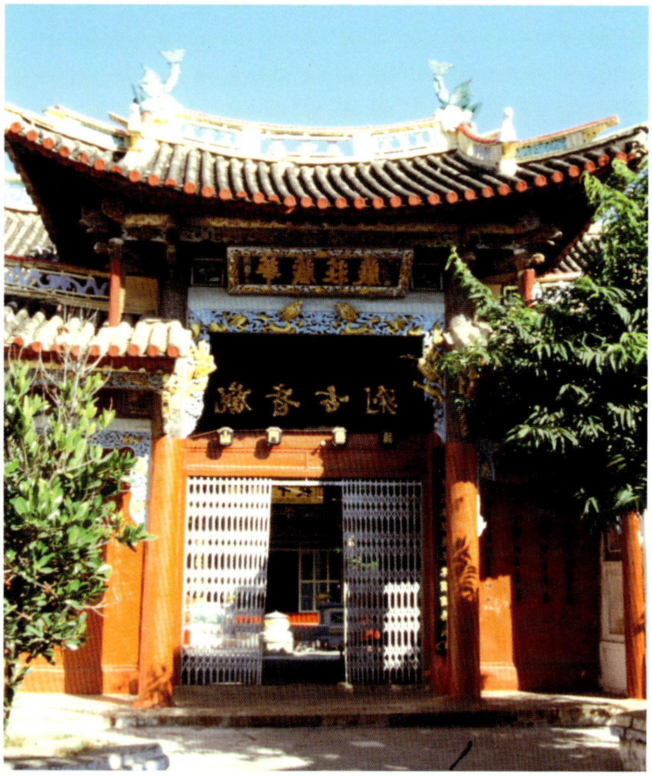

291 The front entrance to the Chinese temple built in 1773.

> *The Directors of the Chamber of Commerce have, therefore, to urge that a communication be made by Her Majesty's Government to Lord Elgin, calling his Lordship's immediate attention to the expediency of the western half of the Chinese Empire being opened to our commerce, overland; by arranging that the Chinese frontier city of Esmok* [Simao] *shall be made an open inland mart, under such regulations and provisions as may be in the circumstances advisable.*[17]

In 1862 Britain and Burma concluded a commercial treaty. It was the aim of the British to embark on trade with China via the Shan States and within a year various British trade organisations were showing interest. The President of the Cotton Supply Association sent a letter in 1863 enquiring about cotton production in Muong Nai, Keng Tung and Keng Hung. The British believed they could increase their share of trade by importing manufactured goods via India and Burma. However, the market for British goods was small, and as stated earlier, overland routes were difficult and at times dangerous for those without experience and transport costs were high. It became evident that the local elite was not particularly interested in a new range of imports. McLeod reported:

> *Though all our piece goods are admired, yet from the Tsobua [saopha] downwards they have no inclination to part with their money; and if anything foreign is seen in their possession, one may be pretty certain it has been given to them.*[18]

In terms of supplies for arts and crafts, in the nineteenth century the Shan States could draw on a variety of local materials. Iron was mined in Keng Hung and there were silver mines in Muong Laem that produced silver that was over ninety-five per cent pure. Small amounts of gold were panned in the Shan river beds, and rubies and sapphires were mined at several sites, Mogok being the most productive. Jade, jadeite and amber were mined in the northern Shan States. There were extensive teak forests that provided wood for building and hardwoods like *yamane (Gmelina arborea)* for general carving, and *yindaik (Dalbergia cultrate)* for fine intricate work.[19] The trees that produce the sap for lacquer *(Melanorrhoea usitata)* grew wild in the drier forests of the Shan States. Orpiment *(arsenic trisulphide)* for yellow lacquer pigment and other lacquer dyes were also available locally. Clay for pottery could be dug from special sites and bamboo for making baskets and mats grew abundantly. Cotton, hemp and indigo grew locally and other dyes were obtained from fruit, core wood and bark. Although many raw materials were available for producing high quality art and craft objects, there was always a market for imported dress and textiles.

Clothes and household textiles used for everyday were made of homespun cotton but people of all classes bought some foreign goods for their best dress. One of the main imports was silk because production was limited and could never meet local demand. Textiles and dress produced for the elite involved imported raw Chinese silk, transported in unprocessed bundles weighing about two viss each.[20] Once it was cleaned, processed and spun, a smooth, shiny thread resulted. This was in contrast to Shan silk that had a distinctive slub and softer sheen. In practical terms, Chinese silk was easier to process because the filaments were less prone to tangling and in terms of status it was viewed by the Shan elite as a luxury item, more sophisticated than silk produced in the villages.

Raw Chinese silk was cleaned dyed and woven, mainly for making women's skirts and blouses, men's sarongs and turban cloths. Other imports included silk and satin piece goods, velvet and flowered tinsel cloth. Lengths of floss silk embroidery, plain silk ribbons, sewing thread, sequins, and gold and silver metal thread were used to trim women's ankle-length skirts, blouses and jackets, and male court coats. Ribbons, lengths of embroidery and sequins were also popular for decorating pillows, and the end panels of floor cushions. The Ho imported ready-made Chinese silk turban cloths, large straw hats and quilted jackets of glazed indigo cotton, produced in Sipsong Pan Na and southern Yunnan For the winter months they suppllied the Shan elite with Chinese silk jackets, lined with fur. The best quality fur was a grey colour and came from a rare indigenous civet cat. The second rank was brown and white from an animal described by McLeod as "about the size of a dog" and the cheapest was sheepskin.[21] They also carried household items like felt and wool carpets, and Chinese glazed pottery, copper and iron pots and utensils. The iron utensils were probably purchased, or bartered from the Wa whom the Ho merchants encountered on route from Dali.

Ho merchants who travelled to the port of Moulmein purchased Indian muslins and cambrics, printed calico and other cotton piece goods, and Burmese silk that they sold on the return journey through the Shan States. These items were bought by the Shan to make blouses, shirts and jackets and turban cloths. Cheaper plain cotton was used for lining. The Ho bartered some goods for raw cotton and dyestuffs, betel, gum, stick lac, wild animal skins and bones and ivory. Shan forest products were valued in China as ingredients for herbal medicines.

Many Shan women gave up weaving when imported mill cotton came down in price to match the cost of local hand-woven cloth. The Tai Khoen women of the Keng Tung valley bought Chinese silk turban cloths and the Tai Lue bought plain cotton and silk piece goods to make jackets and blouses, dyeing the fabric to the colours they preferred. In contrast the Tai Neua of the northern Shan States continued to weave cotton for clothing, although Sir George Scott thought this had more to do with the high cost and poor quality of imports available to them.[22]

Burmese traders carried goods from Moulmein to the Shan States, particularly muslins, Manchester cotton, flannel, lace trimmings, printed cottons, Indian silks and brocades, and silk and cotton handkerchiefs. They also carried floral rugs, velvet, velveteen, satin, aniline dyes, needles, sewing thread, umbrellas, paper fans and combs. They took back to Burma from the Shan States rice, raw cotton, betel, stick lac and tobacco. A few Burmese caravans went as far as Luang Prabang to sell cottons, velvets and trimmings and to buy some French manufactured goods.[23]

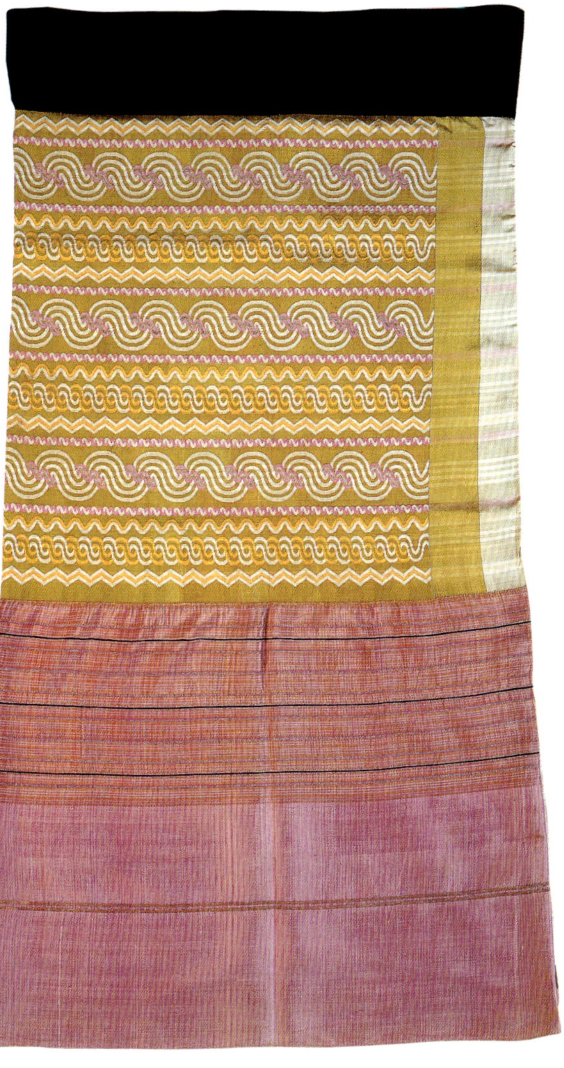

292 An ankle-length silk skirt made near Amarapura, and exported to the Shan States. The central panel is *acheik-luntaya.*

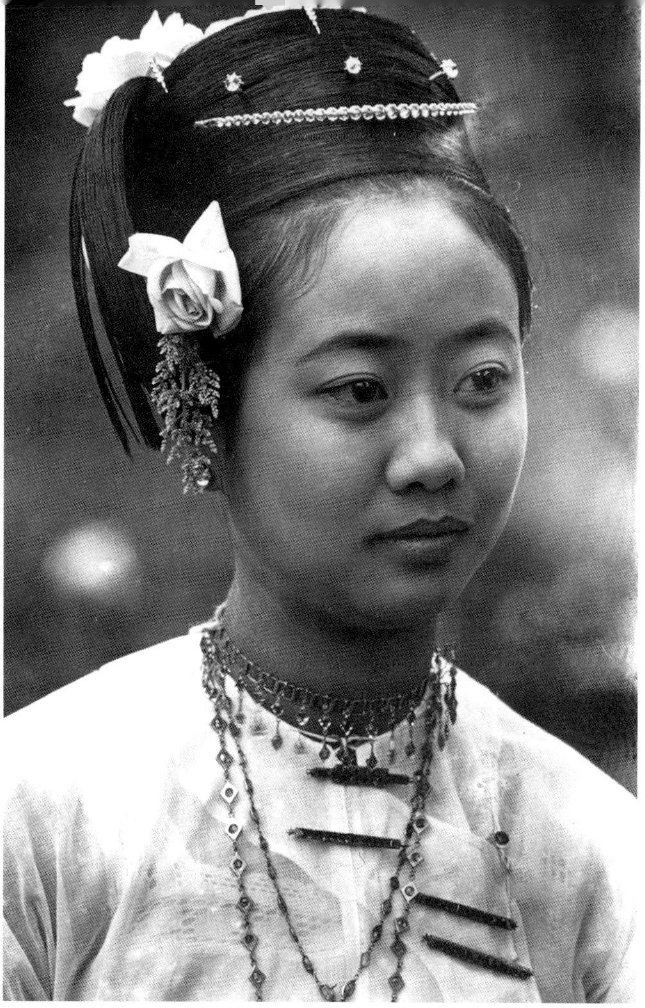

293 A Shan woman wearing necklaces, brooches and hair jewellery, traded throughout the Shan states. *(The Green Centre for World Art at The Royal Pavilion Art Gallery and Museums, Brighton, P0090)*

Shan merchants made good profits from the work of artisans which they marketed in Burma and Lan Na. There was a demand for Shan metal work, particularly niello, cloisonné and repoussé used to decorate silver and gold regalia, swords and scabbards, and drinking vessels.[24] Shan lacquer ware, produced mainly in Laikha and Keng Tung, fetched good prices, particularly lacquer betel boxes, food containers and cups. Shan traders also carried local pottery, ironware, homespun cotton cloth, mulberry paper, Shan tea and citrus fruits. Embroidered shoes with leather soles and leather sandals, mostly made in Hsipaw, were exported to Chiang Mai and other Lan Na towns. Cane products and bamboo mats were sold in the western Shan States where they were not produced, and were also marketed in Burma. On their return journeys the Shan traders bought high quality hand woven textiles from the villages around Chiang Mai and Lamphun. Women's skirt lengths from Lan Na were in demand throughout the Shan States and fetched a high price. The British engineer Holt Hallett named Ban Nang Eng to the south of Chiang Mai as an important source of these skirts.[25]

If the Shan caravans went to Burma they brought back mill cotton and silk and cotton piece goods, betel, dried fish and agricultural products that did not grow at home. They also purchased Burmese silk textiles, particularly silk ikat fabric from Inlay Lake, and silk *acheik-luntaya* from Amarapura and Mandalay, fabrics worn by royalty and the elite.

The major export from the Shan States to China was a short staple variety of raw cotton *(Gossypium herbaceum)*. It was a vital source of revenue. After harvesting, the cotton was pressed into bales, wrapped in cotton cloth and bound tightly with strips of bamboo. The bales were weighed in pairs so that they were evenly balanced for the mules to carry. The average weight was fifty to eighty viss. On his journey from Keng Tung to Keng Hung, McLeod encountered a group of Chinese cotton traders.

> *The plains near the villages are seen dotted over with white patches (all cotton being packed in coarse white cloth), marking their encamping ground, and their mules grazing in all directions. The men also wander about, leaving their goods under the guardianship of fierce Tartar dogs, who well perform the duty entrusted to them.*[26]

McLeod also met Chinese porters with cotton on their backs, noting that they covered the same distance each day as the mules.[27] The price paid for raw cotton in the 1830s was sixty ticals of Chinese silver per one hundred viss of cleaned cotton.[28] Since some Shan States were subject to periodic drought, leading to a shortage of rice, raw cotton and tea *(miang)* provided alternative commercial crops that could be bartered for rice grown elsewhere.

The range of imported goods available in the Shan States increased in the third quarter of the nineteenth century and much was written on the changes that this brought. McLeod had said in the 1830s that there was little demand for imported textiles except red mill cloth that he described as "shani," and in the villages through which he passed, most women had looms and wove cloth in season. However, by the 1880s there were so many imports that some foreigners like Sir George Scott, who had come to appreciate Shan arts and crafts, were concerned for local producers. Scott thought that the fabrics coming from India and Europe were inferior to locally woven textiles. He described the imports as "gaudy calicoes and cheap Manchester fabric." He lamented their replacing indigenous fabrics particularly those worn for religious ceremonies and village festivals.[29] He noted that mill cotton sold well even though indigenous cotton was more durable. He predicted that women who were still weaving distinctive forms of Lue, Khoen and Neua dress, would eventually give because imports were so cheap.

Hsipaw where women produced finely woven cotton for jackets and blouses, provided a picture in microcosm of what was happening in the hills and valleys. Shan women gave up weaving when cheap imported calico became readily available. The Kachin who produced hand-woven vegetable dyed cloth lengths to trim their skirts, and make fringes for their bags, began to substitute strips of imported mill cotton, garishly dyed wools, and manufactured braids. During the late nineteenth century commercial dyes replaced most locally-produced dyes. This was also seen as a regressive step.

> *German aniline dyes are replacing the delicate and artistic tints which may be seen in Shan woven-work made on the hand-looms a few years ago, when the weavers made their own dyes from leaves and the bark of trees... The articles once manufactured by Shans are now supplied by Germany. They no longer dye thread in different colours for their woven work because they can buy German twists and yarns of brilliant colours in any quantity.*[30]

Mrs Leslie Milne provided an account of the Shan markets at the end of the nineteenth century:

> *Shoes and matches come from Japan, also some thin cotton materials. Silks for embroidery, tinsel thread, small porcelain bowls, copper cooking pots, and brass lamps are of Chinese*

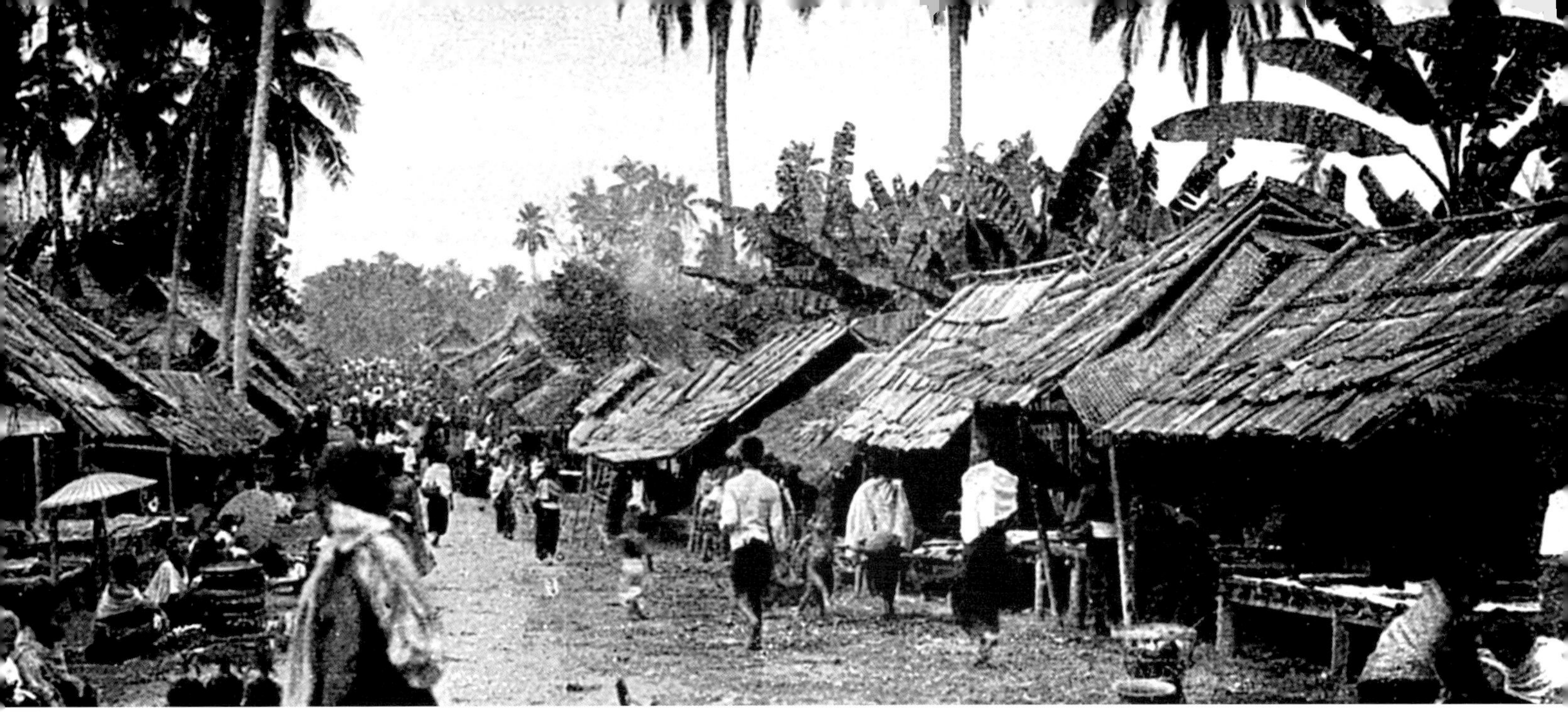

294 A small village market in the Shan states. Goods are laid out on low wood and bamboo tables.

manufacture. Cotton goods and coarse muslins come from India. Kachins can buy the cheap German red flannel which ornaments their jackets, also the scarlet braid which, when cut into lengths of a few inches, is made into fringe, to decorate their bags; common glass beads...amber, green, crimson, milkwhite...all are German.[31]

In contrast to the comments made by Sir George Scott who had regretted the flooding of local markets with imported textiles, Leslie Milne took a more practical view:

Shans show wisdom in preferring cheap velvets and silks, which cost little yet look pretty. There are no chest-of-drawers or wardrobes, though in a few houses there are wooden boxes, in which the best dresses for festival occasions may be kept, but as a rule wearing apparel is thrown over ropes stretched across the rooms, and when so treated, an expensive velvet or silk becomes marked and soiled quite as quickly as one that has cost little. Even with the greatest care, during the rainy season, articles of clothing, whether of good or of shoddy material, become mildewed and spoilt...Each woman sews her own clothes so there are no dressmaker's bills.[32]

Although there were European imports, British goods did not compete effectively.

There are practically no articles of British manufacture in the country districts of the Northern Shan States except a few needles and reels of Paisley thread.[33]

The optimistic predictions of the British and the French, who had explored the Shan States for markets in the nineteenth century, were not realised. Most goods that competed successfully with locally made products came from the factories of China, India, Germany and Japan. Although the Shan markets were flooded with cheap foreign imports, there was a market for traditional Shan arts and crafts commissioned as donations to Buddhist temples as a way of making merit. Goods were also produced for the homes of the elite. Shan silver ware, lacquer ware, woodcarving and metalwork was in demand througout the twentieth century.

Endnotes

1 Grabowsky and Turton, *The Gold and Silver Road of Trade and Friendship,* Chiang Mai, 2003, p. 364.
2 McLeod quoted in Grabowsky and Turton, p. 369.
3 *Ibid.* p. 79.
4 *Ibid* p. 213.
5 George Scott, *Burma: A Handbook of Practical Information* London 1906 reprint Orchid Press, Bangkok, 1999, p. 318.
6 R. Sethakul, *Political Relations between Chiang Mai and Kengtung in the Nineteenth Century,* PhD. dissertation, University of Illinois, 1989.
7 Leslie Milne and Wilbur Cochrane, *Shans at Home,* 1910, reprint Paragon Books, New Yok, 1970, p. 167.
8 Mcleod quoted in Grabowsky and Turton, p. 327.
9 This is particularly interesting because the usual red dye (*krang*) does not take well on cotton. Presumably they were using another source.
10 Grabowsky and Turton, 2003.
11 *Ibid,* p. 181.
12 Holt Hallett, *A Thousand Miles on an Elephant in the Shan States,* Edinburgh and London 1890, reprint White Lotus, Bangkok, 1988, p. 208.
13 M. Ferrars and B. Ferrars, *Burma,* London and New York, 1901, reprint Ava Press, Bangkok, 1996, p. 146.
14 Grabowsky and Turton, 2003, p. 305.
15 E. A. Blundell 'Additional Instructions to Lieutenant McLeod, relative to the Shan States of Zimmay and Laboung; dated 25th November 1836, quoted in Grabowsky and Turton, 2003, p. 257.
16 Maurice Collis, *Lords of the Sunset: A Tour in the Shan States,* 1938, reprint Ava Press, 1996, p. 204.
17 Letter from the President of the Manchester Chamber of Commerce to Lord Palmerston July 12th 1860. India Office Collections, The British Library, London.
18 McLeod quoted in Grabowsky and Turton, 2003, p. 309.
19 Sylvia Fraser Lu, *Burmese Crafts: Past and Present,* Kuala Lumpur, 1994, p. 92-93.
20 A viss weighs 1.65 kilos.
21 Grabowsky and Turton, 2003, p. 354.
22 Scott, 1999.
23 Martha Bassenne, *Au Laos et Au Siam,* Paris, 1912, reprint as *In Laos and in Siam,* (trans. W. Tips), White Lotus Press, Bangkok, 1995.
24 Keng Tung silversmiths exported silver goods to Chiang Mai until the early nineteenth century when, during raids on Keng Tung they were captured and forcibly resettled in Chiang Mai.
25 Hallett, 1988, p. 87.
26 Grabowsky and Turton, 2003, p. 365.
27 *Ibid,* p. 487.
28 One tical weighed approximately 15 grams.
29 George Scott, *Burma and Beyond,* London, 1932.
30 Milne and Cochrane, 1910, p. 139.
31 *Ibid,* p. 137.
32 *Ibid,* p. 138.
33 *Ibid,* p. 137.

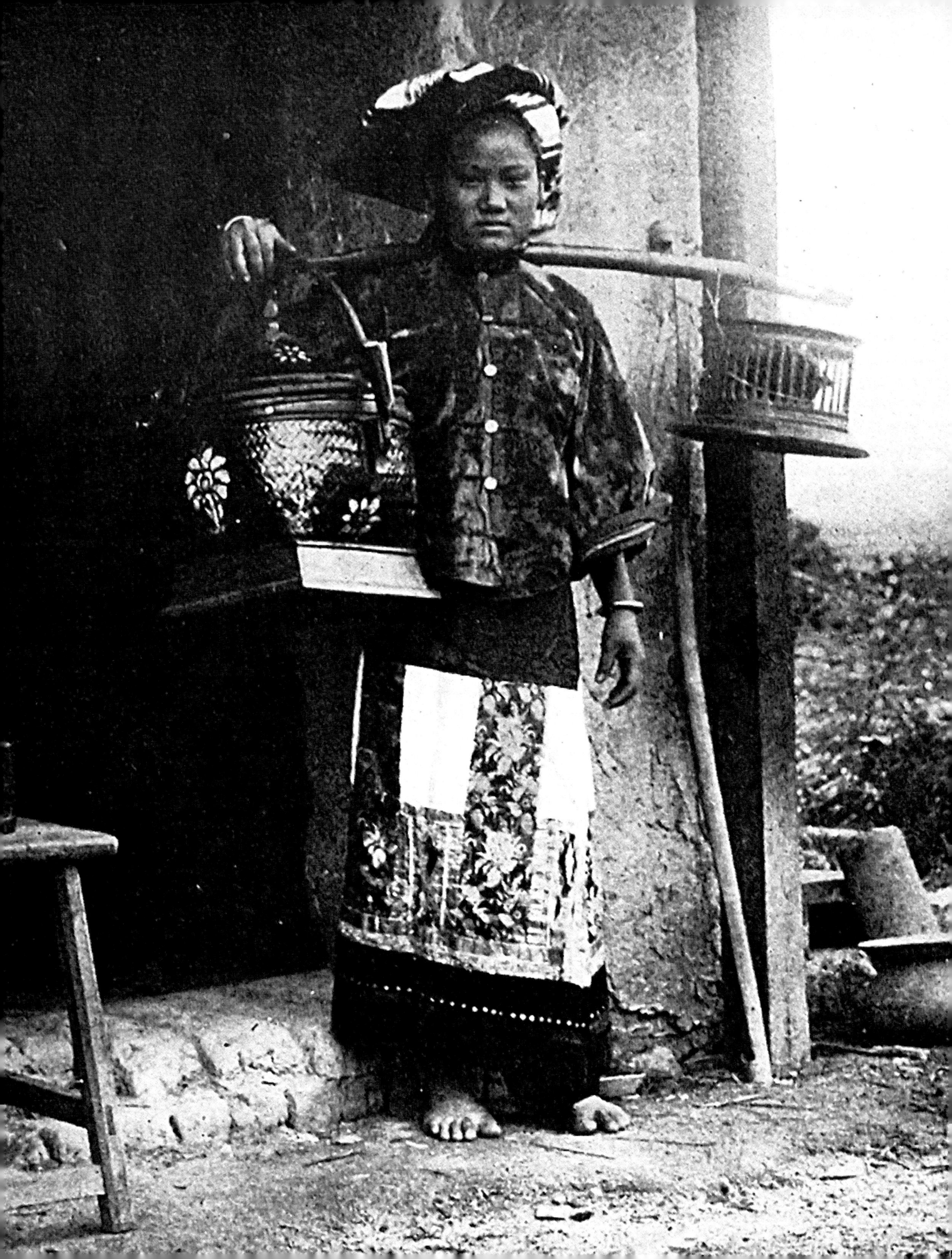

Conclusion

This book highlights the history, art and culture of the valley residents of the Shan States who claim affinity with the people of neighbouring Lan Na (north Thailand), Sipsong Pan Na (Xishuangbanna Autonomous Prefecture) and Western Laos (Lan Xang). The valley dwellers throughout this region of inland Southeast Asia share a language with variations in dialect, and analogous religious scripts, and there are common features in their art and architecture and in their social customs. They practice a similar form of Theravada Buddhism and uphold customs associated with ancestor spirits. Their interaction with hill dwellers was an important element in the development of a unique Shan culture.

The redrawing of state boundaries at the end of the nineteenth century, followed by their closure in the early twentieth century, deprived the people of contact for many years. In more recent times inter-state mobility has returned and the people of Lan Na, Sipsong Pan Na and Western Laos have been able to rebuild and strengthen cultural ties. It has been difficult, and at times impossible, for the people of the Shan States to engage in this dialogue due to political pressure exerted from outside.

This book is illustrated with examples of Shan arts and crafts, and architecture. The monks are custodians of the monastery buildings and their contents but in spite of their vigilance thousands of Shan art treasures and antiques that should be held in museums and public institutions for all to see, have been smuggled out of the country and sold to foreign dealers. There is little conservation of secular buildings. Many wonderful examples of Shan architecture, including teak palaces, have been torn down. Rows of elegant wooden shop houses have been replaced by hideous concrete structures that spoil the urban landscape, as they do in much of inland Southeast Asia. Many fear for the future of Shan artists and artisans. Some families continue to run successful workshops and provide beautiful hand-made objects for the monasteries, for local patrons and for the tourist market. However, the cost of raw materials such as metal, glass for inlay, and gold leaf continues to rise as local currency falls in value. Cheap mass-produced plastic goods from China have replaced many local products that were previously made by hand. Fortunately a distinctive Shan cuisine survives. Delicious noodles, specialist Shan meat and fish dishes and mouth-watering desserts made of sticky rice and coconut, are among the local delicacies available on market stalls.

The production of hand woven textiles has been badly affected by the influx of garish synthetic fabrics. Village weaving traditions have disappeared in many areas. This is not an irreversible process. In other parts of Southeast Asia there has been a great revival in the production of hand-woven silks and cottons, on sale in specialist shops and on stalls in local markets. They are catering to discerning local people, and tourists from all over the world who appreciate beautiful textiles. It would be possible for a renaissance to take place in the Shan States if there was political will and an enlightened tourist industry. There should be a Shan arts and crafts museum as a resource for future designers, artisans, scholars and students, and as a centre of interest for the public, and for tourists. This has been successfully achieved in other parts of Southeast Asia.

One of the obstacles to achieving any of these goals is the current plight of the people. Whole communities of valley dwellers in the Shan States have been relocated far from their homelands. Those who remain struggle to keep their unique customs alive. Others treasure their heritage and preserve its traditions while living overseas. This is not a unique situation. In the past when the Khmer Rouge tried to destroy the cultural heritage of Cambodia, it was a small number of artists, artisans, monks and lay people who kept the culture alive. When peace was restored it was their expertise that helped the Cambodian people rebuild their identity by connecting with the past. This could be a model that gives heart to the people of the Shan States.

295 A woman in Shan dress with lacquer baskets on a pole.

296 (Overleaf) The interior of the Shan Palace Museum, Yawnghwe.

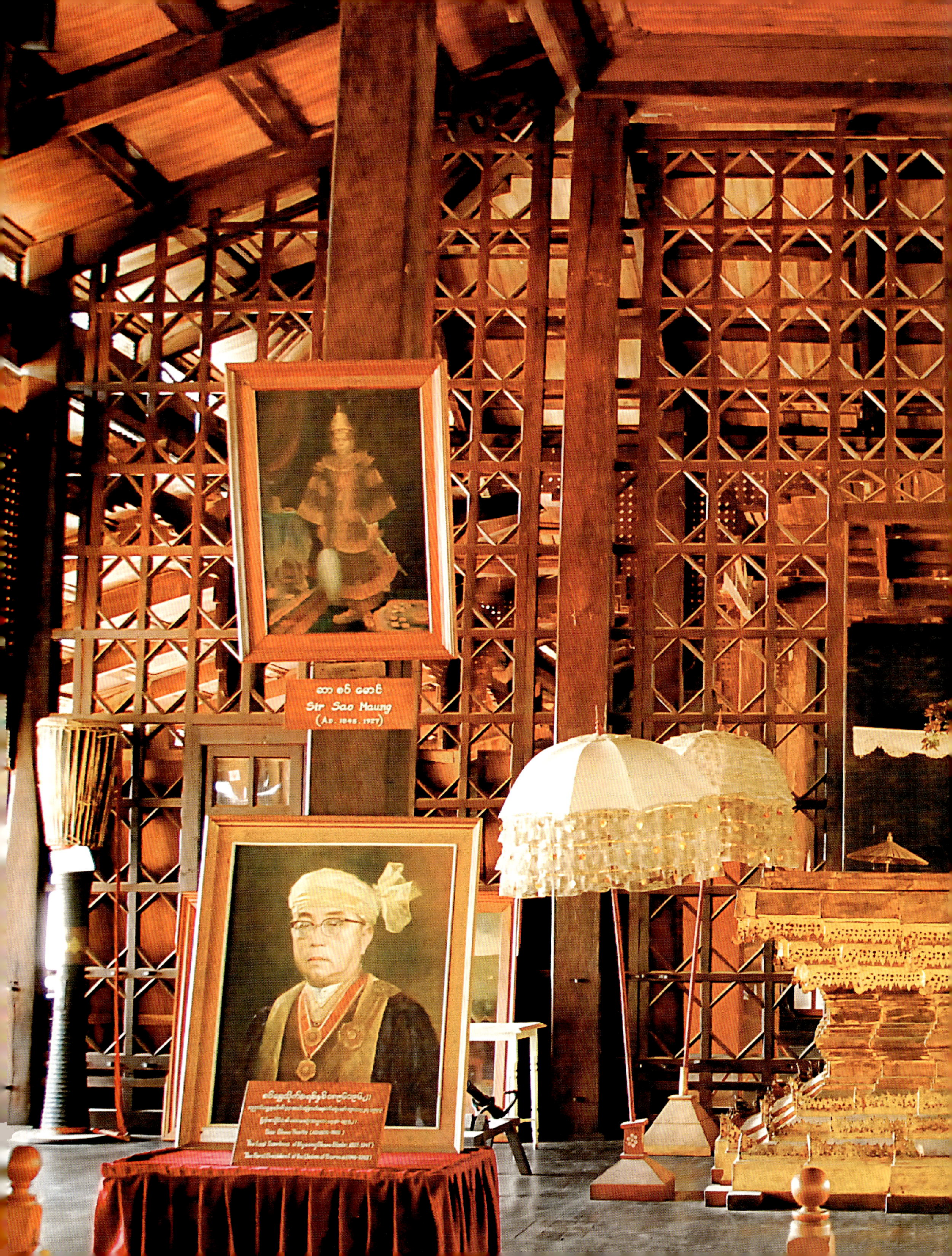
Sir Sao Maung

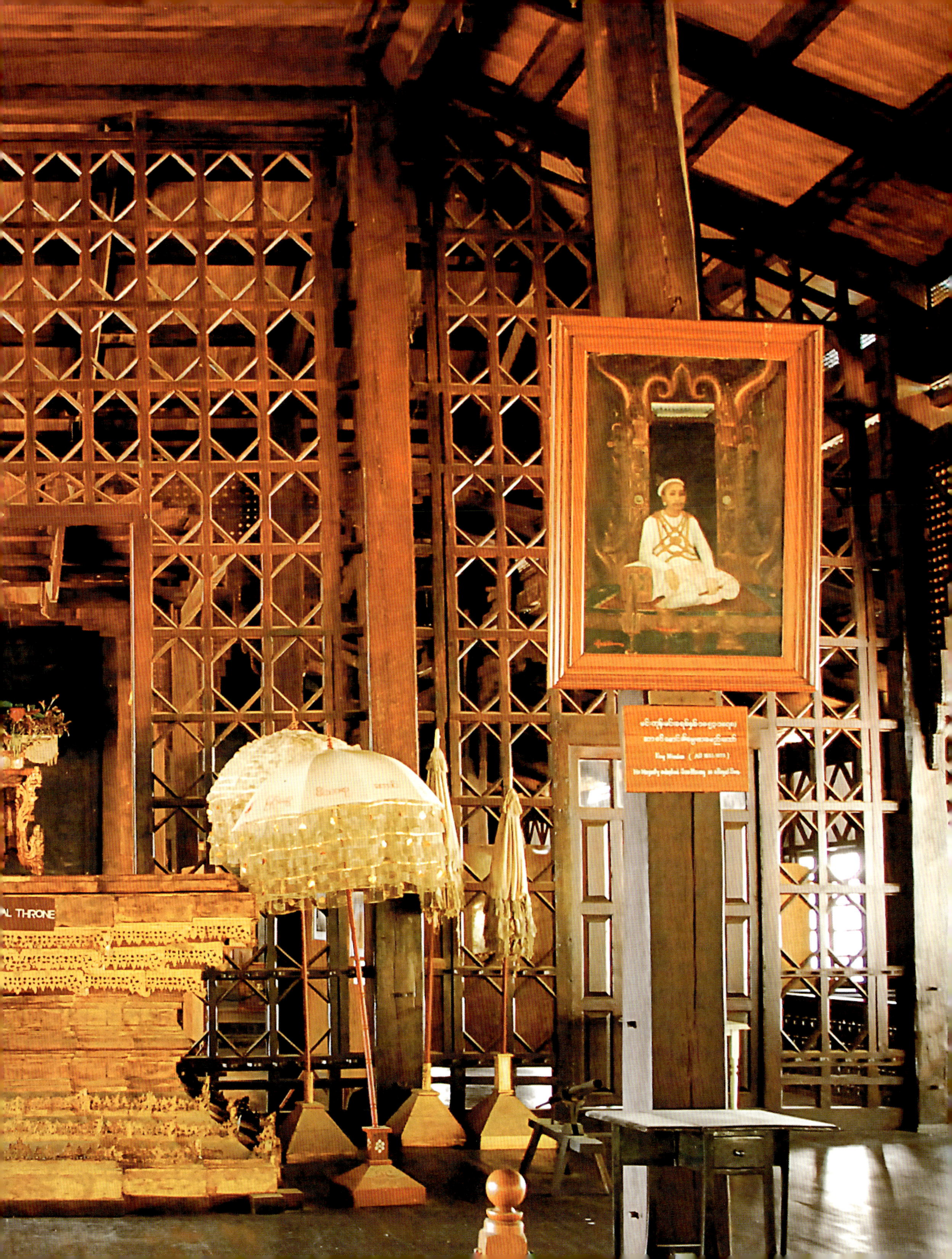
AL THRONE

Ruling Family of North Hsenwi*

Hkun Sang Ton Hung
North Hsenwi State ruled 1888-1916

- Wife1: Nang Nang, *Daughter of Sang Hai, Divorced 1888*
- Wife2: Nang Ywet, *Mahadevi*
  - Nang Hseng U *(F)*, *1900-1972 (married E. T. D Gaudoin)*
    - (child)
    - (child)
    - Nang Htwe Kham (Nancy) *1923-*
    - (child)
    - Nang Sein Myint (Elaine) *1928-became Sao Sa-Mee Daw when adopted by Sao Hom Hpa*
    - (child)
    - Nang Sumpu *(Eleanor 1933-)*
  - Nang Hkam Hkam *(F)*, *1891-1933*
  - Nang Hkam Seng *(F)*, *1885-1927*
- Wife3: Nang Hkam Ai, *Daughter of Sang Hai*
- Wife4: Nang Hkam Kut, *Daughter of Sang Hai, Sao Nang Zoo (keeper of the seal)*
- Wife5: Nang Arm, *Daughter of Hkam Kwe Ai Htamong of Mong Yaw*
  - **Sao Hom Hpa**, *ruled 1925-1959*
    - *1925 married Sao Thu Thiri Mahla of Hsipaw, mahadevi 1925*
    - *married 1933 Sao Ven Tip of Keng Tung mahadevi 1937*
  - **Sao Hman Hpa**, *married Sao Thu Zanda (Hsipaw) 1905-1978*
    - **Sao Hkam Hip Hpa (Ivan)**, *(adopted by Sao Hom Hpa) 1927- married 26.08.1950 Erica May Florence Wootton*
      - Sao Hkam Vai Hpa (Stephen Christopher Hpa) *16.06.1951-*
      - Sao Hkam Hom Hpa (Darryl Colin Hpa) *30.06.1953-*
      - Sao Hpa Hkam Nun (Mark Dana Hpa) *04.03.1958-*
      - Sao Hkam Pung Hpa (Barry Lindsay Hpa) *18.06.1960-*
    - Sao Shwe Ong (Patricia) *1928-*
    - Sao You Pa Kya Yi (Nancy) *1929-*
- Wife6: Nang Ai, *Daughter of Pu Kye of Mong Yaw*
- Wife7: Nang Hkam Hsa, *Daughter of Pu Lol Hsalng Ai Hsa Tin Tat Village Mong Yaw*

* Hsenwi was divided into North and South Hsenwi in 1888.

Ruling Family of Yawnghwe

Sao Hsi Hseng Hpa
said to have established the present town of Yawnghwe in 1369

Hso Hseng Hpa ruled 1434-1477

Hso Hung Pa
ruled 1477-1518

Hso Yawb Hpa
ruled 1518-1559

Saw Maw Hkam
ruled 1559-1574

Sao Hkun Hom Pa
ruled 1574-1608

Sao Htoi Hkam
ruled 1608-1615 (State administered by his grandmother during his minority)

Sao Hpai Hkam,
ruled 1615. Died the same year without issue. (State administered by Nang Nung Pe up to 1618 and by others (names not known up to 1630)

Son married to Mong Mit saohpa's daughter

Sao Awng Hkam
ruled 1630-1658

Sao Hsu Wa ruled 1663-1687

Sao Hkam Hom Hpa ruled 1658-1663

Sao Hkun Daung Sa ruled 1687-1695

Sao Hkam Leng ruled 1695-1733

Sao Hkam Lin ruled 1733-1735

Sao Hsiton Sa ruled 1737-1746

Sao Htawk Sha Sa
ruled 1735-1737

Sao Hpom Maka Sa
ruled 1761-1762

Sao Mong Hkawn
(Maung Myo)
appointed saohpa of Kengtung in 1730.

Sao Hke Hsa Wa
ruled 1746-1758

Sao Naw Mong Hsa Kun
ruled 1758

Sao Yawt Hkam
ruled 1758 - 1761

Sao Yun ruled 1762-1815

Sao Pya

Sao Naw Mong
ruled 1818-1821

Nang Hseng Pu

Sao Se U, ruled 1) 1815-1818
2) 1821-1862

Sao Hkun Shwe (in charge of Lawksawk State 1847 to 1850)

Sao Hsu Dewa

Sao Hom ruled 1852-1858

Sao Naw Hpa ruled 1858-1864

Nang Shwe Bin

Sao On ruled 1885-1897

Sir Sao Mawng
ruled 1) 1864-1885
2) 1897-1926

Sao Chon

Sao Shwe Thaike ruled 1927-1959
became first President of Burma in 1948

Sao Hseng Hpa
kyemong (heir apparent)

Ruling Family of South Hsenwi

* Hsenwi was divided into North and South Hsenwi in 1888.

- **Sao Hwe Hking**, saohpa of Hsenwi
  - **Hseng Naw Hpa** ruled 1846-1891
    - Nang Tin, the Theinni Mibaya of King Mindon
    - Nang Chang Yi
    - **Sao Naw Mon** ruled 1888-1913
      - *Wife2* Nang Htun Hsa of Hoya
        - **Sao Song** ruled 1913-1924
          - *Wife1* Nang Htun Hka, Mahadevi (Niece of late Laihka saohpa)
          - *Wife2* Nang Seng Man of Hoya
          - *Wife3* Nang Hseng Hsa of Hpatang
          - *Wife4* Nang Hkam Hsa of Man Se
            - Sao Hsoe Hom ruled 1949-59
          - *Wife5* Nang Hseng Awn of Mong Sit
          - *Wife6* Nang San Pao of Man Seng
          - *Wife7* Nang Myawaddi of Loikaw and Yawnghwe
          - *Wife8* Nang Hkam Ing of Mongyai
          - *Wife9* Nang Sam Ku of Hoya
            - **Sao Naw Sing Hseng Hung** ruled 1924-1926
          - *Wife10* unknown name

Ruling Family of Hsipaw from 1767

- **Sao Myat Hsan Te** ruled 1767-
  - Sao Shwe Kye
  - Sao Hksi Hpya
  - Sao Hkun Paw
    - **Sao Kya Tun** nephew of Sao Hkun Paw ruled 1902-1906
      - **Sao Hkun Hseng** ruled 1886-1902
        - **Sir Sao Che** ruled 1906 - 1928
          - **Sao Ohn Kya** ruled 1928-1938
            - The state administered by Mr HM Bazett after 1938. Japanese occupation 1942-45
              - **Sao Kya Saing** ruled 1947-1959
        - Sao Lu
        - Sao O

Ruling Family of Keng Tung

- **Sao Hsam** or **Sao Sam Hpi**
  - Sao Mong Sin
  - Sao Mong Myo
    - **Sao Kawng Tai** ruled 1787-1804
    - **Sao Maha Hkanan** ruled 1813-1857
      - **Sao Maha Hpom** ruled 1857-1875
      - **Sao Hkam Hsen** *alias* Sao Mong ruled 1876-1881
      - **Sao Kawng Tai** ruled 1881-1886
        - Sao Nang Tip Htila
        - **Sao Kawng Hkam Hpoo** ruled 1887-1897
        - **Sao Kawn Kiao Intaleng** ruled 1897-1935
          - <u>*Wife2*</u> Nang Hpawng
            - **Sao Kawn Tai** ruled 1937 (assassinated 1937)
              - **Sao Sai Long** ruled 1947-1959
            - Sao Mom Intra
            - Sao Mon Hkun Mong
            - Sao Nang Wo Sawan
            - Sao Nang Weng Kiao
            - Sao Ingta Rop *alias* Sao Kun Suick
          - <u>*Wife3*</u> Nang Wo Tip Long
            - d. Sao Nang Weng Kiao b.1904
          - <u>*Wife4*</u> Nang Leng
          - <u>*Wife5*</u> Nang Yong
            - **Sao Boon Wart** administrator under Japanese rule 1942-1945
          - <u>*Wife6*</u> Nang Wo Tip Nol
        - Sao Nang Hkam Hkam
  - **Sao Mong Hsam** ruled 1742 - 1786

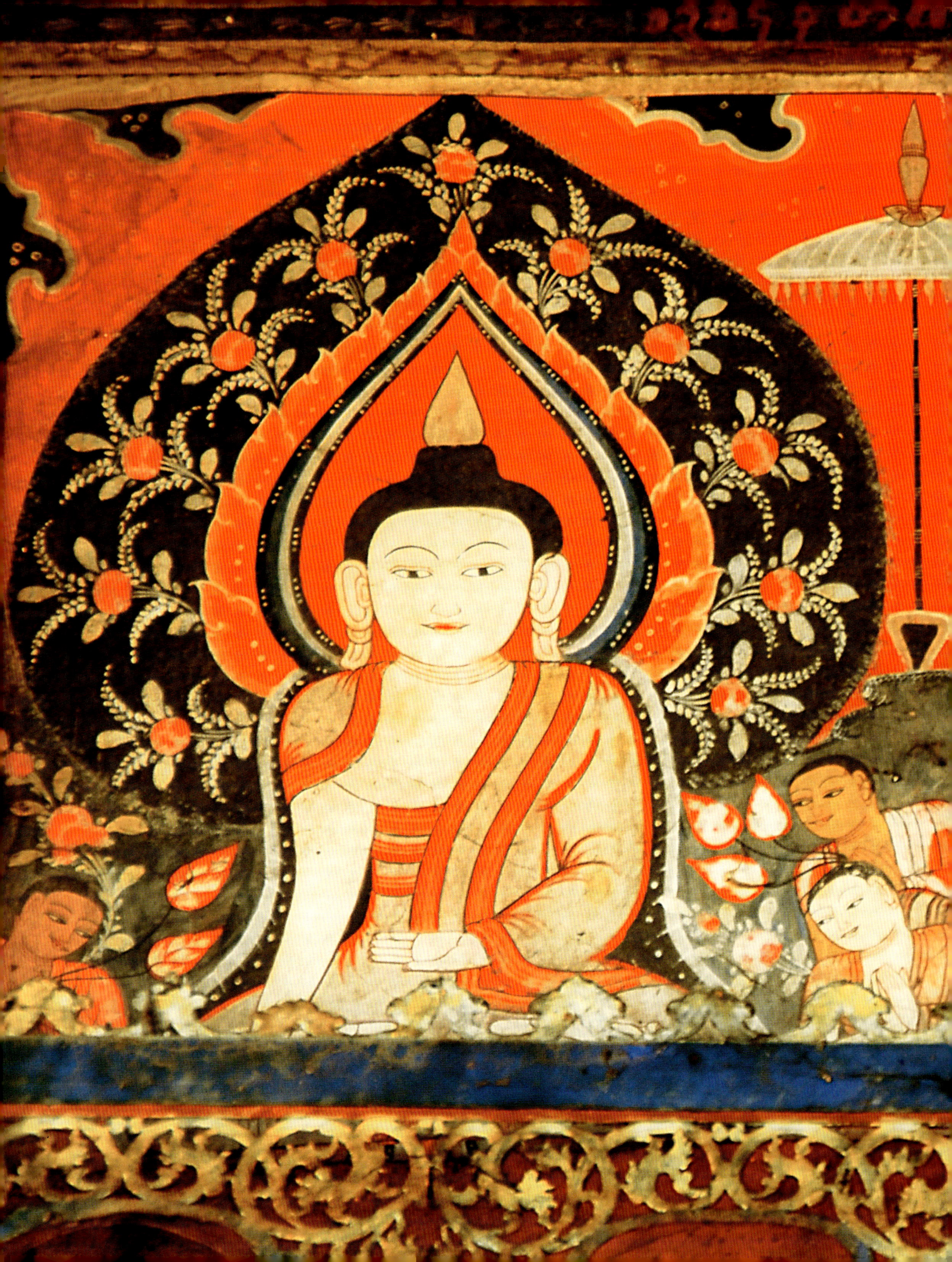

PLANT DYES

Colour	Botanic name	English Name	Part used
red/pink	*Caesalpinia sappan*	sappan wood	corewood
red/pink	*Areca catechu*	betel nut	nut
red	*Carthamus tinctorius*	safflower	flowers
red	*Morinda citrifolia*	Indian mulberry	wood bark roots
red	*Baccaurea sapida*	Burmese grape	wood
red	*Bixa orellana*	annatto	seeds
yellow	*Tamarindus indica*	tamarind	leaves
yellow	*Garcinia mangostana*	mangosteen	sap
yellow	*Cudriana javanensis*	mulberry	corewood
yellow	*Aegle marmelos*	bael fruit tree	fruit seedpods
yellow	*Curcuma longa*	turmeric	rhizome
yellow	*Nyctanthes abortristis*	night-flowering jasmine	corolla
yellow	*Rauwenhoffia siamensis*	Rauwenhoffia	bark
yellow/brown	*Artocarpus integrifolius*	jackfruit	corewood
khaki	*Oroxylon indicum*	sword-fruit tree	bark
khaki	*Tectona grandis*	teak	corewood
green	*Terminalia belerica*	myrobalan	bark, fruit
green	*Terminalia catappa*	wild almond	leaves, bark
green	*Ananas sativa*	pineapple	leaves
green	*Garcinia tinctoria*	sour mangosteen	corewood
green	*Sesbania grandiflora*	leguminous tree	leaves
black	*Harrisonia perforata*	bitter bark	fruit
black	*Piper methysticum*	pepper	root
black	*Psidium guajava*	guava	fruit
black	*Diospyros mollis*	ebony	fruit
brown	*Rhisophora mucronata*	mangrove	wood
brown	*Peltophorum inerme*	pea family	bark
brown	*Acacia catechu*	cutch	wood
orange/gold	*Lawsonia inermis*	henna	leaves
orange	*Bixa orellana*	annatto	seedpods, leaves
blue	*Indigofera tinctoria*	indigo	stem, leaves

INSECT DYES

red	*Lakshadia chinensis*	shellac	insect resin

The Shan States in the Nineteenth Century[1]

State	**Title of Ruler**	**Size** (in square miles)	**Population**
Hkamti Long	*saohpa*	not recorded	Shan[2], Kachin Khunung
Hohsa	*myosa*	not recorded	Shan and Neua
Ho Pong	*myosa*	231	Shan and Karen
Hsahtung (Thaton)	not known	471	Karen and Shan
Hsamongkham (Hsaimoung)	*myosa*	297	Karen, Shan and Danu
Hsawnghsup	*saohpa*	530	Shan and Chin
Hsenwi (north)[3]	*saohpa*	6,330	Lue, Neua, Kachin and Wa
Hsenwi (south)	*saohpa*	2,400	Shan, Kachin and Neua
Hsipaw	*saohpa*	4,524	Shan and Palaung
Kengkham	*myosa*	167	not given
Kehsi Mansam	*myosa*	632	Shan and Yang Lam
Keng Hung[4]	*saohpa*	not recorded	Neua and Lue
Keng Tung	*saohpa*	12,000	Khoen, Lue, Wa, Neua, Lao and Palaung
Keng Lon	*myosa*	43	Shan and Yang Lam
Kyawkku	*ngwegunhmu*	94	Danu and Karen
Kyong	*ngwegunhmu*	24	Danu
Lahsa	not recorded	not recorded	Shan and Neua
Laika	*saohpa*	1,433	Shan and Yang
Lawksawk	*myosa*	4,048	Shan
Loi Ai	*ngwegunhmu*	200	Karen
Loi Long	*myosa*	1,600	Shan and Karen
Tawng Peng	*saohpa*	800	Palaung, Kachin and Shan
Loi Maw	*ngwegunhmu*	49	Karen
Mawson	*ngwegunhmu*	40	Danu and Karen
Maw	*myosa*	550	Danu and Burmese
Mawkmai	*saohpa*	2,787	Shan and Karen
Mawnang	*myosa*	40	Shan, Danu, and Karen
Manglon	*saohpa*	3,000	Shan, Yang Lam, Palaung, Chinese and Wa
Muong Hsu	*myosa*	164	Shan and Yang Lam

State	Title of Ruler	Size (in square miles)	Population
Muong Khwan	not recorded	not recorded	Neua
Muongkung[5]	*saohpa*	not recorded	Shan and Karen
Muong Mit	*myosa* (*saohpa* from 1924)	3,500	Kachin, Shan and Palaung
Muong Nai	*saohpa*	2,717	Shan
Muong Nawng	*myosa*	1,575	Shan
Muong Pai	*saohpa*	660	Shan and Karen
Muong Pan	*saohpa*	2,300	Shan, Lue and Khoen
Muong Pawn	*saohpa*	371	Palaung, Shan and Yang
Muong Singh	*saohpa*	not recorded	Lue
Muong Sit	*myosa*	303	Shan and Karen
Muong Yong	*saohpa*	not recorded	Lue
Muong You	*saohpa*	not recorded	Lue
Namkhai	*ngwegunhmu*	75	Karen
Namkhok	*myosa*	106	Shan
Nam Tok	*myosa*	106	Shan
Nawngwawn	*ngwegunhmu*	42	Shan
Pangmi	*ngwegunhmu*	29	Danu and Karen
Pangtara	*ngwegunhmu*	200	Kachin, Karen and Danu
Putao	*saohpa*	not recorded	Kachin
Pwela	*myosa*	102	Kachin, Danu and Karen
Sakoi	*myosa*	102	Shan and Karen
Samka	*saohpa*	357	Shan
Singkaling Hkamti	*saohpa*	1,925	Shan and Kachin
Wanyin	*myosa*	219	Shan
Yawngwhe	*saohpa*	2,400	Shan, Intha, Karen and Indian
Yengan	*ngwegunhmu*	400	Shan

Endnotes

1 Adapted from a list by Sir George Scott (1900).
2 Scott was using the term Shan for the Tai Yai.
3 Hsenwi was divided into North Hsenwi and South Hsenwi in 1888.
4 Also called Chieng Rung, Keng Hung and by the French, Xienghong.
5 Also called Muong Kung Ma.

Glossary

acheik: an undulating line pattern.

acheik luntaya: an undulating line pattern worked in tapestry weave.

akyok-won: Burmese term for a Lord Chamberlain.

appliqué: the sewing of one fabric onto another.

balanced plain weave: a term used when the weft passes under and over the warp (over-one, under-one) and the threads are of the same size and interlaced with equal spacing.

betel *(piper betle):* a leaf chewed with other ingredients including areca palm nut *(Areca catechu)* tobacco and white lime.

betel set: a set of containers for storing the ingredients listed above. Betel sets, made in gold, silver or lacquer were a symbol of status among the Shan rulers.

bodhisattva: a being destined to be a Buddha who serves as a guide to others seeking Enlightenment.

bodhi tree *(Ficus religiosa):* the tree provided shade for the Buddha while he meditated and attained Enlightenment. The distinctive heart-shaped leaves are reproduced in the arts and crafts of the Shan States.

chao: Tai term for a prince commonly used in Lan Na and the eastern Shan States.

chao fa: Tai term for a prince used in Lan Na and the eastern Shan States.

chao muong: Tai term for the ruler or ancestor spirit of the *muong.*

couching: threads are laid on the surface of fabric and sewn down with an embroidery stitch using another thread.

Danu: a term used to describe people of Shan and Burmese origin.

deva: a celestial being in the lower heavens of the Buddhist cosmology.

devaputta: a celestial guardian figure.

discontinuous supplementary weft: weft threads are inserted into a ground weave by hand.

duwa or ***dwa:*** term for a Kachin chief.

du-yin thin-daing: a jacket with a stiff curved bodice forming part of Burmese court dress.

dye: a colour-producing compound that can be chemically bonded to fibres. Some dyes were extracted from plants, animals and minerals. Others were chemically manufactured.

ein-gyi: a blouse or jacket.

embroidery: the embellishment of cloth with needle-worked stitches.

float weave: *see* twill.

gatha: numbers, letters and symbols read as magical incantations.

glazed cotton: fine woven cotton with the surface burnished with starch.

hamsa: a semi-divine bird.

haw: Shan term for a palace.

hintha: another term for the mythical hamsa bird.

hka-yan-kyo: a stiff apron worn as part of Burmese court dress.

hmanzi-zi shwei-cha: lacquer inlay.

hpa hoi: man's shoulder sash.

hsaung-ma-gyi: a reception hall in a monastery.

hsaya-daw: the head monk of the monastery.

hse: a cotton tunic.

hta-mein: a flat rectangle of cloth wrapped around the waist to form a woman's ankle-length skirt.

htan-sin: a type of sedan chair.

hti: a tiered finial.

hyasa: a tattoo artist.

ikat: a resist process of dyeing and painting selected areas of yarn before weaving. In the Shan States, weft ikat is the most common technique.

indigo: a dye plant containing the colouring agent indigotin which produces a blue colour.

ingwet: a magic formula prepared by a shaman.

Kachin: a term used to describe people living in the hills of the northern Shan States and Bhamo and Katha.

kadaw: a ceremony of respect and allegiance.

Karen: hill dwellers living in the hills that border the Salween and Pai Rivers. Some Karen settled at lower altitude.

kinnari: a mythical bird with a human face.

kong moo: Shan term for a stupa.

lac *(Coccus lacca):* a red dyeobtained from insects.

lacquer: made from the resin of the tree *Gluta usitata.*

Lan Na: an inland kingdom that is now part of Thailand.

***luntaya* trans:** "woven with one hundred shuttles" denoting a type of tapestry weave.

mae posop: the rice goddess.

mahadevi: title given to a Shan princess.

makara: a mythical animal with the head of an elephant and the body of a dragon or serpent.

man hpaya: dry lacquer technique.

mauk you: a close-fitting cap with a stiff neck shield.

Mon: valley-residing people who speak a Mon-Khmer language.

mordant: chemical substances that help bond dyes to fibres.

muk-toe: a dome-shaped hat.

mulberry *(Corpha umbraculifera)* : the inner bark is used for making Shan paper.

muong: a power centre or sphere of influence, usually a city-state.

myin-she: a tiered military robe.

myosa: a minor ruler or governor who was a tax collector, often called "Eater of the Town".

nadaug: a pair of trumpet-shaped earplugs.

naga: a mythical sea dragon or serpent associated with water and fertility.

nandadevi: a Burmese title for a princess.

nat: a spirit associated with pre-Buddhist beliefs.

neem *(Azadirachta indica):* neem resin is used in the lacquer process.

ngwegunhmu: a minor chief.

pah-soe: a lower garment worn by Burmese men.

Palaung: a group mainly inhabiting the northern Shan States.

parabeik: a folding manuscript made of palm leaves or mulberry paper.

pazun-zi: woven tinsel cloth used for court dress and for wall hangings *(shwe chi doe).*

phii muong: the guardian spirits of the *muong.*

plain weave: each weft thread passes over and under each warp thread and the procedure is reversed in the following row.

plying/plied yarns: the process of twisting together single yarns (e.g. two threads=two ply, three threads=three ply). Shan weavers often twisted different coloured threads together in the warp or in the weft, or in warp and weft.

prasad: a tiered roof on a monastery or a palace.

pwe leun ha: the water festival held on the night of the full moon of the New Year.

pyatthat: a multi-tiered spire, also called *hti.*

pyathat-hsaung: main shrine area in a monastery.

quilting: layers of fabric stitched together.

repoussé: punching a design into relief on a metal surface.

sandadevi: a Burmese title given to a princess.

saohpa: Shan word for a prince.

selvedge: the edge of a fabric where the yarns reverse direction.

seua pat: a side-fastening blouse

shaman: an expert in spirit religion (animism).

Shan: Tai of the Shan States.

shan baung-bi: a set of leg tattoos.

Shan trousers: wide-legged trousers that tuck at the waist.

shwe bon nidan: Burmese rules governing the display of court regalia.

shwe chi doe also called *kalaga:* appliqué work embellished with sequins, coloured glass and stones and gold and silver metal thread.

shwe hintha: magical golden bird.

shwe-hpo-thong-hsin: a set of sash-like panels forming part of Burmese court dress.

shwe zawa: gilded lacquer.

sibon: a female headdress.

singha: a mythical lion.

sin mai kam: a tubular skirt worn in the eastern Shan States.

sin man: irregularly-spaced horizontal stripes in a woman's skirt.

sin pong: evenly-spaced stripes in a woman's skirt.

stupa (kong moo) : a monument, originally a burial mound that enshrined relics of the Buddha and marked important Buddhist sites. Shan stupa had a characteristic elongated shape.

seua kop long daeng: a lined jacket.

sulyar: an embroidered scarf.

supplementary weft: extra threads woven in the ground weave.

Tai: people inhabiting Assam, the Shan States, south-west China, Laos and Thailand who share a common heritage. Many sub-groups have been identified.

Tai Khoen: Tai inhabiting the central and eastern Shan States and parts of Lan Na.

Tai Lao: Tai inhabiting Laos and north-east Thailand.

Tai Lue: Tai inhabiting Sipsong Pan Na, the eastern Shan states and Lan Na.

Tai Neua: Tai inhabiting Sipsong Pan Na.

Tai Yai, (also called Shan Proper or Tai Ngio), inhabiting the Shan States and western Lan Na.

Tai Yuan: Tai inhabitants of Lan Na.

tapestry weave: a plain weave of discontinuous weft.

Tavatimsa Heaven: a heaven in the Buddhist cosmology.

tawmaw: a temporary Shan building.

teen jok: patterned section on the hem of a tubular skirt.

thakin-ma: a title meaning "madam".

thayo: relief-moulded lacquer.

Thudhamma Buddhism: a Burmese form of Buddhism.

tical: a weight, approximately 15 grams.

tribute: a form of tax or service provided to a ruler.

tribute ceremony: a ceremony when subjects pledge allegiance to a ruler.

tsaloe: a set of gold chains with repoussé bosses associated with sumptuary law.

twill: weft threads alternate over more than one warp thread and then under one thread. 1/3 is the most common twill woven in the Shan states.

viss: a weight equalling 1.65 kilos.

Wa: people from the Mon-Khmer linguistic group thought to have pre-dated the Tai in the Shan States.

warp-faced plain weave: the number of warp threads per centimetre is more than the number of weft threads.

weft-faced plain weave: the number of weft threads per centimetre is more than the number of warp threads.

yamane: a Shan hardwood used for carving.

yantra: mystical symbolic diagrams.

yin: a palanquin.

yindaik: a wood for carving, similar in texture to ebony and sandalwood.

yin hlwan: a set of stiff attachments forming part of Burmese court dress.

yin-zi: a rectangular breast cloth.

Yuan sect: a form of Theravada Buddhism practised in parts of inland Southeast Asia.

yun: a general term for lacquer.

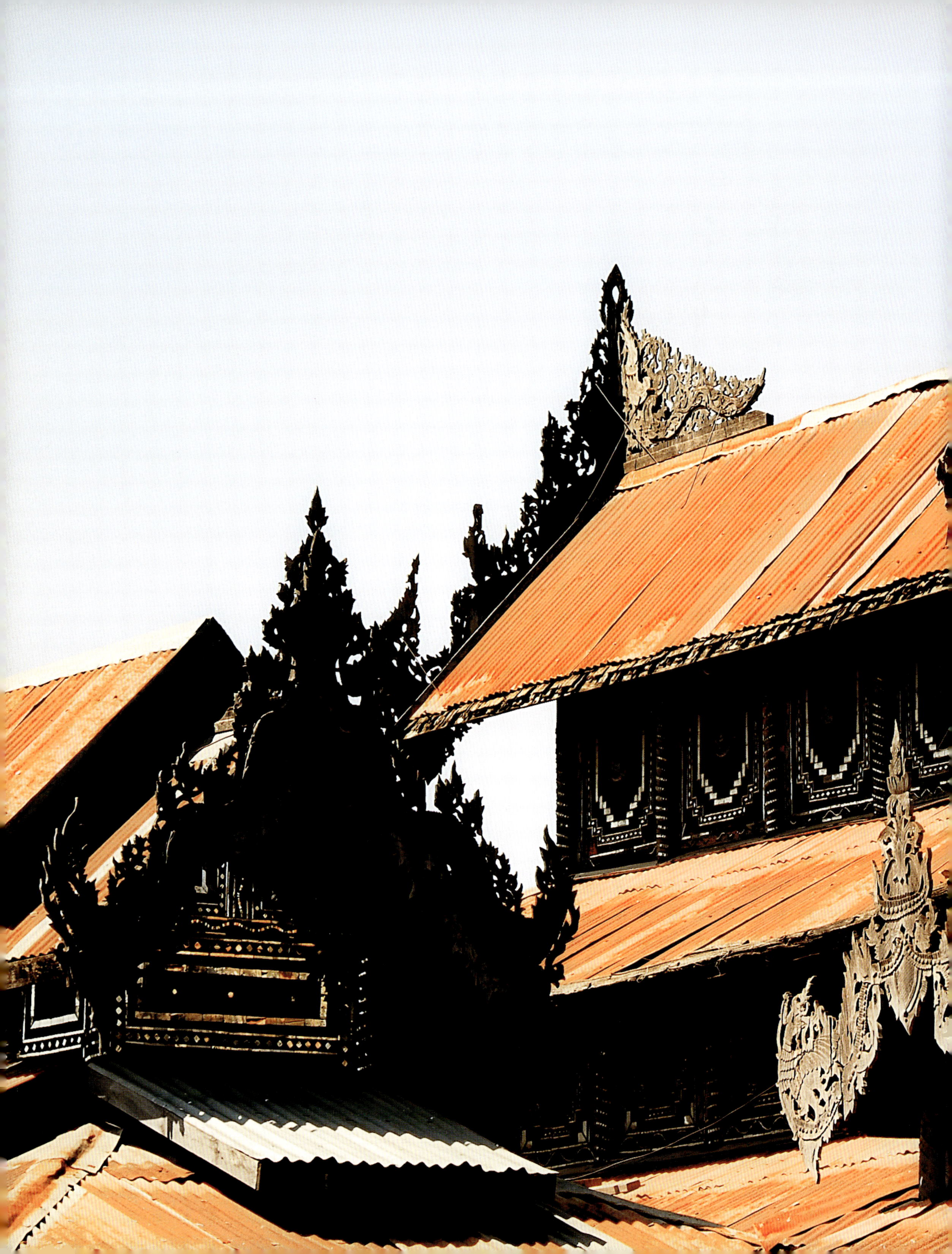

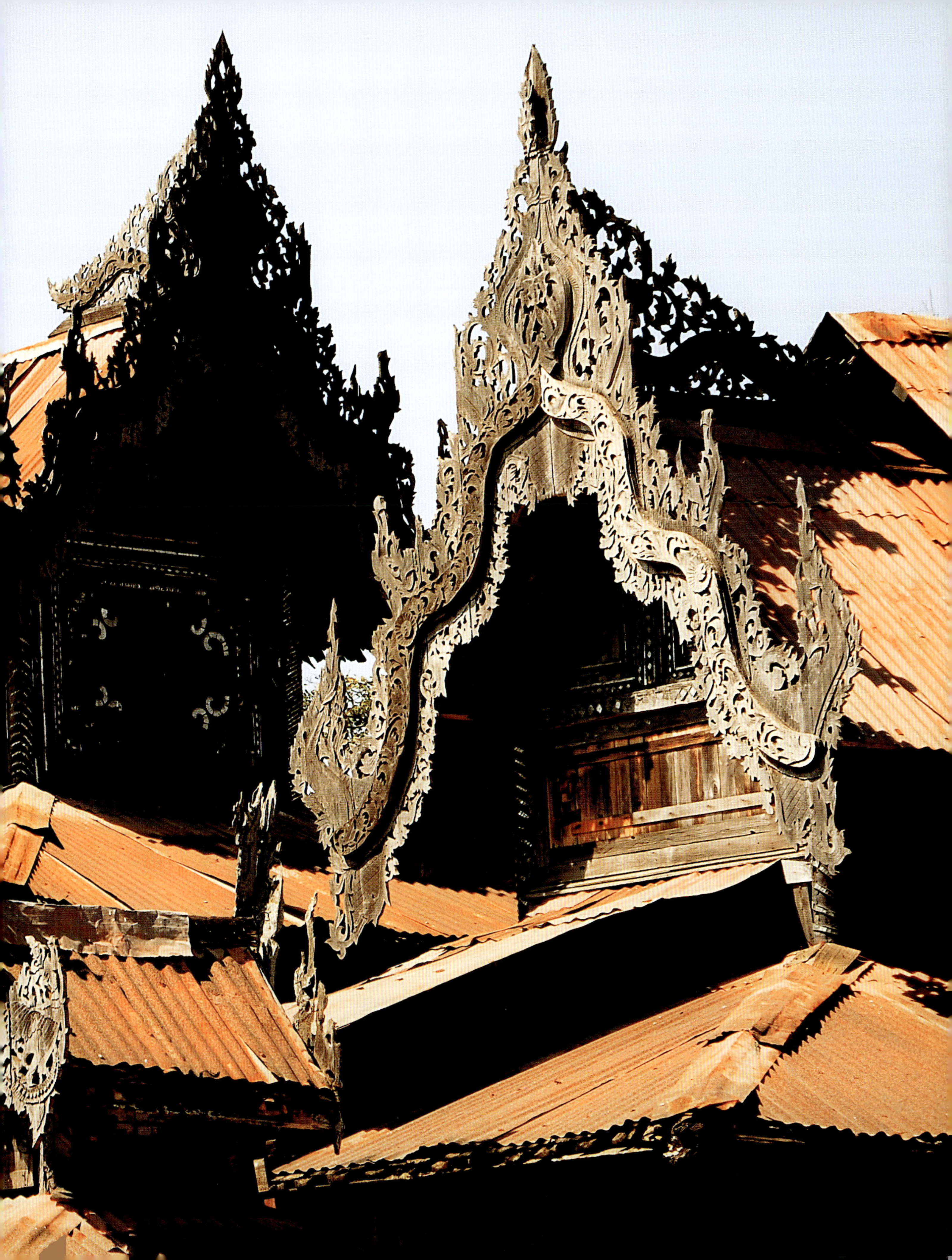

Bibliography

Abhakorn, Ruyaya, 'Chiang Tung and the Thai State Before 1948'. Proceedings of The 16th Conference of the International Association of Historians of Asia, Kota Kinabalu, Sabah, Malaysia, 2000.

Adams, Nel, *My Vanished World*, Horseshoe Publications, Cheshire, UK, 2000.

Anderson, John, *Mandalay to Momein*, Macmillan and Co. 1876.

Anonymous, 'The Helen K. Hunt Collection', *Burmese Art Newsletter*, Dept. of Visual Arts, Denison University, Granville, Ohio, Vol. I, no. 4, June 1969.

Archer, W.J., *Report on a visit to Kengtung in May-June 1888,* Home Correspondence, Vol. 104, October 1888.

Aung Thwin, Michael, 'Kingship, the Sangha and Society in Pagan,' in K.R. Hall and J.K. Whitmore (eds.), *Explorations in Early Southeast Asian History: The Origins of Southeast Asian Statecraft,* Center for Southeast Asian Studies, Northern Illinois University, DeKalb, Illinois, 1976.

Bailey, J.T., 'Burmese Textiles', *Burma Art Newsletter*, Dept. of Visual Arts, Denison University, Granville, Ohio, Vol. 1 no. 4, June 1969.

Barnes, Ruth and Eicher, Joanne, *Dress and Gender: Making and Meaning in Cultural Contexts,* Berg, Oxford and New York, 1992.

Bassenne, Martha, *Au Laos et Au Siam,* Paris, 1912, reprint (trans. W. Tips) *In Laos and in Siam*, White Lotus Press, Bangkok, 1995.

Blundell, E. A. (ed.), 'An Account of Some of the Petty States Lying North of the Tenasserim Provinces (drawn from the journals and reports of D. Richardson Esq. Surgeon of Tenasserim Provinces)', *Journal of the Asiatic Society of Burma*, Vol. 58, 1836.

Blurton, T. Richard 'Looking Very Gay and Bright – Burmese Textiles in the British Museum', *Apollo*, November 1999.

———————— 'Scarlet, Gold and Black: the Lacquer Traditions of Burma (in (ed.) Stadtner, Donald, M., *The Art of Burma* Marg Publications, Vol. 50, Bombay, 1999.

Bock, Carl, *Temples and Elephants, Travels in Siam 1881-1882,* Oxford University Press, 1884, reprint Oxford University Press, 1986.

Burney, Henry, 'Some Account of the Lacquered or Jappaned Ware of Ava', *Journal of the Asiatic Society of Bengal*, No. 5, May 1832.

Cady, J.F., *A History of Modern Burma,* Cornell University Press, Ithaca, 1958.

Cannadine, David, *Ornamentalism*, Oxford University Press, New York, 2001.

Chamberlain, James R., 'A new look at the history and classification of the Tai languages,' in Jimmy G. Harris and James R. Chamberlain (eds.), *Studies in Tai Linguistics in Honor of William J. Gedney*, Central Institute of English languages, Office of State Universities, Bangkok, 1975.

Chao Tzang na Yawnghwe 'The Shans and the Shan States: An Introduction', Chiang Mai, n.d.

Churatana, P. and Wyatt, D., (eds and trans.) *The Nan Chronicle,* Data paper 59, Southeast Asia Program, Cornell University, Ithaca, 1966.

Chutintaranond, Sunait and Tun, Than, *On Both Sides Of The Tenasserim Range: A History of Siamese-Burmese Relations,* Institute of Asian Studies, Chulalongkorn University, Bangkok 1995.

Collis, Maurice, *Lords of the Sunset: A Tour in the Shan States,* London: Faber and Faber, 1938, reprint, Ava House, Bangkok 1996.

Colquhoun, Archibald, R., *Amongst the Shans,* London 1885, reprint Paragon, New York 1970.

Conway, Susan, *Power Dressing: Lanna Shan Siam*, James H.W. Thompson Foundation, Bangkok 2004.

———————— 'The Saopha at Home and Abroad' in *Through the Thread of Time*, (ed. Jane Purananda) James H.W. Thompson Foundation, and River Books, Bangkok, 2004.

———————— 'Court Dress, Politics and Ethnicity in the Shan States' in *Burma Art and Archaeology* Blurton, T. Richard and Green, Alexandra, (eds.), The British Museum Press, London, 2002.

————————*Silken Threads Lacquer Thrones,* River Books, Bangkok, 2000.

————————*Thai Textiles*, British Museum Press, London, 1992.

Cordwell, J. M., 'The Very Human Arts of Transformation,' in J. Cordwell and R.A. Schwarz (eds.), *The Fabrics of Culture: the Anthropology of Clothing and Adornment*: Mouton Press, The Hague, 1979.

Cordwell J.M. and Schwarz R.A., *The Fabrics of Culture: the Anthropology of Clothing and Adornment*, Mouton Press, The Hague, 1979.

Coronation Durbar Illustrated, 1903, Wieleand Klein, Madras, 1903.

Correspondence between Sprye and Gladstone on The Commercial Opening of The Shan States and Western Inland China, London 1865, Shelf mark 8235K24, The British Library.

Cort, Mary Lovina, *Siam: The Heart of Farther India*, Anson, D.F. Randolph and Co., New York, 1886.

Crawfurd, John, *Journal of an Embassy from the Governor General of India to the Court of Ava in the year 1827*, London, 1829.

De Carné, Louis, *Voyage en Indo-Chine et dans l'Empire Chinois*, 1872, Dentu Ed., Paris, reprint *Travels on the Mekong* White Lotus Press, Bangkok, 1995.

Dell, Elizabeth (ed.), *Burma: Frontier Photographs*, Philip Wilson Publishers, London, 2000.

Dell, Elizabeth and Dudley, Sandra (eds.) *Textiles from Burma*, Philip Wilson Publishers, London, 2003.

Di Crocco, V., 'Arts and Crafts : Shan Lacquerware' in Inglis, Kim (ed.), *Myanamar Style, Art, Architecture and Design of Burma*, Bangkok, 1998.

Dodd, William Clifton, *The Tai Race: Elder Brother of the Chinese,* The Torch Press, Cedar Rapids 1923, reprint White Lotus Press, Bangkok 1996.

D'Orleans, Henri, *From Tonkin to India by the Sources of the Irawadi*, London, 1895.

Dudley, Sandra 'Whose textiles and whose meanings' in *Textiles from Burma*, Elizabeth Dell and Sandra Dudley (eds.), Philip Wilson Publishers, London, 2003.

Eicher, Joanne (ed.), *Dress and Ethnicity* Berg Press, Oxford and Washington, D.C. 1995.

Eicher, Joanne and Sumberg, Barbara, 'World Fashion, Ethnic, and National Dress,' in J. Eicher (ed.), *Dress and Ethnicity* Berg Press, Oxford and Washington D.C., 1995.

Eicher, Joanne and Roach-Higgins M.E., 'Describing and Classifying Dress: Implications for the Study of Gender,' in R. Barnes and J.B. Eicher (eds.), *Dress and Gender: Making and Meaning in Cultural Contexts* Berg Press, Oxford and New York, 1992.

Elliott, Patricia, *The White Umbrella*, Post Books, Bangkok, 1999.

Erikson, Thomas Hylland, *Ethnicity and Nationalism: Anthropological Perspectives,* Pluto Press, London, 1993.

Ferrars, Max and Ferrars, Bertha, *Burma,* Sampson Low, Marston and Co., London and New York 1901, reprint Ava Press, Bangkok. 1996.

Fielding-Hall, H. *Palace Tales,* Harper and Brothers 1900, reprint White Lotus Press, Bangkok, 1997.

Fitch, Ralph, 'The Voyage of M. Ralph Fitch, Merchant of London,' in R. Hakluyt (ed.), *The Principal Navigations, Voyages, Traffiques and Discoveries of the English Nation 1599,* Vol. 5, James MacLehose and Sons, Glasgow 1903-1905.

Franklin, Frances and Swallow, Deborah, 'Identifying With The Gods,' *Hali Annual,* London, 1994.

Fraser-Lu, Sylvia, *Splendour in Wood,* Orchid Press, Bangkok, 2001.

——— *Burmese Lacquerware,* The Tamarind Press, Bangkok, 1996.

——— *Burmese Crafts Past and Present,* Kuala Lumpur 1994.

——— *Handwoven Textiles of Southeast Asia,* Oxford University Press, Singapore, 1988.

——— 'Burmese Manuscript Chests', *Arts of Asia,* Vol. 14, no 3 (May-June 1984).

——— 'Kalagas: Burmese Wall Hangings and Related Embroideries', *Arts of Asia,* Vol. 12 no. 4 (July-August, 1982).

Garnier, Francis, *Voyage d'Exploration en Indo Chine,* Paris, 1885, reprint W. Tips (trans), *Further Travels in Laos and in Yunnan: The Mekong Exploration Commission Report 1866-1868,* White Lotus Press, Bangkok, 1996.

Gilhodes, Charles A. *The Kachins* 1922, reprint White Lotus Press, Bangkok, 1996.

Ginsburg, Henry, *Thai Manuscript Painting* The British Library, London, 1989.

Grabowsky, V. 'Forced Resettlement Campaigns in Northern Thailand, During the Early Bangkok Period' in *Fifth International Conference on Thai Studies,* School of Oriental and African Studies, London, 1993.

Grabowsky, V., and Turton, A., *The Gold and Silver Road of Trade and Friendship,* Silkworm Books, Chiang Mai, 2003.

Grant Brown, R., 'The Lady of the Weir', *Journal of the Royal Asiatic Society,* July 1916.

Grant, Colesworthy, *A Trip to Rangoon in 1846,* London 1853.

Green, Colonel James H., 'The Tribes of Upper Burma north of 24 degrees Latitude and Their Classification', Rangoon, Burma, M.A. thesis, University of Cambridge, 1934.

Griswold, A.B. and Prasert na Nagara, 'An Inscription from Keng Tung 1451 AD' *Journal of the Siam Society,* No. 66, January 1976.

Hall, D.G.E., *A History of South-East Asia,* Macmillan, London, 1955, reprint 1968, 1977.

——— *Burma,* The Anchor Press Ltd, London, 1956

Hallett, Holt, *A Thousand Miles on an Elephant in the Shan States,* Blackwood and Sons, Edinburgh and London, 1890, reprint White Lotus Press, Bangkok, 1988.

Hanson, O., *The Kachins: Their Customs and Traditions,* American Baptist Mission Press, Rangoon, 1913.

Harvey, G.E. and Barton, G.E., 'Mengmao Succession,' Burma Secretariat file, Imprint No. 99 H.P.D. 29.10.30, Rangoon, 1930.

Heine-Geldern, Robert, 'Conceptions of State and Kingship in Southeast Asia', *Far Eastern Quarterly,* Vol. II, 1942.

Hildebrand, Mr., 'British Policy and the Shan States 1886-1942,' Foreign Office Report F.O. 69/65:16, 1875, Public Records Office, Kew, London.

Hill, Ann M., 'Familiar Strangers: The Yunnanese Chinese in Northern Thailand,' Ph.D. dissertation, Center for Southeast Asian Studies, University of Northern Illinois, DeKalb, Illinois, 1982.

Hobsbawm, Eric and Ranger, Terence, *The Invention of Tradition,* Cambridge University Press, Cambridge 1983.

Hoskins, Janet, *Biographical Objects,* Routledge, New York 1998.

Howard, Constance, *The Constance Howard Book of Stitches,* Batsford, London, 1979.

Htin Aung, Maung, *A History of Burma,* Columbia University Press, New York, 1967.

Htun Yi, U, *Nanthon Yin Paribhawga Hnint Wutsah-sinyinhmu* [Vehicles, Furniture and Costumes of Royalty], Seinpanmying, Rangoon, 1984.

Innes, R.A., *Costumes of Upper Burma and the Shan States in the Collections of Bankside Museum,* Bankside Museum, Halifax 1957.

——— *Non European Looms,* Calderdale Museums, Calderdale 1977.

Isaacs, Ralph and Blurton, T. Richard, *Visions from the Golden Land: Burma and the Art of Lacquer,* British Museum Press, London, 2000.

Keyes, Charles, 'Kin Groups in a Thai-Lao Community,' in G. William Skinner and A. Thomas Kirsch (eds.), *Change and Persistence in Thai Society: Essays in Honor of Lauriston Sharp,* Cornell University Press, Ithaca, 1975.

——— 'Buddhism and National Integration in Thailand' in *Visakha Puja,* B.E.1514, Bangkok 1971.

Khampaeng Thipmuntali, 'The Tai Lue of Muang Singh' in Grant Evans (ed.) *Laos Culture and Society,* Chiang Mai, 1999.

Kingdom Ward, Frank, *In Farthest Burma: The Record of an Arduous Journey of Exploration and Research Through the Unknown Frontier Territory of Burma and Tibet,* London, 1921.

Kruamas, Woodtikarn, 'Textiles in Mae Chaem: Rituals, Revitalization and Reproduction', Center for the Promotion of Arts and Culture, Chiang Mai University, Chiang Mai, Thailand.

Leach, Edmund R. *Political Systems of Highland Burma,* G. Bell, London, 1954.

Le Bar, Frank M., Hickey, Gerald C. and Musgrave, John, *Ethnic Groups of Mainland Southeast Asia,* Human Relations Area Files Press, New Haven, 1964.

Lefèvre, E., *Un Voyage au Laos,* Plon, Nourrit et Cie, Paris, 1898, reprint *Travels in Laos* W. Tips (trans.), White Lotus Press, Bangkok, 1995.

Lefevre-Pontalis, Pierre, *Travels in Upper Laos and on the Borders of Yunnan and Burma,* W. Tips (trans.), White Lotus Press, Bangkok, 2000.

Letter from Burney to Blundell dated Rangoon June 20th 1834, ORC BUR MSS 2, India Office Library, The British Library.

Lewis, Paul and Elaine, *Peoples of the Golden Triangle,* Thames and Hudson, London, 1984.

Ling-Roth, H., *Studies in Primitive Looms,* Bankfield Museum, Halifax 1918, reprint Ruth Bean, Bedford, 1978.

Lowndes, Captain, 'British Burma Journal of Captain Lowndes whilst on a Mission to the Zimme Court,' [Lowndes Journal] Foreign Office Report 69/55, March 27-May 30 1871, Public Records Office, Kew, London.

Luce, G.H., 'The Early Syam in Burma's History', *Journal of the Siam Society,* Vol. XLVI, 2 Nov, 1958.

Mabbett, I. W., 'Introduction: The Comparative Study of Traditional Political Institutions,' in Mabbett, (ed.), *Patterns of Kingship and Authority in Traditional Asia,* University of Kent, Kent, 1985.

Maha Dhamma Thinkyan, *Sasana Lankaya Satan,* Hanthawaddy Press, Yangon, 1928.

Malinowski, Bronislaw, *Magic, Science and Religion and Other Essays,* Beacon Press, Boston, 1948.

Mangrai, Sao Saimong, 'Form of Sanad Granted to the Sawbwa of Keng Tung 1889' in 'The Shan States and British Annexation', Cornell Dept. Asian Studies, Southeast Asia Program, Ithaca, Data paper no. 57, 1965.

——————————— (trans) 'The Padaeng Chronicle and the Jengtung State Chronicle translated', in A. Becker, P. Hook, J. Musgrave and T. Trautman (eds.), University of Michigan Papers on Southeast Asia, no 19, Center for South and Southeast Asian Studies University of Michigan, Ann Arbor, Michigan, 1981.

Marshall, P.J., 'Empire and Authority in the Late Eighteenth Century' in *Journal of Imperial and Commonwealth History*, Vol. XV, 1987.

Htin Aung, Maung, *Folk Elements in Burmese Buddhism*, Oxford University Press, 1962.

McLeod, Captain W.C., 'A Journal kept by Captain W.C. McLeod, Assistant to the Commissioner in the Tenassarim Provinces during his Mission to the Frontiers of China, 1836-1837', The British Library, India and Oriental Collections, London.

Melchers, K. William, 'The Thai invasion of Keng Tung during the reign of Rama III' in Ronald Renard (ed.), *Anuson Walter Vella*, Center for Asian and Pacific Studies, University of Hawaii at Manoa, Honolulu, 1986.

Milne, Leslie, *The Home of an Eastern Clan*, Oxford 1924, reprint White Lotus Press, Bangkok, 2004.

Milne, Leslie and Cochrane, Wilbur, *Shans at Home,* John Murray, London 1910, reprint Paragon Book Reprint Corps, New York, 1970.

Mitton, G.E. (Lady Scott) (ed.), *Scott of the Shan Hills,* Murray, London, 1936.

Moerman, Michael, 'Who are the Lue: ethnic identification in a complex civilisation', *American Anthropologist,* Vol. 67, 1965.

——————————— 'Chiangkham's Trade in the Old Days', in G. Skinner and A. Thomas Kirsch (eds.) Change and Persistence in Thai Society: Essays in Honor of Lauriston Sharp, Cornell University, Ithaca, 1975.

Nai Banchaphumasathan, 'Report of Nai Banchaphumasathan,' in The National Library, Bangkok, files of Krom Mahatthai M65/2, trans. and ed. by Constance M. Wilson in *The Burma-Thailand Frontier Over Sixteen Decades*, Ohio University, Athens, 1985.

Nash, J.C. 'Living with Nats: An Analysis of Animism in Burman Village Social Relations', Anthropological Studies in Theravada Buddhism, Culture Report Series 13, Southeast Asian Studies, Yale University, 1966.

Nathalang, Siraporn, 'Tai Creation Myths: Reflections of Tai Relations and Tai Cultures', in Tai Culture, International Review on Tai Cultural Studies, Vol. II, No. 1, Berlin, June 1997.

National Museum, Yangon *The Myanmar Regalia and Royal Household Articles*, Government of Myanmar, Yangon, n.d.

Newsletter of the National Museum Volunteers, Bangkok, 'The Abbot's Cremation and the Hatsadiling' Bangkok, No 10, October 2004.

Parker, E.H., 'The Early Laos and China' in *The China Review*, Sept-Oct 1890.

Phasuk, Santanee and Stott, Philip *Royal Siamese Maps,* River Books, 2004.

Phayre, Sir A., *History of Burma,* London 1883, reprint Susil Gupta, London, 1967.

Po, San C. *Burma and the Karens*, 1928, reprint White Lotus Press, Bangkok, 2001

Prangwattanakun and Cheesman, *Lan Na Texiles Yuan Lue Lao*, Chiang Mai Center for the Promotion of Arts and Culture, Chiang Mai University, Chiang Mai, 1987.

Ratanaporn, Sethakul, 'Political Relations Between Chiang Mai and Kengtung in the Ninteenth Century,' in Prakai Nontawasee (ed.), *Changes in Northern Thailand and the Shan States, 1886-1940,* Institute of Southeast Asian Studies, Singapore, 1988.

Reid, Anthony, *Slavery, Bondage and Dependency in Southeast Asia* University of Queensland, St. Lucia, 1983.

——————— *Southeast Asia in the Age of Commerce 1450-1680, Vol. 1, The Land Below the Winds* Yale University Press, New Haven 1988.

Rhum, M,. 'The Ancestral Lords' report no. 29, Monograph Series on Southeast Asia, Center for Southeast Asian Studies, Northern Illinois University, DeKalb, 1994.

Richardson, David, 'Journal of Missions to the Shan States, Siam and Ava', Manuscript no. 30.354, 1830-1836, Western Manuscript Dept., The British Library, London.

———————————- 'Burma Siam Frontier,' India Office Political and Secret Dept. India Office Collections, 1837, The British Library, London.

Roach-Higgins, M. E. and Eicher, J.B., 'Dress and Identity' in *Clothing and Textile Research Journal,* Vol. 10, No. 4, 1992.

Rooney, Dawn F., *Betel Chewing Traditions in South-East Asia,* Oxford University Press, Kuala Lumpur 1993.

Russell, Susan (ed.), *Ritual, Power, and Economy: Upland-Lowland Contrasts in Mainland Southeast Asia*, Monograph Series, Center for Southeast Asian Studies, Northern Illinois University, DeKalb, 1989.

Sadan, Mandy 'The Kachin Photographs in the J.H. Green Collection: a contemporary context' in Dell, Elizabeth (ed.) *Burma Frontier Photographs,* Merrell, London and The Green Centre for Non-Western Art, Brighton 2000.

Sai Aung Tin, 'The Tai Ethnic Settlement in the Hkamti Long Area' in *Myanmar Historical Journal,* No. 5, June 2000.

Sai Kham Mong, 'Buddhism and the Shans' in *Myanmar Historical Research Journal*, No. 7, June 2001.

Sangermano, Vincenzo, *The Burmese Empire A Hundred Years Ago*, Westminster, 1893.

Saw Khin Gyi, 'History of the Cis-Salween Shan States 1860-1900', M.A. thesis, Arts and Science University, Mandalay, 1973.

Schneider, J. and Weiner, A., *Cloth and Human Experience,* Smithsonian Institution Press, Washington D.C. and London, 1989.

Schomburgk, R. H., 'A Visit to Xieng Mai, the Principal City of the Laos of the Shan States,' *Journal of the Royal Asiatic Society of Bengal,* Vol. 32, 1863.

Scott, J.G., *Burma and Beyond* ,Grayson and Grayson, London, 1932.

—————- *Burma A Handbook of Practical Information* 1906, reprint Orchid Press, Bangkok, 1999.

Scott J.G. and Hardiman, J.P., *Gazeteer of Upper Burma and The Shan States,* Vols. 1-V Superintendent of Government Printing, Rangoon, 1900, 1901.

Seidenfaden, Erik, 'The Lawa: an additional note', *Journal of the Siam Society,* Vol.13, 1923.

Sethakul, Ratanaporn, 'Political, Social and Economic Changes in the Northern States of Thailand Resulting from the Chiang Mai Treaties 1874 and 1883,' Ph.D. dissertation, Dept. History, University of Illinois, Illinois, 1989.

——————— *Prebuddhistic Beliefs of the Peoples of Western and Central Indo-China* Oriental Literature Publishing House, Moscow, 1958.

Shway Yoe, (Sir James Scott), *The Burman, His Life and Notions,* Macmillan, London 1882, reprint New York 1963.

Simatrang, Sone, (ed.), *Burmese Design Through Drawings,* The Toyota Foundation, Bangkok 1993.

Singer, Noel, F., 'Palm Leaf Manuscripts of Myanmar,' *Arts of Asia,* Jan.-Feb. 1991.

——————————- 'Jengtung Lacquerware', *Arts of Asia,* Vol. 21, no.5. Sept.-Oct. 1991.

Snodgrass, J.J., *Narrative of the Burmese War,* John Murray, London, 1827, reprint, Bangkok, 1997.

Spiro, Melford E., *Burmese Supernaturalism,* Chicago, 1967.

Steinberg, David J. (ed.), *In Search of Southeast Asia,* University of Hawaii Press, Honolulu 1971, reprint 1987.

Sunait, Chutintaranond, and Than Tun, *On Both Sides of the Tenasserim Range: History of Siamese-Burmese Relations,* Asian Studies Monographs No. 050, Chulalongkorn University, Bangkok, 1995.

Symes, M., *An Account of an Embassy to the Kingdom of Ava sent by the Governor-General of India in the year 1795,* London, 1800, reprint, Madras, 1995.

Talbot-Kelly, R., *Burma.* A.C. Black Ltd., London, 1905.

Tan-kim-yong, Uraivan, 'Resource Mobilization in Traditional Irrigation Systems of Northern Thailand. A Comparison between the Lowland and the Upland Irrigation Communities', Ph.D. dissertation, Cornell University, Ithaca, New York, 1983.

Taylor, R., 'Change in Thailand and the Shan States 1886-1940,' School of Oriental and African Studies, London, 1997.

Thao Sittimongkhon, 'The Report Of Thao Sitthimongkhon On The Re-establishment Of Chiang Rai And Its Borders,' in Constance M. Wilson and Lucien M. Hanks, *'The Burma-Thailand Frontier Over Sixteen Decades: Three Descriptive Documents,'* Monograph in International Studies, Southeast Asia Series, No. 70, University of Ohio, Athens, 1985.

Thawi Sawangpanyangkoon (trans.), *The Xishuangbanna Chronicle*, Chiang Mai 1990.

Tilly, Harry, L., *Wood-carving of Burma*, Superintendent of Government Printing and Stationary, Rangoon, 1903.

Tin Myaing Thein *Old and New Tapestries of Mandalay*, Oxford University Press, 2000.

Trant, T.A., *Two Years in Ava from May 1824 to May 1826 by an Officer on the Staff of the Quartermaster General's Department*, John Murray, London 1826.

U Aye Myint (trans. U Thanoe), *Burmese Design Through Drawings,* Silpakorn University, Bangkok, 1993.

Webb, J., 'Burma and Southeast Asia,' Lecture to the Royal Asiatic Society, London, 1983 (n.p.).

Weiner, A. and Schneider, J. (eds.), *Cloth and Human Experience*, Smithsonian Institution Press, Washington, DC 1989.

Wilson, Constance, M. and Hanks, Lucien, M., *'The Burma-Thailand Frontier Over Sixteen Decades: Three Descriptive Documents,'* Monograph in International Studies, Southeast Asia Series, No. 70, University of Ohio, Athens, Ohio, 1985.

Wilson, Verity, *Chinese Dress,* Victoria and Albert Museum, London, 1986.

Winichakul, Thongchai, *Siam Mapped: A History of the Geo-body of a Nation*, Silkworm Books, Chiang Mai, 1994.

Wyatt, David, *Temple Murals as an Historical Source: The Case of Wat Phumin*, Nan Thai Studies Section, Faculty of Arts, Chulalongkorn University, Bangkok 1993.

Wyatt, David and Aroonrut, Wichienkeeo (trans. and eds.), *The Chiang Mai Chronicle* Silkworm Books, Chiang Mai 1995.

Wyatt, James and Wardwell, Anne, *When Silk Was Gold: Central Asian and Chinese Textiles,* The Metropolitian Museum of Art, New York 1997.

Young, George, 'The Hill Tribes of Northern Thailand' in *The Journal of the Siam Society*, 1962.

Younghusband, G.J., *Eighteen Hundred Miles on a Burmese Tat*, Allen and Co, London, 1888.

Yule, Capt. Henry, *A Narrative of the Mission Sent by the Governor-General of India to the Court of Ava in 1855,* London 1858, reprint Oxford University Press, Kuala Lumpur, 1968.

Yunnan People's Publishing House, *The Folk Arts of Yunnan Ethnics* Yunnan People's Publishing House, Kunming, n.d. (in Chinese).

Zhu Liangwen, *The Dai*, Bangkok: D.D. Books, Bangkoki and The Science Technology Press, Kunming, 1993.

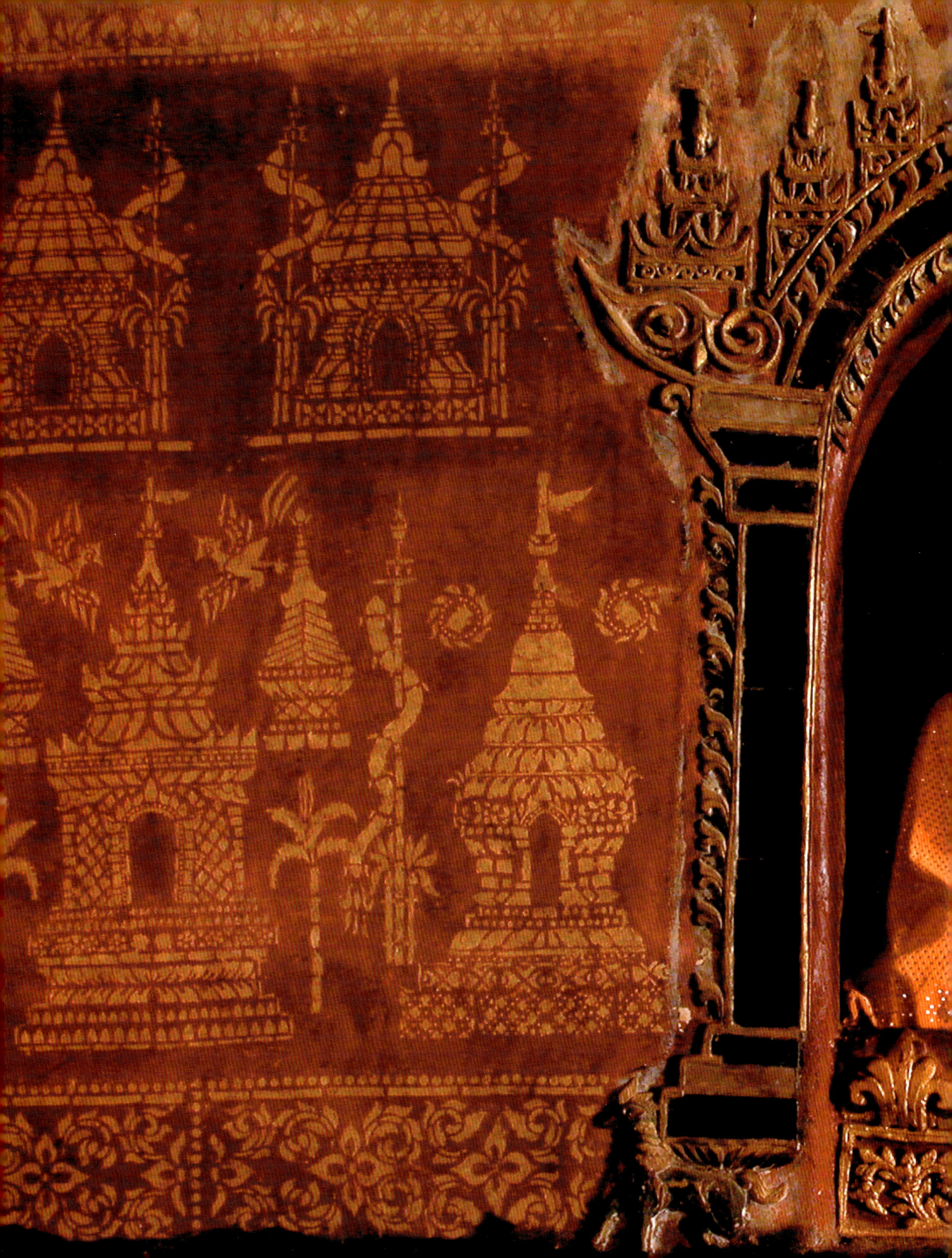

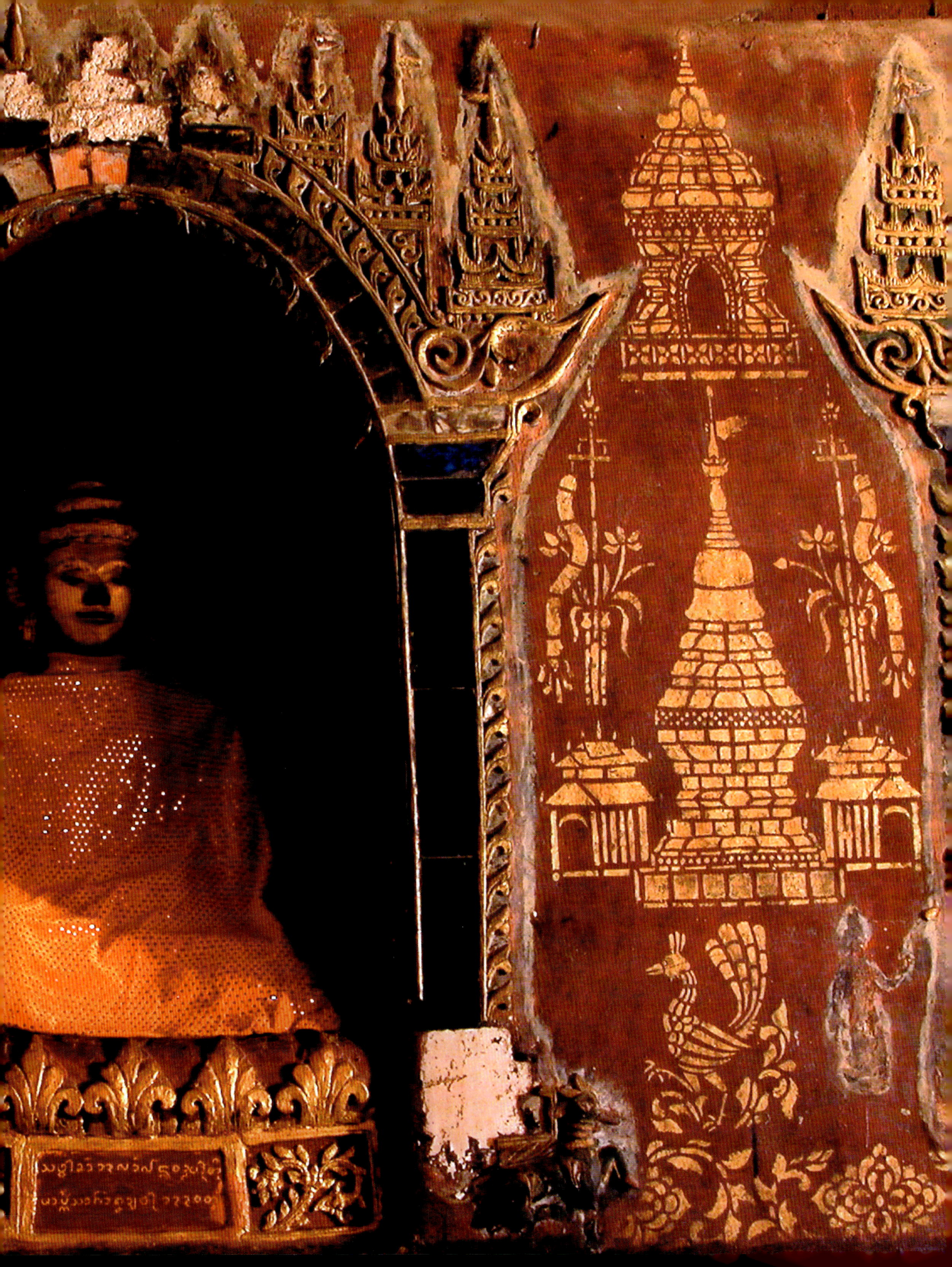

Index

Illustration page numbers are in bold.

Photo Credits

Akadet Nakbunlung collection: pages 27, 50, 56, 60, 70, 71 (top), 150 (top), 156 (bottom).

Ashmolean Museum collection, Oxford: page 73.

***Burma* by Ferrars and Ferrars:** page 80 (top).

***Burma and the Art of Lacquer* by Issacs, R. and Blurton, T. R.:** page 157.

Denison University collection, Ohio: pages 52, 53, 54, 55 (left & bottom), 85 (top), 81, 87, 88 (top), 96, 100, 147.

Duangjit Thaveesri collection: pages 102 (top), 125 (middle).

Fowler Museum for Cultural History, University of Los Angeles: page 74.

The Green Centre for World Art at the Royal Pavilion Art Gallery and Museum, Brighton: pages 58 (top), 59 (right), 71 (bottom), 79, 80 (right), 83 (bottom), 84, 89 (bottom right), 91, 95 (top), 173, 184.

Milne & Cochrane: page 9, 83 (top), 103, 120, 138, 181, 148, 172 (top), 175 (top), 181, 186.

Nel Adams (Sao Noan Oo): pages 63, 68 (bottom), 153 (top).

The Oriental and India Office Collection, The British Library, London: pages 12, 42, 43, 44 (left), 57, 58 (bottom), 66, 67, 68 (top), 75, 93, 94 (top), 95 (bottom), 97, 105, 178, 179.

Paisarn Piammattawat: pages 2, 5, 6, 14 (top), 21, 22, 23 (top), 24 (left), 62, 69 (top left), 76, 124, 126-128, 133, 135, 140, 141, 156 (top & middle), 157 (left), 158 (top right & left), 159, 162-3, 164-6, 167, 168, 169 (top), 170, 171, 180, 188-189, 194, 200-201, 206-207, 211-2.

Paothong Tongchua collection: pages 69 (top right), 88 (right).

Private collection: pages 26 (top), 46, 47, 78, 82, 85 (bottom), 86, 89 (all except bottom right), 90, 98, 99, 101, 106-115, 122, 131 (bottom), 131 (top), 132, 136, 139, 144 (left), 145, 149, 150 (bottom left), 151, 152, 153 (bottom), 155 (bottom), 158 (middle), 160, 161, 177, 183.

Sao Hkam Hip Hpa: pages 92 (top).

Shan Palace Museum: pages 16, 34, 59 (left), 65, 69 (all except middle), 92 (bottom), 95 (right), 116, 119, 125 (top left), 134, 158 (left).

Susan Conway: pages 11, 13, 14 (below), 15, 19, 20, 22, 23 (below), 24 (right), 25, 26 (bottoms), 28, 29, 32, 33, 35, 36, 38, 40, 44 (right), 48, 51, 85 (top), 117, 118, 121, 123, 125 (top right and bottom), 129, 130 (right), 142, 143, 144 (right & bottom), 150 (bottom right), 154, 155 (top),169 (bottom), 172 (bottom), 174, 175 (middle & bottom), 176, 182.

Survey of India Offices, Calcutta: page 102 (bottom).

The Victoria and Albert Museum, London: pages 55 (right), 61, 130 (left).

White Lotus: pages 37, 45, 72, 80 (bottom left), 94 (bottom), 104, 185.

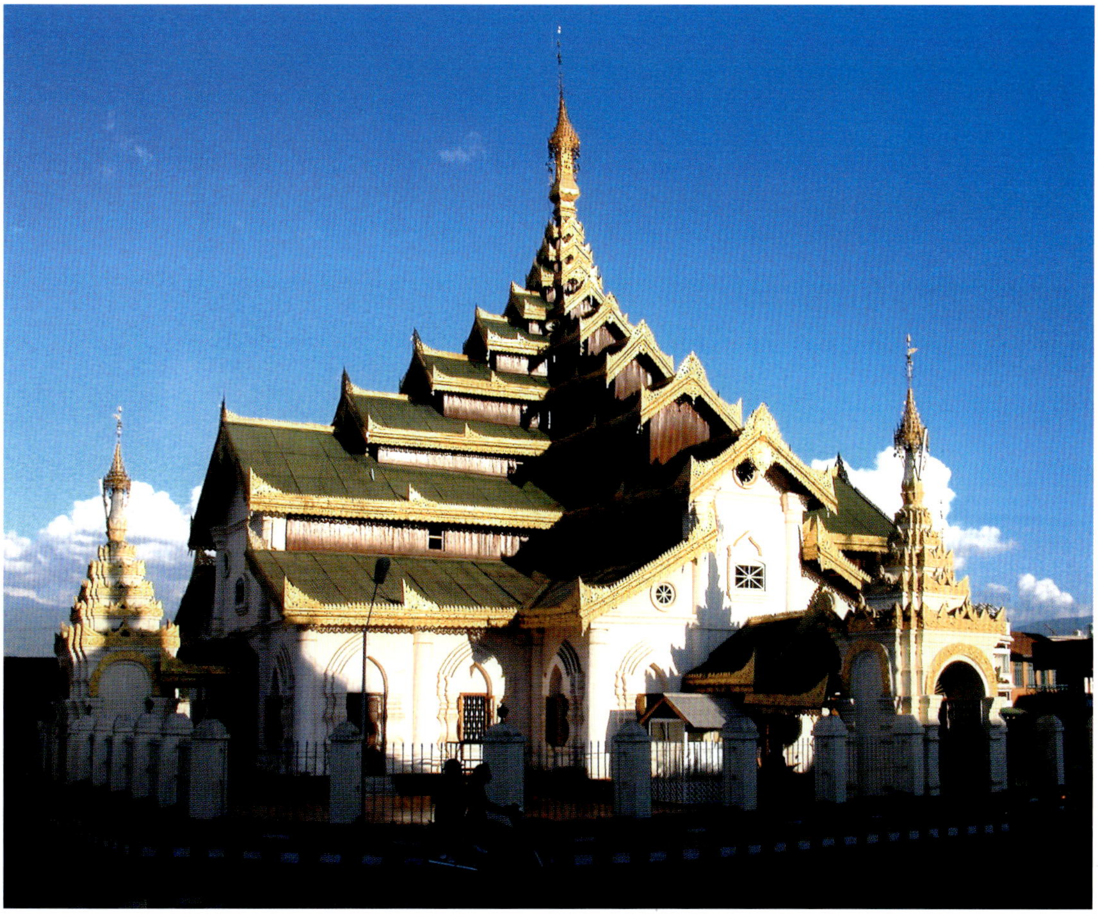

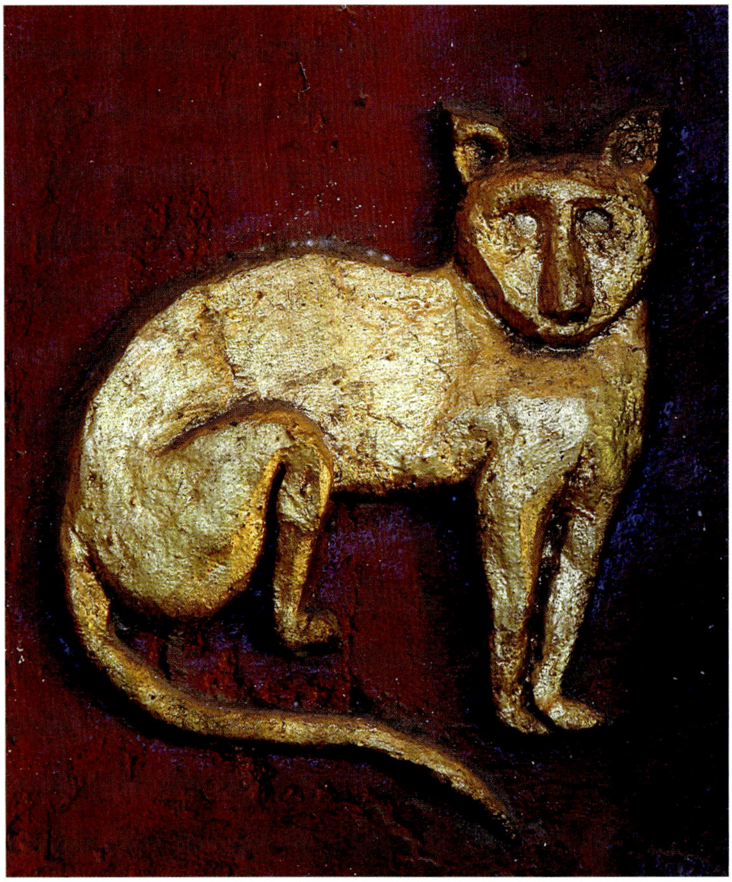